D1234513

HISTORY OF THE POPES
VOL. XXX

PASTOR'S HISTORY OF THE POPES

THE HISTORY OF THE POPES. Translated from the German of LUDWIG, FREIHERR VON PASTOR. Edited, as to Vols. I.–VI. by the late FREDERICK IGNATIUS ANTROBUS, and, as to Vols. VII.–XXIV. by RALPH FRANCIS KERR, of the London Oratory, and Vols. XXV.–XXXII. by DOM ERNEST GRAF of Buckfast Abbey. In 32 Volumes.

Vols. I. and II.	A.D. 1305–1458
Vols. III. and IV.	A.D. 1458–1483
Vols. V. and VI.	A.D. 1484–1513
Vols. VII. and VIII.	A.D. 1513–1521
Vols. IX. and X.	A.D. 1522–1534
Vols. XI. and XII.	A.D. 1534–1549
Vols. XIII. and XIV.	A.D. 1550–1559
Vols. XV. and XVI.	A.D. 1559–1565
Vols. XVII. and XVIII.	A.D. 1566–1572
Vols. XIX. and XX.	A.D. 1572–1585
Vols. XXI. and XXII.	A.D. 1585–1591
Vols. XXIII. and XXIV.	A.D. 1592–1604
Vols. XXV. and XXVI.	A.D. 1605–1621
Vols. XXVII to XXIX.	A.D. 1621–1644
Vols. XXX. to XXXII.	A.D. 1644–1700

The original German text of the *History of the Popes* is published by Herder & Co., Freiburg (Baden).

THE
HISTORY OF THE POPES

FROM THE CLOSE OF THE MIDDLE AGES

DRAWN FROM THE SECRET ARCHIVES OF THE VATICAN AND OTHER
ORIGINAL SOURCES

FROM THE GERMAN OF THE LATE

LUDWIG, FREIHERR VON PASTOR

TRANSLATED BY

DOM ERNEST GRAF, O.S.B.

MONK OF BUCKFAST

VOLUME XXX
INNOCENT X. (1644-1655)

B. HERDER BOOK CO.
15 & 17 SOUTH BROADWAY,
ST. LOUIS, MO.
1940

Imprimi potest
Sublaci, ex Proto-Coenobio Stae Scholasticae,
die 23 Julii 1939.
L. Emmanuel Caronti, O.S.B., Abbas Generalis.

PRINTED IN GREAT BRITAIN

To His Eminence
CARDINAL MERRY DEL VAL
the last Roman caller
at the deathbed of my beloved husband,
in token of reverence,
Constance Pastor.

MOTTO.

Comment peut-on être chrétien sans être catholique ? Et comment peut-on être catholique et refuser au pape l'entière soumission qui lui est due ?

Queen Christine of Sweden, *Pensées, éd. De Bildt*, p. 34.

CONTENTS OF VOLUME XXX.

FOREWORD TO THE GERMAN EDITION.

EVEN one glance at the title page of the present volume suffices to show that this time the author strove to condense the vast material much more than had been his wont. When he had kept his seventieth birthday in 1924, he remarked that after this each year, as it came, would have to be viewed as a gift, as a kindly favour of Providence, which one should accept gratefully but on which one could not count. If many of the latter volumes had embraced the life of but one Pope, such fullness of treatment had been justified because there was question of climaxes in the story of the later papacy. Now, however, less important matter must be ruthlessly eschewed so as to make it possible to complete the history of the Popes, for up to the last, the great historian of the Roman Pontiffs cherished the hope of being able to complete what had been his life-work. A word of encouragement from Pius X., whom he held in highest reverence, gave him courage to undertake the seemingly impossible and he did his utmost to realize his noble ambition. Once again he strained his incomparable capacity for work to the utmost limit ; from the mountain of material collected during fifty years of tireless toil, he omitted everything that would have led him too far.

The widow of the deceased historian, Her Excellency Baroness Constance Pastor, has religiously taken up the literary inheritance and entrusted its publication to competent persons. Volume XIV. appears as it was found, in two sections (in the German original), the only thing missing being the introduction and in Chapter VI. of Book II. the section dealing with Alexander VII.'s patronage of learning together with some concluding remarks on the smaller churches of Rome, and the secular buildings erected by that Pope. Both sections were completed by Fr. Kneller (Munich) on the basis of notes left by the author. Most of the missiological part is based on work by Professor Schmidlin (Münster). In the second half of this volume, and in all subsequent ones, the authors of the few sections which are missing in the MS. will be given, so that the deceased may not be held responsible for what is not from his pen.

We are greatly indebted to Fr. Kneller and Dr. W. Wühr (Munich) for the great care they have bestowed on the publication of the work.

The publishers will deem it an honour and a privilege to issue in rapid succession the remaining volumes (XIV². ; XV. and XVI.) of which, except for a few gaps, they have the author's complete MS.

FREIBURG IN BREISGAU.   THE PUBLISHERS.
Autumn, 1929.

COLLECTIONS OF ARCHIVES AND MANUSCRIPTS REFERRED TO IN VOLUMES XXX., XXXI. AND XXXII.

AIX (Provence)—Méjanes Library.
AREZZO—Bibl. della Fraternità di S. Maria.
ARICCIA—Chigi Family Archives.
AVIGNON—Bibl. de la Ville.

BERLIN—State Library.
BOLOGNA—State Archives.
—— University Library.
BREGENZ—City Library.
BRESCIA—Bibl. Queriniana.

CAMPELLO near Spoleto— Campello Archives.
CAPUA—Archiepiscopal Library.
COMO—Monti Archives.
CORTONA—Communal Library.

EINSIEDELN—Stiftsbibliothek.
EMPOLI VECCHIO—Azzolini Archives.

FLORENCE—State Archives.
—— Magliabecchi Library.
—— Marucelliana Library.
—— National Library.
—— Riccardiana Library.
FRANKFURT A. M.—City Library.
FREIBURG I. BR.—University Library.

GENOA—Civic Library.
—— University Library.
GUBBIO—L. Benveduti Library

HAGUE, THE—Library.
HANNOVER—Library.

INNSBRUCK—Pastor Library.

LODI—Communal Library.
LONDON—British Museum.
LYONS—Library.

MANTUA—Gonzaga Archives.
—— State Archives.
MASSA—State Archives.
MODENA—State Archives.
MONTE CASSINO—Library.
MONTPELLIER—Library.
MUNICH—State Archives.
—— State Library.

NAPLES—National Library.
—— Bibl. della Società di storia patria.

ORVIETO—Piccolomini Archives.
OTTENSTEIN (Schloss)— Lamberg Archives.

PADERBORN — Theodorianische Bibliothek.
PARIS—Archives of Foreign Affairs.
—— National Library.
PARMA—State Archives.
PERUGIA—Communal Library.
PISTOIA—Fabroniana Library.

RAVENNA—Bibl. Classense.

xiii

COMPLETE TITLES OF BOOKS QUOTED IN VOLUMES XXX., XXXI. AND XXXII.

Abhandlungen der Kgl. bayr. Akademie der Wissenschaften. Philos.-philol. u. hist. Kl. Munich, 1827 *seqq.*

Abhandlungen der Kgl. böhmischen Gesellschaft der Wissenschaften Prague, 1841 *seqq.*

Acta historica res gestas Poloniae illustrantia. Vols. 3–7 (1674–1683). Cracow.

Actes et mémoires des négociations de la paix de Nimègue. 7 vols., 3rd edit. La Haye, 1697.

Ademollo, A., Giacinto Gigli e i suoi Diarii del sec. xvii. Florence 1877.

Ademollo, A., La quistione dell' indipendenza Portoghese in Roma 1640–1670. Florence, 1878.

Ademollo, A., Il matrimonio di suor Maria Pulcheria, al secolo Livia Cesarini. Memorie particolari. Rome, 1883.

Ademollo, A., I Teatri di Roma nel secolo decimosettimo. Rome, 1888.

Aiazzi, G., Nunziatura in Irlanda di monsignor G. B. Rinuccini. Florence, 1844.

Allgemeine Deutsche Biographie. Vol. 1–56. Leipzig, 1875 *seqq.*

Alveri, G., Roma in ogni stato. Rome, 1664.

Amabile, L., Il s. Officio della Inquisizione in Napoli. 2 vols. Città di Castello, 1892.

Amayden Teodoro, La storia delle famiglie Romane. Con note di C. A. Bertini. 2 vols. Rome, 1910 and 1914.

Amayden Teodoro, De pietate romana libellus. Rome, 1625.

Analecta iuris pontificii. Dissertations sur divers sujets de droit canonique, liturgie et théologie. Rome, 1855 *seqq.*

Analectes pour servir à l'histoire ecclésiastique de la Belgique. 3rd ser. Brussels-Leipzig-Louvain, 1905–1914.

Anecdotes sur l'état de la religion dans la Chine (par Villermaule). 7 vols. Paris, 1733–1742.

Angeli, D., Le chiese di Roma. Rome.

Angelo, M. D', Luigi xiv. e la S. Sede. (1689–1693.) Rome, 1914.

Annalen des Hist. Vereins für den Niederrhein. First and following numbers. Cologne, 1855 *seqq.*

Annales de la Société d'émulation de Bruges. Vol. 1 *seqq.* Bruges, 1839.

Annales de la Société des soi-disants Jésuites. Paris, 1764–1771.

Annales de St.-Louis des Français. Vol. 1 *seqq.* Rome, 1896 *seqq.*

Archiv für katholisches Kirchenrecht. Vol. 1 *seqq.* Innsbruck, 1857 *seqq.*

Archiv für österreichische Geschichte. Vol 1 *seqq.* Vienna, 1865 *seqq.*

Archivi italiani, Gli. Vol 1 *seqq.* Naples, 1914 *seqq.*
Archivio della R. Società Romana di storia patria. Vol. 1 *seqq.*
    Rome, 1878 *seqq.*
Archivio storico dell' arte, pubbl. per Gnoli. Vol 1 *seqq.* Rome,
    1888 *seqq.*
Archivio storico italiano. 5 ser. Florence, 1842 *seqq.*
Archivio storico Lombardo. Vol 1 *seqq.* Milan, 1874 *seqq.*
Archivio storico per le provincie Napolitane. Vol 1 *seqq.* Naples,
    1876 *seqq.*
Archivium Franciscanum historicum. Vol 1 *seqq.* Quaracchi,
    1908 *seqq.*
Archenholtz, Mémoires concernant Christine reine de Suède.
    4 Vols. Amsterdam, 1751.
Argentré Carolus du Plessis d'. Collectio iudiciorum. Paris, 1724.
Arnauld Antoine, Œuvres complettes. 43 Vols. Paris, 1783.
Arnauld Henri, Les négociations à la cour de Rome et en différentes
    cours d'Italie. 5 Vols. Paris, 1748.
Artaud de Montor, A. F., Histoire du Pape Pie VII. 2 Vols.
    Paris, 1836.
Arte, L', seguito dell' Archivio storico dell' arte. Vol 1 *seqq.*
    Rome, 1898 *seqq.*
Arte e storia. Vol 1 *seqq.* Florence, 1882 *seqq.*
Astráin, A., S.J., Historia de la Compañia de Jesús en la Asistencia
    de España. Vols. 1–7. Madrid, 1902 *seqq.*
Ateneo Veneto., Rivista mensile. Vol. 1 *seqq.* Venice, 1812 *seqq.*
Atti della Reale Accademia nazionale dei Lincei. Roma. (Memorie
    1870 *seqq.* Classe di scienze morali, storiche e filologiche,
    1885 *seqq.* Rendiconti, 1901 *seqq.*)
(*D'Avrigny*), Mémoires chronologiques et dogmatiques pour
    servir à l'histoire ecclésiastique depuis, 1600, jusqu'en 1716.
    4 Vols. 1739.

Bain, F. W., Christina, Queen of Sweden. London, 1890.
Balan, P., Storia d'Italia. 7 Vols. Modena, 1875–1890.
Baldinucci, F., La Vita di Giov. Lorenzo Bernini, translated into
    German and edited by A. Riegl. Vienna, 1912.
Bangen, J. H., Die römische Kurie, ihre gegenwärtige Zusam-
    mensetzung und ihr Geschäftsgang. Münster, 1854.
Barozzi, N., e *Berchet, G.*, Le relazioni degli stati Europei lette al
    senato degli ambasciatori Veneziani nel sec. xvii. First
    series : Spain, 2 Vols. Venice, 1856–1862 ; 2nd series :
    France, 3 Vols., between 1857–1863 ; 3rd series : Italy,
    Vol. 1, Turin, about 1862 ; Relazioni di Roma, 2 Vols.,
    about 1877–9 ; 4th series ; England, Vol. 1, about 1863 ;
    Turkey, 1 Vol., about 1871–2.
Bartoli, Opere. Vol. 25. Turin, 1838.
Batterel, Louis, Mémoires domestiques pour servir à l'histoire,
    publiées par A.-M.-P. Ingold. 4 Vols. Paris, 1902–5.
Bäumer, S., Geschichte des Breviers. Freiburg, 1895.
Baumgartner, A., Geschichte der Weltliteratur. 5 Vols. Die
    französische Literatur. Freiburg, 1911.

Bayle, Dictionnaire historique et critique. 4 Vols. Rotterdam, 1697.

Beani, G., Clemente IX. Notizie storiche. Prato, 1893.

Bellesheim, A., Geschichte der katholischen Kirche in Irland von der Einführung des Christentums bis auf die Gegenwart. 2 Vols. 1509–1690. Mayence, 1890.

Bellori, G. P., Le vite dei pittori, scultori ed architetti moderni. Rome, 1672. (Quoted from the Pisa edition, 1821.)

Benedetti, M. de, Palazzi e ville reali d'Italia. First and following numbers. Florence, 1911 *seqq.*

Benigni, U., Die Getreidepolitik der Päpste. Translated into German by R. Birner. Edited by G. Ruhland. Berlin, 1898.

Benkard Ernst, Giovanni Lorenzo Bernini. Frankfurt, 1926.

Bergner, H., Das barocke Rom. Leipzig, 1914.

Berichte des Historischen Vereins für Bamberg. Vol. 1 *seqq.* Bamberg, 1834 *seq.*.

Berichte und Mitteilungen des Altertumsvereines zu Wien. Vol. 1 *seqq.* Vienna, 1856 *seqq.*

Bernhardy, A. A., Venezia e il Turco nella seconda metà del sec. xvii. Florence, 1902.

Bernino Domenico, Memorie historiche raccolte da D. B. di ciò che ha operato contro li Turchi il Sommo Pontefice Innocenzo undesimo. Naples, 1695.

Bernino Domenico, Historia di tutte l'heresie. 4 Vols. Rome, 1705–9.

Berteaux, E., Rome de l'avènement de Jules II. à nos jours. Paris, 1905.

Berthier, J. J., Innocentii PP. XI. epistolae ad principes. 2 Vols. Rome, 1891–5.

Berthier, J. J., L'église de la Minerve à Rome. Rome, 1910.

Bertolotti, A., Alcuni artisti Siciliani a Roma nei secoli xvi e xvii. Palermo, 1879.

Bertolotti, A., Artisti Belgi e Olandesi in Roma nei secoli xvi e xvii. Florence, 1880.

Bertolotti, A., Artisti subalpini in Roma nei secoli xv, xvi e xvii. Turin, 1877. (Mantua, 1884.)

Bertolotti, A., Artisti Bolognesi in Roma, in Atti d. R. Deput. di stor. patria d. Romagna, 1886.

Bertrand, Jos., La mission de Maduré d'après des documents inédits. 3 Vols. Paris, 1847–1854.

Biaudet Henri, Les Nonciatures apostoliques permanentes jusqu'en 1648. (Annales Academiae scientiarum Fennicae, serie B, Vol. 2, 1.) Helsinki, 1910.

Bibliofilo. Giornale dell' arte antica e moderna. 11 Vols. Florence, 1880–1890.

Biermann, B. M., Die Anfänge der neuern Dominikanermission in China. Münster, 1927.

Bigge, La guerra di Candia negli anni 1667–9. Turin, 1901.

Bildt, Baron Ch. de, Christine de Suède et le card. Azzolino. Lettres inédites, 1666–8. Paris, 1899.

Bildt, Baron Ch. de, Svenska minnen och märken i Rom. Stockholm, 1900.

Bildt, Baron Ch. de, Un banchetto al Quirinale nel seicento. Rome, 1901.

Bildt, Baron Ch. de, Christine de Suède et le conclave de Clément X. 1669–1670. Paris, 1906.

Bildt, Baron Ch. de, Les médailles Romaines de Christine de Suède. Rome, 1908.

Biographie nationale, publiée par l'Académie Royale de Belgique. Vol. 1 *seqq.* Brussels, 1866.

Biographie universelle ou Dictionnaire historique. Paris, 1847 *seqq.*

Bischoffshausen S. Frh. v., Papst Alexander VIII. und der Wiener Hof (1689–1691). Stuttgart, 1900.

Bittner, L., Chronologisches Verzeichnis der österreichischen Staatsverträge. 2 Vols. (1526–1947). Vienna, 1903–9.

Blok, P. J., Geschichte der Niederlande. 5 Vols. Gotha, 1912.

Blume, Fr., Iter Italicum. 4 Vols. Halle, 1824 *seq.*

Boligno, L., La Sicilia e i suoi cardinali. Palermo, 1884.

Böhn, M. v., Lorenzo Bernini : Seine Zeit, sein Leben, sein Werk. Bielefeld, 1910.

Bojani, F. de, Innocent XI. Sa correspondance avec ses Nonces. 3 Vols. Rome, 1910–1912.

Bollettino d'arte. Vol. 1 *seqq.* Rome, 1907 *seq.*

Bollettino Senese di storia patria. Vol. 1 *seqq.* Siena, 1894 *seqq.*

Bonamici (= Bonamicius Philippus), Vita Innocentii XI. Rome, 1776. (German edition, Frankfurt-Leipzig, 1791.)

Bonanni, Ph., Numismata Pontificum Romanorum quae a tempore Martini V. ad annum 1699 vel autoritate publica vel privato genio in lucem prodiere. 2 Vols. Rome, 1699.

Bonanni, Ph., Numismata templi Vaticani historiam illustrantia. 2nd edition. Rome, 1700.

Bonn, M. J., Die englische Kolonisation in Irland. 2 Vols. Stuttgart, 1906.

Borboni, Giov. Andr., Delle statue. Rome, 1661.

Bossi Gaet., La Pasquinata : " Quod non fecerunt barbari, fecerunt Barberini." Ricerche storiche. Rome, 1898.

Bossuet, Correspondance, see *Urbain.*

Bossuet, J. B., Œuvres. Nouvelle édition. 43 Vols. Versailles, 1815–1819.

Bourlon, J., Les assemblées du Clergé et le Jansénisme. Paris, 1909.

Bremond, Histoire de sentiment religieux en France. Vols. 1–5. Paris, 1916–1920.

Briggs, M. S., Barockarchitektur. Berlin, 1914.

Brinckmann, A. E., Platz und Monument. Berlin, 1908.

Brinckmann, A. E., Barockskulptur. 2 Vols. 2nd edit. Berlin, 1921.

Brinckmann, A. E., Stadtbaukunst. 2nd edit. Berlin, 1922.

Brinckmann, A. E., Barock-Bozzetti italienischer Bildhauer. Frankfurt, 1923.

Brom, G., Archalivia in Italië. 3 Vols. 's Gravenhage, 1908–1914.

Brosch, M., Geschichte des Kirchenstaates. Vol. 1. Gotha, 1880.
Brosch, M., Oliver Cromwell und die puritanische Revolution. Frankfort sur M., 1886.
Brosch, M., Geschichte Englands. Vol. 7. Gotha, 1891.
Brucker, J. (*S.J.*), La Compagnie de Jésus. Paris, 1919.
Bullarium Congregationis de Propaganda Fide. 7 Vols. Rome, 1839 *seq.*
Bullarium Romanum. Bullarum, Diplomatum et Privilegiorum Sanctorum Romanorum Pontificum. Taurinensis editio, locupletior facta collectione novissima plurium Brevium, Epistolarum, Decretorum Actorumque S. Sedis. 24 Vols. Augustae Taurinorum, 1857 *seqq.*
Bulletin de la Commission Royale d'histoire de l'Académie de Belgique. Vol. 1 *seqq.* Brussels, 1834.
Bulletin de littérature ecclésiastique. Vol. 1 *seqq.* Toulouse, 1877 *seqq.*
Bulletijn der Maatschappij van Geschied-en Oudheidkunde te Gent. Vol. 1 *seqq.* Ghent, 1914 *seqq.*
Bullettino della Commissione Archeologica Comunale. Vol. 1 *seqq.* Rome, 1872 *seqq.*
Burckhardt, J., Cicerone. Anleitung zum Genuss der Kunstwerke Italiens. 8th edit. 1901.
Bussi, Istoria di Viterbo. Rome, 1742.

Cabrol-Leclerq, Dictionnaire d'archéologie chrétienne et de liturgie. Vol. 1 *seqq.* Paris, 1903 *seqq.*
(*Cadry*), Histoire du livre des Réflexions morales. Vols. 2–4. Amsterdam, 1730–4.
Calisse, Carlo, Storia de Civitavecchia. Florence, 1898.
Campana de Cavelli, Les derniers Stuarts et le château de St.-Germain en Laye. 2 Vols. Paris, 1871.
Campello Giov. Batt., Diario del conte G. B. Campello. Pontificato di Innocenzo XII., edito dal Conte Paolo Campello in Studi e documenti di storia e di diritto VIII–XII., XIV. (1887–1893).
Campori, G., CIII. Lettere inedite di Sommi Pontefici scritte avanti e dopo la loro esaltazione. Modena, 1878.
Cancellieri, Fr., Storia dei solenni possessi dei Sommi Pontefici detti anticamente processi o processioni dopo la loro coronazione dalla basilica Vaticana alla Lateranense. Rome, 1802.
Cancellieri, Fr., Il Mercato, il lago dell' Acqua Vergine ed il Palazzo Panfilliano nel Circo Agonale detto volgarmente Piazza Navona descritti. Rome, 1811.
Cancellieri, Fr., Lettera di F. C. al ch. sig. dott. Koreff sopra il tarantismo, l'aria di Roma e della sua campagna ed i palazzi pontefici dentro e fuori di Roma, con le notizie di Castel Gandolfo e de'paesi circonvicini. Rome, 1817.
Canecazzi, G., Papa Clemente IX. poeta. Modena, 1900.
Capece Galeota, N., Cenni storici dei Nunzii Apostolici di Napoli. Naples, 1877.
Cappelli, E., L'ambasceria del Duca di Créquy alla corte pontificia. Rocca S. Casciano, 1897.

Carabelli, G., Dei Farnese e del ducato di Castro e di Ronciglione, Florence, 1865.
Cardella, L., Memorie storiche de' cardinali della s. Romana Chiesa. 10 Vols. Rome, 1782–1797.
Carini, Isid., La Biblioteca Vaticana, proprietà della Sede Apostolica. Rome, 1893.
Carte Strozziane, Le. Inventario. 1st Series. 2 Vols. Florence, 1884.
Catholic Encyclopedia, The. Vol. 1 *seqq.* New York, 1907 *seqq.*
Cecchelli, C., Il Vaticano. Rome, 1928.
Celli, A., Storia della malaria nell'Agro Romano. Opera postuma, con illustr. del Dr. P. Ambrogetti. Città di Castello, 1925.
Cerri, U., Estat présent de l'Église Romaine dans toutes les parties du monde. Amsterdam, 1716.
Chantelauze, Le card. de Retz et sa mission diplomatique. Paris, 1878.
Charavay, Et., Inventaire des autographes et documents historiques réunis par M. Benjamin Fillon, décrits par Ét. Ch. 3 Vols. Paris, 1879–1881.
Chattard, G. P., Nuova descrizione del Vaticano. 2 Vols. Rome, 1762.
Chéruel, see *Mazarin.*
Chinazzi, Sede vacante per la morte di Urbano VIII. Rome, 1904.
Chledowski, C. v., Rom. 2 Vols. Munich, 1912.
Ciaconius, Alph., Vitae et res gestae Pontificum Romanorum et S. R. E. Cardinalium . . . ab August. Oldoino S.J. recognitae. 3rd and 4th Vols. Rome, 1677.
Ciampi, J., L'Epistolario inedito di Fabio Chigi, poi Papa Alessandro VII., in Atti dei Lincei, Sc. Mor. 3rd ser., 1 (1877).
Ciampi, J., Innocenzo X. Pamfili e la sua corte. Rome, 1878.
Ciampi, S., Bibliografia critica delle corrispondenze dell'Italia colla Russia, colla Polonia, etc. 3 Vols. Florence, 1834–1842.
Cicogna, E. A., Delle iscrizioni Veneziane raccolte ed illustrate. Venice, 1824–1853.
Cicognara, Storia della scultura italiana. Venice, 1813.
Civezza, see *Marcellino*
Civiltà Cattolica. Vol. 1 *seqq.* Rome, 1850.
Claretta, G., La regina Cristina di Suezia in Italia. Turin, 1892.
Clementi, F., Il carnevale Romano nelle cronache contemporanee. Rome, 1899.
Cochin, C., *Henri Arnauld*, évêque d'Angers, 1597–1692. Paris, 1921.
Colantuoni, R., La chiesa di S. Maria del Popolo. Rome, 1899.
Colasanti, G., Le Fontane d'Italia. Milan, 1926.
Collectanea S. Congregationis de Propaganda Fide, seu decreta, instructiones, rescripta pro apostolicis missionibus. Vol. 1 of years 1622–1866. Rome, 1907.
Collectio Lacensis, Acta et decreta s. Conciliorum recentiorum (1682–1870). 7 Vols. Freiburg, 1870–1890.

Colombo, G., Notizie biografiche e lettere di Papa Innocenzo XI.
  Turin, 1878.
Colonna, P., Fr. Massimo. Rome, 1911.
Conclavi de' Pontefici Romani. New Edition. Cologne, 1691.
Congregationis sac. rituum. Eminentiss. et reverend. d. card.
  Ferrario. Romana. Beatificationis et canonizationis ven.
  servi Dei Innocentii Papae XI., positio super dubio an sit
  signanda commissio introductionis causae in casu, etc.
  Rome, 1713. (Citato : Proc. Summ.)
Conring, H., Commentar. historic, de electione Urbani VIII. et
  Innocentii X. Helmstedt, 1651.
Conti, G., Firenze dai Medici ai Lorena 1670–1727. Florence,
  1909.
Coppi, A., Discorso sulle finanze dello Stato Pontificio dal secolo
  XVI. al principio del XIX. Rome, 1855.
Cordara, I., Historiae Soc. Iesu Pars. 1–2. Rome, 1750.
Coste, Pierre, Saint Vincent de Paul. Correspondance, Entretiens,
  Documents. 14 Vols. Paris, 1920 *seqq.*
Courrier de l'art. Chronique hebdomadaire. 10 Vols. Paris,
  1881–1890.
Cousin, V., *Jacqueline Pascal*, in Études sur les femmes illustres
  et la société du xvii. siècle. Paris, 1849.
Coville, H., Études sur Mazarin et ses démêlés avec le Pape
  Innocent X. Paris, 1914.
Coyer, Histoire de J. Sobieski. Paris, 1761.
Crétineau-Joly, J., Histoire de la Compagnie de Jésus. 6 Vols.
  3rd ed. Paris, 1851.
Cupis, C. de, Le vicende dell'agricoltura e della pastorizia
  nell'Agro Romano e l'Annona di Roma. Rome, 1911.

Daru, P. A. N. B., Histoire de la République de Venise. 8 Vols.
  3rd ed. Paris, 1826.
Degert, A., Histoire des Séminaires français jusqu'à la Révolution.
  2 Vols. Paris, 1912.
Dejean, E., Un prélat indépendant au xviie siècle : Nicolas
  Pavillon, évêque d'Alet 1637–1677. Paris, 1909.
Demaria, G., La querra di Castro e la spedizione de'presidi
  1639–1649, in Miscellanea de storia italiana XXXV. Turin,
  1898.
Dengel, Ph. I., Geschichte des palazzo di S. Marco, genannt
  Palazzo di Venezia. (Taken from the work : Der Palazzo
  di Venezia in Rom.) Leipzig, 1909.
Denis, P., Nouvelles de Rome. 1. Paris, 1913.
Denzinger, Henr., et Bannwart, Clem., S.J., Enchiridion
  symbolorum definitionum et declarationum de rebus fidei et
  morum. 16th ed. Freiburg, 1928.
Desmarais, Regnier, Histoire des desmêlés de la cour de France
  avec la cour de Rome au sujet de l'affaire des Corses. 1707.
Deutsche Literaturzeitung. Vol. 1 *seqq.* Berlin, 1880 *seqq.*
Deutsche Rundschau, edited by Rodenberg. Vol. 1 *seqq.* Berlin,
  1874 *seqq.*

Diarium Europaeum. 45 Vols. (1657–1681). Frankfort s. M., 1659 *seqq.*

Dictionnaire apologétique de la foi Catholique. Vol. 1 *seqq.* Paris, 1911 *seqq.*

Dictionnaire de théologie catholique, edited by Vacant-Mangenot. Vol. 1 *seqq.* Paris, 1903 *seqq.*

Doeberl, M., Entwicklungsgeschichte Bayerns. Vol. 1, 2nd ed. Munich, 1916.

Döllinger, J. J. J., Kirche und Kirchen, Papsttum und Kirchenstaat. Historisch-politische Betrachtungen. Munich, 1861.

Döllinger, J. J. J., Beiträge zur politischen, kirchlichen und Kulturgeschichte der sechs letzten Jahrhunderte. Vols. 2 and 3. Ratisbon and Vienna, 1863–1882.

Döllinger, J. J. J., Akademische Vorträge. Nördlingen, 1888.

Döllinger, J. J. J., Geschichte de Moralstreitigkeiten in der römisch-katholischen Kirche seit dem 16. Jahrh, ed. together with Reusch. Nördlingen, 1889.

Domarus, K. v., Pietro Bracci. Strassburg, 1915.

Dreiss, Mémoires de Louis XIV. 2 Vols. Paris, 1859.

Droysen, J. G., Geschichte der preussischen Politik. 14 Vols. 1855–1886.

Drugulin, W. E., Allgemeiner Porträt-Katalog, 1860.

Dubruel, M., Innocent XI. et l'extension de la Régale, in Revue des quest. hist. Vol. 81 (1907).

Dubruel, M., La Congrégation particulaire de la Régale sous Innocent XI. et les papiers d'Agostino Favoriti et de Lorenzo Casoni aux Archives Vaticans, in Revue des quest. hist. Vol. 87 (1909).

Dubruel, M., L'excommunication de Louis XIV., in Études. Vol. 137 (1913).

Dubruel, M., La querelle de la Régale sous Louis XIV. (1673–6) in Revue des quest. hist. 3rd ser. Vol. 1. Paris, 1922.

Dubruel, M., En plein conflit, in Bullet. de la Société Archéol. de France. March, 1925, July, 1926.

Dudik, B., Forschungen in Schweden für Mährens Geschichte. Brünn, 1852.

Dudon, P., Le quiétiste espagnol Michel Molinos (1628–1696). Paris, 1921.

Duhr, B. S. J., Jesuitenfabeln. 3rd ed. Freiburg, 1892.

Duhr. B. S. J., Geschichte der Jesuiten in den Ländern deutscher Zunge. 3 Vols. Ratisbon, 1921.

Dumas, H., Histoire des cinq propositions de Jansénius. 3 Vols. Trevoux, 1703.

Dumont, Jean, Voyages en Rome, en Italie, en Allemagne, à Malte et en Turquie. 4 Vols. The Hague, 1699.

Du Mont de Carels-Croon, Corps universel diplomatique. Vol. 7. Amsterdam, 1728 *seqq.*

(*Dupac de Bellegarde*), Histoire abrégée de l'église métropolitaine d'Utrecht, principalement depuis la révolution arrivée dans les VII. Provinces-Unies des Pays-Bas sous Philippe II. jusqu'à présent. Utrecht, 1765.

Dupin, Louis Ellies, Histoire ecclésiastique du dix-septième siècle. 4 Vols. Paris, 1713 *seqq.*

Dvorák, Geschichte der italienischen Kunst. Munich, 1928.

Egger, H., Römische Veduten. Vienna and Leipzig (1911).

Egger, J., Geschichte Tirols. 3 Vols. Innsbruck, 1872–1880.

Ehrle, Fr., Dalle carte e dai disegni de Virgilio Spada, in Memorie della Pontif. Accademia Rom. di Archeol. Rome, 1927.

Ehses, St., und Meister, A., Nuntiaturberichte aus Deutschland, 1585(1584)–1590. Görres-Gesellschaft ed. Ser. 1, Die Kölner Nuntiatur. Parts I and II. Paderborn, 1895–9.

Eisler, Alex., Das Veto der katholischen Staaten bei der Papstwahl. Vienna, 1907.

Encyclopædia Britannica. By a Society of Gentlemen in Scotland. 3 Vols. Edinburgh, 1771.

Erdmannsdörffer, Deutsche Geschichte. Vol. 1. Stuttgart, 1892.

Erythraeus, Ianus Nicius, Epistolae ad Tyrrhenum. Coloniae Ubiorum, 1645.

Escher, Konrad, Barock und Klassizismus. Studien zur Geschichte der Architektur Roms. Leipzig (1910).

(*Este, R. d'*), Mémoires de m. le cardinal Reynaud d'Este depuis l'an 1657 jusques au dernier de septembre 1673, jour et an de sa mort. 2 Vols. Cologne, 1677.

Estrées, Fr. A., Mémoires du maréchal d'Estrées sur la régence de Marie de Médicis (1610–16) et sur celle d'Anne d'Autriche, published by P. Bonnefon. Paris, 1910.

Études (Periodical), 6th ser. Paris, 1856 *seqq.*

Études Franciscaines. Revue mensuelle. Vol. 1 *seqq.* Paris, 1899 *seqq.*

Euringer, S., Die Obelisken Roms. Augsburg, 1925.

Evelyn, J., Diary and Correspondence of J. E. 4 Vols. London, 1850–1857.

Faillon, Vie de M. Olier, fondateur du séminaire de Saint-Sulpice. 3 Vols. Paris, 1873.

Falda, G. B., Le Fontane di Roma nella piazze e luoghi publici della città. Rome (1675?).

Farges, Louis, Recueil des Instructions données aux ambassadeurs et ministres de France depuis les traités de Westphalie jusqu'à la révolution française. Vols. 4 and 5. Poland. Paris, 1888.

Fea, C. D., Nullità delle amministrazioni capitolari abusive. Rome, 1815.

Fea, C. D., Storia dell'Acque in Roma e dei condotti. Rome, 1832.

Fénelon, Œuvres, éd. Gosselin and Caron. 35 Vols. Versailles, 1820–1830.

Felix, Ravenna. Vol. 1 *seqq.* Ravenna, 1911 *seqq.*

Feret, P. La Faculté de théologie de Paris et ses docteurs les plus célèbres. Époque moderne. Vol. 1 *seqq.* Paris, 1900.

Ferrari, Giulio., La tomba nell'arte italiana dal periodo preromano all'odierno, Milan.

Ferrari, Giulio, Lo stucco nell'arte italiana. Milan (s.a.)

Fester, Die Augsburger Allianz. Munich, 1893.

Fiedler, Jos., Die Relationen der Botschafter Venedigs über Deutschland und Oesterreich im 17. Jahrh. Vols. 2 (Fontes rerum Austriacarum 2nd part. Vol. 27). Vienna, 1867.

Flassan, Gaétan de Raxis, Histoire générale de la diplomatie française. 6 Vols, 2nd ed. Paris, 1811.

Fleury, Claude, Historia ecclesiastica. 91 Vols. Augsburg, 1768.

Floquet, P. A., Bossuet, précepteur du Dauphin. Paris, 1864.

Foley, H. (S.J.), Records of the English Province of the Society of Jesus. 7 Vols. London, 1877 *seqq.*

Fontaine Jacques de la SS. D. N. Clementis Papae XI. Constitutio " Unigenitus " theologice propugnata. 1–4, Rome, 1717–1724.

Fontes rerum Austriacarum. 2nd part : Diplomata et Acta, edited by the historic Commission of the Imperial Academy of Sciences. Vienna, 1849 *seqq.*

Forcella, V., Iscrizioni delle chiese e d'altri edifici di Roma dal secolo xi. fino ai giorni nostri. 14 Vols. Rome, 1869–1885.

Fraknói, W., Relationes cardinalis Buonvisi anno 1686. (Monumenta Vaticana Hungarica, 2nd ser., Vol. 2. Budapest, 1886.

Fraknói, W., Papst Innozenz XI. (Benedikt Odescalchi) und die Befreiung Ungarns von der Türkenherrschaft. Hungarian version by Peter Jékel. Freiburg, 1902.

Franziskanische Studien. Vol. 1 *seqq.* Münster, 1914.

Fraschetti, St., Il Bernini. Milan, 1900.

Frey, D., Beiträge zur römischen Barockarchitektur, im Jahrbuch für Kunstgeschichte, 1924.

Frey, D., Michelangelo-Studien. Vienna, 1920.

Friedensburg, W., Regesten zur deutschen Geschichte aus der Zeit des Pontifikats Innozenz X. (1644–1655). Reprint from Quellen und Forschungen aus italienischen Archiven, Bd. 4–7. Rome, 1904.

Fueter, E., Geschichte der neueren Historiographie. Munich, 1911.

Gaedeke, Arn., Die Politik Österreichs in der spanischen Erbfolgefrage. 2 Vols. Leipzig, 1877.

Galeotti, L., Della sovranità e governo temporale dei Papi. 3 Vols. Paris, 1846.

Gams, P. B., Die Kirchengeschichte von Spanien. 3 Vols. Ratisbon, 1862.

Gams, P. B., Series episcoporum ecclesiae catholicae quotquot innotuerunt a beato Petro apostolo. Ratisbon, 1873.

Garampi, G., Saggi di osservazioni sul valore delle antiche monete pontificie. Con appendice di documenti. s. l. e. s. a. (Rome, 1766.)

Gardiner, S. R., History of the Great Civil War, 1642–9. 4 Vols. London, 1893.

Gardiner, S. R., History of the Commonwealth and Protectorate, 1649–1656. 4 Vols. London, 1894–8.

Gärtner, C., Corpus iuris ecclesiastici catholicorum novioris quod per Germaniam obtinet. 2 Vols. Salzburg, 1797–9.

Garzoni, Pietro, Istoria della Repubblica di Venezia in tempo della sacra lega contra Maometto IV. e tre suoi successori. Venice, 1705–1716.

Gastaldi, Hieron., Tractatus de avertenda et profliganda peste politico-legalis. Bononiae, 1684.

Gazier, A., Histoire générale du mouvement janséniste depuis ses origines jusqu'à nos jours. 2 Vols. Paris, 1924.

Geijer, E. G., Geschichte Schwedens. German trans. : Vols 1–3. Vols. 4–6 by F. F. Carlson ; Vol. 7 by L. Stavenow. Hamburg-Gotha, 1832–1908.

Gerberon, G., Histoire générale du Jansénisme. 3 Vols. Amsterdam, 1700.

Gérin, Ch., Recherches historiques sur l'assemblée du clergé de France de 1682. Paris, 1869.

Gérin, Ch., L'ambassade de Lavardin et la séquestration du nonce Ranuzzi (1687–9) in Revue des quest. hist. Vol. 16 (1874).

Gérin, Ch., Le Pape Innocent XI. et la révolution anglaise de 1688. Vol. 20 (1876).

Gérin, Ch., Le Pape Innocent XI. et la révocation de l'Édit de Nantes. Vol. 24 (1878).

Gérin, Ch., L'expédition des Français à Candie en 1669. Vol. 25 (1879).

Gérin, Ch., La mission de M. de Lionne à Rome en 1655. Vol. 26 (1879).

Gérin, Ch., Le Pape Innocent XI. et l'élection de Cologne en 1688. Vol. 33 (1883).

Gérin, Ch., Le Pape Innocent XI. et le siège de Vienne en 1683 d'après des documents inédits. Vol. 39 (1886).

Gérin, Ch., Louis XIV. et le Saint-Siège. 2 Vols. Paris, 1894.

Giornale Ligustico di archeologia, storia e letteratura. Vols. 1–25. Genoa, 1875–1898.

Giornale storico della letteratura italiana, diretto e redatto da *A. Graf, F. Novati, R. Renier.* Vol. 1 seqq. Rome-Turin-Florence, 1883 seqq.

Giussani, Il Conclave di Innocenzo XI. Como, 1901.

Giustificazione della Bolla della Santità di N. S. Papa Innocenzo XI. sopra l'abolitione de' pretesi quartieri e dell'editto con il quale la chiesa di S. Luigi è stata sottoposta all'interdetto. (Edition of the date of Innocent X. in the possession of the Swedish envoy, Baron de Bildt.)

Gori, F., Archivio storico, artistico, archeologico e letterario della città e provincia di Roma. Vols. 1–4. Rome and Spoleto, 1875–1883.

(*Gosselin, J. E. A.*), Histoire littéraire de Fénelon. Lyons–Paris, 1843.

Gothein, M. L., Geschichte der Gartenkunst. Vol. 1. Jena, 1914.

(*Gramont, A.*), Mémoires du mareschal de Gramont, Duc et Pair de France. Paris, 1716.

Graesse, J. G., Trésor de livres rares et précieux. 7 Vols. Dresden, 1859–1869.
Grauert, W. H., Christina, Königin von Schweden, und ihr Hof. 2 Vols. Bonn, 1837–1842.
Gregorovius, F., Die Grabmäler der römischen Päpste. Leipzig, 1857.
Grisar, H., Geschichte Roms und der Päpste im Mittelalter. Mit besonderer Berücksichtigung von Kultur und Kunst nach den Quellen dargestellt. Vol. 1. Freiburg, 1901.
Grottanelli, L., La regina Cristina di Svezia in Roma. Florence, 1890.
Gruber, Ioh. Dan., Commercii epistolici Leibnitiani P. 12. Hanover and Göttingen, 1745.
Grünhagen, C., Geschichte Schlesiens. 2 Vols. Gotha, 1884–6.
Gualdo, Priorato Galeazzo, Historia della sacra real Maestà di Cristina Alessandra regina di Suetia. Venice, 1656.
Guarnacci, M., Vitae et res gestae Pontificum Romanorum et S. R. E. Cardinalium a Clemente X. usque ad Clementem XII. 2 Vols. Rome 1751.
Gugielmotti, Alb., Storia delle fortificazioni nella spiaggia Romana. Rome, 1880.
Gugielmotti, Alb., La squadra permanente della marina Romana. Storia dal 1573–1644. Rome, 1882.
Gulielmotti, Alb., La squadra ausilaria della marina Romana a Candia ed alla Morea. Storia dal 1644 al 1699. Rome, 1883.
Guhrauer, G. E., Leibniz's deutsche Schriften (s.l.), 1838.
Guidi, Aless., I paesi dei Colli Albani. Roma, 1880.
Guidi, M., Le Fontane barocche di Roma. Zurich, 1917.
Gurlitt, Cornelius, Geschichte des Barockstiles in Italien. Stuttgart, 1887.

Hamel de Breuil, Comte Jean du, Sobieski et sa politique de 1674 à 1683. In Revue d'hist. diplom. VII.–VIII. (1893–4).
Hammer-Purgstall, J. Frh. v., Geschichte des osmanischen Reiches. 4 Vols., 2nd ed. Pest, 1834–6.
Hanisch, Erdm., Die Geschichte Polens. Bonn-Leipzig, 1923.
Hanotaux, G., Recueil des Instructions données aux ambassadeurs et ministres de France depuis les traités de Westphalie jusqu'à la Révolution française. Vols. 6 and 17. Rome, Paris, 1888, 1911.
Hardouin, I., Conciliorum collectio regia maxima. 12 Vols. Paris, 1715.
Harnack, Ad., Lehrburch der Dogmengeschichte. 3 Vols., 4th ed. Tübingen, 1909–1910.
Hase, K. A., Kirchengeschichte auf Grundlage akademischer Vorlesungen. 3 Vols. Leipzig, 1885–1892.
Heeckeren, E. de, Correspondance de Benoît XIV. Vol. 1 (1742–9). Paris, 1912.
Heimbucher, M., Die Orden und Kongregationen der katholischen Kirche. 3 Vols., 2nd ed. Paderborn, 1907–1908.

Hempel, E., Carlo Rainaldi. Ein Beitrag zur Geschichte des römischen Barocks. (Diss.). Munich, 1919.

Hempel, E., Francesco Borromini. Vienna, 1924.

Hergenröther, J., Katholische Kirche und christlicher Staat in ihrer geschichtlichen Entwicklung und in Beziehung auf die Fragen der Gegenwart. Historisch-theologische Essays und zugleich ein Anti-Ianus vindicatus. 2nd section. Freiburg, 1872.

Hergenröther, J., Handbuch der allgemeinen Kirchengeschichte. Restated by *J. P. Kirsch*. 4 Vols., 6th ed. Freiburg, 1924–5.

Hermant, G., Mémoires sur l'histoire ecclésiastique du xviie siècle (1630–1663). Edited by Gazier. 6 Vols. Paris, 1905–1910.

Hermelink, H., Reformation und Gegenreformation. Tübingen, 1911.

Herzog, see Real-Enzyklopädie.

Hilgers, J., S.J., Der Index der verbotenen Bücher. Freiburg, 1904.

Hiltebrandt, Ph., Preussen und die römische Kurie. Vol. 1 (1625–1740). Berlin, 1910.

Hiltebrandt, Ph., Die Anfänge des direkten diplomatischen Verkehrs zwischen dem Päpstlichen und dem Preussischen Hofe. (Quellen u. Forsch. aus ital. Archiven XV., 2.) Rome, 1913.

Hiltebrandt, Ph., Die kirchlichen Reunionsverhandlungen in der zweiten Hälfte des 17. Jahrhunderts. (Bibl. des preuss. Hist. Instituts in Rom. 14). Rome, 1922.

Hinschius, P., System des katholischen Kirchenrechts. 6 Vols. Berlin, 1869 *seqq.*

Hippeau, C., Avènement des Bourbons au trône d'Espagne. 2 Vols. Paris, 1875.

Histoire des conclaves depuis Clément V. jusqu'à présent. Cologne, 1703.

Histoire des intrigues galantes de la Reine Christine, etc. Amsterdam, 1697.

Historisch-politische Blätter für das katholische Deutschland. Vol. 1 *seqq.* Munich, 1838 *seqq.*

Hjärne, H., Sigismunds svenska resor. Upsala, 1884.

Hoffmann, Theob., Entstehungsgeschichte des St. Peter in Rom. Zittau, 1928.

Huber, A., Geschichte Oesterreichs. Vol. 5. Gotha, 1893.

Hubert, E., Les Pays-Bas Espagnols et la République des Provinces Unies. La question religieuse et les relations diplomatiques, in Mémoires de l'Académie Royale de Belgique. 2nd ser. Vol. 2. Brussels, 1907.

Hughes, Thom., History of the Society of Jesus in North America, colonial and federal. Text, 2 Vols. London, 1907, 1917 ; Documents, 2 Vols., same, 1907, 1910.

Hülsen, Chr., Forum und Palatin. Munich (1926).

Huonder, A., Der chinesische Ritenstreit. Aix-la-Chapelle, 1921.

Hürben, J., Handbuch der Schweizergeschichte. 2 Vols. Stans, 1901–1909.
Hurter, H., Nomenclator literarius theologiae catholicae. 5 Vols., 3rd ed. Innsbruck, 1903 *seqq.*

Jahrbuch, Historisches, der Görres-Gesellschaft. Vols. 1–46. Münster and Munich, 1880–1928.
Jahrbuch der preussischen Kunstsammlungen. Berlin, 1880 *seqq.*
Jahrbücher, Preussische. Vol. 1 *seqq.* Berlin, 1858 *seqq.*
Jahrbücher für Schweizerische Geschichte. Vol. 1 *seqq.* Zurich, 1876 *seqq.*
Jann, A. O., Die katholischen Missionen in Indien, China und Japan. Ihre Organisation und das portugiesische Patronat vom 15. bis ins 18. Jahrh. Paderborn, 1915.

Ilg, Geist des hl. Franziskus Seraphikus, dargestellt in Lebensbildern aus der Geschichte des Kapuzinerordens. 2 Vols. Augsburg, 1876–9.
Immich, Max, Zur Vorgeschichte des Orleansschen Krieges. Heidelberg, 1898.
Immich, Max., Papst Innozenz XI., 1676–1689. Beitrag zur Geschichte seiner Politik und zur Charakteristik seiner Persönlichkeit. Berlin, 1900.
Immich, Max., Geschichte des europäischen Staatensystems von 1660–1789. Munich-Berlin, 1905.
Inventario dei monumenti di Roma. Vol. 1. Rome, 1908–1912.
Iorga, N., Geschichte des osmanischen Reiches nach den Quellen dargestellt. Vol. 3. Gotha, 1910.
Israel, F., Adam Adami und seine " Arcana pacis Westfalicae ". Berlin, 1910.
Ius Pontificium = Iuris Pontificii de Propaganda Fide. Pars 1. Vols. 1–7. Rome, 1886 *seqq.* (If not otherwise stated, the quotation is from Part I.)
Iusti, K., Velasquez und seine Zeit. 2 Vols., 3rd ed. Munich, 1922.

Károlyi, Árpád, Buda és Pest visszavivása 1686 ban a kétszázados emlékünnepély alkalmára Budapest fövárosa megbizásábál irta Dr. A. K. Budapest, 1886.
Karttunen, Liisi, Les Nonciatures Apostoliques permanentes de 1650 à 1800, in Annales Acad., scient., Fennicae. Ser. B, Vol. 5, No. 3. Geneva (Helsinski), 1912.
Katholik, Der. Zeitschrift für katholische Wissenschaft und kirchliches Leben. Ann. 1 *seqq.* Strassburg and Mayence.
Katholische Missionen, Vol. 1 *seqq.* Aix-la-Chapelle, 1873 *seqq.*
Katona, Steph., Historia critica Regum Hungariae. 41 Vols. Pest, 1779.
Keyssler, J. G., Neueste Reise durch Deutschland, Böhmen, Ungarn, die Schweiz, Italien und Lothringen. 3 Vols. Hanover, 1740.
Kirchenlexikon, Freiburger, oder Enzyklopädie der kathol. Theologie und ihrer Hilfswissenschaften. Edited by H. J.

Wetzer and B. Welte.   12 Vols.   Freiburg, 1847–1856.
2nd ed. begun by Card. Hergenröther, continued by Fr. Kaulen.
12 Vols. Freiburg, 1882–1901.
Klopp, Onno, Der Fall des Hauses Stuart und die Sukzession des
Hauses Hannover in Grossbritannien und Irland.   14 Vols.
Vienna, 1875–1888.
Klopp, Onno, Das Jahr 1683 und der folgende grosse Türkenkrieg
bis zum Frieden von Carlowitz.   Graz, 1882.
Klopp, Onno, Corrispondenza epistolare tra Leopoldo I Imperatore
ed il P. Marco d'Aviano cappuccino.   Graz, 1888.
Kluczycki, Fr., Acta regis Ioannis III. ad res anno 1683, imprimis
in expeditione Viennensi illustrandas.   Cracow, 1883.
Knuttel, W., De toestand der Katholieken onder der Republiek.
Vol. 1.   The Hague, 1892.
Köcher, A., Geschichte von Hannover und Braunschweig 1648–
1714.   2 Vols. (up to 1674).   Leipzig, 1884–5.
Köhler, Kurt, Die orientalische Politik Ludwigs XIV., ihr
Verhältnis zu dem Türkenkrieg von 1683.   (Diss.).   Leipzig,
1907.
Kolde, Th., Beiträge zur bayrischen Kirchengeschichte.   Vols.
1–18.   Erlangen, 1894 *seqq.*
Kratz, W., Landgraf Ernst von Hessen-Rheinfels und die deutschen
Jesuiten.   Freiburg, 1914.
Kunstchronik und Kunstmarkt.   Leipzig, 1866–1926.

Laborde, J. J., Athènes aux XVe., XVIe., XVIIe. siècles.   2 vols.
Paris, 1855.
Laemmer, H., Analecta Romana.   Kirchengeschichtliche
Forschungen in römischen Bibliotheken und Archiven.
Eine Denkschrift.   Schaffhausen, 1861.
Laemmer, H., Monumenta Vaticana, historiam eccles. saec. XVI.
illustrantia.   Freiburg, 1861.
Laemmer, H., Zur Kirchengeschichte des 16. und 17. Jahrh.
Freiburg, 1863.
Laemmer, H., Meletematum Romanorum mantissa.   Ratisbon,
1875.
Lancellotti, Fil. di, Secondo Centenario della liberazione di
Vienna dall'assedio dei Turchi (1683–1883).   Rome, 1883.
Lancellotti, Fil. di, Pel secondo Centenario della cacciata dei
Turchi da Buda.   Rome, 1886.
Lanciani, R. A., Ancient Rome in the light of recent Discoveries.
London-Cambridge, 1888.
Landau, Markus, Rom, Wien, Neapel während des spanischen
Erbfolgekrieges.   Leipzig, 1885.
Lang, Ch., Catalogue of the curious and valuable Library of Ch.
P. L.   London, 1842.
Lauer, Ph., Le Palais du Latran.   Paris, 1911.
Launay, A., Histoire générale de la Société des Étrangères.
Paris, 1894.
Lavisse, E., Histoire de France.   Vol. 1 *seqq.*   Paris, 1901 *seqq.*

(Le Camus, Ét.) Lettres du cardinal Le Camus, évêque et prince de Grenoble (1632–1707). Published by P. Ingold. Paris, 1892.

Legrand, E., Bibliographie hellénique ou Description raisonnée des ouvrages publiés en grec par les Grecs au XVIIᵉ. siècle. 4 Vols. Paris, 1894–6.

Legrelle, A., La diplomatie française et la succession d'Espagne (1659–1725). 4 Vols. Paris, 1888–1892.

Lehmann, M., Preussen und die katholische Kirche seit 1640. Vol. 1–9, Leipzig, 1878–1902.

Lemmens, L., Acta s. Congregationis de Propaganda Fide pro Terra Santa. Quaracchi, 1921–2.

Lemmens, Leonh., Geschichte der Franziskanermissionen. Münster, 1928.

Le Roy, A., Un Janséniste en exil. Correspondance de Pasquier Quesnel. Paris, 1909.

Letarouilly-Simil, Le Vatican et la basilique de St.-Pierre de Rome. 2 Vols. Paris, 1882.

Levinson, A., Nuntiaturberichte vom Kaiserhof Leopolds I. 1st Part : February, 1657–December, 1669, in Archiv. für österr., Geschichte CIII. (1913) ; 2nd Part : May, 1670–August, 1679, ibid. CVI. (1918).

Linage de Vauciennes, P., Différend des Barbarins avec le Pape Innocent X. Paris, 1678 *seqq.*

Lingard, John, A history of England from the first Invasion by the Romans. Vols. 7–9. London, 1838 *seqq.*

Lippi, M. G., Vita di Papa Innocenzo XI., ed con aggiunte a cura del P. Fr. G. Berthier. Milan, 1899.

Litta, P., Famiglie celebri italiane. Disp. 1–183. Milan and Turin, 1819–1881.

Lundorp, M. C., Acta publica. Frankfurt, 1621–5.

Lünig, I. Chr., Publicorum negotiorum ab Aug. Romanorum Imperatore . . . Sylloge. 2 Vols. Frankfurt-Leipzig, 1694–1702.

Lünig, I. Chr., Deutsches Reichsarchiv. 24 Vols. Leipzig, 1710–1722.

Lünig, I. Chr., Litterae procerum Europae. Vols. 2 and 3. Leipzig, 1712.

Lünig, I. Chr., Orationes procerum Europae eorumque ministrorum ac legatorum. Vols. 2 and 3. Leipzig, 1713.

Lünig, I. Chr., Europäische Staatskonsilia. 2 Vols. Leipzig, 1715.

Lünig, I. Chr., Codex Italiae diplomaticus. Frankfurt-Leipzig, 1725–1735.

Lünig, I. Chr., Bibliotheca deductionum S. R. I. Leipzig, 1748.

Maas, P. O., Cartas de Cina, Documentos inéditos sobre misiones franciscanas del siglo XVII. 2 Vols. Seville, 1917.

Mabillonius, I., Iter italicum, in Museum italicum I., i. Paris, 1724–1789.

Macaulay, Th. B., History of England from the Accession of

James II. 5 Vols. London, 1848–1861. (In German, Leipzig, 1860–1, Brunswick, 1868.)

Macchia, Relazione del P. Sforza Pallavicino con Fabio Chigi. Turin, 1907.

Mackintosh, J., History of the Revolution in England in 1688. London, 1834.

Maes, C., Curiosità di Roma. 2 Vols. Rome, 1885.

Magni, G., Il barocco nell'architettura a Roma. Turin, 1911.

Malvasia, C. C., Felsina pittrice. Vite de'pittori Bolognesi. 2 Vols. Bologna, 1841.

Manni, D. M. Istoria degli Anni Santi. Florence, 1750.

Marcellino da Civezza (O. F. M.), Storia delle missioni francescane. Vol. 2, 1st Part. Prato, 1883.

Marchesan, A., Lettere inedite di O. Rinaldi. Treviso, 1896.

Marchesi, Buonaccorsi G. V., Antichità del Protonotariato Apostolico Participante. Fayance, 1751.

Margraf, J., Kirche und Sklaverei seit der Entdeckung Amerikas. Tübingen, 1865.

Mariéjol, Histoire de France. (Histoire de France by Lavisse. Vol. 6.) Paris, 1904.

Marini, G., Memorie istoriche degli archivi della Santa Sede. Ed. A. Mai. Rome, 1825.

Marsand, A., I manoscritti italiani della Regia biblioteca Parigina. 2 Vols. Paris, 1835 *seqq.*

Martin, V., Le Gallicanisme et la Réforme catholique. Essai hist. sur l'introduction en France des décrets du concile de Trente 1563–1615. Paris, 1919.

Martinelli, F., Roma ricercata nel suo sito e nella scuola di tutti gli antiquarii. Rome, 1644.

Maura, Gamazo G., Carlos II. y su corte. 2 Vols. Madrid, 1911–1915.

Maurer, Jos., Kardinal Leopold Graf Kollonitsch, Primas von Ungarn. Innsbruck, 1887.

Maynard, Les Provinciales ou les Lettres écrites par L. de Montalte, et leur réfutation. 2 Vols. Paris, 1851.

Mazarin, G., Lettres du card. Mazarin pendant son ministère, recueillies et publiées par M. A. Chéruel (s. l). 1835.

Mazure, F. A. J., Histoire de la révolution de 1688 en Angleterre. 3 Vols. Paris, 1825.

Mazzatinti, G., Inventari dei manoscritti delle biblioteche d'Italia. Turin, 1887.

Mazzuchelli, G. M., Gli scrittori d'Italia. 2 Vols. Brescia, 1753.

Mededeelingen van het Nederlandsche Historisch Instituut te Rome. Vol. 1 *seqq.* 's Gravenhage, 1921 *seqq.*

Meiern, I. G., Acta pacis executionis publicae. 2 Vols. Hanover-Göttingen, 1737.

Mejer, O., Die Propaganda, ihre Provinzen und ihr Recht. 2 Vols. Göttingen, 1852.

Mélanges d'archéologie et d'histoire. (École Française de Rome.) Vol. 1 *seqq.* Paris, 1881 *seqq.*

Mémoires de l'Académie de Marseille.   2nd Series, Vol. 1 *seqq.*
Marseilles, 1846 *seqq.*
Menčik, F., Volba Papeže Innocence X.   Prague, 1894.
Menéndez, y Pelayo M., Historia de los heterodoxos españoles.
2 Vols. Madrid, 1880–1.
Mention, L., Documents relatifs aux rapports du clergé avec la
royauté aux XVII. et XVIII. siècles. Vol. 2 : 1705–1789.
Paris, 1903.
Mentz, G., Johann Philipp von Schönborn, Kurfürst von Mainz,
Bischof von Würzburg und Worms 1605–1675.   2 Vols.
Jena, 1896–9.
Menzel, K. A., Neuere Geschichte der Deutschen von der Reforma-
tion bis zum Bundesakt. 12 Vols. Berlin, 1826–1848.
Mergentheim, Leo, Die Quinquennalfakultäten pro foro externo.
2 Vols. Stuttgart, 1908.
Metzler, I., Die Apostolischen Vikariate des Nordens. Paderborn,
1919.
Meyer, Albert de, Les premières controverses jansénistes en
France (1640–9).   Louvain, 1917.
Michael, E., Ignax von Döllinger. Innsbruck, 1891.
Michaud, E., Louis XIV. et Innocent XI.   4 Vols. Paris,
1882–3.
Michaud, E., La politique de compromis avec Rome en 1689.
Le Pape Alexandre VIII. et le Duc de Chaulnes, d'après les
correspondances diplomatiques inédites du Ministère des
Affaires étrangères de France. Berne, 1888.
Mignanti, F. M., Istoria della sacrosancta patriarcale basilica
Vaticana. Rome, 1867.
Mignet, F. A. M., Notices et mémoires historiques.   2 Vols.
Paris, 1843.
Mirbt, C., Quellen zur Geschichte des Papsttums und des römischen
Katholizismus. 4 ed. Tübingen, 1924.
Miscellanea di storia ecclesiastica e studii ausiliari. Quad. 1–8.
Rome, 1899–1901.
Miscellanea di storia italiana. Turin, 1833–1880.
Mitteilungen des Instituts für österreichische Geschichtsforschung.
Vol.1 *seqq.* Innsbruck, 1880 *seqq.*
Mitteilungen des Vereins für die Geschichte der Deutschen in
Böhmen. Vol. 1 *seqq.* Prague, 1862.
Mitteilungen des k. u. k. Kriegsarchivs.   Vol. 1 *seqq.* Vienna,
1876–1914.
Mitteilungen des Vereins für Geschichte der Stadt Wien. Vol. 1
seqq. Vienna, 1919 *seqq.*
Month, The, Vol. 1 *seqq.* London, 1864 *seqq.*
Monumenta ordinis fratrum Praedicatorum historica.   Vol. 1
seqq. Louvain, 1896 *seqq.*
Moran, P. F., Spicilegium Ossoriense. 3rd Series. Dublin, 1874–
1884.
Moroni, G., Dizionario di erudizione storico-ecclesiastica da
San Pietro sino ai nostri giorni. 109 Vols. Venice, 1840–
1879.

Mourret, F., Histoire générale de l'Eglise. L'Ancien Régime. Paris (1912).
Moüy, Ch. de, L'ambassade du Duc de Créqui. 2 Vols. Paris, 1893.
Mozzi, Luigi, Storia delle revolutioni della chiesa d'Utrecht. Vols. 1-3. Venice, 1787.
Müllbauer, Max, Geschichte der katholischen Missionen in Ostindien von Vasco di Gama bis zur Mitte des 18. Jahrhunderts. Munich, 1851.
Muñoz, Ant., Roma barocca. Milan-Rome, 1919.
Muñoz, Ant., Sei e settecento Italiano : Francesco Borromini. Rome, 1921. Pietro da Cortona, *ibid.*. 1921. Bernini, *ibid.* 1925.
Muratori Il. Vol. 1 *seqq.* Rome, 1892 *seqq.*
Mussi, Alcune memorie di conclavi del secolo XVII. Assisi, 1915.

Narducci, H., Catalogus codicum manuscriptorum in Bibliotheca Angelica. Rome, 1893.
Navenne, F. de, Rome et le Palais Farnèse pendant les trois derniers siècles. 2 Vols. Paris, 1923.
Newald, Joh., Beiträge zur der Belagerung von Wien durch die Türken im Jahre 1683. 2 Vols. Vienna, 1883-4.
Nibby, A., Le mura di Roma. Rome, 1820.
Niceron, J. P., Nachrichten von den Begebenheiten und Schriften berühmter Gelehrten. Part 23. Halle, 1749-1771.
Nippold, F., Die römisch-katholische Kirche im Königreich der Niederlande. Leipzig, 1877.
Noack, Fr., Das Deutschtum in Rom seit dem Ausgang des Mittelalters. 2 Vols. Stuttgart, 1927.
Nöthen, C. M., Geschichte aller Jubeljahre und ausserordentlichen Jubiläen der katholischen Kirche. Ratisbon, 1875.
Nouvelle Revue historique de droit français et étranger. Vol. 1 *seqq.* Paris, 1877 *seqq.*
Novaes, G. de, Storia de' Pontefici. Vols. 8 and 9. Siena, 1805.
Numizmatikai Közlöny. Vol. 1 *seqq.* Budapest, 1902 *seqq.*
Nuova Antologia di lettere, scienze ed arti. Vol. 1 *seqq.* Florence-Rome, 1866 *seqq.*
Nuovo Archivio Veneto. Vol. 1 *seqq.* Venice, 1891-1921.

Oberbayrisches Archiv für vaterländische Geschichte, Vol. 1. Munich, 1839 *seqq.*
Odhner, Die Politik Schwedens im westfälischen Friedenskongress. Gotha, 1877.
Ortolani, S., S. Giovanni in Laterano. Rome (1925).
Ottieri, Fr. M., Istoria delle guerre avenute in Europa. Rome, 1728.
Oud, Holland, Nieuwe Bijdragen voor de Geschiedenis der Nederlandsche Kunst. Vol. 1 *seqq.* Amsterdam, 1883 *seqq.*
Ozzola, L., L'arte alla corte d'Alessandro VII. im Arch. della Soc. Rom. di storia patria XXXI.

Pagliucchi, P., I castellani del Castel S. Angelo. 2 Vols. Rome, 1928.

Pallavicino, Sf., Della vita di Alessandro VII. 2 Vols. Prato, 1839–1840.

Parent, P., L'architecture des Pays-Bas méridionaux au XVI.- XVIIIᵉ. siècles. Paris, 1926.

Pascoli, L., Vite de' pittori, scultori ed architetti moderni. 2 Vols. Rome, 1730–1742.

Pasini, Frassoni, Armorial des Papes. Rome, 1906.

Pasolini, P. D., 18 documenti inediti su Alessandro VIII. Imola, 1888.

Pasolini, P. D., Ravenna e le sue grandi memorie. Rome, 1912.

Passeri, G. B., Vite de' pittori, scultori ed architetti che hanno lavorato in Roma, morti dal 1641 fino al 1673. Rome, 1772.

Pastor, L. von., Die Stadt Rom zu Ende der Renaissance. 4th and 6th ed. Freiburg, 1925.

(Patouillet, Louis), Dictionnaire des livres jansénistes. 4 Vols. Antwerp, 1752.

Periodico della Società Storica per la provincia e antica diocesi di Como. Vol. 1 *seqq.* Como, 1878.

Péterffy, C., Sacra concilia ecclesiae romano-catholicae in regno Hungariae celebrata ab anno MXVI. usque ad annum MDCCXV. Viennae Austriae, 1742.

Petrucelli, della Gattina F., Histoire diplomatique des conclaves. Vol. 2 *seq.* Paris, 1864 *seq.*

Pflugk-Harttung, I. v., Iter Italicum, Stuttgart, 1883.

Pflugk-Harttung, I. v., Weltgeschichte. Neuzeit. Berlin, 1908.

Philippson, Das Zeitalter Ludwigs XIV. (Anthology by Oncken.) Berlin, 1879.

Philipuccius, Franc. Xav. (S.J.), De Sinensium ritibus politicis acta seu Praeludium ad plenam disquisitionem, an bona vel mala fide impugnentur opiniones et praxes missionariorum Societatis Iesu in regno Sinarum ad cultum Confucii et defunctorum pertinentes. Paris, 1700.

Phillips, G. J., Kirchenrecht. Vols. 1–7. Ratisbon, 1845–1872. Vol. 8, 1st section of *F. H. Bering*, ibid. 1889.

Phillips, G. J., Das Regalienrecht in Frankreich. Halle, 1873.

Piccolomini, P., Corrispondenza tra la corte di Roma e l'Inquisitore di Malta durante la guerra di Candia 1645–1669. Florence, 1908.

Picot, Essai historique sur l'influence de la religion en France pendant le XVIIᵉ siècle. Vol. 1. Louvain, 1824.

Pieper, A., Die Propaganda-Kongregation und die Nordischen Missionen im 17. Jahrh. Cologne, 1886.

Pieraccini, G., La stirpe de' Medici di Cafaggiolo. 3 Vols. Florence, (1924–5).

Pierling, P., Rome et Démétrius. Paris, 1878.

Pierling, P., Saxe et Moscou. Paris, 1893.

Pierling, P., La Russie et le Saint-Siège. Études diplomatiques. Vol. 4. Paris, 1907.

Piolet, J.-B., Les Missions catholiques françaises. 6 Vols. Paris, 1902–1903.
Pirenne, H., Geschichte Belgiens. Vol. 4. Gotha, 1909.
Platner-Bunsen, Beschreibung der Stadt Rom, von Ernst Platner, Karl Bunsen, Eduard Gerhard und Wilhelm Röstell. 3 Vols. Stuttgart and Tübingen, 1829–1842.
Platzhoff, W., Ludwig XIV. das Kaisertum und die europäische Krisis von 1683, from the Hist. Zeitschr. Vol. 121 (1920).
Polidori, P., De vita et rebus gestis Clementis Undecimi . . . libri sex. 1727.
Poncelet, Alfred, La Compagnie de Jésus en Belgique (1907).
Posse, H., Der römische Maler Andrea Sacchi. Leipzig, 1925.
Pray, Georg, Geschichte der Streitigkeiten über die chinesischen Gebräuche. 3 Vols. Augsburg, 1791.
Pribram, A. F., Franz Paul Frh. v. Lisola (1613–1674) und die Politik seiner Zeit. Leipzig, 1894.
Pribram, A. F., Venezianische Depeschen vom Kaiserhofe. II., 1 : 1659–1661. Vienna, 1901.
Proc. Summ., see Congregationis.
Pufendorf, S. de, De rebus gestis Friderici III. electoris Brandenburgici, post primi Borussiae regis commentariorum libri 3 complectentes annos 1688–1699, ed. E. F. de Hertzberg. Berlin, 1784.
Puyol, Edmond Richer, Étude sur la rénovation du Gallicanisme au commencement du XVIIe siècle. 2 Vols. Paris, 1876.

Quartalschrift, Römische, für christliche Altertumskunde und für Kirchengeschichte. Ed. by A. de Waal, H. Finke, and St. Ehses. No. 1 *seqq.* Rome, 1887.
Quartalschrift, Tübinger Theologische. No. 1 *seqq.* Tübingen, 1819.
Quellen und Forschungen aus italienischen Archiven und Bibliotheken. Ed. by Preuss. Hist. Institut. Vol. 1 *seqq.* Rome, 1898 *seqq.*

Ranke, L. v., Französische Geschichte vornehmlich im 16. und 17. Jahrh. Vol. 3, 2nd ed. Stuttgart, 1855.
Ranke, L. v., Englische Geschichte. Vol. 1 *seqq.* Berlin, 1859 *seqq.*
Ranke, L. v., Die römischen Päpste in den letzten vier Jahrhunderten. 1st and 3rd Vols., 6th and 7th ed. Leipzig, 1885.
Rapin, R., Histoire du Jansénisme. Ed. by Domenech. Paris, 1861.
Rapin, R., Mémoires sur l'Eglise et la société, la cour, la ville et le Jansénisme, ed. by L. Aubineau. 3 Vols. Paris, 1865.
Raess, A., Die Konvertiten seit der Reformation nach ihrem Leben und aus ihren Schriften dargestellt. 13 Vols. Freiburg, 1866–1880.
Rassegna Nazionale. Vol. 1 *seqq.* Florence, 1879 *seqq.*
Ratti, N., Delle famiglie Sforza-Cesarini, Savelli, Peretti, Montalto, etc. 2 Vols. Rome, 1794.
Real-Enzyklopädie für protest. Theologie und Kirche, founded

on and edited by J. J. Herzog. 23 vols, 3rd ed., by A. Hauck. Leipzig, 1896–1909.

Recherches de science religieuse. Vol. 1 *seqq.* Paris, 1910 *seqq.*

Recueil des Instructions, see Farges, Hanotaux.

Redlich, Osw., Geschichte Oesterreichs. Vol. 6. Oesterreichs Grossmachtbildung in der Zeit Kaiser Leopolds I. (Allg. Staatengeschichte, 1, 25). Gotha, 1921.

Renazzi, F. M., Storia dell'Università degli studi di Roma detta communemente la Sapienza. 4 Vols. Rome, 1803 *seqq.*

Reniger, von Reningen, Die Hauptrelation des kaiserlichen Residenten in Konstantinopel R. v. R. 1649–1666. Ed. by A. Veltzé. (Mitteil. des k.u.k. Kriegsarchivs N.F. 12.) Vienna, 1900.

Renner, V. v., Wien im Jahre 1683. Vienna, 1883.

Repertorium für Kunstwissenschaft. Vol. 1 *seqq.* Stuttgart, 1876 *seq.*

Reumont, A. v., Die Carafa von Maddaloni. 2 Vols. Berlin, 1851.

Reumont, A. v., Bibliografia dei lavori pubblicati in Germania sulla storia d'Italia. Berlin, 1863.

Reumont, A. v., Geschichte der Stadt Rom. Vol. 3. Berlin, 1870.

Reumont, A. v., Geschichte Toskanas. 1st Part. Gotha, 1876.

Reusch, H., Der Index der verbotenen Bücher. 2 Vols. Bonn, 1883–5.

Revue des questions historiques. Vol. 1 *seqq.* Paris, 1866 *seqq.*

Revue des questions scientifiques. Vol. 1 *seqq.* Louvain, 1877 *seqq.*

Revue des sciences religieuses. Vol. 1 *seqq.* Paris, 1921 *seqq.*

Revue d'histoire de l'église de France. Vol. 1 *seqq.* 1910 *seqq.*

Revue d'histoire diplomatique. Vol. 1 *seqq.* Paris, 1887 *seqq.*

Revue d'histoire ecclésiastique. Vol. 1 *seqq.* Louvain, 1900 *seqq.*

Revue d'histoire ecclésiastique Suisse. Vol. 1 *seqq.* Stans, 1914 *seqq.*

Revue d'histoire et de littérature religieuses Vol. 1 *seqq.* Paris, 1897–1922.

Revue historique. Vol. 1 *seqq.* Paris, 1876 *seqq.*

Revue Thomiste. Vol. 1 *seqq.* Paris, 1893 *seqq.*

Reymond, U., Le Bernini. Paris, 1910.

Reyssié, F., Le cardinal de Bouillon, 1647–1714. Paris, 1899.

Ricci, C., Geschichte der Kunst in Norditalien. Stuttgart, 1911.

Ricci, C., Baukunst und dekorative Skulptur der Barockzeit in Italien. Stuttgart, 1912.

Riezler, S., Geschichte Bayerns. Vols. 5–7. Gotha, 1903–1913.

Rinaldi, E., La fondazione del Collegio Romano. Memorie storiche. Rome, 1914.

(*Rinckh Euch, Gottl.*), Leopolds des Grossen Röm. Kaysers wunderwürdiges Leben und Thaten. Leipzig, 1708.

Ritter, M., Deutsche Geschichte im Zeitalter der Gegenreformation und des Dreissigjährigen Krieges (1555–1648). 3 Vols. Stuttgart, 1889–1908.

Rivista di artiglieria e genio. Rome, 1884–1905.

Rivista del Collegio Araldico. Vol. 1 *seqq.* Rome, 1903 *seqq.*

Rivista Europea. 3 Serien. Milan, 1834–1847.

Rivista storica Benedittina. Vol. 1 *seqq.* Rome, 1906 *seqq.*
Rivista storica italiana. Vol. 1 *seqq.* Turin, 1884 *seqq.*
Rocco (Cocchia) da Cesinale, Storia delle missioni dei Cappuccini. 3 Vols. Paris, 1867.
Rochemonteix, Camille de, S.J., Les Jésuites de la Nouvelle-France au XVIIᵉ. siècle. 3 Vols. Paris, 1895.
Röder, von Diersburg Ph., Des Markgrafen Ludwig Hermann von Baden Feldzüge wider die Türken. Karlsruhe, 1859.
Rodocanachi, E., Le Capitole Romain antique et moderne. Paris, 1904.
Roma. Rivista di studi e di vita Romana, diretta da Carlo Galassi Paluzzi. Rome, 1922 *seqq.*
Romanin, S., Storia documentata di Venezia. 10 Vols. Venice, 1853–1861.
Rose, H., Spätbarock. Munich, 1922.
Roskovány, Aug. de, Monumenta catholica pro independentia potestatis ecclesiasticae ab imperio civili. 6 Vols. Fünfkirchen-Pest-Vienna, 1847–1865.
Rossi, G. G., Il nuovo teatro delle fabriche ed edificii in prospettiva di Roma moderna sotto il pontificato di N. S. P. Alessandro VII. Rome, 1665.
Rousset, C., Histoire de Louvois et de son administration politique et militaire. 4 Vols. Paris, 1886.
Ruggieri, G. S., Diario dell'Anno del santo giubileo (1750) s.l. nè a.
Ruhemann, Alfr., Die Pontinischen Sümpfe. Ihre Geschichte, ihre Zukunft. Leipzig, 1900.
Rushworth, J., Historical Collections of private Passages of State. 8 Vols. London, 1659.

Saggiatore, Il, Giornale Romano di storia, letteratura, etc. Rome, 1844–6.
Sägmüller, Joh. Bapt., Die Papstwahlbullen und das staatliche Recht der Exklusive. Tübingen, 1892.
Saint-Amour, L. G., Journal de ce qui s'est fait à Rome dans l'affaire des cinq propositions (s.l.), 1622.
Sainte-Beuve, C. A., Port Royal. 4th ed. Paris, 1878.
Saint-Disdier, T. de, Histoire des négociations de la paiz de Nimègue. Paris, 1680.
Saint-Simon, Duc de, Mémoires sur le règne de Louis XIV., ed. by A. de Boislisle. 21 Vols. Paris, 1879–1909.
Salvandy, N. A. de, Histoire de Pologne avant et sous le roi Jean Sobiesky. 3 Vols., 2nd ed. Paris, 1830.
Salzburger Chronik für Stadt und Land. Vol. 1 *seqq.* Salzburg, 1865 *seqq.*
Sardi, G., Il cardinale G. B. Spada e il conclave del 1670. Lucca, 1920.
Sattler, Ehr. Fr., Geschichte des Herzogthums Würtemberg unter der Regierung der Herzogen. 14 Vols. Ulm, 1769–1784.
Sauer, Aug., Rom und Wien im Jahre 1683. Ausgewählte Aktenstücke aus römischen Archiven. Vienna, 1883.

Sayous, Le cardinal Buonvisi, Nonce du Pape, et la croisade de Bude 1684-6, in Acad. des sciences morales et politiques. Paris, 1889.

Schäfer, H., Geschichte von Portugal. 5 Vols. Hamburg, 1836 *seqq.*

Scheible, I., Die gute alte Zeit. Stuttgart, 1847.

Schill, Andr., Die Konstitution Unigenitus, ihre Veranlassung und ihre Folgen. Freiburg, 1876.

Schlegel, Joh. Car., Kirchen und Reformationsgeschichte von Norddeutschland und den Hannoverschen Staaten. 2 Vols. Hanover, 1828-9.

Schmerber, Hugo, Betrachtungen über die italienische Malerei im 17. Jahrh. Strassburg, 1906.

Schmidl, I., Historiae Societatis Jesu provinciae Bohemiae Pars I.-IV. Prague, 1747-1759.

Schmidlin, J., Geschichte der deutschen Nationalkirche in Rom. S. Maria dell'Anima. Freiburg, 1906.

Schmidlin, J., Die Restaurationstätigkeit der Breslauer Fürstbischöfe nach ihren frühesten Statusberichten an den römischen Stuhl. Rome, 1907.

Schmidlin, J., Katholische Missionsgeschichte. Steyl (1925).

Schmidt, Julian, Geschichte des geistigen Lebens in Deutschland von Leibniz bis auf Lessings Tod, 1681-1781. 2 Vols. Leipzig, 1862-4.

Schröckh, Kirchengeschichte. 3 Vols. Leipzig, 1805.

Schudt, L., Giulio Mancini. Viaggio per Roma per vedere le pitture. Leipzig, 1923.

Schweizerische Rundschau. Vol. 1 *seqq.* Stans, 1900 *seqq.*

Scuola Cattolica, La, 4th Series. Vol. 1 *seqq.* Milan, 1902 *seqq.*

Séché, L., Les derniers Jansénistes. 3 Vols. Paris, 1891.

Serafini, C., Le monete e le bolle plumbee pontificie del Medagliere Vaticano. 4 Vols. Rome, 1910 *seqq.*

Serbat, L., Les assemblées du clergé de France. Paris, 1906.

Sfondrati, Coel., Gallia vindicata. St. Gall, 1687.

Shea, History of the Catholic Missions in the United States. 1854.

Sickel, Th. v., Römische Berichte. 5 Parts (Sitzungsber. der Akad. 133, 135, 141, 143, 144). Vienna, 1895-1901.

Simeoni, Francesco I. d'Este e la politica italiana del Mazarino. Bologna, 1922.

Siri, Vitt., Il Mercurio. Casale, 1668.

Sol, E., Les rapports de la France avec l'Italie d'après la série K des Archives Nationales. Paris, 1905.

Sommervogel, C., S.J., Bibliothèque de la Compagnie de Jésus, p.p. de Backer. New Ed., 9 Vols. Brussels-Paris, 1890-1900.

Sotwell, Nathanael, Bibliotheca Scriptorum Societatis Iesu. Rome, 1676.

Spicilegio Vaticano di documenti inediti e rari estratti dagli archivi e dalla bibl. della Sede Apost. Vol. 1. Rome, 1890.

Spillmann, Joseph, S.J., Geschichte der Katholikenverfolgung in

England 1535–1681, 4th Part. Die Blutzeugen unter Jakob I., Karl I. und dem Commonwealth 1603–1654. Freiburg, 1905.

Spittler, C. Th. Frh. v., Geschichte des Fürstentums Hannover. 2 Vols. (Complete works, Vols. 6–7.) Stuttgart-Tübingen, 1828–1835.

Steinberger, L., Die Jesuiten und die Friedensfrage in der Zeit vom Prager Frieden bis zum Nürnberger Friedensexekutions-hauptrezess. 1635–1650. Freiburg, 1906.

Steinhuber, Andr., Geschichte des Kollegium Germanikum Hungarikum in Rom. Vol. 2, 2nd ed. Freiburg, 1906.

Steinmann, Ernst, Die Plünderung Roms durch Bonaparte. Leipzig (1917).

Stieve, F., Abhandlungen, Vorträge und Reden. Leipzig, 1908.

Stimmen aus Maria-Laach. Vol. 1 *seqq.* Freiburg, 1871 *seqq.*

Straganz, Max, Illustrierte Weltgeschichte. 4 Vols. Vienna (1910–1914).

Streit, R., Bibliotheca Missionum. Monasterii, 1916 *seqq.*

Studi e documenti di storia e diritto. Pubblicazione periodica dell'Accademia di conferenze storico-giuridiche. No. 1 *seqq.* Rome, 1880 *seqq.*

Studiën, Nieuwe theologische. Vol. 1 *seqq.* The Hague, 1918 *seqq.*

Studien und Kritiken, Theologische. Vols. 1–70. Hamburg, 1828–1897.

Sylvius, Lodewijk, Historien onses Tyds. Amsterdam, 1685.

Synopsis Actorum S. Sedis in causa Societatis Iesu. 1605–1773. Louvain, 1895. (Ed. as MS., not for sale.) Quoted as : Synopsis II.

Taja, Agostino, Descrizione del Palazzo Apostolico Vaticano. Posthumous work, revised and enlarged. Rome, 1750.

Tcharykow, N., Une ambassade Russe à Rome au XVIIe. siècle : Paul Menzies de Pitfodels. (Extract from Cosmos Catholicus, 1901.)

Terlinden, Le Pape Clément IX. Louvain, 1904.

Tesori della corte Romana in varie relationi. Brussels, 1672.

Theatrum Europaeum. Vols. 3–21 (1633–1718). Frankfurt, 1639–1738.

Thein, Papst Innozenz XI. und die Türkengefahr im Jahre 1863. (Diss.). Breslau, 1912.

Theiner, Aug., Monuments historiques relatifs aux règnes d'Alexis Michaelowitsch, Féodor III. et Pierre le Grand Czars de Russie. Rome, 1859.

Theiner, Aug., Vetera monumenta Poloniae et Lithuaniae gentiumque finitimarum historiam illustrantia maximam partem nondum edita, ex tabulariis Vaticanis deprompta, collecta ac serie chronologica disposita ab A. Th. Vol. 3 : A Sixto PP. V. usque ad Innocentium PP. XII. 1585–1696. Rome, 1863.

Thieme, U., and *Becker, F.*, Allgemeines Lexikon der bildenden

Künstler von der Antike bis zur Gegenwart. Vol. 1 *seqq.* Leipzig, 1907 *seqq.*

Thomas, A., Histoire de la Mission de Pékin. Paris, 1923.

Thürheim, A. v., Feldmarschall Ernst Rüdiger Graf Starhemberg. Vienna, 1882.

Tiraboschi, G., Storia della letteratura italiana. 10 Vols. Modena, 1772 *seqq.*

Titi, F., Descrizione delle pitture, sculture e architetture esposte al pubblico in Roma. Rome, 1763.

Tomassetti, Giuseppe, La Compagna Romana antica, medioevale e moderna. Vols. 1–4. Rome, 1910 *seq.*

Tomba, Ph. N., Arcivescovi di Bologna. Bologna, 1787.

Tourtual, F., Geschichte des Westfälischen Friedens. Münster, 1874.

Trenta, Memorie per servire alla storia politica del card. Franc. Buonvisi. 2 Vols. Lucca, 1818.

Turba, G., Venetianische Depeschen vom Kaiserhofe. 3 Vols. Vienna, 1889–1895.

Uebersberger, H., Russlands Orientpolitik in den letzten zwei Jahrhunderten. Vol. 1. Stuttgart, 1913.

Ughelli, F., Italia sacra, sive de episcopis Italiae et insularum adiacentium rebusque ab iis gestis opus. Ed. 2, ed. N. Coletus. 10 Vols. Venice, 1717–1722.

Ungarische Revue. 15 Vols. Budapest-Leipzig, 1881–1895.

Urbain, Ch., and *Levesque, E.,* Correspondance de Bossuet. Paris, 1909 *seqq.*

Vachon, M., La France et l'Autriche au siège de Vienne en 1683 d'après des documents tirés des Archives du Ministère des Affaires étrangères in La Nouvelle Revue XXIII. (1883).

Valiero, Andrea, Historia della guerra di Candia. Venice, 1679.

Vancsa, Geschichte der Stadt Wien. 4 Vols. Vienna, 1909.

⟨*Varet*⟩, Relation de ce qui s'est passé dans l'affaire de la paix de l'Eglise sous le Pape Clément XI., avec les lettres, actes, mémoires et autres pièces qui y ont rapport. 2 Vols. (s.l.), 1796.

Visco, E., La politica della S. Sede nella rivoluzione di Masaniello. Da documenti dell'Arch. Vatic. Naples, 1923.

Vita d'arte. Rivista mensile d'arte antica e moderna. Vol. 1–6. Siena, 1908–1913.

Viti, Mariani, La Spagna e la S. Sede. 1 : Il matrimonio del Re di Spagna con D. Maria Anna arciducessa d'Austria, 1646–9. Rome, 1899.

Voss, H., Die Malerei der Spätrenaissance in Rom und Florenz. 2 Vols. Berlin, 1920.

Wagner, F., Historia Leopoldi Magni caes, aug. 2 parts. Aug. Vindel, 1719–1931.

Wahrmund, I., Das Ausschliessungsrecht (ius exclusivae) bei den Papstwahlen. Vienna, 1899.

Walewski, A. v., Geschichte der Heiligen Ligue und Leopolds I. (1657–1700). Cracow, 1857.

Weech, F. v., Badische Geschichte. Karlsruhe, 1890.

Weisbach, W., Der Barock als Kunst der Gegenreformation. Berlin, 1921.

Weiss, J. B. v., Lehrbuch der Weltgeschichte. Vol. 5. Vienna, 1884.

Weiss, Karl P., Antonio di Escobar y Mendoza als Moraltheologe in Pascals Beleuchtung und im Lichte der Wahrheit. Klagenfurt, 1908.

Werner, Carl, Franz Suarez und die Scholastik der letzten Jahrhunderte. 2 Vols. Ratisbon, 1861.

Widmann, H., Geschichte Salzburgs. 3 Vols. Gotha, 1907.

Wiedemann, Th., Geschichte der Reformation und Gegenreformation im Lande unter der Enns. 5 Vols. Prague, 1879–1886.

Wieselgren, H., Drottning Kristinas bibliotek ich bibliotekarien fore hennes besättning i Rom. Stockholm, 1901.

Wölfflin, H., Renaissance und Barock, 4th ed., by Rose. Munich, 1926.

Wurzbach, C. v., Biographisches Lexikon des Kaisertums Oesterreich. 60 Vols. Vienna, 1856–1891.

Zaleski, K. St., Jesuici w Polsce. Vol. 1–4. Lwów, 1900–5.

Zaluski, Andr. Chr., Epistolarum historico-familiarium tomus I., continens acta regum Michaelis et Joannis III. Brunsbergae, 1709.

Zeitschrift des Aachener Geschichtsvereins. Vol. 1 *seqq.* Aix-la-Chapelle, 1880 *seqq.*

Zeitschrift für Aszese und Mystik. Vol. 1 *seqq.* Innsbruck, 1925 *seqq.*

Zeitschrift für die Geschichte des Oberrheins. Ed. under the Badischen Hist. Kommission. Vol. 1 *seqq.* Freiburg, 1886–1892 ; Karlsruhe, 1893 *seqq.*

Zeitschrift für Geschichte der Architektur. Vol. 1 *seqq.* Heidelberg, 1907 *seqq.*

Zeitschrift für die Geschichte und Altertumskunde Ermlands. Vol. 1 *seq.* Mayence and Braunsberg, 1860 *seqq.*

Zeitschrift für katholische Theologie. Vol. 1 *seqq.* Innsbruck, 1877 *seq.*

Zeitschrift für Kirchengeschichte, ed. by Brieger. Vol. 1 *seqq.* Gotha, 1877 *seqq.*

Zeitschrift für Missionswissenschaft und Missionsgeschichte, ed. by J. Schmidlin. Vol. 1 *seqq.* Münster i. W., 1911 *seqq.*

Zeitschrift für osteuropäische Geschichte. Vol. 1 *seqq.* Berlin, 1910 *seqq.*

Zeitschrift für Schweizer Kirchengeschichte. Vol. 1 *seqq.* Stans, 1907 *seqq.*

Zeitschrift für vaterländische Geschichte und Altertumskunde. (Westfalens.) Münster, 1838 *seqq.*

Zeitschrift, Historische, ed. by H. v. Sybel. Vol. 1 *seqq.* Munich-Leipzig, 1859 *seqq.*

Zentralblatt für Bibliothekswesen. Vol. 1 *seqq.* Leipzig, 1884.

Zinkeisen, J. M., Geschichte des osmanischen Reiches in Europa. Vol. 5. Gotha, 1857.

Zivier, Ezech., Neuere Geschichte Polens. Vol. 1 *seqq.* (Heeren, Geschichte der europäischen Staaten 1, 39.) Gotha, 1915 *seqq.*

TABLE OF CONTENTS OF VOLUME XXX.

INNOCENT X. 1644–1655.

INTRODUCTION.

CHAPTER I.

THE CONCLAVE OF 1644.—INNOCENT X. AND THE PAMFILI.

CHAPTER II.

MAZARIN AND INNOCENT X.—THE INTRIGUES OF THE BARBERINI—THE IMPRISONMENT OF CARDINAL RETZ—RELATIONS WITH SPAIN AND PORTUGAL—THE RISING AT NAPLES.

CHAPTER III.

THE PEACE OF WESTPHALIA AND RELIGIOUS CONDITIONS IN GERMANY AND HOLLAND—THE ENGLISH CATHOLICS UNDER CROMWELL—IRELAND'S FIGHT FOR FREEDOM ; HER DEFEAT.

CHAPTER IV.

INNOCENT'S WORK WITHIN THE CHURCH—THE JUBILEE
YEAR.

CHAPTER V.

JANSENISM IN FRANCE ; AND THE NETHERLANDS.

CHAPTER VI.

INNOCENT X.'S RELATIONS WITH VENICE—THE
PONTIFICAL STATES—DEATH OF THE POPE.

CHAPTER VII.

INNOCENT X. AS A PATRON OF ART.

LIST OF UNPUBLISHED DOCUMENTS AND EXTRACTS FROM ARCHIVES IN APPENDIX.

INNOCENT X. 1644–1655.

INTRODUCTION.

THE powerful progress of the Catholic Church in the era of the Catholic reform and restoration, which constitutes one of the most wonderful spectacles in the whole history of the Church, comes to a standstill in the second half of the 17th century, when a period of decline follows. Thus the reign of Urban VIII. marks a turning point in the same way as, a century earlier, that of Paul III. had ushered in such a crisis.

The cause of this decline is not to be looked for in the leaders of the religious movement, the Popes ; on the contrary, it is due to such altered conditions as would have prevented even a Pius V. or a Sixtus V. from accomplishing what they did in their time. By the middle of the 17th century the state of the world had undergone a profound change. Germany which—were it only because of its Emperor—the nations had looked upon as the hub of the world, no longer counted as a great Power. Though under Ferdinand II. it looked repeatedly as if the imperial power were about to reassert itself, the Peace of Westphalia put an end to all such hopes. The Empire had resolved itself into a couple of hundreds of States and miniature States which obeyed the Emperor when it suited them, whilst their isolation and impotence left them helplessly at the mercy of their all-powerful western neighbour. Germany was notably paralysed by its religious divisions. Luther was mistaken when he imagined that his death would be the death of the papacy : a large part of Germany remained Catholic. However, Luther's opponents were likewise disappointed in their hope that Germany would return to the ancient faith. The Peace of Westphalia recognized the religious cleavage as insurmountable and definitive, and both parties dropped the principle that full political privileges could only be enjoyed by those who clung to the true religion. Contrasts have now become petrified ; German Catholics and German Protestants now have their own separate territories and face each other like two hostile peoples ; thus when it chanced that foreign co-religionists were oppressed, it might happen that a Protestant government would practise reprisals on their own Catholic subjects and vice versa. Moreover, in the sociological sphere, the humiliating realization of the country's depopulation and impoverishment after the war weighed heavily on the nation and stifled all enterprise. If a German wrote poetry, it was in a French metre ; if a prince raised some luxury building, at the expense of his impoverished subjects, France gave the impulse and supplied the model. When the new learning essayed its first steps, Germany was splendidly represented by her Copernicus and her Keppler. After 1650 she may indeed boast yet another great scholar and historian in the person of Leibnitz, the co-discoverer of the infinitesimal calculus, but in the proper sphere of the natural sciences Otto von Guerike was for a long period the only inventor whose name history has recorded. The dis-spirited Germans had lost all self-reliance, all consciousness of the former greatness of their country. In such a mood how could they have asserted themselves abroad ? A large section of the nation was, as it were, under a kind of religious necessity to look on the Catholic Middle Ages, that is the great centuries of German hegemony, as an era of darkness and barbarism, and if the mere name of the Emperor was still surrounded by a kind of luminous halo, it called forth no more than vague, melancholy memories and a longing that its bearer might awake from slumber.

Like Germany, Spain too had fallen from her pinnacle. Under Charles V. and Philip II. that country had enjoyed its century of hegemony in Europe, but with the 17th century there began a period of decline into ever-increasing political impotence. It is remarkable that it was just then that with Lope and Calderon, Spanish poetry attained its highest efflorescence, as did painting with Velasquez and Murillo. But in Spain literature and art were chiefly rooted in the deep and intimate Catholic faith of a people which had decisively rejected the religious innovations as soon as these sought to strike root, and thus preserved the inestimable blessing of religious unity ; no literature or art is so deeply stamped with the imprint of Catholic religious feeling as the Spanish.

On the whole France also had preserved religious unity. During the Huguenot wars that country was, as it were, the tongue of the balance. Had France at that time swerved towards Protestantism, the consequences would have been incalculable ; in that eventuality the Reformation would in all probability have swept over the whole of Europe. This was not to happen. The French people itself had no love for the new religion ; it wanted to be and to remain Catholic and it compelled its reluctant King to become a Catholic. The horror of the Huguenot wars only served to fan the Catholic spirit and when the dice had been cast in favour of the old religion, there passed over the land a Catholic spirit like a warm breath of spring. Priests, splendidly endowed, energetic and full of religious enthusiasm, arose ; the secular clergy became once more conscious of its lofty vocation ; the religious Orders were rejuvenated ; new religious institutions for educational and charitable purposes arose on all sides and the laity, too, gathered its strength in the service of the Church. The achievements of the humanistic age, in alliance with Catholic mentality, issued in an efflorescence of French literature which in Bossuet, Fénelon, Bourdaloue, Massillon, gave expression to Catholic thought. The poets of the period of Louis XIII. and XIV., Corneille, Racine, Molière, Lafontaine, are classics even at this day ; Poussin, Claude Lorrain, Le Sueur are the finest flowers of French painting, Descartes with his new philosophical views, together with Viète, Fermat, and Pascal, is a pioneer in the sphere of mathematics which he enriched with a new branch, that of analytical geometry. In the theological field a new science arose with Petau, that of the history of dogma, which was carried still further by Morin and Thomassin. Critical patristic studies owe to Fronton du Duc, Sirmond and Labbe a development which, towards the close of the century, and thanks to the French Benedictines, laid the foundations of the modern historical method. Bossuet first sought to carry light and order into the medley which men call the history of the world. Distinguished minds of foreign lands, such as Huygens and Cassini, if they would be put on the candlestick, must needs repair to Paris where the Academy of Science and that of Inscriptions, the Observatory and the rich collections, opened their doors to them. More obvious than these achievements in the intellectual order was the way in which Colbert raised France's trade and industry ; Louvois created the modern army organization and by feeding troops from magazines, made possible the mobilization of large masses ; Vauban laid down the foundations of the modern art of fortification, whilst under generals such as Condé, Turenne and Catinat, France marched from victory to victory in the opening years of Louis XIV.'s reign.

However, the authors of these brilliant achievements, who thereby made of France the first country in the world, were only the stars that prepare the rising of the sun itself, at whose appearance, as willing planets, they ranged themselves in a luminous setting around one man, the real luminary among these lesser lights—the youthful Louis XIV. A born ruler, full of great plans and designs, bent on extending the realm and humiliating Germany and Spain, a prince who really worked and governed as his own minister and only allowed the decrees of his ministers to be issued in his own name, handsome and energetic, a king in his appearance and in his every gesture, the twenty-three year old ruler quickly became the pride and the idol of the French who basked in his glory and who, because they stooped before him as the expression and embodiment of France, felt themselves exalted above all other nations.

It was unquestionably an advantage for the Catholic cause that the most powerful King of Europe, the richest country in the world and the most brilliant literature of the period, should be on the side of Catholicism. This is proved by the numerous conversions among the upper classes in Germany

and in the ranks of intellectual men. None the less the rule
of the *roi soleil* proved a calamity for the Church. Louis XIV.
was the most determined representative of State absolutism
and the very brilliance with which he embodied the new
conception of the State led to its triumph, for the other
princes, even the Catholic ones, proved only too ready pupils
of the great Louis. If Louis did not say in so many words,
" L'État, c'est moi ! " he certainly said it equivalently and
took it for his line of conduct. According to him all right is
vested in the State and all authority proceeds from the
Sovereign, nay, he even owns all that the country owns,
not excluding the property of the Church.[1] The aim of his
policy is the honour of the nation whilst the glory of the
nation is the greatness of the King.[2] Accordingly the great
mass of the people and its welfare are of much less consequence. The Sovereign may pour out its blood in endless
wars, provided his greatness is assured ; it may be impoverished by crushing taxation, so long as the ruler lives
in splendour in castles that surpass all the wonders of the
world. In effect Louis XIV. was the only man who counted
in France ; the wars of the Fronde had broken the power
of the nobles and the fall of La Rochelle that of the Huguenots ;
the States General had not been convened since 1614, and
Parliament only dared move after the death of Louis XIV.
Hence there remained only one power that could act as a
brake, the Church, " whose greatest enemy," in view of his
principles, Louis was bound to become, one, too, whose
action was fraught with greater danger than open violence.[3]

Absolutism was everywhere bent on domination, even in

[1] Les rois sont seigneurs absolus et ont naturellement la
disposition pleine et libre de tous les biens, tant des séculiers que
des ecclésiastiques, pour en user come sages économes, c'est à
dire selon les besoins de leur État. Louis XIV. in DREISS, I, 209 ;
E. LAVISSE, *Histoire de France*, VII, 1, Paris, 1905, 391.

[2] CH. KOCH, *Das unumschränkte Königtum Ludwigs XIV.*
(Progr.), Berlin, 1888 ; P. SSYMANK in *Hist. Vierteljahrschr.*, II.
(1899), 39–71 ; LAVISSE, *loc. cit.*, 119 *seqq.*

[3] O. KLOPP, *Fall des Hauses Stuart*, I, 346 ; X., 200.

the religious and spiritual sphere. Such aims were all the more natural in France as Gallican teaching was gaining ground. Spain too had its Cæsaro-papalism, but this was derived from papal concessions and Philip II. carried it into effect because he imagined that, in the event of the downfall of the Roman Curia, he would be called upon to assume the care of the Catholic Church.[1] French Gallicanism was a quite different thing. In so far as it looked for theoretical foundations at all, it based itself not on papal privileges, its claim was that it preserved the original conditions of the primitive Church. In the Gallican view the Roman See had by degrees subjected all the nations to itself, France alone had preserved the conditions which generally obtained throughout Christendom in the 6th century[2]; hence the genuine Catholic Church was found exclusively on the soil of ancient Gaul. Such views explain Louis XIV.'s conduct towards the Pope. He acknowledged the Pope's precedence in the purely spiritual sphere, but this " purely spiritual " sphere was by him set within very narrow boundaries, and all that went beyond them he felt justified in resisting as Roman pretensions. Hence the attitude towards Alexander VII. and Innocent XI., as if the Pope were a foreign enemy whom one could not confine too sternly within his own boundaries.

In the other great European courts, and even in the little ones, this striving for the complete autonomy of the State found a willing echo, especially when, after the Peace of Utrecht, the Spanish war of succession, the great civil war between the Catholics, the Protestant Powers, England, Holland, Prussia, began to rise. Politics became completely secularized, regard for right and justice sank into the background and the Pope's influence was almost completely eliminated. No papal delegate was present at the Peace of the Pyrenees and that of Monzón. Such a representative appears for the last time at the congresses of Aix-la-Chapelle and Nymegen, but thereafter the men in power thought that

---

[1] *Cf.* P. LETURIA in *Estudios eclesiasticos*, January, 1929, 106–114.

[2] PHILLIPS, *Kirchenrecht*, III., Ratisbon, 1848, 339 *seqq.*

they might dispense with the Pope's mediation.[1] Rome ceased to be the centre of gravity of European politics ; in the great crises of modern history she either plays no rôle at all or only a very limited one. Henceforth the importance of the nunciature reports lies solely in the fact that they proceed from men well able to judge the events they record.

Thus by 1650 the European situation had undergone a great change, one very unfavourable to the Church and the papacy : in the North there was Sweden, the deadly enemy of Catholicism ; Germany and Spain, with their conservative principles pushed into the background ; in the centre of western Europe, France still Catholic but already, under Richelieu, dangerously near a schism and, moreover, the second home and the true focus of one of the most dangerous heresies, Jansenism, one all the more to be feared, as it not only avoided open rupture with the Church but, on the contrary, by various subterfuges, preserved the appearance of submission whilst it claimed to be the genuine orthodox Church, as against the ' Molinists '.

Grievous peril thus brooded over the Church. However, Providence is never asleep. Youthful Louis XIV. may indeed have cherished the dream of acquiring Spain by marriage, winning the imperial crown of Germany and, by establishing real imperial rule, of paving the way for world power. What became of such dreams ? Louis was to learn by bitter experience that the sword is not the only weapon. His arrogance arrayed all Europe against him and he owed it solely to the lack of unity among his opponents if the last of his campaigns ended not unsuccessfully. To this must be added the impoverishment of the land, the embitterment of the people against the *roi soleil* it had at one time idolized, misfortune upon misfortune in his own family, no heir to make it worth while to toil during a whole lifetime, nor any successors to the men of genius who had shed such lustre upon the beginning of his reign.

[1] At the Peace of Utrecht Passionei was only papal agent and at the Congress of Cambrai the participation of a papal envoy was imposed by force by Dubois.

Nor did Louis succeed in enforcing his will on the Pope. Gallicanism was a half-truth and self-contradictory. If in the early Christian centuries the influence of the Roman See was less to the fore, it was nevertheless there ; if Rome gave a free hand to an Athanasius or a Cyril of Alexandria in the distant East, it was because there was no need to interfere, whilst all the time she was fully conscious that she had the right to intervene. Louis XIV. himself had to experience the inconsequence of Gallicanism : again and again he had need of the Pope, both in dogmatic disputes and otherwise, and when faced with insoluble complications he had to request the Pope to speak the decisive word.[1] For all that anti-Roman tendencies and encroachments on the Church's sphere grew constantly. Things came to such a pass that in the 18th century it was no rare thing for Bishop's letters to be burnt, or the Last Sacraments to be administered by order of the police, until at last, by the civil constitution of the clergy, a new ecclesiastical order was dictated by the authority of the State alone and without reference to either Bishops or Pope. However, this extreme

---

[1] " Cette domination du roi, cependant, n'était pas, ne pouvait être complète. Le gallicanisme, placé à mi-chemin entre le schisme et l'infaillibilité papale, était un système plein d'inconséquences, qui devait inévitablement un jour se briser contre la logique d'airain de Rome. Même à son apogée, il ne savait pas se passer de Rome. A chaque instant le pouvoir royal avait besoin de ce pape, qu'il combattait si volontiers et avec tant d'obstination. Il fallait souvent solliciter à Rome, quand on aurait voulu commander. On le voyait chaque fois qu'il s'agissait d'une question d'hérésie ou de doctrine, ou simplement d'un chapeau de cardinal. De là une sourde irritation dans l'esprit du roi, qui sentait qu'il y avait à l'intérieur même de cet État, qu'il identifiait avec soi-même, une autre puissance imposant des limites à la sienne. De là aussi cette inconséquence dans les relations avec le pape, mélange de menaces et de sollicitations, de violence et de déférence, de corruption scandaleuse et de persécution mesquine." (HANOTAUX, Recueil, I, CIX. CH. DE. BILDT, Christine de Suède et le Conclave de Clément X. (1669–1670), 60.)

measure of Cæsaro-papalism provided the occasion for the papacy's supreme triumph. When Napoleon resolved to put order into the religious chaos, he saw himself impelled to invoke the Pope, thereby supplying the opportunity for a display of pontifical power of unprecedented magnitude in the whole history of the Church.

Even in his political contests with the Popes, Louis XIV. experienced unforeseen disappointments. True, he forced Alexander VII. to yield in the dispute over the Corsican guards, so as to preserve the States of the Church from an invasion of the King's soldiery, but no one can admire the brutal conduct of an arrogant youth towards a father and an aged man. However, this did not put an end to all conflicts. After a short period of peace under Clement IX. they were renewed under his successor, eighty-years-old Clement X., and they became extremely acute under Innocent XI. On the other hand this was the moment for the beginning of an extremely interesting spectacle. On one side Europe's mightiest King, in all the force of his manhood, relying on a trained army and all the arts of policy and diplomacy, glorified by poets as the one who saw more clearly than the Pope and who sustained the whole structure of religion,[1] and this

---

[1] Thus Racine in 1689 in the prologue to *Esther* has this address to God :

> De ta gloire animé, lui seul de tant de rois
> S'arme pour ta querelle, et combat pour tes droits . . .
> Tout semble abandonner tes sacrés étendards.
> Et l'enfer, couvrant tout de ses vapeurs funèbres,
> Sur les yeux les plus saints a jeté ses ténèbres.
> Lui seul, invariable et fondé sur la foi,
> Ne cherche, ne regarde et n'écoute que toi ;
> Et bravant du démon l'impuissant artifice
> De la religion soutient tout l'édifice.
> Grand Dieu, juge ta cause. . . .

The fabulist Lafontaine also wrote of Innocent XI. (Letter of August 18, 1689, to Prince De Conti, *Œuvres complètes*, éd. C. H. Walckenaer, II, Paris, 1838, 743) :

embodiment of all the worldly greatness of the period faced
by an unarmed old man, a Pope in whom, on the whole,
there was nothing of the skilled statesman or the wily diplomatist. Simple and straightforward, but consequent, the Pope
defended what he knew to be the cause of right and justice,
ready, if need be, to die a martyr to his cause.[1] " To this we
are called," he wrote to Louis, " and we do not value our
life more than ourselves ; not alone with constancy, but even
with joy, we must bear tribulations for justice' sake and
glory in them and in the cross of Jesus Christ."[2] He would
sooner be flayed alive, like the Apostle St. Bartholomew, than
consent to anything that could redound to the injury of the
Holy See.[3] Such speech, no doubt, would meet with but

> Celui-ci véritablement
> N'est envers nous ni saint ni père.
> Nos soins, de l'erreur triomphants,
> Ne font qu'augmenter sa colère
> Contre l'ainé de ses enfants.

[1] " His policy presents no surprising features, on the contrary,
amid the incredible intrigues of the 17th century and the constantly changing relations between the various States, it is
remarkable by reason of its simplicity and constancy. It is
characterized by the sense of justice that inspired its guide, by
the firmness with which he met encroachments on the pontifical
power and suppressed abuses, and above all by the high aim that
he had set himself . . ." (M. IMMICH, *Zur Vorgeschichte des
Orleanischen Krieges*, Heidelberg, 1898, XVI., *seq.*).

[2] Neque tamen ullum inde incommodum aut periculum,
nullam, quantumvis saevam atque horribilem tempestatem
pertimescimus.   Ad hoc enim vocati sumus, neque facimus
animam Nostram pretiosiorem quam Nos, probe intelligentes
non forti solum, sed etiam laeto animo subeundas tribulationes
propter justitiam, in quibus et in cruce Domini Nos unice
gloriari oportet. Brief of Dec. 29, 1679, in BERTHIER,
I, 330.

[3] che più tosto si sarebbe lasciato scorticare, come s. Bartolo-
meo, che fare o consentire a cosa pregiudiciale alla S. Sede
Apostolica et alle ragioni della medesima. Process of Beatification, *Informatio*, Testimony of Maracchi.

little understanding on the part of the diplomatists, it might even call forth their sneers. But the incredible happened : it was not the unworldly ascetic who was beaten in the dispute ; moral victory would have been his in any case. On other questions also Louis XIV.'s endeavours failed owing to the opposition of the Pope, as the King's efforts for the Electoral See of Cologne ; in the dispute over the freedom of the quarter he also gave in after the death of Innocent XI. ; he restored the confiscated papal possessions in France, viz. Avignon and Venaissin ; the convocation of a General Council was now without point, and under Innocent XII. Louis had to give up the four Gallican articles of 1682 ; the quarrel over the *régale* met with a solution with which Rome could, on the whole, be satisfied.

But we have not yet as much as hinted at Innocent XI.'s greatest triumphs. From beginning to end his government was inspired and dominated by the lofty thought of uniting Christendom for a grand struggle against the traditional enemy in the East—at first sight, and judged by appearances, a hopeless undertaking in view of the utterly secular policy of the States at the time, an enterprise that must have looked like a dream of long ago, which only an unpractical idealism could think of evoking ! However, though Innocent XI. did not realize all he would have wished to accomplish, he could nevertheless register many successes. The salvation of Europe and the anti-Turkish league are for the most part his work ; he was the real soul of the opposition against the rising tide of Islam. Great events rapidly succeeded each other during his pontificate ; the deliverance of Vienna, the conquest of Ofen, the Grand Alliance. The new Austro-Hungarian Imperial State was a result of the wars of the time, and a stop was put for ever to the conquest of the Osmanlis.[1] Even in purely secular matters and in affairs of State the greater political wisdom was on the side of the unpolitical Pope. If France had not robbed his plans of complete success, there would have remained no Eastern question and Europe

---

[1] IMMICH, *Zur Vorgeschichte*, XVII.

would have been spared incalculable complications.[1]   The
reign of Innocent XI. is the epilogue of the age of the
great reforming Popes of the 16th and 17th centuries.
Whereas under Urban VIII. and Alexander VII. and even
after them, Rome, notwithstanding its continual decline in
the political sphere, still remained the centre of the civilized
world, chiefly by reason of its great creations in the artistic
field, up to the French Revolution the Apostolic See knew
indeed excellent priests but no longer any great men.   The
most remarkable Pope of the period was Benedict XIV., a
scholar whose works are not yet out of date, a man of high
and liberal spirit, whose ready repartee could be pungent ; he
knew how to yield but likewise how to go cautiously forward.
For the rest the 18th century is one of the saddest in the
history of the Church, and outwardly one of steady decline.
To the three hostile forces of the 17th century, viz.
Jansenism, Gallicanism, Cæsaro-papalism, a fourth came
to be added, viz. an infidel philosophy, deism, naturalism,
rationalism, which only worked themselves out completely
in the 19th and 20th centuries.   Its aim was to attack
and to undermine Christianity in its foundations.   Added
to this was the fact that the other hostile powers became
even more aggressive than in the past.   The French Parliament, which under Louis XIV. had sunk into political
insignificance, acquired new strength during the Regency and
permitted itself, as the guardian of Gallicanism, encroachments
on the ecclesiastical sphere such as the *roi soleil* would not have
dared to perpetrate.   Jansenism seemingly vanished after
Clement IX., but under Clement X., through Quesnel, it
became a fresh and even greater danger ; under Louis XIV.
it had been opposed by the Government, but now it was the
object of the solicitous protection of Parliament.   By then
State absolutism had become an established thing ; it might

---

[1] " Il faut le dire, à l'honneur de la diplomatie pontificale, que
c'est à Rome qu'on a premièrement compris l'importance de
la question de l'Orient.   Que de maux auraient été épargnés à
l'Europe si la voix des papes avait été mieux écoutée ! " BILDT,
loc. cit., 4.

be said that the princes vied with one another in making the Pope feel his political impotence ; thus Clement XI., in the course of his long and peaceful pontificate, found himself, during the Spanish war of succession, between France and Austria as between the hammer and the anvil ; Benedict XIII. had to become reconciled to the *Monarchia Sicula* so long opposed, whilst Clement XII. was forced to make fresh concessions. It looked as if the papacy's very power to live was to be tested and the fact that it stood the test is one of the most memorable facts of all history. The great pioneers of royal absolutism, Richelieu, Mazarin, Louis XIV., however clear and far-sighted they may have seemed, failed to perceive that by exaggerating the royal prerogatives they conjured up the revolution, and that by setting at nought the most legitimate authority of all, that of the Church, they were undermining all authority, theirs included. Royal absolutism dug its own grave ; when it fell, its fall included that of Gallicanism and Jansenism. For a time it looked as if the deluge was about to sweep away the papacy too. However, the nadir of its depression in the 18th century also marks the starting point of a fresh and unexpected rise, even though not in the political sphere. In the 19th century the papacy remained as a world power with which every State had to reckon, and though it may no longer intervene in world politics, the nations have nevertheless been taught that it would be greatly to their advantage if there still existed a peaceful power, enthroned above the strife of parties, with its superiority and impartiality recognized by all.

When Pius VI. died in captivity, men wrote the epitaph of the papacy, for they fancied that it would rise no more. If ever prophecy was stultified, it was this one.

CHAPTER I.

The Conclave of 1644. Innocent X. and the Pamfili.

WHEN Urban VIII. died on July 29th, 1644, the Cardinals' first care was to remove the mercenaries, French for the most part, who had been enrolled for the recently concluded war of Castro. This seemed all the more urgent as the Grand-Duke of Tuscany and the Viceroy of Naples had drawn up their troops along the borders of the States of the Church and were threatening to take action unless the foreign soldiery was disbanded and Taddeo Barberini deprived of his command. The Emperor's representative, Savelli, worked in the same sense. In the end it was decided that the foreign troops should be evacuated towards Bologna whilst Taddeo Barberini should remain General of the Church, but his authority was to be limited by two Cardinals who were to be placed by his side.[1] These measures had a calming effect on the people, for in Rome the situation had taken on so warlike a character that all the palaces had been put in a state of defence.[2]

On August 9th the Cardinals went into conclave.[3] Contrary

[1] Report of Cardinal Harrach to Ferdinand III., dat. Rome, August 6, 1644, State Archives, Vienna.

[2] See the report in PETRUCELLI, III., 91 ; I. NICII ERYTHRAEI, *epist.* LXVIII. *ad Tyrrhenum* ; COVILLE, 3 *seq.*, 13 *seq.*

[3] *Cf.* on the conclave of Innocent X., H. CONRING, *Comment, hist. de electione Urbani VIII. et Innocentii X.*, Helmstadt, 1651 ; *Conclavi*, II., 356–499 ; PETRUCELLI, III, 95 *seqq.* ; WAHRMUND, *Ausschliessungsrecht*, 128 *seq.* in *Sitzungsberichten der Wiener Akademie*, Hist. Kl. 122 and 170 ; EISLER, 48 *seq.*, 88 *seq.* ; a diary of Cardinal E. A. Harrach on the conclave of 1644 in Harrach Archives, Vienna. *Cf.* F. MENCIK, *Volba Papeze Innocence X.*, *Praze*, 1894, where the election capitulation (*cf. Quellen u. Forsch.*, XII., 299) is given on p. 42. Its date (Sept. 10, 1644) can be ascertained from the copy in *Boncompagni Archives*,

to what had been planned at first,[1] it was not held at the
Quirinal nor at the College of the Jesuits, but notwithstanding
the objections of the physician Collicola, who warned against
the " miasmas and the risk of infection ", at the suggestion
of the two Francesco Barberini and in accordance with
established custom, it was held at the Vatican.[2] The electoral
hall remained open all day, thus enabling the envoys of the
Emperor and those of the Kings of Spain and France to
confer with the Cardinals.[3] In view of the great heat the cells
had been made more spacious than usual.[4]

The Sacred College consisted of 62 members[5]; six were
absent, viz. the Spaniards Borgia and Sandoval, the French
Mazarin and La Rochefoucauld and the Italians Spinola and
Orsini. Most of the 56 Cardinals who took part in the
election were Italians. There were among them only the
three Spaniards Albornoz, Cueva, and Lugo, the two French-
men Alphonse Louis Richelieu and Achille d'Estampes de
Valençay and the German Harrach. Sixteen Cardinals were
Romans, viz. Lante, Crescenzi, Pamfili, Rocci, Cesi, Verospi,
Montalto, Panciroli, Mattei, Altieri, Teodoli, Rapaccioli,
Antonio Barberini, Colonna, Gabrielli, Rondinini ; seven
were Florentines, viz. Capponi, Francesco Barberini, Sacchetti,
Machiavelli, Falconieri, Medici and the elder Antonio
Barberini. There were also five Genoese, viz. Spinola,
Costaguti, Durazzo, Donghi and Grimaldi. To these must
be added three Milanese—Roma, Trivulzio and Monti ; two

Rome, C. 20. A few relevant letters in MARCHESAN, *Lettere
inedite di O. Rinaldo*, Treviso, 1896, and CHINAZZI, *Sede vacante
per la morte di Urbano VIII.*, Rome, 1904. Register of *spese
occorse per il conclave 1644* in Arch. Doria-Pamfili, Rome, 1-5.

[1] See *Conclave di Innocenzo X.*, Vat. 8781, Vat. Lib.

[2] *Cf.* CELLI, *Storia della malaria nell'Agro Romano*, Città di
Castello, 1925.

[3] *Avviso* of August 13, 1644, Papal Secr. Arch. ; *Avvisi*, 96.

[4] *Avviso* of August 6, 1644, *loc. cit.*

[5] Not 61 as given by CIACONIUS (IV., 642-3). *Cf.* the authentic
data in the *Pianta del conclave d'Innocenzo X.*, ed. Calisto Fer-
ranti, Rome, Piazza Navona, Vat. Lib.

Venetians, viz. Cornaro and Bragadino ; two Neapolitans, viz. Brancaccio and Filomarino. Siena was represented by Cennini and Bichi, and Ferrara by Bentivoglio and Rossetti.

The only survivor of Gregory XV.'s Cardinals was Cueva. Seven owed their elevation to Paul V., viz. Lante, Crescenzi, Cennini, Bentivoglio, Roma, Capponi and Medici ; all the others were created by Urban VIII.

Previous to the opening of the conclave the following were spoken of as *papabili* : Lante, Crescenzi, Bentivoglio, Capponi, Sacchetti, Mattei, Pamfili, Rocci, Maculano, Altieri,[1] and besides them also Spinola, Monti and Roma. Concerning the latter everybody took it for granted that if he were elected he would make an end of nepotism, for he gave nothing to his relatives but bestowed all he had on the Church and on the poor. In view of his eighty years Cennini could not be seriously considered ; Pamfili had a reputation for ability but he was definitely rejected by France and even in the Sacred College he had many opponents. Giulio Sacchetti had the best prospects ; he was a priest of blameless life, liberal and highly cultured, the only thing against him being the circumstance that he was not yet sixty years old. Sacchetti was likewise on excellent terms with Mazarin, a circumstance which everybody thought sufficient by itself to range the Spaniards against him.[2]

---

[1] *Avviso* of Aug. 6, 1644, Papal Sec. Arch. Altieri fa gran rumore e se non fosse giovine et sano, potrebbe facilmente colpire (Fr. Mantovani, report of August 6, 1644, Modena State Archives).

[2] See O. Rinaldi's letters of July 30 and August 6, 1644, in A. MARCHESAN, *Lettere inedite di O. Rinaldi*, Treviso, 1896, 23 *seq.*, 28 *seq.* For Sacchetti see MORONI, LX., 100 ; PALLA-VICINO, *Alessandro VII.*, I., 55. Alaleone calls him *vir summae virtutis et incomparabilis doctrinae et vitae integritatis* (* *Diarium*, Vat. Libr.). G. B. TARABUCCI wrote of Sacchetti in 1643 : *" Ha in grado eminente tutte le qualità desiderabili in un cardinale papabile : età provetta, bontà di vita, dottrina, cortesia, piace-volezza, prontezza, grande sincerità di spirito, in somma degno del pontificato " (*Stato della corte di Roma nel 1643*, Gonzaga Archives, Mantua). Franc. Mantovani, envoy of Este, says of Sacchetti : " Gode un aura grande e forse si parla troppo di

On the other hand Sacchetti's most intimate friends were
the Barberini. How close these relations were, as well as
the Cardinals' artistic sense, appears even at this day in his
Villa of Castel Fusano, near Ostia, situated in a magnificent
pine forest planted by himself and now the property of the
Chigi. Pietro da Cortona, Andrea Sacchi, Baldassare and
Francesco Lauri had adorned it with paintings.[1] In the
gallery on the second floor, where maps painted on the walls
recall the extensive travels of his highly cultured brother
Marcello, at one time depositary of the Apostolic *Camera*
under Urban VIII., one may see in the corners by the side
of Sacchetti's arms, those of Cardinals Francesco and Antonio
Barberini and those of Urban VIII. over the main entrance,
so that one has the impression of being in a property of the
Barberini. The gravity of Sacchetti's character appears from
Oderico Rinaldi's remark to the effect that he did not move
a finger to secure his election.[2] The data of the diplomatic
reports on the strength of the various parties differ greatly ;
it was thought that France could rely on 4–6 votes and Spain
on 8–24 ! One and the same Cardinal was often reckoned
as belonging to opposite parties.[3] On the whole the following

lui." Of Pamfili the same writes : " Lodano i suoi meriti e
l'habilità, ma li si oppongano la rozzezza della natura e l' [gap]
della cognata. Li Francesi poi l'escludono apertamente . . . e
nel s. collegio ha più di dieci cardinali che li sono contrarii "
(*report of August 6, 1644, State Archives, Modena).

[1] CAMPORI, *Lettere artist.*, Modena, 1866, 505 ; PASCOLI,
Vite di pittori, II., Rome, 1730 ; POSSE, *Einige Gemälde des
A. Sacchi*, in *Mitteilungen der sächsischen Kunstsammlungen*,
III. (1912). According to the *Documents of the Sacchetti
Archives, Pietro da Cortona received 100 scudi on Sept. 7, 1626 ;
Andrea Sacchi 60 scudi on April 3, 1628 ; Andrea Camassei
25 scudi on Nov. 24 and Pietro Berrettini da Cortona 266½ scudi
in 1630 for their paintings *in casale di Ostia*. *Cf.* the rare work
*Villa Sacchetta Ostiensis cosmographicis tabulis et notis per
Ioannem Tomcum Marnavitium illustrata. Rusticanis legibus
officinarumque inscriptionibus annotata*, Rome, 1630.

[2] MARCHESAN, *Lettere inedite di O. Rinaldi*, 28.

[3] COVILLE, 9–10.

parties may be said to have constituted themselves, viz. the old Cardinals, Urban VIII.'s Cardinals, those who entertained French or Spanish sympathies.

The Spanish-Imperial party was headed by Cardinal Albornoz who was also the depositary of " the secret of the Catholic King ". In addition to the Spanish nationals, Cardinals Medici, Este, Trivulzio, Colonna and Harrach also belonged to this party, whilst that of the old Cardinals, led by Cardinal Mattei, was also closely allied with it. The party of Urban VIII.'s nephews was led by Cardinal Francesco Barberini, but he could only rely with certainty upon barely one half of the forty-four Cardinals who owed the purple to the late Pope.[1] All the same he was strong enough to prevent at any time the elevation of any one candidate unacceptable to himself. The French party was headed by the youthful Antonio Barberini, Cardinal Protector of France, and by Richelieu, Mazarin's confidant.

The two nephews of Urban VIII. fully realized how much they had exploited to their advantage the exceptionally long pontificate of their uncle ; they were afraid of being called to account, hence they were anxious to secure the election of a Pope of whose favour they could feel assured. At bottom they did not care whether the Pontiff leaned towards France or Spain, so long as he guaranteed their security. In order to preserve the greatest freedom of action, the nephews wrapped their plans in deepest mystery.[2] They were by no means in complete agreement as to their candidate ; Francesco's first choice was Giulio Sacchetti and after him Giambattista Pamfili, but Antonio Barberini, and with him all the French, definitely declined the latter whereas they were

---

[1] *" Per certissimo si dice che l'Eminenza Sua non ha seguito sicuro se non di 26 voti, et se durerà nelle sue stitichezze, correrà rischio di provare una ribellione totale e che si faccia il Pontefice senza di lui, perchè insofferibile la sua irresolutezza." Report of Fr. Mantovani dated Aug. 20, 1644. Modena State Arch.

[2] At the opening of the conclave, Mantovani *reports on Aug. 10, 1644 : " Barberini haveva dichiarato la sua intentione con le creature, di chi se dolevano assaissimo." State Arch., Modena.

very keen on Sacchetti.[1] At the imperial court, where there
was much dissatisfaction with Urban VIII.'s attitude during
the Thirty Years' War,[2] little attention had been paid to the
papal election. In vain Savelli asked for fuller instructions,
neither he nor the Protector of the German nation, Cardinal
Colonna, succeeded in obtaining them. All that Savelli
secured was the dispatch of a special Spanish plenipotentiary,
Count Sirvela, who reached Rome shortly before the opening
of the conclave.[3]

On the other hand the leader of France's policy, Cardinal
Mazarin, displayed all the more zeal. As early as February 1st,
1644, he had instructed the French envoy in Rome to work,
in the first instance, for Bentivoglio and in the second for
Sacchetti, but to oppose with all his might, secretly, but if
necessary openly, the election of Pamfili.[4] The instructions
were repeated after the death of Urban VIII., on August 11th.
However, the execution of this programme was hampered by
the circumstance that the French ambassador, the Marquis
Saint-Chamond, was both new to his post and sickly, whilst
Cardinal Valençay could not be depended upon. Only of
Richelieu, Bichi and Grimaldi could Mazarin be quite sure ;
but the wily politician did not despair ; he sent money to
Rome and ordered Admiral De Brézé to be prepared to appear
before Civitavecchia. He also sent to Rome a report of the
victory near Freiburg (August 3rd and 5th).[5]

[1] See *Conclavi*, II., 357 *seq.* ; *Report of Marchese Cesare
Guerrieri on his *obbedienza* embassy in 1645, Gonzaga Archives.
Mantua ; WAHRMUND, *Ausschliessungsrecht*, 130 *seq.* Cardinal
Antonio Barberini had grievously offended Pamfili (SIMEONI,
Francesco I. d'Este e la politica italiana del Mazarino, Bologna,
1922, 55).

[2] See *Considerazioni e prognostici per la sede vacante di
Urbano VIII.* in *Cod.* 1172, of Bibl. Riccardiana, Florence.

[3] WAHRMUND, 129.

[4] Mazarin's hostility towards Pamfili was not exclusively due
to the insinuations of Cardinal Antonio Barberini, but was also
based on the fact that Pamfili was closely allied to Cardinal
Panciroli whom the French Cardinal considered as a personal
enemy. SIMEONI, 55.   [5] COVILLE, 5 *seq.*, 12.

An enormous sensation was created when, at the very
beginning of the conclave, the leader of the Spaniards,
Albornoz, openly pronounced the exclusion of Sacchetti.
The old Cardinals, and not a few of those of Urban VIII.,
such as Cesi and Mattei, took the side of the Spaniards.
Barberini nevertheless upheld Sacchetti and sought to induce
Albornoz, though in vain, to withdraw the exclusion. When
asked on what grounds Sacchetti was to be excluded, Albornoz
declared that his sovereign was not bound to give explanations on the subject, that it must suffice that he did not
trust him : all the Cardinals must reckon with this. As a
matter of fact not a few theologians were of opinion that they
were bound to take that fact into account ; thus the confessor of the conclave, the Jesuit Valentino Magnoni, thought
that it was not possible to resist the will of so powerful a
King without imperilling the Church, hence they must choose
the lesser evil. This view was opposed by some of the
Cardinals. For the time being Barberini upheld Sacchetti's
candidature, but Count Sirvela informed the Spanish Cardinals
that if they supported Sacchetti, they ran the risk of forfeiting
the favour of the King of Spain and with it their benefices
and pensions.[1]

Nothing was more unwelcome to Cardinal Sacchetti from
the first than the ardour of the French in supporting him.
A report circulated in the conclave that money had come
from Paris in furtherance of his election, nay, it was even
affirmed that Mazarin had written a letter to Sacchetti in
which he addressed him as Pope.[2]

By degrees the difficulties of Sacchetti's candidature had
manifestly become so great that Barberini saw himself compelled to consider that of Pamfili and in this sense he got in
touch, by letter, with the French ambassador. However,
even though Antonio Barberini was now prepared to resign
himself to Pamfili's election, Saint-Chamond declared that

---

[1] EISLER, 93, 95 seq., 97.

[2] *Memorie del conclave d'Innocenzo X. scritte dal card.
Lugo in Barb. lat., 4676, p. 255 seqq., Vat. Lib.

he could not possibly go against the will of his King.[1] Accordingly another effort had to be made to bring off Sacchetti's election, but at the ballot of August 30th only twelve Cardinals declared themselves in his favour whereas the three-quarters' majority which was required for the election was thirty-eight.[2]

This failure led to a new phase of the conclave. The candidature of Pamfili, whose prospects had been serious from the beginning of the conclave,[3] was now definitely put forward. Cardinal Francesco Barberini got in touch with Lugo [4] and the latter removed Antonio Barberini's last scruples so that thereafter the latter strove to shape circumstances in such wise as to remove every appearance of the election being directly aimed against France.[5] To gain time he began by urging the election of Maculano.[6] Meanwhile he sought to win over Bichi with the promise of a French archbishopric. Bichi declined. Much depended on the French ambassador, but the latter declared that he must first consult Paris. Mazarin replied in a letter of September 19th in which he emphatically pronounced against the candidature of Pamfili.[7] However, Mazarin's objections came too late ; even before

---

[1] COVILLE, 17. The *Report of Cesare Guerrieri mentioned in note 1 of p. 19 knows nothing of this.

[2] EISLER, 98.

[3] In a MS. entitled *Caratteristica dei papabile, from an imperialist source, we read of Pamfili : " Potrà egli correr la sua fortuna essendo di gran letteratura e di profondo sapere." State Archives, Vienna.

[4] *Memorie del card. Lugo, loc. cit.

[5] COVILLE, 19.

[6] CHINAZZI, 44 seq. From the letters of Michelino here given, which are preserved in the Archives Sforza-Cesarini, Rome, it appears that an attempt was made to overthrow Maculano, a Capuchin, by recalling a certain trial before the Inquisition which, however, in no way touched the Frate. Fr. Mantovani wrote on Aug. 6, 1644 : *" Maculano non ha applauso nel senato apostolico, e dicono che Pio v fu eletto per la santità della vita e Sisto v per la letteratura : parti che non militano nel frate presente." State Arch., Modena.

[7] COVILLE, 19-21.

he had penned his reply Pamfili's election had taken place on September 14th. How was it that events thus precipitated themselves ?

September has the reputation in Rome of being the unhealthiest period of the year and the Cardinals were terrified at the prospect of having to remain together, within the narrow confines of the conclave, even during that month.[1] It soon looked as if their fears were to be realized. The first to fall ill with malaria was Bentivoglio (he died on September 7th) and after him Cardinals Mattei and Gabrielli and lastly also Francesco Barberini. Like his colleagues, Francesco had to leave the conclave, but before doing so he passed on the leadership of the party to his brother Antonio so that the latter found himself at the head of both the French party and that of the nephews.[2]

Mazarin's reply to Saint-Chamond's consultation could not arrive in Rome before September 23rd, but in view of the great heat and the bad state of health of the Cardinals, it was impossible to draw out the conclave for so long. In these circumstances Saint-Chamond suffered himself to be persuaded by the Marquis di San Vito, Cardinal Teodoli's brother, to discuss the eventual election of Pamfili[3] and on this basis Antonio Barberini forthwith announced that France had withdrawn its opposition to Pamfili.

A particular circumstance caused Barberini to hurry his negotiations in favour of Pamfili. This was that at one scrutiny old Cardinal Cennini, who was no friend of his, and who had supported Spain, had secured 25 votes. Antonio realized that further delay would be highly dangerous, hence he decided to act without waiting for Mazarin's reply.[4] On the evening of September 13th a decisive conversation took

---

[1] On Aug. 24, 1644, Fr. Mantovani reports : *" Molti scommettono che non havremo Papa per tutto Settembre." State Arch., Modena.

[2] *Memorie del card. Lugo, *loc. cit.*, Vat. Lib. ; *Conclavi*, II., 473 *seqq.* ; EISLER, 101.

[3] COVILLE, 22, 42 *seqq.*

[4] EISLER, 101-2.

place in Spada's cell between Antonio Barberini, Rapaccioli and Facchinetti.[1] Lugo was informed in the morning and Facchinetti treated with Albornoz. The conditions were as follows : The Spanish party would maintain towards the *pratica* for Pamfili the same attitude as that for Maculano ; should France feel injured by Antonio's action, the Barberini would be assured of Spain's protection. Albornoz accepted these conditions and promptly obtained the assent of fifteen of his followers.[2] The Cardinal likewise sent word to the Spanish ambassador, but the latter's distrust was such that he only saw in the whole thing a manœuvre the object of which was to weaken the Spanish party and to push through Sacchetti's candidature.[3] On the morning of September 15th Lugo repaired to Pamfili's cell, to inform him of his impending election to the papacy. He recommended to him, in the first instance, the interests of the Church and peace between the princes, and lastly the House of the Barberini. In the ensuing scrutiny Pamfili was elected by a large majority, only the French Cardinals Valençay and Richelieu as well as Bichi, Grimaldi and Maculano having voted against him.[4] The thunder of the guns of Castel S. Angelo and the clanging of the bells of the city proclaimed to the Romans that St. Peter's Chair was once more occupied.[5] The new Pope took the name of Innocent X.[6] in view of the fact that his family had settled in Rome under Innocent VIII. ; for his motto he chose the words of 2 Kings iii, 9 : " Give to thy servant an understanding heart to judge thy people." [7]

The Romans were overjoyed that a fellow citizen was to

[1] *Memorie del card. Lugo, *loc. cit.*

[2] EISLER, 102–3.

[3] *Memorie del card. Lugo, *loc. cit.*

[4] COVILLE, 22. Interesting details on the scrutiny in *Memorie del card. Lugo (*loc. cit.*).

[5] A. TAURELLI, *De novissima electione Innocentii X.*, Bononiae, 1640, 24 *seq.* ; NOVAES (X., 8) mentions similar writings.

[6] It was at first thought that he would take the name of Clement IX. ; see Harrach's report of September 15, 1644, in MENCIK, 47.

[7] CIACONIUS, IV., 643.

wear the tiara. Cardinal Harrach expressed his satisfaction
at the election of a Pope who was not only a great lover of
peace, but likewise well disposed towards the House of
Habsburg ; the Spanish party, he wrote, notwithstanding
its weakness, may well boast of having not only paved the
way for a good Pope, but one whom France had excluded
and whose attainment of the supreme dignity looked like
a miracle.[1] The coronation took place on October 4th [2]
and on November 23rd the Pope took possession of the
Lateran. According to custom many triumphal arches had
been erected and these were adorned with pompous inscriptions, pictures and statues ; one arch was especially admired,
even by the Pope himself ; it had been erected on the Capitol,
from a design of the architect Carlo Rainaldi. Between the
Arch of Titus and the Colosseum the Jews had spread sixty
tapestries bearing texts from the Old Testament.[3]

Giambattista Pamfili was sprung from a very ancient family
of the delightful hill town of Gubbio. In the last quarter of
the 15th century one branch of the family settled in
Rome. Camillo Pamfili, whose brother Girolamo became a
Cardinal under Clement VIII., married Maria Flaminia del
Bufalo. Four sons sprang from this union : Pamfili, Giam-
battista, Angelo Benedetto, Alessandro, and two daughters,
Prudenzia and Agata who both took the veil.[4]

---

[1] Harrach's report, *loc. cit.*

[2] Cf. *Relazione delle ceremonie per la coronazione di P. Innocenzo
X.*, Rome, 1644. *" Fu tanto il concorso del popolo, che non
ci è memoria di cosa simile " (Fr. Mantovani on October 5, 1644,
State Archives, Modena).

[3] CANCELLIERI, *Possessi*, 208 *seqq.*, 248 *seq.*, 251 *seq.*, 255 *seq.*
To the reports here indicated must be added an *Avviso* of
November 26, 1644, Papal Secret Archives. EVELYN, *Diary*,
118 *seq.*, also gives a description of the *possesso*.

[4] On Innocent X.'s family and antecedents, *cf.* besides the
Venetian embassy reports in BERCHET, *Roma*, II., 50 *seqq.*,
67 *seqq.* : A. TAURELLI, *De novissima electione Innocenti X.*,
Bononiae 1644 ; F. F. MANCINI, *Compendio della vita di Papa
Innocenzo X.* (copy in Bibl. Casanatense, Rome) ; N. A. CAFERRIUS,

The family coat of arms showed a dove with an olive branch in its beak surmounted by three golden lilies.[1] The family mansion stood near the Pasquino in the Piazza Navona. Here Giambattista Pamfili was born on May 7th, 1574 and three days later he was baptized in the parish church of S. Lorenzo in Damaso.[2] His uncle Girolamo undertook to educate the bright youth[3] and in all probability it was due to him that his pupil ended by embracing the ecclesiastical state. After taking a doctorate in both laws at the Roman University, he was ordained priest on September 27th, 1597. In 1601 Clement VIII. made him a consistorial advocate. When uncle Girolamo was raised to the cardinalate, Giambattista succeeded him, on June 9th, 1604, as auditor of the Rota. At that time he became an intimate friend of his colleague

Synthema vetustatis sive flores historiarum, Romae, 1667 ; CIACONIUS, 570 *seq.* ; AMEYDEN, ed. Bertini, II., 124 *seqq.* ; for BAGATTA, *Vita di Innocenzo X.* (in PLATINA-PANVINIO, *Vite,* ed. Venezia, 1730) see MAZZUCHELLI, III., 63 ; for his correction of the name of the Pope's mother : *Lettere di Michele Giustiniani,* Roma, 1675, 7 ; *Spicil. Vat., I., Roma,* 1890, 116 *seq.* (excellent data from Vat. MSS.) ; CIAMPI, *Innocenzo X.,* 14 *seq.* Much is to be added to the judgment passed by ZWIEDINECK-SÜDENHORST (in *Hist. Zeitschr.,* LII., 118 *seqq.*) and by EHRLE (*Spada,* 2, note 2) on the defects and qualities of Ciampi's biography of the Pamfili Pope. Ciampi is very far from having made adequate use of the Roman material ; from the Papal Secret Archives he quotes nothing and from other collections of MSS. for the most part only secondary details ; the Doria-Pamfili Archives, which he should have used in the first instance, were closed to him. Innocent X.'s sister Prudenzia died on April 25, 1650, at S. Marta. Alaleone describes her as " femina maximi spiritus et incomparabilis prudentiae et pietatis et erga omnes benevolissima " (*Diarium,* Vat. Lib.).

[1] PASINI FRASSONI, *Armorial des Papes,* Rome, 1906, 43 *seq.*

[2] Baptismal register in Archives of S. Lorenzo in Damaso, I., 170 ; copy in Doria-Pamfili Archives, 93–46.

[3] These and the following dates in MSS. *Notes to BRUSONI, Historia d'Italia* in Doria-Pamfili Arch., 93–46, p. 61 *seq.*

Ludovisi, the future Pope Gregory XV.[1] A mighty quarto
volume in the family archives bears witness, even at this
day, to his activity as auditor.[2] Small wonder that on
March 26th, 1621, Gregory XV. appointed the keen and
skilful auditor nuncio in Naples, a post he retained for four
years.[3] Without sacrificing any of the Church's rights,
Pamfili knew how to avoid disputes with the Government.[4]
When Urban VIII. sent his nephew Francesco Barberini to
France and Spain, Pamfili was assigned to him as *datarius*.
In this capacity he won the confidence of the nephew to such
an extent that the latter hardly undertook anything without
his advice.[5] The Pope was so pleased with his services that
he gave him the title of Patriarch of Antiochia and on May 30th,
1626, he entrusted to him the difficult Spanish nunciature.[6]
At Madrid everyone remarked on his reserve and reticence.[7]
Against the will of the Spanish minister Olivares, Urban VIII.

---

[1] *Cf.* Accarisio, **Vita Gregorii*, XV. (*cf.* our data XXVII.
Appendix 5).

[2] **Decisioni rotali in sua* [G. B. Pamfili] *ponenza*, 1605–1617.
Doria-Pamfili Arch., 1–8.

[3] See besides, Biaudet, 206 ; N. Capece Galeota, *Cenni
storici dei Nunzii Apost. di Napoli*, Napoli, 1877, 50 *seqq.* The
*reports of Pamfili in *Barb.*, 7467–7477, Vat. Lib. An **Inventario
di mobili di proprietà di G. B. Pamfili nella nunziatura di Napoli*,
in Doria-Pamfili Arch., 1–5. *Ibid.*, unsigned. **Lettere del card.
G. B. Pamfili* (original), among them a number addressed to his
brother Pamfilio, beginning April 3, 1621 (" Hiersera giunsi
in Napoli ") up to 1641. Other *letters, 1621–1646, *ibid.*, 1–4.
Here also the *original of Pamfili's Instruction as nuncio in
Naples signed by Card. Ludovisi ; the same also in Papal Sec.
Arch. *Misc.* A, II., T 177, p. 93 *seqq.*, and *Ottob.* 2206, p. 212 *seqq.*,
Vat. Lib. ; it treats of immunity, faculties and *spolia*.

[4] A. Contarini in Berchet, II., 68.

[5] *Ibid.*

[6] Biaudet, 207 ; *reports in *Barb.* 8326–8343, Vat. Lib.
Cf. Papal Sec. Arch., *Nunziat. di Spagna*, 66ª, 71, 274 ; *Nunziat.
diverse*, 119–121.

[7] See report in Justi, *Velasqueq*, II., 181, n. 1.

admitted him, *motu proprio*, into the Sacred College.[1] At first
Pamfili was retained *in petto* at the creation of August 30th,
1627 ; his nomination was only published on November 19th,
1629, S. Eusebio being assigned to him for his titular church.
He tarried for a time in Madrid and it was only on July 6th,
1630, that he received the red hat at the hands of Urban VIII.
In Rome he worked assiduously in various Congregations,
especially in that of the Council of which he was Prefect.
It was said that he was wont to speak very freely to Urban
VIII. and that he sought to dissuade him from embarking
on the Castro war, the unfortunate issue of which he foresaw.[2]
Already in 1632 he was deemed worthy of the papacy [3]
whereas a few years earlier he had had no prospects whatever.[4] As nuncio his rigidity earned for him the nickname
of *Monsignor non va*—" Monsignor, it is impossible." As a
Cardinal he became even more strict.   He was ever most
cautious and even in the Congregations he would not obstinately maintain his own opinions.[5]   With the Spaniards
he was on good terms.   His prospects of attaining the supreme
dignity rose so high that by 1640 he was considered one of the
chief *papabili*.[6] Three years later the Mantuan envoy gave
it as his opinion that Pamfili excelled both in questions of
Canon Law and in affairs of State.[7]

The new Pope, though seventy years of age, enjoyed the
best of health, thanks to his imperturbable nature.   A contemporary thus describes his outward appearance : " He is

---

[1] *Spicil. Vatic.*, I., 116, and BERCHET, I., 278. *Cf. Colección de
docum. inéd.*, LXXXVI., 169.

[2] **Note* on Brusoni in Doria-Pamfili Arch., 93–46, p. 116b.

[3] Report of Peter von Quren, Canon of Trèves, in *Hist. Jahrb.*,
X., 562.

[4] BERCHET, I., 279.

[5] A. CONTARINI in BERCHET, II., 69.

[6] BERCHET, II., 30.

[7] *" Card. Pamfilio Romano è un soggetto eminente, non
solo nelle materie legali, ma anche in quelle di stato." G. B.
TARABUCCI, *Stato della corte di Roma nel 1643*, Gonzaga Archives,
Mantua.

tall and thin, has small eyes, large feet, a thin beard, an
almost olive green complexion, his head is bald " [1]—that is,
he was no less ugly than Leo X. Just as the latter had the
good fortune to have his portrait painted by Raphael, so
Innocent X. by Velasquez. In 1650 that great master was
treading for the second time the classic soil of the Eternal
City where he witnessed the solemn functions of the jubilee
year and frequented the Roman artists, especially Pietro da
Cortona, Bernini, Algardi, Salvatore Rosa and Nicolas Poussin.
It was on this occasion that Velasquez painted in a short
space of time and without the Pope having given him a single
sitting, the marvellous portrait which at once called forth
the wonder of all Rome whilst it roused the resident artists
to the greatest admiration.

The plan of the picture does not differ from the usual
papal portraits. Innocent X. is seated in an armchair lined
with red plush. The right hand, on which is seen the fisher-
man's ring, hangs over the arm of the chair with extraordinary plastic effect whilst the left holds a sheet of paper
bearing the name of Velasquez. The dazzling whiteness of
the rochet, the red mozzetta, the red round cap, the so-called
camauro, stand out against the background of a crimson
curtain. The colours are singularly fresh—white, grey and a
symphony of every shade of red; the characterization is
unsurpassed. Whereas Raphael beautified and idealized the
unpleasing appearance of Leo X, though without falsifying it,
Velasquez gives a realistic portrait of the Pamfili Pope, so
that if one has once seen this jewel of the Doria gallery, it is
impossible ever to forget it : it is one of the most magnificent
papal portraits.[2] The head is that of a seventy-three years
old man of coarse, unpleasing features, but the fresh complexion and the piercing, searching glance of the blue-grey
eyes show the essential youthfulness of the old man who fixes
on the beholder a keen, thoughtful, questioning glance.

---

[1] CIAMPI, 14, note 3.

[2] GENSEL (*Velasquez*[2], Stuttgart, 1908, XXII.) calls it the most
magnificent male portrait in existence. *Cf.* JANSSEN, *Briefe*,
ed. Pastor, I., Freiburg, 1920, 226.

There is a fascination in this look, proceeding from the depths of the character of the suspicious, secretive old Statesman and characterizing the whole man.[1] *Troppo vero !*—too true ! the Pope is reported to have said ; however, he was so delighted with the work that he bestowed on Velasquez, who refused to accept money, a gold chain with a medal bearing his portrait and recommended him to Philip IV. for a Spanish knighthood.[2] Other aspects of Innocent X.'s character, his dignity and his coldness tinged with kindliness—are faithfully reproduced in the plastic works of contemporary Roman sculptors, especially in Algardi's great bronze statue in the palace of the *Conservatori*.[3] The Pope's grave, sullen features also appear in the powerful bust of the Bologna museum, likewise a work of Algardi. As regards ruthless vividness of conception and characterization,[4] the busts of the Doria gallery in Rome, executed after a model by Bernini, one in

---

[1] IUSTI, *Velasquez*, II., 183 ; TOMASETTI, *Velasquez a Roma* in the periodical *Cosmos catholicus*, 1899, October ; BERUETE, *Velasquez*, Paris, 1898, 118 ; CALVERT, *Velasquez*, London, 1908, 115 *seq.* ; E. STOWE, *Velasquez*, 61 ; A. ARTIOLI, *Il ritratto meraviglioso* in *Arte e Storia*, XXIX. (1910), 10 *seqq.* According to Iusti, p. 190 *seq.*, of the copies only the half-length portrait in Apsley House is certainly by Velasquez and probably also the so-called sketch in the Eremitage at Petrograd. Iuste sees in the Eremitage sketch a copy by the master, Beruete a pre-liminary sketch ; VOLL (*Velasquez*, Munich, 1913) is undecided, as is Gensel ; *loc. cit.*, XXII. (here, plate 82, reproduction of the Eremitage sketch). Beruete does not think the Apsley House portrait is authentic. Iusti considers as the best copy by another hand the picture in Lord Bute's gallery in London. An old copy is also in the museum of Stockholm. *Cf.* also AUG. MAYER, *Gesch. der span. Malerei*, Leipzig, 1922, 414.

[2] IUSTI, II., 231. The *recommendation of Card. Panciroli, dated December 17, 1650 (Papal Sec. Arch.), in XXX., Appendix I.

[3] *Cf.* below, ch. VII.

[4] *Cf.* BERGNER, 97, who considers Bernini's conception to be more calm and objective and more feelingly rendered than by the Spanish masters, as regards the forehead, eyes, and nose.

marble, another in bronze and a third in bronze and marble,[1]
vie with the work of Algardo and even with that of Velasquez
himself.   The marble bust in particular is a masterpiece of
its kind.   It impresses by its simplicity and repose ; it shows
a resigned old man, shut up within himself, but conscious that
he is the master.   The beholder has an impression that the
Pope, in the midst of the difficulties created for him by the
great Powers and by his own family, with shrewd deliberation
overlooks many things which he cannot alter, though without
forgoing his own point of view.   The eyes, which gaze into
the distance, seem to express the weariness of the old man
and his annoyance at the endless quarrels between the Pamfili.
The contemplative nature of Innocent X., his distrust as well
as his real kindliness, are reflected in that look.   The ugliness
is attenuated, yet so that the resemblance does not suffer.[2]

[1] Also in the Palazzo Doria a coloured terracotta bust by
Algardi ; cf. Iusti, II., 185. Muñoz (in Annuario dell'Accad. di
S. Luca, 1912, Roma, 1913, 43) was the first to make known
Algardi's bust. On the statue in the Capital, see below ch. VII.
The bust of Innocent X. in the museum of Ravenna can hardly
be ascribed to Bernini. Of the London bronze bust (see C. Drurye
E. Fortnum, Catalogue of the Bronzes in the South-Kensington
Museum, London, 1876, 7) there is a marble copy in the Palazzo
Doria-Pamfili in Rome, together with other busts of the Pope.
Another bronze bust of Innocent X. also attributed to Algardi,
found its way into the Metropolitan Museum of New York,
in 1907. Among other busts mention may be made of a marble
one in Piazza Navona, a large one, of white marble, in the right
aisle of the Lateran basilica and another in the Villa at S. Martino
al Cimino with an inscription printed by Bussi, 332 ; cf. Boll
d' Arte, VII. (1913), 261. On Algardi's bust in Trinità de'Pellegrini
(see Forcella, VII., 211), cf. below ch. VII. The terracotta bust
of Innocent X. in the Lib. Vallecelliana is a fine piece of work. It
bears the following inscription : " Ioaneus Gambassi civis
Volaterranus cecus fecit." On Cieco da Gambassi (Gonnelli),
see Thieme, XIV., 370.

[2] Reymond, Bernini, 108 and plate XV. ; cf. also Brinckmann, Barockskulptur, II., 246. The bust is now in the private
apartments of Prince Doria, which are not easy of access. On

The masterpieces of Bernini and Velasquez gather together all the characteristics on which contemporary observers dwell ; between them we get a full length picture of the very complicated nature of Innocent X.

Without a doubt the Pamfili Pope possessed many excellent qualities.[1] Moderation characterized his manner of life ; he readily granted audiences and heard everyone patiently. He assisted punctually and with great dignity at all ecclesiastical functions, even the Lenten and Advent sermons. He was genuinely pious and had a keen sense of justice and order. People saw a happy omen of his great love of peace in his arms which showed a dove with an olive branch.[2] The Pope applied himself diligently to affairs but owing to his being a late riser he was for the most part forced to work far into the night, all the more so as he wished to study and to examine personally all the more important documents, and he was slow in making up his mind. All this was in keeping with his mistrust of everyone, especially his entourage, a trait by which he himself embittered his existence. This,

Innocent X.'s coins, cf. SERAFINI, IV., 238. A beautiful medal of the Pope by J. J. Kormann in NOAK, Deutschtum in Rom., I., Berlin, 1927, 140. In his catalogue, XVIII., p.108 seq., E. LANGE registers a great number of prints of Innocent X.

[1] In addition to the Venetian embassy reports in Berchet and the reports of the envoy of Lucca in Studi e documenti, XXII., 218 seq., cf. on the bright and dark spots of Innocent X.'s character the exhaustive *report of Leonard Pappus to Ferdinand III., dat. Rome, September 26, 1652, State Arch., Vienna. See also *Avviso of May 18, 1647, Papal Secr. Arch. (" propriissimo della Sua Santità il pensar assai et il risolver poco ") ; ARNAULD, Négociations, II., 383 ; *Fr. Albizzi to Chigi, dat. Rome, September 24, 1644, Cod. A. III., 55 of Chigi Library ; CIACONIUS, IV., 660 seq. ; SERVANTIUS, *Diaria for December 12, 1644, Papal Secr. Arch. ; DE ROSSI, *Istoria, Vat. Libr., and the *material of Girolamo Brusoni for a Vita d'Innocenzo X., in Doria-Pamfili Archives, 93–46, 4. Fr. Mantovani already complains of Innocent X.'s slowness in his *reports of October 19 and November 5, 1644, State Archives, Modena.

[2] See Harrach's report of September 15, 1644, in MENCIK, 47.

no doubt his greatest fault, joined to his violence, made it difficult to treat with the sulky man with whom favour and displeasure were subject to rapid fluctuations according to the impression of the moment. The diplomatists likewise complained of his obstinacy in debate and the skill with which he knew how to hide his real opinions. Parsimony, which the financial situation fully justified, he carried to great lengths [1]; always suspicious, he had the treasure kept not in Castel S. Angelo but in his own apartments.

Innocent X.'s Italian temperament showed itself both in his parsimony and in his strong attachment to his family ; of the latter trait he gave public proof during the solemn progress to the Lateran when, contrary to the ceremonial, he had the procession halted in front of his parents' house in the Piazza Navona, to enable him to give his blessing to his little niece who was held at a window by her nurse.[2]

Innocent X. would not be taught by the difficulties in which Urban VIII. became involved in consequence of his reckless nepotism, and it never entered his mind to do away with the post of a Cardinal nephew reputed indispensable for running the court. It was the misfortune of the Pamfili Pope that the only person in his family circle possessed of the requisite qualities for such a position, was a woman, viz. his sister-in-law Olimpia Maidalchini-Pamfili, whereas all the nephews whom he successively adorned with the purple proved utter failures.[3]

Donna Maidalchini, born at Viterbo in 1594,[4] was first

---

[1] *" Ha il Papa soppresso diversi uffici a Palazzo che portavano via da cento mila scudi, compresovi ancora gli emolumenti che si sono sminuti al generale di s. Chiesa." Fr. Mantovani on October 8, 1644. State Arch., Modena.

[2] See the Diary of Deone (AMEYDEN) in CIAMPI, n. 1.

[3] IUSTI, II., 182.

[4] Olimpia's fortress-like Gothic palace at Viterbo is to-day the *Ospizio degli Esposti*. On Olimpia's country residence at S. Martino al Cimino and its decoration, see CIACONIUS, IV., 648 ; CHLEDOWSKI, II., 246 ; EHRLE, *Spada*, 11, 13 ; CIAMPI, 205 ; BUSSI, *Istoria di Viterbo*, Rome, 1742, 331 *seq.*

married to Paolo Nini. She contracted a second marriage with the Pope's elder brother Pamfilio Pamfili to whom she bore a son, Camillo, in 1622, and subsequently two daughters, Maria and Costanza. The former was married in 1644 to Prince Nicolò Ludovisi.[1]

Olimpia, whose energetic, resolute but anything but attractive features are admirably portrayed in Algardi's bust in the Doria Gallery,[2] was a very gifted woman [3] but exceedingly ambitious and domineering.[4] She had had a rich dowry ; she accordingly managed to become the most important person in the Pamfili family. Her clerical brother-in-law, Giambattista, she supplied with the requisite funds to enable him to rise, thereby putting him under great obligation to her. The influence she exercised over him continued even when Giambattista had to leave Rome : both as nuncio at Naples and at Madrid he kept up a lively correspondence with his shrewd sister-in-law.[5] On one occasion, whilst at Madrid,

[1] CIAMPI, 11 *seq.* The Pope officiated at Costanza's wedding on December 21, 1644, in the Sistine Chapel (SERVANTIUS, *Diaria*, Papal Secr. Arch.). Twenty-six persons were present at the wedding breakfast, among them being Cardinals Medici, Barberini, Colonna, Orsini and Este (*Avviso* of December 24, 1644, *ibid.*).

[2] CIAMPI, 200, and below, ch. VII ; reproduction in MUÑOZ, *Roma*, 319. Perhaps an even more unpleasant impression is conveyed by the portrait of Olimpia with little Olimpuccia in the private apartments of the Palazzo Doria-Pamfili, reproduced by CHLEDOWSKI, II., 236.

[3] All the contemporaries insist on this fact ; it is also emphasized in the *" Instruttione del sig. Baili de Valencè, ambasciatore Christ. a Roma al suo successore "* (1653), of which there exist numerous manuscript copies (Rome, Chigi Library, N. III., 88. *Barb.*, 53, 32 ; *Ottob.*, 2175 (also in Bibl. communale of Verona). The Lyons Library has a * detailed report, in 3 vols., on his Roman embassy, by Henri d'Estampes-Valençay. Valençay's reports in GÉRIN, I., and CHANTELAUZE, II., 315 *seqq.*

[4] See Venetian reports in BERCHET, II., 50, 69 *seq.*, 101 *seq.*

[5] Part of these *letters (original text) in the *Lettere del card. G. B. Pamfili*, T. IV., in Doria-Pamfili Archives ; they include *a letter, partly in code, dated Naples, February 15, 1625.

he sent her a gift of luxury articles and some glass-ware.[1]

Hence it was not surprising that on the elevation of her brother-in-law to the papacy, Olimpia should have acquired considerable importance.[2] " Olimpia's influence," so the Florentine envoy wrote on February 11th, 1645, " grows daily ; she visits the Pope every other day and the whole world turns to her." [3] But there were not wanting enemies who, by word of mouth and in writing, spread such evil reports that Olimpia lodged a complaint with the Governor of Rome, whereupon a number of arrests were made.[4] However this did not put an end to the libels.[5] Later writers have woven divers myths around the Pope's relations with his sister-in-law, even representing them as criminal ; these assertions are calumnies ; the best information goes to show that there is not a word of truth in the whole myth.[6] However,

---

[1] *" Invio a V.S. certi galantarie e de' vetri." Letter from Madrid, dat. May, 1627, *ibid.*

[2] Prince Andrea Giustiniani, husband of her daughter Maria, became castellan of S. Angelo as early as October 5, 1644 ; *cf.* PAGLIUCCHI, II., 77 *seq.*

[3] State Archives, Florence, *Lett. di Roma*, F. 3373.

[4] *Report of Florentine envoy dat. June 24, 1645, *ibid.*

[5] One of these publications bore the title : *La Olimpiade del governo del Pontefice Innocenzo X.* *Report of the Florentine envoy of June 26 and July 1 and 23, 1645, *loc. cit.*

[6] Niceroni (*Notices of the Writings of famous scholars*, III., 326) already describes Gualdi's *Vita di Donna Olimpia Maidalchini* (Cosmopoli, 1666, and often reprinted, last of all in Rome in 1849[!], translated into French by Renoult, Leyden, 1666) as a romance and an extravagant libel. For all that SCHRÖCKH Kirchengesch., III., Leipzig, 1805, 393) thought that the story was substantially true seeing that it had never been contradicted. RANKE (III., 172) examined it briefly with the above result. *Cf.* also E. ROSSI in the periodical *Roma*, V. (1927), 385 *seqq.*, where, on p. 391 light is thrown on Ameyden's inventions (*cf.* on Ameyden our data, XXIX., Appendix 25). ADEMOLLO (*I narratori*) della vita di Donna O.P., in the *Rassegna settimanale*, 1878, No. 6, p. 94 *seq.*) has established the fact that not G. Leti but

Olimpia's excessive influence over the aged Pontiff is only
too well established. It did grave injury to his prestige for
soon all Rome knew how much in all temporal matters a
word of the wily intriguer weighed with Innocent X. The
nobility, ambassadors, Bishops, Cardinals showed the utmost
regard for Olimpia and strove to secure her goodwill by means
of rich presents, an easy matter in view of the woman's great
covetousness. Even some of their Eminences adorned their
apartments with Olimpia's portrait. She made frequent
appearances at the Vatican and the Pope on his part often
called on her.[1] From time to time the artful woman made
as if she were about to retire, but this she did merely in order
to save appearances. The truth was that the Pope attached
great weight to her opinion, especially in family matters,
yet, self-willed as he was, he would often refuse her most
persistent requests.[2]

Whilst this strange relationship arose, Innocent X. took an
important step for the development of an institution which
was destined, in course of time, to do away with nepotism,
in that, for the first time, he named as Secretary of State a
Cardinal who did not belong to his own family. His choice
fell on Giovanni Giacomo Panciroli, a former auditor of the
Neapolitan and Spanish nunciature who had only received the
purple in 1643. Panciroli's talent and accomplished manners

Gualdi is the real author of the above-mentioned *Vita*, a fact
also insisted upon by DUBARRY (*La belle-sœur d'un Pape*, Paris,
1878). Dubarry wrote a romance about Olimpia and so did
Delécluze, whose work is based on a second revision of Gualdi's
Vita which appeared at Florence in 1781. In France Olimpia
was represented as a poisoner ; see RENÉE, *Nièces de Mazarin*,
5th edit., 219. *Cf.* also the anecdote in J. RACINE, *Œuvres
complètes*, ed. Mesnard, V., Paris, 1887, 168. Roman satires against
Olimpia in CIAMPI, 142 *seq.* ; one such in the library of St. Gall ;
see catalogue of its MSS., 409.

[1] *Cf.* *Diary of Deone (Ameyden) and the *Avvisi* in Papal
Sec. Arch. ; Giov. Giustinian in BERCHET, II., 102 ; PALLA-
VICINO, *Alessandro VII.*, I., 190.

[2] EHRLE, *Spada*, 5 *seq.* ; *cf.* E. ROSSI, *loc. cit.*, 390.

made him an excellent interpreter of the papal policy. Both he and the datarius Cecchini were assigned apartments in the Pope's palace. Innocent X. attached great weight to his opinion.[1] Besides Panciroli, who surrounded himself with excellent secretaries,[2] there also arose a Cardinal nephew in the person of Camillo, Olimpia's son.[3]

Camillo had at first been destined for the post of a lay nephew. On September 27th, 1644, the Pope had named him General of the Church, on October 1st Commander-in-Chief of the papal fleet and the Guards as well as Governor of the Borgo and the chief fortresses of the Pontifical States.[4] Soon, however, Camillo laid aside all these offices in order to become a Cardinal nephew. On November 14th, 1644, he was raised to the Sacred College [5] when the full tide of papal favours poured itself over him. In that same year, 1644, he was given the legation of Avignon, the supreme superintendence of the Papal States and an abbey at Capua ; to this came to be added in the ensuing years a great number of benefices and other favours. He also became Prefect of Briefs and of the *Segnatura delle grazie.*[6]

---

[1] CIACONIUS, IV., 627 ; Venetian reports in BERCHET, II., 52, 71.

[2] *" Ha chiamati a se buoni segretari, onde si spera rinoverà quell'antica e buona scuola e dei Feliciani e degli Aguchia." Fr. degli Albizzi to Chigi, dat. Rome, September 5, 1644. Cod. A. III., 55, Chigi Library, Rome.

[3] The title was no longer *Cardinal Padrone* but *Cardinale sopraintendente agl' affari maggiori* ; see FILIPPO DE ROSSI, *Istoria giornale della corte de Roma scritta negl' anni 1653 e 1654,* Vat. 8873, Vat. Libr. Numerous *letters of congratulation to Camillo Pamfili on the occasion of the election of Innocent X. in Rospigliosi Archives, Rome, 207, n. 2.

[4] See *Index bullarum expeditarum ad favorem card. Pamphili, Doria-Pamfili Archives, 1–9.

[5] Acta consist., Papal Secr. Arch. It is impossible to control the assertions of Deone (Ameyden) in his *Diario (see CIAMPI, 123) and the *Avvisi* on the proceedings at the consistory.

[6] *Index bullarum ad fav. card. Pamphili, *loc. cit.*

The new Cardinal nephew was by no means destitute of talents [1] ; he was fond of poetry and the plastic arts and had such a grasp of technical problems as to enable him to submit a plan for galleys at Civitavecchia.[2] In the Secretariate of State it was his duty to sign letters and dispatches, as had been done by former Cardinal nephews ; incoming correspondence came to him and Panciroli, and the ambassadors had to present themselves before both Cardinals.[3]

At first Camillo performed his duties with assiduity, but as Innocent X. did not suffer him to have any influence,[4] his zeal soon cooled [5] until it gave out altogether. If this circumstance alone was bound to annoy the Pope, his displeasure was further increased when he learnt that Camillo was resolved to lay aside the purple and to marry a beautiful, wealthy and gifted young widow—Olimpia Aldobrandini, Princess of Rossano.[6] This plan was vehemently opposed by Olimpia Maidalchini who feared that her position would be shaken by a sister-in-law of a higher social rank and of outstanding intellectual gifts. Accordingly she did all in her power to thwart the projected alliance and she persisted in her opposition even after Innocent X. had yielded to his nephew's importunity. In view of the fact that the Pope had previously dissuaded his nephew from taking priest's orders, people surmised that he had from the first looked on the cardinalate as no more than a transition and that there had existed between the Pontiff and Camillo a secret understanding concerning the match.[7]

---

[1] Portrait by G. B. Gaulli in the Doria Gallery ; see Voss, *Malerei*, 587. Another portrait now in the museum of the Hispanic Society of America, New York ; *cf.* Iusti, *Velasquez*, II.[3], 179.

[2] Ciampi, 122.

[3] *Cf.* Richard in *Rev. d'hist. eccl.*, XI. (1910), 735.

[4] *Avviso* of January 26, 1647, Papal Sec. Arch.

[5] See the report of the envoy of Lucca in *Studi e docum.*, XXII., 219.

[6] *Cf.* Savelli's *report to Ferdinand III., dat. January 5, 1647, State Archives, Vienna.

[7] See above, p. 36. *Cf.* reports in Coville, 144 *seq.*

In a consistory of January 21st, 1647, the Pope granted the requisite dispensations and accepted Camillo's resignation of the cardinalate.[1] Even after the marriage contract had been concluded, on February 2nd,[2] Olimpia continued to give public expression, in all sorts of ways, to her strong disapproval.[3] In vain the Pope sought to calm her.[4] Neither she nor Innocent X. assisted at the wedding of Camillo and Olimpia Aldobrandini which took place, very quietly, on February 10th, 1647, at the Villa Torre Nuova, six miles outside Rome.[5] The young couple immediately withdrew to the Castle of Caprarola and thence to Frascati, a circumstance that gave rise to all kinds of rumours.[6] For the time being the couple had to remain out of Rome as the jealousy of Olimpia could not endure the presence of her sister-in-law in the city.[7]

In the sequel Olimpia's influence grew as much as her wealth, for the money-loving woman exacted good payment for the smallest service, and since everyone knew how well she could manage Innocent X., thanks to her knowledge of the latter's peculiar character, and that her opinion had great weight, the whole world turned to her and gold flowed to her in an ever growing stream. She was frequently closeted for as long as four to six hours with the Pope who did nothing of importance without consulting her.[8] Even Cardinal Panciroli

---

[1] *Acta consist.*, Papal Sec. Arch. *Cf.* Camillo's declaration together with other details regarding this affair in *Cod.* N. III., 69, p. 305, of the Chigi Libr., Rome. To escape his having to surrender the red hat in person Camillo left Rome ; see Savelli's report to Ferdinand III., January 19, 1647, State Archives, Vienna.

[2] SERVANTIUS *Diaria*, Papal Sec. Arch.

[3] *Avviso* of February 2, 1647, *ibid.*

[4] *Avviso* of February 9, 1647, *ibid.*

[5] Savelli's *report to Ferdinand III., dat. January 9, 1647, State Arch., Vienna ; ADEMOLLO, *Gigii*, 121.

[6] *Avvisi* of February 16 and March 6, 1647, Papal Sec. Arch. ; Deone in CIAMPI, 131 ; Gigli in CANCELLIERI, *Mercato*, 108.

[7] ARNAULD, *Négociations*, IV., 25 ; *cf.* 116.

[8] *Cf.* *Avvisi* of May 18, June 22 and July 27, 1647, Papal Sec.

kept on good terms with her. The two joined forces when
the question arose of giving a successor to Camillo Pamfili ;
in effect, on October 7th, 1647, Francesco Maidalchini,
Olimpia's seventeen years old nephew, was raised to the
cardinalate.[1] However, to the Pope's painful surprise,
Francesco proved utterly unfit for the position of a Cardinal
nephew, a fact which created great difficulties in the transac-
tion of business.[2] Even Innocent X. was forced to see that
a more capable person must be found for treating with the
ambassadors. Panciroli induced the Pope to entrust this
post to the thirty years old Camillo Astalli, a distant relative
of Olimpia.[3] To the general amazement Innocent, always
hasty and capricious, bestowed on Astalli, on one and the
same day (September 19th, 1650), the purple, his name, his
arms and all the privileges of a nephew ; at the same time
he made him a present of the palace in Piazza Navona and
the Villa before Porta S. Pancrazio.[4] It was generally believed
that Olimpia, who had at one time secured for Astalli the

Arch. *" Se raccontare se volesse i casi della sua nauseante
ingordigia da lei esercitata," says Fr. de Rossi of Olimpia, " se
ne empirebbero i volumi (*Istoria, Vat. 8873, Vat. Libr.).

[1] See *Acta consist., Papal Sec. Arch. ; F. de Rossi, *Istoria
Vat. 8873, Vat. Lib.

[2] See A. Contarini in BERCHET, II., 72 seq. ; ibid., 126 seq.
Maidalchini's limited intellectual gifts roused the irony of
Pasquino ; but his conduct was blameless and his liberality
great ; cf. besides STEINHUBER, I.², 398, *Scrittura politica
soprà il conclave da farsi (a. 1689), Liechtenstein Archives,
Vienna.

[3] De Rossi *Istoria (Vat. 8873, Vat. Libr.), according to whom
Astalli's elevation was thought of already in 1647. Cf. also
G. Riccardi's *" dissertation on the College of Cardinals in 1652 ",
in Cod. C. III., 60, Chigi Library, Rome.

[4] *Acta consist., Papal Sec. Arch. ; AMEYDEN, *Diary, Barb.
4819, Vat. Lib. ; Gigli in CANCELLIERI, Mercato, 109 ; CIAMPI,
150 ; Giustinian in BERCHET, II., 127 ; *Diary in Cod. 93-46 of
Doria-Pamfili Archives ; DENIS, I., 255 seq. Magalotti says
in his *" Osservazioni sopra la futura elezione del S. Pontefice ",
that people could not understand how Innocent X. could have

post of a consistorial advocate and later on a clericate of the *Camera*,[1] had brought about the rise of this mediocre personage. In point of fact Olimpia had had nothing to do with it ; her prestige, which in June, 1649, was still such as to enable her, with the help of Panciroli, to bring about the fall of the influential datarius Cardinal Cecchini,[2] had begun to wane already in the autumn of that year.[3] She now fell into complete disgrace for, roused by her sons-in-law Giustiniani and Ludovisi, she had allowed herself to be carried away by perfect fits of fury on account of Astalli's elevation. The Pope, in consequence, forbade her the Vatican. Even before this occurrence, Panciroli had counselled such a step by dwelling on the scandal which Olimpia's rule created everywhere, especially in Germany.[4]

In October Olimpia's fall was looked upon as definite. The Princess of Rossano was triumphant,[5] and with good reason. Three months after Olimpia's fall, at the request of his sister Agata, a nun in the convent of Tor de' Specchi, Innocent received Camillo Pamfili back into his good graces. When, on January 8th, 1651, the latter presented himself at an audience with his two years old little son, the Pope was unable to restrain his tears. To the child he gave a silver statue of his patron Saint, John the Baptist.[6] On January

hit on Astalli ; Magalotti sees in it a sudden *capriccio, Cod. C. III.*, 60, Chigi Libr.

[1] *De Rossi, *loc. cit.*

[2] *Cf.* FUMI in *Arch. Rom.*, X., 317 *seq.* The resignation of the Dataria which Cecchini offered at once, was only accepted by Innocent X. on September 15, 1652, together with a declaration of complete disgrace ; see Servantius, *Diaria, loc. cit.* ; *De Rossi, *loc. cit.*

[3] DENIS, I., 154.

[4] PALLAVICINO, *Alessandro VII.*, I., 155 *seq.*, whose account is confirmed by *De Rossi (*loc. cit.*). *Cf.* also Giustinian in BERCHET, II., 103, and *Arch. Rom.*, X., 318.

[5] See *Diaro* del a. 1650 (by Ameyden) *Barb.* 4891, p. 118, Vat. Lib.

[6] Servantius *Diaria, loc. cit.*, who remarks : " Post spatium tandem quinque annorum Camillus Pamphilius nepos Papae

20th it was learnt that Camillo's wife had been with the Pope for three hours and had received rich presents from him [1] ; shortly before she had given birth to her second child.[2] Thereafter she visited the Pope almost every week and won a not inconsiderable influence, whereas Camillo had none at all.[3]

Old Cardinal Panciroli had hoped, after Olimpia's fall, to retain his influence with the Pope through Astalli who owed him everything. In this he was greatly deceived ; very soon he had to realize that Astalli would not be guided by him, on the contrary, grown proud by reason of his sudden exaltation, the latter broke with him and in the end became a successful rival. Together with Camillo Pamfili he intrigued against Panciroli.[4] The latter's bad state of health also helped to contribute to a gradual estrangement between him and the Pope.[5] No one sympathized with the Secretary of State, had he not prepared a similar fate for so many others ? Almost in disgrace, Panciroli died on September 3rd, 1651.[6] It became evident that Cardinal Pamfili could not carry out unaided the duties of a Secretary of State ; his inexperience and indolence were such as to cause Innocent X. to regret his elevation. Moreover the Pope did not really trust him and repeatedly reproached him with being far more

ob dimissam card. dignitatem contumax fuit a gratia pontificis et modo extra urbem exul, modo vero Romae ignotus privatim vitam duxit una cum principessa Rossano eius uxore."

[1] Servantius *Diaria, loc. cit.

[2] According to *records in the Dora-Pamfili Archives the following children were born to Camillo and Olimpia Aldobrandini : 1, Giov. Battista, born June 24, 1648 ; 2, Flaminia, b. January 5, 1651 ; 3, Benedetto (a future Cardinal), b. April 25, 1653 ; 4, Teresa, b. October 16, 1654. On the splendid palace erected by Camillo in 1662 at Valmontone, see TOMASSETTI, III., 457.

[3] De Rossi, *Istoria, Vat. 8873, Vat. Lib.

[4] See the *Dissertations by Magalotti and G. Riccardi quoted above, p. 39, nn. 3 and 4 Chigi Lib., Rome.

[5] PALLAVICINO, Alessandro, VII., I., 156.

[6] Servantius, *Diaria, loc. cit. Cf. Giustinian in BERCHET, II., 94 seq. ; Arch. Rom., X., 318 seq.

interested in the affairs of the Pamfili than in those of the Pope. Cardinal Borghese, he remarked, though sprung from the House of Caffarelli, became a complete Borghese.[1] Outwardly, however, Pamfili enjoyed all the prerogatives of his position ; he occupied the apartments set apart for the nephews and was given rich benefices.[2]

Nevertheless a new Secretary of State had to be appointed. Astalli sought in vain to direct the choice to his cousin Francesco Gaetani or to the very gifted Decio Azzolini. Cardinal Spada, whom the Pope often consulted in the most important affairs, proposed Fabio Chigi, until then nuncio in the Rhineland.[3] To this Innocent agreed. He did not know Chigi personally but he set great value on his reports.[4] In the first days of October, 1651, Chigi left Aix-la-Chapelle, where he had lodged with the Canons Regular. Whilst Chigi was still on the way, Astalli sought to circumvent his appointment and to prejudice the Spanish ambassador, the Duke of Infantado, against him, but all in vain.[5]

---

[1] De Rossi, *Istoria*, Vat. 8873, and *Diaro* del. a. 1650 (Ameyden), *Barb.* 4819, Vat. Lib. *Cf.* Giustinian in BERCHET, II., 127 *seq.* In the *Instruttione del sig. Baili de Valencè*, quoted p. 33, n. 3, we read : " Il card. Pamfilio è adottivo e adiettivo nella casa del Papa, e buon per lui, se assieme colla berretta se gli fosse potuto dare il cervello. Nel principio non era in grazia, ed in progresso di tempo ha vacillato di tal maniera che talvolta parse stabilito sicuramente e talaltra, vicino a' precipitii et alle ruine. Non sono in lui qualità singolari, e certo che sarebbe stato proclive a' passatempi piuttosto che adattato al negotio, quando non l'havesse ritirato il genio del Papa. Di amore è piutosto francese, ma non sa pigliare la congiontura di mostrarlo all'occorrenza ; è romanesco nè mai è partito da Roma. *Ottob.* 2175, p. 7[b], Vat. Lib.

[2] *De Rossi, loc. cit.* On November 21, 1650, Cardinal Pamfili had received the Avignon legation. *Acta consist.*, Papal Sec. Arch.

[3] PALLAVICINO, I., 157 *seq.*

[4] *Cf.* De Rossi, *Istoria, Vat. 8873, Vat. Lib.

[5] Infantado's conduct was wholly in keeping with the intentions of his sovereign who invited him to support Chigi in a

Chigi, who was preceded by an excellent reputation, reached Rome on the last day of November.[1] At their very first meeting the Pope was completely won over by him, consequently the last minute intrigues against him also failed completely. About the middle of December he took up residence at the Vatican. Both the party of Cardinal Pamfili and that of the Princess of Rossano sought to win him over but Chigi would ally himself to neither. As Secretary of State, he declared, it was his duty to mind political and ecclesiastical affairs, not those of a particular family.[2]

When, at the beginning of February, 1652, Pamfili, by order of the Pope, informed Chigi of his impending elevation to the Sacred College, the latter replied that he would be far better able to serve His Holiness in his present condition. On the same evening Chigi had an audience with the Pope. Of what Pamfili had told him he never said a word, so that Innocent X. thought that the Cardinal had failed to carry out his instructions. When he was informed that this was not so, he exclaimed : " I have never yet met such a man ! " On the eve of his elevation to the cardinalate, which took place on February 19th, 1652, Chigi remarked to a friend that if he could strike out his name from the list, he would do so since dignities merely added to responsibility.[3]

Previous to his nomination as a Cardinal Chigi had rendered the Pope a signal service when he exposed the shameful conduct of the Sub-datarius Francesco Canonici, surnamed Mascambruno, whom Innocent X. held in great esteem. To enrich himself Mascambruno had not scrupled to falsify documents for which he surreptitiously obtained the papal signature.[4] He was tried together with his accomplices ;

*letter in code dated Madrid, November 29, 1651. Arch. of the Spanish Embassy, Rome.

[1] " Personnage discret, sage, spirituel et sans vicieuse ambition, homme d'intelligence et de probité," writes Gueffier, the French Resident, CHANTELAUZE, *Ritz.*, II., 340.

[2] PALLAVICINO, I., 166–170.

[3] *Ibid.*, 172.

[4] See *Scritture contro Msgr. Mascambruno, Barb.* 5323,

on April 15th, 1652, severe sentences were passed. Mascambruno was executed and died repentant.[1]

The fall of Mascambruno, who had been hostile to Olimpia,
proved very advantageous to the latter,[2] but she benefited
even more by the constant disputes between Camillo, the
Princess of Rossano and Cardinal Pamfili, disputes that greatly
vexed the Pope. Thus it came about that Innocent's attachment to his sister-in-law, which had never been wholly
extinct, came once more to life ; her shrewdness, so he
thought, would restore peace in the family. The majority
of the Cardinals and the other prelates also favoured a pardon,
for, they remarked, Olimpia would have been taught by misfortune and would henceforth keep within becoming bounds.
Chigi alone thought otherwise, but his warnings were not
heeded.[3] After the Pope's sister Agata had brought about a
reconciliation between the two rivals, the Princess of Rossano,
on March 11th, 1653, conducted Olimpia into the presence
of the Pope who received her graciously.[4] The last state,

p. 188–211, and Chigi Library, N. III., 69, p. 570–595 ; G. B.
RINALDUCCI, *Prosperità infelice di Francesco Canonici detto
Mascambruno* (Bibl. Casanat., X., VII., 46, Urb. 1728 and
Barb. 4898, Vat. Lib. ; Archives of the Spanish Embassy, Rome ;
Magl. Cl., XXV., n. 457, National Lib., Florence), anonymous,
printed with variants in *Miscell. di varia lett.*, V., Lucca, 1765.
Cf. *Römisches Tagebuch* in Cod. 93–46 of Doria-Pamfili Arch. ;
PALLAVICINO, I., 186 seq. ; BERCHET, II., 149 ; CIAMPI, 154 seq. ;
REUSCH, Index, II., 495, 1225 ; DÖLLINGER-REUSCH, Moralstreitig-
keiten, I., 604 ; CHANTELAUZE, loc. cit., 383 seq., 393 seqq., 403
seqq., 435 seqq., 463, 465 seqq., 469 seqq., 474 seq.

[1] "*In atrio Turris Nonæ," says Servantius (*Diaria), who
describes Mascambruno as " ingeniosissimus, habilissimus et
cujuslibet licet maximi negotii capax " (Papal Sec. Arch.).
The sentenza of April 15, 1652, in Arch. of the Spanish Embassy,
Rome. Cf. *Decio Memmoli, Relaz. della morte di Fr. Mascam-
bruni, in Barb. 4885, Vat. Lib.

[2] De Rossi *Istoria, Vat. 8873, Vat. Lib.

[3] PALLAVICINO, I., 191 seqq.

[4] Servantius *Diaria, Papal Sec. Arch. ; Gigli in CANCELLIERI,
Mercato, 110, and CIAMPI, 166.

however, was destined to be worse than the first : Olimpia's influence waxed greater than ever [1] and she exploited it as before. One of the victims of her intrigues was Cardinal Pamfili whom the Pope had mistrusted already for some time by reason of his relations with the Medici and the Spaniards. On February 2nd, 1654, it was decided to remove him from Rome by offering him the see of Ferrara. When Pamfili declined, he was forced to leave the Eternal City ; his disgrace was public and he forfeited everyone of his positions and dignities. In July, 1654, a similar fate overtook Niccolò Ludovisi. Cardinal Chigi, who had vainly endeavoured to save Pamfili, was now entrusted with the duty of signing dispatches in the latter's place. However, this extension of power was only apparent for Olimpia was bent on undermining his position after she had unsuccessfully attempted to make this strong and honourable character subservient to her interests.[2]

How successfully Olimpia undermined Innocent X.'s confidence in Chigi is shown by the fact that the final decision concerning the nomination of Cardinals in March, 1654, was made without the Secretary of State having been consulted, and since on this occasion the purple was bestowed on Decio Azzolini,[3] Secretary of the *cifra*, an avowed follower of Olimpia, it was thought that he would also obtain the Secretariate of State. However, Innocent X. could not part with Chigi, but Olimpia at least secured this much, namely that Azzolini

---

[1] "*Erario unico onde uscivano le grazie," says De Rossi (*Istoria, loc. cit.*).

[2] PALLAVICINO, I., 194, whose account is confirmed by De Rossi, *Istoria (Vat. 8873, Vat. Lib. Cf. also DENIS, I., 302 ; ADEMOLLO, Gigli, 113 seqq. ; CIAMPI, 169 seqq., 376 ; Quellen und Forschungen, IV., 243 ; PICCOLOMINI, Corrisp. tra la corte di Roma e l'Inquisitore di Malta, II., Florence, 1910, 7 ; on Ludovisi's fall, cf. GUGLIELMOTTI, 135.

[3] Azzolini, born 1612 (see MORONI, III., 314 seq. ; G. de MINICIS, Notizie biogr. del card. D. Azzolino, Fermo, 1858), was also Secretary of the Epistolae ad principes since 1653. His predecessors in that office were, from 1644–7, Gaspar de Simeonibus, and from 1648–1653, Franc. Nerlius. Papal Sec. Arch.

should always be present at the audience of the Secretary of State.[1] Had Innocent's life been prolonged Chigi would probably have been overthrown, for Olimpia was unwilling to share her influence with anyone. Innocent X. ended by painfully realizing that he had become " a tool of a woman's greed for power and gold " ; but how was he, an octogenarian and one who had always found it difficult to make up his mind, to muster sufficient strength to break these unworthy shackles, which could not fail to injure the prestige of the Holy See ? Olimpia's avarice revealed itself in most revolting fashion after the Pope's demise (January 7th, 1655) : the woman who owed to the dead man such vast sums of money [2] refused, as did Camillo Pamfili, to pay for the customary wood and lead coffins so that, after it had been exposed in St. Peter's, the body had to be kept for several days in a damp corner of the sacristy and to be buried in the most simple manner imaginable [3] : " a stern warning for the

---

[1] PALLAVICINO, I., 206 seq.

[2] See Arch. Rom., IV., 252 seq., 259 ; CIAMPI, 337 seqq., 344 seqq. Cf. *Avviso of May 18, 1647. Papal Sec. Arch.

[3] De Rossi, *Istoria, Vat. 8873, Vat. Lib. ; PALLAVICINO, I., 213 ; Gigli in NOVAES, X., 60, and CANCELLIERI, Mercato, 115 ; *Deone's *diary in Cod. 93–46 of Doria-Pamfili Archives, Rome. On January 13, 1655, Riccardi, the Florentine envoy, wrote : " *Il Papa non è ancora sotterrato, perchè non si trova chi voglia fare la spesa. D. Camillo dice di non havere havuto niente da Sᵃ Bⁿᵉ e toccare di farlo alla Sig.ᵃ Donna Olimpia ; et essa dice : che ella non è l'herede. E così Sᵃ Bⁿᵉ se ne sta là in un canto, in una cassaccia." On January 30, 1655, the same wrote : " *Dopo la morte del Papa la Sigᵃ Donna Olimpia ha detto che ella resta più... mortificata del modo che tiene Maidal-chini, essendo unito con i suoi nemici, che della morte del medesimo Papa e delle tante pasquinate e scritture uscite contro di lei. Che sebbene gli era stato innanzi detto che il card.ˡᵉ suo nipote era stato guadagnato dalli Spagnuoli e dai Fiorentini, non l'haveva mai creduto, se non quando l'ha visto." The same on the same day : " *[D. Olimpia]) si chiama malissimo sodisfatta del signor card.ˡᵉ suo nipote che (come si scrisse) ella cacciò di case e gli fece mettere le sue masserizie in casa del signor principe Ludovisio;

Popes," says Cardinal Pallavicino, "one showing what
gratitude they may expect from relatives for whose sake they
have often enough risked both honour and conscience." [1]

e intendo che in conclave egli continui a dir male della zia, come
faceva di fuora." State Archives, Florence.

[1] PALLAVICINO, *loc. cit.* On Olimpia's end, *cf.* CIAMPI in
N. Antologia, 1877.

CHAPTER II.

Mazarin and Innocent X.—The Intrigues of the
Barberini—The Imprisonment of Cardinal Retz—
Relations with Spain and Portugal—The Rising at
Naples.

(1.)

Innocent X.'s election meant a sensible defeat for Cardinal
Mazarin, the leader of France's policy. He had done his
utmost to procure the tiara for a friend of his and now he
had to witness the elevation of the very Cardinal whom he
had expressly excluded, and it had so happened that the
Cardinal Protector of France, Antonio Barberini, and even
the French ambassador had substantially contributed to
bring it about !

For a moment Mazarin seriously considered whether France
should not refuse to recognize the new Pope on the plea that
his election was illegal, but in the end he shrank from taking
so dangerous a course.[1] He began by venting his tremendous
anger on those whom he regarded as the authors of the
election. In October, 1644, Antonio Barberini was deprived,
in brutal fashion, of his Protectorate of France, an event
which caused an enormous sensation in Rome.[2] About the
middle of December the French ambassador, Saint-Chamond,
was recalled from his post. The punishment was excessive
forasmuch as Saint-Chamond was guilty, not of treason, but
merely of grave imprudence. Accordingly the latter thought
that he might successfully invoke the clemency of the King
and Queen, but Mazarin would not be softened. The whole
affair weakened the prestige of Innocent X. inasmuch as it

---

[1] See Mém. du P. Rapin, I., 89 ; Coville, 27 *seq.* ; cf.
Bougeant, *Hist. des guerres et négotiat. qui précéd. le traité de
Westphalie*, IV., Paris, 1759, 59.

[2] See *report of Card. Harrach to Ferdinand III., dat. Nov. 19,
1644. State Archives, Vienna.

created a suspicion that he had obtained the papacy through some intrigue.[1] For the rest, Mazarin was soon made to feel that his punitive measures had isolated France in dangerous fashion, for the Barberini now turned to Spain.[2] Thereupon the Cardinal-Minister promptly changed his tactics. In November, 1644, Monsieur de Grémonville, until then accredited to Venice, was dispatched to Rome for the purpose of offering to the Pope the homage of the French royal couple. He was to seize the opportunity to obtain the elevation to the cardinalate of Michel, Mazarin's brother, on the ground that by this means the Pope would best refute the accusation of partiality towards Spain.[3] At the same time Mazarin resigned the Abbey of Corbie, reputed the second richest in the realm and yielding 12,000 scudi a year, in favour of Cardinal Camillo Pamfili. The latter accepted the gift, but his uncle remained deaf to Grémonville's prayers and representations. Michel Mazarin's candidature for the red hat failed completely, he himself contributing not a little to this result by his impetuosity and want of tact.[4]

At the promotion of March 6th, 1645, eight new Cardinals were proclaimed, all of them excellent men, but favouring Spain and hostile to the Barberini.[5] France's representatives, who had already made bitter complaints,[6] became still louder

---

[1] COVILLE, 37 seqq.

[2] COCHIN, H. Arnauld, 67. Simeoni (above p. 19, n. 1) justly remarks (p. 56) that Mazarin's policy towards Rome was from the first " meschina e personale ".

[3] Instruction of Dec. 26, 1644, in ARNAULD, Négociations, I., 128 seqq., 137 seqq. When informing the Queen-Regent Anne of his election, Innocent X. had assured her that he would not forget the honours paid to him by Louis XIII. during his stay in France. Letter of Sept. 16, 1644, in FILLON, n. 2457.

[4] COVILLE, 55 seqq. On Mich. Mazarin, cf. G. de MUN in Rev. d'hist. dipl., IV. (1904), 497 seqq.

[5] The hostility of the newly elect towards the Barberini is insisted upon by the Florentine envoy in his *report of March 12, 1645. State Arch., Florence, loc. cit.

[6] *Avviso of Feb. 23, 1645, Papal Sec. Arch.

with their protests.[1] As for Mazarin, when he was informed,
his fury knew no bounds.   Henceforth, he muttered, he
would change his tune. Even Queen Anne spitefully remarked
that the Pope was mistaken if he imagined that he could
treat great kings like the small prelates of the Roman court.
In Paris there was talk of a schism. Grémonville was ordered
to adopt a manner that would frighten Rome ; the nuncio
also had to hear many remarks to the same effect.[2]

Mazarin's speeches and writings of the period bear witness
to his rage. Many people, he remarked, had their own ideas
about the election of Innocent X. ; until now he had kept
silent and enforced silence, but those who roused him would
have cause to regret it.[3]   Nor was he content with words.
On March 27th, 1646, Grémonville was ordered to betake
himself at once to Venice.   This interruption of diplomatic
relations did not as yet imply a complete rupture because
the nuncio stayed on in Paris and a number of French agents
remained in Rome, but they only dealt with secondary
matters, not with affairs of State. Mazarin maintained
contact with Rome only in so far as this made it possible for
him to create difficulties for Innocent X.

Michel Mazarin was indemnified by his elevation to the
archiepiscopal see of Aix which had just then become vacant
and the Pope was compelled to approve the nomination.[4]

---

[1] *Avviso* of March 11, 1645, *ibid.* ; *report of Savelli, April 15,
1645, State Arch., Vienna. Cf. also the *letter of the Secretary
of State to Rinuccini dated April 10, 1645 : " Fu inviata a
V. S. la Rosa Pontificia, acciò ella compiacesse di presentarla
in nome di Nostro Signore alla Maestà della regina di Francia ;
ma perchè sono giunte lettere da quel Monsignor Nunzio, nelle
quali avvisa che si mostri in quella corte molto sentimento per
non esser stato posto nella promotione il Padre Mazzarino, sarà
bene che ella non pigli in modo alcuno risolutione di presentarla
se non vede acquietato il disgusto, et non sia più che certo che il
dono potesse essere accettato volentieri.   Il che si lascia alla
molta prudenza di lei." Papal Sec. Arch.

[2] COVILLE, 57 *seqq.*

[3] *Lettres du card. Mazarin*, éd. Chéruel, II., 131, 135.

[4] COVILLE, 60 *seqq.*

But this was not revenge enough for Mazarin. He sought to create opponents for Innocent X. in Rome itself. To this end he resolved to make his peace with the Barberini. This was not easy because as soon as the latter realized that Mazarin needed them, they changed their tactics, seeking to get the utmost in return for as little as possible.[1] However, in the end events compelled the Barberini to accept so powerful a patronage. Besides, they were not united among themselves and their counsels were divided.[2]

Such was the hatred which Urban VIII.'s nephews had drawn on themselves in Rome that according to a report of the envoy of Este in October 1644, everyone wished to see them punished. The Romans witnessed with satisfaction the depressed air of those who had once been so proud.[3] In these circumstances it was no small comfort for the latter, when it was reported that the new Pope was prepared to forgive them.[4] But after a long period of suspense between hope and despair, the Barberini were forced to realize that they would be called to account for the enormous wealth they had accumulated during the reign of Urban VIII. In March, 1645, Cardinal Giustiniani said that the Pope was bound in conscience to try the Barberini and to punish them should their guilt be established.[5]

When in June, 1645, an inquiry was begun into the administration of public money during the war of Castro, the memory of the fate of the relatives of Paul IV. must have haunted Urban VIII.'s nephews like a nightmare.[6] However,

---

[1] *Ibid.*, 70 *seq.*

[2] See the interesting *report of Walter Leslie to Ferdinand III., dated Rome, May 5, 1645, State Arch., Vienna.

[3] *Report of Fr. Mantovani of October 5, 1644. State Arch., Modena.

[4] *Report of Fr. Mantovani of October 19, 1644, *ibid.*

[5] *Report of the Florentine envoy, March 30, 1645, State Arch., Florence, *loc. cit.*

[6] See *the reports of the Florentine envoy of June 3, 11, 24, 1645, State Arch., Florence. Cf. P. LINAGE DE VAUCIENNES, *Différend des Barberini avec le pape Innocent X.*, Paris, 1678. A

it was very difficult to bring home to the Barberini any real defalcations for they had covered themselves betimes with divers decrees of Urban VIII. Innocent X. himself said as much to the Florentine envoy who reported that the Pope was particularly incensed against Antonio Barberini.[1] The Pope's anger so alarmed the latter that the threatened man, who of all his brothers had always entertained the strongest sympathy towards France,[2] decided on a desperate step. On the evening of September 28th, 1645, he let it be known that he was about to drive to Monterotondo whither his servants had preceded him. In reality, disguised beyond recognition, he repaired to Santa Marinella, a small hamlet on the coast between Palo and Civitavecchia, where, accompanied by only one servant, he embarked on a small boat with the intention of sailing for Genoa, but a violent storm compelled him to seek shelter in the harbour of Leghorn, from whence, disguised as a sailor, he safely reached the

---

*Discorso per eccitare Innocenzo X. ad procedere contro i Barberini (written shortly after the death of Urban VIII.) in Barb. 5650, p. 90 seqq. Vat. Lib.

[1] See the *letter of the Florentine envoy, July 5, 1645 : " Mi disse [il Papa] ancora che havea fatto vedere le spese fatte a la Camera di tanti milioni, e che non può ritrovare niente da potere attaccare i Barberini, havendo bene aggiustato le scritture. E dicendogli io : B^{do} P^e, gli è una gran cosa quello raconta il sig. Card^e Cornaro pubblicamente, che venendo egli a Roma poco tempo prima che morisse Papa Urbano, egli fu a baciargli i piedi, e S. St^à gli disse : Sig. Card^{le}, siamo stati assassinati da nostri nepoti, che ci hanno fatto far la guerra e perdere la vita e la riputazione ; da che si vede chiaramente, dissi io, che Papa Urbano fu aggirato ; e per capriccio de' Barberini, e non del Papa, è stato rovinata la Chiesa Apostolica e lo Stato ecclesiastico. Mi rispose S. St^à : V. S. dice bene ; ma si sono aggiustati e fortificati con brevi, bolle e chirografi, che non si può far niente a voler far la giustizia . . ." State Arch., Florence.

[2] *" Cardinal Antonio has French sympathies and imagines he cannot live unless he becomes reconciled with France," W. Leslie wrote on May 5, 1645, to Ferdinand III. State Arch., Vienna.

coast of Provence.[1] He sent his excuses to the Pope for his disappearance without farewell audience ; the motive of his departure, he claimed, was the desire to clear himself in France of the accusations of which he was the object.[2]

Both Cardinal Francesco and Taddeo Barberini made common cause with their brother when, on October 15th, they put up on their palaces the arms of France.[3] Thus the alliance of the Barberini with Mazarin, which had seemed unlikely only a short while ago, became suddenly an accomplished fact : it also bore an anti-papal character. In vain Innocent X. admonished the King and Queen of France and Mazarin not to shelter the Barberini [4] ; so far from complying with the request, Mazarin invited Antonio to Piedmont, after which he sent-ironical congratulations to the Pope on so happy a solution. When the French minister was informed that Francesco and Taddeo had likewise sought French protection, he exulted. The Venetian envoy Nani, who saw him after the reception of this piece of news, wrote : " I have never seen him so jubilant, not even after the greatest victories." [5] In effect, nothing could have been more agreeable to Mazarin, for the Barberini had become his unconditional allies and this in such circumstances as compelled them to serve all his interests.

Thereafter the arrogance of the French Government knew no bounds. On November 16th, 1645, the French Chancellor,

[1] On the flight, see the letter in GUALDO PRIORATO, *Scena d'huomini illustri*, Venice, 1659 ; and TOMMASO RAGGI, *Fuga de' Barberini*, in *Cod.* 3481 of the Bibl. Casanat., Rome ; also the *Avvisi* in *Arch. Rom.*, III., 26 *seq.*, and *Collección de docum. inéditos*, LXXXVI., 217.

[2] Innocent X. told this to Savelli, Ferdinand III.'s representative ; see the latter's *report of October 7, 1645, State Arch., Vienna.

[3] Only on his official residence in the Cancelleria did Antonio not put up the French arms ; Savelli's *report of October 21, 1645, State Arch., Vienna.

[4] COVILLE, 89 ; *Annales de St. Louis*, II. (1897), 361 *seq.*

[5] See *Corresp. de Mazarin*, II., 252 ; COVILLE, *loc. cit.*

speaking in the name of the King at a crown council, addressed to nuncio Bagno a speech full of invectives, which was a real masterpiece of its kind.   He began with the ironical remark that their Majesties found it hard to understand that Innocent X. should request them to " oppress " the Barberini, seeing that these were being so badly treated in Rome.   The Curia was dominated by the Spaniards, the French were relegated to the background, as was shown by the refusal of the purple to Mazarin's brother.   However, the King was not embarrassed for there were a hundred ways in which he could reward Mazarin's faithful services.   He then went on to complain about the intrigues in Rome which included even the prospect of the assassination of Mazarin.   Not without reason the Spaniards had proclaimed that a blow would be struck in France.   In view of all this it could not be expected that the French Government should sacrifice the Barberini.   Antonio's secret journey was justified ; he would not have received permission had he asked for it.   The speech ended with a threat to the effect that their Majesties might be compelled to seek means by which to protect their good name.   After the Duke of Orleans and the Prince of Condé had expressed their approval, Mazarin concluded with the blunt and unequivocal statement that the King would know how to avenge a persecution of the Barberini.[1]

This pronouncement was also made known to the Venetian ambassador and to the representatives of Tuscany and Florence,[2] and copies were circulated both in France and in Rome.   Contemporary Italian and French publications, both for and against Mazarin, show how excited public opinion had become.   Thereafter the conflict was passionately discussed in endless publications.[3]   With a view to alarming the Pope

---

[1] ARNAULD, *Negociat.*, I., 141 *seq.* ;   COVILLE, 90 *seqq.*

[2] See Bagno's *report dated Paris, November 24, 1645, in *Nunziat. di Francia*, 92, Papal Sec. Arch.

[3] COVILLE, 93.   Italian *documents from *Cod*. I., III., 87 of Chigi Libr. enumerated by CIAMPI (31, n. 2).   Partly the same *documents, but others also bearing on this point in *Barb.* 4673,

Mazarin caused the rumour to be circulated that the Barberini would be indemnified out of the revenues of Avignon and that there was a possibility of convening a Council of all the anti-papal malcontents.[1] Yet shortly afterwards he told the nuncio that though he was held but of little account at the Roman court, he would nevertheless prohibit a book by Salmasius against the Pope's primacy which was being circulated in Paris from Holland, so that all might see the high regard in which the Apostolic See was held in France.[2]

Meanwhile a Congregation had been set up in Rome, presided over by Cardinal Sforza, for the purpose of examining expenditure in connexion with the war of Castro. In obedience to an autograph letter of October 20th and a decree of December 16th, 1645, the Barberini submitted their books to an examination, but there were many gaps and errors in their accounts. Consequently their bank deposits were sequestrated and they themselves subjected to surveillance.[3] Thereupon Cardinal Francesco as well as Taddeo Barberini, the latter with his four children, fled in the night of January 16–17th, 1646, to France where Mazarin had offered them an asylum. Taddeo remained in Provence. On March 1st Francesco reached Paris, where Antonio had met with a solemn reception on the part of Mazarin already on January 6th.[4] Even before the flight of the two Barberini, vehement

5112, 5257, 5393. The *Fuga del cardinale Antonio male inter-pretata e peggio calunniata*, by the Genoese Raffaelo della Torre, was printed at Perugia in 1646. Of the *Relazione della fuga di Barberini nel pontificato di Innocenzo X.*, in *Cod.*, 277 of the library of Aix I have in my possession a contemporary copy bought in 1902 in Rome. A *Discorso contro il card. A. Barberini fuggito da Roma*, in *Ottob.* 1289, p. 27 *seqq.*, Vat. Lib.

[1] Bagno's *report of November 24, 1645, *loc. cit.*

[2] Bagno's *report of December 8, 1645, *loc. cit.*

[3] See LINAGE DE VAUCIENNES, 32 *seq.*, 52 *seqq.* ; COVILLE, 96 *seqq.* The autograph of October 20, 1645, is in *Barb.* 4903, n. 2, Vat. Lib.

[4] COVILLE, 103 *seqq.* ; FRATI, *Una fuga storica* (account from the University library of Bologna), in *N. Antologia*, 1911. As yet unpublished are *the report of Servantius (*Diaria*, Papal

altercations had taken place at a consistory between the Pope and Cardinal Grimaldi, when the latter had insinuated that, if need be, France would give them armed assistance. Besides Grimaldi, six other Cardinals spoke in favour of the Barberini. They were : Valençay, Rocci, Rondinini, Rapaccioli, Lugo and Colonna.[1]

When the Barberini, notwithstanding every precaution, made good their escape, the Pope fell into the greatest consternation.[2] He referred to the matter in a consistory on February 5th, 1646, when he pointed out that by their unlawful flight the two Cardinals had spontaneously avowed their guilt.[3]

Thereafter the Barberini were treated as *contumaces* ; accordingly all their possessions were sequestrated, their palaces seized and their offices disposed of.[4] There was little sympathy for them ; a large section of the nobles and the majority of the people were against them ; their fate was deemed a just retribution. Already on February 20th, when a meeting on the Capitol decreed the abolition of the tax on flour, which had been introduced by Urban VIII., a suggestion was made that the consequent loss of revenue should be covered with Taddeo's property. If the protest of Anne Colonna, Taddeo's plucky wife who had remained in Rome, could not prevent the abolition of the tax, it at least prevented this use of her husband's possessions.[5]

Sec. Arch.) of January 18, 1646 ; T. RAGGI, *Fuga de'Barberini* (above, p. 53, n. 1) ;   the *Avvisi* of January 20 and 24, 1646 (Papal Sec. Arch.) which give many details of the flight, as well as Savelli's *reports of January 17 and 20, 1646, State Arch., Vienna.

[1] *Avviso* of January 13, 1646, Papal Sec. Arch.

[2] *Avviso* of January 20, 1646, *ibid.*

[3] *Acta consist.* (where the Pope's speech is given in full), *Barb.* 2928, Vat. Lib. *Cf.* also DENIS, I., 21 *seq.*, 27.

[4] LINAGE DE VAUCIENNES, 72 *seqq.* ;   COVILLE, 108 ;   *cf.* Savelli's *report of February 5, 1646, State Arch., Vienna.

[5] Deone (Ameyden) in RANKE, III., 27 and 169, (*on Ranke's superficial and erroneous use of Ameyden *cf.* ADEMOLLO, *Macinato*

On the previous day a Bull had been published forbidding the Cardinals to leave Rome without the Pope's express permission ; those who contravened this order were to be punished with confiscation of their property ; if one of them stayed away from Rome for more than six months, he would forfeit all his benefices and offices and in case of obstinacy, after the lapse of a further three months, even the cardinalitial dignity, without the possibility of reinstatement.[1]

Publication of the Bull was forbidden in France, and when it was nevertheless passed from hand to hand, Mazarin summoned to the defence " of the rights of the King and the liberties of the Gallican Church " both Parliament and clergy ; these bodies proved only too subservient to the wishes of the Government. There was even question of a refusal of obedience and a schism.[2] But as Innocent X. remained firm, Mazarin resolved to have recourse to extreme measures, namely to armed force. True, the Pope was to be attacked only indirectly inasmuch as the French advanced on the fortresses on the coast of Tuscany occupied by the Spaniards. In this way Mazarin hoped to hit the Pope in a threefold manner : in his friends, the Spaniards, in his nephew, Prince Ludovisi who, under Spanish suzerainty, ruled over the territory of Piombino, and lastly in his own security since it was an easy thing for the French to invade the States of the Church from Tuscany.[3]

Connected with these plans was the mission of the Abbé St. Nicolas, Henri Arnauld, a brother of the famous Jansenist. He had been dispatched about the middle of December, 1645, by Mazarin, with mission to intrigue against Spain at the smaller courts of Italy. In Rome Arnauld was to agitate in favour of the Barberini and to induce the Pope, on the plea of the Church's interest, to recognize the separation

di Roma, in Riv. Europ., 1877, II., 442) ; *Savelli's *report of February 24, 1646, loc. cit.; DENIS, I., 26 ; ibid., 30, on A. Colonna's successful protest ; cf. also CIAMPI, 106.

[1] Bull., XV., 441 seqq. ; cf. HINSCHIUS, I., 349.

[2] COVILLE, 109 seqq.

[3] COVILLE, 118 seqq. ; SIMEONI, 80

of Portugal and Catalonia from Spain by recognizing the episcopal nomination that had been made there. In addition to all this, not the least duty of Arnauld was to further certain private interests of Mazarin, especially the extradition of Count De Beaupuy, who had had a hand in the conspiracy of the Duke of Beaufort and who had fled into the States of the Church, and, lastly, the bestowal of the red hat on Michel Mazarin.[1]

At Parma Arnauld achieved nothing. Modena gratefully accepted Cardinal Rinaldo Este's nomination as Protector of France at the Curia, but they would await more propitious times before siding with France. From the Grand Duke Ferdinand II. of Tuscany Arnauld likewise only obtained fair words.[2]

Arnauld reached Rome on March 17th, 1646, where he was given lodgings at the palace of Cardinal Este[3]; four days later Este himself arrived. Innocent X. imagined that it was Mazarin's intention, through Arnauld, to resume the diplomatic relations which had been interupted, but the latter had strict orders not to seek an audience. Arnauld at once put himself at the head of the French party and established close contact not only with Este and Valençay, but likewise with Cardinal Grimaldi, who was particularly hostile to the Pope.[4] The general excitement is revealed by an incident which came like a prelude to the war of the French against the Spaniards in Italy.

On March 24th, 1646, there arrived in Rome as *obbedienza* ambassador, Cabrera, Admiral of Castile.[5] From the first

---

[1] ARNAULD, *Négociat.*, I., 161 *seqq.*; COCHIN, H. Arnauld, 68 *seqq.*

[2] COCHIN, 70 *seqq.*

[3] At the end of February, 1646, Card. Este had had the imperial arms removed from his palace, retaining only the French and the papal ones, a fact which caused a sensation. Savelli's *report of February 24, 1646, State Arch., Vienna.

[4] COVILLE, 123 *seqq.*

[5] The Spanish ambassador Sirvela left Rome in August, 1645; Cabrera's wife made her entry into Rome together with her

Cabrera struck a most arrogant attitude ; he caused it to be rumoured that he would not call on Cardinal Este and would not greet him should he happen to meet him. The Cardinal promptly replied that he would compel him to do so. Cabrera, who had had several thousand men dispatched from Naples to Rome, boasted that he would make a prisoner of Este. The latter refused to be intimidated. He made arrangements with the French party and likewise raised a few thousand armed men.[1] Cardinal Grimaldi also took 200 mounted men into his service.[2] Consequently the Pope took measures for the preservation of tranquillity.[3]

On April 29th Cabrera decided to call on Cardinal Lante, Dean of the Sacred College. Innocent X. sought to persuade Este not to leave his house that day, but the Cardinal would not hear of it. Thus it came about that, on returning from his visit, Cabrera fell in with Este in the Piazza of the Gesù. A bloody encounter took place between their respective suites, in which the Spaniards were worsted.[4] The incident was soon disposed of through the Pope's mediation but Cabrera, who had become the butt of Pasquino's gibes, had now but one thought, namely to get out of Rome as quickly as possible.[5] A quite disproportionate importance was attached

husband, " che non più si è veduta in questa città " ; she was greeted by Olimpia Pamfili before Porta S. Giovanni. Savelli's *report of March 24, 1646, State Arch., Vienna ; cf. *Avviso of March 31, 1646, Papal Sec. Arch.

[1] COVILLE, 124-5 : *Writings on the dispute in Cod. N., III., 69, of Chigi Lib., Rome.

[2] Savelli's *report of May 19, 1646, loc. cit.

[3] ARNAULD, Négociat., II., 122.

[4] Besides ARNAULD, Négociat., I., 155 seq. ; II., 3 seq., 22 seq., 112 seq., 116 seq., 145 seq., and the reports used by COVILLE (125 seq.), cf. also Savelli's letter of May 3, 1646, loc. cit.

[5] Cabrera journeyed to Loreto on June 4 ; on May 2 Count Oñate, the new Spanish ambassador, arrived in Rome ; see *Avvisi of June 9 and July 7, 1646, Papal Sec. Arch. An ironical poem L'Amirante fugitivo, in Cod. N. III., 69, p. 255 seq. of the Chigi Library, Rome. Cf. also SIMEONI, 83.

to this trifling incident. The French in Rome raised shouts of victory and there was no less enthusiasm in France ; Mazarin himself, though as a rule a past-master in self-control, paid exuberant compliments to Este.[1]

A more serious drama opened on the confines of the States of the Church. On May 10th the French took the fortresses of Talamone and S. Stefano ; five days later the trenches of Orbetello were forced whilst the fleet advanced as far as Civitavecchia. These first successes, together with the incident in Rome, appeared to lend support to Mazarin's diplomacy. He hoped to intimidate Innocent X. and accordingly allowed Arnauld to seek an audience. The latter saw the Pope on June 7th and 11th, but for the Barberini he could obtain nothing.[2]

About the middle of June the military situation of the French grew worse. Admiral De Brizé was killed in a fierce naval engagement with the Spaniards and the fleet, though victorious, returned to Provence. The French also fared badly before Orbetello which was being gallantly defended by the Neapolitan Carlo della Gatta[3] : their ranks were decimated by fever. In these circumstances Arnauld, naturally enough, could do nothing for the Barberini. On July 16th the French were compelled to raise the siege of Orbetello, to the huge satisfaction of their enemies in Rome.[4]

This defeat in Italy gave fresh courage to Mazarin's enemies in France, so much so that in Rome his fall was deemed imminent. However, the Cardinal succeeded in stifling the

---

[1] COVILLE, 126.

[2] ARNAULD, *Négociat.*, II., 287 *seqq.*, 294 *seqq.* CHÉRUEL, II., 196 *seqq.* ; COVILLE, 127 *seqq.* ; COCHIN, 81 *seqq.* Orbetello, "*guerra propria di Mazarino*," Chigi says in *Diario* of his stay at Münster, Chigi Lib. ; see XXXII., Appendix 2.

[3] CAPECELATRO, *Istoria dell' assedio posto ad Orbetello dal principe Tommaso di Savoia*, edit. by Prince Belmonte, Naples, 1857 ; ADEMOLLO, *L'Assedio di Orbetello dell a' 1646*, Grosseto, 1883. *Versi satirici sopra il campo e guerra d'Orbetello* in *Cod. N. III.*, 69, p. 597, of the Chigi Library. *Cf.* also CERBONI, *Eritreo*, 96.

[4] CHÉRUEL. II., 212 *seqq.* ; COVILLE, 130 ; COCHIN, 84.

discontent and the upshot of it all was the decision to equip another fleet and to resume military operations in central Italy.[1] The idea was to intimidate the Pope and this was fully realized. Even before the French troops had effected a landing opposite the isle of Elba on September 17th, Innocent unexpectedly sent for Cardinals Este and Grimaldi, when he informed them that he had made up his mind to grant a pardon to the Barberini ; they might repair to Avignon and all that had been confiscated should be restored to them.[2]

Thereupon Mazarin's attitude underwent a complete change. His friendliness was such that one hardly knew him. He protested that he was the most reliable and most sincere servant of the Holy See, spoke with enthusiasm of universal peace, of a league of all the princes against the common enemy of Christendom and of the undying glory of the present pontificate.[3] Nor was he content with words ; when Piombo fell on October 11th, 1646, out of regard for the Pope, Ludovisi was allowed to retain his principality, of course under the overlordship of the Most Christian King. Lastly Mazarin promised to send an ambassador who would be acceptable to the Pope in every respect.[4] It was not easy to find such a person. Many undesirable candidates offered their services, whereas those who were offered the honour sought to escape it Thus the Cardinal of Lyons and the Marquis of Noirmoutiers declined. Finally the choice fell on the Marquis of Fontenay-Mareuil, who demurred at first on the plea of age and health, but ended by accepting.[5]

[1] COVILLE, 131 seqq.

[2] Besides the accounts consulted by COVILLE (137), cf. Servantius, *Diaria (Papal Sec. Arch.) on September 17, 1646, and Savelli's *letter of September 22, 1646, to Duke Maximilian of Bavaria, Epist., II.–III., Papal Sec. Arch. A *Discorso addressed to the Pope, praying him not to pardon the Barberini, to the injury of the Apostolic Camera, in Barb. 5748, Vat. Lib.

[3] Letters to a Roman confidant, October 13 and 15, 1646, in COVILLE, 138.

[4] Ibid., 138-9.

[5] Ibid., 142-3. Fontenay-Mareuil had been French ambassador in Rome, 1639-1644 ; cf. BAGUENOT DE PUCHESSE in Rev. des

Mazarin's inquiry whether Fontenay would be agreeable to the Holy See, promptly met with an affirmative reply, in fact Rome awaited his arrival with impatience.[1] Innocent had long desired the resumption of normal diplomatic relations with France and just then he had additional grounds for it ; in view of the intrigues of the French Jansenists [2] a great deal depended on the attitude of Mazarin.

Some time elapsed before Fontenay reached Rome. The difficulties in the mutual relations were happily removed by concessions on both sides. The first thing to be dealt with was Ludovisi's position at Piombino, then the full pardon of the Barberini, towards whom there appeared to have been a certain cooling off on the part of Mazarin, for in February, 1647, he had written to Arnauld that it was not worth while, for their sakes, to become involved in fresh complications. In the end Innocent X. gave leave to Francesco Barberini to return to Rome.[3]

On May 24th, 1647, Fontenay made his entry into the Eternal City, with a magnificent retinue. Cardinal Este went out to meet him with eighty-four carriages and escorted him into the presence of the Pope. In order to impress the Spaniards the greatest possible pomp was likewise displayed on the occasion of the visits to Olimpia and the Princess Ludovisi.[4]

Fontenay met with an all the more friendly reception from the Pope as shortly before, in connexion with the Jansenist affair, Mazarin had adopted a line of conduct which earned for him a special Brief of praise and thanks.[5] However, Mazarin demanded something in return, viz. the red hat for

quest. hist., XVIII. (1875), 160, and the Mémoires de Fontenay-Mareuil, éd. Michaud-Poujolat, 2nd series, V. (1837), though these are not always reliable.

[1] COVILLE, 143.
[2] Particulars in Ch. VI.
[3] COCHIN, 94.
[4] Servantius *Diaria, Papal Sec. Arch. ; COVILLE, 149 ; COCHIN, loc. cit.
[5] Text in Annales de St. Louis, II. (1897), 362 seq.

his brother Michel. Though he was well aware of the obstacles,[1]
he nevertheless hoped for speedy success, seeing that it was
precisely Fontenay that had obtained it for himself under
Urban VIII. However, at all times undecided, Innocent X.
hesitated even more in this instance—notwithstanding the
pressure of the French agents—for Mazarin's brother was a
very mediocre personality [2]; moreover the representatives
of the Emperor and Spain opposed the promotion.[3] The
Pope complained that the French diplomatists gave him no
peace [4] but in the end Fontenay, whom the Pope always
treated in the friendliest fashion, obtained his assent to
Michel's promotion ; and since no time limit was fixed, its
execution could be delayed indefinitely. For the rest Michel,
who came to Rome against Mazarin's will, spoilt his cause
by numerous imprudences, and the Spanish party, still very
influential with the Pope, continued to make energetic
remonstrances.

At this time certain agitations at Naples held everyone
in suspense. Mazarin was suspected—assuredly not without
good reason—of having a hand in the risings. By reason of
the feverish excitement which the events of Naples called
forth, every favour done to one party was construed into an
act of hostility towards the other. If Innocent X. named a
Cardinal at the request of France, he must needs appoint
another to please Spain. A considerable time had to elapse
before the answer concerning Mazarin's promotion could
arrive, accordingly the Spaniards did not despair of inducing
the Pope to change his mind.[5] Other difficulties were due to
Mazarin himself. He who always protested that he asked
nothing for his own, now insisted that his brother should be
raised to the cardinalate on the recommendation of the
King of Poland, whereas Innocent would rather have a

---

[1] *Cf.* Venetian report in BERCHET, II., 54 *seqq.*

[2] COVILLE, 165, 170 *seqq.*

[3] See Savelli's *report of August 31, 1647, State Arch.,
Vienna.

[4] COVILLE, 172.

[5] *Ibid.*, 173 *seqq.*, 175.

recommendation from the French Queen-Regent. At the end of September Mazarin suddenly announced that he would be satisfied with any mode of promotion that was agreeable to the Pope ; accordingly on October 7th, Michel Mazarin was at last raised to the Sacred College. The event was a considerable diplomatic triumph for Mazarin, whilst it also satisfied a desire of his heart. He was anxious to create for his family as splendid a position as Richelieu had done for his ; ambition of this kind characterizes the upstarts of every age, but in the 17th century this passion was even more imperious for it was the only guarantee against the whims and storms of fate.[1] Mazarin himself was not to be spared the experience.

Disagreements with the Apostolic See by no means came to an end with the elevation of Michel Mazarin who, in point of fact, died as early as August 31st, 1648.[2] On February 27th, 1648, Cardinal Francesco Barberini had returned to Rome. His brother Taddeo had died in Paris the year before.[3] Cardinal Francesco met with a kindly welcome from the Pope [4] as did Cardinal Antonio who returned to Rome on

---

[1] COVILLE, 165 seqq., 175 seqq. On Mich. Mazarin, cf. DE MUN in Rev. d'hist. dipl., XVIII., 497–530.

[2] Mich. Mazarin succumbed in his palace on the Quirinal to a fever which he caught at Palidoro on his return to Rome. Servantius *Diaria, Papal Sec. Arch.). "*Quanto s'è travagliato per vestirlo di porpora, e poi non ha potuto terminare l'anno delle sue grandezzi," Fr. Albizzi wrote to Chigi as Mazarin lay on his death-bed, dated Rome, August 29, 1646, Chigi Lib., Rome. Cod. A. III., 55.

[3] Taddeo's somewhat plain sepulchre (by Bernardo Cametti, a pupil of Bernini) in S. Rosalia, close to the family palace, at Palestrina (cf. Zeitschr. für bild. Kunst., new series, XXV. [1914], 326), shows how much the splendour of the family had waned. The coffin stands in the adjoining mausoleum.

[4] "*Fuit receptus maxima cum benignitate . . . confabulantes super mediam horam " (Servantius *Diaria, Papal Sec. Arch.). Cf. DENIS, I., iii.; ARNAULD, Négociat., V., 413 ; Miscell. di stor. ital., XV. (1875), 199.

July 12th, 1653, when the people greeted him with enthusiasm.[1]
A painting entitled " The Sacrifice of Diana ", for which
Cardinal Francesco gave a commission to Pietro da Cortona—
the most vivid modern representation of a Greek sacrifice—
was intended as an allegory of the return of his family from
exile.[2] But as all the wishes of the Barberini were by no
means fulfilled, they repeatedly invoked France's patronage
with the Pope.[3] To this annoyance others came to be added.
In April, 1648, the French Government conceived the notion
of publishing the condemnation which Parliament had
passed the year before on a papal censure of certain Jansenist
writings. A strong protest by the papal nuncio followed.
Not long afterwards the French ambassador in Rome gave
grave offence by sheltering a criminal accused of sacrilege
and robbery.[4]

However, these disputes were not remotely comparable to
the previous ones when Mazarin, by means of brutal attacks,
forced the Pope to a kind of capitulation. The warlike
conflagration which had broken out in Italy at that time had
done much to increase the minister's unpopularity in France.
Everyone could see how this upstart put his personal gain
before that of the State and it was generally felt that he made
war in his own interest, not that of France.[5] To begin with,
the Italian Mazarin was hated as a foreigner whilst the
greed that caused him to pile up gold for himself still further
alienated all hearts. The enormous expenditure on the
army and the consequent intolerable taxation, brought about
the triumph of his enemies, the so-called *Fronde*, in the
autumn of 1648. Banished as an enemy of the State, at the
beginning of 1649, Mazarin was forced to leave Paris and in

---

[1] *Servantius, *loc. cit.* Antonio's audience with the Pope on
July 14 lasted two hours, *ibid.*

[2] Voss, *Malerei*, 545, on the picture in the Barberini Gallery.

[3] *Cf.* the *Brief to Louis XIV. of June 11, 1650. *Epist.*, IV.–VI.,
Papal Sec. Arch.

[4] Coville, 185 *seq.*

[5] Gérin, I., 3 *seqq.*

February of the following year even France itself. He withdrew to Brühl, near Cologne,[1] from where he kept in close touch with Queen Anne. In the end he came out triumphantly from the dangerous struggle.[2] During those troubles Innocent X. did all he could to preserve the Church in France from injury.[3]

Innocent X. was fully justified when, at the beginning of 1651, he remarked that from the beginning of his pontificate Mazarin had been a stumbling block in the relations between France and Rome ; from him had proceeded every unpleasantness and every dispute ; that minister would end by ruining both France and the Holy See.[4] In December, 1651, the tension was such that the French ambassador, Valençay, ceased to seek audiences with the Pope.[5]

When the nuncios of Vienna, Madrid and Paris were changed in the autumn of 1652, Innocent X. named Neri Corsini, Archbishop of Damietta, for France. Although the French ambassador in Rome described the new nuncio as worthy of confidence,[6] Corsini was arrested on landing at Marseilles and interned in a monastery. In an audience on November 25th Valençay endeavoured to justify this action

[1] By a *Brief of July 8, 1651, Innocent X. approved Mazarin's leaving France as this would preserve his ecclesiastical dignity from injury (*Epist.*, IV.–VI., Papal Sec. Arch.). *Ibid.*, under date of October 23, 1651, *the Pope's congratulations to Louis XIV. on his assumption of the reins of government, with an exhortation that he should defend the Church and honour the Holy See.

[2] " *S'egli esce con riputazione, sarà il compimento delle sue fortune," Fr. Albizzi wrote to Chig on February 27, 1649, from Rome. Chigi Lib., *Cod.* A. III., 55.

[3] See the *Brief to the French clergy dated May 20, 1652, Papal Sec. Arch., *loc. cit.*

[4] See Valençay's letter dated Rome, November 13, 1651, in CHANTELAUZE, *Retz.*, II., 338.

[5] See Gueffier's letter dated Rome, December 18, 1651, *ibid.*, 461.

[6] GÉRIN, I., 21. On N. Corsini *cf.* MORONI, XVII., 280 *seq.*, 285 *seq.*

and in doing so adopted a grossly offensive attitude towards the Pope.[1] It was solely due to the unfavourable military situation—the Spaniards had just recaptured Barcelona—that Corsini recovered his freedom and was allowed to proceed to Avignon. However, France's policy towards Rome remained unaltered and a fresh conflict broke out within the same year.

October, 1652, witnessed the restoration of royal absolutism, before which disappeared both the aristocracy and Parliament. Only one man remained as Mazarin's competitor : this was Jean François Paul de Gondi, known as Cardinal de Retz.[2] Born in 1613 and destined, against his inclination, for the ecclesiastical state, Retz had been given a Canon's stall at Notre Dame when he was only thirteen. In 1643 he became coadjutor to his uncle, the Archbishop of Paris, with the title of Archbishop of Corinth. Talented and endowed with high political ability, but restless, immoral and an adherent of the Jansenists, Retz headed the Fronde between 1648 and 1649. But it was hoped that he might be won over and the King proposed him for the cardinalate which he received on February 19th, 1652. However, Retz continued an irreconcilable opponent of Mazarin whom he was anxious to succeed at all costs. He believed that the purple would protect him in his intrigues, but Mazarin, who in his disputes with the Pope had often threatened to free the French from

---

[1] GÉRIN, I., 22 seq., for Valençay's report of November 25, 1651. *Instruction for Corsini in State Lib., Vienna 5645, p. 28 seqq.

[2] CHANTELAUZE, Le card. de Retz et l'affaire du chapeau, Paris, 1878 ; NORMAND, Card. de Retz, ibid., 1895 ; RANKE, Französ. Gesch., III., 71 seqq., V., 199 seq. ; FUETER, Historiographie, 156 seq. ; Œuvres de Retz, éd. FEILLET, GOURDAULT, and CHANTELAUZE, 10 vols., Paris, 1872–1896. CH. COCHIN, who died in 1918, intended to write a new life of Retz ; the following fragment of his papers has been published : Suppl. à la corresp. du card. de Retz, Paris, 1920, with an appendix on his elevation to the cardinalate. See also D. OGG, Card. de Retz, London, 1912 ; BATTIEOL, Le card. de Retz, Paris, 1927.

" the Roman phantom ", was not the man to allow himself
to be frightened by an obstacle of this kind.[1] In a secret
memorandum he advised the King to have the Cardinal
arrested.   Retz allowed himself to be deceived : on the
occasion of a call at the Louvre, December 19th, 1652, he
was arrested and taken to the dungeon of Vincennes.[2] The
Cardinal-Minister wished the public to believe that he had
had nothing to do with this act of violence ; but there can
be no doubt that it was he who had instigated the arrest.
His enemy and rival should be kept in custody for as long as
seemed good to him, irrespectively of the circumstance that
the Pope alone has jurisdiction over the members of the
Sacred College.[3]

The French ambassador in Rome began by boldly denying
the act of violence ; it was not likely, he declared, that a
Cardinal would throw a colleague into prison.[4] But the
Pope had been fully informed of the incident by the Paris
nuncio, Bagno, whose report dated December 27th, 1652,[5] he
communicated to the College of Cardinals at a consistory
held on January 8th, 1653.[6] By special courier the Pontiff
sent a fatherly letter to the young King, Louis XIV., urging
him to set at liberty a man who had been unjustly imprisoned
and whom he himself had recommended for the purple.[7]
Though some of the Cardinals, for instance Capponi, sought
to defend the action against Retz, the majority thought

[1] CHANTELAUZE, Retz, I., 477.

[2] Ibid., 477-8.

[3] GÉRIN, I., 27.

[4] Ibid., 28.

[5] Cf. " *Ristretto delle lettere per il negotiato fatto da Mons.
Nunzio Apost. per la liberatione del card. di Retz ", Miscell.
Clement., XI., t. 123, p. 106 seqq,. Papal Sec. Arch.

[6] *Acta consist., loc. cit., Papal Sec. Arch. ; cf. *Card. Colonna's
report to Ferdinand III., dated Rome, February 7, 1653, State
Arch., Vienna.

[7] " *Regi Francorum," dated January 20, 1653, Epist., IX.,
Papal Sec. Arch., ibid., same date, a similar *Brief to the Queen-
Regent Anne.

otherwise. Cardinals Colonna and Trivulzio counselled the severest counter-measures, but Cornaro recommended moderation [1] and the Pope referred the matter to a special congregation.

Mazarin, who had returned to Paris in triumph on February 3rd, 1653, became more powerful than ever,[2] a circumstance that was decisive for Retz' fate. To the representations of the French episcopate, when it spoke up in defence of ecclesiastical immunity, Mazarin only replied in general terms. The nuncio, who on March 3rd and 4th was at length received by the King and Queen, likewise failed to obtain anything.[3] Domenico Marini, Archbishop of Avignon, whom the Pope dispatched as nuncio extraordinary, was refused admittance at court.[4] To justify his conduct Mazarin referred to former imprisonments of Cardinals, as Balue and Klesl. The nuncio's suggestion to send Retz to Rome to have his guilt examined by the Pope, Mazarin rejected on the ground that Retz would go on agitating from there by means of his skilful pen.[5]

When, in July, the prisoner declared his readiness to furnish hostages until he should have reached Rome, Mazarin came forward with a fresh demand : this was that Retz should resign his coadjutorship with the right of succession to the archiepiscopal See of Paris. This Retz emphatically declined to agree to—he would rather remain in prison for ten years and die there, he declared.[6]

Meanwhile the Jansenists had expressed their sympathy with the imprisoned Cardinal. Mazarin seized the occasion

---

[1] De Rossi, *Istoria, Vat. 8873, Vat. Lib.

[2] DONAVER, Il card. Mazzarino, Genoa, 1884, p. 274, for report of Genoese envoy on Mazarin's return.

[3] See Bagno's *reports of January 30, February 28, March 5, 1653, in *Ristretto, etc., Papal Sec. Arch.

[4] Bagno's *reports of April 4 and May 30, 1653, loc. cit. The *Briefs which the Archbishop was to hand to the King, Queen Anne and Mazarin, in Epist., IX., Papal Sec. Arch.

[5] Bagno's *letters of May 9 and 16, 1653, loc. cit.

[6] Bagno's *letter of July 11, 1653, ibid.

to enforce with all his energy the papal Bull of May 31st, 1652, condemning the five theses of Jansenism. In a consistory of September 22nd the Pope expressed his satisfaction, but refused to drop the affair of the imprisoned Cardinal for in this matter an inalienable prerogative of the Holy See was at stake.[1] On September 24th the Paris nuncio was instructed to make representations to the King on the scandal and the injustice of detaining a Cardinal for so long a time in an unhealthy dungeon, and on the fact that the prisoner had not even been confronted with his judges ; as for the promise that in the event of his acquittal, Retz would not return to France, it could not be given.[2] The nuncio's representations, though supported by special Briefs to the King, Queen Anne and Mazarin [3] proved unavailing.[4] Even the Pope's proposal to allow Retz' trial to be conducted in France by the Archbishop of Avignon was rejected by the Government. Yet even so Rome did not desist in its efforts and in March and April, 1654, the nuncio was again instructed to intervene on behalf of the prisoner.[5]

Meanwhile the situation underwent a change inasmuch as in consequence of the death of his uncle, on March 21st, 1654, Retz became Archbishop of Paris. A renunciation of the dignity was now extorted from the prisoner to which Cardinal Este strove in vain to obtain Innocent X.'s assent.[6] On August 8th Retz succeeded in breaking prison and escaping into Spain.[7] He now declared his resignation to be null and void and appointed a Vicar General. The Pope,

---

[1] GÉRIN, I., 32.

[2] The *Brief for Bagno, dated September 24, 1653, with the exhortation : " Viriliter age," in *Epist.*, X., Papal Sec. Arch.

[3] Text of *Briefs, *ibid.*

[4] See Bagno's *report of December 29, 1653, in *Ristretto*, etc., *loc. cit.*

[5] Instructions for Bagno, March 16, and April 6, 1654, *ibid.*

[6] *Letter of the Secretary of State to Bagno, June 8, 1654, in *Ristretto*, etc., *ibid.*

[7] See L. MAÎTRE, *L'évasion du card. Retz hors du château de Nantes d'après des documents nouveaux*, Nantes, 1903.

who learnt of the escape on September 4th,[1] approved his step in a letter in which he congratulated Retz on his deliverance and assured him of his protection.[2]

The report of his opponent's escape hit Mazarin as news of a lost battle might have done. He now did his utmost to deprive Retz of his archiepiscopal dignity; the Cathedral Chapter, which had at first sided with Retz,[3] was forced to nominate Vicars Capitular as if the See were vacant! At the same time orders were issued for the rearrest of Retz.[4]

The French ambassador in Rome, Valençay, had been recalled at the end of 1653. So as to avoid the semblance of a diplomatic rupture, François Bosquet, Bishop of Lodève, was dispatched to the Pope. Bosquet's first audience was a very stormy one. Unheard of things were happening in France, Innocent X. exclaimed, for there nuncios were being expelled and Cardinals imprisoned.[5] When, a little later, the Pope had calmed down, Bosquet entertained hopes of a compromise; however, this proved impossible owing to the fact that the Pope refused to accede to Mazarin's demand for the removal of Retz from the archiepiscopal see of Paris. Mazarin nevertheless hoped to gain his point through the new Secretary of State, but in this respect he deluded himself.[6]

Bosquet had already left Rome when Retz arrived there on November 30th, 1654. The Pope gave orders for his reception with all the honours due to a Cardinal. On December 1st Retz had an audience lasting an hour and a quarter.[7] What he told the Pope confirmed Innocent X.'s bad opinion of Mazarin. The latter now dispatched to Rome one of his

---

[1] On Bagno's *report in code dated August 14, 1654 (Papal Sec. Arch., *Nunziat. di Spagna*), we read: " decifrato 4 settembre."

[2] *Brief of September 30, 1654, *Epist.*, X., Papal Sec. Arch.

[3] See Bagno's *reports, dated Paris, August 14 and 22, 1654, *ibid.*, *Nunziat. di Spagna*.

[4] Bagno's *reports, Paris, August 28, September 4, 1654, *ibid.*

[5] GÉRIN, 153.

[6] *Ibid.*, 35 *seqq.*

[7] Servantius, *Diaria, ibid.*

most daring and most unscrupulous agents, Hugues de
Lionne, for the purpose of negotiating the deposition of his
enemy from the archiepiscopal See of Paris.[1] However,
Innocent X. had died before Lionne reached the Eternal
City.

(2.)

Innocent X., in view of the struggle which France and
Spain were waging against each other in every quarter and
with unexampled bitterness, remarked on one occasion that
it was not easy for him to keep his equilibrium seeing that
he had to walk for ever as on a silken thread.[2] The truth of
these words is shown by a glance at the Pope's relations with
Spain.   French diplomatists, foremost among them being
Mazarin, never wearied of accusing Innocent X. of partiality
towards that nation whilst in Spain the opposite view
prevailed, viz. that the Pope did not sufficiently consider
the Catholic King and was too accommodating towards
France.[3] Now, as in the days of Urban VIII., the cabinets
of Madrid and Paris were each equally insistent that the
Pope should take its part, an action which could not be
reconciled with his duty as the universal father of Christendom.

[1] GÉRIN, I., 43.
[2] COVILLE, 148.
[3] See Giustinian in BERCHET, *Relaz.*, *Spagna*, II., 182 ;
BASADONNA, *ibid.*, 220 *seq.*   Chigi fared like Innocent X. ; on
December 7, 1646, the former wrote to Melzi from Münster :
" *Giustiniani says you are Spanish ! Io non mi curo di niente
per me.   Finchè visse Urbano, gridavano gli Spagnoli che io era
Francese, per due anni d'Innocenzo gridavano i Francesi che io
era Spagnolo, dipoi ritornan gl'altri come prima et invece di
conciliarsi il Papa e gli altri principi italiani gli irritano.   Avanti
quattro mesi si diceva, che per perseguitare i Barberini S. Stà
prolongava le guerre, hora si dice, che per restituirgli guasta la
pace.   Io non credo che si guasti, se non col abbandonare la
religione cattolica, come si fa, e vorrei essere in Persia in cambio
d'essere qua." *Cod.* A., I., 23, Chigi Library.

Each Government watched with Argus' eyes Rome's every step to see whether it was in its favour or not. On the occasion of any important decision, especially when it was a question of the appointment of Cardinals, a bitter struggle always broke out at the Curia between the French and the Spanish diplomatists. To satisfy both parties was impossible and the Pope had to resign himself to reclamations both from France and from Spain.

If, on the whole, Innocent X. inclined rather towards Spain, the reason is not difficult to see. Mazarin's brutal treatment of him might indeed intimidate him and compel him to yield for the moment, but it could not win him over. The cautious, slow temperament of the Pope was in sympathy with the Spanish character rather than with the restless nature of the French. Innocent X. had likewise grateful recollections of the support he had received from Spain ever since his nunciature in that country. Philip IV.'s preponderance in Italy lay heavily in the scales. Any Pope would have to reckon with a King who was master of Milan and Naples.[1] Lastly, notwithstanding the decline of Spanish power, its significance for the Catholic Church remained very great.

It is, however, a mistake to think that Innocent X. favoured the Spaniards unduly. If these, because of the share they had had in Innocent's elevation, imagined that the new Head of the Church would at all times energetically promote their particularist interests, they were soon undeceived.[2] A signal proof of this is the testimony of the Venetian envoy, Giustinian, who expressly states in his report of 1651 that every observer of the Pope's conduct since his elevation, had to admit that he had shown no undue partiality toward Spain.[3] Giustinian further relates that every Spanish ambassador in Rome, beginning with Count Oñata, then

---

[1] Giustinian in BERCHET, Roma, II., 131 seq., 151.

[2] See Maffei's report in PELLEGRINI, Relazioni inedite degli ambasciatori Lucchesi alla corte di Madrid, Lucca, 1909, 79.

[3] Giustinian, loc. cit.

Cardinal Albornoz and lastly the Duke of Infantado, had complained to him of the anything but accommodating disposition of Innocent X. not only in important but even in small matters : of all the ambassadors those of Spain had received fewest favours. For the prevailing notion that Innocent X. was Hispanophil, these diplomatists had nothing but bitter scorn.[1] There were two affairs in particular in which Innocent X. was supposed to have shown special preference for Spain, viz. his attitude towards Portugal and his conduct during the sedition in Naples. In the days of Urban VIII., Innocent X. had been a member of the Congregation dealing with Portuguese affairs.[2] Accordingly for him there was nothing new in the question whether the Apostolic See should recognize King John IV. of Braganza whom, after eighty years of subjection to Spain, Portugal had put at its head, and at the same time grant him the right to nominate Bishops. In Portugal it was said that under Urban VIII. Cardinal Pamfili had favoured a compromise.[3] At the beginning of 1645 Nicolas Monteiro, Prior of Sodofeita, came to Rome as representative of the Portuguese clergy in order to promote John IV.'s nominations to the vacant sees.[4] By this means it was hoped to obtain his recognition as King of Portugal, a step to which Spain offered the most determined opposition. The Pope was determined to dissociate the political aspect of the matter from the ecclesiastical one ; hence he resolved himself, as Head of the Church, to appoint the Bishops, *motu proprio*, without any reference to the right of royal nomination. Accordingly, in May, 1645, he filled, *motu proprio*, the vacant sees of Guarda, Miranda and Viseu.[5] Spain had no cause to complain of this proceeding

---

[1] *Ibid.*

[2] *Cf.* our data, XXIX., 203.

[3] See *Cifra* of the sub-collector Girolamo Battaglia, dated Lisbon, April 28, 1645, *Nunziat. di Portogallo*, 24, Papal Sec. Arch.

[4] ADEMOLLO, *Indipendenza Portoghese*, 67.

[5] See *Acta consist.*, *Barb.* 2918, P. 1, Vat. Lib. *Cf.* FEA, *Nullità delle amministrazioni capitolari abusive*, Rome, 1815, 76.

since it had likewise been in force during the Spanish occupation of Portugal.[1] However, the King of Portugal, who had recently threatened with a national council [2] and in June, 1645, had arbitrarily appointed Bishops for Lisbon, Evora and Braga,[3] whose confirmation by the Pope was not to be expected, now, at the instigation of Mazarin, opposed this solution, which he had seemed willing at one time to agree to.[4]

There now broke out a diplomatic struggle at the Curia on the subject of the recognition of John IV. Whereas the Spanish ambassador, Count Sirvela, offered the strongest opposition to it, the demand found a most enthusiastic advocate in the French ambassador, Grémonville, who had arrived at the beginning of 1645.[5] Neither the French nor

News of the Pope's action *" fu inteso con qualche comotione " the nuncio of Naples, Altieri, writes on May 23, 1645, Altieri Archives, Rome, XX., A. 3. On May 29, 1645, the Secretary of State wrote to Rinuccini on the Pope's action : " Hanno procurato questi signori ministri del Re di Spagna di far che N. S. si astenesse da ogni sorte di propositione, mentre non si proseguiva nel possesso, che tuttavia dicono che civilmente ritiene il Re loro nella provista di quelle Chiese ; ma N. S. ha voluto in questo sodisfare alla propria coscienza e al precetto di Christo signor nostro : Pasce oves meas, senza riparare ad altro interesse humano, e le ha proposto come di suo proprio moto. Subodoratasi la risolutione dai signori cardinali spagnuoli, si come poi si è veduto, dovettero havere per bene di non intervenire quella mattina nel concistoro, per non esser posti in necessità di approvare questa risolutione, che essi impugnavano, lodando la provista, come è solito di farsi nella provisione di tutti li vescovati, e disapprovandola per non intaccare il rispetto et la riverenza dovuta a Nostro Signore. Di tutto questo si dà parte a Vostra Signoria per sua notitia." Rospigliosi Arch., Rome.

[1] See *Cifra al Nuntio di Venetia, October 14, 1645, Nunziat. di Venezia, Papal Sec. Arch.

[2] Ibid.

[3] Cifra of G. Battaglia, dated Lisbon, June 6, 1645, loc. cit.

[4] SCHÄFER, Portugal, IV., 538. Ismael Bullialdo's memorial was printed in 1653.

[5] ADEMOLLO, 68-9.

the Spaniards were really interested in the affair ; each party pursued its own particularist political aim and their meddling could but injure the interests of the Church. What the French aimed at was revealed by Grémonville's demand for the admission of an *obbedienza* embassy whose members had already been named by the Portuguese King.[1]

Fearing lest the Pope should yield to the powerful pressure of the French, the Spanish party in Rome had perpetrated an act of violence. In the first days of April, 1645, Monteiro's carriage was attacked in the Ripetta by twenty armed Spaniards who killed the steward of the Portuguese agent. When the police intervened all the Spaniards gathered in arms before the palace of their ambassador.[2] It was soon seen that the latter had himself had a hand in the affair. Thereupon the Pope no longer received him in audience and this attitude he maintained even when Cardinal Medici pleaded on behalf of Sirvela.[3] Thus much did the Pope connive with the Spaniards' act of violence, though the enemies of the Holy See at Lisbon sought to persuade John IV. that this was so, in order to induce him to expel the papal sub-collector Girolamo Battaglia.[4]

Even Spain's representatives at Naples had to admit that the Pope's treatment of Sirvela was fully justified ; for all that they sought to excuse the ambassador and to induce the Pontiff, through the nuncio, to pardon Sirvela. All was in vain.[5] Meanwhile the ambassador had gone to Frascati, Cardinal Albornoz transacting current business in the meantime. Sirvela ended by realizing that his position at the Curia had become untenable : on August 5th he left Rome

[1] *Ibid., loc. cit.*

[2] Besides the partial and exculpating reports of Ameyden in ADEMOLLO, 68, *cf.* *Avviso of April 8, 1645, Papal Sec. Arch., and Savelli's *report of April 8, 1645, State Arch., Vienna.

[3] *Avviso of April 29, 1645, *loc. cit.*

[4] *Cf.* *Cifra of G. Battaglia, dated Lisbon, June 6, 1645, *loc. cit.*

[5] *Cf.* Altieri's *reports, Naples, April 22, May 22 and 23, June 3, 1646, Altieri Arch., Rome.

without a farewell visit to the Pope.[1] The question of replacing
him at the embassy raised many difficulties. In September
the Bishop of Pozzuoli told the nuncio of Naples that if the
Duke of Medina de las Torres were to come to Rome, the
Pope would treat him worse than even Sirvela.[2] Eventually,
towards the end of the year, Count Oñate was appointed
Spanish ambassador in Rome.[3]

The struggle for John IV.'s right of nomination, which
included his recognition as King, continued during the
following year. The French supported it in every way whilst
the Spaniards fought it no less obstinately. Innocent X.
maintained the principle that his position as common father
of all Christians laid on him the duty of impartiality in the
dispute. Nor could he be made to swerve from his determination by the circumstance that John IV. sought to force him
to accept an embassy by expelling the Apostolic sub-collector
Girolamo Battaglia from the realm in November, 1646.[4]
The King also sought the opinion of scholars and universities
on the question of further forcible measures. In 1647 he
presented to the Pope, through his agent Nuno da Cunha,
a memorial in the concluding paragraph of which he stated
that some very learned men had assured him that in a case
of urgent necessity, like the present one, the Chapters were
qualified to elect the Bishops whom the sovereign had
nominated. The Portuguese Inquisition condemned this
thesis which was defended by the one-time Calvinist Ismael
Bullialdo. The Pope, the Inquisition declared, as Head of the
Catholic and Roman Church, possessed full monarchical

---

[1] Cf. ADEMOLLO, 72. Altieri *reports Sirvela's departure for
Spain from Naples, February 8, 1646, loc. cit.

[2] *Altieri's report of September 9, 1645, ibid.

[3] *Altieri's report of December 31, 1645, ibid.

[4] See SIRI, Mercurio, VIII., 701 ; ADEMOLLO, 73. An attempt
had been made before this to remove Battaglia, the Pope's
faithful informant, from Portugal, by proposing to him a mission
to Rome, a task which, failing a command by the Pope, he was
bound to decline. *Cifra of G. Battaglia of June 27, 1645, Papal
Sec. Arch.

power and was the fount of all ecclesiastical jurisdiction, which could only be conveyed to the ministers of the Church by his express will and consent. Thereupon the King desisted from his purpose [1] and when in March, 1652, Mazarin provoked an intervention of the French hierarchy in favour of the Portuguese right of nomination,[2] the action, in view of the circumstances, could only do harm. A memorial presented at Rome by the Estates of Portugal in 1653 also remained without result.[3] Whatever may have been the arrogance of the friends of John IV. at the Curia,[4] the Portuguese Government was shrewd enough to refrain from going to the extremity of filling the vacant sees independently of the Pope.   There can be no doubt that the Spaniards benefited by the fact that the Portuguese problem remained unsolved, though this was certainly not due to any consideration for them,[5] on the contrary, the failure of every attempt at a compromise must be ascribed to the conduct of the King of Portugal and his friends the French. For a long time the Pope hoped for a satisfactory solution. In 1651 the Venetian envoy, Giustinian, asserted that he knew from an excellent source that Innocent X. was for ever considering how he might fill the vacant Portuguese sees and so happily settle the disputes to which those vacancies had given rise.[6]

No less anxiety for the Pope arose out of an anti-Spanish revolt in neighbouring Naples.[7] Its cause was the intolerable

----

[1] SCHÄFER, IV., 540 *seq.* A *eulogy of the " episc. Aegitanen. Inquisit. Portug.", of October 15, 1650, in *Epist.*, VII.–VIII., *loc. cit.*

[2] The document is in FEA, *Nullità delle amministrazioni capitolari abusive,* 45 *seqq.*

[3] SCHÄFER, IV., 540 *seq.*

[4] ADEMOLLO, 75.

[5] This is stressed by Giustinian in BERCHET, *Relaz.*, Rome, II., 133. SCHÄFER's contrary view (IV., 536 *seq.*) is based on an anonymous report the passionate partiality of which is so manifest that one is amazed that Schäfer should follow it unreservedly.

[6] Giustinian, *loc. cit.*

[7] G. PRIORATO, *Massaniello*, Paris, 1654 ; PALERMO, *Narraz.*

burden of taxation arbitrarily laid on the people, so that
Dante's words were applied to the Viceroy, Rodrigo Ponce
de León, Duke of Arcos : " *Dopo il pasto ha più fame che
pria*—he is more hungry after eating than before." In consequence of excessive taxation, risings occurred in May,
1647, first at Palermo and in other towns of Sicily. The
movement soon spread to Naples. It was directed not only
against the excessive imposts of the Spanish Government
but equally against the privileged nobility. Its leader was
Masaniello, a man of the lowliest origin, a native of Amalfi
and a fishmonger by trade. Masaniello went about bare-
footed, dressed in a white shirt and white trousers—the
uniform of the fisherfolk—without covering on his head.
He quickly became the idol of the people and the terror of
the Viceroy. An armed mob noisily surrounded the Viceroy's
palace who had to flee for his life into a neighbouring
monastery. The anger of the populace vented itself in an
appalling fury of destruction. In order to avoid bloodshed
the Cardinal Archbishop Filomarino, an excellent man who
was also most highly esteemed by the people, intervened
in an effort to bring about an accommodation between the
rebels and the Viceroy.[1] The Cardinal was soon forced to
realize how difficult it was to calm such an angry sea. The
people's demands grew daily, but Filomarino did not lose
heart. On July 11th he succeeded in wresting extensive concessions from the Government by means of a pact the terms

e documenti, in *Arch. stor. ital.*, IX. (1846) ; SAAVEDRA DE RIVAS,
Insurrection de Naples en 1647, Paris, 1849 ; REUMONT, *Carafa*,
II., 109 *seq.* ; CAPASSO, *La casa e la famiglia di Massaniello*,
Naples, 1893, and the works on Massaniello quoted in n. 2, p. 80.
To these must be added the monograph by E. VISCO : *La politica
della S. Sede nella rivoluzione di Masaniello. Da documenti dell'
Arch. Vatic.*, Naples, 1923.

[1] See Filomarino's report to Innocent X., dated July 8, 1647,
in *Arch. stor. ital.*, IX., 379 *seqq.*, and VISCO, 22 *seq.*, 25, 191 *seq.*
(Altieri's report of July 9, 1647). On Filomarino's attitude see
DE BLASIIS, in *Arch. Napolet.*, VI., 774 *seq.*, and especially
VISCO, 20 *seq.*, who pays a high tribute to the Cardinal.

of which he published in the Cathedral on July 13th.[1] The
fishmonger saw his wildest dreams fulfilled, but he fell a
victim to megalomania and was assassinated in a monastery
on July 16th.[2] It is not certain whether the bloody deed was
inspired by the Viceroy and a former follower of Masaniello,
the aged Giulio Genoino. The hope of Filomarino and
Innocent X. that the rebellion was now at an end,[3] remained
unfulfilled. The revolt flared up once more. Again Filomarino,
supported by the nuncio Emilio Altieri, took up the task of
mediation, and on this occasion he spoke some bitter truths
to the foolish Viceroy. " I know," Filomarino wrote to the
Pope on July 19th, " that my province is solely the ecclesiastical government, but in order to prevent the destruction
of this unhappy city, I have been compelled to venture into
the political arena." [4] The troubles continued throughout
August, as did the work of pacification of the indefatigable
Filomarino [5] to whom the Pope dispatched a laudatory Brief.
At the beginning of September, 1647, the Cardinal brought
about a fresh compromise, but the excitement would not die
down in Naples. On September 13th a manifesto summoned
the populace not to trust the Viceroy and by means of a
fresh rising either to win independence or to proclaim the
Pope immediate Sovereign of Naples.[6]

[1] Filomarino's reports of July 12 and 16, 1647, *loc. cit.*, 381
seq., 386 ; Visco, 28 *seq.*

[2] The chief source on the rising is the *Diario of* FRANC.
CAPECELATRO, I., Naples, 1850. Among the more recent writers
on Masaniello, *cf.* REUMONT, *Die Carafa von Maddaloni*, vol. II.,
the monographs of CAPASSO (Naples, 1919) and SCHIPPA (Bari,
1925) (*Arch. stor. Napolet.*, 1926, 394 *seqq.*). See also the article
by NIEHUES in *Jahrbuch des westfäl. Vereins für Wissenschaft und
Kunst*, 1874 ; letter of the Duke of Arcos to the Duke of Parma
on the death of Masaniello in *Arch. stor. Napolet.*, XXXII., 4.

[3] VISCO, 30, 31.

[4] *Arch. stor. ital.*, IX., 387 *seq.*

[5] *Ibid.*, 390 *seq. Cf.*, 351, the report of Vinc. de' Medici, Altieri's
reports in VISCO, 196 *seqq.* The laudatory *Brief to Filomarino,
July 20, 1647, in *Epist.*, II.–III., Papal Sec. Arch.

[6] VISCO, 39–40.

It has been made a reproach to Innocent X. that he did not take advantage of so favourable an opportunity. However, though tortured on the one hand by a fear of the revolt spreading to the States of the Church, and on the other grievously afflicted by the injury done to the Church at Naples,[1] he was equally unwilling to abandon the impartiality which he had hitherto observed and allow himself to be dragged into so dangerous a venture. Thereupon it was seriously contemplated at Naples to invoke the help of France.[2] Spain, however, was first on the spot. In the first days of October, 1647, a Spanish fleet appeared before Naples. It was under the command of Don Juan, a natural son of Philip IV. But the people of Naples had no intention to surrender, they accepted battle. During the bombardment of the city the papal nunciature was hit several times.[3] The Spaniards bombarded indiscriminately not only the quarters of the city which were in the hands of the rebels but those also which had remained loyal to the king. Innocent X. instructed the nuncio to work for an accommodation, but his efforts were in vain.[4] The upshot was that Naples declared itself independent of Spain. The royal arms were torn down and in some districts of the city the cry was raised : " Long live France ! " [5]

From the very beginning of the outbreak the Spanish ambassador in Rome, Oñate, had requested the Pope to proceed against the rebels with the penalties of the Church. His demand fell on deaf ears. Since it was by no means immediately evident that right was on the side of the Spaniards, the Pope could not unconditionally pronounce in their favour. Nor did he allow himself to be induced by the representations of the French ambassador, Fontenay, to assert his right as feudal overlord of Naples and to claim the kingdom for the States of the Church, as was desired by many people in Naples,

[1] *Ibid.*, 45 *seq.*, 53, 134 *seq.*

[2] *Ibid.*, 56 *seq.*

[3] *Ibid.*, 59.

[4] *Ibid.*, 62 *seq.*

[5] See Hermes Stampa's report of September 27, 1647, in *Arch. stor. ital.*, IX., 400.

where the Pope was still very popular from the time of his nunciature.[1] However, Innocent X. continued in his impartial attitude. The bombardment of the city was openly condemned in Rome. The Pope, so the Secretary of State wrote to the nuncio on October 27th, 1647, was greatly surprised that the representatives of the King of Spain only sought salvation by means of guns and rifles and that they had given free vent to the nobility's thirst for vengeance. Weeks ago the Holy Father had offered his mediation but the Spanish authorities would not hear of it ; all they thought of was to cool their ardour for revenge, heedless of the fact that the burning of houses and churches, the breaking of the enclosure of nuns' convents and the profanation and violation of churches were the order of the day. Yet Catalonia showed them what came of the use of force ! The Secretary of State ended by expressing his amazement at the fact that in view of such conditions in a city not far removed from Rome, it had not entered the mind of any one of Spain's representatives to invoke the Pope's mediation, which would obviously have been the proper thing to do.[2]

The position of the nuncio Altieri, difficult enough in itself, was rendered still more so by the circumstance that his own brother was implicated in the troubles.[3] The Spaniards were annoyed with Altieri and reproached him with arbitrariness. In Rome also the nuncio had given offence. To a letter of vituperation of the Secretary of State, dated October 26th, Altieri replied that it was solely at the request of the Viceroy and of Cardinal Trivulzio that he had sought to mediate, because the Spaniards were dissatisfied with Filomarino ; in future he would refrain from participating in any negotia-

---

[1] See Filomarino's report of July 12, 1647, *ibid.*, 384 ; *cf.* also Visco, 70, and the report of A. Contarini in BERCHET, *Relaz.*, Rome, II., 77.

[2] *Cifra al Nuntio di Napoli* of October 27, 1647, in Visco, 138 *seq.*

[3] See N. CAPECE GALEOTA, *Cenni storici dei Nunzii Apost. di Napoli*, Naples, 1877, 56.

tions.[1] To a fresh exhortation, dated October 27th, Altieri replied on November 12th that he had obeyed at once ; that he had never assumed the smallest obligation in the Pope's name ; that he had always been at pains not to offend either party and not to jeopardize the papal authority.[2]

Altieri failed to give satisfaction to the Viceroy [3] quite as much as to the Curia, so that he conceived an increasing distaste for his post. Already at the end of October he had asked permission to leave Naples and to betake himself to some other town of the realm. No sooner was this granted,[4] than he changed his mind once more. On January 4th, 1648, the Secretary of State wrote to him : " If you think it better to remain at your post, the Holy Father allows you to do so ; but His Holiness wishes that in future you refrain from issuing manifestos to the people or, in general, from publishing anything at all, seeing that this gives rise to false interpretations and misunderstandings." [5]

The Curia's policy was to wait for events to develop, and it pursued this course even when the situation became increasingly unfavourable to the Spaniards.[6] Maintenance of this standpoint was rendered very difficult in consequence of the pressure of the French ambassador Fontenay and the rest of France's supporters in Rome, and because a number of Cardinals urged the Pope to intervene.[7] The French had openly hailed the outbreak of the revolt and had immediately

[1] " *Hora mi asterrò da ogni trattato per conformarmi col commandamento che V. E. me ne fa." Altieri's report of November 2, 1647, Altieri Arch., XX., A. 3.

[2] Altieri's *report of November 12, 1647, loc. cit.

[3] See Cifra al Nuntio di Napoli, December 7, 1647, in VISCO, 142.

[4] Cifra of November 2, 1647 ; ibid., 139 seq.

[5] Cifra in REUMONT, Carafa, II., 192. In a Cifra of February 15, 1648, Altieri was ordered to defer his departure on account of the arrival at Naples of Oñate (VISCO, 144).

[6] See the *reports of L. Allacci to Fabio Chigi, dated Rome, January 18 and 31, 1648, Cod. A., III., 59, of Chigi Lib.

[7] Giustinian in BERCHET, Roma, II., 132.

established relations with the rebels.[1] They pressed Mazarin
to give direct support to the insurrection, but this the Cardinal
Minister deemed too risky ;   open participation, he feared,
would induce the Viceroy to become reconciled with the
rebels.[2]   '

The Spaniards' bombardment of the city from the *castelli*
led to a complete break with Spain and to a powerful increase
of Francophile feeling in Naples.   The leaders explained to
the populace that, unless they were willing to submit once
more to the Spaniards, only three courses were open to them :
viz. to offer the crown either to the Pope, their feudal overlord, or to the King of France, or to proclaim a republic.[3]
They chose the latter. They would not hear of the papal
peace mediation proposed by Innocent X.,[4] instead they
invoked the help of the ambitious Duke Henry II. of Guise
who was in Rome at the time in connection with the dis-
solution of his marriage.   Guise has asserted that the Pope
had encouraged him to put himself at the head of the rebels.
Though Siri, who was anything but friendly to the Pope,[5]
already described this assertion of Guise as a lie, it has been
repeated in our own days.[6]   In reality at that moment the
Pope was anything but prejudiced in favour of France. It was
precisely just then (November, 1647) that Innocent X. was
reported to have said that every one of France's gains
was the Roman Church's loss, and only on Spain could the

---

[1] See Savelli's *report of November 2, 1647, State Arch.,
Vienna ; *cf.* Fr. Albizzi's *letter to Chigi, Rome, November 2,
1647, in which he says : " la monarchia di Spagna divenuta
un panno fracido, che s'egli ricuce in un luogo, s'apre in un
altro." *Cod.* A., III., 55, Chigi Lib.

[2] RANKE, *Französ. Gesch.*, V., 176.

[3] RANKE, *Französ. Gesch.*, V., 176.

[4] **Cifre al Nuntio di Napoli*, of November 9 and 15, 1647,
Papal Sec. Arch. *Cf.* VISCO, 74 *seq.*, 140 *seq.*

[5] SIRI, *Mercurio*, Casale, 1668, 520, against *Mém. de feu M.
le duc de Guise*, Paris, 1668.

[6] ZÖPPFEL-BENRATH, in HERZOG, *Realenzyclopädie*, IX (1901),
142.

Holy See securely rely.[1] This remark has come down to us only from Spanish sources and may very properly be questioned ; for all that it contains a kernel of truth, for now as always there was no one Innocent X. was more afraid of than his old opponent Mazarin. Consequently he preferred Spanish to French domination in Naples.[2] He could only view with grave misgivings the negotiations which his bitter enemy, Cardinal Grimaldi, and Du Plessis-Besançon conducted at Naples in the spring of 1648 by order of Mazarin. The object of these discussions was not the consolidation of the Neapolitan republic or the setting up in authority of the ambitious, unreliable Guise ; Mazarin's scheme was to transfer the crown of Naples from the King of Spain to his pupil Louis XIV, who, so he asserted, had numerous claims to it.[3] However, this plan which, had it succeeded, would have altered the whole course of history, was to prove a complete failure.

On January 30th, 1648, Spain had signed a treaty of peace with the Republic of the Netherlands. Secure from that side she cherished the hope of continuing the war against France with better prospects of success. On April 5th the Spaniards succeeded in recovering Naples where the new Viceroy Oñate, hitherto ambassador in Rome, to whom Innocent X. expressed his high hopes,[4] re-established the sovereignty of Philip IV. on easy terms. Guise had committed the imprudence of leaving the city for an expedition against the island of Nisida ; he now thought of fleeing into the Abruzzi, but he fell into the hands of the Spaniards near Capua.[5]

---

[1] Deone (Ameyden) in CIAMPI, 38.

[2] Giustinian in BERCHET, *Spagna*, II., 182 ; *cf.* VISCO, 72.

[3] RANKE, *loc. cit.*, 179 ; VISCO, 73.

[4] VISCO, 94.

[5] LOISELEUR et BAGUENAULT DE PUCHESSE, *L'expédition du duc de Guise à Naples*, Paris, 1875, and CARUTTI in *Arch. stor. ital.*, 3rd series, XXII., 497 *seq*. How anti-Spanish most of the Cardinals were is shown by the fact that only five of them were present at the *Te Deum* sung at S. Giacomo on the occasion of the

Mazarin, however, did not consider this occurrence sufficient reason for giving up his intentions with regard to Naples. As early as May, the French in Rome spoke of a new fleet about to sail for Naples ; in view of the scarcity of provisions this caused the Spaniards not a little anxiety.[1] At Naples a real famine prevailed. Innocent X. sanctioned the export of provisions both for the Spaniards and the French. Now, as always, he would not side with either party.[2]

For the success of his enterprise against Naples Mazarin reckoned particularly on the nobility of that city, for he imagined that nothing but fear of the preponderance of the popular party had driven them back into the arms of Spain. In this he was mistaken for now both the nobility and the upper middle class felt that they were once more under obligation to the Spanish Government.[3] When in September Prince Tommaso of Savoy appeared before Naples with a French fleet, no one stirred. When French troops were landed at Salerno, they received no support and were defeated by the Spaniards.[4] The revolutionary fire was spent and Philip IV. found himself freed from the fear of losing his South-Italian possessions.

Innocent X's joy over the end of the Neapolitan complications is intelligible enough.[5] How easily these troubles might have spread to the Papal States ! Moreover the revolution had had a paralysing effect on trade and industry in Rome.[6] But the mere fact that Spain retained Naples gave

---

capture of Naples (viz. Cueva, Montalto, Cesi, Lugo, Colonna). Deone, *Diario*, in *Cod.* XX., III., 26., Bibl. Casanat.

[1] *Cf.* L. Allacci's *letter to F. Chigi, dated Rome, May 9, 1648, in *Cod.* A., III., 59, of Chigi Lib.

[2] Giustinian in BERCHET, Rome, II., 132 *seq.*

[3] RANKE, *loc. cit.*, 184 *seq.*

[4] GARIGNANI in *Arch. stor. Napolit.*, VI., 661 *seq.* ; *cf.* IX., 485 *seqq.*

[5] Servantius *Diaria*, April 8, 1648, Papal Sec. Arch. ; *cf.* also *Brief to Philip IV. of May 20, 1648, in *Epist.*, IV.–VI., *ibid.* ; also VISCO, 104 *seq.*

[6] Deone *Diario*, 1648, in *Cod.* XX., III., 21, *loc. cit.*

satisfaction to the Pope inasmuch as in the circumstances, the choice lay between French and Spanish hegemony in Italy, hence the Pope was bound to prefer the weakened domination of Spain to France's rising and disturbing power.[1] Moreover, Catholic interests were, on the whole, better safe-guarded by Spain than by France.[2] On the other hand Innocent X. could not approve the cruel severity with which the Spaniards re-established order in a land ruined by the rebellion.[3]

On the conclusion of the exhausting struggle with the Dutch Republic and the reconquest of Naples, a new period opened for Philip IV., so sorely tried, even in his domestic life. On October 6th, 1644, the King had lost his wife Elizabeth Bourbon, daughter of Henry IV. Though pressed by the Cortes, Philip did not, for the time being, contemplate a second marriage. Ever since 1645 Innocent X. had been endeavouring, through his nuncio Giulio Rospigliosi, to persuade the King

---

[1] A picture of the relations of the Italian States with Spain is drawn in " *Lettera di confidenza scritta in cifra della Maestà di Filippo IV., Re della Spagna, al conte Ognate vicere dii Napoli, fedelmente tradotta dallo Spagnuolo in Italiano," dated Madrid, September 18, 1649, in *Cod. lat.* 12547, p. 355 *seq.* of the Bibliothèque Nationale, Paris. The letter, which is also found in *Cod. ital.* 341 of the City Library, Munich, with date of September 27, 1649, is interesting in itself, but apocryphal ; *cf.* REUMONT, in *Arch. stor. ital.*, N.S. XVII. (1863), P. 2, 140 *seq.*

[2] *Cf.* the *letter of Fr. Albizzi to F. Chigi, dated Rome, September 7, 1647, in *Cod.* A., III., 55, of the Chigi Lib.

[3] VISCO (p. 11–12) examines Innocent X.'s conduct during the Neapolitan troubles and expresses the opinion that on this occasion the Pope showed true greatness : " Non solo prova dolore alla vista del popolo oppresso, quanto sdegno, nel dover riconoscere così abbietto e feroce quel governo straniero, sotto il quale sono costretti a vivere i miseri Napoletani. Innocenzo X. non volle Napoli per sè nè per i Francesi, poichè vide che l'unica soluzione per il momento era il ristabilimento del governo spagnuolo, ma ne desiderò sempre un vero e profondo migliora-mento. La sua voce fiera di protesta si eleva sola tra tutti i principi d'Europa contro i crudeli rigori usati dal conte d'Ognate

to overcome this reluctance.[1] The Pope had in view, in the
first instance, the daughter of the Archduchess Claudia of
Innsbruck but when, in February, 1646, the Council of
State discussed the marriage of his son Baltasar Carlos, the
King would not have his own re-marriage mentioned. However, the heir to the throne died unexpectedly on October 9th,
1646, after a short illness. Thereupon the King felt compelled
to contract a new alliance in order to prevent the extinction
of the Spanish Habsburgs in the male line. On November 19th,
1646, the nuncio, after a previous understanding with the
minister Luis de Haro, represented to the King in such
forcible fashion the complications that were bound to arise
should he die without an heir, that Philip IV. yielded.[2]

The heir to the throne had been betrothed to Marianne,
daughter of the Emperor Ferdinand III. and Princess Maria,
Philip IV.'s sister, born in 1635. The imperial ambassador
suggested that the King should step into his son's place, but
against this proposal there militated the princess' tender age
and the near kinship. However, all the ministers whom the
King consulted spoke in favour of an alliance with the
Emperor's daughter for which there existed also political
motives of the greatest weight. The King was attracted to
such a union by his great affection for his sister Maria who,
twenty years earlier, had gone to Vienna as a bride : in
Calderon's words, Germany was now to make a return to
Spain for this gift.[3]

The marriage treaty was signed on April 2nd, 1647, and the
wedding celebrated, by proxy, at Vienna in November of
the following year. In December, 1648, the new Queen repaired
to Trent where she was delayed until the spring of 1649 by

verso i ribelli e la fede mancata da Filippo IV. alle giurate
capitulazioni e al perdono generale."

[1] For what follows cf. the work of VITI MARIANI : *La Spagna
e la S. Sede. I : Il matrimonio del Re di Spagna con D. Maria
Anna arciducissa d' Austria,* 1646–9, Rome, 1899, 21 *seqq.* This
work is based on documents in the Papal Sec. Arch.

[2] *Ibid.,* 28 *seqq.*

[3] *Ibid.,* 30 *seqq.* ; *cf.* IUSTI, *Velasquez,* II., 137, 285.

the circumstance that the Master of the Ceremonies, the Duke of Nájera y Maqueda, only arrived with her suite at the end of April. Count Lumiares brought to the Queen a portrait of Philip IV. adorned with twenty-two diamonds. On June 23rd she finally arrived at Milan whither Cardinal Montalto had repaired by order of the Pope.[1]

Innocent X., who had taken the liveliest interest in the match, was anxious to give expression to his joy by sending a legate *a latere*. For this mission his choice fell on Cardinal Ludovisi who was also the bearer of the Golden Rose for Marianne. Wearisome and protracted disputes arose with the Spaniards with regard to the legate's entry into Milan, for the former were unwilling to pay to the Pope's representative the honours which the Holy See had to insist upon. In that era of conflicts over questions of etiquette enormous weight was attached to matters of this kind. The affair was further complicated by the jealousy that existed between the Duke of Nájera y Maqueda and the Governor of Milan, Marchese di Caracena.[2]

Cardinal Ludovisi set out from Bologna on July 9th. No sooner had he arrived on Spanish territory, at Cremona, than it was seen that the Spaniards were unwilling to abide by the terms of their agreement with the Pope concerning the reception of the legate. They only yielded when the Cardinal threatened to return to Bologna. On August 3rd the Cardinal legate was at length able to make his solemn entry into the capital of Lombardy. The Spaniards now courted oblivion for their former conduct by heaping honours on the legate. The Cardinal offered to the Queen, in the name of the Pope, not only the Golden Rose but other presents also, among them the relics of St. Beatrice in a silver shrine.[3] Queen Marianne set out from Milan on August 9th and on the 25th she embarked at Finalmarina. A fleet of forty-four ships, commanded by Don Juan, escorted her. She landed at

[1] See Collección de docum. inéditos, LXXXVI., 641 *seq.* ; VITI MARIANI, 32 *seqq.*, 39 *seqq.*

[2] VITI MARIANI, 44 *seqq.* ; FRIEDENSBURG, *Regesten*, V., 63.

[3] VITI MARIANI, 55 *seqq.*, 61 *seqq.*, 67.

Denia and reached Navalcarnero on October 6th, two and a half years after her betrothal. On the following day the Cardinal of Toledo celebrated, in the utmost privacy, the marriage of the fourteen years' old princess with the king, twenty-six years her senior.[1] The external celebrations were reserved for the entry into Madrid which took place on November 15th. According to the reports of nuncio Rospigliosi, the magnificence displayed on that occasion surpassed anything ever seen before. Architects, sculptors and poets had vied with one another ; the scheme for the triumphal arches which glittered with gold, each of which cost 25,000 scudi, had been suggested by Calderon. The statues and paintings which adorned them represented Spain's possessions in the four quarters of the globe. "The court was determined to show," so we read in a report of Basadonna, the Venetian ambassador, "that they could still perform miracles at a time when everybody thought they lay prostrate."[2]

In view of the financial straits of the Spanish State, Madrid had always been anxious to obtain revenues from ecclesiastical sources, from subsidies by the clergy and from the so-called *cruzada* ; under Philip IV. this tendency was stronger than ever. In this respect Innocent X. granted all that could be conceded[3] ; consequently he could not but feel all the more deeply hurt by the constant encroachments on the Church's sphere and the manifold injuries done to ecclesiastical jurisdiction and immunity which the Spanish authorities allowed themselves especially at Milan and Naples. Complaints on this subject began as early as 1645[4] and they continued throughout his pontificate, though a settlement was usually secured.[5]

---

[1] *Ibid.*, 42–3, 81–2.

[2] *Ibid.*, 84 *seqq.*, and IUSTI, *Velasquez*, II., 286 *seq.*

[3] *Cf. Bull.*, XV., 331 *seqq.*, 342, 347 *seqq.*, 350 *seqq.*, 377 *seq.*, 465 *seqq.*, 559 *seqq.*, 661, 665.

[4] *Brief to Philip IV., September 30, 1645, in *Epist.*, I., Papal Sec. Arch.

[5] *Cf.* besides the *reports of Rospigliosi in *Nunziat. di Spagna*,

A more serious conflict arose towards the end of Innocent X.'s pontificate. After the Spaniards had reconquered Barcelona in 1652, they demanded from the Pope that Philip IV. should once more have the right of nomination to vacant bishoprics. In view of the fact that the struggle for Catalonia was by no means at an end, Innocent X. refused, on the ground that it was necessary first to see who would secure the mastery there, France or Spain. As a result of this incident and various fresh encroachments on ecclesiastical jurisdiction, especially at Naples,[1] a tension existed between Madrid and Rome which was further increased by a fresh incident.[2]

Francesco Gaetano, Archbishop of Rhodes and a nephew of Cardinal Pamfili, had been nuncio in Spain since September, 1652, in succession to Rospigliosi. Gaetano proved unequal to this difficult post.[3] Complaints reached Rome concerning the conduct of the nunciature and Gaetano failed to carry out the Pope's instructions with a view to the recovery of the ecclesiastical revenues of Cardinal Barberini. Consequently Innocent appointed a new nuncio for Spain in the person of Camillo Massimo to whom he granted the title of Patriarch

Papal Sec. Arch., *ibid.*, 347, the *letters of the Secretary of State to Rospigliosi, especially those of December 16, 1645, January 5, March 23, May 11, June 8, July 19, August 30, 1647, June 18, October 30 and 31, 1651, as well as the *Cifre al Nuntio di Napoli* of June 6, 1647, July 25, 1648, and December 21, 1650, *Nunziat. Napol.*, 39 A., *ibid.* Cf. also *Arch. stor. ital.*, IX., 344. Also a *dissertation of Carolus Maranta, " pro libertate ecclesiastica," directed against an ordinance of the Spanish authorities at Naples, January 4, 1652, dealing with the conflicts of jurisdiction with Archbp. Filomarino of Naples, *Cod.* 12547, p. 365 *seqq.*, in National Lib., Paris; see DE BLASIIS in *Arch. stor. Napolet.*, VI., 758 *seq.*

[1] See *warning Brief of March, 1653, to Philip IV. in which the blame is laid on the King's ministers (" Acria timemus, sed, ut ait etiam Bernardus, quia acriora (divine chastisements) timemus "). *Epist.*, IX., Papal Sec. Arch.

[2] DENIS, I., 207, 286.

[3] *Cf.* MEISTER in *Röm. Quartalschr.*, VII., 466 *seq.*

of Jerusalem. However, Cardinal Trivulzio, at that time Spanish ambassador in Rome, was a strong opponent of the new nominee, owing to his being a partisan of Olimpia and the Barberini ; he declared the appointment null because it had been made without previous agreement with the King of Spain. Innocent X. would not admit the existence of an obligation in this respect and ordered Massimo to set out for his post.[1]

On his arrival in Spain in February, 1654,[2] the new nuncio was informed that the King would not receive him. Though every prince was perfectly free in the choice of his ambassadors, the Madrid Cabinet declared, the Spanish nuncio was no mere political official ; in view of the wide range of his faculties in regard to ecclesiastical administration and jurisdiction the King could only accept a person agreeable to himself.

Innocent soon learnt that this action was Spain's revenge for his conduct in respect to the Catalonian bishoprics as well as for the fact that on March 25th, 1653, he had married his niece Olimpiuccia Giustiniani to Matteo Barberini and granted the purple to Carlo Barberini on June 23rd.[3] Moreover it was evident that France's " bad example " had also contributed to this result, the latter having just then refused to accept Domenico Marini as nuncio.[4] More than by all this the Pope, who on October 31st had appointed a new nuncio for Spain, in the person of Francesco Mancini,[5] was greatly annoyed by the conduct of nuncio Gaetano who was determined to remain at his post at any cost and who, accordingly, was secretly in league with the Spanish Government. The Pope's command to hand over to Massimo a third of the

---

[1] PALLAVICINO, I., 306 seqq. On C. Massimo see MORONI, XLIII., 230 seq.

[2] His *correspondence in Nunziat. di Spagna, 107 and 108, Papal Sec. Arch.

[3] *Cifra del Fiscale (of the nunciature), dated Madrid, February 18, 1654, in Nunziat. di Spagna, 107, loc. cit.

[4] See above, p. 69.

[5] *Brief to Philip IV. of October 31, 1654 (duplic. et tripl., Nov. 2, 1654), Epist., X., Papal Sec. Arch.

revenues of the nunciature he executed only very imper-
fectly.[1]   Thereupon the Pope gave orders for the Spanish
nunciature to be closed. On December 13th Mancini informed
Gaetano of this decision [2] ; the command to take his departure
which he received at the same time, Gaetano likewise refused
to obey, notwithstanding the exhortations of Cardinal
Sandoval [3] ; he was, however, compelled to close the nunciature
since his jurisdiction had been withdrawn. Massimo now hoped
to be received at least as nuncio extraordinary,[4] but the
Spanish Government put off a decision in the matter for it
had been informed of Innocent X.'s fatal illness.

---

[1] PALLAVICINO, *loc. cit.* Gaetano affirms in a *letter of June 3,
1654, that he had done everything to remove the " impediments "
against Massimo ; but Massimo himself, in a *letter of March 1
1654, declares that Gaetano had worked against him in order
to maintain himself at his post. *Nunziat. di Spagna*, 107, Papal
Sec. Arch.

[2] See Mancini's *report, dated Madrid, December 16, 1654, *ibid.*

[3] See Mancini's *report, Madrid, December 25, 1654, *ibid.*

[4] *Letter of Massimo, January 3, 1655, *ibid.*

CHAPTER III.

The Peace of Westphalia and Religious Conditions in Germany and Holland—The English Catholics under Cromwell—Ireland's Fight for Freedom; Her Defeat.

(1.)

Of all the diplomatic representatives of Urban VIII. the Cologne nuncio, Fabio Chigi, Bishop of Nardò, had the most difficult task of all, for it was his duty to represent the Holy See in the supremely important peace negotiations at Münster.[1] A skilful diplomatist and an accomplished gentleman, Chigi won for himself an honourable position in that assembly which eventually grew into a European congress, but the Spaniards were at first dissatisfied with his attitude because his foremost concern was always the good of the Church, not the particularist interests of individual States.

With the election of Innocent X. the Spaniards believed

---

[1] For Chigi's *reports and correspondence during the period of the congress (in the Papal Sec. Arch. and the Chigi Lib., Rome), see XXX, Appendix 2. At Münster Chigi lodged at the Convent of the Friars Minor, as an inscription recalls to this day ; see *Zeitschr. des westfäl. Gesch. Ver.*, 3 series, II., 372. The dwelling was damp and dingy and as a southerner he suffered not a little from the German climate (Tourtual, 25 *seq.*). *Viaggio che fece Msgr. Ill. da Colonia a Münster, 1644 (departure from Cologne, March 14) in Q., II., 48, p. 183–7 of Chigi Lib. " *Discessi aspero coelo et infirmo corpore, convalui utcunque . . . Huius tractatus a divini numinis imploratione facto exordio feliciter atque alacriter fundamenta iacere videbamur, cum repente cessatum est ab eo fervore et lente coeptum progredi." Chigi to Erycius Puteanus, Münster, May 26, 1644, *Barb.* 2575, Vat. Lib.

the time had come when they might use the papal diplomacy for their own ends, but Chigi was not the man to lend himself to such manœuvres. A partisan neither of Spain nor of France, he deemed it his first duty to labour for the Church.[1] The Spanish ambassador in Rome, Count Sirvela, at the instigation of the Spanish plenipotentiary at Münster, Diego Saavedra and the one-sided Hispanophile Cardinal Rossetti, pulled every imaginable string in order to get the new Pope to remove Chigi from his post. But it was precisely this passionate persistence which set the Pontiff thinking. He asked to see the reports of the Cologne nuncio ; after studying them he remarked to the Secretary of State, Panciroli : " Chigi is the right man ! " and to Sirvela he said that the Holy See had no better nuncio than Chigi.[2] A Brief of October 5th, 1644, confirmed Chigi in his position as the Holy See's representative at the peace congress. That document describes his task negatively rather than positively : he was to further peace with all his might, yet so that religion and the Church suffered no injury ; he must neither consent to, nor even merely connive at, what might be in any way incompatible with the prerogatives and the welfare of the Church, on the contrary, he should boldly and with all his might stand up for her defence and, if necessary, withdraw from the deliberations, for human considerations must give way when one's duty to God is at stake.[3]

Chigi's patience was put to a fresh test even after the imperialists had at last opened the way for the beginning of the discussions properly so called by their proposals of November 23rd and December 4th to the Swedes and the French. " Here," he wrote to a friend at the close of 1644, " labour, discussions and sittings are on the increase but we make no progress ; often I go home at night my head burning with the discussions and the heat of the stove, so that I am

---

[1] See Chigi's letter of February 11, 1645, in BROM, III., 391. *Cf.* above, p. 72, n. 3.

[2] PALLAVICINO, I., 126 *seq.*

[3] BROM, III., 388-9.

only able to write a couple of lines. May the name of the Lord be blessed." [1]

From the first Chigi kept in close touch with the representative of Venice, Alvise Contarini, his fellow mediator. Their mutual relations were so friendly that between them they frequently displayed greater harmony than the plenipotentiaries of one and the same Power, who often quarrelled among themselves. [2]

On a motion of the imperial delegates, the sole object of the discussions was to be peace between the Empire and the Kings of France and Sweden, and the determination of boundaries. However, very soon the Swedes, in concert with the French, demanded not only an increase of their territories but likewise effective influence on the new internal constitution of the German Empire, hence they insisted on all the Estates of the Empire being invited to take part in the peace negotiations. The Emperor resisted this demand but in the end he was forced to give way and to summon to the peace congress all the Estates entitled to vote. As a result business, the slowness of which Chigi lamented, was bound to become even more involved. [3]

In the first days of June, 1645, Chigi wrote to his friend the Jesuit Sforza Pallavicino : " We have reached port ; three days hence the French and the Swedes will come out with their peace conditions. Great dangers will then arise for the Church for I foresee that the Swedes will reveal the purpose for which they went to war, because so long as they needed France's money and support, they pretended to have none but political motives. Pray ! " [4]

The peace proposals which the French delegates presented at Münster on Trinity Sunday, 1645 (June 11th), through Chigi and Contarini, whilst the Swedes presented theirs to the imperialists at Osnabrück, are justly described by Chigi

---

[1] Chigi to Albizzi, *ibid.*, 390.

[2] See Contarini's report in *Fontes rer. Austr.*, II., 26, 28.

[3] *Letter to Pallavicino, April 28, 1645. *Cod.* A., II., 28, Chigi Lib.

[4] *Letter of June 9, 1645, *ibid.*

as the high demands of a victor.[1] Both Powers demanded a general, unlimited amnesty, including Bohemia, the restoration of all the Estates of Empire to the condition of 1618, a guarantee of the constitution of the Empire, abolition of the custom hitherto observed of choosing a successor to the Emperor under the title of King of the Romans during the lifetime of the Emperor, the preservation of all the liberties of the Estates of the Empire, especially in respect of their right to enter into alliances with foreign Powers for the purpose of their security, lastly an indemnity for expenses incurred, guarantees for the future and payment for their armies as well as for their allies, especially for Hesse and Transilvania. The French left it to the Swedes to present the demand made in the interest of the Protestants for a definitive settlement of all ecclesiastical conflicts over the religious peace and the holding of Church property. The Imperialists were well justified when they remarked that by peace conditions such as these the Empire would not be reformed but destroyed. The Swedes openly avowed that they had waged a religious war and that now they were resolved on making a peace that would redound to the damage of the Catholics. Chigi felt obliged to delay expressing his opinion for fear of losing France's confidence in his capacity as a mediator, all the more so as just then relations between Rome and Paris had become such that an interruption of diplomatic intercourse had ensued.[2]

Most of the summer of 1645 was spent in endless disputes over preliminaries in connection with which the ceremonial, titles and visits gave rise to no small difficulties.[3]

Special difficulties arose for Chigi as the Pope's delegate with regard to immediate contact with Protestants. During his six years' stay in Germany he had made it a strict law unto himself, especially out of consideration for his dignity

---

[1] *Letter to Pallavicino of June 23, 1643, *ibid.*

[2] *Ibid.*, *cf.* also Chigi's *letter to Ropigliosi, nuncio in Madrid, June 11, 1645, Cod. A., I., 25, Chigi Lib., and *ibid.*, A., I., 22, *Albizzi's letter of June 16, 1645.

[3] *Chigi to Sf. Pallavicino, June 19, 1645, *ibid.*

as representative of the Apostolic See, to avoid all contact with people who denounced the Pope as Antichrist. By this rule he resolved to abide now also, for attempts to approach him had been made, from political motives, first by the delegates of the Duke of Brandenburg [1] and after them by those of the Dutch Republic who had arrived in 1646 for the peace negotiations with Spain. However, Chigi very skilfully avoided giving offence by brusquely repelling the above-named Powers, for such conduct might have done grievous injury to the Church. He likewise avoided intercourse with those who had fallen away from the Church, lest they should be able to say afterwards that he had angered them by threats or cajoled them by promises and flatteries. He knew his History, hence he was well aware of the accusations of which his predecessors, Cardinals Contarini and Cajetan, had been the objects in this respect. Accordingly he decided on a middle course, that is, neither to allow himself to be carried too far by the Protestants—conduct that might have been mis-interpreted later on—nor to repel them altogether. He was careful to remove, by his general attitude, any offensiveness there might have been in this reserve. He avoided most scrupulously any offensive expression and showed a conciliatory disposition. If a non-Catholic delegate wrote to ask a favour he replied, not indeed in writing but by ful-filling the request. If a Protestant man of letters, duly recom-mended, expressed a desire to have speech with him, he granted the request on condition that controversial questions were not discussed and that the interview took place in presence of witnesses. By this prudent and conciliatory attitude, which clearly evidenced both his devotion to the Church and his freedom from hatred or contempt for those who did not share his religious convictions, he won the respect and even the veneration of many Protestants.[2] However, this reserve which he had imposed on himself,

---

[1] Cf. HILTEBRANDT in Quellen u. Forsch., XV., 360 seq.; PALLAVICINO, I., 132 seq.; BROM, III., 482 seq.

[2] PALLAVICINO, loc. cit., cf. TOURTUAL, 23.

robbed him of any influence he might have had on the Protestant delegates, and 1e would surely have been better advised had he unhesitatingly treated with them, as did the Jesuits of Münster.[1]

Though the Turkish peril counselled haste, the negotiations at Münster made no progress,[2] the real cause of the delay being the hope cherished by each party, that the military situation might shift in its own favour.

On September 25th, 1645, the delegates of France and Sweden were made acquainted with the Emperor's answer to their demands. It fixed 1630 as the year of the amnesty, Bohemia and the imperial Hereditary States being excluded. With regard to the question of religion, the Emperor declared his readiness for an amicable settlement, only it must be brought about in conformity with the Constitution of the Empire. He would tolerate alliances of the Estates of Empire with foreign Powers in so far as these were not directed against himself and the Empire and injured neither the public tranquillity nor the oath which bound each Estate of Empire to the Emperor and the Empire. The proposal not to choose a successor during the Emperor's lifetime was irreconcilable with the Golden Bull and the rights of the Electors. With regard to Spain, before concluding peace, the Emperor must have a guarantee that neither France nor Sweden would lend help to his enemies ; only then could he give the desired promise not to intervene in Franco-Spanish disputes. It was not the affair of France or Sweden to demand compensation, but rather the Emperor's, for the violent and unprovoked invasion of the Empire and his Hereditary States. A compromise was being negotiated with the Landgravine of Hesse, but as for the Prince of Transilvania, he was neither one of the Estates of Empire nor a German ally of Sweden.

So as to be prepared for any emergency in respect of the religious questions, Chigi drew up in December 1645, a protest against any direct or indirect injury to the Church

---

[1] DUHR, II., I, 488.
[2] *Cf.* Chigi's *letter to Sf. Pallavicino, August 11, 1645, *loc. cit*.

as a result of the treaty of peace. As a model he made use of a similar document with which Cardinal Truchsess had protested, on March 23rd, 1555, against a religious settlement within the Empire which favoured the Protestants.[1] As for the proper moment at which to make his protest, Chigi determined it in concert with Contarini who promised his support.[2]

Not long afterwards, the Protestant princes and towns presented to the Councillor of Empire at Mayence and to the imperial delegates their very considerable demands, styled by them "religious grievances", to which the Catholics, on February 8th, 1646, replied with their counter-claims.[3] The Protestants demanded from the Catholics unprecedented sacrifices, viz. abolition of the ecclesiastical reservation which represented the best bulwark against further secularizations ; the abandonment by them of all Church property usurped after the treaty of Passau in 1552 ; the free practice of their religion by the Protestant subjects of Catholic princes, whereas the same right was to be denied to Catholic subjects ; lastly in regard to religion and property, restoration of the situation as it existed previous to the outbreak of the great war in 1618.

One thing was in favour of the Catholics, namely the circumstance that in this question the two most powerful Protestant princes pursued opposite aims. The Elector of Saxony did not wish to go beyond the Peace of Prague, would not hear of linking himself to the Swedes and refused to assume the presidency of the Protestant separate assembly. Nor was the Duke of Brandenburg prepared to take his place for he knew well how much the Lutherans were opposed to him by reason of his being a Calvinist ; moreover he was bound to consider the Emperor because the Swedes threatened

---

[1] *Cf.* our data XIV., 339.

[2] Chigi's letter to C. Pamfili, December 15, 1645, in CIAMPI, 55. The text of the *protest (undated) in *Cod.* A. I., 45, p. 60b-61, Chigi Lib.

[3] MEIERN, *Acta*, II., 522 *seqq.*, 540 *seqq.* ; GÄRTNER, VII., 237 *seq.*

his interests in Pomerania. Consequently the Protestant princes, counts and towns saw themselves compelled to stand up for their demands without the support of the two Electors. However, the advantage the Catholics might have derived from this circumstance was neutralized by the fact that they too were not united and that the Swedes gave unconditional support to all the demands of the Protestants. Although, in the great question as to how far they might go in their concessions to the Protestants, the Catholics firmly held to the fundamental principles, in regard to their application to German conditons, the opinions of the princes, Statesmen and theologians diverged considerably.[1] The more intransigent clung firmly to the lofty but by then unattainable ideal of unity in the Catholic faith and they condemned any concession of importance to the Protestants, even at the risk of wrecking the peace. This group, which had found a resolute spokesman in the Dillingen Jesuit Henry Wangnereck and strong backing from nuncio Chigi, included in the first instance the Bishop of Osnabrück, Franz Wilhelm von Wartenberg, a cousin of Maximilian of Bavaria, the delegate of the Bishop of Augsburg, Henry von Knäringen, the first Spanish delegate, Count Peñeranda, the Benedictine Adam Adami who represented the threatened monasteries of Württemberg and the delegate of the Catholic council of Augsburg, Dr. Johann von Leuxselring.

This intransigent group was faced by another set of men more opportunist, yielding and conciliatory, who, taking into account existing circumstances, were for peace at any price, even that of wide concessions in the religious sphere. This view was defended by the Elector Maximilian of Bavaria, his confessor, the Jesuit Johann Vervaux, a native of Lorraine, and by Count Maximilian von Trauttmansdorff, first master

---

[1] *Cf.* for what follows the work (based on extensive research in archives), of L. STEINBERGER, *Die Jesuiten und die Friedensfrage*, 1635–1650, Freiburg, 1906. This work adds considerably to our knowledge ; also RITTER in *Hist. Zeitschr.*, C. (1908), 253 *seqq.* See also F. ISRAEL, *Adam Adami und seine Arcana pacis Westfalicae*, Berlin, 1910.

of ceremonies and a trusted councillor of Ferdinand III.,
who arrived at Münster, on November 29th, 1645, at the
head of the imperial delegation and armed with the most
ample powers.

The divisions among the Catholics, the slow progress
of the negotiations, Trauttmansdorff's tendency to influence
the Swedes by satisfying the Protestants so as to isolate
the French, the great dangers for the German Catholics which
became increasingly threatening, and lastly the unfavourable
turn of the war after the battle of Alerheim in August, 1645,
and even more so after the junction of the French army
with that of the Swedes which was effected in August of the
following year—all this filled Chigi's heart with bitter grief.
In confidential letters to friends he poured out his heart.
He expected no good from this peace, he wrote to Sforza
Pallavicino on February 9th, 1646, and wished himself out
of Münster.[1] In a letter of April 6th to Francesco Albizzi
he wrote that there was truth in what the people were saying
just then ; namely that hell must be empty since all its
denizens had come to Münster to prevent a true peace.[2]
Again and again he begs Pallavicino's prayers ; this he did
with special insistence during the conferences, with a view
to a compromise, which were held at Osnabrück from
April 12th to May 5th, 1646, between the representatives
of the Catholics and the Protestants. Chigi did his utmost
to induce the Catholic delegates to oppose a determined
refusal to the Protestant demands, but he found that many
of the adherents of the ancient Church had become greatly
dispirited.[3] The course of the negotiations was such that
on April 27th the nuncio came to the sorrowful conclusion
that all his representations and protests were unvailing to
prevent a most grievous injury being done to the Catholic
religion.[4] In a letter of the same date Chigi laments the great

[1] *Letter in Cod., A. II., 28, Chigi Lib.

[2] Ibid., *Cod., A. I., 22.

[3] Chigi's *report to the Secretary of State, April 13, 1646, in
Paci, 20, Papal Sec. Arch.

[4] *Cod., A. II., 28, loc. cit.

readiness with which people spoke of the necessity of throwing everything overboard to save what remained.[1] Chigi's fears grew when, on May 19th, Count von Trauttmansdorff was charged to continue the negotiations with the Protestants at Osnabrück. The Count was full of the best goodwill in the world but he was only moderately endowed, credulous, timorous, and burning with a misguided keenness for a settlement which Chigi sought in vain to moderate.[2] Trautt- mansdorff showed excessive readiness to yield—the Bishop of Osnabrück was one of those who bitterly lamented the fact—with regard to the definitive cession of Catholic dioceses to the Protestants.[3] Chigi had hopes that on this point the Elector of Bavaria, Maximilian, would support him against the imperial delegate, but he was mistaken : about the middle of May, Maximilian took the side of his imperial brother-in-law in this matter. In view of the fact that both princes based their conduct on the judgment of their respective spiritual advisers, Chigi and together with him the nuncio in Vienna, Melzi, made powerful but fruitless efforts to exorcize from the courts of Vienna and Munich this excessively accommodating spirit.[4] The French delegates had promised to support Chigi in the matter of the dioceses, but from the first the nuncio felt very doubtful whether, in view of her

---

[1] " *La prontezza che si chiama necessitate a far gettito per salvar il resto." *Cod.* A. I., 22, *loc. cit.*

[2] PALLAVICINO, I., 134 *seqq. Cf.* Chigi's views in his reports to Rome quoted by STEINBERGER, 58, n. 10, and 61, n. 6. The Spanish reports (*Colecc. de docum. inéd.*, LXXXII *seq.*) depict Trauttmansdorff as a man of sanguine disposition who was all too easily deluded by the false promises of his opponents and who allowed them to see far too much of his own game. Chigi wrote in his *Diarium* : " Trauttmansdorff e Volmar due neofiti [both had been Protestants] non si curano di religione che fredissimamente, solo del patrimonio Cesareo sono zelanti," Chigi Lib.

[3] Chigi's *report to the Secretary of State, May 18, 1646, *Paci*, 20, Papal Sec. Arch. *Cf.* BAUR, Sötern, II., 157.

[4] STEINBERGER, 60-2.

close alliance with the Swedes, France would be able to obtain anything in the face of their opposition.[1] His fears could but be confirmed when he had to witness the fact that France's representative, the Duke of Longueville, who before Chigi posed as a supporter of staunchly Catholic principles, simultaneously endeavoured to bring about the nomination to the coadjutorship of Paderborn of a son of the Calvinist Landgravine Amalia.[2]

When on May 19th the Catholics entrusted to Count Trauttmansdorff the task of continuing the negotiations with the Protestants it was arranged that any terms arrived at should be submitted to them for confirmation. But how did the imperial delegate act? Without consulting the Catholics he guaranteed to the Protestants, for a hundred years, the possession of whatever ecclesiastical property they had held since 1627. This weakness so whetted the appetite of the Protestants that they promptly renewed their demands for possession of all Church property held by them since 1618.[3] "The danger for the Church," Chigi wrote after presentation of the Protestants' demands at Osnabrück on July 29th,[4] "grows daily, but I am helpless; soon no Catholic will be able to feel sure that his nephews, if not his sons, will not become Protestants, so bad has the situation become.[5]

To Chigi's moral sufferings there were added physical ones for he suffered from the climate of Westphalia. He speaks of it in his letters as early as 1646,[6] but since he says

---

[1] "*Non so già, se quando lo vogliono, lo potranno fare, se gli Suedesi prevaglino con le armi." Letter to the Secretary of State, May 26, 1646, *Paci* 20, *loc. cit.*

[2] BAUR, *Sötern*, II., 167.

[3] ISRAEL, *Adami*, 43 *seq.*

[4] Chigi's *report to the Secretary of State, June 29, 1646, *Paci*, 20, *loc. cit.*

[5] *Cod. A. I., 22, Chigi Lib. *Cf. ibid.*, A. II., 29, *letter to the nuncio in Venice, June 22, 1646.

[6] *Letter to Fr. Albizzi, July 13 and 27, 1646, *ibid. Cf.* above, p. 94.

nothing about German cooking, the story that he dispatched to Rome a huge loaf bearing this inscription : *Ecce panis Westphalorum*, is probably an invention.

Whilst the real peace negotiations were in a state of stagnation during the summer of 1646, because everyone was waiting for the issue of the operations in the field,[1] the imperialists went a step further in the path of concessions upon which they had entered, when they decided to consider as the norm for the practice of religion in the Cities of Empire and the ownership of ecclesiastical property the year 1624, that is, a year in which the restoration of confiscated Church property had not yet been enforced. They were prepared to leave Church property in the hands of the Protestants for a hundred years, before the lapse of which a friendly settlement would have to be made. Chigi gave all the support he could to the counteraction of the intransigents,[2] nevertheless in a declaration of November 19th the year 1624 was conceded to the Protestant delegates who had come over to Münster.[3] Chigi was beside himself. Notwithstanding all the assurances with which Trauttmansdorff sought to calm the nuncio, the former had so encouraged the Swedes in the course of his private negotiations, that they cherished the hope of retaining the Church's property not for a hundred years only but for all time ; as a matter of fact this too was granted by the Count on November 30th. He started from the point of view that peace alone could save the Catholic Church in Germany, hence peace must be secured at any cost,[4] and he was prepared for more and more concessions. In view of this fact Chigi and the more determined among the Catholics sought to save the little which it seemed

---

[1] Chigi's *reports in code to the Secretary of State, June 15 and July 27, 1646, *Paci*, 20, *loc. cit.*

[2] Chigi's *report in code to the Secretary of State, November 23, 1646, *ibid.* *Cf.* Chigi's *Diarium* for September 17, 1646, Chigi Lib.

[3] ISRAEL, *Adami*, 45 *seq.*

[4] Chigi's *report in code to the Secretary of State, November 30, 1646, *Paci*, 20, *loc. cit.*

possible to save.[1] Chigi never ceased to warn the Emperor's
representatives.[2] He often wondered that he did not break
down under the weight of his labours and anxieties, he wrote
on December 7th.[3] His one comfort was that Rome was
perfectly satisfied with his conduct. Just as the Secretary of
State had approved his timely protest,[4] so he repeatedly
expressed his unreserved satisfaction with his line of action.[5]
It was realized in Rome that the nuncio strictly maintained
the point of view of the Holy See, which was to preserve
established rights and conditions and where these could not
be saved, at least not to sanction their loss. Particular
instructions were deemed all the more unnecessary as Chigi
possessed so much sound judgment and such wide experience
that details could very well be left to his discretion.[6]

Rome fully shared Chigi's opinion as to the Emperor's
deplorable weakness. With him the Secretary of State condemned a state of mind which caused men to drop that for
which they had so long fought arms in hand,[7] and that
a political theology sought to find a theoretical justification
for this ruinous policy of concession.[8] Chigi was under no
delusion as to the magnitude of the peril which was bound to
arise out of a peace bought at any price.[9] With deepest grief

[1] Chigi's *reports in code to the Secretary of State, December 7
and 14, 1646, *ibid*.

[2] Chigi's **Diarium*, December 3, 1646, Chigi Lib.

[3] *Letter to Albizzi in *Cod*. A. I., 22, *ibid*. On the same
day Chigi wrote to Pallavicino : " *Agli Suedesi offeriscono gli
imperiali grandi stati, e quel che peggio è a costo della religione
cattolica. Io grido alle stelle e le chiamo a vendetta contro
questi pregiuditii." *Cod*. A. II., 29, *loc. cit.*

[4] *Pamfili to Chigi, January 6, 1646, *Cod*. A. II., 47, *loc. cit.*

[5] *Cf.* especially Pamfili's instructions of January 13 and 20,
May 5, June 30, and December 22, 1646, *ibid*.

[6] Pamfili emphasizes the Pope's confidence in Chigi especially
in the *instructions of December 15, 22 and 29, 1646, *loc. cit.*

[7] *Pamfili to Chigi, August 11, 18, 25, 1646, *ibid*.

[8] Pamfili to Chigi, July 7, 1646, in BROM, III., 404.

[9] *Cf.* Chigi's **Diarium*, December 21, 1646, *loc. cit.*

he watched the continuous decline of the Catholic Church
which was about to lose for good to the Protestants three
archbishoprics and thirteen bishoprics, that is, sixteen large
territories with thousands of churches, monasteries and pious
foundations.[1]   The decision was drawing near, Chigi wrote
to Pallavicino on December 14th, perhaps it would come
suddenly ; as long as it had been possible he had issued his
warnings and he would continue to do so, regardless of
persons ; since the cause of God had been abandoned by all,
he could only grieve and protest.[2] Chigi's indignation against
Trauttmansdorff rose so high that in a moment of exasperation
he remarked that the Count would give up St. Peter's in
Rome to the Protestants should they ask for it.   In the
course of his representations the nuncio did not fail to
observe that the policy of the imperialists was a mistake
even from a political point of view, inasmuch as the endless
concessions merely served to sharpen the Protestants'
appetite.[3]

Chigi's ceaseless warnings were exceedingly awkward for
Trauttmansdorff ; accordingly he attempted to silence the
tiresome mentor by informing him that his elevation to the
cardinalate had been proposed in Rome both with a view
to doing honour to the Congress and to rewarding the nuncio's
labours in the cause of a general peace. Chigi bluntly replied
that he would not hear of such an honour, for the cause of
God was being so greatly injured by the proposed peace that
he would consider it a sacrilege to receive any recognition of
whatever kind.   To a French delegate Chigi observed that
what he deserved was not reward but punishment since
he had achieved nothing on behalf of the Catholic cause
which was being neglected by one party and injured by the
other.   In Rome the nuncio pleaded for his recall ; after
vainly working day and night to bring about a tolerable peace
he did not wish, by prolonging his stay, to create an impression

---

[1] See letter of December 11, 1646, in BROM, III., 407.
[2] *Cod. A. II., 28, loc. cit.
[3] Letter of December 19, 1646, in BROM, III., 407-8.

that he approved a settlement which inflicted the most grievous wounds on the Church. Innocent X. refused to listen to his pleading. He bade him hold on forasmuch as his departure would hearten the Protestants whilst his presence would at least lessen the evils that threatened.[1]

A glaring light was thrown on the contrast between the intransigent and accommodating parties in the Catholic body by a pamphlet published at the end of 1646, under the signature of one *Ernestus de Eusebiis*. This pamphlet submits to a close and searching analysis the question how far one might in conscience yield to the demands of the Protestants. For a time the identity of the author remained a secret ; eventually it became known that he was none other than the Jesuit Henry Wangnereck of Lindau. The pamphlet was sent to press without the author's knowledge, probably by the Bishop of Osnabrück, Franz Wilhelm von Wartenberg, as a counterweight to the concessions in the question of the peace by the Munich and Vienna divines, and in order to rouse the conscience of the Catholic princes by means of an uncompromising statement of the principles which had been considered authoritative during the era before the religious divisions.[2]

The publication of the treatise came as a complete surprise for Chigi. For reasons of opportuneness he disapproved of its publication, though not of the contents, although as representative of the Church he rejected more than one concession accepted by de Eusebiis. With a view to preserving the Holy See from the slightest stain, Chigi had striven from the first to prevent even such concessions as the strict Catholic party was prepared to make. He was anxious thereby to strengthen their attitude as much as possible, for he knew only too well how ready human weakness is, in circumstances

---

[1] PALLAVICINO, I., 143–4, who here quotes, in part textually, a *letter of Chigi of December 15, 1646, which I found in *Cod.* A. II., 28, of the Chigi Lib.

[2] STEINBERGER, 63 *seq.* ; RITTER in *Hist. Zeitschr.*, CI., 265 *seq.* ; SOMMERVOGEL, VIII., 982 *seq.*

of such difficulty, to be content with what seems at least tolerable.[1]

Chigi's view was also that of Rome. The Secretary of State, Cardinal Panciroli, expressed the hope that the pamphlet would strengthen the resistance of such Catholics as were too ready to yield to Protestant demands. When he had been informed of the contents of the publication, Innocent X. expressed his approval by sending his blessing to the author.[2]

How well founded Chigi's misgivings were as to the opportuneness of the publication was soon made evident when the Swedes began to use it in order to rouse Protestant feeling. In effect, not content with defending the Catholics' claim to the ecclesiastical possessions of which they had been robbed through an infraction of the religious peace of Augsburg, a claim which could not be legally contested, Ernestus de Eusebiis also condemned that peace itself, and from this he argued that it was morally wrong to agree to a fresh confirmation, not to speak of an extension, of the treaty. The way in which de Eusebiis sought to explain away the awkward fact that even Peter Canisius had declared it lawful to tolerate the religious peace of Augsburg, drew down on him the just blame of a highly placed member of his Order.[3]

---

[1] See Chigi's letter of January 25, 1647, to Panciroli in STEINBERGER, 196 *seq.*

[2] STEINBERGER, 75.

[3] *Ibid.*, 76 *seq.* Wangnereck's irreconcilable attitude as an uncompromising protagonist of canon law, is severely condemned by the historian of the German Jesuits. This shows, he says, " the confusion and disaster which the upholding of medieval opinions in an entirely altered situation was bound to cause. Where there existed but the one Catholic religion, such principles might have been defended ; but once the force of circumstances had secured for non-Catholic confessions vast and permanent possessions, opinions of this kind could no longer be maintained, unless there was a willingness to declare a war of all against all and so to put weapons into the hands of other confessions against Catholics. If, in Wangnereck's opinion, it was unlawful for

Naturally enough Count Trauttmansdorff was exceedingly annoyed by de Eusebiis' pamphlet. When the Protestants suggested that the Inquisition should proceed against the unknown author, he expressed the opinion that the book was only scholastic nonsense, that it was, in fact, an extravagance—*Bachantenwerk*. His colleague and successor Isaac Volmar described all such writings as " lauter sofistische *cavillationes* und närrische Träume "—nothing but sophistries and foolish dreams. But the imperial court, where the influential Capuchin Quiroga condemned the pamphlet in the most severe terms, ordered the learned Abbot of the Cistercian monastery of Prague, Johann Caramuel y Lobkowitz, to write a reply, the publication of which Chigi vainly strove to prevent.[1] De Eusebiis' pamphlet had had an enormous circulation and it had swept many fresh adherents into the camp of the intransigents from the ranks of those Catholics who, until then, had been of a more accommodating disposition,[2] but neither this nor any other literary production produced any substantial change in the decision of Münster.

At the beginning of 1647 Chigi did all he could to encourage

Catholics to conclude a lasting peace with Protestants, the latter were bound to conclude that any peace might be broken by the Catholics as soon as they were strong enough to oppress the Protestants with some prospect of success." This opinion of DUHR (II., 1, 482) refers to Wangnereck's " Responsum Theologicum ", written against the Jesuit Vervaux and printed at the beginning of 1648 by the Bishop of Osnabrück, though not in a public press but in a private one, so that it only circulated among Catholics. On the strife between the Jesuits of moderate opinion and the extremists, in which the moderates were in the majority, *cf*. STEINBERGER, 76 *seqq*. In the end the General of the Society imposed a penance on Wangnereck but the Curia's pressure forced him to revoke it (*ibid*., 136).

[1] STEINBERGER, 78 *seq*., 80 *seq*. Steinberger had no access to the Chigi Library ; *Cod*. A. III., 69, contains *Caramuel's letters to Chigi from 1647 to 1649, which cannot be further considered here.

[2] STEINBERGER, 73.

the more intransigent Catholics to resist the imperialists'
policy of concessions so as to save at least some of the
threatened bishoprics. The cession of Bremen and Verden
was to be condemned for its own sake, he said, but even more
so because of the deplorable precedent it established. In his
direct appeals to Trauttmansdorff the nuncio observed that
such trafficking with bishoprics was an infamy, quite as much
as if for fear of the Swedes the Emperor were to deny the
Catholic faith.[1] When Trauttmansdorff and the French
promised to save at least the bishoprics of Osnabrück and
Minden, the nuncio, who was accurately informed by Wartenberg, knew only too well the value of such comfort.[2]

The Catholic position became worse when, at the negotiations
which opened at Osnabrück on February 7th, 1647, not only
the Catholics yielded to the imperialists but the Protestant
delegates acted in the same way towards the Swedes, whereupon the latter took charge of the discussions whilst remaining
all the time in close touch with a committee of Protestants.

Chigi had persuaded the strictly Catholic deputies to go to
Osnabrück in order to restrain the imperialists from making
concessions.[3] He remained in close touch with them through
Wartenberg,[4] but he soon learnt that they were able to do
so little that in their disappointment they had withdrawn
once more. In effect, on March 9th the Swedes renewed their
demand for the unconditional surrender of all Church property which had been in Protestant hands in 1624 ; on this
they insisted with the utmost obstinacy.[5] Trauttmansdorff,
for his part, maintained that the success of the Franco-
Swedish arms forced him against his will to give way, whilst
he pointed out that by their treaties of neutrality Cologne
and Bavaria had deserted the Emperor.[6]   The Elector

---

[1] See Chigi's *report in code, January 18, 1647, *Paci*, 21,
Papal Sec. Arch.

[2] See Chigi's *report in code, February 8, 1647, *ibid.*

[3] *Cf.* Chigi's *report in code, January 18, 1647, *ibid.*

[4] *Cf.* Chigi's *report in code, March 8, 1647, *ibid.*

[5] RITTER, *loc. cit.*, 263 ; *cf.* ISRAEL, *Adami*, 57 *seq.*

[6] Chigi's *report in code, March 8, 1647, *Paci*, 21, *loc. cit.*

Maximilian of Bavaria had imagined that with the conclusion
of an armistice with the Swedes, on March 14th, at Ulm, he
was furthering the cause of peace, but in reality that treaty
rendered it more remote, for now the demands of the Swedes
and the Protestants grew beyond all bounds.[1]   They now
hoped to wrest from the Emperor freedom to practise their
religion for the heretics of the Imperial Hereditary States,
viz. the so-called autonomy, by which, according to a remark
of the Swedish delegate Salvius, the roots of Austria's power
would be gradually eaten into.[2]   This danger of a political
order did not escape Trauttmansdorff ; he declared that he
would refuse to sign a contract of the kind even if he were a
prisoner at Stockholm ; the Emperor could not possibly
forgo in his Hereditary States the right embodied in the
axiom : *Cujus regio ejus religio,* to which even the most
insignificant lords laid claim.[3] When the Swedes stuck to their
demands, Trauttmannsdorff left Osnabrück for Münster on
April 24th.   However, negotiations were not broken off.   In
May an agreement was reached concerning the religious
situation of the subjects within the Empire.   In the first
days of June the representatives of Sweden and the
Protestants repaired to Münster for further negotiations.
The draft of the peace treaty which the imperialists drew
up in the chancellery of Mayence on June 3rd, represented
their definitive concessions to the Protestants : the year
1624 was to be considered as the norm for the ownership of
Church property.   The eight monasteries in Württemberg
and the diocese of Minden which, like Osnabrück, still had a
Catholic Bishop, were now sacrificed though in November
they had been excepted from the cession made by the
Catholics. Other concessions followed. As late as November
the right had been insisted upon for the Catholic authorities
to expel their Protestant subjects.   This right was now

---

[1] STEINBERGER, 98 *seq.*

[2] ODHNER, *Die Politik Schweden's im westfäl. Friedenskongress,*
Gotha, 1877, 203 note.

[3] MENZEL, VIII., 186 *seq.* ; HUBER, V., 605.

subjected to a threefold limitation : 1° Those subjects
who had had the exercise of their religion at any period of the
year 1624, were to retain it ; 2° those who up to the year of
the peace had been subjects of Catholic princes, without the
right of practising their religion, were to enjoy freedom of
conscience but without the practice of religion ; 3° those
who only adopted the Protestant confession after the year of
the peace, or who came into the country as Protestants,
might be banished, but only after a time limit of ten years
which in cases of exceptional difficulty, could be prolonged
for a further period of five years. These three limitations were
not to apply to the Imperial Hereditary States and the whole
agreement was to be in force not only until the restoration of
religious unity at some future date, but " for ever ".[1]

This draft was submitted for examination to the Catholic
Estates on June 12th. The more intransigent among the
Catholics, headed by Wartenberg and Adami and warmly
supported by Chigi, naturally refused to assent to the
arbitrary procedure of the imperialists, though they feared
already then that, as at Prague, the head of the Empire
would force them to yield. Trauttmansdorff declared that
his master was the Emperor of the Protestants as well as of
the Catholics, hence he was bound to consider his non-
Catholic subjects.[2]

Chigi's efforts to strengthen the Catholics in their resistance
received support from the Spanish ambassador, and even
from the French. The latter sought to delay the conclusion
of peace until such time as the Emperor should have dropped
the Duke of Lorraine and promised, not only as Emperor but
as Sovereign of Austria also, to give no further assistance
to the Spaniards.[3]

If all Catholics were united, Chigi wrote on June 14th, they

---

[1] RITTER, loc. cit., 275–6.

[2] Chigi's *report in code, June 14, 1647, Paci, 21, loc. cit.
Cf. Adami's *report to Chigi, June 29, 1647, in Cod. A. III., 69,
Chigi Lib.

[3] HUBER, V., 605.

would influence the deliberations to a considerable degree ; they could force the Portestants to drop some of the demands which Trauttmannsdorff had already conceded.[1] Presently the Count himself was to realize whither his weakness was leading him, when the Swedes came forward with fresh and impossible demands as, for instance, that their Queen should be given the first place on the secular princes' bench and that they should have an Elector of their own. They likewise meant to insist on their demand for private Protestant services in the Emperor's Hereditary States. Thereupon Trauttmansdorff threatened his departure, a step for which he had long ago obtained Ferdinand III.'s permission.[2] From Trauttmansdorff's son Chigi learnt that the Count had remarked that he would not be able to show himself at court unless he had concluded peace [3] ; accordingly he sought to bring pressure to bear on the intransigent Catholics not only by means of promises but likewise by threats, a proceeding to which Wartenberg offered strong opposition.[4]

On July 16th the Count carried out his long standing threat to take his departure. The Protestants would have liked all the envoys of the Electors, princes and cities to press him to remain, but this the strict Catholics would not do [5] ; the latter in fact now began to hope if not for complete success, then at least for a considerable lowering of the Protestant demands, a thing which in their and Chigi's opinion, had to be secured, if necessary, by force of arms. A favourable turn for the Catholics did not seem impossible now that Cologne and Bavaria stood once more by the Emperor's side and the Swedes had been forced to evacuate Bohemia. In August Chigi exerted himself more than ever in order to fan the opposition to the Protestant demands, on the basis of the arguments expounded by Ernestus

---

[1] *Paci*, 21, p. 274, Papal Sec. Arch.

[2] HUBER, V., 605-6.

[3] Chigi's *report in code, June 14, 1647, *loc. cit.*

[4] Chigi's *report in code, June 28, 1647, *ibid.*

[5] Chigi's *report in code, July 19, 1647, *ibid.*

de Eusebiis ; these efforts were eagerly seconded by Wartenberg and Adami.[1] A memorial, in the drawing up of which
Adami had the principal share and which the Catholics
presented on October 7th, rejected a notable part of the concessions made to the Protestants up to that time.[2] " More
could not be secured," Chigi wrote to Rome, " because the
Catholics are not united and are no less threatened by their
co-religionists than by their enemies."[3] He had previously
reported, in August, that the delegates of the Bavarian
Elector and the Bishops of Salzburg, Bamberg, Würzburg
and Fulda, had been instructed to yield to the imperialists
as much as possible.[4] The Catholics experienced a sensible
loss through the death, on October 9th, of the Elector of
Mayence, Anselm Casimir von Wambold, whose representative, notwithstanding all the efforts of Bavaria, had
hitherto sided with the stricter party.[5]

However, a decision could only be brought about by the
attitude adopted by the Emperor and Bavaria.   On
October 15th Ferdinand III. directed his envoys Lamberg
and Crane to explain to the Catholics that he intended to
abide by the concessions already made ; should they refuse
to yield he, as head of the Empire and in virtue of his supreme
imperial power, would take such steps for the tranquillity of
the Empire as he would be able to answer for to God and the
world ; he had done all that was possible, but in view of the
superiority of the enemy it was necessary to give way. The
Elector Maximilian was of the same opinion ; though one of
the chief promoters of the edict of restitution he now threw
away all the advantages it had hitherto yielded. He counselled
the Emperor to come to terms with France, Sweden and the
Protestants, assuring him that the more important among the
Catholic Estates would side with him.[6] In a subsequent

---

[1] Chigi's *reports in code, August 9, 16, 23, 1647, *ibid.*
[2] ISRAEL, *Adami*, 65.
[3] Chigi's *report in code, October 25, 1647, *Paci*, 21, *loc. cit.*
[4] Chigi's *report in code, August 9, 1647, *ibid.*
[5] MEIERN, IV., 816 *seq.* ; ISRAEL, *Adami*, 66 *seq.*
[6] MEIERN, IV., 777.

letter to Ferdinand III., dated October 21st, Maximilian's exhortations to peace were mingled with undisguised threats.[1] When the imperial plenipotentiaries at Münster, the Count of Nassau and Isaac Volmar, in obedience to their sovereign's command, urgently pleaded with the Catholic delegates to yield, they pointed to the fact that the Catholic fighting forces were hopelessly inadequate, notwithstanding a few isolated successes, and that if they continued the struggle they would have to expect far worse conditions; since everybody was weary of the war, let them also change their minds, else the Emperor would have to act in the fulness of his personal power.[2]

Though taken by surprise by this declaration the stricter Catholic party did not lose heart and maintained its opposition. The representative of Cologne declared: " We are subject to the Emperor in worldly matters but not in ecclesiastical questions." [3] This firm attitude infuriated not only the Protestants and the Swedes, but even the imperialists. Volmar so far forgot himself as to exclaim that " for the sake of a few stinking Abbots " one could not delay the peace any longer ! [4] On November 14th he left Osnabrück for further negotiations. By Chigi's advice the Catholics followed him for the purpose of restraining the imperialists from making too sweeping concessions.[5] However, this turned out to be impossible. Bavaria, utterly exhausted, pressed for peace at any price quite as much as the Emperor, for both Powers saw the hopelessness of any attempt to reduce the demands of their opponents to more reasonable proportions by force of arms. For all that the intransigent Catholics, who hoped for a favourable turn from a fresh military enterprise,

---

[1] Sattler, *Gesch. Württembergs*, VIII., *Beil.* 62.   Riezler (V., 647) observes : " Maximilian, for the sake of peace, sacrificed to France and the German Protestants both his national sentiments and his religious convictions."

[2] Israel, *Adami*, 67 *seq.*

[3] Chigi's *report in code, November 1, 1647, *loc. cit.*

[4] Israel, *Adami*, 69.

[5] Chigi's *report in code, November 15, 1647, *Paci*, 21, *loc. cit.*

continued their opposition. To compel them to yield, recourse
was had, without scruple, to any means, even the worst.
When threats failed Volmar did not shrink from a clumsy
lie. To some Catholic delegates he declared that the papal
nuncio was not against concessions being made to the
Protestants ! [1]

At that time the staunch Catholic deputies Adami,
Leuxselring, together with Wartenstein ironically styled the
triumviri,[2] saw themselves threatened even in their personal
safety : the Swedish envoy Salvius declared that these
zealots might be silenced with a musket-shot.[3] In order,
as it were, to add weight to these threats, the servants of
Adami and Leuxselring were subjected to severe ill-treatment ;
after that the intransigents, feeling no longer safe, returned
to Münster.[4] It was an evil omen for them that at that time,
through the influence of Bavaria, the Bishop of Würzburg,
Johann Philipp von Schönborn, was raised to the archiepiscopal see of Mayence, for Schönborn was exceedingly
compliant in matters of religion.[5] Already in 1643 his representative, Vorburg, had said at Frankfort that the ecclesiastical reservation must be allowed to lapse in regard to its
retrospective effects, whereas at that time Maximilian was
ready to go on with the war for another hundred years rather
than make such a concession.[6] Now, however, the ruler of
Bavaria told Chigi and the Pope that it was better to save
what could be saved than to run after what was lost at one's

---

[1] Chigi's *report in code, November 29, 1647, *ibid.*

[2] PUFENDORF, *De rebus gestis Frederici Wilhelmi electoris
Brandenburgensis. Berolini*, 1695, 170 ; *Mitteil. des Hist. Vereins zu
Osnabrück*, XII., 328 ; ODHNER, *Schwedens Friedenspolitik*, 122.

[3] Chigi's *report in code, November 15, 1647, *loc. cit.*

[4] ISRAEL, *Adami*, 70, 73.

[5] Chigi's *report in code, December 6, 1647, *Paci*, 21, *ibid.* ;
CONTARINI in *Fontes rer. Austr. Dipl.*, XXVI., 328. *Cf.* MENTZ,
Schönborn, I., 34 *seq.*, 41 ; also PALLAVICINO, II., 187.

[6] MENTZ, *loc. cit.*, 34. In 1646 Schönborn was also in favour
of abandoning to the Protestants what had been conceded to
them by the religious peace and the peace of Prague ; see *ibid.*

present risk.[1] At the beginning of May the Emperor and
Bavaria had the support of the Eectors of Mayence and
Trèves as well as that of the delegates of Salzburg, Bamberg,
Würzburg, Liège, Freising, Münster, Ratisbon, Hildesheim,
Eichstätt, Worms, Bâle, Spires, Paderborn and Fulda ; some
others, such as the delegates of the Teutonic Knights and those
of Strassburg and Passau, were still undecided.   The only
ones who remained intransigent were, in addition to Warten-
berg and Adami, the envoys of Neuburg, Augsburg, Trent,
Brixen and the representatives of a few of the lesser Catholic
Estates of Empire.[2]

After the Emperor's command, by letter of February 15th,
1648, to yield all along the line, Chigi too felt that, humanly
speaking, there was no longer any hope.[3]   In November,
1647, he had written to a friend that he was resigned and ready
to bear with patience the cross God laid on him, however
heavy it might be. However keenly he longed for his Tuscan
home, he would prefer to it, if it were God's will, the swamps
of Westphalia as if they were so many jewels.[4] Without
considering the protests of the strictly minded Catholics who
had returned to Münster, the imperialists negotiated with the
Swedish envoys at Osnabrück from February 28th onwards,
whilst plenipotentiaries of the Protestants and of those
Catholics who favoured a compromise waited in an adjoining
room.[5] In view of the fact that the Swedes displayed great
arrogance and threatened to have recourse to arms,[6] a compromise on the ecclesiastical questions was arrived at already
on March 24th : this deed was entered, almost unaltered, in
the peace treaty. In it a few concessions were made to the
Catholics.[7] It was an important clause that in the Emperor's

---

[1] December, 1647 ; cf. RIETZLER, V., 648.

[2] Chigi's *report in code, January 11, 1648, Paci, 22, loc. cit.

[3] Chigi's *report in code, February 28, 1648, ibid.

[4] Letter of November 22, 1647, in CAMPORI, CIII. Lettere
inedite di Sommi Pontefici, Modena, 1878, 47 seq.

[5] ISRAEL Adami, 79 seq.

[6] Chigi, *Diarium on February 14, 1648, Chigi Lib.

[7] RITTER, III., 635 seq. ; cf. Hist. polit. Blätter, LI., 570 seq.

Hereditary States the normal year was not to be in force, whilst for Silesia the Peace of Prague was to remain substantially operative.[1] On the other hand a serious retreat of the Catholics before the demands of the Protestants was implied in the settlement in respect of parity in the composition of the Diet of deputies, of the tribunal of the Imperial Chamber and the Imperial Court Council, in disputes concerning questions of religion.[2] The Catholics could view with some indifference the inclusion of the Reformed in the religious peace which was carried through notwithstanding the opposition of the intransigent Lutheran element.[3] But an enormous loss for the adherents of the old faith was implied in the fact that with regard to possession of ecclesiastical property, the year 1624 was fixed upon, with supreme arbitrariness,[4] as the normal year, instead of the Peace of Passau of 1552. Thus all the bishoprics, abbeys and canonries which the Protestants had seized up to that date, were irrevocably lost. Of what use was it that the ecclesiastical reservation was recognized as operative for the future? it no longer had any practical meaning.

In Rome, Chigi's conduct met with complete approval.[5] Bitter regret was felt at the fact that Bavaria pursued its own private interests in preference to those of religion and that Ferdinand and Maximilian were prepared to accept a peace which did such grievous injury to religion when together they might have driven the Swedes from Germany.[6]

In November, 1647, Chigi had asked for copies of the documents attesting the Holy See's protest against the

---

[1] MENZEL, VIII., 190 *seq.* ; HUBER, V., 607 *seq.*

[2] RITTER, III., 637.

[3] H. RICHTER, *Die Verhandlungen über die Aufnahme der Reformierten in den Religionsfrieden auf dem Friedenskongress zu Osnabrück*, 1645–1648, Berlin, 1906.

[4] Cf. *Hist.-polit. Blätter*, LI., 567.

[5] Cf. the *instructions of the Secretary of State of 1647 and 1648 in *Cod.* A. II., 47, Chigi Lib.

[6] Cf. the *instructions of November 2 and December 14, 1647, and March 28, 1648, *loc. cit.*

Interim and the religious peace of Augsburg. He evidently wished to make use of them for the protest which he had prepared long ago; however, the documents were not to be found in Rome.[1]

After the compromise on the religious questions in the spring of 1648, the Swedes haggled throughout the summer with the imperialists about the payment of their troops and the extension of the amnesty to the Emperor's Hereditary States. The discussions were so violent that time and again there was reason to fear that the entire work for peace would be wrecked at the last moment. At last, on August 6th, an agreement was reached, and thus the treaty of peace with Sweden could be confirmed at Osnabrück, with a handshake, by the representatives of the Emperor, the Estates of Empire and those of Sweden.[2] However, Oxenstjerna and Salvius refused to sign until peace should have been made with France also. In this respect the chief difficulty lay in Ferdinand III.'s unwillingness to leave Spain in the lurch. But on this point also both the Elector of Mayence, Johann Philipp von Schönborn,[3] and Maximilian of Bavaria pressed him to yield; they even threatened to come to terms with the Swedes on their own account should he make difficulties.[4]

Thereupon, on September 22nd, the Emperor commanded his envoys to sign the treaty immediately. But at this juncture the representatives of France and Sweden raised fresh difficulties. Only after these had been cleared out of the way, did it become possible to proceed, on October 24th, 1648, to the solemn act with which the peace negotiations were to be closed, namely the signing and exchanging of the documents. Chigi had seen to it that neither his own name

[1] *Instruction of December 14, 1647, *ibid.*

[2] See Chigi's *letter to Abbate Altoviti, August 7, 1648, in *Cod.* A. II., 28, Chigi Lib.

[3] Mentz, *Schönborn*, I., 39.

[4] This was communicated by Chigi in his *report in code of January 10, 1648, *loc. cit.* On the pressure exercised by Maximilian, *cf.* Odhner, 281.

nor that of the Pope appeared in the instrument of a peace by which, as he lamented, a deep wound was inflicted on the Catholic religion every time it was mentioned.[1]

It was not only the compliance of the Emperor, Bavaria and the Elector of Mayence which caused the religious and political clauses of the treaty to turn out to so great a disadvantage for the ancient Church. Of no less consequence was the fact that the hopes which many fervent Catholics in Germany had placed on Catholic France turned out to have been in vain.[2] In this connection a remark of the French ambassador, Longueville, speaks volumes. When there was question of giving the rich abbey of Hirschfeld to the Landgravine Amalia of Hesse-Kassel, a lady who was the object of the ambassador's particular goodwill, Wartenberg represented to him that it did not redound to the honour of the Most Christian King to rob Christ and His Mother of their garments in order to deck out with them a heretical woman. Longueville replied that it was impossible to do too much for so virtuous a lady.[3] The French diplomatists only thought of their political interests and in this respect they secured nearly all they wanted—the Rhine frontier, the utter weakening of the imperial federation and the reduction to impotence of the imperial power. The fate of their German co-religionists left them cold. The Swedes were more far-sighted : whilst pursuing their political ends no less keenly than the French, they at the same time lent the strongest support to their Protestant co-religionists.

[1] *Chigi to Marcello Virgilio Malvezza, December 4, 1648, in *Cod.* A. II., 29, Chigi Lib. *Cf. ibid.*, the *letter to nuncio Bentivoglio at Florence, November 13, 1648. In *Cod.* A. II., 28, p. 350 *seq.* *Elegia Chisii super pacem Westphal, sent to Altoviti on September 18, 1648. To Albizzi Chigi wrote on November 29, 1649 : " Del resto gli fautori dell'infausta pace . . . si avvedran, crede, di aver donato più con essa agli Svezzesi x volte tanto di quel che non potevano havere con la guerra." (*Accad. dei Lincei. Mem., class. di scienze mor.* 3, Series I [1877], 395).

[2] ISRAEL, *Adami*, 60.

[3] See *Adami*, ed. Meiern, Lipsiae, 1737, c. 27.

The Peace of Westphalia, " the worst humiliation Germany
had ever experienced until then,"[1] meant the definitive
wreck of the Catholic restoration the triumph of which had
seemed so near at hand only a score of years earlier. It set
the seal on the system, first introduced by the Protestant
party, of the princes' dominion over religion and conscience.[2] The fresh confirmation of the so-called religious
peace of Augsburg meant the solemn recognition of the
fundamental principle of the new system of territorial
Churches : " Who owns the territory orders the religion,"
a principle with no other check except the basic year 1624.
Apart from the fact of possession guaranteed by this time
limit, every Estate of Empire, even the smallest, secured
the right to determine the faith of its subjects so that every
Catholic could be compelled by his Protestant lord, every
Protestant by his Catholic lord, either to change his religion
or to emigrate. This " right to reform ", which in 1555 had
been guaranteed only to the Catholic Estates of Empire and
to those of the Confession of Augsburg, was now extended to
the followers of Calvin. That which the peace treaty secured
for the victors, the Swedes and the French, in the political
sphere, viz. an extreme weakening of the Empire through
territorial losses and its disintegration into several hundred
small States, was completed by the religious divisions. The
German people, once so strong in the oneness of its faith,
was now definitely split up into Catholics, Lutherans and
Calvinists : the price of the juridical existence of the new
religion was the impotence of the Empire.[3]

An enormous injury to the Church and her rights was
implied in the fact that the peace treaty included the ratification of the treaty of Passau and the religious peace of Augsburg
and that January 1st, 1624, was fixed as the norm for the
practice of religion and the ownership of ecclesiastical goods.

[1] Kaser, *Das Zeitalter der Reformation und Gegenreformation*,
Gotha, 1922, 204.

[2] Döllinger, *Kirche und Kirchen*, 58 seq.

[3] Opinion of Stegemann, *Der Kampf um den Rhein.*, Berlin,
1925, 236.

In consequence of the latter disposition only the following free cities remained Catholic in their entirety : Cologne, Aix-la-Chapelle and a few small towns of Empire in Swabia. As against this the Protestants became sole masters at Hamburg, Lübeck, Goslar, Mühlhausen, Nordhausen, Worms, Spires, Wetzlar, Swäbisch-Hall, Heilbronn, Reutlingen, Wimpfen, Schweinfurt, Nuremberg together with its considerable territory, Ulm and Lindau. Frankfort on the Main remained almost wholly Protestant but the Collegiate Church of St. Bartholomew, in which the election and coronation of the Emperors was wont to take place, as well as a few other churches, were left to the Catholics. The same thing happened at Ratisbon where Protestants were in the majority. In the religiously mixed Cities of Empire, Augsburg, Dinkelsbühl, Ravensburg, Biberach and Kaufbeuren, the posts of councillors and other offices were to be equally divided between the Catholics and the Protestants.[1]

Even more sensible were the losses of the Catholic Church with regard to ecclesiastical property with which, as Chigi lamented, the congress trafficked in a manner that cried to heaven,[2] so much so that a contemporary could write : " To pass the time, these gentlemen play with bishoprics and monasteries as boys play with nuts and marbles." [3] Only the four archdioceses of Mayence, Trèves, Cologne and Salzburg were saved from the wreck, together with the dioceses of Bamberg, Würzburg, Worms, Eichstätt, Spires, Strassburg, Constance, Augsburg, Freissing, Ratisbon, Passau, Trent, Brixen, Bâle, Liège, Chur, Hildesheim, Paderborn,

---

[1] Whilst at Augsburg Maximilian insisted on the execution of the clauses of the peace treaty concerning religious parity and withheld his protection from recalcitrant Catholics, he resisted with the utmost energy the Swedish demands for the free exercise of their religion by the Protestant subjects of the Upper Palatinate which had only been re-Catholicized since January 1, 1624. RIEZLER, V., 652 seq ; DOEBERL, I. (1906), 567 seq.

[2] *Chigi to Abbate Altoviti, August 28, 1648, Cod. A. II., 28, Chigi Lib.   [3] Adami, ed. MEIERN, c. 26.

Münster and Osnabrück, though for the latter place the truly
monstrous arrangement was made that the see should always
be held alternately by a Catholic and a Protestant Bishop ! [1]
Of the abbeys the following remained in Catholic hands :
Fulda, Stablo, Korvei, Prüm, Kempten, Ellwangen, Berchtes-
gaden, Weissenburg, and the two principalities of the Teutonic
Order and the Order of St. John.   On the other hand the
Catholics lost besides the vast bulk of the " mediate " ecclesiastical possessions which had been appropriated by the
princes and the towns, the " immediate " archbishoprics
of Magdeburg and Bremen and the bishoprics of Lübeck,
Halberstadt, Verden, Meissen, Naumburg, Merseburg, Lebus,
Brandenburg, Havelberg, Minden, Kammin, Schwerin, the
Abbeys of Hirschfeld, Walkenried, Gandersheim, Quedlin-
burg, Herford and Gernrode.

In presence of these gigantic losses, which were now legally
sanctioned by the treaty of peace, the Pope and his representative would have failed in their duty had they remained
silent.   The fact that Chigi had stayed away from the decisive
negotiations [2] achieved as little as did the protests of about a
score of Catholic Estates.[3]   Consequently, foreseeing what was

---

[1] " Scelerata alternativa," Chigi calls these dispositions in
his *report in code of October 16, 1648 (Papal Sec. Arch.).   *Cf.*
F. FRECKMANN, *Die capitulatio perpetua und ihre verfassungs-
geschichtliche Bedeutung für das Hochstift Osnabrück* (1648–1650),
Osnabrück, 1906.

[2] See Chigi's *report in code, October 25, 1648, *loc. cit.*

[3] ISRAEL, *Adami*, 81 ; WIDMANN, *Salzburg*, 297 *seq.*   Chigi
would have liked the Catholics to refrain from signing ; this he
says himself in his *report in code of October 16, 1648.   On
October 30 he wrote to Rome : " Quanto a questa soscrittione,
io nel male godo che tanti buoni cattolici habbiano protestato,
i quali saranno forse due dozzine.   Ho obligatione a Monsignore
vescovo d'Osnaburgh, che ha tenuto saldo, e a quei di Trento
e di Brissenone, che son dependuti da me espressamente.   Ancora
l'arciduca Leopoldo per quello di Argentina e di Alberstat, ha
rimesso il suo agente al consiglio di Mgr. vescovo d'Osnaburgh,
et con questo ha fatto le sue proteste, le quali tutte si può sperare
in Dio che gioveranno in qualche tempo . . ."   Chigi Lib., *loc. cit.*

to come, Chigi had drawn up from the beginning a general
protest against every injury that might be done to the Church
and to her rights [1] ; its definitive form had been left to his
discretion by Rome.[2]   Even before the conclusion of the
negotiations, on October 14th, 1648, Chigi made a solemn
protest which he repeated on October 26th.[3] In it the nuncio
called to witness the delegates of the Catholic Powers, and
Contarini in particular, that lest by his presence he should have
seemed to give some kind of approval to the negotiations,
he had mostly absented himself from them and had refused
to sign them.

The first protest, that of October 14th, was approved by
the Pope as soon as he received the text of it, in fact the
Pontiff exhorted Chigi to repeat it publicly on some future
occasion seeing that, as a result of the deplorable compliance
of the Catholics, the agreements were doing grievous injury

---

[1] See above, p. 119.

[2] PALLAVICINO I., 137.   *Cf.* BROM III., 451, 456.

[3] Both protests are printed in CONRING, *De pace perpetua,*
Helmstadii, 1657, 116 *seqq.* ; *De pace civili, ibid.,* 1677, 371 *seqq.*
The protest of October 26, 1648, in Italian, in PALLAVICINO,
I., 138 *seq.,* in Latin, in BROM, III., 448 *seq.,* and previously in
POLLIDORUS, *Vita F. Chisii,* in *N. Raccolta d'opusc. scientifici,*
IV., Venezia, 1758, 315 *seq.* On October 16, 1648 (*decif. Nov.* 6)
Chigi reports to Rome : " *Publicandosi assai chiaramente
i pregiuditii fatti alla religion cattolica dagli Stati cattolici in
Osnaburgh, sotto la guida del Magontino e del Bavaro, ho stimato
bene far nuova protesta con solenne istromento nella forma, che
rappresenterà la copia autentica che mando, riserbandomi a farne
altra, se quà ancora siano i medesimi ratificati o soscritti, come
par che siano pronti a fare." On 30 Oct. he writes : " *Mando
i fogli, co quali mando anco la nuova protestazione che ho stimato
bene reiterare per altro pubblico instrumento ch'è l'unico rimedio,
che dopo ogni opera adoperata, perchè non seguano i pregiuditii
alla s. religione, potiamo adoperare con gli huomini che per
preservare la ragione e per consolare in parte il zelo sanctissimo
di S. B^{ne}, già che per altro non potrà godere intiero di questa
pace . . ." *Paci* 24, Papal Sec. Arch.

to the Catholic religion.[1] For these reasons, the Secretary of
State wrote on November 14th and 21st that the Pope could
derive no pleasure from the settlement, though he appreciated
Chigi's conduct most highly.[2] There is as yet no mention in
these Briefs of a protest by the Pope. Rome precipitated
nothing. It was only in January, 1649, that a congregation
of Cardinals, presided over by the Pope, decided that Chigi's
protests should be confirmed by a solemn Bull though the
nuncio was instructed to keep this document secret for the
time being.[3] Chigi made a third protest on February 19th,
1649, on the occasion of the ratification of the treaty of
peace.[4] All three protests were approved in Rome by all the
Cardinals,[5] and this approval was renewed in March.[6]

[1] " *É alla S^{tà} Sua sommamente deplorabile il danno che alla
religione cattolica reca la facilità de' cattolici nelle continue
cessioni che sempre con augmento si stabiliscono a favore degli
heretici per il capitolato della pace fra le corone collegate e
l'imperio, e V. S. ha corrisposto al desiderio del suo ministerio
nell'astenersi dalla mediatione e nel fare solenne protesta a
pregiuditii della nostra s. fede. Egli dove proseguire," etc.
Panzirolo a Chigi, dated November 7, 1648, Cod. A. II., 47,
Chigi Lib.

[2] The *letter of November 14, 1648, in Cod. A. II., 47 (loc. cit.) ;
that of November 21, in BROM, III., 449 seq. The peace was at
once universally condemned in Rome, see Servantius, *Diaria,
Papal Sec. Arch., and Deone, *Diario, 1649, Cod. XX. III., 21,
Bibl. Casanat. The reproach passivity here made against Chigi
was quite unjustified.

[3] " *Nella congregazione fu col parere di 9 cardinali deliberato
da S. S^{tà} di confermar con una bolla apostolica in amplissima
forma li protesti di V. S., questo però finchè non si mandi ad
effetto, dovere ella tenerlo in se." Panzirolo a Chigi, January 9,
1649, Cod. A. II., 47, Chigi Lib.

[4] Text in GARAMPI, 94.

[5] " *Nella congregatione di stato tenutasi avanti N. S. furono
lette le proteste fatte e reiterate costì e commendate da tutti
signori cardinali, come prima erano da N. S. state approvate."
Panzirolo to Chigi, January 9, 1649, loc. cit.

[6] Panzirolo a Chigi, *cifre of March 6 and 13, 1649, Cod. A. II.,
47, loc. cit.

In view of the fact that most of the delegates, even Contarini himself, had left Münster, Chigi also begged to be allowed to return to Italy. Permission was given him on September 11th, 1649, but it was at once cancelled,[1] inasmuch as the French desired the presence of a papal representative in view of the peace negotiations between France and Spain, a happy issue of which Innocent X. also had very much at heart. Consequently Chigi decided to go to Aix-la-Chapelle, but a serious illness prevented him from doing so at the beginning of November, as he had intended, so he only got there a month later.[2] In consequence of the peace being so unfavourable to the Church, he left very quietly on December 13th, 1649.[3] The famous baths and the mild climate of the imperial city agreed with him so well that he decided to stay. [4] But though his great diplomatic skill won him the continued confidence of both hostile Powers, all

---

[1] PALLAVICINO, I., 145 seq., where there is also Chigi's letter to the Emperor, dated May 7, 1649, refusing the present intended for him, since it was a principle with him to decline even the smallest gift; cf. BROM, III.,454 seq. Cf. also Chigi's *letter to M. V. Malvezzi, dated Aachen, December 24, 1649, loc. cit. Cf. a letter of the same date to Albizzi in Atti dei Lincei, Scienze mor. Mem., I., 396.

[2] MACCHIA. Relazioni del P. Sforza Pallavicino con Fabio Chigi, Torino 1907.

[3] See his letter of December 24, 1649, in MACCHIA, loc. cit., and in CIAMPI, Epistolario, 395. Cf. REUMONT, Fabio Chigi (Papst Alexander VII.) in Deutschland, Aachen, 1885, 15 seq.

[4] Cf. besides the letters published by CAMPORI (CIII. Lettere, 52 seq.), Chigi's *reports to Panciroli, 1650–1651, in Paci, 26–8, Papal Sec. Arch. These reports substantially supplement Reumont's data in the work quoted in the preceding note, who for Chigi's relations with Mazarin and the Dane Corfits Ulfeldt also uses the letters in Ciampi. Chigi's recall to Rome only occurred on September 9, 1651 (BROM, III., 475). Chigi *reports on his journey in a *letter to Albizzi, dated Frankfort, October 14, 1651. Cod. A. I., 22, loc. cit. On memories of Alexander VII. at Aachen cf. J. LAURENT, Aachener Stadtrechnungen aus dem. 14 Jahrb., Aachen, 1866, 45.

his efforts to reconcile them failed.[1]   The papal intervention
was completely put in jeopardy when Mazarin requested the
Dutch to mediate.[2]   Although the situation looked hopeless,
the Pope, to leave nothing undone, issued on November 26th,
1650, a fresh exhortation to peace to the Kings of France and
Spain, to Olivares, Mazarin and other influential personalities.[3]   Chigi's happy solution of the difficulties in connexion
with the election of a co-adjutor for Trèves was a fine success
for him,[4] but his pleasure was completely spoilt for him by
his having to witness the execution of the fatal peace of
Westphalia.   His letters of the period are full of bitter laments
over the " tragedy of Germany ", an ever recurrent theme
in them being his grief that it was chiefly Bavaria which, by
its readiness to yield, induced the Protestants to demand ten
times more than they had dared at first.[5]

Meanwhile the Bull protesting against the peace treaty was
still being withheld, for its publication would have raised grave
dangers so long as the Swedish troops remained in Germany.
The imperial ambassador Savelli, in defence of the Emperor,

---

[1] PALLAVICINO, I., 148.   Cf. MACCHIA, 65.   On March, 1650,
Chigi *wrote to L. Allacci : " Dissi, nisi videro et tetigero. Così
è stato, perchè dopo tre mesi non se ne parla più e le parti non
pensano che alla campagna."   Arch. of Greek College, Rome.

[2] BROM, III., 465.

[3] *Epist., VII.–VIII., Papal Sec. Arch.   On December 30,
1653, Innocent X. renewed his exhortations to peace in *Briefs
addressed to the Kings of France and Spain (ibid.).

[4] PALLAVICINO, I., 150 seq. ;   BAUR, Sötern, II., 286 seq.,
335 seq. ;   REUMONT, loc. cit., 28 seq.

[5] Cf. Chigi's *letters to Albizzi, dated Aachen, January 14,
March 12, and September 17, 1650, Chigi Lib.   On June 24,
1651, Chigi *writes to Albizzi from Aachen (ibid., Cod. A. I., 22) :
" Quella infame pace di Munster che tanto cede agli heretici,
dopo haver essi eseguito eccessivamente tutto ciò che era a lor
pro, e dopo haver impedito l'esecuzione di quel poco che era a
favor dei cattolici restato, ecco che hanno rotta sfacciatamente
assalendo Brandeburg gli stati di Giuliers all'improvviso.
O tempora, o mores ! "   On July 29, 1651 he writes to *Albizzi :

pleaded his difficult position [1] whilst at the same time he
drew a forceful picture of the strength of the enemy and the
weakness of the Catholics who, he told Innocent X., would
presently appeal to Rome for assistance. In order to get the
Bull suspended he had recourse to the support of Cardinal
Capponi whom the Pope held in high esteem at that time.
The Cardinal drew attention to the advantages which would
accrue to religion in the Imperial Hereditary States out of the
peace ; these would outweigh the loss of the North German
dioceses which could only be held by means of an endless war.
Savelli believed that in this way the Pope would become
reconciled to the peace treaty for the unfavourable clauses
of which Bavaria was held chiefly responsible, as a result of

"Ho fatto una solenne risata in leggere, che si trovasse prelati,
che facessero condoglienza, con la S^{tà} di Papa Urbano VIII.
per la morte del Re di Suetia parendomi una scempiaggine
dello stile di quelli che diceva : mi Papezzo, mi Papezzo,
e non volendo sospettare di altro senso maligno che havesse
il complimentatore sotto la maschera di quella semplicità.
Certo è che io trovai in Germania 12 anni sono religiosi gravi
che havevano prestato fede a relationi di Hollanda, che ivi si
fosse un reggimento con le chiavi e con le api : tanto sono stolidi
anco i men mal sensati. Ma quanto al lodare l'imperatore ed
il Duca di Baviera, e che hanno fatto bene a far questa pace e
che non potevano far altrimenti, e che Caramuel parla da S. Tommaso, si sparge che siano prelati e cardinali, e molti, e così si
scrive poi in Germania, contro le quali voci io sgrido e contradico
più di prima, come ho pur accennato a Palazzo più volte. Sia
benedetto il cardinal di Cueva che si serviva di vomitorio il
leggere le due paci di Münster." On October 25, he writes :
" *In Francoforte mi scusai di dar audientia a quei deputati
principali autori della pace di Munster." On Maximilian's determined attitude towards the execution of the peace in the Upper
Palatinate and at Augsburg, see RIEZLER, V., 651 *seq.*

[1] " *Di che S. B. se ben non contenta non ha ricusato affatto
di appagarsene, sapendo quanto sia il zelo di V. M. Ces. e di
tutto l'august. suo sangue verso la religione et rispetto verso
la S. Sede." Savelli to Ferdinand III., dated Rome, March 6,
1649, State Arch., Vienna.

its forcing the Emperor to yield.[1]   Grave accusations were
also made at the Curia against the Elector of Mayence.[2]

After the evacuation of Germany by the Swedes had begun,
as a result of the decree for the execution of the peace treaty
published at Nuremberg on June 26th, 1650, the Pope gave
orders, on August 20th, for his protest against the peace
treaty to be sent to all the nuncios so that they might publish
the judgment of the Holy See.[3] However, this was not done in
the form of a solemn Bull, as had at first been intended, but
by a simple Brief.[4] Chigi's proposal of the publication of a
fourth protest was declined by Rome.[5] The Brief, retrodated
to November 26th, 1648,[6] did not condemn the peace as such,
nor all its articles, but only those which injured the Church.
The agreements and decisions arrived at at Osnabrück and
Münster, the document states, have given great pain to the
Pope because they gravely curtail and injure the Catholic
religion and its exercise, the Apostolic See, the Roman Church
and its subordinate Churches, the ecclesiastical state, the

---

[1] This according to a hitherto unknown *report of L. Pappus to
Ferdinand III., of September 20, 1652, in State Arch., Vienna.

[2] Deone *Diario, 1649, Cod. XX. III., 21, of Bibl. Casanat.

[3] Panciroli to Chigi, August 20, 1650, in BROM, III., 463.

[4] The frequently made statement, the most recent instance
being MIRBST (Quellen, 202), that Innocent X. had protested
with a Bull, is erroneous ; the document is a Brief dated Romae . . .
sub annulo piscatoris.

[5] " *Io proposi 3 settimane fa di fare una quarta protesta
contro la esecuzione della pace, come havevo fatte le tre ante-
cedenti contro la sottoscrittione di Osnabruk, contro altra di
Munster e contro la ratificazione dei principi stessi, e ne chiedeva
la formula a palazzo ; ben è vero che voleva attendere che fossero
gli Suedesi usciti di Germania per liberarne che doppo essa non
facessero renuntiare gli stati cattolici anco a questa, come ultimamente si fecero renuntiare a Norimberga alle altro tre." Confidential letter of Chigi to Albizzi, assessore del S. Officio,
September 17, 1650, Cod. A. I., 22, Chigi Lib.

[6] MEIEREN, Acta pacis execut. publ., II., Göttingen, 1737,
781 seq. ; Bull., XV., 603 seqq. (with several misprints which
alter the meaning), and elsewhere ; see MENZEL, VIII., 242.

jurisdiction, liberties, privileges, possessions, goods and rights of the Catholic Church. They surrender for all time to the heretics and their successors the property of the Church seized by them. In a number of localities the adherents of the Confession of Augsburg obtain the free exercise of their heretical religion and the right to erect churches ; they share with the Catholics a great many dioceses and other ecclesiastical dignities and benefices as well as the right of first requests (*jus primarum precum*) which the Apostolic See had granted the Emperor Ferdinand. As against this We are precluded from our rights in regard to the *Annates*, pallium fees, the papal months and reservations in the ecclesiastical property of the followers of the Confession of Augsburg ; confirmation of elections or postulations to the confiscated archbishoprics and bishoprics and prelatures is attributed to the secular authorities of the aforesaid Confession ; many archbishoprics, bishoprics, abbeys, bailiwicks, commendas, canonries, and other ecclesiastical benefices and properties are granted in perpetuity as secular fiefs to heretical princes and their heirs, the ecclesiastical right of nomination being revoked." The extension of the College of Electors and the bestowal of a new electoral title, the eighth, to a Protestant prince, is disapproved and a protest lodged against it by reason of its having been done without the consent of the Holy See. Finally the Brief declares null and void the clause by the terms of which no law, be it ecclesiastical or civil, general or particular, no conciliar decree, monastic Rule, oath, concordat with the Pope or any secular or ecclesiastical decree, dispensation, absolution or exception of any kind could be adduced, heard or received against the peace and any of its articles.[1]

Other princes also raised their protests, as for instance Duke Charles of Mantua, Duke Charles of Lorraine, the King of Spain, the Archbishop of Salzburg and others. All these protests, like that of the Pope, had not for their object the

[1] Research in the archives was made on this point in Rome ; *Arch. Rom.*, III., 27 *seq.*, 30 *seqq.*

peace itself but merely some of its clauses. Since these inflicted so enormous an injury on the Church, its Head could not have remained silent without failing in his duty, hence the blame to which Innocent X. was subjected by reason of his protest [1] was quite unjustified [2] and even non-Catholics have slowly come to see that in his position the Pope could not have acted otherwise.[3] The papal protest yielded no practical result. The Emperor Ferdinand forbade its publication,[4] the Archbishop of Trèves being the first, but also the last German Bishop to publish it.[5] A number of theologians also were of opinion that in practice the papal condemnation of the peace amounted to no more than a censure or a disapproval.[6]

[1] List of polemical writings in CONRING, *loc. cit.*; SCHRÖCKH, *Kirchengesch.*, III., Leipzig, 1805, 402 *seq.* The *Examen Bullae* of John Hoornbeeck (Ultraiecti, 1653) comprises 300 pages.

[2] PHILLIPS, *Kirchenrecht*, III., 450 *seq.*, 476; DÖLLINGER, *Kirche u. Kirchen*, 49 *seq.*; HERGENRÖTHER, *Kirche und Staat*, 703–711; MALET, *Hist. dipl. de l'Europe au 17e et 18e siècles*, I., Paris, 161. *Cf.* also GRAUERT, *Königin Christine*, I., 251 *seq.* The protest was likewise justified on the ground that since the peace there existed the possibility of a Protestant Emperor; see GÜNTER, in *Hist. Jahrbuch*, XXVII., 380.

[3] K. A. MENZEL writes (VIII., 244) that " the Pope was only anxious to fulfil the duty of his office and to do, as Head of the Church, what no head of any other body could have omitted in similar circumstances without rendering himself liable to the reproach of neglect of duty." HILTEBRANDT (*Quellen und For-schungen*, XI., 321) says that " from the standpoint of view of the Curia Innocent X.'s protest was a natural step." See also ERDMANNSDÖRFFER, *Deutsche Gesch.*, I, Stuttgart, 1892, 6 *seq.*, and PFLUGK-HARTTUNG, *Weltgeschichte, Neuzeit*, II., 101 *seq.*

[4] MEIERN, VI., 794. When the Vienna nuncio handed the protest to the Emperor, it seemed to the Venetian ambassador " che non malvolentieri la ricevè " (*Fontes rer. Austr. Dipl.*, XXVI., 395).

[5] BAUR, Sötern, I., 291.

[6] DÖLLINGER, *Kirche und Kirchen*, 62; HERGENRÖTHER, *Kirchengesch.*, III[5]., 744.

Notwithstanding the enormous gains which the Peace of Westphalia guaranteed to the Protestants, the latter remained unsatisfied. They regretted, on the one hand, the maintenance of the ecclesiastical reservation which put a stop to further secularizations, and on the other the decision in regard to the Protestants in the imperial Hereditary States. When the Emperor began to carry the latter into effect by means of the edict on religion of January 4th, 1652,[1] strong complaints and protests were raised by the Protestant party and these came up for discussion at the Diet of Ratisbon, the first to be held after the conclusion of peace.

The Pope's representative at that assembly was the new nuncio in Vienna Scipione d'Elce, Archbishop of Pisa, a splendid man,[2] whose task it was to prevent further injury to the Catholic cause.[3] In April, 1653, a warning letter in the same sense was dispatched to the Emperor.[4] Before the Diet opened the discussion of questions of religion, the nuncio, toward the end of August, issued yet another solemn protest dated May 17th, 1653, against those clauses of the Peace of Westphalia which were to the disadvantage of Catholics.[5]

---

[1] WIEDEMANN, V., 25 seq.; MENZEL, VIII., 277 seq.; GRÜNHAGEN, II., 318 seq.; STIEVE, Abhandlungen, 293 seq.; LEHMANN, Preussen, I., 55 seq.

[2] Cf. Fontes rer. Austr. Dipl., XXVI., 406. Since some time already Ferdinand III. had kept no ambassador in Rome; relations between the two courts were not lively; see ibid., 395.

[3] Cf. ELCE's *report, dated Ratisbon, April 28, 1653, Barb. 6112, p. 41 seq., Vat. Lib. Copies of all Elce's *reports from 1652–1657 also in Cod. 33 D., 19–20 of Corsini Library, Rome (cf. LÄMMER, Zur Kirchengesch., 170 seq.) and Barb. 6109–6112, loc. cit. In the latter codex, p. 132 seqq.: *Osservazioni hist. delle cose più notabili occorse in Germania et alla corte dell'imperatore durante la nunziatura di Msgr. arcivescovo di Pisa. See also FRIEDENSBURG, Regesten, VI., 103, 105, 107, 110 seq. Elce's *Diarium nuntiat. apud imperatorem, 1652–1658, in Vat. 10423, p. 105–318, Vat. Lib.; *Letters of Elce during his nunciature in Vat. 10440, ibid.

[4] See ELCE's *report of April 7, 1653, Corsini Lib.

[5] On September 1, 1653, Elce *reports from Ratisbon to

Besides the situation within the Empire, religious conditions in Bohemia and Hungary also claimed the nuncio's anxious attention just then. In Bohemia, where merchants from Hamburg sought to spread Protestantism, the Capuchin Valerian Magni [1] and the Jesuits showed great zeal, in the spirit of the Catholic restoration. The Jesuits counselled gentleness in the attempts at conversion ; so did Cardinal Harrach, but the latter's adviser, Caramuel y Lobkowitz, and the lieutenants were for stern measures. Though the Emperor Ferdinand gave his approval to the lieutenants' proposals, he nevertheless substantially altered some of their provisions.[2]

Like the Peace of Westphalia, the religious compromise

Cardinal Pamfili : ' Ancorchè non si sia ancora stabilito in Dieta il punto della deputazione per le cose ecclesiastiche, nondimeno potendo essere che segua ad ogn'hora e si dia principio al trattato di questa materia, stimai bene due giorni sono di fare la mia protesta alla presenza di due notari et di quattro testimonii nella forma che mando qui acclusa a V. Emza e perchè mi è stato confermato da molti che nelle capitolazione giurate dal Re de' Romani in Augusta e non pubblicate però sin'hora in Dieta, vi sia stata tra l'altre cose aggiunta l'osservanza dell'instrumento della pace di Munster e di tenerla per leggi fondamentali dell'imperio, mi è parso d'inserirvi quelle parole che l'Emza Vra vedrà lineate, senza venire a maggior specificatione dell'atto così consigliato da questi bene affetti alla Santa Sede, per non esservi esempio che nelle capitolationi passate li ministri apostolici habbino mai interposte simili proteste, non ostante vi fussero inscritti punti pregiuditiali alla religione. Ma, se giudicherà bene Vostra Eminenza che se ne debba fare maggior dichiaratione, starò attendendo i suoi comandamenti, già che conservo appresso di me la protesta, senza haverla per anche publicata. *Barb.* 6112, p. 66[b]-7, Vat. Lib. Cf. Lundorp, VII., 717 ; F. Garampi, 94.

[1] Lämmer, *Zur Kirchengeschichte*, 170.

[2] Scmidl, V., 661 *seqq.*, 668 *seqq.*, 672 ; Rezek in *Mitteil. des Vereins für die Gesch. der Deutschen in Böhmen*, XXXI., Lit. 16 ; Radda, *Zur Gesch. des Protestantismus in Teschen*, Teschen, 1885 ; Redlich, VI., 219 *seqq.* ; Kröss in *Zeitschr. für Kath. Theologie*, XL., 772 *seq.*

realized in Hungary by means of the Peace of Linz and the Recess of Empire (Reichsabschied) of 1647, satisfied neither Catholics nor Protestants. It guaranteed to the Protestants and Calvinists a legal status and considerably extended the concessions already granted to them but failed to meet all their wishes inasmuch as the Catholic Church preserved her dominant position, whilst the most dreaded of their enemies, the Jesuits, whom it had been hoped to uproot, also retained their possessions and all their strong positions. The clergy, trained as they had been by the Jesuits, co-operated with them whilst the Primate, George Lippay, was resolved to work in the spirit of Pázmány. In 1649 Lippay founded a general Seminary for the Hungarian clergy at Tyrnau, its direction being entrusted to the Jesuits.[1] The Jesuits displayed great activity not only at Tyrnau, the heart of Catholic Hungary, but likewise at Pressburg, Ödenburg, Raab, Warasdin, Agram, Trentschin, Neusohl, Kaschau and Ungvár. Despite every obstacle they were indefatigable in strengthening the faithful, supporting the waverers and bringing back the apostates. They even succeeded in getting a foothold in the Turkish territory of Fünfkirchen, and their missionary activity also extended itself to Moldavia.[2] Innocent X. had shown his concern for the Catholics of that province already in 1645 [3] ; he also supported the Franciscans in Wallachia.[4] Amid the appalling misery and decay of the ravaged German Empire, the Jesuits, with undismayed courage, were busy rebuilding what had been destroyed and, notwithstanding every difficulty, they continued their pastoral, educational and scientific

---

[1] KRONES in *Archiv. für österr. Gesch.*, LXXIX (1893), 281 *seqq.*, 307 *seqq.* On Lippay see FRIEDENSBURG, *Regesten*, V., 68, 100, 102.

[2] KRONES, *loc. cit.*, 311 *seqq.*, 321 *seqq.*, 324 *seq.*, 339 *seq.*, 345 *seq.* Cf. *id., Zur Gesch. des Jesuitenordens in Ungarn seit dem Linzer Frieden*, Vienna, 1893.

[3] *Brief to " princeps Moldaviae ", May 20, 1645, *Epist.*, I., Papal Sec. Arch.

[4] *Brief to " princeps Walachiae ", May 20, 1646, *Epist.*, I. *loc. cit.*

work. The most recent research has shown how, true to their old ideals, wherever they laboured, they worked most beneficially for the well-being of a generation that had sunk to a very low level.[1]

Innocent X. gave particular support to the Jesuit seminaries at Braunsberg, Vienna, Prague, Olmütz, and Dillingen,[2] for he knew how much depended on the formation of a well-trained clergy. With a view to a general regeneration of the German clergy he addressed, on April 4th, 1652, a circular letter to the German Bishops, exhorting them, by means of synods and visitations, to see to it that the reform decrees of Trent were carried into effect.[3] During the latter stages of the Thirty Years' War the ecclesiastical authorities had sought to stem the moral decay of the population by means of popular missions [4]; now that peace had been restored, missionaries, especially Jesuits, with the encouragement of the Bishops, zealously devoted themselves to the unobtrusive and exacting task of giving such missions.[5] Ecclesiastical restoration began on all sides. In the dioceses of Münster, Paderborn and the part of the diocese of Cologne situate on the right bank of the Rhine, the Franciscans established new convents and wherever this was at all possible, they likewise founded mission stations in the Protestant districts.[6]

[1] See the documented presentment in Duhr, *Geschichte*, III., 660 *seqq.*

[2] *Chirografo d' Innocenzo X. con l'ordine fermo per le provisioni de' seminarii, June 12, 1646, Arch. of Propaganda 362, p. 17.

[3] *Deutsche Geschichtsblätter* by Tille, XVI, (1915), 10 *seqq.* The reform was also furthered by the efforts of the Swiss nuncios to secure for the stricter Order of the Jesuits in the Canton of Lucerne some of the rights enjoyed by the Cistercians, which led to dissensions that brought to light Innocent X.'s opposition to France; *cf.* V. Liebenau in *Jahrbücher für Schweizer Gesch.*, XI. (1886), 167 *seqq.*, 184.

[4] Duhr, *Gesch.*, II., 2, 38 *seqq.*

[5] Duhr in *Hist. Iahrb.*, XXXVII. (1916), 601; *id. Gesch.*, III., 660 *seqq.*

[6] *Hist.-polit. Blätter*, LXXXVII., 312; Woker, *Gesch. der norddeutschen Franziskanermissionen*, Freiburg, 1880.

One of the most remarkable phenomena of the period following the Peace of Westphalia is the return to the ancient Church of many distinguished and influential men in Germany. In the course of a few years the following were converted : the Silesian Christoph, Count of Rantzau, the Westphalian Johann von der Recke, George Christian, Landgrave of Hesse, John Frederick, Duke of Brunswick-Lüneburg, Duke Ulrich of Württemberg and his daughter Mary Anne, Ernest, Landgrave of Hesse-Rheinfels, a great-nephew of bigamous Philip of Hesse, the Governor of Silesia, Count von Wetzhausen, George Frederick Philip von Griesheim, Gustaf Adolf, Count zu Nassau-Saarbrücken, the Chancellor of Mayence, Johann Christian von Boyneburg, the archæologist and historian Heinrich Julius Blume, the Countesses Palatine Elizabeth Amalia and Anna Sophia, the celebrated poet and controversialist Angelus Silesius, author of the lofty didactic poems of the " Cherubinische Wandersmann ", Count Johann Ludwig of Nassau-Hadamar, the Lutheran preacher Heinrich Schacht and many others.[1]

Thus the converts were for the most part highly cultivated men and members of the upper clases,[2] of whom many lived

---

[1] *Cf.* Räss, VI., 366 *seq.*, 401 *seq.*, 449 *seq.*, 456 *seq.*, 465 *seq.*, 501 *seq.*, 513 *seqq.*, 526 *seqq.*, 536 *seqq.*, 558 *seqq.*, 572 *seqq.* ; VII., 1 *seqq.*, 528 *seqq.*, 551 *seq.* Also Erdmannsdörfer, I., 480 *seqq.* ; *Allgem. Deutsche Biogr.*, III., 222 *seq.*, X., 187, XIII., 157 *seq.*, XIV., 177 *seq.* ; Heinemann, *Braunschweig*, III., 130 *seq.* ; *Hist.-polit. Blätter*, XCVII., 790 *seq.* ; Köcher, *Gesch. von Hannover*, I., 351 *seq.*, II., 32 *seq.* ; W. Kratz, *Landgraf Ernst von Hessen-Rheinfels und die deutschen Jesuiten*, Freiburg, 1914 ; on A. Silesius see the monographs by Lindemann (1876), Seltmann (1896), Kralik (1902), and G. Ellinger (1927). *Cf.* Richstätter in *Stimmen der Zeit.*, CXI. (1926), 377 *seqq.*, and in *Zeitschr. für Aszese und Mystik*, III. (1928), 79–85. A Brief of September 13, 1651, to George Christian of Homburg, Landgrave of Hesse, congratulating him on his conversion, in Friedensburg, *Regesten*, V., 91 ; *ibid.*, 114 on the Princess of Darmstadt.

[2] Harnack (*Dogmengesch.*, III., 691) gives as one reason of

in circumstances that rendered conversion not easier but more difficult ; thus Alexander Heinrich, son of Duke Alexander of Sonderburg, who came over with his wife, forfeited his inheritance and became so destitute that he had to appeal to the Pope for help.[1] In the case of Boyneburg, a man distinguished both as a statesman and a scholar, it was the idea of the necessity of the unity of the Church that led to his conversion [2] ; he was also influenced by certain efforts to bring about reunion such as those pursued at that time by George Calixt. That scholar and professor at the University of Helmstedt, who in the course of four years' travelling for purposes of study, had become personally acquainted with Catholic countries and who had made a thorough study of Christian antiquity, no longer stood on the platform of orthodox Lutheranism. In 1645 he openly advocated his views at the peace conference convened at Thorn by Ladislaus, King of Poland ; they were to the effect that all those who held fast to the Scriptures and the Apostles' Creed, or more accurately to the faith of the first five centuries, must be considered as brethren in the faith and cannot be excluded from salvation.[3] In the case of more than one German convert Prince of that period, especially in that of John Frederick, Prince of Brunswick, and the Landgrave Ernest of Hesse-Rheinfels, the change of religious conviction was furthered by travel in Catholic countries, especially in Italy, where they saw Catholic personalities and Catholic institutions in a

these conversions the fact that at that period Catholicism kept better pace than Protestantism with the progress of cultivated circles.

[1] FRIEDENSBURG, *Regesten*, V., 80.

[2] MENTZ, II., 279, who insists that Boyneburg was moved by real conviction and not by any personal consideration.

[3] *Cf.* E. L. TH. HENKE, *Georg Calixt und seine Zeit.*, Halle, 1853–1860 ; *Freib. Kirchenlex.*, II[2]., 1711 *seqq.* On the *colloquium* of Thorn, *cf.* the specialized works of IKIER (Halle, 1889) and IACOBI (Gotha, 1895). Reasoned decision of Propaganda on disputations with Protestants in *Collect. Propag.*, I., 30 *seq.*

light that differed greatly from what they had been taught in their youth.[1]

When Prince John Frederick of Brunswick, whom the Pope recommended to the Emperor in a special Brief,[2] informed his brothers in a letter from Rome, dated December 29th, 1652, of his reception into the Catholic Church which had taken place secretly in February, 1651, he gave as his reason his realization of the unity of the Catholic Church, a Church that was in agreement with the ancient teaching of the Fathers and the Scriptures in her moral teaching, her customs and her Sacraments, under one visible supreme Head, whereas in the opposite camp, disunion prevailed and each day witnessed fresh divisions which were bound to lead to the utter destruction and ruin of their beloved German fatherland. John Frederick was refused permission to practise the Catholic religion in private so that he had to resign himself to live abroad.[3] In like manner Landgrave Ernest of Hesse-Rheinfels, intellectually the most distinguished prince of his time, was shaken in his convictions by his repeated stays in Catholic countries, though he had been brought up along strict Calvinist lines and his tutor had taken the utmost care that he came under no Catholic influence. He laid his scruples before three divines, viz. Calixt of Helmstedt, Crocius of Marburg, and Haberkorn of Giessen, and summoned them to enter into a disputation with the Capuchin Valerian Magni on some of the controverted questions. Haberkorn alone consented to do so but broke off the discussions because of Valerian's attacks on Luther. Thereupon, in his joy at having found in the old Church sure teaching as against the divided opinions of Protestantism, Ernest, together with his wife, made profession

---

[1] MENZEL, VIII., 298.

[2] FRIEDENSBURG, *Regesten*, V., 95 ; *cf.* 103, on the bestowal of canonries. This shows the erroneousness of KÖCHER's assertion (*Allgem. Deutsche Biographe*, XIV., 178) concerning Innocent X.'s utter indifference towards these converts.

[3] J. K. SCHLEGEL, *Kirchengesch. von Norddeutschland*, III., Suppl. 14 ; KÖCHER, II., 372 *seq.*

of the Catholic faith on Trinity Sunday, 1652.[1] He wrote to
the Pope to inform him that he had openly professed the faith
from which his fathers had strayed and that he had returned
to the Lord to whom they had become disloyal. Innocent X.
congratulated him in a Brief, exhorting him at the same time to
persevere in his resolve.[2] The conversion of the Landgrave,
who admitted the Jesuits into the county of Katzenelnbogen,
nearly cost him his territory ; though he escaped this extremity
he forfeited his rights as a sovereign.[3] The nuncio in Vienna,
Scipione d'Elce, energetically intervened on behalf of Ernest.[4]

These conversions could have no substantial bearing on the
religious situation in the Empire, were it only that since the
Peace of Westphalia the year 1624, which had been agreed
upon as the norm, had force of law. Landgrave Ernest told the
celebrated Lukas Holste in February, 1654, that his efforts to
bring the Lutheran and Calvinist preachers to a better frame
of mind had proved fruitless ; alone Georg Calixt had deigned
to send a reply. The Landgrave nevertheless resolved to get
his confessor to publish a book entitled *Invitation to the Catholic
Faith*. He was however, of opinion that the Holy See should
concede Communion under both kinds as well as the marriage
of priests after the manner of the Greeks. In his letter he
likewise expressed the hope that the King of Denmark and
the Queen of Sweden, " both potentates of extraordinarily
high gifts," would come to see the futility (*ineptias*) of the
Protestant teaching.[5] In the case of Queen Christina of Sweden
that hope was fulfilled but Innocent X. lay on his death-bed
when news of that event reached Rome.

---

[1] STRIEDER, *Hessische Gelehrten-Geschichte*, III., Göttingen,
1783, 413 *seq.* ; MENZEL, VIII., 301 *seq.* ; ROMMEL, *Leibnitz und
Landgraf Ernst von Hessen*, 2 vols., Frankfort, 1847 ; RÄSS,
VI., 465 *seq.*, and especially KRATZ, *loc. cit.*

[2] Brief of February 17, 1652, in FRIEDENSBURG, *Regesten*,
V., 98.

[3] MENTZ, II., 205.

[4] See the *Osservazioni*, 188, Vat. Lib., quoted above, p. 133, n. 3.

[5] Original of *letter, dated Rheinfels, February 16, 1654, in
Barb. 3631, n. 64, Vat. Lib.

On January 30th, 1648, a peace treaty between Spain and the United States of the Netherlands was signed at Münster, but that settlement was so disadvantageous for the Catholic Church in Holland that on this occasion also the nuncio lodged a protest in the name of the Pope.[1] The Spaniards had almost completely kept the negotiations from the knowledge of the representative of the Holy See,[2] because they could obtain no advantage for religion. As a matter of fact Spain ended by renouncing its full sovereignty over the almost wholly Catholic parts of Brabant, Flanders and Limburg, which it ceded to the States General, and for its own territory it consented to silent toleration of Protestantism. This situation was ruthlessly exploited by the States General. Scarcely had the Treaty of Münster been signed when the Bishop of Ghent saw his diocese swept by a flood of preachers, whereas at the very same time Holland refused to admit Spanish priests, even though they were duly provided with passports.[3] Already in May, 1648, an order of the States General had been issued throughout the newly acquired provinces for the removal from the churches of images, statues and other ornaments. At Bois-le-Duc all Church property was confiscated and the expulsion of priests and religious was a daily occurrence. All the remonstrances of the Spanish Government on the subject proved as unavailing [4] as the protest against the illegal oppression of the Catholics in the county of Lingen. Nevertheless nuncio Chigi continued to work in favour of the Dutch Catholics by diplomatic means [5] but the results amounted to next to nothing.

In July, 1648, a synod of Dutch preachers expatiated on the dangers threatening from Rome and demanded fresh measures against the Catholics, but the States General declared that the

---

[1] This protest, which was strictly kept secret for the sake of the Dutch Catholics who were already hard pressed enough, has only become known through BROM (III., 437 seq.), ibid., 489.

[2] BROM, III., 425 seq.

[3] HUBERT, 113, 158.

[4] HUBERT, 115 ; cf. BROM, 439 seqq.

[5] BROM, III., 446 seq., 451 seq.

ordinances of August 30th, 1641, were adequate, in fact they agreed to a few " mitigations " of the decisions taken at that date : thus collections for Catholic purposes were no longer to be punishable by death and arrested Jesuits were not to be whipped out of the country ; they were merely banished.[1] In 1651 the preachers raised fresh cries of alarm on the plea that there was reason to fear that, as in Ireland, the Catholics were planning a massacre of the Protestants ; accordingly they demanded the withdrawal of the few privileges still enjoyed by the former as well as new penal laws and compulsory attendance at Protestant services.   However, the States General rejected these measures as impossible of execution.

Though the preachers never ceased to clamour for the destruction of the Catholics, the Government refused to stir ; there can be no doubt that this was due to consideration for the interests of trade.[2] The condition of the Catholics in the Dutch Republic nevertheless remained an anxious one and it became increasingly difficult to minister to their spiritual needs.   When, in 1649, James de la Torre, Archbishop of Ephesus and Coadjutor of Rovenius, the Vicar Apostolic, wished to hold a confirmation at Zijdewind in North Holland, the Catholics had to guard him from insults. The consequence was the banishment of the Archbishop and the Catholic priest, the destruction of the chapel and a fine of 8,300 florins for the burgher who had called upon the Catholics to protect their chief pastor.[3] The tribulations of the Dutch Catholics continued during the ensuing years.[4]

(2.)

Far worse were the sufferings of the Catholics in many parts of Great Britain, but there also they maintained

---

[1] Even the representative of the province of Holland protested against this measure ; *cf.* KNUTTEL, I., 251.

[2] HUBERT, 250, 253 *seq.*

[3] See *Bijdragen voor de geschiedenis van het bisdom Haarlem,* III., 161 *seqq.* On Jesuit missions in Holland, *cf.* PONCELET, *Les Jésuites en Belgique,* 33 *seqq.*

[4] BLOCK, V., 53, 133.

themselves with " wonderful fortitude ".[1] In the first years of
Innocent X. that unhappy monarch, Charles I., had given his
Catholic subjects some hope of religious toleration, as he had
done under Urban VIII. On one occasion, in the year 1646,[2]
he observed to his Catholic wife that if the adherents of the
old faith would stand by him with all their hearts, he would
promise them freedom of conscience on his royal word. At
the beginning of June, 1647, he caused a letter to be presented
to Innocent X. through Somerset, in which he prayed for
pecuniary assistance and hinted at recognition by himself both
of papal supremacy and the Catholic faith.[3] The Pope replied
that since his assistance was chiefly given to Catholic princes,
he prayed that God would enlighten the King so that he might
find the way to the true Church.[4] When a *rapprochement* took
place between Cromwell and the King, Charles I. and his
army were inclined to extend the general religious freedom to
those Catholics also who were prepared to take a modified oath
of allegiance. A draft for an oath of this kind, after it had been
examined by some Catholic theologians, was dispatched to
Rome for the Pope's approval, together with a petition bearing

[1] This is the opinion of the strict Protestant MEYER (*Propaganda*, II., 9).

[2] March 12, 1646, GARDINER, *Civil War*, II., 443.

[3] LINGARD, X., 418 *seq.* In 1645 Glamorgan showed to the
Irish nuncio Rinuccini the heading of a royal letter which reads
thus : " Beatissimo Patri Innocentio Decimo " (AIAZZI, 81).
A royal letter of recommendantion for Glamorgan to Rinuccini
of April 30, 1645, *ibid.*, 82. Already on May 10, 1645, the nuncio
of Naples was told in a *letter that the English oath was being
studied by the Inquisition (*Nunziat. di Napoli*, 39 A., Pap. Sec.
Arch.). A letter from London, July 19, 1647, according to which
the Independents were ready to grant limited religious liberty
also to the Catholics, is found in RANKE, *Engl. Gesch.*, III[3]., 281.

[4] *Brief of June 29, 1647, in *Innocentii X. Epist.*, II.–III.,
188, Pap. Sec. Arch. The hope of the conversion of Charles is
also expressed in Servantius, *Diaria of March 12, 1649, Pap.
Sec. Arch. The Catholic zeal of the Duchess of Buckingham
is commended in a *Brief of June 24, 1647, in *Innocentii X.
Epist.*, II.–III., 186, *ibid.*

the signatures of fifty laymen.[1]   Rome, however, could not
countenance the fact that laymen should presume to decide
whether in certain circumstances the Pope could absolve
subjects from their oath of allegiance to the secular power,
hence the Roman Congregation rejected the petition.[2]

On the other hand after Urban VIII.'s death, Charles I.
no longer counted so far as the destiny of England was
concerned.   Shortly before Innocent X.'s elevation the
battle of Naseby, June 14th, 1645, had dealt a decisive blow
to English kingship.   From that moment Cromwell gradually
became the real master of the country and though he lacked
the royal title, he gathered more power in his hand than any
English King had ever wielded [3] ; in fact the title " Emperor
of the British Isles " was actually suggested as an appropriate
one.[4]

Cromwell's conduct after his victory could but fill the
Catholics with anxious forebodings.   On October 14th, 1645,
his victorious army stood before the magnificent, strongly
fortified castle of Basing House.   Its owner, the Catholic
Marquis of Winchester, had remained loyal to the King ;
" Loyalty House " was the Marquis' favourite name for
his castle whereas his enemies nursed a particular hatred for
it as " a nest of Romanists " ; as for Cromwell, he looked upon
himself, during the siege, as God's champion against the
powers of darkness, against the idolaters sheltering behind
these walls with their idols. " Let them that make them become
like unto them, and all such as trust in them," he quoted from
the psalm, in order to justify what followed the storming of
the place.   After the fall of the place there was no longer
question of sparing the lives of either men or women.   Six
out of the ten priests who had found a refuge in the castle
were killed on the spot, the others were reserved for the gallows
and the knife and about a hundred of the defenders of the

---

[1] GARDINER, Civil War, III., 187.

[2] GARDINER, Commonwealth, I., 90 ; REUSCH, Index, II., 335.

[3] SAGREDO in LINGARD, XI., 55.

[4] A. D. MEYER, in Quellen und Forschungen aus italienischen
Archiven, X., Rome, 1907, 235.

castle were massacred.[1] A contemporary newspaper says that
" the enemy desired no quarter and I believe that they had
but little offered them ; you must remember what they were ;
they were most of them Papists ; therefore our muskets and
our swords did show but little compassion ".[2]

On the other hand the fears to which these events were
bound to give rise were only partially realized in the sequel.
In 1646 three priests were indeed executed because of their
priesthood but after that, up till 1679, only the years 1651
and 1654 witnessed the death of one priest each, out of all the
Catholic clergy.[3] But the position of the Catholics remained
an exceedingly difficult one. To what extent they had been
impoverished, as a result of the plunderings and violences of
the Civil War, is shown by an appeal addressed by the English
Jesuits to the other Provinces of the Order in 1645. Their
friends, we read, had been robbed by Parliament either of a
large part of their property or even of the whole of it, so that
they were no longer in a position to give the assistance on
which they had to depend both at home and in Flanders ;
though 200 Jesuits still exercised their sacred functions,
as best they could, from their hiding places and amid great
privations, there was no possibility of providing for the
maintenance of the remaining eighty ; hence the foreign
Provinces were asked to find employment for them either as
teachers or in ministering to English Catholics abroad.[4]
Ten years later, in the year of Innocent X.'s death, we learn
from a Jesuit report from Lancashire and Staffordshire that the
Fathers could be sure neither of revenue nor alms, by reason
of the bad times and because the Catholics were ruined.[5]
Yet, as another report informs us, notwithstanding the
inhuman robberies committed by the heretics, and the
utter destruction of their possessions, the faithful continued

---

[1] GARDINER, *Civil War*, II., 344-7.
[2] *Ibid.*, 347, n. 2.
[3] SPILLMANN, IV., 309, 319, 320 *seqq.*
[4] FOLEY, VII., 1 ; CXLIII., *seq.*
[5] *Ibid.*, CXLVII.

most loyally to do their duty to God and His ministers.[1]
In 1653 the College of Saint-Omer [2] still numbered 126 pupils,
mostly from the best families, " so little do English Catholics
allow themselves to be deterred by the unhappy times from
procuring the best education for their children."

Meanwhile the religious divisions among the Protestants
were taking the most ominous forms. " At this time of law-
lessness," Baillie wrote in 1643, " the disunion of the people
grows week by week. The party of the Independents is on the
increase, that of the Anabaptists is even more so, and both
are surpassed by that of the Antinomians." [3] A publication of
the time enumerates the following contemporary sects :
the Independents, Brownists, Millenarians, Antinomians,
Anabaptists, Arminians, Libertines, Familists, Enthusiasts,
Seekers, Perfectists, Socinians, Arians, Antitrinitarians,
Antiscripturists, Sceptics.[4] As early as 1641 [5] the Venetian
ambassador, Giovanni Giustiniani, expressed the opinion that
in point of fact the religious disorders could hardly grow worse ;
persons from the dregs of the populace and even women
appeared in the pulpit ; there were as many religions as there
were heads and any opinion is tolerated so long as it is not
Catholic. The idea of universal toleration was bound to arise [6]
but it is characteristic that a publication which went furthest
in its demand for religious freedom nevertheless excludes
Catholics, and this on the plea that they were idolaters, though
the writer was in favour of the fines for non-attendance at
Anglican services being remitted.[7] Among all the contemporary
advocates of liberty of belief Jeremy Taylor is the only one to

---

[1] *Ibid.*

[2] Annual report, *ibid.*, 1169.

[3] GARDINER, *Civil War*, I., 314.

[4] LINGARD, X., 192 note.

[5] BROSCH, *Cromwell*, 211.

[6] A. D. MEYER, *Der Toleranz gedanke im England der Stuarts :*
Hist. Zeitsch., CVIII. (1912), 254–294 ; GARDINER, I., 324–344 ;
II., 136–140.

[7] Thus the author of *Liberty of conscience or the sole means to
obtain peace and truth*, in GARDINER, I., 342.

concede to Catholics a qualified toleration.[1] In 1649 General Fairfax and his officers demanded from Parliament the abolition of all penal laws in connection with religion, with the exception, however, of Catholics, Anglicans and such sects as despise God or His word ; however, a petition of Cromwell of the same period makes no mention of a limitation of this kind.[2]

There are other reasons for thinking that in point of fact Cromwell was by no means opposed to the concession of liberty of religion.[3] Even as a military commander he had for ever the name of God and Scripture texts on his lips, after the manner of the Puritans, but if a man could serve his purposes he did not narrowly inquire into his religious opinions.[4] On one occasion, in 1652, he observed that he would rather see Islam tolerated than a child of God persecuted,[5] though it is not clear what he understood by a child of God.   This observation was made by him during the discussion of a bill which, contrary to custom, did not expressly mention Catholics and Anglicans as excluded from religious toleration. However, the bill was conceived in the spirit of John Owen who was unwilling to grant to Catholics the right of freely holding religious assemblies.[6] In order to calm Protestant excitement which had arisen in consequence of rumours of fresh conspiracies by the Catholics, Cromwell had a priest executed in 1654, precisely because of his priesthood,[7] and on occasion he would indulge in violent language against the Pope.[8]

---

[1] MEYER, *loc. cit.*, 269.   To the question of his opponent Cheynell, whether he admitted that anyone can be saved whether he lives and dies as a Turk, a Papist or a Socinian, Chillingworth, the champion of Tolerance answers : That he neither condemned nor absolved. GARDINER, I., 332.

[2] GARDINER, *Commonwealth*, I., 192.

[3] *Ibid.*, II., 223 ; III., 107.

[4] GARDINER, *Civil War*, II., 217 *seq.*, 295.

[5] *Ibid.*, 30.

[6] GARDINER, *Civil War*, II., 26.

[7] *Ibid.*, 462 ; LINGARD, XI., 23.

[8] LINGARD, XI., 79, 108.

As a matter of fact on more than one occasion his words and
actions belied all he had said in favour of religious toleration.[1]

Whatever may have been Cromwell's personal opinions,
Parliament refused to grant toleration to the adherents of the
old religion. When after Charles I.'s defeat a compromise had to
be negotiated between the Presbyterians and the Independents,
Cromwell brought in a bill which the House of Lords passed
on October 13th, 1647 ; by its terms Presbyterianism was to
have a privileged position though in such wise that those who
held other opinions were not interfered with, so long as they
did not disturb the peace, but even so toleration was withheld
from those who professed the " popish religion ", all those
who did not take the standpoint of the Apostles' creed and the
adherents of doctrines whom the law barred from the Communion. The fines for non-attendance at Church were to be
maintained.[2]

The bill failed to pass through the Lower House, though it
gave rise to a curious discussion.[3] The Independent Selden
demanded toleration even for Catholics, since they too believed
in Jesus Christ, whilst his sympathizer Marten asked why
Catholics should not be tolerated, seeing that the Presbyterians
were.   They were told that Catholics were idolaters and
acknowledged a foreigner as their Head.   Whereupon Selden

[1] W. HOLDEN HUTTON (*The English Church from the accession
of Charles I. to the death of Anne,* London, 1903, 150 *seqq.*) thus
judges the tolerance of Cromwell : " It is difficult to avoid the
dilemma of either convicting him of gross inconsistency or
regarding him as a pure opportunist.   Passage after passage
from his letters and his speeches may be quoted to show his
assertion of the right to complete freedom in belief. . . . But, on
the other side, there are words as strong and acts much stronger.
. . . The possession of religious ideals different from his own was
an intolerable crime in his eyes.   He could never really allow
freedom of belief to Irish Romanists, or Scottish Presbyterians,
or English Churchmen. . . . The Puritan position, as he himself
saw it, was the only real Christianity for him."

[2] GARDINER, *Civil War,* III., 210 *seqq.*

[3] *Ibid.*, 212 *seq.*

observed on the next day that veneration of Saints was not the same thing as adoration of Saints, whilst Marten told the Presbyterians that he preferred a single tyrant in a distant country to one in every parish and that the Protestant clergy fought the Catholic clergy solely because of their superior morality.[1] It goes without saying that these arguments proved unavailing. The Catholics, who had flocked in large numbers to the sitting, had presented a petition in which they sought to refute one of the most odious calumnies against their religion, that is, they protested against the accusation that according to Catholic teaching it was lawful to resist or to kill an excommunicated King. The petition was not even accepted.[2]

Nevertheless some hope seemed to dawn for the adherents of the ancient faith when on September 27th, 1650, Parliament repealed the penalties for non-attendance at Protestant services. Henceforth no one was to be fined for such neglect, provided he attended some religious service or other on Sundays and on holy days established by law, but in view of the fact that the prohibition of the Mass was maintained, this alleviation could not be of any great value for Catholics.[3] In February of that year the oaths of supremacy and allegiance were replaced by an assurance of loyalty to the Republic but the oath of 1643 was maintained; by this oath all those doctrines were denied which were considered as specifically Catholic dogmas, namely the Pope's supremacy, transubstantiation, Purgatory, adoration of the Host, veneration of the crucifix and the Saints, justification by good works.[4] When the

[1] That the Protestant clergy detested the Catholic priests simply on account of their superior chastity. *Ibid.*, 212.

[2] *Ibid.*

[3] GARDINER, *Commonwealth*, I., 396.

[4] " I, A. B., do abjure and renounce the Pope's supremacy and authority over the Catholic Church in general, and over myself in particular. And I believe, that there is not any Transubstantiation. . . . And I do also believe, that there is not any Purgatory, or that the Consecrated Host, crucifixes or images ought to be worshipped. . . . And I also believe, that salvation cannot be merited by works; and all doctrines in affirmation

royalists attempted a rising, a proclamation of April 26th, 1655, demanded the oath not only from the laity but from the priests also and the Jesuits ; anyone refusing it was held to be a papist, forfeited two-thirds of his property and nearly all civil rights.[1] Consequently it was of no advantage that the laws against non-attendance at church no longer existed since the Catholics' money was taken from them on the ground of their refusal to abjure papal authority.[2] In 1650 the Government's revenue from confiscated Catholic property amounted to £62,000, the revenue from thirteen districts not being included in this total.[3] The possessions of the Catholics were considered a fruitful source from which the Government might relieve its need of money.[4] By a law of the same year, 1650, the same reward was promised for the discovery of priests or Jesuits and those who sheltered them as for the capture of a highwayman. Judges and accusers were once more busy ; Catholics might have their houses searched at any hour of the day or night ; however, only one of the arrested priests, Peter Wright, died at the executioner's hand, the others were deported.[5] In 1655 a fresh decree ordered all priests, under pain of death, to leave the Kingdom, and all Catholics were banished to within twenty miles of the capital.[6] In the so-called " Instrument of Government " which established Cromwell's Protectorate in 1653, the adherents of the old religion were excluded from toleration [7] ; the same applies also to the Constitution of 1657.[8]

of the said points, I do abjure and renounce, without any equivocation, etc."   RUSHWORTH, *Historical Collections*, V., 141 ; *The Month*, LXXXIV. (1895), 191 ; AIAZZI, 482–6. *Cf.* POLLEN in *The Catholic Encyclopedia*, XI., 179 ; BRIDGETT in *The Month*, *loc. cit.* ; GARDINER, *Commonwealth*, II., 322 ; LINGARD, X., 128.

[1] GARDINER, *loc. cit.*, III., 225 ; LINGARD, X., 393.

[2] GARDINER, *Commonwealth*, III., 224.

[3] LINGARD, X., 399.

[4] *Ibid.*, 397.

[5] *Ibid.*, 399.

[6] *Ibid.*, XI., 53.

[7] *Ibid.*, 18.   [8] *Ibid.*, 97. *Cf.* HUGHES, II., 55.

When after a ten years' interruption, Venice sent an ambassador to London, from September, 1655, till February, 1656, the latter reported home that the intention of the English Government was to rob the Catholics of their property whilst letting them have as many Masses as they might wish for.[1] Thus under Cromwell's Government the situation of the Catholics seemed to have become somewhat easier. In the following year [2] the French ambassador, Bordeaux, inferred from the forbearance of the Government, the number of priests in London, the crowds that attended the Embassy chapels, that it appeared that under the Protector, Catholics were better treated than under the governments that had gone before. This did not prevent the arrest, on one occasion, of 400 Catholics as they left the Venetian Embassy Chapel.[3] Inroads into the possessions of Catholics continued even beyond Innocent X.'s pontificate. When, in 1657, they were threatened with a fresh enforcement of the laws of 1655, they ended by offering to buy themselves off with a gift of £50,000 a year ; however, Cromwell demanded £80,000.[4]

After the execution of Charles I., his son, the future Charles II., disputed the Protector's power for some time. Towards the Pope and the Catholics he adopted at that time the same attitude as his father. In 1649 he dispatched to Rome Robert Meynell, with letters of recommendation [5] to all such persons as, in his judgment, might further his hope of recovering the throne. In a letter of Lord Cottington to Cardinal Capponi, the young prince promised to show favour to his Catholic subjects if the Pope were willing to lend him pecuniary assistance ; as a matter of fact he also hoped to influence the Catholic Powers in his favour through the Pope.[6]

---

[1] *Sagredo* in GARDINER, *loc. cit.*, 225.

[2] October 5 (September 25), 1656, *ibid.*, 226.

[3] *Ibid.*, 225.

[4] The successor of the Venetian ambassador Sagredo, the agent Giavarina, on October 5, 1657, in BROSCH, *Cromwell*, 429, note.

[5] Of July 28 (August 7), 1649, in GARDINER, I., 79.

[6] *Ibid.*, 219.

However, these efforts proved unfortunate for the young
pretender, for a memorial apparently addressed to Innocent X.
by Meynell, fell into the hands of the republicans and its
publication [1] could not but grievously damage the royal cause
in the eyes of the Protestants.[2] The document stated that it
was a well-known fact that Charles had cherished sincere
leanings towards the Catholic faith, even whilst his father was
alive ; he had accordingly promised to the Irish Catholics
not only freedom to practise their religion but even the
restoration of their property.[3] At that time the young prince
was under the most diverse influences and it cannot be said
that he stood like a rock among these contrary currents.
In 1650 the royalists of London advised him to give to the
Catholics a secret promise of religious freedom [4] whilst the
Scottish divines described such a step as sinful.[5] Charles fell
back on equivocations : to the Cavaliers, who took up his
cause, he promised freedom of conscience [6] but to the Scots
the execution of the anti-Catholic laws, with the exception
of the agreements with the Irish.[7] After his defeat by Cromwell
at Worcester in 1651 and during his flight, he had some
discussions with a Catholic priest to whom he gave to understand that he would return to the ancient Church if the
Pope would take up his cause.   Innocent X. did not allow
himself to be deluded, though Charles renewed his promise to
protect the English Catholics and the Irish, if the Pope
and the Catholic Powers would intervene on his behalf.[8]

---

[1] On July 16, 1650.

[2] GARDINER, *Commonwealth*, I., 299 *seq.* On the authenticity
of the document, *ibid.*, 300, note.

[3] LINGARD, XI., 70 *seq.*

[4] GARDINER, I., 217 *seq.*

[5] *Ibid.*, 220.

[6] *Ibid.*, 221.

[7] *Ibid.*, 226.

[8] *Ibid.*, II., 95. *Cf.* LINGARD, XI., 70, note. According to the
contemporary testimony of the archæologist Thomas Blount
(*ob.* 1679), it was the Catholics who helped the young King
on his adventurous flight for safety : " To which I shall add

Even before this he had held out similar promises to the Catholics.[1]

(3.)

The opening years of Innocent X.'s reign were decisive ones both for the fate of Charles I. and for Catholic Ireland. Until then the fortune of arms had smiled on the Irish; apparently little was to be feared from a divided England, and Catholic worship was once more publicly celebrated. But instead of commanding England's respect by a firm and decided attitude and thus compelling her to concede religious liberty, as the Old-Irish and the papal envoy Scarampi desired, recourse was had to the weakly contrivance of negotiations with the King and the Viceroy.[2] These negotiations continued even after the armistice of Castlemartin in 1643. At Oxford Charles I. had only given vague promises, and on September 6th, 1644, the negotiations were resumed at Dublin with his representative, the Viceroy Ormond. The

---

but this one circumstance, that it was performed by persons for the most part of that religion which has long suffered under an imputation (laid on them by some mistaken zealots) of disloyalty to their sovereign." BLOUNT, *Boscobel*, I., edit. by C. G. THOMAS, London, 1894, 78. *Cf. The Month*, CXLVII. (1926), 212.

[1] GARDINER, I., 270.

[2] *Cf.* Vol. XXIX., 337 *seqq.*, of this work and the Report of Rinuccini, in AIAZZI, 391-3. *Ibid.*, on p. 397 we read : " Io trovai nel ingresso le cose spirituali in buonissimo termine e l'esercizio della religione splendido e bene ordinato." *Cf.* " *Rerum Hibernicarum ab initio postremi belli gestorum et praesentis status epitome ad Innocentium X. auctore Carolo Francisco Invernitio Mediolanensi," 1645, *Barb.* 2242, Vatican Library. There it is stated, p. 51[b], that after the cessation of the persecution a great many religious returned to Ireland : 1,000 (?) Franciscans, 400 Dominicans, 40 calced and 20 discalced Carmelites, 40 Capuchins, 80 Augustinians, 10 Benedictines, 60 Cistercians ; the Jesuits worked with great success, especially among the young. The Pope is asked to help Ireland ; he would suffer great loss if Parliament and the Scots were victorious.

Irish demanded the repeal of all the laws against their religious freedom and against appeals to Rome, as well as the suppression of the Statute of *Praemunire*.   Meanwhile one party headed by Muskerry was of opinion that the anti-religious laws would fall into abeyance of their own accord once Charles I. had again a free hand, hence all they demanded was a guarantee for the safety of Irishmen's life and property. Thereupon Charles instructed Ormond to promise that, to begin with, the penal laws would not be applied and as soon as he should have recovered his throne, with the help of the Irish, he would abolish them altogether, but the Statute of *Praemunire* would have to remain.[1]   Ormond did not relish the risk of acting as a go-between in negotiations of this kind, consequently he offered his resignation to the king, but all that Charles would consent to was to appoint Herbert, Earl of Raglan, as his assistant.   With Raglan a fresh personality appears on the stage which once more involved the Pope in the Irish complications.

Raglan, since the beginning of 1645 Earl of Glamorgan, was a fervent Catholic and like his father, the Marquis of Worcester, an enthusiastic champion of the King, convinced as he was that in serving the latter, he was defending a righteous cause against the forces of revolution.   To free his Church from the fetters of anti-religious laws, to equip an Irish army for the support of the King in England, to arm half Europe on his behalf—these were Glamorgan's chivalrous plans, or rather dreams.   Charles I. approved his efforts : through this Catholic mediator he hoped to win the confidence of the Irish and once they were won over by his promises, his Irish regiments would be free for employment in England. For the realization of his plans Glamorgan set his hopes on the Pope and the Catholic princes, for Charles I. himself had no money for such far-reaching plans.   However, if the King's position was hopeless, were it only because of his lack of money, it was made worse by the circumstance that the task of raising an Irish army was entrusted by him to Ormond, who

---

[1] GARDINER, *Civil War*, II., 114 *seq.*

was hopelessly unequal to the task, as well as by his constant fear of offending the English by his reliance on the Irish. This was made evident shortly before Urban VIII.'s death. On May 13th, 1644, the commander of the English and Scottish troops, Monroe, had taken Belfast. To oppose him the supreme council of the allied Catholics placed the whole of its fighting power at the disposal of the Viceroy Ormond, but the latter did not dare to accept the offer without being ordered to do so by the King and Charles lacked the courage to give the order.[1] Thus were the Irish taught that they had nothing to hope from negotiations with the King.

On April 1st, 1644, under the Great Seal, Charles I. appointed Glamorgan commander of three armies which were to consist of Englishmen, Irishmen, and foreign mercenaries. He was authorized to raise money from the royal domains and to bestow titles of nobility at his discretion, his son was to be given the hand of the Princess Elizabeth, with a dowry of three hundred thousand pounds, whilst Glamorgan himself would become Duke of Somerset and a member of the highest Orders. For his negotiations with the Pope and the Catholic princes, who would have to contribute thirty thousand pounds a month for the maintenance of the army, Glamorgan was given royal letters in which he himself was to insert the names : this precaution would enable the King to deny his servant, should the affair come to light, a subterfuge of which Charles did eventually avail himself.[2] On January 12th, 1645, the King granted an even wider concession : any faculty, even if conveyed by word of mouth alone, was to have the same efficacy as if it had been given under the Great Seal, even if it should go beyond the letter of the law.[3] The Supreme Council of the Irish Confederates were satisfied with these powers : at Kilkenny, on August 25th, 1645, they entered into a secret understanding with Glamorgan which guaranteed to the Irish Catholics freedom of religion and the possession of all

---

[1] *Ibid.*, 109–111.
[2] *Ibid.*, 117 *seqq.* ; LINGARD, X., 165, 410.
[3] LINGARD, X., 411.

churches not actually in the hands of the Protestants ; in return they bound themselves, and that openly, to raise ten thousand men for the King and to devote two-thirds of the Church's property to his defence.[1]

It is possible that when he made these concessions Glamorgan exceeded his powers [2] ; however, be this as it may, they would not be considered adequate in as much as, for one thing, they rested on a secret, not a public treaty and, secondly, because they did not settle the burning question of the Church's property.   Moreover Ormond raised objections against the agreement which led to the further concession that future royal guarantees in respect of religion would be considered as an integral part of the agreement just concluded and that instead of any formal guarantees the Irish should be satisfied with Ormond's written assurance that the Catholics would not be molested in their possession of the churches they held at the time, until Parliament should give a definitive judgment.[3] The papal envoy Scarampi attached no value to these agreements, on the contrary he now despaired of the possibility of obtaining anything for the Catholics by political action ; accordingly he made it his chief concern to further the religious life in Ireland, and this he did with success.[4]   In Rome also the agreement was criticized on the ground that it only bore the King's signature.[5]

Meanwhile the situation had undergone a change in so far as the Pope's influence in Irish affairs had become more effective. On the other hand Queen Henrietta's pleadings with Innocent X. met with but small success. From Paris she did all she could for her husband, pleaded with Queen Anne and Mazarin for support, promised freedom of conscience to the English and Irish Catholics in Charles I.'s name and dispatched

[1] LINGARD, X., 166 ; BELLESHEIM, *Irland*, II., 403.

[2] According to GARDINER (II., 119) the plenipotentiary powers did not refer to the conclusion of peace but to the negotiations with the Pope and the Catholic Powers.

[3] LINGARD, X., 167.

[4] BELLESHEIM, II., 405.

[5] *Ibid.*, 425.

Kenelm Digby to the Pope as her personal envoy. In Rome, Digby raised hopes of the King's conversion, but all he obtained from the Pope was twenty thousand crowns to buy ammunition for the army.[1] The Irish were more successful ; already at the end of 1644 they had dispatched Richard Bellings to Rome to request the Pope and Propaganda [2] to send a formal nuncio to Ireland. Thereupon Scarampi was recalled on May 5th, 1645, though at the Pope's request he remained until the middle of 1646 as adviser to Battista Rinuccini, Archbishop of Fermo, who had been appointed nuncio.[3]

Rinuccini set out in the first days of April, 1645, but he only landed on Irish soil on 21st October. He was detained for a long time in Paris where Queen Henrietta, advised as she was by friends of Ormond and full of prejudices against the Irish, refused to give audience to the papal representative, whilst Mazarin put off paying the subsidies destined for the Irish.[4] Twelve days before his departure from France the nuncio dispatched to Ireland a ship with a cargo of arms, whilst he personally took charge of considerable sums of money.[5] Later on, too, Innocent X. supplied the Irish with considerable subsidies [6] and Spain also lent them aid.[7]

---

[1] GARDINER, II., 121, 127, 378.

[2] On November 23, 1644, BELLESHEIM, II., 409.

[3] *Ibid.*, 406.

[4] *Ibid.*, 415 *seqq.* About Rinuccini. *Cf.* G. AIAZZI, *Nunziatura in Irlanda di Monsignor G. B. Rinuccini*, Firenze, 1844. His Instruction (AIAZZI, XXXV. *seqq.*, LIII., *seqq.*) was written by Albizzi, as the latter informed *Chigi on July 7, 1644 (Bibl. Chigi, Rome, A. III., 55). *Letters of recommendation for Rinuccini to the Bishops and clergy of Ireland in the *Epist.*, I., p. 18, Pap. Sec. Arch., to the Governor of Belgium of March 2, 1645, *ibid.* It was feared in Rome that Queen Henrietta would not accept the present of the Golden Rose (the Secretary of State to Rinuccini, July 3, 1645, Rospigliosi Archives, Rome).

[5] BELLESHEIM, II., 420.

[6] *Ibid.*, 440, 450. *Cf.* AIAZZI, XV. On the readiness of the Pope to support Ireland see *Brief of March 25, 1644, to the Spanish nuncio in *Nunziat. di Spagna*, 347, Pap. Sec. Arch.

[7] See p. 158.

Rinuccini's reports give a very clear idea of the Irish situation ; they draw a gloomy picture of division and discord. Two parties stood face to face : on the one hand the Old-Irish, keenly religious and putting all their hopes solely on decisive action and the exploitation of the successes so far achieved ; on the other hand there were the Anglo-Irish, that is, the descendants of Englishmen who had come into the country during the Middle Ages, had acquired Church property during the period of the religious troubles which they were afraid they would have to surrender should the Church in Ireland be once more publicly recognized. Englishmen in thought and feeling, what they wanted before all else was peace and reconciliation, and their influence, Rinuccini reports, was great. The Supreme Council of the Confederates consisted almost exclusively of Anglo-Irishmen ; it was due to their influence that the armistice came about during which the war fever abated, though in its place the strife between the two parties raged all the more fiercely in meetings, sermons and pamphlets. One of the two leading Irish generals, Eugene O'Neill, was on the side of the Old-Irish whilst the other, Preston, sided with the Anglo-Irish.[1]

The arrival of the nuncio, though seemingly so ardently longed for, came as a heavy blow for the less intransigent party, so much so that Bellings, whose secret instructions ordered him to request the dispatch of a nuncio, remained almost speechless for several days on hearing that a nomination had actually been made.[2] On the other hand the real cause of

The *Letter of the Secretary of State to Rinuccini on July 3, 1645, lays stress on the fact that the Pope does not pursue political aims in Ireland, but " solamente la propagazione della religione cattolica senza un minimo pensiero di pregiudicare al dominio temporale di chi si sia ". Rospigliosi Archives, Rome.

[7] BELLESHEIM, II., 450.

[1] Report of Rinuccini after his return from Ireland in AIAZZI, 391–4. Limerick remained outside the Catholic confederation ; ibid., LV. Innocent X. *commends the city on March 19, 1646, for giving up its neutrality. Epist., II.-III., 31, Pap. Sec. Arch.

[2] AIAZZI, 394 seq.

the dissensions had been fully grasped in Rome and the nuncio was accordingly empowered to drop the restoration of Church property.[1] However, a great many Irishmen were not interested in dispensations and spiritual favours. The Old-Irish, Rinuccini wrote, saw in the nuncio the minister of God and the Young-Irish the dispenser of a prince's money [2] and they would rather have had papal subsidies than a papal nuncio. They did not dare to publish the armistice with Ormond till after Rinuccini's arrival for fear the papal envoy might return at once to Rome with the money of which he was the bearer.[3]

Another serious difficulty, according to Rinuccini, arose out of the fact that the Supreme Council of the federated Irish included forty persons, unanimity of votes was required for the validity of its decisions, and small matters as well as big ones were submitted to its decisions, with the result that its members were overwhelmed with work, and since the Council was bound to deal with Ormond, it showed a tendency to send as envoys men that were acceptable to him, hence only friends of Ormond were admitted into the Council; in consequence of this conduct the Old-Irish were further irritated and the cleavage between the two parties grew steadily.[4]

On reaching Ireland the nuncio had some serious representations to make, in connection with the peace negotiations. To the Supreme Council he pointed out what a bad impression would be made throughout the whole world if, in the published peace conditions, the Catholic Irish did little more than lightly allude to religion.[5] He found Glamorgan willing to fall in with his views. The Earl was prepared to promise in the

---

[1] " Per istimolare viepiù i cattolici alla concordia e proseguire nell'impresa, assicuri tutti coloro che posseggono beni ecclesiastici, che non li verranno tolti, nè per motivo di essi soffriranno veruna molestia, ma anzi saranno loro confermati . . ." Secret Instruction of Rinuccini in AIAZZI, LV. ; cf. XLVII.

[2] Ibid., 395.

[3] Ibid., 396.

[4] Report of Rinuccini of March 1, 1646, ibid., 104 seq.

[5] Report of December 23, 1645, ibid., 76 seq.

name of the King that in future the Viceroy of Ireland would always be a Catholic, that the Bishops would sit in the Irish Parliament, and many more things of this kind.[1]

However, the conversations soon came to an unexpected termination. This was due to the agreement with Glamorgan coming to the knowledge of the English Parliament. About the middle of October, 1645, the titular Archbishop of Tuam was killed in an affray. In his carriage was found a copy of the agreement. To save appearances Ormond had the Earl arrested,[2] whilst in a message to both Houses of Parliament, Charles I. told the falsehood that he had given Glamorgan no powers beyond the levying of troops, nor authorized him to enter into any negotiations without Ormond's knowledge; that he acknowledged no agreement with the Irish Catholics and had ordered proceedings to be taken against Glamorgan. When Ormond reminded him of the wide powers granted by him to the Earl of Glamorgan, the King replied that he had no recollection of his having done so; he may possibly have accredited Glamorgan with the Irish but he had never authorized him to enter into negotiations without Ormond's knowledge.[3]

Whilst this letter was being written by the King to Parliament, Glamorgan had already been set at liberty on bail. In order to justify himself, he made public a secret clause of the treaty which stated that the King was not to be bound beyond his own good pleasure.

Even now Glamorgan continued to negotiate with the nuncio. The discussions turned round a peace project devised by Kenelm Digby, Queen Henrietta's envoy, and Innocent X.[4] The draft demanded for the Irish complete freedom to practise their religion, restoration of Church property, an independent Parliament and the admission of Catholics to all offices.

---

[1] *Ibid.*, 76; GARDINER, *Civil War*, II., 406 *seq.*

[2] Rinuccini, January 1, 1646, in AIAZZI, 85; BELLESHEIM, II., 424 *seq.*; LINGARD, X., 167.

[3] LINGARD, X., 171 *seq.*; *cf.* 408–419, where the proofs of Charles' duplicity are grouped together.

[4] AIAZZI, 459 *seqq.*, 462 *seq.*; *cf.* 96.

A yearly subsidy was guaranteed to the King but religious liberty was likewise demanded for English Catholics. Glamorgan allowed himself to be persuaded to withdraw his draft in favour of that of the Pope,[1] in fact he even wished to go to Rome in order to lay the Irish situation before the Pontiff.[2] Meanwhile, no decisive result could be reached in Glamorgan's negotiations with the Supreme Council, because Rinuccini was not in possession of the original text of Digby's peace plan ; none the less the Supreme Council insisted, notwithstanding the nuncio's arguments to the contrary,[3] on concluding peace before the arrival of the papal formula.[4]

On March 18th, 1646, Glamorgan learnt that the King had publicly disavowed both his person and his peace proposals.[5] Thus there was an end to his rôle as a mediator even though for the time being he himself did not take the King's declaration too seriously. In any case there could be no question of sending an Irish army to England as Glamorgan had planned.[6] The King had practically lost all authority, so that nothing was left to Ormond except to choose whether to throw in his lot with the Puritans in England or the Catholics of Ireland. He adopted the latter alternative ; accordingly, on March 28th, 1646, peace was concluded between him and the Irish Supreme Council. By its terms the Catholics were relieved from the oath of supremacy and from all such penalties, fines and such disadvantages as profession of the Catholic faith entailed. Thus was peace at last realized after endless discussions and plannings, but it was a peace that could not give universal satisfaction. The concessions in the religious sphere only eased the situation of individual Catholics, as a body, Catholics were not guaranteed the possession of their churches and other Church property, in fact, the final settlement of the religious question was deferred until a message should have come from the King. It is easy to see the reasons why such a peace was kept secret, especially from the nuncio ; it was only made

---

[1] *Ibid.*, 94 *seq.* ; *cf.* 91.

[2] *Ibid.*, 159 ; GARDINER, II., 421.

[3] AIAZZI, 99. [4] *Ibid.*, 98. [5] GARDINER, II., 422.

[6] *Ibid.*, 423, 425 *seq.*

M

public on July 30th, 1646, when it was criticized from all sides.[1]

The disappointment of the clergy was all the more bitter as during the whole of 1646 the Catholic cause had prospered and as recently as June 5th, 1646, O'Neill had won a brilliant victory over the Scotch at Benburb in Ulster.[2] The Archbishop of Dublin and Cashel, together with six Bishops and six Provincials of Orders lamented the event in a letter to Louis XIV. who had sent important contributions.[3] The Irish people would not allow the treaty to be read and the clergy refused to pay its taxes.

In view of such a situation the Supreme Council had to make very large promises in the hope of winning over Rinuccini,[4] but it was in vain that it invoked the help of Ormond, now its confederate.   Kilkenny indeed gave the Viceroy a solemn reception, but the assembly of nobles convened at Cashel refused to admit him, and Clonmel shut its gates against him. On the other hand the nuncio entered Kilkenny at the head of an army, the peace treaty was declared null and void, the Supreme Council thrown into prison and another elected in its place on 26th September.[5] This attitude of the Catholics was to a large extent the result of a convention of the clergy which had opened at Waterford on 12th August ; that assembly declared that the peace treaty was incompatible with their previous oath, namely that they would do all that was in their power for the preservation of religion. Rinuccini dispatched his auditor, Massari, Dean of Fermo, to Rome, to report to the Pope.[6]

[1] GARDINER, II., 540 ; Report of Rinuccini about the peace, Waterford, August 16, 1646, in AIAZZI, 153–7.

[2] BELLESHEIM, II., 433. Rinuccini sent the captured standards to Rome where they remained in St. Peter's till the pontificate of Alexander VII. ; *ibid.*, 434.

[3] *Ibid.*, 427.

[4] GARDINER, II., 541 *seq.*

[5] *Ibid.*, 543 *seq.* ; AIAZZI, 158.

[6] Rinuccini, August 16 and September 12, 1646, in AIAZZI, 155 *seq.* ; BELLESHEIM, II., 435.

Thus was Ormond forced to realize that his attempt to lean on the Catholics had failed. Accordingly he passed over to the parliamentary side, ready either to prosecute the war or to withdraw from his post at a sign from Parliament, should the King consent to his resignation. This clause delayed his retreat for a considerable time.[1]

If in 1646 the position of the Irish was a favourable one,[2] it grew steadily more and more desperate in the following year. It was a bad omen when an advance on Dublin failed in December, 1646,[3] and this not least in consequence of the lack of concord between the two army leaders Preston and O'Neill, in fact the former went so far as to contemplate sending O'Neill and the nuncio as prisoners to Dublin.[4] A grave danger likewise arose out of the fact that since February 6th, 1647, Ormond was negotiating with the English Parliament with a view to surrendering to the latter Ireland's strong places. On June 28th, 1647, he surrendered Dublin to the enemies of his King in return for a large sum of money; having done so he left Ireland. Henceforth Catholics were forbidden, under pain of death, to spend were it only one night in the Irish capital, and death and confiscation of property was to be the penalty for harbouring a Jesuit or a priest.[5] To fill the cup of misfortune Preston suffered a defeat near Trim in the second half of the year; Taafe was defeated at Knocknamus[6] and the Province of Munster was ravaged with fire and sword by the parliamentary troops under Inchiquin. Appalling horrors marked the storming of Cashel; after the fall of Cork all Catholics were forced to leave the city and none might buy the right to stay even at the price of apostasy.[7] To save itself the Supreme Council conceived the

---

[1] GARDINER, II., 545 seqq.

[2] Rinuccini in AIAZZI, 287.

[3] Report on this of December 29, 1646, in AIAZZI, 177–183. Cf. GARDINER, II., 576; LINGARD, X., 191.

[4] BELLESHEIM, II., 437.

[5] Ibid., 440, 442.

[6] Ibid., 442, 447.

[7] Ibid., 442 seqq., 444 seq.

idea of looking for a patron abroad. To this end it was decided
to dispatch envoys, of course in vain, to Innocent X.,
Louis XIV. and Philip IV. Rinuccini neither favoured nor
discountenanced the plan of papal patronage, but the Secretary
of State instructed him [1] that in view of the jealousies of the
Princes, the great distance and the exhaustion of the pontifical
exchequer, the plan could not be carried out. The Ormondists
desired a French protectorate in the hope of bringing over to
England the Prince of Wales who was staying with Queen
Henrietta in France, and to whom Ormond would have acted
as companion and guide.[2] Rinuccini was but little pleased
with the choice of the envoys who were to go to France
because two of their number, Muskerry and Browne, were
opponents of his and only the third, Antrim, belonged to his
party ; however, he obtained a promise from the General
Assembly that no decision affecting religion would be made
without the Pope's consent.[3]

Meanwhile Muskerry and Browne were pressing Queen
Henrietta to appoint Ormond lieutenant without waiting for
the Pope and to sanction an understanding between Inchiquin
and the Confederates. The Queen gave her consent and pawned
jewels to the value of thirty thousand pounds for the support
of Ormond.[4] Shortly before this Inchiquin, until then a bitter
enemy of the Irish, had unexpectedly gone over to the King's
side : accordingly Ormond's party resolved to conclude an
armistice with him. Vainly did the opposite party urge that
this was precisely the right moment for attacking Inchiquin
and rendering him harmless ; if this were done the other
commanders of the parliamentary troops would not be able
to hold the field for long. Rinuccini, who was unwilling to be

[1] On July 22, 1647, in AIAZZI, 475 *seq.*

[2] BELLESHEIM, II., 447.

[3] GARDINER, III., 355, 413. The nuncio did not expect anything from the Queen : " Quanto alla Regina non bisogna sperar
mai de lei se non concetti perniciosi alla religione, poichè è
totalmente in mano di Germen [Jermyn], di Digby e d'altri
eretici." January 29, 1648, in AIAZZI, 294.

[4] GARDINER, III., 414.

present at the negotiations at Kilkenny, vainly urged his objections in writing : the fatal treaty was concluded, which four Irish Archbishops and ten Bishops described as the ruination of the Catholic religion and their native land. The Supreme Council countered their further declaration that the armistice could not be observed with a safe conscience by ordering General Preston to take forcible proceedings against the recalcitrants.[1]

The course of events made it evident that the ruin of Ireland could not be long delayed. None of Rinuccini's counsels and warnings had borne fruit ; believing his personal safety threatened, he took to flight and on May 27th, 1648, he pronounced a sentence of excommunication and interdict against the adherents of the armistice.[2] The Supreme Council appealed against this sentence, the immediate result being that the national defect of the Irish, lack of unity, broke out into enmities which created irretrievable confusion. Seven of the Bishops supported the nuncio, seven were against him, some defended the justice of the censures whilst others condemned them. The dispute spread to the Orders ; divines and canonists argued for and against the nuncio whilst the common people no longer knew whom to believe.[3] Rinuccini had to flee a second time from Preston ; he crossed the Shannon by night in disguise and sought a refuge in Galway.[4] His attempt to convene a synod there was frustrated by the Supreme Council who barred the roads and threatened him with imprisonment.[5] Galway had to endure all the horrors of a siege until it surrendered, and its besieger, Clanricarde, withdrew after payment of a ransom.[6] In addition to all this Irishmen now turned their weapons against Irishmen. O'Neill concluded an armistice with the parliamentary generals, Jones and Monk respectively, in Dublin and Ulster, Preston

---

[1] BELLESHEIM, II., 451 seq.
[2] Ibid., 452.
[3] Ibid., 452–8.
[4] Ibid., 453.
[5] Ibid., 457.
[6] Ibid., 458 ; LINGARD, X., 289.

allied himself with Inchiquin in support of the Supreme
Council against O'Neill, in fact things came to such a pass that
the ablest of all the Irish generals, O'Neill, was denounced as a
rebel and a traitor.[1]

The Holy See had good grounds, in a Brief of August 18th,
1648, to exhort the Supreme Council to concord.[2] An embassy
composed of the Bishop of Ferns and Count Nicolas Plunkett
which had set out for Rome in February, brought this message
from Rome to Ireland towards the end of November. It came
much too late,[3] the ground was prepared for Ormond. On
September 29th, 1648, the latter returned to Ireland. At
Kilkenny he was solemnly received by the Archbishops of
Tuam and Cashel and by them installed in his office as Viceroy.[4]
Rinuccini, who had been ordered by the Supreme Council to
leave Ireland, now announced that since the Holy See kept
no nuncios with Protestant rulers, his nunciature was at an
end. He left Ireland on March 2nd, 1649 [5] : his mission had
been a complete failure. Innocent X. nevertheless gave him
a kindly reception [6] whilst a few Irish Bishops proposed him
for the cardinalate [7] and the Bishop of Clonfert described
him to the Pope as " the luminary and pillar of the struggling
Irish ".[8]

On January 19th, 1649, the Catholic Confederates concluded
a treaty of peace with Ormond in which the latter guaranteed
liberty of conscience and an independent Irish Parliament.
In return the Confederates were to furnish Ormond with an
army of fifteen thousand foot and five hundred horse, to be
employed, in the first instance, in the conquest of Dublin.[9]

---

[1] LINGARD, X., 289.

[2] *Epist., IV.-VI., n. 41, Pap. Sec. Arch.

[3] BELLESHEIM, II., 459 seq.

[4] Ibid., 458.

[5] Ibid., 459, 461.

[6] Ibid., 462 ; cf. 466.

[7] Ibid., 468 seq.

[8] Ibid.

[9] GARDINER, Commonwealth, I., 14 seq., 23 ; LINGARD, X.,
290.

Of the rights of the Church in Ireland there is no mention in the treaty ; all that it grants to the Catholics is the possession of their churches until such time as the King would give a definitive judgment. The Archbishop of Tuam and seven other Bishops forthwith proclaimed the peace by means of pastoral letters.[1]

(4.)

Thus the whole of Ireland had taken sides against Parliament and in favour of the King. The commanders of the parliamentary army, Jones at Dublin, Monk at Belfast, Coote in Londonderry, were almost completely confined within the area of these towns, nearly the whole of the rest of Ireland stood by the King and a considerable army was about to be placed under the command of the royal lieutenant. The Prince of Wales was invited to cross over to Ireland and he seemed not unwilling to accept the invitation.[2]

The English Parliament anxiously watched these developments. In close proximity to England a dangerous Power seemed to be rising and the threatening spectre of the invasion of the country by the hated bands of wild Irishmen appeared to take a tangible form. The peril had to be conjured and Ireland so utterly crushed that she would never rise again. Parliament indeed adopted a resolution that the natives of Ireland were neither to be exterminated nor deprived of their possessions,[3] but the mere fact that such a resolution was deemed necessary speaks only too eloquently. For the subjection of Ireland choice was made of England's most tried military captain, Oliver Cromwell, and Cromwell was prepared for every violence, nor did he for a moment entertain the notion of restoring peace by means of negotiations and treaties with the Irish Catholics. He assumed the supreme command on March 30th, 1649, but refused to embark until

[1] BELLESHEIM, II., 460.
[2] LINGARD, X., 291.
[3] GARDINER, I., 30.

he had assured himself that adequate supplies had been provided for his troops. This entailed a delay of several months during which Parliament, by a series of negotiations, prevented the Irish from striking an immediate blow. A Catholic of the name of Winter, who was loyal to the King, was dispatched to the Confederates with promises of freedom of religion on condition that they rejected the Pope's claim to intervene in secular matters and raised an army of ten thousand men for the Republic.[1] The proposals of the envoy of the Catholics of Ulster, the Cistercian Abbot Crelly, got at least a hearing, though in the end Parliament rejected the proposal of religious toleration for the Irish Catholics.[2] So the decision was left to the sword. On August 15th, 1649, Cromwell landed at Dublin [3]; Ireland's doom was about to be sealed.

Shortly before this time the royalists, under Ormond, had undertaken an attack on the Irish capital, but they were defeated in the neighbourhood, at Rathmines, by the parliamentary general Jones.[4] However, Ormond did not despair. In order to keep open the road to Dublin, he strengthened the garrison of Drogheda, hence Cromwell's first blow was directed against that unhappy town. At the third assault his troops penetrated into the city after promising to spare the lives of all who surrendered.[5] However, once the place was in their power, and whilst a remainder of the garrison was climbing the near-by hill, Cromwell ordered a general massacre. Thereupon sword and pike raged against the dense masses of the fleeing garrison. About a thousand fell near St. Peter's church whilst eighty sought refuge in the tower. Fire was set to the tower when some thirty unhappy men perished in the flames whilst the rest, who had escaped to the roof, met with a violent end there. The heads of the friars in particular were smashed indiscriminately. It is not known how many among the civilian population fell under the sword. Even on the

---

[1] LINGARD, X., 292 ; GARDINER, I., 92.

[2] GARDINER, I., 92 seq., 104.

[3] Ibid., 118.

[4] Ibid., 113 seq.

[5] Ibid., 131, note.

following day a few surviving officers were massacred in cold blood.[1] Cromwell justified these horrors with the plea that such severity would deter others from offering resistance and thus bloodshed would be avoided, moreover this butchery was a judgment of God on those who, in 1641, had killed so large a number of Protestants.[2] However, so appalling a slaughter was calculated to fill the rest with a stronger determination than ever to sell their lives as dearly as possible.[3] In the opinion of a weighty historian,[4] " it is most unlikely that even one of the defenders of Drogheda had had a share in the Ulster butchery." Some of the survivors who had sought a refuge in two towers were more mildly treated by Cromwell. When they were at last forced to surrender only the officers of one of the towers were put to death whilst every tenth man of the rest and the entire garrison of the second tower were shipped to the Barbados islands.[5]

After this Cromwell turned to the coastal town of Wexford whose inhabitants had inflicted severe damage on English maritime trade. After the capture of the town the horrors of Drogheda were repeated. At Wexford priests and friars were massacred without pity and a general butchery followed which Cromwell and his officers refused to stop. A number of the unhappy people sought to escape by water but the overcrowded boats overturned and three hundred of the helpless fugitives were drowned. In his revolting Puritan jargon Cromwell threw the responsibility for his deeds of horror on divine justice.[6]

Cromwell then turned South, to Munster, where the Protestants were strong whilst Inchiquin's troops only

---

[1] *Ibid.*, 131–7.

[2] *Ibid.*, 138 *seq.*

[3] *Cf. ibid.*, 140, 175.

[4] *Ibid.*, 139.

[5] *Ibid.*, 134 *seq.* On the evidence of Anthony Wood, *ibid.*, 135, note 1.

[6] *Ibid.*, 140–8. " The horrors of the Irish war turn the judgment of even well-meaning biographers against the general," says WOLF MEYER-ERLACH (*Cromwell*, Munich, 1927, 28).

reluctantly fought by the side of their Catholic allies and
many officers had a traitorous understanding with Cromwell.[1]
The first place he encountered in his advance was the small
town of New Ross. Its commander declared his willingness
to admit him on condition that the garrison might freely
withdraw together with such citizens as chose to accompany
them, and that those who remained should enjoy freedom of
conscience. " I don't meddle with anyone's conscience,"
Cromwell replied, " but if by freedom of conscience is meant
freedom for the Mass, there can be no such liberty wherever
the Parliament of England is in power."

When Cromwell left Ireland on May 26th, 1650, the subjuga-
tion of the whole island was only a question of time. The
English were amply provided with everything whereas
the Irish lacked indispensables ; thus, for instance, during the
siege of Clonmel the Irish garrison fought heroically but in
the end it had to make its escape under cover of the night
because its stock of powder was exhausted.[2]   Moreover on
November 6th, 1649, the Irish lost their best general, O'Neill,
by death.[3] Cromwell's successor Ireton, and after the latter's
death on December 2nd, 1651, Ludlow, took one strong place
after another, and by the beginning of 1653 nearly all the Irish
army leaders had surrendered.[4] By then Ireland had suffered
the loss of a third of its population not only by the sword but
probably quite as much through lack of food, a situation
which was systematically brought about [5] by the English
cutting down the growing corn in the fields : on one occasion
eighteen thousand sickles were dispatched to them for that
purpose.[6]

Besides hunger and pestilence England's mightiest ally was
the lack of unity among the Irish. Their one rallying centre
was the Bishops but even they were divided in consequence

[1] GARDINER, I., 105 seq.
[2] Ibid., 174.
[3] Ibid., 155 seq.
[4] Ibid., II., 36–63.
[5] Ibid., 62.
[6] BELLESHEIM, II., 532.

of their attitude for or against Rinuccini. In the long run
the prelates could not fail to realize the disastrous consequences
of such a situation, hence at a meeting at Clonmacnoise they
issued a manifesto to the nation [1] in which they declared that
henceforth there would be no discord among them where the
rights of the Church were concerned, and that in future they
would stand as one man for the King and their people.
Shortly before, the assembly had warned the people against
Cromwell as the latter aimed at no less, so they declared,
than the destruction of the Catholic religion by means of
massacre, banishment and expropriation of the Catholics.
By the terms of a parliamentary resolution their possessions
were already forfeit and it was only a question of carrying
the decision into effect ; for considerations of prudence the
common people were being spared for the time being, but
once the conquest was completed, they too would be dis-
placed by English immigrants. The number of those who
had been transported to Barbados provided an eloquent
commentary on the last point.[2]

No one knew better than Cromwell that this language was
the plain truth, without any exaggeration whatever, but
perhaps for that very reason he decided " to enlighten a
deluded and misguided people " by means of a public explanation.[3] According to him the English were peaceful lambs
who had come over to Ireland, bringing with them nothing
but blessings. Profound peace had reigned in the land until
the wild natives suddenly fell upon and massacred their
benefactors and thus brought upon Ireland all the calamities
that have befallen it ever since.

Whether by such phrases Cromwell succeeded in quieting
his own conscience is an idle question ; words from his
mouth had long ceased to impress the Irish and to this day
his name is held in execration in Ireland.[4] Unfortunately the

---

[1] Of December 13, 1649, *ibid.*, 486 ; GARDINER, *Commonwealth*,
I., 162.

[2] *Ibid.*

[3] In January, 1650, *ibid.*

[4] BONN, II., 21.

words of the Bishops remained likewise without effect. Once again the prelates intervened in the destinies of Ireland when at an assembly at Jamestown, on August 12th, 1650, they dealt with the evil genius of the Irish rebellion, Ormond, the equivocal representative of the King, by forbidding, under pain of excommunication, all intercourse with him.[1]   In effect Ormond was compelled to give up his post and to leave the country, his place being taken by Lord Clanricarde, a Catholic.[2] However, this change of personnel could no more alter the fate of Ireland than the appeals for help to the Duke of Lorraine.[3] The subjection of Ireland went on apace and on its completion there took place what the Bishops had predicted for the unhappy land.

As the prelates had reminded their flocks, a parliamentary resolution had been passed in the course of the year following the rising of 1641, by the terms of which two and a half million acres of Irish soil were declared forfeit in favour of the men who would advance money to the Government for the conquest of Ireland.[4] As the triumph of Parliament was drawing near, the execution of this measure was being studied.[5] On April 17th, 1652, a meeting of officials and citizens prayed that action be taken, otherwise they would have to fear the anger of God inasmuch as England had treated the Irish too leniently.[6] Accordingly, on August 12th, 1652, Parliament passed an act of expropriation [7] which, assuredly, was well calculated to allay all the scruples of these tender consciences. The act was Ireland's death warrant. It divided its inhabitants into eight classes ; the first five included all those who had been in any way concerned in the rising and the bloodshed of 1641 ; as such the following were singled out before the rest :

[1] GARDINER, *loc. cit.*, II., 40.

[2] *Ibid.*, 44.

[3] *Ibid.*, 44 *seq.* ; BELLESHEIM, 498 *seqq.*

[4] BONN, II., 7.

[5] Since 1651 ; GARDINER, III., 297.

[6] *Ibid.*, 303.

[7] Table of contents, *ibid.*, 298 *seqq.* ; BONN, II., 29 *seqq.* ; text in LINGARD, X., 422–8.

the members of the General Assembly of Kilkenny, the Jesuits and other priests instigated by the Pope and a list of others mentioned by name. Other classes included those who had killed or had had a share in the killing of any man, not in battle, especially if the victim was an Englishman, and lastly those who did not lay down their arms within twenty-eight days. These five classes were condemned to lose life and property ; in this way sentence of death was passed in cold blood on over one hundred thousand persons.[1] Of persons not included in these five classes a small number, who had held higher offices, were condemned to banishment and the loss of two-thirds of their landed property ; in exchange for the remaining third, land of equal value would be assigned to their families at Parliament's pleasure. The soldiers of the regular army were also allowed to exchange the third of their property in the same way, on condition that they laid down their arms. Persons who had resided in Ireland since the rebellion and had not taken sides with Parliament between August, 1649, and March 1st, 1650, were assigned land in some part of Ireland to the value of two-thirds of what they had owned until then. Lastly there came a milder disposition for those whose possessions amounted to less than ten pounds. They were to forfeit neither life nor goods provided they did not fall into any of the above classes and that they laid down their arms. The preamble of the Act contains the not superfluous remark that it was not Parliament's intention to destroy the whole Irish nation and that this was the reason why the common people were more leniently dealt with.

However, considerations such as these could scarcely benefit anyone except those whose only crime was that they had served in the Irish army.[2] But it was precisely these people whom it was hoped to get rid of by the offer of emigration. In effect some 34,000 Irish soldiers chose to leave a country

[1] " No such deed of cruelty was ever contemplated in cold blood by any State with pretence to civilization," says GARDINER (III., 299). BONN tries to find excuses (II., 31 note).

[2] GARDINER, III., 302.

which was no longer theirs and to take service with the
armies of France, Spain, Austria and Venice.[1] On January
6th, 1653, a decree was published ordering all priests to
leave the country within twenty days, under pain of being
treated as traitors.[2] A reward of five pounds was promised to
anyone capturing a priest. " Three beasts we have to destroy,"
Major Morgan observed in Parliament in 1657, " the first is
the wolf, the second the priest, the third the Tory." [3] The
name " Tory " was given to those Irishmen who, when
driven from their own homesteads, withdrew into the bog
and joined forces with robber bands ; they became objects
of such terror for those who had deprived them of their
property that a price of fifty pounds was placed on the head
of a Tory.[4] In order to get rid of yet more Irishmen, they
were packed in large numbers on boats that carried them off
to the West Indies, more particularly to Barbados. From
a Government ordinance of March 4th, 1655, we learn that
in the course of the four previous years 6,400 men, women
and children were taken across seas ; poor people, we read
in this document, should be attracted into lonely places and
then taken aboard ship by force.[5] Ostensibly only tramps
and beggars, workless and unemployed were to be transported
to America,[6] but a similar fate befell even persons of the more
privileged classes.[7] Once arrived in the colonies the victims
of transportation were first compelled to work for some years
in order to pay for the cost of the voyage [8] ; after that they
were put out to service, but for a time at least their lot was
worse than that of real slaves.[9] Recourse was had to yet

---

[1] *Ibid.*, 297 ; LINGARD, X., 365 *seq.*

[2] BELLESHEIM, II., 517.

[3] *Ibid.*, 519.

[4] LINGARD, X., 369.

[5] BELLESHEIM, II., 530 *seqq.*

[6] GARDINER, III., 331 *seq.*

[7] BELLESHEIM, *loc. cit.*

[8] GARDINER, III., 332.

[9] *Ibid.*, 162, note. GARDINER denies that those thus deported
could be regarded as slaves ; but from the texts quoted by him

another means with a view to procuring a preponderance of Protestants and Englishmen in Ireland. In 1654 all the Catholic inhabitants of Kilkenny, Wexford and Clonmel, with few exceptions, were compelled to take up their abode outside the city walls. In 1655 a decree was published ordering all " papists and other superfluous Irishmen " to be driven from Dublin, and in the same year every healthy Irishman was ordered to leave the city of Galway.[1] In addition to all this the greater part of the cost of the subjection of Ireland, which amounted to 3,509,396 pounds, namely the sum of 1,942,548 pounds was to be raised by the Irish themselves,[2] that is, by the Irish who, on the Royal Commission's own evidence,[3] were reduced to feed on herbs and carrion in their uncultivated, ravaged land, who died of hunger on the highways, and whose abandoned children fell a prey to the wolves. " Taxation," a contemporary writer of the name of Gookin reports,[4] " takes all they possess, and when want has turned them into robbers and ' Tories ', they are hunted with fire and sword. Failure to denounce a Tory leads them to the gallows at the hands of the English, denunciation brings them death at those of the Irish, and if anyone with a heart in his breast shows them the small meed of pity that the law allows, he is accused of favouring the Tories."

For a time the colonization law of 1652 presented the English Statesmen with almost insuperable difficulties. It

(*ibid.*, 161, note 2) it is clear that traders sold Irishmen in America whom they had bought in Ireland at 20 shillings per head (BELLES-HEIM, II., 527). RICHARD BAGWELL (*Encyclopædia Britannica*, XIV.[11], 778) reckons that 9,000 Irishmen were deported to the West Indies " practically into slavery ". The texts in BELLESHEIM prove nothing as to the conditions beyond seas, but they do prove the atrocities committed by the Government in Ireland.

[1] GARDINER, III., 335. " To weaken Papists and to strengthen Protestants was the chief object of the Government in Dublin and Westminster," says GARDINER (*ibid.*, 335 *seq.*).

[2] *Ibid.*, 306 *seq.*

[3] *Ibid.*, 307 *seq.*

[4] *Ibid.*, 307.

was easy, on paper, to condemn one hundred thousand people to the gallows, but it was not possible to carry out the sentence in practice. A tribunal was set up for the purpose of punishing those involved in the murders of 1641, and this body shed blood enough on its tour of the country,[1] though it is unlikely that the number of the victims went much beyond a few hundreds.[2] Colonization itself made no progress until Cromwell took the matter into his own hands. Besides the " Knights of fortune " it was necessary to provide land for the soldiers of the British army which was breaking up ; to make room for them, the natives of Ulster, Leinster and Munster were to be transported to barren Connaught and Clare, in the West of Ireland.[3] However, this plan also could not be carried into effect for Connaught and Clare could not absorb such a multitude of exiles and though the new proprietors from England were afraid of their Irish neighbours, they had to admit that without native labour there could be no agriculture in Ireland ; accordingly the authorities contented themselves with settling in Connaught the Irish landowners and the few remaining soldiers of the Irish army,[4] though this was no real solution of the problem. The ghost of murdered Ireland was about to haunt the murderer for centuries to come.[5]

---

[1] *Ibid.*, 296 *seq.* LINGARD, X., 364 *seq.*

[2] Perhaps " 200–300 notorious criminals ", says GARDINER (III., 312).

[3] Acts of Parliament of September 26, 1653. GARDINER, III., 311 ; BONN, II., 45 *seqq.*

[4] GARDINER, III., 306–341.

[5] Since the end of the Middle Ages, says KATTENBUSCH in *Studien und Kritiken*, the story of Ireland is the " story of great misery, of the gradual but conscious destruction of an ancient and rich civilization by a people in whose way that civilization stood ".

CHAPTER IV.

INNOCENT'S WORK WITHIN THE CHURCH—THE JUBILEE YEAR.

(1.)

WITH regard to Innocent X.'s purely spiritual activities [1] mention must be made, in the first instance, of his efforts on behalf of the religious Orders. The reform of the Benedictine Congregation of Montecassino falls into the opening period of his pontificate.[2] The Society of the Clerics Regular of the Pious Schools founded by Joseph Calasanzio was subjected to a visitation and approved as an Association of secular clerics. In 1647 Innocent dissolved the union between the Doctrinarians and the Somaschans so that the former became once more an independent body.[3] The Pope also approved the reform of the Calced Carmelites of Monte Santo in Sicily. In France he united, in 1646, the Congregation of Val des Ecoliers with that of St. Geneviève of Paris. In 1647 he approved the Congregation of Priests of the Blessed Sacrament founded in 1623 by Christoph d'Authier at Marseilles ; these priests devoted themselves to the work of popular missions and the conduct of Seminaries. The founder of the Eudists,

---

[1] About the additions of feasts in the Calendar made by Innocent X., see BÄUMER, *Brevier*, 511.

[2] See *Bull.*, XV., 329.

[3] See HEIMBUCHER, II., 274, 341. On April 14, 1646, the nuncio in Poland was informed that the measure concerning the *Scuole pie* had been taken by a Congregation after mature consideration ; on June 9, 1646, the Secretary of State writes that the Jesuits have had no part in it (Nunziat. di Napoli, 39 A., Pap. Sec. Arch.). On the interests of Poland in the clerics of the *Scuole pie*, see A. CHECCUCCI, *Alcune lettere di S. Giuseppe Calasanzio*, Roma, 1852, 5 *seq.*, 13 *seq.*

Jean Eudes, received the Pope's encouragement in his under-takings.[1] He also warmly praised and encouraged the Congregation of secular priests founded by Bartholomew Holzhauser (*obiit* 1658), the object of which was to repair the ruins of the Thirty Years' War by renewing and furthering the priestly life, but the Society never received canonical approbation. The Cologne nuncio Sanfelice and the Elector of Mayence, Johann Philipp von Schönborn, gave their encouragement to the Association.[2] The Jesuits received a Brief on January 1st, 1646, shortly before the election of the new General Vincenzo Carafa ; this document ordered the holding of a General Congregation every nine years whilst it restricted the Superiors' term of Office to three years, with the sole exception of the novice master.[3]

In Italy there existed a great many monasteries which no longer fulfilled their original purpose owing to the small number of their inmates. The Pope sought accurate information on the situation which was fraught with serious drawbacks, and he set up a special Congregation to deal with the matter.[4] Reforms began in 1649.[5] In 1650 and 1651 a number of Societies were suppressed, among them the Clerics Regulars of the Good Jesus which had shrunk to only ten members,[6] and on October 15th, 1652, a Bull was published ordering the suppression of such Italian monasteries as, owing to reduced membership, no longer fulfilled the aim of their original founders ; their property was to be applied by

---

[1] See *ibid.*, I., 413 ; II., 18, 364, 371, 373.

[2] See HUNDHAUSEN in *Freib. Kirchenlex.*, VI.[2], 185 *seq.*

[3] See *Bull.*, XV., 436.

[4] See *Bull.*, XV., 647 ; De Rossi, *Istoria, Vat.* 8873, Vatican Library. On this matter, *cf.* also the " *Relatione dello stato della religione de' chierici regolari Teatini fatta l'anno 1650 ", Theatine Archives, Rome, *Cass.*, 38, compiled in consequence of the Bull of December, 1649.

[5] See Deone, *Diario*, 1649, *Cod.* XX., III., 21, Bibl. Casanat., Rome.

[6] See *Bull.*, XV., 372, 670, 677 *seqq.*

the Bishops to other pious purposes.[1] There can be no doubt
that the measure was fully justified, yet it failed to please
the various Italian Governments whose Cæsaro-papalistic
ambitions had involved them in many disputes with the
Pope.[2] The Republics of Venice and Genoa offered open
resistance and some heated remonstrances ensued. To
the Genoese ambassador the Pope bluntly declared that the
Republic was not at all interested in the reform of the
monasteries ; all it aimed at was to make itself independent
in the ecclesiastical sphere, as Henry VIII. had done in
England. When the Genoese ambassador referred to the
" proverbial piety " of the Genoese, Innocent X. interrupted
him with the words " What piety ? We are not speaking of
the churches, pious foundations and other external manifesta-
tions, but of submission to the Apostolic Authority to which
your Government seeks to subtract itself by all manner of
pretexts and artifices ".[3]

Though the Governments of Florence, Savoy, Parma,
Modena and Lucca outwardly submitted to the Bull, they
left nothing undone to frustrate its effect.[4] At Naples the
measure had already been carried into effect and the Bishops
had taken over the property of the suppressed monasteries,
when the Viceroy unexpectedly intervened and claimed the
property for the State on the plea of the lack of the *Exequatur*.[5]
In the sequel there were those in Rome who demanded that

---

[1] See *ibid.*, 696 *seqq.* Cf. *Arch. Rom.*, XXXII., 218.

[2] *Cf.* BERCHET, II., 136, 152 *seq.* On the conflict with the nuncio
in Florence, see REUMONT, *Toskana*, I., 515 ; for that of Genoa,
see *Riv. Europea*, 1878, V., 692. See also *Cifre al Nuntio di
Torino of 1645 in *Nunziat. di Napoli*, 39 A, Pap. Sec. Arch.,
and the Brief to Duke Carlo Emanuele of September 18, 1649,
Epist., IV.-VI., *ibid.*

[3] See NERI, *Corrispond. di F. Raggio*, in the *Riv. Europea*,
1878, V., 691. *Cf.* also PALLAVICINO, *Alessandro VII.*, I.,
408 *seq.*

[4] See DE ROSSI, *Istoria, Vat.* 8873, Vatican Library.

[5] See *ibid.* Cf. PADIGLIONE, *Bibl. di Museo Naz. di S. Martino*,
Naples, 1876, 349.

Naples should be laid under an interdict.[1] However, things did not go so far and Philip IV. promised the nuncio to remedy the situation.[2]

(2.)

The jubilee of 1649, proclaimed by the Bull of May 4th, 1649,[3] and carefully prepared for,[4] opened on Christmas Day. It proved an inspiring manifestation of Catholic life. The Pope opened the Holy Door at St. Peter's in person whilst a similar ceremony was being carried out at St. Paul's by Cardinal Lante, at the Lateran by Cardinal Colonna and at St. Mary Major by Cardinal Maidalchini. Such was the concourse at St. Peter's that the military had to be called out to maintain order, whilst at St. Mary Major, where this precaution had not been taken, Cardinal Maidalchini was in danger of being crushed by the crowd.[5]

Innocent X. eagerly participated in the exercises prescribed for gaining the Indulgence : he visited the four prescribed churches on no less than sixteen occasions and not even bad weather deterred him from making these visits. In order to set a good example all the Cardinals, even the eighty years old Lante, made their visits to the churches on foot. Cardinals Giovan Battista Altieri, Francesco Rapaccioli, Juan de Lugo, Vincenzo Maculano and Luigi Capponi preached at S. Marcello,

---

[1] See DE ROSSI, *Istoria, loc. cit.

[2] *Letter of the Spanish nuncio, dat. Madrid, 1653, August 6, Nunziat. di Spagna, 105, Pap. Sec. Arch.

[3] See Bull., XV., 628 seqq. (cf. 632 seqq.) ; G. S. RUGGIERI, Diario dell' anno del S. Giubileo 1650, 2 seqq. On October 15, 23 and 25, 1649, respectively, Briefs were sent to the Emperor, to all the Catholic Princes and to the Bishops exhorting them to promote Jubilee pilgrimages to the utmost of their power. Epist., IV.-VI., Pap. Sec. Arch.

[4] See Deone, *Diario, Cod. XX., III., 21, Bibl. Casanatense, Rome.

[5] See Servantius, *Diaria, Pap. Sec. Arch. Cf. also the copper-plate engravings of FR. BOSONI.

and the Pope also summoned distinguished preachers from outside Rome.[1]

On January 20th, 1650, the Pope received in solemn audience the Duke of Infantado, Philip IV.'s ambassador, who displayed characteristic Spanish pomp on the occasion.[2] His suite consisted of 300 carriages whilst the extraordinary envoy of the Spanish King's wife, Marianna of Austria, came with a suite of 160 carriages when he presented himself for his audience on January 28th.[3]

Notwithstanding the continuation of the war between France and Spain and the tension in Italy arising out of Spanish military preparations, crowds of pilgrims came from all parts, among them even princely personages. Thus spring saw the arrival of the sons of the Grand Duke of Florence, Princes Matthias and Leopold, who travelled incognito. The Princes spent some time in Rome and for five days (20–25th April) they lodged at the Vatican.[4] Princess Margaret of Savoy arrived in May ; she was dressed and travelled as an ordinary pilgrim and lodged at the Convent of Tor de' Specchi. It is related that it was with difficulty that Olimpia succeeded in persuading the Princess to receive her.[5]

During the Holy Week and Easter services the splendour and majesty of the Church's liturgy were seen in all their

[1] See the *Avvisi of 1650, especially that of December 3, Pap. Sec. Arch. Cf. Deone, January 12, 1650, in CIAMPI, 74, and *Diario, Barb. 4819, March 12, 1650, Vatican Library ; MANNI, 200 seq.

[2] Cf. Deone, *Diario, loc. cit.

[3] See RUGGIERI, 36, 38. Cardinal Albornoz, who had represented Spain up till then, died towards the end of 1649, as also the representative of the Emperor, Duke Federigo Savelli ; Deone writes : " *ambedue i più esperti ambasciatori che vedesse mai Roma " (Diario, loc. cit.).

[4] See *Report of Vinc. Roseo, dated 1650, April 9, Gonzaga Arch., Mantua ; Servantius, *Diaria, Pap. Sec. Arch., and Alaleone, *Diarium, Vatican Library.

[5] See Servantius, loc. cit., *Alaleone, loc. cit. ; RUGGIERI, 134 ; ADEMOLLO, G. Gigli, 123 seqq.

overwhelming grandeur. The Pope took a personal part in all the functions ; on Maundy Thursday he performed the ceremony of the washing of the feet in the Sala Ducale but he likewise washed the feet of poor pilgrims in the hospital of Trinità de' Pellegrini.[1] The many Confraternities of the Eternal City vied with one another in the adornment of their churches. The altar of repose in the Spanish national church of S. Giacomo surpassed even that of the Vatican basilica ; hundreds of lamps and candles formed a resplendent crown of glory around it. The Pantheon, the interior of which was adorned with religious pictures and thousands of lights, presented a fairylike spectacle. At the Good Friday procession the magnificent new banners of the Campo Santo attracted much notice ; 12,500 pilgrims were counted in the procession of the Confraternity of Trinità de' Pellegrini.[2]

Universal admiration was aroused by the decoration of Piazza Navona for the procession which was held there by the Spanish Confraternity of the Resurrection in the early hours of Easter Sunday morning (April 17th). This ceremony, in which the Spanish ambassador was wont to take a conspicuous part, had fallen into abeyance during the pontificate of Urban VIII. The Roman Carlo Rinaldi turned the ancient *circus* of Domitian into a court surrounded by columns entwined with garlands of foliage and illumined by 1,600 lights. Choirs of singers were stationed in the centre. At each end rose a magnificent pavilion given by the Castilians and the Aragonese ; in one was seen a figure of the risen Saviour, in the other that of His Blessed Mother. A contemporary declared that this exhibition, of which a copper engraving by Dominique Barrière has preserved a faithful picture, was by itself alone worth the journey from Spain to Rome.[3]

---

[1] See RUGGIERI, 75, 78 *seq.*

[2] See DE ROSSI, *Istoria, Vat.* 8873, Vatican Library ; Deone, *Diario, loc. cit.* ; RUGGIERI, 78 *seq.,* 81.

[3] See *DE ROSSI, loc. cit.* ; Deone, *Diario, loc. cit.* ; RUGGIERI, 88 ; JUSTI, *Velasquez,* II., 166 *seq.* ; HEMPEL, *Rainaldi,* 26 *seqq.*

Already by Easter the number of pilgrims was reckoned at 70,000.[1] May witnessed the arrival of Confraternities from all parts of Italy, each with its own insignia and accompanied by the clergy and the civil authorities ; the insignia of the Orvietans were the most admired of all.[2] Unfortunately some regrettable quarrels and collisions occurred between the various Confraternities on account of questions of precedence and even here the great political divergences manifested themselves ; thus the Archconfraternity of the Madonna del Gonfalone was favoured by the French whilst that of S Marcello enjoyed the support of the Spaniards. Regrettable incidents were also provoked by the conduct of Spanish recruiting agents. When these interfered even with some of the pilgrims, the latter beat them with their own silver-mounted sticks off St. Peter's square and dragged them to prison. The following threat was posted up on Pasquino : " Masaniellos are born in Rome also ".[3] The resentment of the Romans against the Spaniards rose so high that the latter scarcely dared to show themselves in the streets and the Pope experienced the utmost difficulty in maintaining order and tranquillity.[4] Though such incidents were bound to disturb the devotion of the pilgrims, they did not spoil the general impression of the jubilee. " If the innovators could see the devotion of the crowds, which included many men of education, as they went their way to the various shrines, they would not attack the institution of the jubilee," we read in the diary of a Roman of the time [5] ; in fact more

[1] See *DE ROSSI, loc. cit.

[2] Deone in CIAMPI, 75. RUGGIERI (103 seqq.) has very detailed accounts of all the entries. Cf. RIVETTI, Viaggio di un prete Bresciano a Roma nel 1650, in Brixia sacra, IV. (1913), 32 seqq.

[3] See DE ROSSI, loc. cit. ; ADEMOLLO, G. Gigli, 84 seqq. ; JUSTI, II., 165.

[4] Cf. the detailed description in Servantius, *Diaria on July 28, 1650, loc. cit., and the *Diario of AMEYDEN, loc. cit., p. 84 seq.

[5] *Diario in Barb. 4819, p. 56ᵇ, Vatican Library. Cf. also MANNI, 196, 202 seq.

than one non-Catholic visitor to Rome, such as Duke Johann Friedrich of Brunswick and Count Christoph of Rantzau, were so favourably impressed that they returned to the ancient Church.[1]

The total number of pilgrims was estimated at 700,000 [2] everyone of whom stayed in the Eternal City for at least a fortnight. The consequence was that prices rose at first, but the Pope intervened in order to save the pilgrims from being imposed upon. For poor Bishops he had set aside a special hospice in the Borgo.[3] As at former jubilees, this time also the hospice of Trinità de' Pellegrini distinguished itself; eventually a bronze bust of Innocent X. by Algardi was put up in the hostel in memory of the Pope's benefactions.[4] Even Olimpia put herself at the service of benevolence; she got forty-two ladies to collect money for the maintenance of the pilgrims; between them they collected 16,582 scudi, a sum sufficient to shelter and entertain in the above-mentioned hospice, for the space of three days, 226,711 men, 81,822 women and 25,902 convalescents.[5] The other Roman Confraternities also provided so generously for the entertainment of outside Confraternities affiliated to them, that a contemporary observed that on occasions like this the Romans did not only gain much, but they likewise expended much.[6]

The Pope did all in his power to assure the importation of

---

[1] *Cf.* above, p. 137.

[2] *Avviso* of December 31, 1650, Pap. Sec. Arch.

[3] See RUGGIERI, 15 *seq.*, 19 *seq.*, 21 ; NOACK, *Deutschtum in Rom*, 56.

[4] RUGGIERI, 75.

[5] See NOVAES, X., 32. According to the list in the appendix of Ruggieri the total expenses of the hospice amounted to 28,808 scudi, of which 26,539 scudi could be covered by alms. An engraving of FR. BOSONI represents the " funzioni principali, che si esercitano dalla arciconfraternità della S. Trinità di Roma nel albergare i peregrini 1650 ".

[6] DE ROSSI, *Istoria, loc. cit.* The engraving of FR. BOSONI represents " il modo che tengono le arciconfraternite e compagnie spirit. di Roma in alloggiar le compagnie aggregate, 1650 ".

provisions. On the occasion of his visits to the churches he showed such willingness to listen to those who drew near to him that the pilgrims were filled with admiration.[1]　On November 24th, 1650, he reduced the number of the prescribed visits to the churches and at the conclusion of the jubilee he extended it to the whole Catholic world for the following year.[2]

(3.)

In nine creations Innocent X. raised forty prelates to the purple ; most of them Italians.[3]　At his first creation, on November 14th, 1644, the red hat was bestowed on his

---

[1] DE ROSSI, *loc. cit.*

[2] See Servantius, **Diaria*, Pap. Sec. Arch. ; MANNI, 208 (here also particulars on the Jubilee coins). *Cf.* also BARBIER DE MONTAULT, *Une médaille du Jubilé de 1650*, Beauvais, 1900. The publications on the Jubilee are enumerated in MANNI (208 *seq.*). On the directors of the pilgrimages and on the publications on the Jubilee, see SCHUDT, *Mancini*, 126 *seq.* ; *Zeitschrift für Kunstgesch.* of SAUER, 1928, as also NOGARA, *Anno Santo*, Roma, 1928, 1092 *seq.* In the year 1650 appeared the following interesting work from the point of view of the history of art : " **Descrittione* delle pitture più insigni che si trovano nelle chiese di Roma come nelli palazzi e faciate di essi con li nomi dell' ecc. pittori che l'hanno depinte, compresovi il palazzo Pontificio Vaticano con la dichiaratione di alcune statue e nomi d' architetti," *Ottob.* 2975, Vatican Library. Here we read : " A mezzo Borgo Nuovo vi è una facciata di chiaroscuro con una Venere — è disegno di Santio."

[3] *Cf.* for what follows, CIACONIUS, IV., 667–705 ; CARDELLA, VII., 51–120. For G. C. Medici, see REUMONT, *Toskana*, II., 435, and G. PIERACCINI, *La stirpe de' Medici di Cafaggiolo*, II., 553 *seq.* Quite void of historical value is *La balance des cardinaux vivants*, Paris, 1652 (see about this satire, *Lettres de Richelieu*, II., 558, n. 2), in Italian *Genevra*, 1650, under the name of G. Leti, Castellana (Ginevra, 1656) ; *cf.* CIAMPI, 398. Retz' opinion on the Cardinals of Innocent X. in his *Mémoires*, II., 314.

nephew Camillo Pamfili and Gian Carlo Medici, the art-loving
brother of the Grand Duke of Tuscany, evidently because
Tuscany had furthered Innocent X.'s election. Medici had
previously nursed very different plans ; his worldly sentiments
and loose morals made him so unworthy of this high distinction
that he was eventually compelled to leave Rome. At this
first creation the Datarius Domenico Cecchini was named *in
petto* ; his elevation was not published till March 6th, 1645.[1]
Seven Cardinals were created on the same occasion : all of
them were thought to be decided supporters of Spain but
undoubtedly worthy of the high dignity to which they had
been raised ; they were the Bolognese Niccolò Albergati, a
kinsman of Gregory XV. and Archbishop of his native city ;
the Roman Tiberio Cenci, Bishop of Iesi ;   the Neapolitan
Pier Luigi Carafa, who had for many years successfully held
the nunciature of Cologne under the pontificate of Urban
VIII.,[2] after which he had done excellent work in his diocese
of Tricarico ; the Genoese Orazio Giustiniani, at first Bishop
of Montalto, then of Nocera, a warm friend of the Oratorians ;
Alderano Cibo, a scion of the princely House of Massa-
Carrara,[3] Innocent X.'s maggiordomo ; the Roman Federigo
Sforza and Benedetto Odescalchi of Como. Francesco Maria
Farnese, reserved *in petto*, was proclaimed on December 14th,
1645.

The Pope's former relations with Poland—as Cardinal he
had been Protector of that Kingdom—explain the elevation,
on March 28th, 1646, of John Casimir, King Sigismund III.'s
son who, however, had to lay aside the purple on July 6th,
1648, when he was elected King of Poland.[4]

---

[1] Cf. *Arch. Rom.*, X., 308 *seq.* On Tuscany's good relations
with Innocent X., see the *Report of the Florentine ambassador
of February 1, 1645, State Archives, Florence.

[2] Cf. the present work, Vol. XXVIII., 162 *seqq.*

[3] Cf. L. Mussi, *Il Cardinal Alderano dei principi Cibo-Malaspina*,
Massa, 1913 ; E. Jovy, *Les archives du card. A. Cibo à Massa*,
Paris, 1918.

[4] See Theiner, *Mon. Pol.*, III., 439 *seq.*, 457 ; Ciaconius,
IV., 678 ; *Appendix* to Ciaconius, 26 *seq.* Cf. Pallavicino,

Another great creation of Cardinals took place on October 7th, 1647. On this occasion Mazarin, after protracted efforts, at last obtained the red hat for his brother Michel, since 1645 Archbishop of Aix.[1] The Spaniards had opposed him up to the last, but in vain ; all they secured was the nomination of Antonio d'Aragona, a candidate agreeable to their King though for the time being reserved *in petto*.[2] Of those raised to the Sacred College on this occasion only the Roman Francesco Savelli and the Venetian Cristoforo Vidman could be described as adherents of the House of Habsburg ; the rest were politically neutral : they were Francesco Cherubini, formerly Innocent's auditor during his nunciatures at Naples and Madrid [3] ; the Genoese Lorenzo Raggi, and the youthful Francesco Maidalchini. Camillo Astalli's elevation to the Sacred College on September 19th, 1650, has already been mentioned.[4]

All these creations were, however, insufficient to fill the gaps in the Church's supreme senate for from the time of Innocent X.'s election to the beginning of 1652, the death had taken place of no less than twenty Cardinals.[5] Accordingly,

I., 293 ; DAROWSKI, in the periodical *Przeglad polski*, 1897, II., iii. See also LÄMMER, *Zur Kirchengesch.*, 150 *seq.*

[1] *Cf.* above, p. 63.

[2] Published March 14, 1650.

[3] GIUSTINIAN calls Cherubini " un' angelo di bontà ". BERCHET, II., 157.

[4] *Cf.* above, p. 39.

[5] In 1645 died : F. de la Rochefoucauld, P. P. Crescenzi, Fr. Cennini, G. Borgia ; in 1646 : Valençay, D. Spinola, A. Barberini ; in 1647 : Fr. M. Farnese ; in 1648 : M. Mazarin and L. Falconieri (on the latter's marble tomb, see FORCELLA, VII., 39) ; in 1649 : A. Spinola, D. Giustiniani and Egidio Albornoz ; in 1650 : G. Mattei, M. Teodoli, C. Monti and Ant. de Aragonia ; in 1651 : Panciroli and C. Rocci ; in 1652 (January 20) : G. Verospi. See CIACONIUS, IV., 706, who also gives the names of those who died later. (On the tomb of Cardinal Bichi, who died in 1657, see TAURISANO, *S. Sabina tav.*, 20.) Not a few of these Cardinals left an excellent reputation behind them. Servantius, who is often very severe (*Diaria, Pap. Sec. Arch*).,

in a large scale creation of February 15th, 1652, Innocent X.
sought to complete the Sacred College once more.[1] A few
foreigners among the new members of the College of Cardinals
owed their elevation to consideration for the Great Catholic
Powers.   To France's and Spain's recommendation was due
the bestowal of the purple on the Archbishop of Paris, Gondi,
and on the Spanish Dominican Domingo Pimentel whose
tomb, designed by Bernini, may be seen in the church of the
Minerva in Rome.[2] The Emperor succeeded in forcing through
the nomination of the Landgrave Frederick of Hesse, a great-
nephew of Philip, the author of the religious cleavage in his
territory.[3] The remaining seven Cardinals were all Italians,
and among them the Secretary of State Chigi and the Auditor
of the Rota Pietro Ottoboni were by far the most distinguished
figures :   the former was destined to ascend the See of
Peter under the name of Alexander VII., the latter under
that of Alexander VIII.   Gian Girolamo Lomellini, Luigi
Alessandro Omodei and Marcello Santa Croce had rendered
distinguished services in the administration of the Pontifical
States.   Jacopo Corrado of Ferrara was distinguished both

praises Falconieri as " vir prudentissimus et maximae expecta-
tionis " ; of Spinola he says : " eius integerrima vita, qua ipse
magis cardinalatus dignitatem illustravit quam purpura ipsum
decorasset." Of Mattei he says : " Vir fuit summae virtutis,
maximi ingenii et prudentiae et non mediocris doctrinae.
Maioribus potitus est Sedis Apostolicae oneribus, et numquam
lassus, semper autem vigilans adhuc in minoribus Status ecclesiastici quietem sustinuit et ab omni perturbatione totis animi
viribus defendere studuit maxime dum pestis anno 1630 totam
fere depopulabatur Italiam ; tunc enim tanta fuit eius diligentia
et virtus, ut ex ipsius vigilantia maior pars ecclesiastici Status
propriam usque adhuc recognoscat integritatem."

[1] *Cf.* CIACONIUS, IV., 686.   See also the *dissertation of
G. RICCARDI of 1652, in *Cod.* C., III., 60, Chigi Library, Rome.

[2] See BERTHIER, *L'église de la Minerve à Rome*, Rome, 1910,
257 *seq* ; REYMOND, 111.

[3] See FRIEDENSBURG, *Regesten*, V., 95, 97 *seq.*, 99, 106 ; NOACK,
in *Zeitschr. für die Gesch. des Oberrheins*, LXXX. (1928),
341–386.

for his knowledge of the law and the holiness of his life.[1] Baccio Aldobrandi owed his elevation to his being a kinsman of Olimpia Aldobrandini. Two Cardinals reserved *in petto* were proclaimed on March 2nd, 1654 : they were the Genoese Lorenzo Imperiali who had forced seditious Fermo to surrender, after which he had become Governor of Rome, and Gilberto Borromeo, Secretary of the *Consulta*. On June 23rd, 1653,[2] in order to seal his reconciliation with the Barberini, the Pope bestowed the purple on Carlo Barberini.[3]

Innocent X.'s last creation, on March 2nd, 1654, added seven new members to the Sacred College. Unfortunately among them there were two whose elevation to so high an honour was as worthy of blame as the disastrous nominations of papal nephews. Carlo Gualtieri of Orvieto, a protégé of Cardinal Pamfili, was too young, whilst Decio Azzolini, sponsored by Olimpia, was indeed richly endowed,[4] but his moral conduct was not irreproachable.[5] On the other hand the remaining five were excellent men. Prospero Caffarelli and Ottavio Acquaviva d'Aragona had successfully worked in the administration of the Pontifical States ; Carlo Pio of Savoy, a nephew of Cardinal Carlo Emmanuele, had served Innocent X. in the capacity of treasurer. Giambattista

---

[1] See BERCHET, *Relaz. Roma*, II., 270 *seq*. The King of Poland, John Casimir, had used his influence on behalf of M. Santa Croce ; see THEINER, *Mon. Pol.*, III., 475.

[2] Not on February 19, 1652, as Cardella states (VII., 83) ; see *Acta consist.*, Pap. Sec. Arch.

[3] " *Il Tobia. Composizione musicale per Oratorio," was dedicated to Carlo Barberini by Benedetto Salvetti. *Barb.* 3661, Vatican Library.

[4] DE ROSSI (**Istoria*) extols his " vivacità innarrabile del suo spirito e leggiadro intelletto ". *Vat.* 8873, Vat. Library.

[5] See PALLAVICIO, I., 206. For Azzolini, *cf.* BILDT, *Christine de Suède et le card. Azzolino*, Paris, 1899. For the medals of Azzolini, see BILDT, *Les médailles Romaines de Christine de Suède*, Rome, 1908. A bust of Gualtieri from the Cappella del Corporale is now in the museum of the cathedral of Orvieto.

Spada[1] had been recommended to the Pope by Cardinal Francesco Barberini whilst Francesco Albizzi's excellent qualities were sufficient recommendation. Under Urban VIII. the latter had held the post of an assessor of the Inquisition and had accompanied Cardinal Ginetti on his legation to Germany. Innocent X.'s attention had been drawn to him by his great services to the Church as Secretary of the Congregation set up to deal with Jansenism.[2]

(4.)

As regards missionary work throughout the world, the pontificate of Innocent X. is less important than the reign of his predecessors Gregory V. and Urban VIII., but the Pamfili Pope nevertheless earnestly watched and furthered the cause of the apostolate to the heathen, hence the missions were able to register considerable progress during his reign.

With the foundation and endowment of Propaganda under his two predecessors, the foundation had been laid down, as far as Europe was concerned, of a new orientation and a more powerful development of missionary enterprise, but under Innocent these beginnings were to attain a much wider expansion. In this respect there was no pause even when, in 1649, the death occurred of Francesco Ingoli, the indefatigable secretary of Propaganda and its quickening spirit. His inspiration opened the new paths along which it was desired to develop missionary activities. Ingoli's plan was to place the missions under the immediate direction of Propaganda, to render them independent of the Colonial Powers, to employ secular priests and to create a native clergy in missionary countries.[3] Propaganda's vigilance over the missions extended likewise to the papal Colleges for the training of priests ;

---

[1] Cf. our account about him in Vol. XXVIII, 51. Extensive biography by SARDI, *Il cardinale G. B. Spada e il conclave del 1670*, Lucca, 1920, 6 *seq.*, 20 *seq.*

[2] Exact data about the Cardinals of the promotion of 1654 are given by De Rossi, *Istoria*, *loc. cit.* About Albizzi, *cf.* also below, Ch. VI.

[3] See KILGER, in *Zeitschr. für Missionswiss.*, XII., 27.

these institutions were to remain subject to canonical visitations.[1] Innocent X. appointed Dionisio Massari to succeed
Ingoli as Secretary to Propaganda. During the stay in France
of Cardinal Antonio Barberini,[2] Urban VIII.'s nephew,
Ludovico Capponi became Prefect of Propaganda, but on his
return Antonio Barberini resumed that position and retained
it until his death in 1671.[3]

Although we do not hear of any financial assistance of
Propaganda by the Pope, he nevertheless strengthened its
authority and confirmed its powers. In the Philippines the
decisions of Propaganda had been described as no more than
the opinions of some Cardinals ; thereupon Innocent X.
confirmed anew Urban VIII.'s decision that the decrees of
the Prefect and Secretary of Propaganda possessed the weight
of Apostolic Constitutions and were to be strictly observed
by all concerned.[4] The palace which served as Propaganda's
headquarters was further enlarged.[5] A number of ordinances

---

[1] See *Visite*, 26 *seq.* Archives of Propaganda, Rome. *Cf.*
" *Instruttione per li Nuntii per visitare i collegi soggetti alle
loro Nunziature conforme all' ordine di S. S^{tà} e della congreg.
di Propag. ", dated 1645, February 25, *Cod.* A. II., 48, p. 136 *seq.*
Bibl. Chigi, Rome. " *Chirografo di N. S. Innocenzo X. con
l'ordine fermo per le provisioni de seminarii sotto li 12 giugno
1646 : Al collegio Inglese in Duaco, già in Reims, scudi 175
moneta il mese." For the seminaries at Fulda, now in Cologne,
146 sc. and 5 soldi, for the seminary at Braunsberg 97 sc. and 10
soldi ; for the poor students of Propaganda 24 sc. ; for the
seminaries in Vienna, Prague, Olmütz, Dillingen, Vilna 115 sc.
respectively (Arch. of Propaganda, Rome, 362, p. 17). " *Stato
della s. congregatione de Propaganda fide of September 19,
1649 " (Expenses and Receipts), *Cod. Barb.* 5086, p. 25^{b}, Vat.
Library.

[2] *Cf.* above, p. 52.

[3] *Cf.* Moroni, XVI., 256 *seq.*

[4] See decree of June 30, 1652, in *Ius pontif.*, I., 280 ; *cf.*
Collectio S. Congregat. de Prop. Fide, I., 35 *seq.*, n. 119.

[5] *Cf.* Castellucci, in *Alma Mater Collegium Urbanum de
Prop. Fide*, 1927, III. (1921), and IV. (1922) ; Hempel, *Borromini*,
157 *seq.*

were issued for the internal consolidation of the institution :
thus the oath of the pupils who were ordained *ad titulum
missionis* (for the missions) was to bind them perpetually to
Propaganda ; in accordance with an ordinance of 1654, the
money for their journey was to be handed to them only on
completion of their studies.[1]

The Pope likewise intervened in the development of the
Carmelite Missionary Seminary in Rome when in 1647 he
approved the decision of the General Chapter to unite the
Seminary and the Provincial house of studies ; however, in
1650 he demanded their severance.[2] The centralization of
the missions to the heathen was decisively furthered by the
foundation of the society of secular missionary priests which
was already preparing in Paris.[3] The first impulse was given
by a Jesuit missionary from the Far East, Alexander Rhodes,
who petitioned Innocent X. to give Bishops to the Church of
Annam for, in the event of the expulsion of the missionaries
by the native Kings, that Church ran the risk of extinction.[4]
At one moment the Pope felt inclined to make Rhodes himself
a Bishop but the latter declined the honour on the ground of
his being a Jesuit ; consequently Innocent X. instructed him
to look for suitable men who might be sent as Bishops to the
Far East.[5] Propaganda amplified this scheme in the sense
that in 1650 it laid before the Pope a scheme for the erection
of twelve dioceses, under one or two Archbishops, and the
training of a native clergy for the Far Eastern Churches.[6]
After a vain search for suitable candidates for the episcopate
in Italy and Switzerland, Rhodes visited Paris in 1653. There

---

[1] See *Ius pontif.*, I., 97, 109, and *Collect.*, I., n. 112–122. About
the studies in the colleges see *Alma Mater*, 55 *seq.*

[2] See *Ius pontif.*, I., 250 *seq.* Cf. KILGER, in *Zeitschr. für
Missionswiss.*, 1915, 213.

[3] *Cf.* CERRI, *Estat présent de l'Église*, Rome, 1677, 300 *seq.* ;
JANN, 215 *seq.*, and KILGER, in *Zeitschr. für Missionswiss.*, 1922,
27 *seq.*

[4] LAUNAY, I., 8.

[5] *Ibid.*, 9.

[6] *Ibid.*, 10.

his fellow Jesuit, Bagot, introduced him to his small sodality of the Blessed Virgin, whose members declared their readiness to work for the spread of the faith and the foundation of new churches.[1] Innocent X., informed by Propaganda, ordered Bagno, the Paris nuncio, to choose from among the French clergy three priests whom he judged the most worthy of the episcopate. Bagno's choice fell on Pallu, De Laval and Pique, whilst the yearly endowment of 600 francs for each of them was soon raised, mainly through the generosity of Richelieu's niece, the Duchess of Aiguillon.[2] Portugal strongly opposed the appointment of French Bishops in territory included in its Patronage. With a view to circumventing this difficulty, the Archbishop of Rheims, together with St. Vincent de Paul and some other priests, petitioned the Pope in July, 1653, to refrain from erecting new dioceses in the Far East, and whilst having the selected secular priests consecrated Bishops, to send them forth merely as delegates of the Apostolic See.[3] The proposal was favourably received in Rome but remained without effect owing to a campaign against the French secular priests and the Pope himself was reported to have said, when commissioning Rhodes, " Above all, no Frenchmen ! " [4] Innocent X. died in 1655, leaving the execution of the project to his successor Alexander VII.[5] On the other hand the foundation of another missionary Society, which was likewise to contribute to the shifting of the centre of gravity of missionary activities towards France, viz. the Lazarists, still falls into the pontificate of Innocent X.

[1] *Ibid.*, 13.

[2] *Ibid.*, 15.

[3] *Ibid.*, 19 *seq.* On the protest of Portugal, *ibid.*, 15 *seq.*, and JANN, *loc. cit.*

[4] LAUNAY, I., 20.

[5] *Ibid.*, 21 *seq.* Rhodes went to Persia in 1654, without having achieved anything in Paris for the execution of the command of the Pope, so that he cannot be regarded as the founder of the Missionary Society of Paris. *Cf.* the controversy about this between HUONDER and SCHWAGER, in *Zeitschr. für Missionswiss.*, 1911, 291 *seq.*

for their founder, St. Vincent de Paul, sent missionaries to Algiers in 1640 and to Madagascar in 1648.[1] Missionary work was likewise greatly furthered when in 1649, at the request of the General of the Jesuits, Innocent X. granted a Plenary Indulgence to all persons who either converted an idolater in the Indies or overseas, or prayed for the conversion of infidels in a Jesuit church after receiving the Holy Eucharist, whilst the Pope also gave extensive faculties to the missionaries of the Society of Jesus.[2] To this period also belong the decisions of Propaganda authorizing missionaries to administer without leave of either Bishops or parish priests, those sacraments the dispensation of which was not the exclusive right of the latter (1647)[3]; another forbade missionaries to abandon their posts even in times of persecution, seeing that it was then that their flocks had most need of their presence (1646); finally it was decreed that the Prefects of Provinces might recall their missionaries to their respective convents after three years so as to preserve the religious spirit (1648).[4]

How firmly the religious Orders, not only the Jesuits but also, and that in a special manner, the Franciscans, clung to their missionary duties and privileges, may be gathered, to give but one instance, from the book of the Franciscan Raymond Caron on the work of evangelization by religious missionaries, in which he discusses the technique of the apostolate.[5] Statistics, obviously incomplete, of the year 1649, enumerate forty-six missions or prefectures subject to Propaganda with over 300 missionaries.[6]

In the East, Jesuits, Franciscans, Capuchins, Dominicans and Carmelites, in conformity with the Pope's efforts for

[1] See below, p. 197.
[2] *Ius pontif.*, I., 276 *seq.*; *cf. ibid.*, 111.
[3] *Collect.*, I., n. 116.
[4] *Ibid.*, n. 109–115.
[5] *Apostolatus evangelicus Missionariorum regularium per universum orbem expositus*, Antwerpiae, 1653. *Cf.* SCHMIDLIN, in *Zeitschr. für Missionswiss.*, I. (1911), 225 *seq.*
[6] See KILGER, in *Zeitschr. für Missionswiss.*, XII. (1922), 27.

reunion, continued to labour for the preservation of unity and the return of the schismatics.[1] Innocent X. confirmed the Constitutions of the Basilians in 1647[2]; the Jesuits established new houses in Ruthenian Poland, as for instance at Kieff in 1645,[3] and in Syria many Jacobites were brought back to Roman unity by Archbishop Andrew Abdelgal of Aleppo, himself a convert.[4] The Patriarch of the Maronites Joseph III. (1622–1647) had pronounced a sentence of excommunication against those Maronites who received the Sacraments at the hands of the missionaries of the Holy See, but in 1646 the Archbishop of Aleppo withdrew the sentence and the dispute itself was settled through the intervention of the French consul.[5] In order to preserve the loyalty of the Maronite people to the Holy See, Innocent X., with the help of a donation of the Maronite Victor Scialac, of Accon, founded and endowed a pontifical Maronite Seminary at Ravenna and placed it under Propaganda.[6] In 1655 the *Catholicos* Philip did homage to the Pope in the name of the

---

[1] The Visitation of the residence of the Jesuits in Constantinople ordered by Propaganda (April 22, 1647), showed that the Jesuits laboured much among the Catholics and also among the Greeks, who liked to go to confession to them. (*Visite*, 29 [1648], Archives of Propag., Rome.) On January 22, 1648, Propaganda bestowed great praise on the Jesuits who had residences also in Smyrna, Naxos, Santorin and Paros. The Visitation of their residence in Chios (May 8, 1648), testifies to the excellent work of the Fathers but also to their poverty ; they were supported only by contributions from the Pope which they received since the time of Clement VIII. (*ibid.*).

[2] *Ius pontif.*, I., 273 seq.

[3] *Cf.* HERGENRÖTHER-KIRSCH, III.[5], 416.

[4] *Cf. ibid.*, 413. A " *Relation de ce qui s'est passé ès missions de Syrie de la Comp. de Jésus de leur commencement [1625] jusques au bout de l'an 1651, in *Cod. Z.* 104 of The Hague Library.

[5] *Ius pontif.*, P. II., 102, n. 197.

[6] *Ius pontif.*, I., 260 seq. ; *Bull. Prop. App.*, I., 237 seq. ; *Bull. Taur.*, XV., 575 seq.

Armenians.[1] Among the Persian Chaldeans 40,000 families
were still Catholic in 1653,[2] whereas the Indian Chaldeans,
the so-called Christians of St. Thomas, at the instigation of
the Dutch, expelled the Jesuits in 1653, when they went over
in large numbers to the monophysite Jacobites.[3] In 1645, on
the advice of Propaganda, Innocent entrusted the administration of the Churches of both Circassias, and of those in
Mingrelia and Abbatia, to a neighbouring Bishop.[4]

In Africa the Copts and Abyssinians had relapsed into
schism so that the *Reformati* and the Capuchins dispatched
thither by Propaganda suffered a Martyrs' death.[5] For the
Christians of Barbary, on the recommendation of Propaganda,
the Pope appointed the French Lazarist Philip Le Vacher,
as Vicar Apostolic of Algiers where this disciple of St. Vincent
de Paul displayed the greatest zeal in ministering to the
Christian slaves and in converting the Mohammedans.[6] On
the coast of Guinea, in addition to the Augustinians (1646),
Spanish Capuchins likewise undertook missionary work under
the auspices of Propaganda, as for example in 1644, at
Commando where they were well received and baptized the
King's son. In 1645, under the Andalusian pro-provincial,
Caspar of Sevilla, they undertook work among the negroes

---

[1] HERGENRÖTHER-KIRSCH, III., 414.   A *Brief to the Shah
of Persia, dated July 13, 1652 (*Epist.*, VII.–VIII., Pap. Sec.
Arch.) recommends missionaries returning to Armenia.

[2] HERGENRÖTHER-KIRSCH, III., 411 *seq.*

[3] *Ibid.*, 410. *Cf.* MÜLLBAUER, 302.

[4] " Sigismundo episcopo Chersonensi in Tartaria Praecopensi,"
Ius pontif., I., 238 *seq.* In the regions of the Caucasus Carmelites
and at times also Jesuits, Capuchins and Theatines were at
work ; see SCHMIDLIN, *Missionsgesch.*, 222. In a *Letter to the
Princeps Mengrelliae (dated February 2, 1646), Innocent X.
expresses his thanks for the friendly reception of the Theatines
and for sending two young Mingrelians who will be educated
at the Propaganda. *Epist.*, II., Pap. Sec. Archives.

[5] See HERGENRÖTHER-KIRSCH, III., 412, 577 ; SCHMIDLIN,
Missionsgesch., 233, 371 ; LEMMENS, 180.

[6] *Ius pontif.*, I., 279, P. II., n. 107. *Cf.* SCHMIDLIN, 372.

of Senegal where they also met with a friendly reception ; in 1648 in Benin, where they converted the King, in Sierra Leone in 1652, with equal success, notwithstanding Portuguese opposition ; in 1655 in Overo where the ruler embraced Christianity.[1] Several large missionary expeditions of Italian Capuchins entered the kingdom of Congo, viz. five Fathers in 1646, thirty-one in 1648, forty-five in 1651, sixteen in 1654. From the Christian Queen Zinga they received powerful support whilst on the part of the Portuguese they met with grievous obstacles.[2] The Portuguese and the Mohammedans between them brought about the ruin of the mission in East Africa, though we read of a short-lived Augustinian mission to Melinda in 1644 and the conversion, by some Dominicans, of the " emperor " of Monomatapa.[3] The Lazarists landed in Madagascar in 1648 but their activity was hampered in many ways as a result of its being involved in France's colonial policy.[4] In India the Jesuits were still making thousands of converts, as in the territory of Madura, in

---

[1] Cf. ROCCO DA CESINALE, III., 502 seq. ; SCHMIDLIN, 229, 372. A decree of Propaganda of 1645 for the Andalusian Capuchins among the Negritos, in Ius pontif., P. II., n. 188.

[2] Cf. ROCCO DA CESINALE, III. ; SCHMIDLIN, 227, 373 ; CIAMPI, 242. Among the rare printed works of the Bibl. Casanatense, Rome, there is a copy of the " Breve relatione della missione dei frati minori Cappuccini al regno di Congo " (Roma, 1649), and " a copia della lettera del Re di Congo a S. Stà ", dated Congo, October 5, 1646. Pontifical Letters to the King of Congo on the dispatch of Capuchins, of November 10, 1645, May 20, 1648, January 14, 1651 and November 21, 1653, in Bull. Congr. Prop. Fide, VII., 24 seqq. In 1653 Propaganda decided that missionaries in the Congo could not exercise any missionary jurisdiction within five hours' walk of the districts of the parish priests without the latter's permission ; Ius pontif., P. II., n. 209.

[3] Cf. PIOLET, Les missions cath. franc., V., 470 ; KILGER, in Zeitschr. für Missionswiss., 1907, 103, and SCHMIDLIN, 231.

[4] SCHMIDLIN, 222, and the bibliography there quoted. A " *Lettera scritta dalli missionarii di Madagascar al sig. Vincenzo di Paolo sup. gen. d. frati delle missioni per darne parte alla S. Congreg. de Propaganda, 1650 ", in Barb. 4546, Vatican Library.

Tanjaur, Sattiamangalam and Tiruchirapalli,[1] in central Cochin, in Travancor, on the fishers' coast, in Canara, Bejapor and Bengal as well as at the court of the Great Mogul.[2] Franciscans, Dominicans, Augustinians, Carmelites, Theatines and Capuchins erected new houses besides the existing ones and made them the bases of their missionary undertakings.[3] Between 1645 and 1646 Fr. Rhodes was expelled from Cochin China where he had achieved splendid successes, but in 1646 two Jesuits returned thither and five others went to Tonkin where, between 1645 and 1646, 24,000 persons received baptism whilst 50,000 were converted in Cochin China, so that in a petition to Innocent X. of the year 1653, the French missionaries spoke of 200,000 Christians in the two kingdoms who were, however, deprived of spiritual help and longed for the advent of new shepherds.[4] On the other hand, of the missions in the islands, the only ones that survived were those in Ceylon where the king or emperor Mutale had been converted in 1644 [5]; in Sanguin where the Franciscans baptized the kings of Colonga and Tabuca [6] and in Solor where the Dominican Juan da Costa established the station of Baju in 1650 and received a number of pagans into the Church. On Timor heavy struggles began with the infiltration of the Dutch in 1648.[7] Lastly in the Philippines, Dominicans and Franciscans, Jesuits and Augustinians laboured together in strengthening the Christians and in an attempt at the definitive defeat of paganism. A decisive step towards this consummation was the act of November 20th, 1645, by

---

[1] See MÜLLBAUER, 204 seq., 208, 214, 225 seq., 228 seq.

[2] Ibid., 279, 284, 287, 294, 296.

[3] Ibid., 325 seq., 334, 341, 346, 352, 354. Cf. 365, on the Indo-Portuguese bishoprics of that time.

[4] LAUNAY, I., 19 seq. Cf. PACHTLER, Das Christentum in Tonkin und Cochinchina (1861), 62 seqq., 163 seq. RHODES caused also an Annamite Catechism to be printed in Rome ; SCHMIDLIN, 254.

[5] SCHMIDLIN, 255.

[6] CIVEZZA, VII., 2, 929 seq. ; SCHMIDLIN, 257.

[7] Cf. BIERMANN, in Zeitschr. für Missionswiss., 1924, 36, 41.

which Innocent X., at the request of the King of Spain, raised the Dominican College of St. Thomas at Manila to the status of a University where grammar, rhetoric, logic, philosophy and theology were taught and the academic degrees could be obtained.[1] In Japan Christianity had been destroyed together with the missionaries so that only a few pitiful remains lingered on in secret, though as late as 1646 Propaganda dispatched thither the secular priest Bonfilz and an Augustinian friar.[2]

In China the number of Christians had risen to 150,000 by 1650 so that in the following year Propaganda was

---

[1] *Bull. Taur.*, XV., 414 ; *Ius pontif.*, I., 242 *seq. Cf.* SCHMIDLIN, 263 *seq.*

[2] SCHMIDLIN, 286. *Cf. Kath. Missionen*, 1922–3, nr. 4. The " *Ragguaglio della missione del Giappone tratto dall'ultima lettera annua del 1649 scritta in lingua Portoghese " says of the College of Macao that " È egli il capo della provincia del Giappone e seminario de' suoi missionanti, campo ancora e teatro in cui essi per apparecchio alle lor gloriose imprese si esercitano, collegio nel quale vivon soggetti di zelo e di fervor si grande che alcuni di lor pregarono instantissimamente quest'anno il Provinciale a far veduta di licentiarli come discoli della Compagnia e dar loro le vesti di secolo, acciochè creduti di non esser dell'ordine potessero acconciatisi per servi a' mercanti Olandesi haver franco passaggio nel Giappone, se bene per saggi riguardi non fu loro in ciò acconsentito. . . . È ivi anche un seminario fondato da un prete Giapponese con capital di dodici mila tais. Quivi s'allevano i putti Giapponesi apprendendo tutto il necessario per ordinarsi sacerdoti e aprendosi il Giappone, entrarvi con la sufficenza sufficiente a predicare e risolver li dubi che occorrono. Si attende in Macao da nostri con sommo studio al bene spirituale de' prossimi, essendovi gran messe di Portughesi e di gente senza conto di altre nationi. Il concorso che in tutte le feste dell'anno è in nostra chiesa per confessarsi sembra un non intermesso giubileo. La pietà in cui per opera della Compagnia son venute le donne e le publiche penitenze che fanno, supera ogni credenza. I più nobili cittadini si ritirano spesso nel collegio a far esercitii spirituali di Sant'Ignatio, e ciò fanno specialmente nella quaresima fin a venti e più insieme." University Library, Freiburg, in Br. *Cod.* 274, p. 94.

considering a plan for a Chinese Patriarchate of twelve
dioceses with two or three archbishoprics.[1]   The Cologne
Jesuit Adam Schall maintained himself at Pekin even after
the overthrow of the Ming dynasty by the Manchurian
Tartars 1644 ; he won the goodwill of the new emperor Shung-
Ti and though love of pleasure prevented the latter's
conversion, he conceived a great esteem for the Christian
religion and frequently visited Schall.   The Jesuit took
advantage of his conversations and his epistolary commerce
with the emperor to wrest from him an ordinance favourable
to Christianity and to win for it the sympathies of the educated
classes.[2]

In southern China the Jesuits succeeded in converting the
emperor of the dethroned Ming dynasty who had fled thither,
together with three other members of the imperial family,
among them the empress' son.   The empress was given the
name of Helena in baptism and her son that of Constantine.[3]
The Vatican Archives still preserve the empress Helena's
letter to Innocent X. written on silk, but by the time that
document reached Rome the Pope was dead.[4]

[1] See *Rapporto delle missioni di Cina, *Scrit. rif.*, 1874, II.,
n. 596, Propaganda Archives, Rome. *Cf.* A. LAUNAY, *Hist. de
la mission de Chine*, Vannes, 1907 ; SCHWAGER, in *Zeitschr.
für Missionswiss.*, 1912, 207 *seq.* ; *Hist.-polit. Blätter*, CXXXIX.,
120 *seq. Cf.* above, p.   .

[2] See SCHALL, *Relatio de initio et progressu missionis Soc. Iesu in
regno Sinarum* (1665) ;   MARTINI, *Brevis relatio de numero et
qualitate christianorum apud Sinas* (1654).   *Cf.* SCHMIDLIN,
273.

[3] *Cf.* SCHMIDLIN, 273 *seq.*

[4] The remarkable *Document discovered by Mgr. Ugolini
(*cf. Antiquitäten-Zeitung*, 1911, 53), the authenticity of which was
attested by the Chinese ambassador in Rome, is in *Arm. VII.,
caps. III., 36, Pap. Sec. Arch., with a latin translation.   The
Empress writes that she learnt the Faith from Fr. Andrew Xavier,
" et ecce credidi " ;   likewise " regina imperatoris mater Maria,
regina eius legitima coniux Anna et filius imperatoris princeps
Constantinus ".   She sends the letter by " P. Andreas Xavier et
Michael Boym, S.J., in aula imperatoris pro tempore assistentes ",

After the heroic martyrdom in 1648 of the Dominican, Blessed Capillas, the Dominican Morales, with three companions and the Franciscan Antonio di S. Maria with two companions, returned to Fukien in 1649. In 1650 the latter went to Shantung where he opened the mission of Tsinanfu and many others.[1]

The controversy concerning the lawfulness of the veneration of ancestors which had begun under Urban VIII[2]., became more acute under Innocent X. At Manila, in the Philippines, the question was eagerly discussed. The Dominican Morales of Macao summed up the controverted points under twelve headings and the Franciscan Antonio di S. Maria did so under fifteen. On the part of the Jesuits it was chiefly Francisco Furtado who made it his business to reply to these writings.[3] A proposal by the Dominican Provincial, Clement Gan, to thrash out the whole question in a joint assembly of theologians of both Orders was declined by the Jesuit Provincial Manuel Diaz on the ground that he had already dispatched to Rome one of his subjects, Alvaro Semedo, with a view to obtaining from Propaganda directions for a uniform line of conduct for the missionaries.[4] Thereupon the Dominicans likewise had recourse to Rome. At a Provincial Assembly at Manila in 1640 they unanimously chose Morales

and she asks him to send more Jesuits (dated November 4, 1650). The *reply of Alexander VII. to " Helena Tamingue Sinarum regina ", dated December 18, 1655, is in *Epist.*, I., 282, Pap. Sec. Arch. *Cf. Arch. stor. ital.*, IV., Series XVII., 157.

[1] See the letters of Antonio of 1649 in MAAS, *Cartas de Cina*, I. (1917). *Cf.* SCHMIDLIN, 257.

[2] *Cf.* the present work, XXIX., 249.

[3] CASTNER, *Relatio ; BIERMANN, 65 ; FURTADO, *Informatio antiquissima*, Paris, 1700. Furtado defends the conduct of the Jesuits in a letter of November 10, 1636, to Vitelleschi, General of the Order (FURTADO, 8–13), and in 1640 he replied to the twelve questions of Morales (*ibid.*, 19–52). Both writings are translated in PRAY, I., 32–49, 51–103.

[4] BIERMANN, 50–63. Little is known of the mission of Semedo ; *cf. ibid.*, 66, n. 52.

for their representative. The latter sailed at once but only reached Rome towards the end of February, 1643 ; by that time Semedo had left the Eternal City.[1] A whole year went by before the seven *qualificators* of the Inquisition began their study of the question at fourteen sittings, from March 22nd to June, 1644. The decision was left to a Congregation of eight members under Cardinal Ginetti and at a later date under Cardinal Espada. Their final decisions were published by Propaganda at whose request the Inquisition had likewise taken up the matter.[2]

The queries which Morales submitted on behalf of the Dominicans and the Franciscans were summed up under seventeen headings ; the first five were concerned with the Commandments of the Church, such as fasting and so forth, the observance of which met with some difficulty on the part of the Chinese neophytes and the levying of taxes ; the two last were about prayers for the dead and the preaching of Christ crucified. The remaining points dealt with the burning question of co-operation in idolatrous acts.[3] The difficulties were presented in the form of queries, not as accusations against the Jesuits. However, a memorial of Morales to Propaganda, which forms a preamble to the seventeen queries,[4] makes some grave accusations against them. Morales starts from the danger of the Chinese missionaries becoming an occasion of spiritual ruin for the souls of the new converts ; in fact according to him that ruin was already at work in consequence of the quarrel of the Jesuits in China with the Dominican and Franciscan missionaries ; the Jesuits, he asserted, did not take to heart Urban VIII.'s warning to the missionaries, to pursue a uniform line of conduct. This

---

[1] BIERMANN, 66.

[2] *Ibid.*, 67.

[3] Decree of Propaganda of September 12, 1645, in *Collectanea*, I., 30–5, n. 114 ; *Bullarium Prop.* (1839 *seqq.*), I., 123 *seqq.*

[4] *Annales de la Société des soi-disans Jésuites*, III., Paris, 1767, 826.

introduction is in keeping with the eighteenth point [1] at the end of the seventeen. That additional point treats of the penalties which those missionaries are said to deserve who do, teach or tolerate any of the things enumerated in the seventeen points. Though the Congregation did not condemn the procedure described in the seventeen points from every point of view, on the whole its decision was in the sense of Morales' memorial : Propaganda's decree of September 12th, 1645 [2] contains a first condemnation of the Chinese rites.

Contrary to subsequent procedure, on this occasion the Congregation did not consider the question whether Morales' accusations were really justified by the facts. The accused denied it ; a pamphlet by the Jesuit Philippucci [3] enumerates no less than forty-two inaccuracies as forming the basis of the accusations. The offerings made to Confucius and to the ancestors were not, in his view, real sacrifices ; those who made them were not priests ; the rooms in which the offerings were presented were not temples with real altars, nor were prayers offered to Confucius and to the ancestors.[4] Philippucci and the Jesuits generally, strongly protested against the most odious accusation of all, which subsequently made the round of the world in Pascal's " Lettres Provinciales " [5] ;

[1] *Annales de la Société des soi-disans Jésuites*, III., 829, and *Morale pratique des Jésuites*, n. XXXI. (ARNAULD, *Œuvres*, XXXIV., 373). According to the *Annales*, III., 829, the intrigues of the Jesuits succeeded in suppressing the 18th question, " dont la resolution les eut notés et fait connoitre pour ce qu'ils ont été dans l'empire de la Chine. Un Prélat de Rome en envoya une copie faite sur l'original même, et c'est sur cette copie que nous donnons au public celle-ci.

[2] *Collect.*, n. 114.

[3] *De Sinensium ritibus politicis acta, seu praeludium ad plenam disquisitionem, an bona vel mala fide impugnentur opiniones et praxes missionariorum Soc. Jesu*, Lugd.-Parisiis, 1700.

[4] *Ibid.*, 13 *seqq.*

[5] Letter 4 (s. l., 1767), p. 54 : " [dans les Indes et dans la Chine], où ils ont permis aux chrétiens l'idolâtrie même par cette subtile invention, etc."

according to Morales the Jesuits allowed the neophytes, in the ceremonial veneration of Confucius and the ancestors, to hide a crucifix amid the flowers or other ornaments, or to hold it in their hand, and to refer to it the homage which they paid in exactly the same manner as the pagans did to the pictures of the ancestors or the idols.[1] Ceremonies also which every beholder could only look upon as pagan, they were accused of attempting to justify in their conscience by means of a purely internal diversion of intention. However, the Jesuits were quite wrongly accused of such revolting duplicity, but it is true that at times when Christian Mandarins had to take an oath in a pagan temple, they had a table placed there with a large crucifix and before this they took the oath, but this was done quite openly.[2]

The Dominicans based these inaccuracies on information concerning the conduct of the Jesuits obtained by them at Tongtou, about the turn of the year 1635. By then they had been a year in China, yet it was only then, and by chance, that they learnt something about the centre and kernel of Chinese life, the worship of ancestors. Thus they had not as yet acquired a deep knowledge of things Chinese and in all probability their acquaintance with the Chinese language and literature was little better. It is true that at a later date, under Clement XI. and Benedict XIV. the Mendicants won their case against the Jesuits, but it is nevertheless regrettable that, notwithstanding their very inadequate information, they threw themselves so suddenly and so precipitately upon the Jesuits and that their irritation against

---

[1] *Collectanea*, n. 114, p. 33 (septimo : the veneration of Chim-hoam ; octavo : public veneration of Confucius).

[2] Biermann, 196 *seq.* ; *Acta Sanctorum Maii Propylaeum, Paralipomena*, Paris, 1868, 144. The Jesuits, says Philippucci (19, n. 20), held the veneration of Confucius which they permitted, to be either lawful or unlawful : if lawful why then this extenuation by means of the hidden cross ? if unlawful, " ista simulatio . . . intolerabilis plane et stultissima videretur, eiusque permissio non esset tam facile sine ullo fundamento in Patres Societatis reiicienda, quasi doctrinam adeo nefariam docerent."

their rivals in the mission field should show itself so plainly. This feeling finds expression in the preamble to the seventeen points [1] and by more than one token it appears that they deemed themselves chosen by God to bring back the church of China into the right path.[2]

All this was bound to make bad blood, hence it was not to be expected that the Jesuits would accept Propaganda's decree of 1645 in silence.   This also Morales reported in Rome in his own fashion [3]; on his part the Franciscan Antonio di S. Maria reported from the Philippines that there were " some religious " there who saw in the decrees of Propaganda no more than private opinions.[4]   Thereupon Innocent X. confirmed anew [5] in general terms and without mentioning the decree of 1645, a decision of his predecessor by the terms of which the duly accredited decrees of that Congregation had the force of Apostolic Constitutions.   For the rest the decree of Propaganda concerning the Chinese rites was not fully carried out even in the missions of the Mendicants,[6] but the Chinese translation for the neophytes mentioned only eight out of the seventeen points and these in a diluted form ; in particular the prohibition " under pain of excommunication " was replaced by the expression that this or that " was not seemly ".[7]

---

[1] See above, p. 202.

[2] " Just as Divine Providence had chosen Francis and Dominic in the 13th century to prevent the ruin of the Church, so were their sons now chosen for the Church in China." Antonio di S. Maria ; *Arch. Francisc.*, IV., 52).

[3] He " warns " Propaganda " not to believe that the Jesuits will submit to the Roman decisions ". BIERMANN, 85, note.

[4] *Ibid.*

[5] On July 30, 1652, *Collect.*, I., 35 *seq.*, n. 119.

[6] PHILIPPUCCIUS, 42.

[7] Translation of the Chinese text in PHILIPPUCCIUS, 40 *seq.* After a few historical data the document states that Innocent X. had issued a decree " inquiens : (1) Christianos regiae Sinarum familiae Ta Mim [the Ming dynasty which still ruled over part of China] maioribus defunctis munera offerre non convenit ; (2)

In South America, where the religious situation was far from uniformly bright, the mission to the pagans was also grievously neglected. In 1645, at the prayer of the Catholics of Pernambuco, Innocent X. forbade the Bishop of San Salvador (Bahia), to compel the latter to present themselves before him when they had to take oaths in connexion with marriage dispensations.[1] Just as the French Capuchins wrested Pernambuco from the hands of the Dutch for the Portuguese and then established themselves there, so did the Portuguese Jesuits rescue Maranhao from the power of Holland in 1644, their reward being the suppression of slavery in 1652.[2] In 1645 twelve Capuchins took over a mission from Propaganda on the Maranhao whilst in 1646 some of their colleagues went to Tuapel and Nahuelgami in Chile.[3]

In the North, Spanish Capuchins penetrated into Darien, (Panama) in 1646 and into Kumana (Piritu) in 1650 ; in

Confucio munera offerre non convenit ; (3) Insuper Chim Hoam munera offerre non convenit ; (4) Tempore praedicationis omnia ad D. N. Iesu Christi Incarnationem, mundi redemptionem et passionem pertinentia convenit promulgare, et Iesu Christi imaginem in Domini altari erigere convenit ; (5) Maiorum defunctorum epitaphium in tabella descriptum exponere christianis non convenit ; (6) Pecuniam alteri foenerare non convenit ; (7) Tempore baptismi convenit, ut sacerdos omnes mulieres sancto oleo vice alterius [sic !] inungat, et sanctum salem gustandum eisdem praebeat, et in earum mortis articulo convenit, ut vice alterius sanctum oleum iis conferat ; (8) Omnibus maribus et feminis christianis diem dominicum et magnos dies festos, abstinentiam a carnibus et ieiunia servare convenit.'' The mention of the Ming dynasty shows that the translation was made immediately after Morales' return and probably by himself. It only came to the knowledge of the Jesuits in 1679 (*ibid.*, 43 *seq.*).

[1] *Ius pontif.*, I., 236 *seq.*

[2] *Cf.* SCHMIDLIN, 330, and the authorities there quoted ; GIUSEPPE DA CASTROGIOVANNI O. M. Cap., *Notizie storiche della missione Cappuccina di Rio de Janeiro*, 1650–1910, Catania, 1910.

[3] ROCCO DA CESINALE, III., 728, and SCHMIDLIN, 305, n. 6, 309, n. 9.

1647 the two Jesuits Grillet and Bachamel went to Guyana.[1]

In Paraguay, in 1647, the Jesuits had twenty-seven Reductions with 300,000 Indians, but they were involved in a fierce contest with the Franciscan Bishop Bernardino de Cardenas of Asunción on account of the latter's pretension to visit their Reductions and to replace the Fathers by secular priests. In 1652 Cardenas left his diocese for good.[2]

A great stir was caused by a dispute which broke out in 1647 in Mexico between the Jesuits and the Bishop of La Puebla de los Angelos, Juan Palafox y Mendoza.[3] Born at Fitero in Spain and sent to Mexico in 1639, armed with extraordinary faculties, Palafox, to the amazement of everybody, deposed the Viceroy and took his place himself ; in addition to this he was also Captain General, Visitor of the Audiencia, Bishop of Puebla and administrator of the archbishopric of Mexico which had become vacant just then. As Visitor, Palafox gave the city of Mexico occasion for grievous complaints to Philip IV. and as Bishop he promptly came in conflict with all the Orders, with the temporary exception of the Society of Jesus. However, his initial friendliness with the Jesuits turned to a profound estrangement in consequence of a dispute over a tenth which he wished to levy from their possessions. On March 6th,

[1] See ROCCO DA CESINALE, III., 712, and SCHMIDLIN, 302.

[2] Cf. STREIT, Bibl. Missionum, II., 455 seqq., 507 seq., 527 ; SCHMIDLIN, 318 ; ASTRÁIN, 568 and 596 ; LEMMENS, 331 ; P. PASTELLS, II., 1–356 (Documents, 1638–54).

[3] ASTRÁIN, V., 356–411 ; EGUREN, Palafox et les Jésuites, Madrid, 1878 ; GENARO GARCIA, Don Juan Palafox y Mendoza, obispo de Puebla y Osma, visitador y virrey de la Nueva España, Mexico, 1918 ; Idem, Documentos inéditos o muy raros para la historia de México, VII. : Don Juan Palafox y Mendoza, su virreinato en la Nueva España, sus contiendas con los P.P. Jesuitas, sus partidarios en Puebla, sus apariciones, sus escritos escogidos, Mexico, 1906 ; STREIT, Bibl. Miss., II., 472 ; Letter of Palafox to Innocent X. of May 25, 1647, ibid., 497, that of January 8, 1649, ibid., 511, 548 seq. Cf. MARIANO CUEVAS, Hist. de la Iglesia en México, III., Tlalpam, 1924, 283–312.

1647, he forbade them to hear confessions and to preach and demanded that they should furnish proof that they had the required faculties. This the Jesuits refused to do ; this was a grave blunder which earned them a severe reprimand from their General. They nevertheless no longer celebrated offices publicly, though at the approach of the first Friday in Lent, which was always observed with particular solemnity, they asked Palafox' permission to preach the customary sermon. Permission was refused. Thereupon the Fathers argued that it was enough to have asked for the permission. The Bishop now laid his case before the general public by publishing a proclamation on March 8th, 1647, to the effect that the Jesuits had no faculties for hearing confessions or preaching, though he himself had at first chosen his own confessor from among them and on his visitations he always took with him a Jesuit as confessor and preacher for the Indians. Palafox now barred the confessional and the pulpit to the Jesuits until they should have asked him for faculties.

In view of the lack of facilities of communications in those days, which often made it difficult to have recourse to Rome, the Jesuits, like the other Orders, enjoyed the right of choosing so-called Conservators who had the power to safeguard their privileges in virtue of special papal faculties. Instead of seeking an amicable settlement with the Bishop, the Jesuits had recourse to this unfortunate remedy and chose two Dominicans for their Conservators. Now although the four Orders established in Mexico, viz. the Dominicans, Franciscans, Augustinians and Mercedarians, as well as the Chapter of Mexico City and finally even the Archbishop of that city, had declared that the situation was such as to justify the appointment of Conservators, their decision was none the less a mistake for Palafox had not gone beyond his rights. Consequently Palafox refused to recognize the Conservators who, on their part, published a manifesto in which they declared that the Bishop had incurred ex-communication—a grievous " exorbitance " as the Jesuit General described it. On April 6th Palafox excommunicated the Conservators.

On June 4th the Bishop reinforced his defence by a most unusual manifestation. On the evening of that day all the bells of the city were rung till far into the night ; no one knew why. On the following morning the bells were again rung for a long time. The whole city flocked to the cathedral ; at the end of High Mass Palafox, escorted by the entire Chapter, seated himself at the entrance of the choir whilst a document was read inculcating obedience to the Bishop and forbidding acknowledgement of the Conservators. After that the Bishop and Chapter went in procession, preceded by a cross covered with a black veil, to a platform from which he gave an explanation of the decree just read. There followed the recitation of the imprecatory psalm (Ps. CVIII.), so called by reason of its terrible imprecations, and at its conclusion the Canons put out the lighted candles they had carried and threw them on the ground. Palafox had not foreseen that the Jesuits would have their windows smashed and that the ordinances of the Conservators would be bespattered with dirt. More serious disorders were only prevented by the intervention of the Inquisition and the Viceroy who extended the royal protection to the Conservators. On June 7th Palafox drove in state through the streets of the city, to the sound of the bells, whilst his partisans hailed him as Viceroy.

Whilst the Viceroy Salvatierro sought to reconcile the disputants, Palafox suddenly disappeared from La Puebla for a whole four months ; no one knew his whereabouts ; he himself left word that he was going away in the hope that his absence would promote the restoration of peace. The Chapter of La Puebla now undertook the government of the diocese in the name of the Bishop and at its request the Jesuits submitted their faculties on July 19th, when the Chapter renewed them. In point of fact sixteen of the twenty-four Jesuits of the city had received their powers from Palafox himself. Until November they exercised their ministry without molestation. Thanks to the mediation of the Viceroy the mutual excommunications were raised by Palafox and the Conservators and on November 27th the Bishop made his solemn entry into La Puebla. Tolerable relations were resumed with the Jesuits and the conflict seemed settled.

In reality it was not so. In May, 1648, a friend of the Bishop, Marcos de Torres y Rueda, Bishop of Yucatan, became Viceroy. Palafox now threw aside all sense of his own dignity and gave full vent to his resentment against the Jesuits. On May 16th he drove through the city in an open carriage, escorted by a crowd of noisy youths, who hailed him with shouts of victory and threw stones against the houses of the friends of the Jesuits. Handbills with the text of alleged excommunications against the Jesuits were scattered and Palafox threatened not to ordain anyone who had studied in their colleges. The hated religious were accused of simony and assassinations and three Canons were detained in incredibly cruel confinement for having protected the Conservators, in compliance with the order of the previous Viceroy.

In September, 1648, a Brief came from Rome, bearing the date of May 14th, 1648,[1] which Palafox considered as a triumph for his cause. In the preceding year he had forwarded to Rome five accusations against the Jesuits, with a request for a papal sentence which, as a matter of fact, was given by a commission of five Cardinals and four assessors.[2] The Brief made a change in the existing law, to the disadvantage of the Jesuits. Gregory XIII. had granted them the privilege of preaching, hearing confessions, saying Mass in their own churches, in any part of those distant countries, without further formality, provided they had been approved by *any Bishop whatever*. Gregory XV. revoked this privilege by insisting on the approval of the Bishop *of the diocese* ; Urban VIII. had excepted the Spanish dominions, hence Gregory XIII.'s privilege had revived. Now Innocent X.'s Brief, as if by inadvertence, failed to mention Urban VIII.'s restriction, and took the standpoint of Gregory XV.'s decision. Thus

---

[1] Reproduced in *Bull.*, XV., 713 *seq.*, and in *Ius pontif.*, I., 253 *seq.*

[2] Spada, Sacchetti, Ginetti, Carpegna and Franciotti ; the assessors were : Fagnani, Maraldi, Paolucci and Farnese.

the privilege of the Jesuits was revoked by this decree, but
it was evident enough that the latter would lodge a protest
against Rome's apparent oversight. Innocent X. also declared
that Palafox was within his rights when he forbade all pastoral
work within his diocese to those Jesuits who refused to submit
their faculties. Consequently the nomination of Conservators
and the latter's sentence and excommunication were likewise
null and void.

In obedience to this Brief, the faculties of the twenty-two
Jesuits in La Puebla were submitted to Palafox ; twelve of
them he renewed at once, the rest he wished to subject to
further study. Palafox might have been satisfied with his
triumph, but he would not be content. He insisted that the
Jesuits should seek public absolution from their excommunication and, as was rumoured by some officials, with a rope
round their necks and a black taper in their hands. However,
things did not go so far. In view of a rumour that the original
text of the Bull had been tampered with, the Jesuits appealed
to the Royal Council which, on the strength of papal
concessions, enjoyed in Mexico the most exorbitant powers
even in the ecclesiastical sphere. That body gave orders to
withhold the Bull and to hand over the deeds to the fiscal.
On February 6th, 1648, Philip IV. recalled Palafox from
Mexico ; in June, 1649, the latter obeyed the order and
returned to Spain. He had been removed from the office
of Visitor of the *Audiencia* already in October, 1647. Before
leaving for Spain he drew up his famous memorandum on
the Jesuits addressed to the Pope. Already at an earlier
date, viz. May 25th, 1647, he had written to the Pope making
accusations which are in part explained by the circumstance
that his quarrel with the hated religious was at its height
just then. In his letter of January 8th, 1649, his accusations
against the Jesuits exceeded all bounds.[1]

---

[1] The authenticity of the letter is proved by ARNAULD. The
author of the *Pratique morale des Jésuites* (ARNAULD, *Œuvres*,
XXXIII., 618 *seqq.*), ASTRÁIN (V., 407 *seqq.*), DUHR (*Jesuitenfabeln*[4], 640 *seq.*, and Cardinal Calini in the process of beatification
of Palafox (in [BOERO], *Osservazioni sopra l'istoria del pontificato*

Meanwhile the discussion of the tiresome business was proceeding in Rome. At the request of the Jesuits all the facts of the dispute were brought together ; out of these fifty-one points thirteen only were recognized as certain by the cardinalitial Congregation (December 17th, 1652).[1] On the whole the thirteen points are not unfavourable to the Jesuits. Thus the first point states that previous to Palafox' prohibition, they had been authorized, either by himself or by his predecessors, both to preach and to hear the confessions of seculars. The last point establishes the fact that the five accusations sent in by Palafox do not prove the Jesuits' guilt, nor did it appear that any one of them had incurred excommunication or that the censures pronounced by the Bishop could be looked upon as justified.

No judgment was pronounced with regard to the past and directions were only given for future conduct. Cardinal Spada [2] wrote to Palafox requesting him privately to give faculties to the superiors of the Jesuits to absolve any of their subjects who might perchance have incurred some censure. Just as the Jesuits were directed to show submission and respect for the Bishop, so was Palafox repeatedly exhorted to treat with due esteem so praiseworthy and useful an Order, and to embrace with fatherly affection a religious Society which had so fruitfully and so laboriously cultivated the vineyard of the Lord.

On the same day a Brief was dispatched to the Jesuits which put an end to the disputes. The Fathers had protested against the Brief of 1648, but the Congregation upheld it on February 14th, 1652. Thereupon they asked once more

---

di Clemente XIV. scritta dal P. A. THEINER, II., Monza, 1854, 261), do not doubt its authenticity. In PALAFOX, Obras, the letter is found in Vol. XI., 63–120, and in ARNAULD, loc. cit., p. 713–760. According to Calini (loc. cit., 263) the letter proves that " Palafoxii in carpenda proximorum fama effrenis malitia, in mendaciis libertas, in conviciis facilitas et obstinatio in sua iniquitate, sine poenitentia factorum et a se scriptorum.".

[1] Published in Obras, XII., 552. Cf. ASTRÁIN, V., 407 seqq.

[2] On December 17, 1652, Obras, XII., 554.

whether the nomination of Conservators had been lawful at least on grounds other than those enumerated in the Brief. On December 17th, 1652, the Congregation replied in the negative and imposed silence for the future. Innocent X. confirmed both decisions on November 17th, 1652, and on May 17th, 1653.[1] Some difficulties subsequently arose in Spain but these were removed by means of a compromise between Palafox and the Jesuits. The former did not return to La Puebla but became Bishop of Osma in Spain where he died in 1659.

For the rest in 1648 Innocent X. confirmed the erection of a Seminary by Palafox and permitted its students to take the doctorate in philosophy, theology and Canon Law at the University of Mexico even though they did not attend the lectures there. He likewise approved the Constitutions of the Congregations of the priests of St. Peter at Los Angeles.[2] Jesuits, Franciscans, Dominicans and Augustinians continued their missionary labours in Mexico; the Franciscans penetrated further into Yucatan and New Leon[3]; in 1648 two Jesuits accompanied Bordel into California whilst Jesuits, Dominicans and Capuchins continued their labours in the French Lesser Antilles.[4]

In British territory in North America, at the request of the Queen of England, the Jesuit mission of Maryland was reopened in 1648 by Fr. Fisher, and that of the Capuchins in Virginia in 1650, but both were soon abandoned once more.[5] In 1645 the Capuchin Prefect Pacificus, in Canada, sent Fr. Archangel to France; the Father was accompanied by an Indian who received baptism whilst in France.[6] By 1650 the Jesuits in Canada had converted almost all the Hurons, the Algonquins and the Montagnais, but during the

---

[1] *Ius pontif.*, I., 281 ; *Bull.*, XV., 705 *seq.*

[2] *Ius pontif.*, I., 257 *seq.*, 267 *seq.*

[3] SCHMIDLIN, 349 ; *cf.* 344, n. 7, and 348, n. 6.

[4] *Cf. ibid.*, 295 *seq.*

[5] SCHMIDLIN, 356, n. 6 ; *Arch. stor. ital.*, LXXVI., 2 (1920), 250 *seq.*

[6] *Cf.* SCHMIDLIN, *loc. cit.*

war with the Iroquois (1646–9) several missionaries suffered martyrdom, a number of stations were destroyed and the Christian Hurons exterminated, except for a small remnant which in 1650 was transported to Quebec.[1] Already in 1646 an assembly of the French clergy had prayed for the establishment of a Canadian bishopric, and for this the Queen and the ecclesiastical council had in view the Jesuits ; but the latter proposed François de Montmorency–Laval who, in effect, was appointed Vicar Apostolic.[2] Laval proved a splendid Bishop whose merits have received sufficient recognition by the fact that in 1890 he was proposed for beatification.[3] That honour was actually bestowed in 1925 on the above-named Jesuit missionaries. Anyone who undertook to live among the Indians of Canada thereby renounced all the comforts and refinements with which two thousand years has embellished life in Europe, and ran the obvious risk of falling into the hands of hostile Indians who then sought to discover, by means of the most exquisite tortures, how much pain the white man could endure. Of this the Jesuit Martyrs of the years 1646–9 had ample experience, but they also endured the most dreadful tortures with a heroism beyond all praise.

[1] SCHMIDLIN, *loc. cit.*

[2] DE LA ROCHEMONTEIX, *Les Jésuites de la Nouvelle France au XVII. siècle*, Paris, 1895 ; SCHMIDLIN, 412 ; A. GOSSELIN, *La mission du Canada avant Mgr. de Laval* (1615–1659), EVREUX, 1909 ; The Jesuit relations and allied documents. Travels and explorations of the Jesuit missionaries in New France, 1610–1671, ed. THWAITES, 73 vols., 1896–1901.

[3] Biography by GOSSELIN, Quebec, 1890. *Cf. The Cath. Encyclop.*, XV., New York [1911], 45 *seq.* Laval was first destined for Tongking ; see above, p. 193.

CHAPTER V.

Jansenism in France and the Netherlands.[1]

(1.)

Urban VIII. had raised his voice against Jansenism as soon as it arose, though without marked success.[2] Under his successors also conditions for the further progress of the new teaching were only seemingly unfavourable.

Counselled as she was by the Marquise de Senecey, the governess of the royal children, Queen Anne of France was a decided opponent of " the disciples of St. Augustine ",[3] but the high functionary, François Daubray, whom she charged with the surveillance of the party, allowed himself to be intimidated by the Jansenists, with the result that he did his duty badly.[4] On the other hand the Queen had the advantage of having Vincent de Paul to advise her with regard to Church appointments, but even he did not succeed in preventing mistakes. Though Anne had promised him to give no preferment to men suspected of favouring the new teaching, the two most powerful patrons of the sect, viz. Jean François Paul de Gondi and Louis Henri de Gondrin de Pardaillan, were respectively named coadjutors of Paris and Sens in 1643 and 1644.[5]

---

[1] For this chapter I had at my disposal many documents from various archives left by the late Professor Schill, who was unfortunately not able to make use of them.

[2] Cf. the present work, Vol. XXIX., 119 seq.

[3] Rapin, Mém., I., 112, 137. Rapin gives an account of Jansenism as it works in practical life. We may trust him for his assertions based on personal observation, but otherwise he is not always reliable. Cf. for his characterization, Bremond, IV., 312 seq.   [4] Rapin, I., 162.

[5] Ibid., 47. On Gondrin see G. Dubois, Alençon, 1902.

The Council of State shared the Queen's religious stand-point. Chavigny, who as castellan of Vincennes and St. Cyran's gaoler, had been won over by the latter for his person and his cause, was the only one of its members to support the party,[1] whilst Henry, Prince of Condé, using Vincent de Paul as his intermediary, was planning measures against the new teaching with the nuncio and chancellor Séguier.[2] Mazarin was but little interested in religious questions. His ambition was to maintain himself in his position, hence his anxiety to stand well with all parties and to play off the one against the other. Even the attitude of the Bishops was not uniformly clear. Though the controversialist François d'Abra de Raconis could write that as against the sixteen Bishops and the twenty Doctors who had praised Arnauld's book on Holy Communion, there were a hundred Bishops and two hundred Doctors who condemned it,[3] it is none the less a sign of the confusion of thought that, as late as 1645, the Archbishop of Auch and the ten Bishops of his Province commanded their clergy to set Arnauld's teaching on Holy Communion before the people.[4] Many of the high prelates were moreover prejudiced in favour of *Petrus Aurelius*, hence for St. Cyran's ideas, forasmuch as he pretended to defend the rights of the Bishops against the regulars. As a matter of fact, France was just then undergoing a movement whose aim it was to limit the privileges of the regulars in favour of the secular clergy. The " disciples of St. Augustine " skilfully exploited this tendency of the period to their own advantage.[5] At the time of Innocent X.'s election most of the senior professors of the Sorbonne were

[1] RAPIN, I., 41.   [2] *Ibid.*, 40

[3] ARNAULD, *Œuvres*, XVI., XLIX.

[4] *Ibid.*, XXVI., XXXIII.

[5] RAPIN, *Mém.*, I., 343 s. " L'on peut dire que ce fut, de toutes leur intrigues, celle qui leur réussit le mieux " (*ibid.*, 344). " Ce fut, à proprement parler, l'intrigue des Jansénistes, qui mit en vogue cet esprit de paroisse qui régna depuis si fort à Paris, par où les curés devinrent si importants qu'ils se firent redouter des grands, respecter des petits, considérer de tout le monde " (*Ibid.*, 485).

still hostile to Jansenius, although the brilliant name of the youthful Arnauld won for him an ever increasing number of followers among the younger ones.[1]

Nor were the parish priests of Paris inclined, at that time, to favour the innovations, hence, if they would win over the masses, it was necessary for the party to get an able Jansenist appointed to some prominent parish in Paris. In this they were successful. Hilerin, curé of Saint-Merry, was tortured by a scruple that he had become a priest without a true vocation ; accordingly Arnauld and De Barcos persuaded him that it was best for him to resign his parish. His place was then taken by Henri Duhamel, the man who had introduced the practice of public penance at Saint-Maurice. Duhamel played no small part in the story of Jansenism in Paris ; it was due to the influence of this clever and persuasive man that the aristocratic world opened its purse for Port-Royal.[2]

On the whole, at the time of Innocent X.'s accession, the new teaching was meeting with more disapproval than favour on the part of leading circles in France. On the other hand the efforts of the opponents of the heresy were hampered in sundry ways, whereas its friends and adherents were united, determined, shrewd and above all, exceedingly active.

Their chief tool was the press. Arnauld and " the gentlemen of Port-Royal " did not write in learned Latin, they wrote in French, and in excellent French. Arnauld's book on Holy Communion was positively devoured and the results soon became apparent. The new reformer alienated priests and people from the altar, as Vincent de Paul lamented in 1648.[3] It is possible that some people in France or Italy drew some benefit from the book, he said, but in Paris for one hundred in

---

[1] " La jeunesse [at the University] court impunément après ces nouveautés," the Jesuit Pintherau tells the older professors in 1646, in PRUNEL, *La renaissance cath. en France au 17e siècle*, Paris, 1921, 285.

[2] RAPIN, I., 60 *seqq.* Duhamel, however, renounced the Jansenistic doctrines some time before his death. DUBOIS, *Hist. de l'abbé de Rancé*, II., Paris, 1866, 17 *seqq.*

[3] To Dehorgny, September 10, 1648, COSTE, III., 372.

whom it had perhaps called forth greater reverence in the
reception of the Sacraments, there were at least ten thousand
to whom it had done harm by frightening them away altogether
from Holy Communion.[1]   For quite ordinary sins the new
reformers often put off absolution.[2]   Even the Easter Com-
munions had diminished : there were three thousand less at
St. Sulpice, whilst the parish priest of St. Nicolas-du-
Chardonnet who visited the households of his parish after
Easter, found that fifteen hundred people had not been to
Holy Communion.   Hardly anyone, or at least only very few
people, went to the Sacraments on the first Sunday of the
month or on feast days, and even in the churches of the Orders
those of the Jesuits were the only ones where things were a
little better.[3]

In 1644 Petau said of the Jansenist teaching on grace that
if Calvin were to return from the grave he would find many
Catholics ready to defend his errors.[4]   It is true that at that
time the " Augustinus " of the Bishop of Ypres could only
find readers among the learned, but three sermons against
Jansenius preached at Richelieu's request by the able theologian Isaac Habert in 1642 and 1643, provided Arnauld with a
suitable pretext for publishing two apologies of Jansenius [5]
in September, 1644, and April, 1645.[6]   According to Arnauld,
Jansenius was " the luminary of scholars, the mirror of
Bishops, a Master of piety ; he appeared as an angel on earth
whose spirit dwelt in heaven, who only looked to God and
found no rest except in the love of the sovereign and
unchanging truth.   In him could be seen the penitential spirit
of a religious, the gravity of a scholar, the courage of a Bishop,
whilst his burning charity made him the father of the poor
and the refuge of those in trouble ".   The Netherlands venerated
him " as Augustine returned from heaven " whilst in France

[1] *Ibid.*, 362.

[2] *Ibid.*, 368.

[3] To Dehorgny, June 25, 1648, *ibid.*, 321.

[4] *De poenitentia*, l. 1, c. 1, n. 3, p. 212.

[5] ARNAULD, *Oeuvres*, XVI., XIII., XVI.

[6] *Ibid.*, 39–312 ; XVII., 1–637.

"his holy teaching", whatever his enemies might say,
"yielded wonderful fruits."[1]   In similar rhetorical phrases,
Habert is then demolished and even now Arnauld describes
Urban VIII.'s Bull as a forgery.[2]   In his defence of Jansenius
against the accusation of heresy he starts from the principle
that the question was not whether this teaching was condemned
by the Bull against Baius, or by the Council of Trent, but
whether it was the teaching of St. Augustine.[3]   Here, then, is a
plain admission that he has given up the Catholic standpoint :
the "disciples of St. Augustine" considered themselves
authorized to follow the views of Augustine without any more
ado, solely because they were taught by him.

True these writings had no direct influence on the masses,
but their elegant French and showy rhetoric succeeded in
rousing enthusiasm for the new teaching in the upper classes.[4]

It is a well-known fact that already at that time the salons
of Paris and the "preciosity" of aristocratic ladies had begun
to exercise great influence upon French intellectual life.
Arnauld conquered these salons for the new teaching and
turned them into so many centres from which it radiated into
wider circles. If even before this "St. Augustine was the only
topic of conversation"[5] in that world, it was still more so
after the publication of Arnauld's new books. Gentlemen at
court and the ladies of the great world discussed, with the air
of experts, grace and predestination, bandied about the
Councils of Arles and Orange, extolled Augustine and damned
Molina. Jansenism became the fashion in leading circles ;
one had to be a supporter of Jansenius if one wished to be
reckoned intelligent and to be considered such it sufficed to
declare oneself in favour of Port-Royal.[6]   Not a few among

---

[1] ARNAULD, *Oeuvres*, XVI., 56, 59 *seq.*

[2] *Ibid.*, XVII., 64 *seq.*

[3] *Ibid.*, 87 *seq.* ; DENZINGER, *Ench. Symb.* (1928), n. 1320.

[4] RAPIN, *Mém.*, I., 95.

[5] "On ne parloit que de saint Augustin dans les ruelles"
(RAPIN, I., 62). On the meaning of "ruelles", *cf.* KREITEN, in
Stimmen aus Maria-Laach., XXVI. (1884), 432.

[6] RAPIN, I., 95 ; *cf.* 22 : " c'étoit être à la mode que d'être de

the most aristocratic ladies and gentlemen built themselves houses in proximity to Port-Royal in order to withdraw
thither at intervals or even altogether.[1] Among them was the
Marquise de Sablé, of whom it was said that by her example
she won almost as many adherents for the new doctrine in the
great world as Jansenius had secured for it by his book among
scholars.[2] However, the approval of the new penitential
teaching did not necessarily imply that this new kind of
solitaries personally took up the works of penance.[3]

The broad masses of the people were not overlooked because
of these aristocratic circles. In 1647 Jean Jacques Olier, the
founder of St. Sulpice, wrote that the new teachers successfully
insinuated themselves everywhere under cover of reform and
piety, and everybody sided with them.[4] One of their chief
means of propaganda was to circulate small books which
were soon in everybody's hands.[5] St. Cyran had composed a
" household theology " which was prohibited by the Archbishop of Paris in 1643 and by Rome in 1654.[6] In 1650 a
" Catechism of Grace " by Feydeau sought to render
" Augustinus " intelligible to the people. The booklet, which
was prohibited in the year of its publication, nevertheless
circulated under divers titles both in France and in the Low
Countries.[7] Numerous biting pamphlets, scattered among the
general public, brought it about that no one cared any longer
to attack the powerful party. Even preachers in their refutations of the new doctrine on grace, no longer dared to designate

---

ce parti là." The Archbishop of Embrun said to the Duke of
Orleans : " que Son Altesse Royale avoit trop d'esprit pour ne
pas être du parti de Port-Royal " (ibid., 135).

[1] Ibid., 172, 211.

[2] Ibid., 175. Cf. VICTOR COUSIN, Mme de Sablé, Paris, 1855.
She is the Parthenie in the novel Grand Cyrus of MADAME DE
SCUDÉRY (PETIT DE JULLEVILLE, IV., 101).

[3] RAPIN, I., 174.

[4] DUBRUEL, in Recherches, VII. (1917), 258.

[5] RAPIN, I., 137.   [6] [PATOUILLET], IV., 83 seqq.

[7] Ibid., I., 226 seqq. Reprint of the Catéchisme de la grâce,
in ARNAULD, Œuvres, XVII., 839-848.

its authors by name [1] and things had come to such a pass that loud murmuring arose if the teaching of Jansenius was attacked in the pulpit.[2] By spreading all manner of calumnies about him, special though fruitless efforts were made to intimidate Olier, whose zeal had preserved the whole of the faubourg Saint-Germain from Jansenism. When his associates wished to defend him, Olier threw their apologies into the fire unread, with the remark : " Do you not know that calumny is the reward with which God is wont to honour the defenders of religion ? " [3] Olier was not the only victim of the party's evil tongues. Port-Royal was an adept at extolling its own people and in reviling its opponents. To-day a man might be an ignoramus ; all of a sudden he got a reputation as a theologian and a preacher, simply by going over to Port-Royal. The broad masses were already impressed by the simple fact that the members of the young sect described themselves as the disciples of the great Augustine and their opponents as the followers of the almost unknown Molina.[4] Great also was the influence exercised by the Abbey of Port-Royal. On one occasion Queen Anne confessed that the strict conduct observed there impressed her not a little, except that she felt repelled by the fact that everybody there spoke ill of those who did not belong to the party.[5] Even the young nuns were brought up with an exaggerated notion of their importance, as if God had specially chosen them to reform His Church ; hence arose a presumption which refused to bow even to papal authority.[6] Nevertheless even genuinely devout people were impressed by the fact that the only topic of conversation at the Abbey was the strictness of life in the early centuries of Christianity, the severity of the primitive penitential system,

---

[1] RAPIN, I., 135, 137.

[2] Olier, in FAILLON, II., 422.

[3] *Ibid.*, 418 *seqq.* ; RAPIN, I., 137, 163.

[4] RAPIN, I., 133, 197.

[5] *Ibid.*, 64.

[6] RAPIN, I., 122. V. COUSIN (JACQUELINE PASCAL[6], Paris, 1869, 9) says of Port-Royal : " Peut-être le don céleste de l'humi-lité lui a-t-il un peu manqué."

the decadence and abuses of later times.[1] Moreover Port-Royal could point to real achievements, even to such a miracle as the fact that, in opposition to the prevailing fashion, the ladies adopted a more becoming attire.[2] Even the Abbey's wealth,[3] the result of the generosity of friends, was held to be a sign of God's particular favour.[4] Port-Royal became one of the sights and it was the fashionable thing to visit the nuns and to lend a wondering ear as they unfolded the mysteries of grace and predestination to their admiring listeners.[5] Madame de Sévigné has left us an enthusiastic account of the visit she made in 1674.[6]

The spread of the new sect was greatly furthered by the troubles of the Fronde : they diverted the attention of the Government so that the " disciples of St. Augustine " had a free hand.[7] As a matter of fact the party welcomed the struggle with the court for Queen Anne was an opponent whilst Mazarin was at least no friend [8] ; moreover the coadjutor of the Archbishop of Paris, the future Cardinal Retz, who was deeply implicated in the intrigues of the Fronde, inclined, from political reasons, towards the Jansenists ; the result was that they supported him and his friends both by their influence and by the considerable sums of money which they received from their own adherents.[9] Queen Anne subsequently

---

[1] RAPIN, I., 64, 134.

[2] Ibid., 333. " Manches à la Janséniste " became the fashion ; ibid.

[3] Ibid., 128, 276, 361, 525.

[4] Ibid., 133.

[5] Ibid., 362, 441.

[6] " Ce Port-Royal est une Thébaide, c'est le paradis, c'est un désert où toute la dévotion du christianisme s'est rangée, c'est une sainteté répandue dans tout ce pays à une lieue à la ronde." Letter of January 26, 1674, Lettres, ed. by MONMERQUE, III., Paris, 1862, 390.

[7] RAPIN, I., 248.

[8] Ibid., 237.

[9] Ibid., 268. " J'ai ouï dire au prince de Conty, au même temps qu'il fut fait généralissime des troupes de Paris, qu'il

observed that the Jansenists had shown so much zeal that in a sense the war was their work, a circumstance which the King would remember at some future day ; in point of fact at court the troubles of the Fronde were spoken of as properly the Jansenist war.[1] Duhamel, the Jansenist curé of Saint-Merry, specially distinguished himself by his zeal for the Fronde.[2]

By degrees the new teaching took firm roots beyond the capital. It was preached at Amiens during the last years of Urban VIII. At the request of Bishop Caumartin, Port-Royal dispatched thither two ex-Jesuits, Labadie and Dabert, but their teaching caused such confusion in the city that the two emissaries had to be barred from the pulpit. Labadie now embarked on an adventurous career. By permission of the Bishop he preached Jansenism at Bazas, but at Toulouse he narrowly escaped being burnt at the stake for a number of misdeeds in a convent of nuns. At Montauban he turned Huguenot and wrote a book to show that Jansenius and Calvin taught the same doctrine. After founding a peculiar sect known for its fanatical and communistic tendencies he died at Altona in 1674, having been expelled, together with his sect, from Holland and Germany.[3]

By 1650 Jansenism had spread to nearly every province of France.[4] Among the religious Orders Bérulle's Oratory in

avoit grande obligation aux Jansénistes, lesquels, pour soutenir le party opposé à la cour et au roy, venoient tous les jours luy offrir leurs suffrages et les bourses de leurs amis pour entretenir la guerre," *ibid.*, 246.

[1] *Ibid.*, 271.

[2] *Ibid.*, 265, 277.

[3] RAPIN, I., 50 ; DE MEYER, 322 *seqq.* ; GOEBEL-FRANK, in HERZOG-HAUCK, *Realenzyklop*, XI.[3], 191 *seqq.*

[4] RAPIN, I., 309 *seq.* On Jansenism in Marseilles see *ibid.*, 228 and p. 167 *seq.*, in Guyenne and at Bordeaux, p. 291, 339, in the neighbourhood of Blois, p. 338 (*cf.* 130), at Angers, p. 340, at Beauvais, p. 344, in Auvergue, p. 346, at Sens, p. 448, at Amiens, p. 527. In the *Excerpta ex actis s. Officii*, 1653–6, f. 896, the *Letter of the Bishop of Verdun (without date), who

particular included many supporters of the new teaching.
The second General, Condren, was an opponent and one of
those who denounced St. Cyran to Richelieu ; the third
General, Bourgoing, bound his subjects to accept the Bull of
Urban VIII. and in a memorial to the Queen he drew up a set
of principles on the administration of the sacrament of
Penance which were diametrically opposed to Arnauld's book
on Holy Communion.[1] However, all this was not enough to
banish the sympathies for the new views which had infiltrated
into the Congregation.[2] At Marseilles in particular the so-called
teaching of St. Augustine was spread by the preaching and
through the school of the Oratorians. The Fathers were held
in high esteem in that city because one of their colleagues,
the saintly Bishop Jean Baptiste Gault, had most successfully
laboured there for the reform of the diocese. However, the
very fervour which he had roused now favoured the spread
of Jansenist rigorism.[3] At Bordeaux an Oratorian parish

asks for a remedy from the Pope against the " nova dissidia " ;
f. 928 seqq., the correspondence between Cardinal Bichi and the
Bishop of Marseilles, January, 1651, about complaints on account
of Jansenistic sermons in a church at Marseilles ; p. 920 : Filleau
(September 22, 1651), forwards an edict of the " lieutenant
criminel " of Poitiers, of August 11, promulgated at his instigation,
according to which the defence of the Jansenist doctrine is
prohibited under pain of a fine of 1,000 livres (Schill). Cf.
A. FÉRON, Contribution à l'hist. du Jansénisme en Normandie
(diocese of Rouen, 1629–1643), Rouen, 1906 ; G. DOUBLET,
Le Jansénisme de l'ancien diocèse de Vence, Paris, 1901 ;
HERSCHER, Analecta Gallicana (diocese of Langres) in Rev.
d'histoire de l'Église de France, 1910 ; ALPHONSE AUGUSTE,
Les origines du Jansénisme à Toulouse, in Bull. de litt. ecclés.,
1916, 262 seqq., 315 seqq.

[1] DE MEYER, 305 seq.

[2] Olier and his Sulpicians were terrified when the Oratorians
tried to establish themselves in their parish. Olier in FAILLON,
II., 432.

[3] RAPIN, I., 288 seq. Cf. Albizzi's report on the Congregation
of Cardinals against Jansenism of June 22 and July 6, 1651, in
Katholik, 1883, II., 290.

priest likewise revealed himself as an adherent of the sect.[1]
At Toulouse, though there existed points of contact for the
new teaching, it did not develop to any extent, notwithstanding
the undecided attitude of Archbishop Montchal.[2] At Cahors,
the splendid Bishop, Alain de Solminihac, successfully closed
his diocese to Jansenism. When one professor of theology,
the Dominican Mesplède, began to expound the new teaching,
Solminihac promptly ordered him to desist and when
he refused to obey, the Bishop forbade his students to attend
his lectures. Another priest felt he ought to preach against
the Dominican but this the Bishop likewise forbade and he
promised himself to defend the honour of the professor if
the latter would bear the attack in silence. Soon Solminihac
was able to write " the fire is out, in a few days no one will
remember it ".[3]

Similar instructions had been issued in Paris [4] but there
the new ideas had struck such deep roots, that the policy of
silence was impossible.[5] In point of fact the new teaching
was making headway beyond the boundaries of France ;
thus, through Flanders it had penetrated to the Rhine [6] and
its progress was particularly marked in Poland. The Queen
of Poland, Marie Louise of Gonzaga-Cleve, a daughter of the
Duke of Nevers, married first to King Ladislaus Sigismund
of Poland and after the latter's death in 1648, to his brother
and successor, John Casimir, had been educated at Port-Royal,
corresponded with Angélique Arnauld and had for her confessor
the Jansenist François de Fleury. In these circumstances
the Latin translation of the book on frequent Communion

---

[1] RAPIN, I., 292.

[2] Alphonse Auguste, loc. cit., 262.

[3] COSTE, III., 348–350.

[4] Prohibitions of the Archbishop of March 4 and December 11,
1643, " d'invectiver " against those who in matters of faith are
of a different opinion ; prohibition of the coadjutor, of November
25, 1644, to speak about grace from the pulpit. ARNAULD,
Œuvres, XVI., XII.

[5] DE MEYER, 144.

[6] RAPIN, I., 310.

received the approval of the Archbishop of Vilna and Gnesen and of one of the latter's suffragans.[1] John Casimir, who had been a Jesuit and a Cardinal (in 1647) before his elevation to the throne, saw this fresh cause of division with great displeasure. Through the nuncio he referred the matter to Rome. By way of reply the Curia forwarded a copy of Urban VIII.'s Bull and held out the prospect of a papal decision on pending questions. The King was not satisfied with this answer.[2] In a letter to the Pope [3] he lamented the divisions at his court and prayed for a speedy explanation as to which side was in the right. The Archbishop of Warsaw also wrote in the same sense to Rome.[4] A reply now came to the effect that Jansenius' work had already been condemned and the nuncio was instructed to use his influence to obtain silence on the subject.[5] Thereupon Urban VIII.'s Bull was published in Poland but the King persisted in demanding a decision on Arnauld's teaching.[6]

Apart from the personal exertions of such eminent men as Vincent de Paul and Olier, the defence against the rising heresy in France was mainly confined within the literary

---

[1] ARNAULD, *loc. cit.*, LXXV.

[2] * Of August 11, 1650, annotation on the back of the report of nuncio Giov. de Torrez of July 2, 1650, in *Excerpta*, 1647–1652, *loc. cit.*

[3] Of September 12, 1650, *ibid.*, in RAPIN, I., 395.

[4] *On September 20, 1650, *Excerpta, loc. cit.*

[5] " Acciochè questa controversia resti totalmente sopita nè si permetta alcuna disputatione in contrario," Instruction of November 19, 1650, in THEINER, *Mon. Poloniae*, III., 466.

[6] The nuncio *on January 7, 1651 (*Excerpta, loc. cit.*). The nuncio constantly praises the Queen's piety ! *" La quale nè può esser devota nè più ossequiosa verso cotesta S. Sede " (on September 17, 1650, *ibid.*). " *Non posso perciò non confessar d'haver sempre conosciuto nella regina uno zelo purissimo, una (bontà) maravigliosa et una pietà senza esempio. . . . M'avvidi che non haveva notizia alcuna di queste dottrine jansenistiche, e ha lasciato affatto anche la lettione del Arnaldo " (on November 5, 1650, *ibid.*).

sphere. Polemical writings for and against the heresy were bandied about by both sides even in the opening years of Innocent X.'s reign, though a change was visible at least in one respect : weary of subterfuges and misrepresentations as well as of the endless personal attacks of the Jansenists,[1] it was precisely the most learned champions of Catholic teaching who despaired of success in a strife in which, in so far as the broad masses were concerned, the decisive factor was not the goodness of the cause, but skill with the pen. Accordingly they now wrote their refutations exclusively in Latin, for the benefit of the learned circles. Thus Habert, who was made Bishop of Vabres in 1645, notwithstanding Arnauld's efforts to blacken his character, published in 1646 a scholarly work on grace which is esteemed even at this day [2] ; in it he refutes

---

[1] They continually accuse their adversaries that they let themselves be guided solely by egoistical motives or that they do not even believe in the righteousness of their cause, and seek to bring them into contempt. Habert and Petau are also haughtily dealt with. One example of these travesties (another in the next note) : Petau had not obtained an episcopal letter of introduction for his work against Arnauld's book on Frequent Communion. Therefore, concludes Arnauld, " la seule qualité de Jésuite (contains according to Petau) une autorité plus vénérable pour la décision des véritéz chrétiennes que celle des évêques " (DE MEYER, 276).

[2] *Theologiae Graecorum Patrum vindicatae circa universam materiam gratiae libri tres*, new edition, Würzburg, 1863. On the work and especially on Habert, see HURTER, *Nomenclator*, II., 65. To what exaggerations his adversaries had recourse in order to disparage the work is shown by the remark of Hermant (IV., 17) : " Il porta le ridicule jusqu'à mettre les sieurs Gamache, Duval et Isambert, docteurs de Sorbonne, ses amis, au nombre des Pères Grecs," ARNAULD, *Œuvres*, XVI., XVII. ; cf. DE MEYER, 195). But Habert states already on the title page of his work that he constantly refers also to the teaching of the doctors of the Sorbonne. In the impugned passage (l. 2, c. 6, Würzburg, 1863, 203), he adduces by way of preliminary to what was to follow, the irrefutable proof that the Sorbonne had always admitted the so-called " sufficient grace ".

the innovators without mentioning their names.[1]   Petau
did the same in 1648.[2]   A book by the Jesuit Etienne
Dechamps, which shows the untenability of Jansenius'
concept of freedom, saw several editions.   Dechamps had very
skilfully chosen his standpoint by taking the field as a defender
of the Sorbonne which, as early as 1560, had condemned the
thesis of the compatibility of freedom and necessity.   This
time Arnauld, always so ready with a reply, deemed it wiser
to forgo a refutation :   Dechamps never received a reply
worth considering.[3]   A work of pure scholarship was furnished
by the Spanish Jesuit, Juan Martinez de Ripalda, when he
added to his great work *De ente supernaturali* (on the super-
natural) [4] a third volume directed against the followers of
Baius.

With a view to safeguarding the mass both of the educated
and the uneducated from the Jansenists, recourse was had
to Rome for a decision by the Apostolic See.   The first to take
this step was Nicolas Sanguin, the excellent Bishop of Senlis [5] ;
he was followed by Abra de Raconis, the Capuchin Yves,
Habert and Petau.[6]   Queen Anne, at the instigation of the
Jesuit De Lingendes, had expressed a desire to write to Rome
already in 1644 but Cardinal Mazarin was opposed to such a
step.[7]

Since there already existed a declaration by the Holy See
on Jansenius' " Augustinus ", Yves, De Raconis and Petau
pressed before all else for a judgment on Arnauld's book on
Holy Communion.   As a matter of fact that dangerous work

---

[1] He occasionally quotes Jansenius, whenever he is able to agree
with him (*loc. cit.*, 238, 323), also Conrius, *ibid.*, 241.

[2] *De lege et gratia*, Paris, 1648 (SOMMERVOGEL, VI., 611).

[3] SOMMERVOGEL, II., 1863.   For Fromond's reply, see
DE MEYER, 464.

[4] *De ente supernaturali*, Bordeaux, 1634, Lyons, 1663, Paris,
1870 and 1871 (SOMMERVOGEL, V., 640).   Other anti-Jansenist
writings in DE MEYER, 452 *seqq.*

[5] RAPIN, I., 87 *seq.*

[6] DE MEYER, 184, 295, 320, 428 ;   SOMMERVOGEL, VI., 614.

[7] RAPIN, I., 66.

had been under examination in Rome for some time already. According to a letter of Bentivoglio's secretary, Lutti, to D'Andilly,[1] Albizzi was of opinion that it should be prohibited owing to the many errors it contained ; consequently, the Jansenist Sinnich felt that it was essential that a theologian should be sent to Rome to defend Arnauld. In effect, by the end of April, 1645, Jean Bourgeois,[2] an able theologian, arrived in Rome as a representative of the party, whilst the Jesuit Brisacier, was simultaneously pressing the authorities to condemn Arnauld. Rome was not long in doubt as to the erroneous assertions in Arnauld's book [3] ; however, not a few French Bishops had given it their approval so that, as the sequel was to show, it was necessary to proceed cautiously.[4] When Abra de Raconis wrote to the Pope, the Assembly of the French clergy of 1645 charged him with having falsely

---

[1] On December 18, 1644, ARNAULD, Œuvres, XXVIII., 642 seq. *On June 26, 1645, a letter from Rome says : From the book on Frequent Communion " si fa un estratto delle propositioni che patiscono qualche difficoltà, perchè si possano qualificare dai qualificatori della S. Congregatione del S. Officio. Qualche tempo vi correrà prima che si aduni tanta Consulta ; onde non vi è pericolo che esca la censura prima che si termini costì l'assemblea dei vescovi di cotesto Stato," Barb. 6105, p. 378 seq., Vatican Library.

[2] HERMANT, I., 330 ; Relation de M. Bourgeois docteur de Sorbonne, contenant ce qui s'est passé à Rome en 1645 et 1646 pour la justification du livre de la Fréquente Communion, in ARNAULD, loc. cit., 674-725.

[3] BOURGEOIS, loc. cit., 684.

[4] GRIMALDI *writes already on April 19, 1644, to the Secretary of State : " Mi sento in obligo di rappresentare a V. E. che trovandosi impiegati oltre 20 dottori di Sorbona 15 preeati, e fra questi alcuni dei più affezionati alla S. Sede et in reputazione di maggior probità, quali conforme mi hanno detto, vivono con speranza che non si farà alcuna proibizione del medesimo libro, la quale non può seguire senza prejudicio della loro reputazione, che prima non sieno avvisati per poter render ragione della loro approvazione. Bibl. Angelica, Rome, S. 3, 1.

accused his fellow Bishops ; they demanded that his Archbishop should proceed against him. De Raconis upheld the
substance of what he had written but was forced to drop some
of his expressions.[1] The Bishops who had approved the book
on Holy Communion wrote a second letter to Rome, July 21st,
1645,[2] in a tone which betrays no desire on their part to be
taught by the Holy See.[3] They take it for granted that
Arnauld's book was daily doing greater good, that its author
was deserving of praise and the Jesuits of blame, whilst by
accrediting Bourgeois as their spokesman, they demanded a
papal pronouncement in this sense. A further letter to
Innocent X., dated March 2nd, 1646, is in a similar strain.
In answer to his report to Rome, de Raconis had received a
Brief [4] ; it was, however, couched in the same general terms
as another addressed at the same time to the Archbishop
of Sens,[5] the leader of Arnauld's episcopal supporters. None
the less the Bishops' new letter [6] takes de Raconis violently
to task for the step he had taken in Rome ; once more they
take it for granted that Arnauld's book is irreproachable,
whereas his opponents are wicked men ; the Bishops finally
summon the Pope at last to raise his voice on behalf of a man
so grievously calumniated. This letter only bore the signatures
of twelve Bishops for the gaps made by death in their ranks
had not been filled. Even more disagreeable for the signatories
must have been the circumstance that their leader, Octave de
Bellegarde, Archbishop of Sens, when on his death-bed, had
rejected Jansenism and charged his entourage to inform the

---

[1] ARNAULD, Œuvres, XXVI., LII.

[2] Ibid., XXVIII., 647.

[3] Cf. the editors of the Works of Arnauld (XXVI., XLVII.) :
" Loin de demander un jugement sur le livre de la Fréquente
Communion, ils reconoissoient que ce jugement étoit déjà porté
en sa faveur par leurs approbations, et ils le confirmoient de
nouveau etc."

[4] *Of October 22, in Innocentii X. Epist., II.–III. (Secretary
Gaspare de Simeonibus), p. 88, Pap. Sec. Arch.

[5] ARNAULD, loc. cit., 649.

[6] Ibid., 650.

Pope of the dangerous plans cherished by St. Cyran, to which his followers were endeavouring to give effect.[1] Nonetheless, all the Bishops of the Assembly of the Clergy in a sense took the side of the signatories, when they sent a deputation to the nuncio to protest against the letter of De Raconis [2] forasmuch as it accused the French Bishops of favouring error and dissension. Both Bagno and Panciroli sought to calm them with general assurances.[3] All this could not fail to convince Rome that the French Bishops must not be roused, all the more so as that loyal son of the Church, Bishop Habert, had expressed a fear that the Assembly of the Clergy was quite capable of giving its approval to Jansenius' " Augustinus ".[4]

A memorial by Cardinal De Lugo [5] conveys a similar warning against the use of sterner measures, lest the party, which still styled itself Catholic, should be driven into open rebellion. Since precisely at this moment the party was trying to give a Catholic meaning to its teaching, the Pope should take them at their word and whilst exhorting them to concord, stress those points in connexion with the administration of the Sacrament of Penance and that of the Eucharist on which there can be no controversy among Catholics, such as, for instance, that there was no law demanding the performance of the penance before the absolution by the priest, or public penance for hidden sins. All these points—Lugo enumerates

---

[1] De Meyer, 356. Nuncio Bagno sent this explanation to Rome on March 26, 1646, *ibid.*

[2] By a decision of February 6, 1646. This explains the exaggerated rumour in the *Diario of Ameyden of 1650 (Barb. 4819, p. 107)* : Incomincia dar pensiero la controversia Janseniana prendendo piede in Francia e stando per questa parte la maggior parte de' vescovi di quel regno, ove sono depositati ducentomila scudi per istampare tutto quello che verrà scritto per questa opinione : cosa che potrà cagionare turbolenze grandi," Vatican Library.

[3] De Meyer, 434.

[4] *Ibid.*, 184.

[5] In Lämmer, *Meletemata*, 391 *seqq.*

six of them—Arnauld seems to deny in some places whilst
he grants them in others ; accordingly, in any future edition
of his book he should be made to make a preliminary statement
that he held these points, as well as to attenuate his eulogy
of Jansenius in so far as the latter's achievements in the sphere
of scholarship were concerned.   Besides the fixed points in
regard to the administration of the two Sacraments, there were
others for which no certain general ruling could be laid down ;
these must be left in every instance to the judgment of the
confessor, as, for instance, the frequency of reception of the
Sacraments.

In Rome there was no inclination to go even as far as Lugo
had counselled. A decision on frequent Communion was only
issued in 1679 and it was not until 1690 that the questions
about Penance raised by Arnauld were authoritatively dealt
with.[1] Another point on which De Lugo states that Arnauld
should be made to speak more clearly in his book, is his
assertion of the quality of the two Apostles, SS. Peter and
Paul. In the preface of his book Arnauld had represented
as models of penance " the two heads of the Church who
constitute but one ".[2]

The unostentatious little paragraph was not so innocent as
it was made to look. The Catholic dogma of the Pope's primacy
over all Bishops is based on the fact that Peter was chosen

---

[1] DENZINGER, *Euchir. symb.*[16] (1928), n. 1147, 1306, 1312
seq. The Jansenists affirmed that Arnauld was not meant in
the condemned propositions (ARNAULD, *Œuvres*, XXVI., XCIII.
seq. DE MEYER, 240, note 2). But who else could have been
meant ? An appeal to Viva (DE MEYER, 241) does not hold good,
because Viva says expressly : " cum theses fere omnes ab
Alexandro VIII. confixæ in Iansenii doctrina et propositionibus
nitantur . . ." (De Iansenii propositionibus universim : VIVA,
Opera, VII., Ferrariae, 1757, 120).

[2] " les deux chefs de l'Église qui n'en font qu'un " (n. 6,
Œuvres, XXVII., 85). The Jansenists asserted that the pro-
position had been added on his own authority by De Barcos,
Saint-Cyran's nephew (*ibid.*, XXVI., LVII. ; DUPIN, *Hist.*,
II., 14).

to be the head of the Church and that Peter's successor in
the Roman See is also his successor as head of the Church.
Now in order to combat the papacy, De Dominis had laid
down two propositions : first that Peter was in all things the
equal of his fellow apostle, hence he was not head of the
whole Church in any higher sense than Paul ; second, that
Peter was not Bishop of Rome in a different sense than
Paul, that is, he was so solely in virtue of his Apostolic office,
not by any special link with Rome.[1]   Was it Arnauld's
intention, with his seemingly casual reflexion, to foster the
rise of similar ideas ?   There was every reason to mistrust
the Jansenists whenever they discussed the nature of the
Church's   authority.   Moreover   the   accusation   against
Richelieu, that he aimed at the establishment of a separate
patriarchate for France, was fresh in everybody's memory.
The notion of two heads of the Church could also be interpreted
so as to provide support for the plan of another Pope on
French soil.[2]

This suspicion was heightened by the publication, in
connexion with Arnauld's thesis, of a number of anonymous
pamphlets which sought to establish the equality of the two
Apostles.   On January 18th, 1645, the Paris nuncio, Bagno,
forwarded a copy of the first of these publications.   A little
later he reported that Duke Henry of Bourbon, a fervent
Catholic, desired to see these new declarations condemned,
that the Queen and Mazarin saw them with displeasure and
that Habert was preparing a refutation of which he forwarded
the proofs to Rome.[3]   At the end of April the Roman envoy
of the Jansenists, Bourgeois,[4] learnt that the proposition
about the two heads of the Church had been condemned
by the Inquisition.   Although, as was asserted, the approval

[1] *Cf.* M. BECANUS, *De republ. eccles.*, l. 2, c. 7, obi. 7 ; l. 3,
c. 2 : *Opera Omnia*, Mogunt., 1649, 1359, 1363.

[2] That such preoccupations were entertained in Rome is
attested by Bourgeois in his " Report " (ARNAULD, *Œuvres*,
XXVIII., 677 ; *cf.* 680).

[3] DE MEYER, 437 *seq.*

[4] Report, *loc. cit.*, 677.

of the sixteen Bishops did not include the preface to Arnauld's book,[1] so that there was no great fear of offending these prelates by the condemnation, Innocent delayed its publication and when De Barcos published a small work on the greatness of the Roman Church, the Pope ordered a fresh examination of the whole affair.[2]

Bourgeois and his ally Duchesne naturally did all they could to prevent a definitive condemnation. In Paris people learned from the Roman newspapers and nuncio Bagno from his letters,[3] that they even spread the report that the equality of the two Apostles was taught by the Sorbonne. This falsehood could only damage their cause. Vincent de Paul reported to Cardinal Grimaldi on the whole question [4] and the syndic of the theological Faculty, Cornet, laid it before the Sorbonne. Contrary to Bagno's expectation, the University had at first hesitated to pronounce on the matter, but it now informed the nuncio that it had nothing to do with the assertions of the two Doctors. Accordingly the Holy See no longer put off the publication of the decree of the Inquisition which bears the date of January 25th, 1647. Arnauld is not mentioned by name but the assertion concerning the equality of the Princes of the Apostles is textually quoted from the book on Holy Communion and declared heretical in that form, or in any other, in so far as it was understood as claiming equality for both Apostles in the government of the Church. The two opuscules of De Barcos and all other writings which maintained the condemned opinion were prohibited.[5]

Rome's wisdom in temporarily refraining from a condemnation of the book on Communion soon became apparent. At the nuncio's request Mazarin had had the papal decree examined and allowed it to be printed and Bagno added to it a letter of his own. It was not long before an anonymous

---

[1] RAPIN, I., 32.

[2] The opinions of the *qualificatori* on this in DE MEYER, 439 *seq.*

[3] RAPIN, I., 116.

[4] On October 4, 1646, *ibid.*, reprinted in COSTE, III., 65 *seqq.*

[5] DENZINGER, *loc. cit.*, n. 1091 ; REUSCH, *Index*, II., 450 *seqq.*

writer, in all probability De Barcos, pounced upon the decree
and heaped injuries on the Pope and the Jesuits. The Government ordered his libel to be burnt, but now Parliament took
action. On May 8th, at a stormy session, Broussel protested
against the promulgation of the decree and the action of the
nuncio whom he accused of arrogating to himself undue
authority. When a deputation of Parliament repaired to
the palace for the purpose of offering its good wishes to the
King and Queen who were about to leave the capital, so
heated an altercation took place between the first president
and the chancellor that the Queen had to call them to order.
Mazarin sought to calm the excitement,[1] but Parliament
would not yield. Two days later, in the great Chamber,
Talon made three protests against the decree of the Inquisition
and the action of the nuncio : the Roman Congregations,
he claimed, were not recognized in France for the country
would not put up with the intolerable Inquisition ; further-
more Bagno styled himself nuncio to the King and the
whole of France whereas his mission was confined to the
person of the King ; lastly he talked as if he had territorial
jurisdiction in France seeing that he spoke of communicating
the papal decrees to the Bishops, and of the " Archives "
of the nunciature, whereas the nuncio in France had no
such thing ; if they allowed these trifles to pass they must
be prepared for bigger things.[2]

The nuncio found a defender against these accusations in
the person of the chancellor. Bagno, the latter explained,
spoke as his five predecessors had done ; the papal decree
had been printed by the King's permission and the expression
" Archives " simply designated the place where the nuncio
kept his papers. After these explanations Mazarin felt he
could impose silence on Parliament and on May 13th, 1647,
the King wrote in this sense from Compiègne. However,

---

[1] Bagno, May 10, 1647, in COVILLE, 155 seq.

[2] Bagno, May 24, 1647, ibid., 156 seq. ; Remontrance de
M. Talon, of May 10, 1647, in ARNAULD, Œuvres, XVII., 822 ;
Arrêt du Parlement of May 15, 1647, ibid., 825.

Parliament did not take the hint ; it decreed that without the King's express permission no one could print any Roman documents and that all copies of the papal decree as well as the nuncio's covering letter must be confiscated. Even these resolutions failed to embarrass the resourceful Mazarin. In fact even before this Talon had himself pointed to a possible way out ; this was that the Paris Parliament should pronounce judgment but that the sentence should not be made public ; in this way they would satisfy the jurists without unduly offending Rome. Mazarin now fell back upon this expedient.[1] A final decision was thus circumvented, for neither the resolution of Parliament nor the royal permission to print the decree of the Roman Inquisition were valid : the one lacked confirmation by the King, and the other that of Parliament. Innocent X. showed himself grateful to Mazarin : in a Brief of March 30th, 1647,[2] he extolled his zeal for religion.

The resolutions of Parliament in no way affected the attitude of loyal Catholics towards the papal decree ; it was repeatedly quoted in subsequent years as a proof of the authority and prestige which the Holy See enjoyed in France.[3] On the other hand the Holy See must have been far more deeply hurt by the fact that Urban VIII.'s Bull against Jansenius' " Augustinus " continued to encounter obstacles in France than by the objections to the decision on the subject of the two heads of the Church. From the first Innocent X. stressed the duty of all theologians to receive the Bull and he ordered a fresh impression of the document ; the decree of the Inquisition of July 29th, 1644, concerning its authenticity, was joined to the Bull and thus enforced anew. However, the measure yielded but small results. The Jansenists at once objected that the decrees of the Inquisition had no binding force in France ; even when the Pope sought to take the sting out of this pretext by

[1] COVILLE, 158–160.
[2] *Annales de St.-Louis*, II., 362.
[3] See below, p. 246.

ordering Bagno, on February 25th, 1645, to communicate the Bull to all the Bishops and the Doctors of Paris, it was not formally received though its doctrinal decisions apparently met with submission. This conduct was likewise adopted by some religious Orders, such as the Discalced Carmelites and the Feuillants, whereas the Superior General of the Oratory, Bourgoing, demanded from his subjects explicit acceptance of the Bull.[1] Even Alexander VIII. found himself compelled to defend the authenticity of the Bull.[2]

(2.)

From the first the Sorbonne had taken an equivocal attitude in the Jansenist controversy. Though pressed by Richelieu to do so, it refused to make a definite pronouncement on the heresy or to receive Urban VIII.'s Bull without reservation.[3] It is true that the older professors did not countenance

[1] DE MEYER, 419–421. *Cf.* above, p. 224.
[2] On December 7, 1690 ; see DENZINGER, n. 1321.
[3] DE MEYER, 124 s., 136 s. " *Trovo che la maggior parte de' dottori della medesima Sorbona concorrono in questo senso di non stimare espediente, almeno per adesso, prescrivere cosa alcuna nè per l'una, nè per l'altra parte, non parendo che in tutto si possa approvare nè rifiutare l'opera del Jansenio." Six members of the Sorbonne had approved the book ; " i suoi scolari di buono et ardente ingegno con difficoltà si n'asterranno dal publicare qualche scritto in sua difesa. . . . Richelieu mostra desiderio, e per sua parte si vanno facendo diligenze, acciò la Sorbona censuri et riprovi l'Augustinus, ma sin ora non trova disposizione a bastanza in quei dottori, la maggior parte de' quali, quando si venga al cimento, inclinerebbe ad approvare che levate alcune poche cose si possa sostenere il libro come dottrina di s. Agostino et altri padri, e v'è stato tra essi che mi ha accennato che in questa controversia sarebbe molto a proposito qualche consulta e resoluzione della S. Sede. Non lascio di farne motivo al card. di Richelieu per intendere più particolarmente in ciò i suoi sentimenti et procurare d'indurlo in quello di V. E., l'impedire di scrivere all'una e all'altra parte " (Grimaldi, June 13, 1642, Bibl. Angelica, Rome, p. 3, 1). On April 1, 1644, Grimaldi *writes (*ibid.*)

the innovations, but in 1645 Sainte-Beuve began to expound Jansenius' teaching on grace and the younger students adopted his views in ever increasing numbers.[1] Care was taken not to state publicly that the doctrine that was being taught was that of Jansenius, and when the necessity arose it was urged in defence of such conduct that on December 11th, 1643, the Archbishop of Paris had forbidden all reference to Jansenius.[2] Arnauld was even then the unquestioned head of the party ; he was represented to the young people as a paragon of ability, learning and genius ; as the brother of Mère Angélique, the principal disciple of St. Cyran and the heir of his spirit, the author of the much read book on Communion and the victim of unjust persecution, he enjoyed unequalled prestige and the splendour of his name won over to Jansenism many of the younger theologians.[3]

Before long they found the courage to say that very soon all the Bishops of the realm would follow the example of the Coadjutor of Paris and the Archbishop of Sens ; that in six years' time the party would dispose of all the episcopal sees of France, when it would allot them to its members. A

---

that the Sorbonne had decided not to accept the Louvain letter (see present work, Vol. XXIX., 126 *seqq.*), apparently because it had been directed to the Rector " ma in effetto per non volere in alcun modo interessarsi nelle opinioni di Jansenio ". Some were for exhorting the Louvain professors to obedience, " ma la determinazione è stato di non fare altro, per tenersi nelli puri sentimenti della chiesa Romana, senza dar alcun segno d'inclinar ad una parte nè all'altra." In 1645 Olier writes to Caulet on Jansenism. " Maintenant cela fait de tels progrès et s'insinue sous le prétexte de la réforme et de la piété si universellement dans les âmes qu'il n'y a rien presentement pour quoy on doive plus prier. Ces opinions ôtent a Dieu tant d'âmes et de serviteurs que cela n'est pas croyable, tout tourne de ce côté la et arrache ainsi mil âmes et mil serviteurs très disposés," *Bullet. de litt. ecclés.*, 1902, 219.

[1] RAPIN, I., 43–6, 113.

[2] *Ibid.*, 93.

[3] *Ibid.*, 113.

spirit of innovation got hold of the young professors ; every thesis had at all costs to contain some novelty, above all something of the Jansenist teaching on grace.[1]

In the spring of 1648 the situation became even more tense. François Véron, first a Jesuit and subsequently parish priest of Charenton, a keen and successful opponent of the Huguenots,[2] now intervened in the controversy on grace. In a book against the Jansenists he explained that their teaching on predestination even to eternal reprobation had already been expounded in the 9th century by the monk Gottschalk and no less than five Councils had condemned it in the same century. Moreover their teaching was a throw-back to Calvinism, which as a matter of fact, had been professed by Arnauld's ancestors. The style of Véron's book was violent and it added to the annoyance of the Jansenists that the sub-title of the book should have described it as " The Gag of the Jansenists " and as such it was hawked in the streets, to the merriment of the populace [3] ; consequently in May, 1647, they sought a judgment of the Sorbonne in their favour. However, the syndic declared that he must first hear the theologians who had approved the book ; as the representative of the latter the Franciscan Charruau spoke in defence of the book under attack and in doing so, made an onslaught on the Jansenists.[4] In the ensuing debate the syndic expressed the opinion that in order to judge Véron it would be necessary to examine Jansenius. Pereyret replied that this would take ten years since it would be necessary to consult the writings of St. Augustine and others. In the end it was resolved to refrain from the examination in question. However, Cornet added, if anyone wished to submit a few propositions to the judgment of the Faculty, he might do so within the ensuing two months.[5]

---

[1] RAPIN, I., 163 *seq.*, 280.

[2] Concerning him FERET, *Un curé de Charenton au 17ᵉ siècle*, Paris, 1881.

[3] RAPIN, I., 227.

[4] *Ibid.*, 229.

[5] SAINT-AMOUR, f. 5.

The Faculty was reluctant to pass sentence on Véron as this was bound to hamper his action against the Huguenots. But for the Jansenists the likening of their master to Gottschalk, and the condemnation of his teaching by five Councils, was all the more serious as just then the Jesuit Sirmond had drawn the attention of the learned world to the condemnation of precisely similar theses in Christian antiquity and in the person of Gottschalk.[1] With a view to facilitating a judgment by the Sorbonne in their sense, they sought to eliminate from the assembly of the Doctors their opponents who, for the most part, were to be found among the religious. As a matter of fact, at the suggestion of the Jansenists Le Roux and Saint-Amour, Parliament re-enacted a parliamentary decision of 1626 according to which only two Doctors from the Mendicant Orders were allowed to take part in the meetings of the Sorbonne. However, the syndic Cornet opposed with all his might a decision which would have delivered the Faculty into the hands of the friends of the Jansenists and which, in point of fact, had not acquired force of law even in 1626. Parliament also no longer insisted on the matter and the troubles of the Fronde drew attention to other things.[2]

Further developments were occasioned by Cornet " a scholar of the old stamp, of the old straightforwardness, the old efficiency, insensible both to flattery and to fear,

---

[1] He published the so-called *Praedestinatus* in 1643 (cf. O. BARDENHEWER, *Gesch. der altkirchl. Lit.*, IV., 520). Writings of HINCMAR of Rheims, 1645, of RABANUS MAURUS, 1647. About the same time as VÉRON's work appeared the *Historia praedestinatiana* of SIRMOND, 1648. To the publication of *Praedestinatus* DE BARCOS answered with success (DE MEYER, 169). The *Historia praedestinatiana* remained unanswered ; it was, however, affected by the condemnation of VÉRON. To the other publications the Jansenists opposed, under the name of the Mint official, MAUGUIN, 1650, a collection of writings also unpublished, of the time of Gottschalk ; in 1655 the Jesuit Cellot wrote fully about Gottschalk, RAPIN, I., 230 *seqq.*

[2] RAPIN, I., 235 *seq.* ; SAINT-AMOUR, f. 7 *seqq.*

one of the greatest ornaments of the Church and of his century ". During the troublous period that was to follow Cornet was to have ample opportunity to justify this tribute paid to him by Bossuet in the funeral oration of his beloved master.[1] At the memorable sitting of the Faculty of July 1st, 1649, Cornet took advantage of the permission to submit some propositions to the Sorbonne's judgment. He began by protesting against the young people's mania for innovations. It had happened that theses which had been struck out by the Faculty nevertheless reappeared on the printed programmes. Others had not dared to go so far, yet they had defended the cancelled theses ; moreover Sainte-Beuve had infringed the rights of the president by speaking from the body of the hall and ordering a disputant to hold his tongue. Things could not go on in this fashion, hence he submitted for examination seven propositions which he requested the Faculty to accept.[2]

The step taken by the syndic was a bold one for the first five out of the seven propositions were taken from the " Augustinus " of the Bishop of Ypres and were its very soul and marrow. They run as follows ; " first, some commandments of God are impossible even for the just, considering their actual strength, even with the best of wills, and the grace which would make them possible is also lacking ; second, in the state of fallen nature we never resist an interior grace ; third, to merit, or to demerit, in the state of fallen nature, a man does not need freedom from necessity, freedom from coercion suffices ; fourth, the Semi-Pelagians taught the necessity of an interior, preventing grace for every action, even for the beginning of faith ; they were heretics forasmuch as they considered grace to be such that the human will can

---

[1] *Œuvres*, XVII., Versailles, 1816, 616, 619. He calls him " protecteur des pauvres et le soulagement des hôpitaux " (*ibid.*, 635) ; he extols his " science exacte et profonde " and his " prudence consommée " (*ibid.*, 626).

[2] SAINT-AMOUR, f. 13 ; RAPIN, I., 280 *seq.* ; [DUMAS], I,, 5 *seqq.*

either co-operate with it or refuse to do so ; fifth, it is a Semi-Pelagian error to assert without qualification that Christ has shed His blood and died for all men ". These are the famous five theses round which so fierce a controversy was about to rage. The other two propositions are unconnected with " Augustinus " and were soon left on one side. Jansenius' name was left out of the five propositions just as his doctrine was taught without his name being mentioned.

Cornet's proposal at once caused a great stir. Sainte-Beuve, Bourgeois and others would not so much as hear of a discussion of the seven points on the plea that they turned on matters where the Church allowed freedom ; what was aimed at was a covert attack on Jansenius ; the examination of Véron's book had been declined because of the difficulty of the task ; was it any easier now, after the lapse of a whole year ? However, in the end Cornet's proposal was accepted by a majority of votes, a committee of eight members was appointed whose duty it would be to report on the theses in question at the next monthly meeting.

Meanwhile minds were further heated by the prompt appearance of three pamphlets against Cornet. The most important had been thrown into the arena by Arnauld from his hiding place.[1] According to him Cornet's aim was nothing less than an attack on the teaching of the great Doctor of the Church, St. Augustine.[2] If he complained of innovations by the young people it was that, owing to his ignorance and violence, St. Augustine's true and old principles seemed to him new.[3] According to Arnauld, behind the syndic stood the Jesuits who made use of him in order to throw the Faculty into confusion and so to hide the shame of their bad principles.[4] Of the five propositions the first had been textually taken from Jansenius and contained the true teaching of St. Augustine whilst the remaining four were intentionally

---

[1] *Considérations sur l' entreprise faite par Maître N. Cornet* (*Œuvres*, XIX., 1 seqq.).

[2] *Ibid.*, 9.

[3] *Ibid.*, 10.

[4] *Ibid.*, 11.

equivocal so as to make it possible to use them against Augustine.[1] The book saw four editions in 1649 and helped not a little to strengthen the resistance of the friends of Jansenius.

August 1st was the day appointed for the sitting of the Faculty at which the report on the seven propositions was to be submitted. At the very outset Chancellor Loisel rose to contest the dean's right to preside. The whole sitting was taken up by this dispute and the seven propositions were not submitted at all.[2] Already three days earlier 62 minority Doctors, all of them secular priests, with the exception of one Augustinian, had had recourse to the means by which it was possible to burke almost any ecclesiastical initiative : viz. they appealed to Parliament because of abuse of ecclesiastical authority. However, at the parliamentary sitting of August 18th President Molé, at one time a friend of St. Cyran's, did not allow the appeal to be discussed. The parties exchanged mutual promises to leave the matter alone for three or four months and meanwhile to seek an understanding.[3]

Some four weeks of the four months' armistice had elapsed when the existence of a draft of a censure became known in which the seven propositions were described as partly heretical and partly as contrary to the Scriptures, or as false and scandalous. The minority at once lodged another appeal. In the judicial proceedings of October 5th the genuineness of the censure was not contested but all attempts at mediation failed so that a discussion of the matter was fixed for the day after the feast of St. Martin.

In the meantime another dispute had thrown more oil on the flames. On October 1st Hallier had been elected syndic in succession to Cornet. Again Saint-Amour, under divers pretexts, lodged an appeal with Parliament and as the price of the recognition of his election, Hallier was challenged to

---

[1] *Ibid.,* 15 *seqq.*

[2] RAPIN, I., 285 ; [DUMAS], I., 9.

[3] SAINT-AMOUR, f. 22 *seqq.* ; RAPIN, *loc. cit.*

carry out the parliamentary resolutions of 1626 [1] against the Mendicants and to give a free hand to the party of the juniors at the Faculty.[2] To this Hallier demurred ; however, the appeal to Parliament was also without result inasmuch as President Molé was not only unwilling to pronounce sentence, but was bent on conciliation.

Thus the dispute was bound to come up once more at the session of the Faculty in which the Jansenists formed a majority. Consequently, at the stormy session of December 1st, the " disciples of St. Augustine " tried a last artifice : if Cornet's seven propositions were to be discussed, they insisted that seven propositions of Molina together with an eighth from the lecture notes of Professor Pereyret should likewise be examined. A committee was to conduct the inquiry in presence of the Coadjutor of Paris, after which the Faculty would give its decision by a two-thirds' majority.[3]

The Faculty accepted the proposed committee, Saint-Amour being one of its nine members. On December 6th a formula was accepted by all, with the sole exception of Saint-Amour's vote.[4] The formula stated that with regard to the propositions in dispute and the Thomistico-Molinist difference of opinion, sufficient provision had been made by the decisions of the Church and those of the Faculty, hence all that was needed was that syndic Hallier should carry them into effect, appealing to the Faculty if he met with difficulties and in urgent cases to his predecessors. In this way Hallier was acknowledged as syndic but it had also been made clear that a condemnation of Jansenius could not be obtained from the Faculty— consequently Cornet's offensive had failed.

If the opponents of the new teaching gave up the hopes of seeing it condemned, their retreat was probably due in no small measure to the warnings of nuncio Bagno. On July 16th, 1649, Bagno wrote to Rome that the plan of the

---

[1] See above, p. 240.
[2] SAINT-AMOUR, f. 36.
[3] *Ibid.*, f. 38 *seqq.*
[4] SAINT-AMOUR, f. 43.

well-disposed professors was not universally approved, for whatever the decision might be, it would meet with much opposition.[1] After the futile August session of the Faculty, he felt convinced that the affair would not be further discussed at the Sorbonne, in fact this was believed to be the better course ; he himself had done all he could to bring about this result.[2] Rome approved the nuncio's action. The Inquisition instructed him to restrain the Sorbonne from passing sentence on the propositions submitted to it and to persuade the Coadjutor of Paris to forbid all preaching for or against Jansenius.[3] As a matter of fact the nuncio did obtain a promise to this effect.[4] On November 9th Bagno felt he might report to Rome that in view of the obstacles put in the way by the opposite party, as well as his own exhortations to the well disposed among the professors, it was practically certain that the Sorbonne would deliver no sentence ; they might reckon on this with all the more certainty as precisely those who had pressed for judgment by the Faculty had now had recourse to Cardinal Roma with a view to a papal decision.[5]

However, by now matters had gone so far that the nuncio could not promise himself that even a papal decision would meet with immediate submission. "The number and the prestige of the so-called Jansenists grow daily," he wrote on

---

[1] " *perchè in qualunque modo che la Sorbona havesse dato fuori il suo parere, per la qualità de' tempi correnti havrebbe havuto molte contradizioni, le quali già sono cominciate." *Nunziat. di Francia*, 98, Pap. Secr. Archives.

[2] " *Si può credere che più non sia per trattarsi di questa materia in detta Sorbona, il che vien creduto per meglio, e io vi son concorso con lo poco che ho potuto." *Ibid.*

[3] *Bagno, November 9, 1649, *ibid.*

[4] *Bagno, November 26, 1649, *ibid.*

[5] *" La detta censura per gli impedimenti procurati dalla parte contraria et esortazioni da me fatte a quelli che con buona intenzione mostravano desiderarla . . . si può quasi fermamente credere che più non sia parlarsene." Bagno, November 9, 1649, *ibid.*

October 22nd, 1649. " Despite the Bull and the papal decrees
they preach, teach and print books in support of that false
doctrine. Some Bishops allow it, others, though more zealous,
do not forbid it because they are unable to obtain the royal
support ; thus there is great danger of a new heresy creeping
into this realm. Though the Queen is opposed to the new
opinions, she takes no steps against them, perhaps because
she doubts whether her commands would be obeyed. Thereupon a few good and zealous theologians of the Sorbonne
sought to obtain from the Faculty a censure and explanation
of the subjoined propositions, in view of the power of their
opponents in Parliament. These theologians likewise requested
me to dispatch to your Eminence a sheet setting forth what,
in their opinion, the Pope might do by way of remedying
this state of affairs. The evil is very great indeed, but unless
the Holy See has the assistance of the King, there is little
hope that it will be obeyed." [1]

Bagno joined to his report the draft of a censure by the
committee of the Faculty as well as some suggestions on the
remedies which the Pope might apply to the dangers that

---

[1] " Giornalmente," he writes on October 20, 1649, " va
crescendo il numero e autorità di quei che qua chiamano giansenisti,
i quali nonostante la bolla e i decreti dei sommi pontefici predicano,
insegnano e stampano libri a favor di quella falsa dottrina con
permissione di alcuni vescovi et senza repugnanza degl'altri,
che sono più zelanti, non potendosi ottener l'assistenza della
autorità di Re. . . . Così esiste pericolo grande di introdurre
una nuova eresia in questo regno. La regina si mostra contraria
a queste nuove opinioni, ma S. M. non piglia resolutione alcuna,
forse per dubbio che li suoi ordini non fussero obbediti. Porro
pensorono alcuni buoni e zelanti theologi della Sorbona . . . di
procurare la censura e dichiaratione dei dubbii, ch'io mando
qui allegati mediante la facoltà perchè i loro avversari sono
potenti nel parlamento. Vengo ricercato da medesimi d'inviare
a V. E. un foglio che contiene quel che li buoni theologi credono
che N. S. potesse fare per provederli. Il male veramente è grandissimo ; ma se l'autorità della S. Sede non è assistita dal Re.
sarà poco obedita." *Excerpta ex actis s. Officii a.* 1647.

threatened.[1]   There was no more powerful means, Bagno
wrote, than the intervention of the Holy See ; since the
decree on the two heads of the Church nothing more had
been written on the subject whereas previously each week had
brought some fresh publication.   If the Pope was willing to
give a decision, he might very well base himself on the propositions recently censured by the committee of the Faculty,
though on that occasion the party used both violence and
cunning to prevent the Faculty from being as much as
informed of the occurrence.[2]   The propositions were so chosen
that their condemnation would be the best antidote against
evil teaching, and without a doubt nearly everyone, or
certainly the majority, would bow to the papal condemnation.[3]
On the other hand, unless God and His Vicar intervened,
that poison would before long run through the whole Faculty
for nearly all the younger Doctors were infected by it and
openly styled themselves Jansenists and " disciples of
Augustine ".

The seven propositions forwarded by Bagno were now
submitted to the consultors of the Holy Office for examination.
However, a prompt decision on the affair was not come to.
The memorandums sent in to the Inquisition show very

[1] " *Commentarius remediorum, quae Romae adhiberi possunt
gravissimis incommodis et periculis, quae iure merito timentur
ex factione sectatorum doctrinae D. Iansenii, etc."   Draft for
the letter of October 22, 1649, ibid.

[2] " *Si vero. . . .   Sedes Romana aliquid de novo statuit,
opportunum forte esset, eas propositiones carpere, quae nuper
a deputatis facultatis theologicae Parisiensis censura affectae
sunt, sed quominus ea censura in publica mensis, ut assolet,
congregatione a tota facultate admitteretur aut etiam ad eam
a deputatis referretur, factionis illius et artibus et vi manifesta
effectum est " (ibid.).   It is therefore not true that the draft of
the censure of the committee of the Faculty was given as a
censure of the Faculty.

[3] " *Nec dubium est, quin, si placuerit SS^{mo} D. N. eas damnare,
aut fere omnes aut certe quam plurimi damnationem amplexuri
sint."   Ibid.

clearly what were the causes of the delay [1] : it was feared lest a condemnation of the first five propositions should prejudice the Dominican doctrine on grace and thus hurt a deserving theological school.   True, most of the consultors rejected all five, or even the seven propositions, though they were unwilling to describe each particular thesis as heretical in every sense.   In his memorandum on the first four propositions [2] the Master of the Palace, the Dominican Candidus, defends them all, though he adds to each of them a note stating that " Jansenius understands this thus ",[3] after which he endeavours to prove from Jansenius' book that the latter held the same opinions as himself.

The problem is very fully discussed in the memorial of Hilarion Rancati, the Cistercian Abbot of S. Croce in Gerusalemme in Rome.[4]   According to Rancati the first five propositions do no more than deny merely sufficient grace. Now the Molinists assert that sufficient grace is a dogma and the Thomists dare not deny it ; when it is objected to them that the denial of sufficient grace was a necessary sequel of physical premotion, they try to evade the arguments of their opponents ; thus they obviously admit that their cause is lost if they are forced to deny sufficient grace.   Jansenius says that he is in agreement with the Thomists, but the latter admit a sufficient grace which empowers man to do what is good and to avoid sin, so that man somehow possesses a real capacity, as well as freedom from coercion, whereas Jansenius denies freedom, power and sufficient grace. Sufficient grace was taught by the Council of Trent and the

---

[1] " *Diversorum vota super 5 propositionibus collecta a fr. Phil. Vicecom. ord. Eremit. S. Aug." Biblia Angelica, Rome, R. 3, 5 f., 1 seqq.

[2] Ibid., f. 155–167.

[3] " Sensus Iansenii est : . . ."

[4] Ibid., f. 41–9. Also in Bibl. Angelica, Rome, S. 3, 1 : *Excerpta ex V. Parte circa librum Iansenii, f. 94–9 (dated October 31 1649), and in Bibl. Casanatense, Rome, X., VI., 34, f. 60–2. Cf. ANG. FUMAGALLI, Vita del P. D. Il. Rancati, Brescia, 1762 ; DE MEYER, 127, n. 2.

provincial Councils of Sens and Cologne of the years 1528 and 1536, hence theologians cannot be prevented from describing Jansenism as a straying from the faith, and in so doing they did no injury to anyone.[1]

Rancati then examines the five propositions one by one and shows that they are all rooted in the denial of sufficient grace, though it could not be denied that Jansenius supported each of them with texts from St. Augustine which are very difficult to explain. As a matter of fact that which theologians say of the Fathers in general, namely that in the heat of the struggle with pagans and heretics they sometimes allowed themselves to be carried too far, is also true of Augustine who in his fight against the Pelagians speaks too unfavourably of free will. Consequently, however much theologians should be left free to censure Jansenius, Rancati is of opinion that the Holy See had better refrain from intervening in an affair which was not as yet ripe for definition.[2] If, however, it was deemed expedient to go further, it should be done only after long and careful study by a number of theologians, including some from the Thomist and Molinist schools,, for the condemnation of Jansenius would necessarily lead to conclusions being drawn concerning the questions which were the object of such lengthy discussions under Urban VIII., seeing that the defenders of physical premotion asserted its necessity no less strongly than Jansenius insisted on the necessity of efficient grace for every good work. Now if this necessity did not do away with sufficient grace in the Thomist system, though it did in that of Jansenius, the difference was verbal rather than substantial, for what the Thomists called sufficient and Jansenism insufficient grace was one and the same thing.

Accordingly Rancati was of opinion that they should be content with the Bull of Urban VIII. ; the most that could

---

[1] " *Censeo proinde dotrinam Iansenii sine iniuria (against a theological school) a theologis affici posse nota erroris in fide."

[2] " *Propterea censerem, liberum maneat doctoribus theologis censuris contra Iansenium uti, Sedis Apostolicae auctoritas in hoc negotio plane adhuc immaturo ne oppigneretur " (*loc. cit.*).

be done would be a prohibition to bring these controversies to the notice of the people. At the conclusion of this examination by the theologians, Rome was sufficiently informed on the nature of Jansenism, yet no public definition ensued. In accordance with Rancati's memorial, nuncio Bagno was instructed, by Innocent X.'s order, to induce the Assembly of the Clergy of 1650 to obey the Bull of Urban VIII. and to demand obedience to it from its subjects.[1] His Holiness would give a decision on the new teaching, the nuncio declared, if the King and a large section of the French hierarchy would press him to do so. Vincent de Paul, who supplies this information,[2] adds that the King was willing to write to the Pope and the first President declared that Parliament would accept the Bull if it was not described as a decree of the Roman Inquisition.

Complete silence was, however, impossible for the Holy See. In 1650, on the feast of St. Louis and in Rome itself, the ex-Oratorian Hersent, the same who had written *Optatus Gallus* against Richelieu, went so far as to preach Jansenism in the presence of three Cardinals, to print his sermon, to dedicate it to the Pope and in the dedication to extol the Bishop of Ypres as a man without his equal and another Augustine. Hersent escaped the order of the Inquisition for his arrest by flight but the Dominican Du Four, who had allowed the sermon to be printed, went to prison in his place.[3]

On the same day on which the Inquisition took action

---

[1] " *Sanctissimus iussit (July 28, 1650), Nuntio rescribi, ut efficaciter interponat officia sua apud Cleri Assembleam, ut non solum sint constanter obedientes Bullae Apostolicae publicatae contra Iansenium, sed ut curent ab eorum subditis eandem obedienter observari. Bagno, April 8, 1650. Biblioteca Angelica, Rome, *loc. cit.*

[2] Letter of April 23, 1651, in MAYNARD, II., 328.

[3] RAPIN, I., 322 seq.; SAINT-AMOUR, 47, 49, 61; AMEYDEN, *Diario, October, 1650, Barb.* 4819, f. 122 seq. (also RANKE, *Päpste*, III.⁸, 96). Two *apologetical writings* by DU FOUR to the Inquisition in *Barb.* 1023, pp. 7–18, Vatican Library.

against Hersent, it also prohibited another small book but one that was of great value for the Jansenists.[1] Their *Catechism of Grace* had already been refuted in a number of publications [2] but the worst thing that could befall it was that a Calvinist professor of Gröningen having translated it into Latin, declared that it confirmed the teaching on grace of the Calvinist synod of Dortrecht ; consequently he expressed his hope that the Jansenists would end by completely dropping the Council of Trent.[3] The University of Louvain had the opuscule translated into Flemish,[4] but the Inquisition prohibited its circulation on October 6th, 1650. The condemnation was a blow for the Jansenists in Gallican France also. Arnauld defended the Catechism from the attacks of the Jesuits [5] and sought to weaken the impression by a special publication.[6] His introduction is noteworthy. He declares that the Pope had no more devoted sons in France than " the disciples of St. Augustine " [7] since it was owing to the Popes that Augustine had become the Doctor of Grace !

However, relations with the Holy See were none too intimate even on the part of those French Catholics who were sincerely attached to the Church. Notwithstanding the

---

[1] On October 6, 1650, ARNAULD, *Œuvres*, XVI., XXI. *Cf.* above, p. 220.

[2] ARNAULD, *loc. cit.*, XX.

[3] [PATOUILLET], I., 228, II., 159 ; ARNAULD, *loc. cit.*, 697.

[4] ARNAULD, *loc. cit.*, XX. The royal Council of Flanders confiscated the *Catéchisme de la grâce* (Report of the Belgian nuncio, September 15, 1650, in *Excerpta ex actis s. Officii 1647–1652, loc. cit.*).

[5] *Œuvres*, XVII., 705 *seqq.*

[6] *Ibid.*, 689 *seqq.* For the same purpose fictitious censures of the University of Salamanca and of the Inquisition were disseminated against a Molinist counter catechism (RAPIN, I., 414), which latter, however, was also suppressed by the Inquisition on October 6, 1650, because it treated of a forbidden subject. *Cf.* REUSCH, *Index*, II., 470.

[7] " qu'il n'y a point de personnes qui soient plus sincerement affectionnées au S. Siège que les disciples de S. Augustin " (*Œuvres.*, XVII., 696).

numerous opponents whom these novelties encountered
among the clergy, at court, at the Sorbonne, and in spite
of the vigour and zeal displayed in resisting them, there
existed a curious shyness to seize the only effective weapon,
viz. a request for a papal definition.[1] Rome was resolved
to continue its waiting policy until a majority of the French
Bishops should request the Holy See to intervene. Hence,
for the time being, nothing was done. Individual Bishops
had appealed to Rome, on their own initiative, against the
innovations, as for instance the Archbishop of Rheims, the
Bishops of Senlis, Chartres, Aire, Riez, Avranches.[2] But
the Assembly of the Clergy of 1650 observed a striking
silence ; moreover, after Condé's arrest on January 16th,
1650, the country's attention was diverted from religious
questions and thus Jansenism spread silently but continuously.[3]

In the universal perplexity as to how to deal with the
rising flood, amid the turmoil of opinions which confused
even Bishops and scholars, a man was found who stood
strong and serene amid the trouble and agitation of his time,
as a lighthouse towers above the surging billows—that man
was Vincent de Paul. Vincent is known to the world as the
apostle of benevolence, but the care of the poor and the
destitute by no means exhausted his charity. His far-reaching
vision embraced all the needs and wants of the Church ;
he examined without prejudice at what point it was necessary,
or possible, to intervene ; having done so he carried through
his carefully considered plans with unfailing determination.
How consistently he had studied the rising Jansenist movement
and with what penetration he saw through the innovation,
is shown by his opinion on Arnauld's book on Communion [4]
which at the time bewitched almost everybody, as well as
his view on Jansenius' teaching on grace.[5] Since as Superior

---

[1] RAPIN, I., 365.

[2] Ibid., 316.

[3] Ibid., 364.

[4] Letter to Dehorgny, September 10, 1648, COSTE, III., 362–
374.

[5] Letter to the same, June 25, 1648, ibid., 318–332.

he was responsible for the Lazarists' attitude towards the burning questions of the day, we need not wonder when he assures us that these were the usual subject of his prayers.[1] As a matter of fact the sure vision with which he discovered the weak points in the long-winded arguments of Jansenius and Arnauld, the superior simplicity which enables him to show convincingly that their teaching was incompatible with the Catholic faith, give the irresistible impression that a judgment so measured and so sure could only have matured in ceaseless, dispassionate reflection under the eye of God. Naturally enough Arnauld's crafty ways found but little favour with Vincent whose favourite virtues were simplicity and straightforwardness.[2]   From his intercourse with St. Cyran he had ascertained the real aims of the sect which Arnauld did not dare to avow ; in fact he remarked on more than one occasion that Arnauld played false and sought to hide his purpose behind fine phrases,[3] nor did he trust the attenuations to which Arnauld condescended in a later work,[4] for the explanations there given, which were insidious enough,

---

[1] *Ibid.*, 330 *seq.* : " Je vous avoue, Monsieur, que j'ai fait quelque petite étude touchant ces questions, et que c'est le sujet ordinaire de mes chétives oraisons.

[2] Jésus, mon Dieu ! serais—je réduit à ce malheur qu'il me fallût faire ou dire quelque chose à votre égard contre la sainte simplicité. . . .   C'est la vertu que j'aime le plus et à laquelle je fais le plus d'attention dans mes actions, si me semble.'' Letter to Ducoudray, November 6, 1634, Coste, I., 284.

[3] " Quoique l'auteur [Arnauld] fasse quelque fois semblant . . ., il est certain néanmoins . . . (*ibid.*, III., 363). Je réponds que ce n'est pas de merveille que M. Arnauld parle quelque fois comme les autres catholiques.   Il ne fait en cela qu'imiter Calvin, qui nie trente fois, qu'il fasse Dieu auteur du péché, quoiqu'il fasse ailleurs tous ses efforts pour établir cette maxime détestable '' (*ibid.*, 365).   *Arnauld refrains from the Sacraments " quoiqu'il fasse semblant, pour mieux couvrir son jeu, d'être fort éloigné de ce dessein '' (*ibid.*, 369).

[4] *La tradition de l'Église* ; see the present work, XXIX., 143, n. 1.

could not clear away existing difficulties.[1] None the less Vincent deprecates any kind of general hue and cry against the new doctrines[2]; on the contrary his Congregation should adopt the following line of conduct : " We never dispute about these things, we never preach about them, we never treat of them in conferences if others do not begin, and if they do we endeavour to speak with the utmost reserve. ' What then ' you will tell me, ' do you forbid all discussion of these topics ? ' I answer ' Yes ' ! " Those who disobeyed were not to go without a penance.[3]

Though Vincent restrained his companions from a method of attack which would only have attracted more attention to the new opinions, he none the less did not wish them to stand by idly. In his opinion a remedy could only come from the Holy See and its intervention was to be brought about at the request of the French Bishops. Yet it did not seem practical to submit to the Assembly of the Clergy, which met in May, 1650, a draft for a collective letter to the Pope ; the consequence would only have been endless and, probably, fruitless discussions and disputes, perhaps even a fresh intervention by Parliament.[4] So there was nothing for it but to undertake the laborious task of winning over the Bishops individually. In concert with some Bishops who had come to Paris before the opening of the Assembly of the Clergy, and with the King's confessor, the Jesuit Dinet, Vincent drafted a letter for Rome the text of which was finally drawn up by Habert, Bishop of Vabres.[5] Some Bishops signed during the Assembly, to the others Vincent addressed a circular letter in February, 1651. The letter states that the dangerous opinions prevalent at the time had already led a goodly number of prelates to write to Rome to request a papal pronouncement on the new teaching. They had been

---

[1] COSTE, III., 323.

[2] " à cor et à cri " ; ibid., 328.

[3] Ibid., 328 seq.

[4] RAPIN, I., 335.

[5] Ibid., 329, 336 ; [DUMAS], I., 12. On the steps which Vincent took in this matter, cf. the compilation in COSTE, XIV., 279 seq.

actuated by the following motives : first, the hope that by this means many people would be confirmed in their loyalty to the traditional teaching ; the effect of the Roman decree on the two heads of the Church had sufficiently shown the power of a papal definition. Secondly, if the evil were tolerated it would spread further. In Rome it was thought that the majority of the French Bishops favoured the new doctrine, hence it was imperative to make it clear that this was the attitude of only a few. Lastly, the Council of Trent decreed that Rome should be appealed to whenever new opinions arose.[1]

The grounds on which Vincent's undertaking, notwithstanding his prestige, encountered great obstacles, appear from a letter of Archbishop Montchal of Toulouse to a fellow-Bishop who, like himself, had withheld his signature.[2] A letter to the Pope, he writes, must be decided upon by the Assembly of the Clergy in the name of all the Bishops. In view of their obstinacy both parties would find all kinds of subterfuges to evade a papal definition. How carefully, to give but one example, both Popes and Councils had avoided to hurt either party, for instance in the controversy on grace between the Dominicans and the Jesuits, or in the question of the Immaculate Conception ! Were they going to force the Holy See to give up such a wise restraint ? Like Montchal, the Bishops of Alet and Pamiers [3] also failed to realize the bearing of the new movement and the reliance they might place on the power of the Holy See ; to them [4] as to others,[5] Vincent had to point out that a papal decision would prevent many, if not all, from adopting the new opinions or lead them to renounce them.

However, as during the internal troubles of the Fronde the growth of the new sect took on more and more alarming

[1] Coste, IV., 148 seq. ; Maynard, II., 326 ; Rapin, I., 318.
[2] Published by A. Auguste in Bullet. de litt. ecclés., 1916, 272.
[3] Letter of end of May, 1651, in Maynard, II., 333.
[4] Ibid., 335 seqq. ; Coste, IV., 204–210.
[5] Vincent to the Bishop of Luçon, April 23, 1651, in Maynard, II., 327 seqq. ; Coste, IV., 175 seqq.

proportions,[1] the number of episcopal adhesions very soon
rose to seventy,[2] until it reached a total of eighty-eight,[3]
among them being the Archbishops of Arles, Bourges,
Narbonne, Bordeaux and Rheims. The Cardinal Archbishop
of Lyons gave as the reason of his refusal to sign the fact
that, as a member of the Inquisition, his rôle was that of a
judge, not an accuser, whilst Harlay of Rouen declared that
he had made his opinion clear enough at his Provincial
Council.[4]

The letter had already been dispatched by Dinet to his
brother in religion Annat, the French Assistant of the General
of the Society, to be forwarded by him to Rome, when the
Assessor of the Inquisition, Albizzi, announced that if it was
to produce its effect, the document must be handed to the
nuncio by the Bishops themselves, without the intervention
of a third party. Most of the Bishops objected to their names
being known even to the nuncio, but Dinet and Vincent
ended by overcoming this difficulty also.[5] The letter [6] begins
by stating that it was the constant tradition of the Church
to lay the more important affairs before the Holy See, and

[1] RAPIN, I., 332.

[2] Ibid., 335.

[3] GERBERON (I., 393) mentions 68 signatories by name.
The original text of Habert's letter is in the Acts of the Inquisition,
with 24 signatures, also copies with the signatures of one or
more Bishops, altogether 39 ; besides a special document which
agrees with Habert's letter of April 25, 1651, signed by 5, and
another signed by 8 Bishops, and by two others on special sheets
(Bibl. Angelica, Rome, S. 3, 1, *Excerpta ex V. Parte circa librum
Iansenii, f. 135 seq., 137, 252). On August 18, 1651, Bagno
transmits further signatures (ibid., 125). Bishop Scarron of
Grenoble, in a letter to the Pope, June 6, 1651, complains of
the growth of Jansenism ; he awaits with impatience the decision
of the Pope. Annales de St. Louis, XI. (1905), 241.

[4] Cf. RAPIN, I., 316.

[5] Ibid., 366.

[6] Latin text in HARDOUIN, Acta Conc., XI., 141 ; COSTE,
IV, 632 ; ARNAULD, Œuvres, XIX., 73 ; translation in [DUMAS],
I., 12 seq. RAPIN, I., 370.

Peter's faith that never fails demanded the maintenance of this tradition. Accordingly, in conformity with tradition, they submitted to Rome the questions connected with the Jansenist controversy. In reality both the Council of Trent and the Bull of Urban VIII. confirming Pius V.'s and Gregory XIII.'s condemnation of Baius, which Innocent X. had enacted anew, should suffice to put an end to the dispute, but since it was not stated what censure falls on each proposition, some thought that room was left for further subtleties and subterfuges. It was hoped that a clear and detailed papal judgment would bring about a change in this respect. The letter then gives the text of the five propositions and prays for a pronouncement on each of them. The authority of the Holy See had been shown quite recently, when it pronounced in the question of the two heads of the Church. Jansenius had himself submitted his work to the judgment of the Holy See. On April 28th, 1651, nuncio Bagno forwarded the document to Rome.[1] Thus the most important step towards warding off the new teaching had been taken and the Jansenists never forgave Vincent de Paul for having been the means of it.[2]

It goes without saying that this action could not long be kept from those Bishops who thought otherwise. On February 20th, 1651, the Archbishop of Embrun and the Bishops of Agen, Châlons, Comminges, Orléans and Valence called on the papal nuncio in Paris to inform him that Habert's letter was no more than a manifesto on the part of a few individual Bishops signed without the knowledge of the Assembly of the Clergy. The movement in France may indeed be fraught with danger, that is, if judgment was passed without hearing both parties. With regard to the theses impugned, they should make sure in what sense they were taught by " the disciples of Augustine " and above all by Augustine himself, lest they should implicate that holy Doctor in a censure

---

[1] Bibl. Angelica, Rome, *loc. cit.*, f. 245.

[2] On their opposition to his canonization, *cf.* [PATOUILLET], I., 178, 330 ; II., 479.

and so should give occasion to the heretics to calumniate the Holy See, as if at present it condemned what it had previously approved.[1] Eight days later the Archbishop of Sens called on the nuncio and represented to him in a haughty tone that in this affair the Pope must proceed after mature reflection and in accordance with the canons ; if he acted otherwise little notice would be taken in France of his decision.[2] Bagno sought to calm the prelates but already in April he had to report renewed pressure on the part of some of the Bishops. He added that the number of the Jansenists grew from day to day, a large section of Parliament and the University, many monasteries and nobles favoured them and there was no doubt that the situation was becoming serious.[3]

Even before the friends of Jansenism among the Bishops had remonstrated with the nuncio, Arnauld, at their instigation,[4] had published a violent pamphlet against his old enemy Habert.[5] The latter, Arnauld declared, had nothing to answer to the two excellent apologies of Jansenius in which he had exposed the falsehoods contained in Habert's inflammatory sermons and the pitiable weakness of his writings, hence he now had recourse to secret tricks and manœuvres to obtain in clandestine fashion the signatures of a few Bishops for a letter with which to deceive the Pope,

---

[1] Letter of the Bishop of Valence to the Archbishop of Toulouse, March 3, 1651, in SAINT-AMOUR, 67 ; RAPIN, I., 336.

[2] RAPIN, I., 337 ; ARNAULD, Œuvres, XIX., x.

[3] " *replicate instanze fattemi di alcuni pochi vescovi di supplicarla di rappresentare a N. S. gl'inconvenienti che possono succedere, quando si facesse alcuna dichiarazione sopra li capi controversi. . . . Si accresce sempre il numero de' Jansenisti, essendo caduto in quest'errore una gran parte del Parlamento e dell'Universià della Sorbona e de' molti monasterii et ancora molte persone nobili che senz'alcun dubbio possono apportare gran danno." Bagno, April 28, 1651, Biblioteca Angelica, loc. cit.

[4] ARNAULD, Œuvres, XIX., viii.

[5] " Observations sur la lettre composée par M. l'évêque de Vabres," ibid., 43–73.

in order that under the name of Jansenius the latter might condemn St. Augustine himself.[1] The propositions attacked by Habert were the very pillars of St. Augustine's teaching which neither Pope nor Council could oppose without sacrificing the infallibility of the Church, which could not condemn to-day what she had taught for 1,200 years.[2] Habert, the servant of the Jesuits,[3] wanted the Church to turn Molinist, for all Europe to see that an assessor and a handful of theologians of the Inquisition were to-day the judges and masters of the Church's teaching and that they were to be honoured above the Fathers, the Popes and the Councils.[4]

Notwithstanding this violent diatribe Habert's letter secured an ever increasing number of signatures. So as not to leave the ground free for their opponents, the Bishops in favour of Jansenism also wrote to the Pope,[5] but their letter, dated April 14th, 1651, bore only eleven signatures.[6] The document, drawn up at Port-Royal,[7] well characterizes the spirit of the party. It tells the Pope in substance how to proceed in this affair ; in fact it utters scarcely veiled threats should he refuse to be taught. The five propositions, the document states, had been brought together arbitrarily and equivocally worded, in order to make of them an apple of discord. The times were not propitious for a solemn definition unless the Pope had the propositions examined, as was done under Clement VIII. and Paul V., in the controversy on grace. If a different procedure was adopted, the defeated

---

[1] *Ibid.*, 43.

[2] *Ibid.*, 56.

[3] *Ibid.*, 51.

[4] *Ibid.*, 70.

[5] [DUMAS], I., 16 *seqq.* ; RAPIN, I., 380 *seqq.*

[6] Namely, those of Archbishop Louis Henri de Gondrin of Sens, Bishops Barth. Delbene of Agen, Gilbert de Choiseul of Comminges, Le Béron of Valence and Die, Delbene of Orléans, Bernard Despruets of Saint-Papoul, Jean Henri de Salette of Lescar, Félix Vialart of Châlons, François de Caumartin of Amiens, Henri Arnauld of Angers, Nicolas de Buzenval of Beauvais.

[7] RAPIN, I., 378.

party might justly complain that it had been condemned
unheard, in consequence of the misrepresentations and
trickeries of its adversaries. They might even add that their
cause had been laid before the Holy See without previous
examination by the Bishops, as was required by the practice
of Christian antiquity, the legitimate order for the judgment
of the universal Church and the customs of the Gallican
Church. The letter goes on to describe for the benefit of the
Romans, by way of a shining example, how the French would
proceed if called upon to deliver judgment in a matter of
this kind. " Equity would compel us to examine with the
utmost care whether the five propositions had not been
arbitrarily brought together, out of hatred for some persons
and for the pleasure of sowing trouble ; it would compel us
to examine in what books, by what authors, in what sense
they were stated, to hear the various parties, to study the
books written on the theses, to distinguish their true, false
or doubtful meaning, to inform ourselves of everything
connected with the dispute from its very beginning. After
that we would inform the Holy See of all we had done in a
matter which touches on the faith, so that our own just
declarations might be confirmed by your Apostolic authority."
On the other hand, the letter proceeds, if direct recourse
was had to the Holy See, by what artifices might not truth
be suppressed, by how many calumnies might not Bishops
and Doctors be blackened, by how many frauds might not
the Pope himself be deceived ? For one party maintained
that the majority of the scholastics, God's goodness and
natural reason were in its favour, whilst those who were
integral followers of Augustine asserted that the questions
in dispute were questions no longer but a matter decided
long since, more particularly by the Council of Trent. For
this reason they were afraid of neither an episcopal nor a
papal sentence, for they felt confident that the Pope would
not swerve in the slightest degree from the teaching of the
holy Fathers and that the Holy See would not be made the
laughing-stock of the heretics. Hence they prayed the Pope
to suffer the continuation, for a short while, of a dispute

which had gone on for centuries without injury to the Church, or to decide it with due regard to legal forms.

Port-Royal did not have to make a long search for someone to hand in the letter of the eleven Bishops. As early as November 1650, ostensibly to accompany a young nobleman, but in reality to spy out the land for the Jansenists, Saint-Amour had been dispatched to Rome, but in view of the strong feeling against the sect called forth by Hersent's Jansenist sermon, he spent the whole of the summer in Venetian territory ; from the Pope he obtained, at a later date, a purely formal audience. Saint-Amour was nevertheless in a position to give his friends one valuable piece of advice, this was that to defend Jansenius they should send a formal embassy to Rome.[1] Notwithstanding every precaution Saint-Amour was in danger of being arrested as a Jansenist, hence on April 13th, 1651, he left in all haste for Genoa.[2]

Meanwhile the dispatch of an embassy to Rome had also been discussed by Cornet's supporters, whereupon Saint-Amour was commissioned by his friends to return to Rome in the capacity of representative of the eleven episcopal supporters of Jansenism, for as their envoy he had nothing to fear.[3] Bishop Henri Arnauld of Angers, brother to the " great " Arnauld, who was known in Rome, supplied him with letters of recommendation to Cardinals Este, Spada and Barberini.[4] Before long, Saint-Amour returned to Rome but, despite the letters of recommendation, Cardinal Este, for his safety's sake, advised him to leave as quickly as possible.[5] From Innocent X., to whom he had presented himself as the envoy of the French Bishops, he received directions than which none could have been unpleasanter for the Jansenists [6] : the Pope referred him to the Assessor of the Inquisition,

---

[1] RAPIN, I., 320, 324, 326, 328.
[2] Ibid., 329.
[3] Ibid., 329, 372 ; SAINT-AMOUR, 83.
[4] RAPIN, I., 373 ; COCHIN, 149 seq.
[5] RAPIN, I., 374 seq. ; SAINT-AMOUR, 86 seqq.
[6] On July 10, 1651, in RAPIN, I., 378.

Albizzi, for everything that had not been settled by Urban
VIII.'s Bull. Albizzi was feared and hated by the party as no
other man. When Saint-Amour hinted that his adversaries
gave themselves the air as if they had the Pope's tongue in
their mouth and his pen in their hand, Innocent pointed to
the crucifix as his counsellor.[1]

To complete the Jansenists' discomfiture the French
ambassador was commissioned by his Government to present
on October 16th, 1651, a petition praying the Pope to pronounce
judgment in the disputes about grace, so that the followers of
Jansenius and Molina should no longer be able to call each
other Pelagians and Calvinists, to the great delight of the
heretics.[2] A second audience with the Pope was hardly more
successful for Saint-Amour. This time he came with a message
from the Bishop of Grasse, Godeau, who exposed to the Pope
familiar grievances of the Jansenists.[3]   Innocent received
Godeau's message very coldly and stopped Saint-Amour
when the latter began to talk of Congregations such as those
held under Clement VIII. Urban VIII.'s Bull could not be
touched, he said, nor could there be question of resuming the
discussions which had taken place under Clement VIII.[4]
When Saint-Amour desired to present a memorial, the Pope
declined it with the remark that he was old and no theologian.[5]
From this Saint-Amour promptly concluded that the Pope
had no intention to pronounce sentence, so he wrote to his
friends in France that they might dispatch their envoys
without hesitation ; a papal sentence, which Port-Royal had
every reason to fear, would not be delivered.[6]

Dispatched by the Jansenists, Doctors Brousse, Lalane and
Angran, as a matter of fact, did arrive in Rome on December
5th, 1651, describing themselves as representatives of the

---

[1] SAINT-AMOUR, 96 *seq.*

[2] RAPIN, I., 383.

[3] SAINT-AMOUR, *Documents*, 6.

[4] SAINT-AMOUR, 149 *seq.* ; RAPIN, I., 384.

[5] " Oltra che son vecchio, non ho mai studiato in theologia."
SAINT-AMOUR, 150.

[6] RAPIN. I.. 384.

Sorbonne. Now it so happened that a month earlier, on being questioned by the new syndic Grandin, the Faculty had protested that Saint-Amour did not represent it [1] and on November 8th, 1651, Hallier had written to the nuncio to put him on his guard against the artifices of the Jansenists ; not more than ten to twelve Bishops and less than twenty of the 460 Doctors of Sorbonne favoured them, Hallier wrote ; moreover it was a deception to pretend that there was only question of continuing the controversy on grace between Dominicans and Jesuits. The nuncio forwarded Hallier's letter to Rome [2] but of this the Jansenist envoys were ignorant ; accordingly, at their first audience with Innocent X., January 21st, 1652, they described themselves as the representatives of the French Bishops. The Pope let this pass and in other ways also he treated them graciously but declared emphatically that he stuck to Urban VIII.'s Bull. [3] Faithful to their instructions, the envoys had prayed for a discussion on the model of the Congregations under Clement VIII. and Paul V., [4] with the object, as openly avowed in a private letter, [5] to delay and impede a definition. The Pope replied in general terms that they would have no reason to be dissatisfied. [6] It was, however, no happy omen for Brousse and his colleagues that at the time of their arrival the former

---

[1] *Ibid.*, 420.

[2] *Ibid.*, 418 *seq.*

[3] *Ibid.*, 431 *seq.*

[4] " *ut distingui et singillatim examinari iubeat [SS. Pont.] varios sensus 5 propositionum aequivocarum et ad fraudem fictarum . . ., atque ut de praedictis sensibus, prout exiget illorum veritas ac aliorum falsitas, sententiam ferri velit, partibus prius in Congregatione tum voce tum scripto coram auditis et omnibus illarum scriptis mutuo communicatis." Bibl. Angelica, Rome, S. 3, 1, *Excerpta ex V. Parte circa librum Iansenii*, f. 261.

[5] Lalane, July 14, 1651, to SAINT-AMOUR : " Faites tous vos efforts possibles afin qu'on ne prononce rien sur les propositions " ; or at least they should try to introduce three clauses into the decision which would have stultified it. RAPIN, I., 373, n.

[6] *Ibid.*, 432.

Cologne nuncio, Fabio Chigi, became Secretary of State, for as a near kinsman of the internuncio of Brussels, Bichi, as well as by his prolonged stay in the North, he was well informed about the Jansenists.[1] For the time being all that the envoys could do was to court prestige by much pomp and display and to try and bring opinion round in their favour by means of personal visits. As a matter of fact they did succeed in influencing in their favour especially the Generals of the Augustinians and the Dominicans.[2]

Meanwhile no steps had as yet been taken in France to send to Rome representatives of the Catholics loyal to the Church. In the end a sarcastic remark in one of Saint-Amour's letters prompted a priest to collect a small sum from his parishioners for the maintenance of representatives in Rome ; he also discussed the matter with Hallier ; thereupon Hallier decided to go himself to Rome as ambassador, taking Lagault and Joisel as his companions.[3] The three men reached Rome on May 24th, 1652, and were soon after received in audience. Hallier explained to the Pontiff that their undertaking had nothing in common with the dispute about grace under Clement VIII. ; they prayed for an examination whether the five propositions had not been condemned long ago and that, if this was the case, the Pope would state it anew.[4] They also requested the Dominicans in Paris to make it clear to their General that the Jansenist dispute had nothing to do with the teaching of the Order of Preachers.[5] They kept out of the way

[1] *Ibid.*, 428 *seq.*

[2] *Ibid.*, 459 *seq.*

[3] *Ibid.*, 430.

[4] *Ibid.*, 486. *" ut examen fiat 5 illarum propositionum . . . excutiaturque num propositiones illae iam ecclesiasticis definitionibus et traditione proscriptae sint. Quod si iam damnatas fuisse constiterit, supplicant S. Sti, ut pro pace et tranquillitate Ecclesiae id novo diplomate velit declarare. Iidem doctores protestantur, se non petere, ut quaestiones controversae inter Dominicanos et Iesuitas . . . ulli examini aut censurae subiiciantur ". Biblioteca Angelica, *loc. cit.*, f. 262.

[5] Letter of Lagault, June 17, 1652, in RAPIN, I., 487.

of the envoys of the friends of the Jansenists and an attempt by the French ambassador to bring the two parties together, proved a failure.[1] At this time Queen Anne wrote to the French ambassador and to Cardinal Barberini, requesting them to urge the Pope to decide the question then pending and recommending Hallier and his fellow delegates to him.[2]

(3.)

On April 12th, 1651, before the arrival of the delegation in the Eternal City and before the French Bishops had drawn up their letter, Innocent X. had taken a decisive step in the Jansenist affair by charging a special Congregation to deal with it.[3] It consisted of Cardinals Roma, Spada, Ginetti and Cecchini with Albizzi as secretary.[4] Roma having died on April 11th, 1652, Spada replaced him as chairman from April 11th, 1652. On April 11th, Cardinal Chigi joined as a new member, and Cardinal Camillo Pamfili on October 30th.[5] Innocent X. had deliberately set up an entirely new Congregation owing to the circumstance that the Inquisition, to whose competence the affair belonged in the first instance, was the object of extreme hatred in France.[6] In like manner he had also deliberately excluded from the deliberations Cardinals Maculano and Lugo, both of them able theologians, but who might be suspected of partiality as being the one a Dominican and the other a Jesuit.[7] It was an important

---

[1] *Ibid.*, 486, 488 *seq.* ; SAINT-AMOUR, 241 *seq.*

[2] RAPIN, I., 494 *seqq.*

[3] The official report of the Roman Office, compiled by Albizzi, is published by A. SCHILL in *Katholik*, 1883, II., 282 *seqq.*, 363 *seqq.*, 472 *seqq.* Cf. SAINT-AMOUR, *Appendix*, 173. RAPIN (II., 2–31, 66–72 81–5), gives " l'histoire du procès-verbal de ce jugement, prise sur les mémoires du Saint-Office que j'ai copiés fidèlement sur l'original qu'on y garde."

[4] SCHILL, 288.

[5] *Ibid.*, 204, 365.

[6] RAPIN, II., 6.

[7] PALLAVICINO, I., 183.

circumstance for the discussions that Chigi had become acquainted with Jansenius' work during his Cologne nunciature and that, on the basis of an examination by two Dominicans of that city, he had been able to form an independent opinion of the book.[1]

The first nine sittings of the new tribunal were of a preparatory nature. With a view to laying down a solid basis, it began by examining the proceedings against Baius. The more important documents concerning the events of Louvain as well as the censures against him by the Universities of Alcalá, Salamanca and Paris were read and the Paris nuncio was instructed to forward an authentic copy of the Paris censure. The Congregation approached its real task in the seventh session. It was resolved that copies of the Roman memorials of 1649 on the five theses should be submitted and further details on the Jansenist dispute obtained from the Belgian nuncio. At these preliminary sittings the measures to be taken against the Archbishop of Malines, the Bishop of Ghent and against Jansenism at Marseilles also came up for discussion[2]; a Jansenist book of devotion was also prohibited.[3]

At its tenth session, September 28th, 1651, the Congregation took up the discussion of the five propositions. The letter of the French Bishops demanding their condemnation was read. It was decided to have them examined by theologians and to submit the list of these theologians, the so-called qualificators. There followed a pause until September 24th, 1652, probably to give the theologians time to study the subject.[4] In the few sessions during that interlude there was only question of the situation in Flanders, a book by one of the Jansenist delegates was prohibited and it was resolved to give an opportunity to the two delegations of the French

---

[1] *Ibid.*, 181 *seqq.*

[2] SCHILL, 287–292.

[3] The so-called *Heures de Port-Royal* or *Heures à la janséniste* (*ibid.*, 291), a misleading translation from the Roman Breviary; *cf.* [PATOUILLET], II., 177 *seqq.*

[4] SCHILL, 293.

Bishops for and against Jansenius to defend their case either
before each of the Cardinals of the Congregation individually
or before all of them assembled in general session.   At the
sessions on 11th and 18th August, Saint-Amour and his
friends, as well as Hallier and his colleagues, were informed
of this decision.   The Jansenist delegates allowed nearly the
whole of July and August to go by without taking advantage
of the offer, though on August 16th they were reminded of
it by order of the Pope.   On August 28th they put their
signatures to two documents, but under various pretexts
its presentation was put off until September 21st.   Neither
document was to the point ; the one traced the history of the
five theses, the other treated of St. Augustine's prestige in
the Church.   Once again they demanded a formal disputation
and that the relevant papers of either party should be communicated to the other.[1]   Albizzi had the impression that their
only aim was to drag out the affair indefinitely.[2]

The Pope had no intention to allow this and the reason for
it was made quite clear to the qualificators before the opening
of the sitting of September 24th, 1652, the first at which they
were present.   A formal disputation, Albizzi explained, only
served to inflame tempers, whilst the mutual exchange of
papers would unduly protract the business.   Meanwhile Spada
requested the Cardinals to declare whether they desired an
opinion on the five propositions solely as they stood, or as they
were understood by Jansenius.   When the qualificators were
questioned, they replied that no more than the text of the
first of the five theses had been communicated to them some
time ago, hence a majority of them were of opinion that the
propositions should be examined only as they stood, for some
of their number had not seen Jansenius' book.   The Cardinals
adopted this view though it was open to anyone to judge the
theses in Jansenius' sense also.[3]   At the very next sitting, on

---

[1] *Ibid.*, 293-7 ; SAINT-AMOUR, 276.

[2] " Relecta quadam scriptura, quae nihil ad propositum,
curabant protrahere negotium, petendo contradictoria et com-
municationem scripturarum." SCHILL, 297.

[3] SCHILL, 297-9.

October 1st, Spada reported that Hallier had objected to the propositions not being examined in Jansenius' sense and Hallier's remonstrances had the support of a learned Carmelite. This view steadily gained ground with the Congregation.[1]

From October 1st onwards the qualificators were the only ones to speak at the sittings of the Congregation. In order to avoid every semblance of partiality against Jansenius, the ordinary qualificators of the Inquisition had been charged to draw up reports.[2] These were taken from the most diverse Orders and belonged to different theological schools. Among them were two Dominicans, the Master of the Palace, Vincenzo Depretis, the General of the Augustinians, Filippo Visconti, whose views closely resembled those of the Dominicans, two Franciscans, the Conventual Modestus Gavazzi of Ferrara and the Observant Luke Wadding. To them were added Raphael Aversa, of the Clerics Minor, the Carmelite Domenico Campanella, the Servite Angelo Maria Ciria of Cremona, the Theatine Tommaso Imbene and the Procurator General of the Capachins, Marco Antonio of Carpineto. There was also included a Jesuit, Sforza Pallavicino, the historian of the Council of Trent.[3] On November 6th, 1652, they were reinforced by the addition of the Discalced Carmelite John Augustine (Tartaglia) of the Nativity.[4] During October, owing to the vacation, only three sittings were held together with the consultors, viz. on 1, 8 and 10, but as the Pope pressed for the termination of the business, two weekly sittings took place from the middle of November, a hitherto unheard of thing in Rome [5]; the labours of the Congregation were not even completely interrupted by the Christmas season.[6]

---

[1] *Ibid.*, 363.

[2] " Ne, si eligerentur aliqui ex iis [from the theologians of the Inquisition], daretur ansa dicendi, fuisse selectos eos, qui contra Iansenium sentiebant." SCHILL, 295 *seq.*

[3] *Ibid.*, 298.   [4] *Ibid.*, 366.   [5] *Ibid.*, 368.

[6] Sessions took place on December 23 and 30 and January 13. SCHILL, 377 *seqq.*

From this time onwards the discussions proceeded as follows : the five propositions were examined one after another and each of the thirteen consultors made his report. After the thirty-seventh sitting, January 20th, 1653, all the five theses were examined in order ; in two further sessions, on February 3rd and 5th,[1] the consultors were given an opportunity to add further remarks to their reports. At first most of the thirteen consultors took advantage of the permission to abstract from the meaning of the propositions in Jansenius, and to consider only their literal sense,[2] but at the sittings of February 3rd and 5th, 1653, only three did so—they were the General of the Augustinians Visconti, and the two Dominicans Candido and Depretis. At the sitting of February 5th, 1653, these three were likewise called upon to give their opinion on Jansenius' meaning, but on February 27th they declared that they were not prepared for this.[3] After that the Cardinals gave orders to all the consultors to examine Jansenius' book [4] and in the sequel the two Dominicans showed that they were acquainted with the work of the Bishop of Ypres.[5]

In point of fact the two Dominicans and the General of the Augustinians adopted a very different attitude from that of the others, as did the two historians among them, the Franciscan annalist, Luke Wadding, and the historian of the Council of Trent, Sforza Pallavicino. The Jesuit Pallavicino showed remarkable moderation ; he qualifies the theses in Jansenius' sense as at most erroneous, and only later on as

---

[1] SCHILL, 475–8.

[2] *Ibid.*, 285.

[3] *Ibid.*, 478.

[4] *Ibid.*, 479.

[5] *Ibid.*, 481. The opinions of the consultors are given in detail in a folio-volume in *the Archives of the Roman Inquisition* which SCHILL was able to consult. " The arguments of the majority endeavour to show for each proposition that it is Jansenistic and they furnish, besides abundant theological matter, the evident proof that their authors had thoroughly examined the work of Jansenius before drawing up their reports." SCHILL, 286, note.

savouring of heresy [1] ; the second proposition he declares
to deserve no censure in itself and equally the fourth, even in
Jansenius' sense.[2] If Pallavicino, notwithstanding his milder
sentence, must be included in the first group of theologians,
since on the whole he too expresses an unfavourable judgment,
the same cannot be said of the other historian, Luke Wadding.
In his opinion none of the five propositions deserve condemnation : of the first and third he says so clearly ; the second
could be saved by making a distinction, in the fourth and fifth
Jansenius was misunderstood.[3] The two Dominican consultors
go still further, in fact the Master of the Palace, Candido,
only drops the second half of the fourth proposition which he
describes as erroneous. According to him the first proposition,
about the impossibility of keeping God's commandments,
is not deserving of censure, on the contrary he holds it to be
true in the highest degree and Catholic. The assertion that
a man never resists interior grace, is equally blameless according to him ; he describes it as true and Catholic ; the same
holds good with regard to the third proposition to which it
is possible to attach a Catholic meaning ; the fifth, viz. that
Christ did not die for all men may be maintained " as probable
and undoubtedly true ".[4] The other Dominican, Depretis,
does not go quite so far but he too is of opinion that the,
condemnation, for instance, of the irresistibility of grace,
would hit the teaching of the Thomists and that of
St. Augustine's later works.[5]   The Augustinian General
Visconti must also be ranked with the defenders of Jansenius,[6]
but not his brother in religion, Bruni.

Thus, though the overwhelming majority of the consultors
was decidedly in favour of Jansenius' condemnation, the final
sentence was not pronounced without his friends having had

[1] *Ibid.*, 364, 373, 379 ; *cf.* for the conclusion of the votes
Schill's remark on page 285.

[2] *Ibid.*, 370, 376.

[3] *Ibid.*, 365, 371, 373, 377, 381.

[4] *Ibid.*, 368, 372, 375, 378, 472.

[5] *Ibid.*, 371 *seq.*

[6] *Ibid.*, 368 *seq.*

their say. His opponents, in their lengthy memorandums, examined the five propositions from every angle, turned them this way and that, and even ended by discovering a sense in which the one or the other might be defended, only that sense was neither the natural one nor that of Jansenius.

After the consultors had stated their opinions before the Cardinals, they were invited, at the forty-first session, to be prepared to expound and substantiate their opinions once again before the Pope himself.[1] This was done between March 10th and April 7th, 1653, in ten Congregations.[2]

The consultors maintained their original opinions in presence of the Pope also. Pallavicino added to his first verdict on the third and fourth proposition that the Pope could pronounce a formal definition on them.[3] Wadding defended Jansenius with energy. On the latter's assertion on the impossibility of keeping the commandments of God he remarked that it could be defended in many senses, including that of the Bishop of Ypres. As for the remaining four propositions, they were not even to be found in Jansenius.[4] An unexpected incident occurred during the discussion of the third proposition, viz. that to merit or de-merit, freedom from necessity was not required, but only freedom from coercion. When the turn of the Dominican Depretis came, he threw himself on his knees, exclaiming that the five propositions were a mere disguise : " let them take care lest by condemning the disguise they condemn Augustine. The third proposition was neither Jansenius', nor was it censurable." Depretis was suceeded by Visconti. " He would speak rather with tears than with words," he said, " for words failed him. Alas ! Augustine is being condemned under the name of Jansenius ! " A second prostration, this time by the Dominican Candido, lent further emphasis to this cry of despair.[5] A further prostration was executed by Depretis

[1] *Ibid.*, 479.

[2] *Ibid.*, 479–487.

[3] *Ibid.*, 483, 485.

[4] *Ibid.*, 480, 482, 484 *seq.*, 487.

[5] *Ibid.*, 484.

at the sitting of April 3rd, during the discussion of the fourth proposition, viz. that the Semi-Pelagians were heretics forasmuch as they denied the irresistibility of grace ; in the mouth of the Semi-Pelagians the statement was heretical but in the mouth of Catholics, according to him, it deserved no censure. On the other hand Visconti argued that if this proposition was condemned, the Jesuits must likewise be condemned. On this occasion Candido merely stated, in a lengthy speech, that he maintained his opinion.[1] In the last session, on April 7th, Visconti asserted [2] that all five theses were defended by St. Prosper, Fulgentius, Thomas Acquinas and by the Scholastics. He then fell on his knees, calling upon the assembly to beware of bringing back the unhappy times when, thanks to the intrigues of Ursacius and Valens, the whole world suddenly discovered that it had become Arian.[3] "May it not have to realize to-day that it has become Semi-Pelagian ! " From which side Visconti feared a catastrophe, who those were who, in his opinion, intended to strike at St. Augustine under the mask of Jansenius, appears from his outburst against the Jesuits at the sitting of April 3rd, and by his remarks, on April 7th, on " convertible " grace.[4] The latter nickname had been coined to designate the Molinist system of grace. This quite unjustifiable dragging in of the chief opponents of Jansenism lends support to the report that many Roman religious had allowed themselves to be influenced by Saint-Amour.[5]

The Jansenist delegates deemed it one of their chief duties to foment anti-Jesuit feeling by means of visits to prelates

---

[1] *Ibid.*, 486.

[2] *Ibid.*, 488.

[3] Allusion to St. Jerome's, *Adv. Lucifer*, n. 19 : " Ingemuit totus orbis (after the events of Seleucia-Rimini) et Arianum se esse miratus est." HEFELE, *Konzilien gesch.*, I.², 722.

[4] SCHILL, 488.

[5] RAPIN, II., 11 *seq. Ibid.*, 13, in the mouth of SAINT-AMOUR the reproach " qu'on ne cherchoit qu'à déguiser le fait au lieu d' éclaircir ".

and monasteries.[1]   A memorial of December, 1652, in which they sought to restrain the Pope from issuing a definition, dwells, in the first part, on the difficulty of the matter.   It then turns on the Jesuits as the chief authors and instigators of a conspiracy whose only aim was to destroy the teaching of St. Augustine.   Hence it was only right that these hidden enemies should appear before the Congregation of Cardinals to meet the accusations of the Jansenists.   Lastly, they demanded that Albizzi, who was hopelessly tied to the Jesuits' apron strings, should cease to be Secretary of the Congregation.[2]   Already before this they had demanded the removal of Albizzi who, they stated, behaved like a Turk towards them ;   at the very least he must be given an assistant Secretary.[3]   Spada replied to these recriminations on the occasion of a visit which Saint-Amour and his friends paid to him.   He assured them on oath that in this affair the Jesuits did not play the part with which they were credited and as for Albizzi, he had no vote and all he did was to take down in writing what was said by the various members.[4]   As the delegates insisted on being confronted with their opponents, Spada replied that neither Pius V. nor Gregory XIII., nor Urban VIII. had reached a decision by means of discussions and that Clement VIII., who tried it, fared very badly. Disputations were excellent things for the schools, as exercises for young people, but no conclusion would ever be reached by their means.   The Church did not dispute, she judged ; once they consented to disputations they would have to allow them to every *frate*.[5]

These exhortations were, however, in vain.   It was the Pope's wish, with a view to providing against future recriminations, that after all the consultors had spoken on the five propositions

[1] They made special efforts with the Roman Dominicans. Lagault, June 17, 1652, in RAPIN, I., 488.

[2] SAINT-AMOUR, 363 *seq.* ;   RAPIN, II., 21.

[3] SAINT-AMOUR, 265.

[4] RAPIN, II., 22 ;   SAINT-AMOUR, 354.

[5] RAPIN, II., 13, 19.

on January 20th, both delegations of the French Bishops should have an opportunity freely to state their respective cases before the Cardinals and the consultors. However, as Cardinal Spada informed the Cardinals of the Congregation on January 27th, Saint-Amour and his associates persisted in declaring that they would only appear at a Congregation at which there would be a formal disputation ; at the same time they repeated their demand with regard to Albizzi ; moreover no Jesuit was to be present.[1] Accordingly the delegates did not appear before the Cardinals. On the other hand Hallier and his companions declared that they had come to Rome to seek instruction, hence they were prepared to obey the directions of the Congregation.[2] Hallier subsequently spoke sharply of the Jansenists in presence of the Cardinals and the consultors.[3] " We raise our voice on behalf of the Church of God against the disturbers of the peace ; on behalf of the faith against innovators ; on behalf of ecclesiastical institutions against troublesome men." The five propositions, he declared, stated, though perhaps not in so many words, the deliberate thought of the Jansenists and they resulted from its two principles, viz. the denial of sufficient grace and the irresistibility of grace. If their opponents attached various meanings to the theses, it was for the purpose of disguising their heresy ; as a matter of fact, there was hardly a single heretical proposition which was not somehow susceptible of a favourable interpretation. In Rome members of the party repudiated the appellation of Jansenists, whilst in Paris they published three apologies and many other writings in favour of Jansenius. Notwithstanding their hostility towards the Molinists, they could not appeal to the Thomists. When Hallier concluded, Joisel spoke of the novelties introduced by the Jansenists in the sphere of morals and ecclesiastical discipline and sketched the activities of the sect from its first beginnings.

---

[1] SCHILL, 473 *seq.* ; RAPIN, I., 499.
[2] RAPIN, I., 474.
[3] *Excerpta*, Bibl. Angelica, Rome, S. 3, 1, f. 931–3.

Finally Langault expatiated on the danger of Jansenism for the whole Church.[1]

For the time being, and in the sequel also, the Jansenist delegates contented themselves, by means of visits, with making friends with the Cardinals and other personages. Thus on February 14th they presented their old demands to Cardinal Chigi, and to the Pope himself in a petition of February 17th.[2] In April, 1653, they received reinforcements from Paris. One of their number, Brousse, had left Rome to escape from the hot season and, by a curious choice, he was replaced by the Oratorian Desmares who had been forbidden to preach on account of his Jansenism, and by Manessier who was barred from the lecture hall for the same reason.[3] However, the new-comers were just as unsuccessful when they had their first audience with the Pope on May 4th, 1653. Innocent X. told them he would restore peace to the Church by other means than disputations.[4] Nor had Saint-Amour's efforts to win over the Dominicans the desired effect, though in May 1652, the General summoned to Rome from Toulouse that fanatical opponent of the Jesuits, Reginald Ravaille [5] who, jointly with a brother in religion, sought to influence the French ambassador. On the other hand Hallier's statement to the Dominicans of Rome that he was far from attacking the Thomists, had no further result. A publication in which the Jesuit Annat dwelt on the difference between the Thomist and the Jansenist teaching on grace was favourably received by the French Dominicans, though not by the Roman ones.[6] For all that Saint-Amour failed to win over the Friars Preacher

---

[1] Letter of Lagault, January 27, 1653, in RAPIN, II., 44, of March 24, 1653, *ibid.*, 48, of the French ambassador, February 3, *ibid.*, 51 *seq.*

[2] SAINT-AMOUR, 393 *seq.*, 396.

[3] *Ibid.*, 428 ; RAPIN, II., 23, 85.

[4] SAINT-AMOUR, 440.

[5] On him, *cf.* A. AUGUSTE in *Bullet. de litt. ecclés.*, 1916, 316 *seqq.*

[6] SAINT-AMOUR, 386 ; RAPIN, II., 64 *seq.*

wholly to his side because he himself did not share their opinions on every point.[1]

Their sad experience in Rome ended by inducing Saint-Amour and his colleagues to alter their policy. After the Congregation had decided, on April 18th, 1653, to hear them if they asked to be heard,[2] they ended by making up their minds to do so and on May 19th they presented themselves before the Pope and the consultors. Lalane spoke first : he commented on the Holy See's duty to safeguard the teaching of St. Augustine. Against this teaching snares were being set. After this exordium he " stormed " [3] for nearly two hours against the Jesuits. Finally he distinguished a threefold sense of the five propositions, the Lutheran-Calvinistic, the Catholic and the Molinist-Pelagian. He and his friends prayed to be allowed to dispute with their opponents on this threefold sense : they would submit to the Pope's verdict.[4] Desmares then expatiated for a further two hours on efficient grace. Lastly the five delegates submitted five papers which they asked permission to have printed, for the purpose of presenting copies to the Cardinals and the consultors. They also prayed for another audience. Innocent answered evasively.[5] Of the five papers only the last two dealt with the business in hand.[6]

Albizzi was now commissioned to draw up a memorial in which, after a general survey of the sessions of the Congregation, he answered the questions whether Jansenius

---

[1] Letter of Lagault, February 24, 1653, in RAPIN, II., 65 : " Ils disent qu'ils craignent en ce rencontre que les Jésuites, à qui ils attribuent la forme de ces propositions, n'en tirent des conséquences contre leurs opinions, et qu'ils ne s'y opposent pas tant pour l'intérêt de la doctrine de Jansénius que pour l'intérêt de leur ordre."

[2] SCHILL, 488.

[3] " debacchatus est."

[4] SCHILL, 489. The *discourse is in *Barb.* 3565, n. 21. Vatican Library.

[5] SCHILL, 491 ; SAINT-AMOUR, 502.

[6] Their titles, *ibid.*

taught the five theses and in what sense ; what censures outstanding theologians, especially from the Dominican school, had passed on them ; whether a definition in the sense of the eighty-six French Bishops was advisable and how it should be worded. On Albizzi's advice prayers were offered in all the churches in Rome. At the last moment the Pope felt perplexed whether to issue a definition and thereby still further provoke the recalcitrants. However, Chigi represented to him that failure to publish a definition after such protracted discussions could not but give rise to the impression that Jansenism had been approved. After Innocent X. had examined the document six times, he decided to issue a definition and charged Albizzi to draw it up. Albizzi's first draft, with its historical introduction on the action of Urban VIII. in the matter, failed to meet with the Pope's approval ; the second, which the Assessor drew up in collaboration with Chigi, was read four times by Albizzi at a Congregation held in presence of the Pope and consisting of Spada, Ginetti and Pamfili : this was done for the purpose of enabling them to suggest further improvements on points of detail.[1] At last, on Whitsun Eve, May 31st, 1653, the Bull was issued ; on June 9th it was published by being affixed at the usual places and on the same day it was dispatched in every direction.[2]

The text of the short Constitution bears evidence of most careful drafting. As the publication of Jansenius' book *Augustinus* had given rise, particularly in France, to a controversy on five propositions,[3] we there read, several Bishops of that country had prayed for judgment by the Pope. Then follows the text of the propositions. The Pope, as having at heart the tranquillity of the Church, had had

---

[1] SCHILL, 491–3 ; PALLAVICINO, I., 184 *seq.*

[2] SCHILL, 493.

[3] " Cum occasione impressionis libri, cui titulus : Augustinus Cornelii Iansenii Episcopi Yprensis, inter alias eius opiniones orta fuerit, praesertim in Galliis, controversia super quinque ex illis. . . ."

these propositions examined and had also personally studied them, and after prolonged prayer, both public and private, he now proceeded to give a declaration and definition. Here follows once more the text of the five propositions, each with its own particular censure. To three of their number some minor censures are likewise affixed, but all are the object of the strongest censure of all ; the fifth proposition is condemned as heretical, at least in one sense, which is obviously that of Jansenius. Accordingly all the faithful and all ecclesiastical Superiors are warned to act accordingly ; the Constitution adds that the condemnation of only these five propositions did not imply approval of the other opinions in Jansenius' book.[1]

The publication of this Constitution is Innocent X.'s most personal merit. When he approached the Jansenist question he soon perceived the tremendous bearing of a movement which affected the innermost core of the Christian life and sought to transplant, on Catholic soil, a but slightly attenuated form of Calvinism. It was an unheard of thing in Rome for a Pope to command a Congregation of Cardinals to hold two sittings a week. They must do all that can be done, he was wont to say, and he himself acted accordingly.

---

[1] *Bull. Rom.*, XV., 720. The *Excerpta of the Bibl. Angelica*, Rome, S. 3, 1, give at the end two drafts of the Constitution. Variants from the printed text : at the beginning : " inter alias eius *pravas* opiniones " ; in the censure of the first proposition : " haereticam " is missing ; the censure of the fifth proposition reads : " hanc propositionem impiam, blasphemam . . . declaramus et uti talem damnamus " ; the last paragraph : " Non intendentes," is missing. *Covering Briefs for the Emperor, for Spain, Poland, the Empire, for the Governor of Belgium, for Bavaria, France, in *Innocentii X. Epist.*, IX., 168 *seqq.*, 177 ; *Answers to letters of thanks : to the Bishops of Meaux, September 13, Grenoble and Noyon, September 29, Sarlat, December 13, 1653, Tulle, March 21, 1654, *ibid.*, X., n. 16, 22, 23, 52, 93 ; to the Dean and Chapter of Poitiers, October 9, 1653, *ibid.*, n. 28 ; to the Universities of Douai and Poitiers, *ibid.*, 95. Papal Secret Archives.

In delivering sentence he wished to take every possible precaution so as to leave no ground for further recrimination. Every University in Europe was asked for its opinion ; the best Roman theologians of every Order were summoned. The Dominicans and Augustinians furnished two each and these could not be suspected of being in favour of Molinism.[1] Whilst the cardinalitial Congregations were in progress, Cardinal Chigi had to make a report each night and this often took from two to three hours.[2] During the final Congregations, in the Pope's presence, he listened with tense attention on each occasion for some four hours ; he took no notice of the suggestions of his sister-in-law, Olimpia, that he should spare himself ; to the French ambassador he even declared that he would deem himself happy if he were permitted to sacrifice his life for the faith in the pursuit of this task.[3] He thought and spoke of nothing else, one of the delegates of the eighty-six French Bishops wrote ; he could have done no more even if the Kings of France and Spain had come to Rome to push the affair.[4] At the first session, on May 27th,

[1] Letter of Lagault, November 20, 1652, in RAPIN, II., n. 11 ; cf. 2, 35.

[2] Lagault, January 20, 1653, ibid., 34, note ; cf. 35, where RAPIN says : " L'on sut qu'il se faisoit rendre compte deux fois la semaine, en deux heures à chaque fois par le card. Chigi."

[3] Ibid., 73 ; Lagault, March 17, 1653, ibid., 68, note. Albizzi also writes : " in quibus [sessionibus] maxima cum attentione et patientia semper fere per quatuor horas SS. D. N. adstitit " (in SCHILL, 488). " Il est attentif à tout ce qu'on lui dit, n'interrompt personne (LAGAULT, loc. cit.). Cf. Lagault and Hallier to St. Vincent de Paul, June 14 and 16, 1653, in COSTE, IV., 607 seqq., 610 seqq.

[4] RAPIN, II., 89. " *Io non so se al nostro tempo sia mai più seguita azzione in cui maggiore evidenza si sia veduta dell'assistenza di Dio ; mentre il Papa, che di professione non era teologo, così sagacemente capiva nulladimeno i sensi dei Consultori, che appena proferiti il repeteva e l'applicazione impiegò all'affare, che volle anco separatamente sentire ciascheduna classe di dottori, con capacitare i medesimi della più sicura interpretazione che si doveva al trattato di S. Agostino e per pienamente quelli

1653, Innocent felt justified in saying that he thought he had employed every means which could be legitimately made use of.[1]

(4.)

On the evening of June 9th, 1653, Saint-Amour and his colleagues were in the very act of drawing up their reports to France when news was brought to them that the Constitution on the five propositions was affixed outside the papal Chancellery. They hastened to the Chancellery but by the time they got there the document had been removed ; so they hurried on to St. Peter's but there it was just being taken down.[2] All they could do now was to report the fact to France and to make ready, in a very depressed state of mind, for their departure. But according to Albizzi the depression of the consultors who had advocated Jansenius' cause, was even greater[3] ; the blow was a particularly hard one for the two Dominicans[4] whose opinions, for the rest, were by no means shared by all their brethren in religion.[5]

Very different were the feelings of the other side. " When

---

sodisfare, patientemente soffrì lo stare cinque e sei hore ben fisse assistente alla discussione del negozio. Questo finalmente a sufficienza digerito, lunedì 7 di giugno, fu publicata un'ampia Costituzione (De Rossi, *Istoria, Vatic. 8873, p. 105, Vatican Library).

[1] SCHILL, 492.

[2] SAINT-AMOUR, 530 ; RAPIN, II., 112.

[3] SCHILL, 493.

[4] As Hallier and Lagault wrote, the Pope reprimanded them ; in Rome it was already said that a decision on physical pre-determination would be made (RAPIN, II., 114, note ; 118, note). Wadding submitted explicitly and unreservedly to the decision of Innocent X. ([DUMAS], III., 92).

[5] RAPIN, II., 38. In Paris the Dominicans Nicolai and Guyard defended Thomism against its supposed affinity to Jansenism (FERET, V., 236, 242 ; HURTER, IV., 39, 67 ; their confrère Alexander Sebille did the same at Louvain (HURTER, III., 1017).

I think of all the plots and intrigues, I can only say : ' It is
the act of God ' ! " Lagault remarked [1] ; " The Dominicans
have done all they could ; a Cardinal of their Order strove
his utmost ; the General of the Augustinians was allied
with them and on top of everything there was a powerful
French plot which time alone will bring fully to light, yet
the Pope has not given way." He wrote even more
enthusiastically on June 9th, when the impression of the
publication of the recent decision was still fresh.[2] He did
not know himself for joy, he wrote. The Constitution could
not be better if he and his friends had had the framing of it.
It contained two master strokes : viz. the name of Jansenius
was in it as well as the condemnation of the fifth proposition
in the sense therein stated ; and when in conclusion the
Pope declared that the remaining propositions of Jansenius,
though not expressly condemned, were not for that reason
approved, he did not know what more could be desired :
" God be praised ! Good-bye, Jansenism ! "

However, these shouts of triumph were premature. The
Jansenist delegates were in no mind to allow themselves
to be taught by the supreme ecclesiastical authority in matters
of faith.[3] In view of the fact that Innocent X. had fixed
June 13th for a farewell audience, their first preoccupation
was what they should do if the Pope insisted on their signing
the definition. They agreed to plead inadequate instructions
from their employers and in the last extremity to sign with
the reservation of the doctrine of efficacious grace and the

[1] On June 30, RAPIN, II., 118, n. 1. " Il ne se peut dire combien
d'obstacles on forma en France, en Espagne, en Flandre, en
Italie et à Rome même, pour s'opposer, combien d'intrigues
on fit jouer dedans et dehors le palais, dans la ville et dans la
maison du pape, pour lui faire changer de résolution, tant par
les dégoûts qu'on lui donnoit de l'affaire en elle—même que par
les défiances qu'on lui vouloit inspirer contre le France." Ibid., 118.

[2] Ibid., 112, n. 1.

[3] This is clear from the statements in SAINT-AMOUR, compiled
by DUMAS (I., 47–51).

teaching of St. Augustine.[1] At their audience, at which they were not requested to sign anything, they asked the Pope, as it were casually, whether he had defined anything on the latter points. The answer could only be in the negative. Thereupon, in reporting to the eleven French Bishops,[2] they stated that the five propositions had only been condemned in the bad sense in which they might be construed, which, in fact, they themselves had condemned. Not only had nothing been done to the prejudice of the propositions, the fully Catholic sense of which they had maintained before the Pope, on the contrary, they may be said to have received papal approbation. They caused their supporters to spread the report in Rome that neither they themselves had been condemned, nor the five propositions as understood by them ; that the Pope had, in fact, declared that he had defined nothing concerning efficacious grace and the teaching of St. Augustine.[3] The delegates, in their letters to their patrons, went so far as to extol divine Providence which had guided their steps to Rome that they might discern truth from falsehood in the presence of the Pope and thereby prevent the condemnation of error from recoiling upon truth.[4] Hence the conduct of the Jansenist delegates, when they thanked the Pope for his definition and promised submission,[5] needs no explanation.

However, the cheerful assurance which the delegates exhibited in public could not easily be reconciled with the speed of their departure, which was such that they did not even take leave from the Cardinals of the Congregation. They only reached Paris about the middle of September. In a letter from Florence they suggested to their friends that, in view of the alleged obscurity of the papal definition, they should pray the Holy See to have the propositions

---

[1] SAINT-AMOUR, 533.
[2] June 16, ibid., 534.
[3] Lagault, June 23, RAPIN, II., 116.
[4] SAINT-AMOUR, 534.
[5] Lagault, June 16, RAPIN, II., 117, note.

which the delegates had submitted, examined in a public Congregation and to allow them to speak in their defence.[1] From Rome their sympathizers wrote that anyone with any degree of education attached but little importance to a censure which, they said, was the result of passion ; let Saint-Amour make sure of the favour of the court—that would be the best deterrent of all.[2] News soon came from Paris that the possible value, for the purposes of the sect, of Innocent X.'s casual remark about St. Augustine, had already been grasped. The Constitution, the message stated, had added to the number of the " disciples of St. Augustine " instead of diminishing it ; all felt a new courage and would exploit the Pope's remark to the utmost.[3]

If these observations enable us to make out the main lines of the developments which were about to ensue, the same is true of a document [4] which Hallier left behind at his departure from Rome on September 6th, 1653. In it he suggested that the conventicles of Port-Royal should be stopped, that the Abbey should be once more placed under Citeaux and the nuns distributed in other convents.

However, the success of these plans depended before all else on the co-operation of the court which, at that very time, had incurred Rome's displeasure by the imprisonment of Cardinal Retz.[5] With a view to conciliating the Pope in these circumstances, the French ambassador in Rome counselled that the sentence against the Jansenists should be received with every mark of respect and that expressions of gratitude should reach the Pope from all sides.[6] The Government was all the more willing to fall in with this

---

[1] Saint-Amour, 549 seq. ; Rapin, II., 121.

[2] Saint-Amour, 554.

[3] Saint-Amour, 558 seq.

[4] " *Acta in Galliis circa Constitutionem damnantem quinque propositiones Iansenii a. 1653-6," f. 751 seq. Archives of the Roman Inquisition. (Papers left by A. Schill.)

[5] Cf. above, p. 68.

[6] Rapin, II., 118.

suggestion as Queen Anne continued in her dislike of the
Jansenists and the youthful King was under the influence
of Jesuit confessors. Hence Bagno was graciously received
when he presented the Constitution on June 3rd and at
the same time requested Mazarin to issue a royal ordinance
in due form for its execution, whilst he prayed for Queen
Anne's protection in view of the opposition [1] which was
already being set on foot by various assemblies and in which
even some Bishops and parish priests seemed to be involved.[2]
A royal ordinance of July 4th " exhorted " the Bishops and
commanded the secular officials to do their part for the
publication and execution of the papal definition.[3] On July
8th Bagno dispatched the customary 124 copies to the Bishops.

A few days later Bagno reported that there was great need
of the help of the secular arm if the Bull was to be carried
into effect. So far the papal Constitution had not encountered
open opposition, but without the King's patronage many
difficulties would be encountered on the part of Parliament
and certain powerful gentlemen who favoured the new
teaching, including even some Bishops. Already some ill-
disposed people were complaining of the fact that the Bull
had been first communicated to the King instead of to the
Bishops ; the expression, " we command," in the royal
ordinance,[4] was disrespectful towards the Bishops ; the five
propositions should have been examined first in France and
only then submitted to the Pope's judgment. Others expressed
their fear that by the present action the way was opened
for the King to decide whether or no Roman ordinances were

---

[1] *Nunziat. di Francia*, 106, Pap. Sec. Arch.

[2] " . . . gli dissi, haver inteso che già si facevano alcune
congregazioni sopra ciò per muover qualche oppositione alla
bolla, giudicandosi che alcuni vescovi e curati di questa città
vi concorrino." *Ibid.*

[3] Thus according to the later text at least : D'ARGENTRÉ,
III., 2, 271 ; [DUMAS], III., 73.

[4] The later text has only : " exhortons et admonestons,"
[DUMAS], III., 74.

to be received ; a French work against the Constitution had
already appeared in print.[1]

The Constitution owed its acceptance by the Bishops solely
to the skill and prestige of the Prime Minister. At Mazarin's
invitation six Archbishops and twenty-six Bishops met on
July 11th at the former's rooms at the Louvre. Since the
judgment on the five propositions, Mazarin urged, was due
to the urgent requests of the King and the French Bishops,
as the Pope himself declared in his Brief to Louis XIV.
and the Bishops,[2] it followed that they were bound not only
to submit to the decision as such, but to thank the Pope
for it.   The Bishops agreed and commissioned Pierre de
Marca, Archbishop of Toulouse, to draw up a letter to that
effect. It was also decided to send a circular letter to all
the Bishops which Bishop Godeau of Grasse was instructed
to write.[3] There was less unanimity when Mazarin ordered
the royal ordinance concerning acceptance of the papal
decision to be read. It was objected that the Constitution
would be forwarded to individual Bishops in any case so
that there was no need to receive it in a body. Mazarin had
the affair put to the vote ; thereupon the Archbishops of
Embrun and Rouen complained that the Constitution had
only been come to by trampling on the rights of the Gallican
Church ; the Bishop of Dol asked that its publication be
put off, in fact there were those who spoke of having the
papal sentence examined by a national council or, alternately,
they suggested that the President of the Assembly should
alone sign the letter to the Pope. Mazarin conceded that in
the royal letter the King's " command " to the Bishops
would be toned down to a " wish " and eventually succeeded
in getting the condemnation of the five propositions accepted.[4]
On July 16th nine Bishops met at Mazarin's residence for

---

[1] *Bagno, July 11, 1653, *loc. cit.*
[2] May 31, 1653, in [DUMAS], III., *Recueil,* 69, 71.
[3] *Bagno, July 18, 1653, *loc. cit.*
[4] RAPIN, II., 130 ; BOURLON, 11 ; *report in *Excerpta, 1653–6,*
f. 812 *seq.* Bibl. Angelica, Rome, S. 3, 1.

the purpose of examining De Marca's and Godeau's letters. Godeau criticized De Marca's draft and succeeded in getting one sentence struck out ; however, even so the text finally agreed upon [1] expressly describes the five propositions as Jansenius' teaching, in fact De Marca draws a parallel between the sentence of Innocent X. and that of Innocent I. against Pelagianism " which was accepted by the Church of that period without hesitation, on the sole basis of the communion and authority of the See of Peter ", for in view of Christ's promises and the action of former Popes, especially that of Damasus I., the Church of that time held it as certain that the dogmatic definitions of the Popes rested on divine authority and accordingly demanded the internal assent of all Christians.[2]

Godeau's circular [3] strikes a different note. It invites the

---

[1] D'ARGENTRÉ, III., 2, 275 *seq.* The *Original letter with 27 original signatures in *Excerpta*, f. 824, *loc. cit.*

[2] In a letter to the Pope of July 19, 1653, De Marca draws special attention to the fact that in these propositions the Gallican doctrine of the superiority of the Council over the Pope has been abandoned : " *Enimvero prae gaudio me continere vix possum, quin Beatitudini Vestrae gratuler, quod eius auspiciis, agente me hac in causa, altera illi laurea placide obvenerit de sententia illa Parisiensium nomine famosa, quae summum de rebus fidei iudicium Papae una cum concilio generali vindicabat. Contrariam epistulae prudens inserui solamque Petri cathedrae communionem et auctoritatem ad damnandas haereses valuisse quondam, eademque nos fide imbutos illam in S. V. hodie colere docui, et ab episcopis ut subscriberetur obtinui. The Bull of Leo X. against Luther had never been published in France, on account of Gallicanism holding sway there, but instead only an extract authorized by the King : " Quae in posterum non sunt subsecutura, postquam non solum exemplo, sed etiam epistolae magisterio, satagente me, contrariam sententiam episcopi profiteantur " (*Excerpta, 1653–6*, f. 829 *seq., loc. cit.*). *Cf.* BOURLON, 12.

[3] About him A. COGNET, *Ant. Godeau, évêque de Grasse et de Vence, un des premiers membres de l'Académie française 1615–1672*, Paris, 1900 ; G. DOUBLET, *Godeau, évêque de Grasse et de Vence 1605–1672*, Paris, 1911–13. Godeau was a good Bishop, but

Bishops, for the sake of concord in the Church, to accept the papal decree and to have it published by the parish priests. However, " such discretion should accompany publication " that no one—presumably the Jansenists included—should have cause to complain.[1] The condemned doctrines could not be defended, nor may anyone depart from the language of the Constitution. About Jansenius not a word : his name is not as much as mentioned.

Rome was naturally dissatisfied with Godeau's equivocations. Lagault wrote from the Eternal City [2] that, in point of fact, the drafting of the circular could not have got into worse hands. None the less from now onwards publication of the papal decree followed quickly enough in individual dioceses ; by the middle of September only a very few Bishops were behind with it [3] and not a few wrote to thank the Pope as, for instance, the Bishops of Noyon, Cahors, Grenoble, Meaux, Poitiers. De Marca's letter was published together with a French translation and with the signatures of sixty-two Bishops.[4] The King himself thanked the Pope for the Constitution ; in a consistory of September 22nd Innocent X. expressed his joy at this action of the monarch.[5]

However, opposition to the papal condemnation was

" il ne sût pas discerner l'hérésie naissante, il flirta avec elle ". (*Rev. d'hist de l'Eglise de France*, IV. [1913], 600.) *Cf.* also BAUMGARTNER, *Weltliteratur*, V., 291 ss.

[1] " *Vous ordonnant en outre de vous gouverner en cette publication avec tant de sagesse, que vous ne donniez sujet à aucun de se plaindre." *Excerpta, 1653–6,* f. 830, *loc. cit.,* 31.

[2] On August 11, 1653, in RAPIN, II., 132.

[3] *Bagno, September 12, 1653, *loc. cit.* Some " l'hanno fatta publicare in lingua latina in alcun luoghi, dove sono poche persone che l'intendono ".

[4] *Excerpta, 1653–6,* f. 886, *loc. cit.*

[5] *Ibid.,* f. 842. *Ibid.,* *Letters of thanks for the decision, from the Bishop of Noyon, August 24, Cahors, September 1, Grenoble, August 10, Meaux, August 3. A printed circular of July 29, 1653, to the Oratory from its General Bourgoing, about the acceptance of the decision, *ibid.,* 872. *Answers of the Pope to the Bishop of Meaux, September 13, 1653, in

anything but dead. From Sullay, the "official" of Paris, Bagno learnt that a number of men of position had urged various objections against publication [1] ; that the Duke of Ventadour, who was a Canon of Notre Dame, had expressed his regret that some members of the Chapter were against the definition and that he had told the Queen that if the King did not punish a few rebellious Jansenists the sect would raise its head once more.[2] The Bishop of Rennes met with no opposition when he expounded to the Sorbonne the royal decree concerning the Constitution, in fact it was embodied in the acts of the University. Bagno, however, was well aware that if there had been no opposition, it was solely because no one had the courage to offer any.[3] "Come what may," the Sorbonnist Taignier wrote,[4] "we allow things to run their course at the Faculty because in existing circumstances it is impossible to do anything without raising a tremendous storm against ourselves and thus creating difficulties for truth." "Christ Himself," he added, "said : 'My hour is not yet come.'" The shrewder ones among the opponents of the Jansenists likewise avoided everything liable to cause friction and the supporters of the Pope acted in like manner. Vincent de Paul paid several friendly visits to Port-Royal after publication of the papal decree,[5] and

---

Innocentii X. Epist., IX., p. 16, to the Bishops of Grenoble and Noyon, September 29, *ibid.*, 22, 23, to the Dean and Chapter of Poitiers, October 9, *ibid.*, 28, to the Bishop of Sarlat, December 13, *ibid.*, 52, to the Bishop of Tulle, March 21, 1654, *ibid.*, 93, to the professors of Douai and Poitiers, *ibid.*, 94 *seq.* Pap. Sec. Archives.

[1] *Bagno, July 25, 1653, *loc. cit.*

[2] " * . . . che se il Re non punisce qualcheduno de' Jansenisti disubbedienti, ritornerà in piedi la loro setta, et che la regina rispose che si farà, quando sarà necessario." *Ibid.*

[3] " *che essendosi molti di contrario senso, alcuno non ha havuto ardire di parlare." Bagno, August 1, 1653, *loc. cit.* ; *Report of Halliers, *Excerpta, 1653–6*, f. 848, *loc. cit.*

[4] July 14, 1653, in RAPIN, II., 127.

[5] MAYNARD, II., 349.

the General of the Jesuits forbade all noisy expressions of satisfaction at the decree on the part of his subjects [1] and Olier was anxious to win over the party by friendliness and straightforwardness.[2]

Thus, at least outwardly, everything was quiet for a time. Angélique wrote that the Jesuits must be allowed to enjoy what they looked upon as their triumph ; God would know how to uphold His truth. The five propositions had been condemned solely because a wrong meaning could be attached to them, but the Pope had protested that he was not condemning St. Augustine ; more they did not ask for.[3] However, though in public the Jansenists observed a policy of silence, they spread in underhand fashion the document presented by them to the Pope in which they had distinguished a threefold interpretation of the five theses, viz. the Calvinistic, the one defended by the delegates and, as they claimed, by St. Augustine and, lastly, one which they attributed to their opponents, the Molinists, and which they had asked the Pope to condemn.

The public attack against the Bull was inaugurated by Antoine Arnauld's brother Henri, Bishop of Angers. When publishing the Bull that prelate made use of the formula drawn up by Godeau and approved at the Bishops' meeting, but with two additional clauses of his own. Whereas Godeau had not said a word about the authorship of the five propositions, Henri Arnauld stated that they were being ascribed to Jansenius. After that the Bishop forbids the extension of the papal condemnation of the five propositions " to the sacred and intangible teaching of the Apostolic See and the Church, which up to the present time the Popes had acknowledged to have been preserved in the writings of

---

[1] RAPIN, II., 137.

[2] " Ma pensée serait, dans ce commencement, de ne point blesser les Jansénistes, mais d'agir envers eux avec douceur et grande ouverture de cœur, pour les attirer à l'union." FAILLON, II., 456.

[3] July 8 and 10 and August 22, 1653, *Lettres*, II., 341, 343, 345, 362.

St. Augustine and which our Holy Father protested that he had no intention to touch ".[1] Language of this kind was bound to give rise to the suspicion that there was an intention to give the partisans of the five propositions a handle, or, as Bagno wrote, " pretexts ".[2] The Bishop of Angers was followed by Bishop Gilbert de Choiseul, of Comminges.[3] After he had published the papal Constitution at a diocesan synod, the Bishop allowed himself to be persuaded that it was possible to deduct from the text of the definition arguments against the teaching of St. Augustine and St. Thomas to which the University of Toulouse was particularly attached. Accordingly he formally forbade all such deductions.[4] In like manner, during the illness of the Bishop or Orleans, his Vicar General forbade preachers and catechists to speak of the five propositions and the papal Constitution, except with such discretion that no one would have reason to complain. What this meant was soon experienced by a Jesuit who, having spoken with some warmth against the propositions, was forbidden the pulpit.[5] In the same way Bishop Buzenval of Beauvais commanded the Constitution to be published in such a manner that no

---

[1] The *pastoral of August 14, 1653, in *Excerpta, 1653-6*, f. 872 (*loc. cit.*). " Propositions que l'on attribue à feu M. Jansenius d'Ipres." Prohibition " de faire retomber cette condamnation sur la doctrine sainte et inviolable du Siège Apostolique et de l'Église que les papes jusqu'à notre siècle on déclarée être enfermée dans les œuvres de S. Augustin et à laquelle notre très— saint et très vénérable Père a témoigné qu'il n'avoit point entendu toucher."

[2] *pretesti. Bagno, September 12, 1653, *Nunziat. di Francia*, 106, Pap. Sec. Arch.

[3] Henri Arnauld, personally of irreproachable conduct (Rapin, I., 340), was a good Bishop, as was Choiseul, subsequently Bishop of Tournai [*ob.* 1689], in spite of his Jansenism and Gallicanism. *Cf.* Desmons, *Gilbert de Choiseul, évêque de Tournai*, Tournai, 1907 ; A. Degert in *Bullet. de litt. éccles.*, Toulouse, 1908, 131-8.

[4] Rapin, II., 164.

[5] *Ibid.*, 165.

one could feel hit by it ; no one was to make use of the five
propositions in order to defend laxity and impenitence.[1]

Archbishop Gondrin of Sens spoke even more clearly than
all the above-named.[2] His pastoral letter begins with a
eulogy of St. Augustine's teaching on grace ; he then goes
on to speak of those who " have recourse to the tricks of the
Semi-Pelagians in order to discredit this teaching ; this they
did when they drew up five propositions susceptible of a
heretical interpretation and ascribed them to the late Bishop
of Ypres, of holy memory ". These ambiguous propositions,
it was said, did not embody the doctrine of St. Augustine
and were equivocally worded out of sheer malice, so as to
secure more readily their condemnation. The Pope had
only condemned them in general terms and without touching
on the doctrine that had been maintained in his presence.
Of course sentence should have been first pronounced by
the French Bishops. Instead of this the episcopate was
being further humiliated from day to day, hence he left it
to the faithful to lament with the groans of the dove and
the feelings of good and loving children, the eclipse and the
abasement both of the episcopal dignity and of the Gallican
Church.[3] The letter ends with an order for the publication
of the Bull with the explicit declaration that it affected neither
the doctrine of efficacious grace nor Augustine, and preachers
were not to pass from the general terms of the five propositions
to the particular meaning which embodies the fundamental
teaching of St. Augustine.

On October 17th the nuncio forwarded the pastoral letter
to Rome. He described it as worse than that of the Bishop of

---

[1] *Ibid.*, 166.

[2] *Ibid.*, 167 *seq.* Printed pastoral of September 23, in *Excerpta*,
1653-6, f. 931, *loc. cit.*

[3] Complaint that the episcopate " s'abbat de jour en jour par
les entreprises de ceux, ou qui en ignorent la grandeur, ou qui
en méprisent la sainteté, ou qui en redoutent la puissance. Nous
nous contentons de laisser aux peuples qui nous sont commis,
à déplorer par des gémissements de colombes et par les sentimens
de bons et tendres enfants l'obscurcissement, etc."

Angers and complained at the same time that the Government took no steps against the largely attended gatherings at Port-Royal, although the King's ministers had been requested to do so ; hence there was reason to fear that within a short time there would be a considerable increase in the number of the Jansenists.[1] In vain had he drawn attention, through Vincent de Paul and the Grand-Penitentiary of Paris, to the pastoral letter of the Bishop of Angers and to the evils to which it may give rise. He had fared no better with regard to the pastoral letter of the Archbishop of Sens. In the opinion of many, the Jansenists had led astray these two prelates in order that they might be in a position to appeal to Parliament on the ground of abuse of office, so soon as the Pope raised his voice. Consequently he recommended that three or four of the best-disposed Bishops of France should be given power to take action against disobedient prelates and priests, though without naming those of Sens and Angers.[2] Soon after Bagno forwarded a list of the most zealous among the French Bishops.[3]

It is not surprising that Rome was indignant at the conduct of the four Bishops. The nuncio was instructed to inform the court that the Pope resented the pastoral letter of Sens as an insult. At the same time the Bishops and Hallier were asked their opinion as to how the Archbishop could be punished.[4] On December 22nd, 1653 a Brief was dispatched

---

[1] " *si può dubitare che in breve tempo siano per maggiormente augmentarsi li seguaci di questi errori." *Nunziat. di Francia*, 106. Pap. Sec. Archives.

[2] *Bagno, November 7, 1653, *ibid.*

[3] They are the Archbishops of Bordeaux, Toulouse, Narbonne, Arles, the Bishops of Le Puy, Saint-Flour, Vabres, La Rochelle, Bazas, Alet, Lodève, Pamiers, Toulon, Langres, Mâcon, Saint-Malo, Meaux, Sarlat (*Bagno, November 14, 1653, *ibid*). The principal Jansenists of the Sorbonne :   Dreux, Sainte-Beuve, Feydeau, Macaron, Carré, Fortin, Loisel, De Lalane, he mentions on November 21 (*ibid.).

[4] *Commission of November 17, 1653, in *Excerpta, 1653–6*, f. 345, *loc. cit.*

to the Bishops of Arles, Annecy, Conserans and Mâcon, instructing them to open an inquiry against the Archbishop. The latter's conduct was generally condemned even in France. The Criminal Court of Poitiers prohibited the "alleged" pastoral letter and threatened to punish those who printed and distributed it.[1] Even the Chancellor and the Keeper of the Seals described it as heretical [2] whilst the King refused to receive the Archbishop.[3]

For all that no decisive measure was taken. "The court," Bagno wrote on November 7th, "was more lavish of words than of deeds.[4] When on December 16th he spoke to the King and Queen of the continual meetings at Port-Royal, of the emisssaries who were being sent out from there to spread the old errors, of the four Bishops who had acted more like wolves than shepherds, he was left with the impression that their Majesties' zeal had waxed cold.[5] Mazarin's answers to his protests were also couched in general terms.[6] Hallier submitted tangible plans to the Minister; they were to the effect that the Constitution should be registered in Parliament and the schools and the community of hermits at Port-Royal suppressed. But even he only obtained vague promises.[7]

However, the prelates of Sens and Comminges judged it

---

[1] *Bull.*, X., 745 ; *Excerpta*, f. 981, *loc. cit.* In the session of the Inquisition of December 9, 1653, general opinion was in favour of censuring the pastoral letter of Sens. *Ibid.*, f. 953.

[2] *Ibid.*, f. 953 ; *Bagno, November 7, 1653, *Nunziat. di Francia*, 106, Pap. Sec. Archives.

[3] *Hallier, January 9, 1654, in *Excerpta, 1653-6*, *loc. cit.*

[4] *Ibid.*

[5] *Bagno, December 19, 1653, *ibid.*

[6] *Bagno, December 20, 1653, *ibid.*

[7] *Hallier to Rome, December 25, 1653, *Excerpta, 1653-6*, f. 989. The "petites écoles" were described by Hallier as seminaries, "quae in hac urbe et circa urbem plura sunt, in quibus et pueri et juvenes primariae nobilitatis et alii ad clericatum formandi recipiuntur," the hermits are called "congregatio ista hominum silvestrium".

expedient to write to Innocent X. On December 31st, 1653,[1] they addressed to the Pope a letter of substantially identical tenor. They expressed their regret at the report which had come to their ears that they had offended the Pope ; would he point out what was wrong in their pastoral letters and hear their explanations ? They would then amend the wrong. But surely it could not be wrong on their part to make a stand for the teaching of St. Augustine and the rights of Bishops. The Pope was naturally not impressed by these explanations. Meanwhile the commission that was to deal with Archbishop Gondrin had been appointed, but it did nothing, though both the King and the Queen renewed to the nuncio the old assurances.[2] Accordingly Hallier suggested at Rome to have the four Bishops tried by their colleagues of their respective Provinces, or Gondrin by the Primate of Lyons ; in any case the matter should not be allowed to drift.[3] However, Gallican pride rebelled at the thought of French Bishops being judged by papal commissaries ; so on the ground of some antiquated judicial enactments a demand was made for a tribunal of twelve Bishops. Rome consented to the appointment of at least eight,[4] and of another seven for the examination of the pastorals of Beauvais and Comminges.[5] However, several of the commissaries refused to act as judges in the affair and Innocent X. died before anything was done.[6]

---

[1] *Ibid., f. 998, 999.

[2] *Bagno, January 23, 1654, Excerpta, 1653-6, loc. cit. ; *Bagno pointed out to their Majesties that of the 125 French Bishops, 121 had done their duty. Ibid.

[3] " *Eo in loco positae sunt res nostrae, i. e. catholicae Ecclesiae, ut ulterius non progredi sit cedere, et Ecclesiae unitatem, fidei integritatem, summi Ecclesiae capitis auctoritatem certo periculo exponere." February 12, 1654, ibid.

[4] Brief of March 16, 1654, Bull., XV, 760.

[5] Brief of October 26, 1654, ibid., 775.

[6] *Mariscotti's report (1668) for Bargellini, Bibl. Casanatense, Rome, X., XVI., 34, p. 154–162. The fact that the Pope issued his Brief " motu proprio " hurt the French. (Ibid.)

It would seem that it was the Princess Guémené who at that time held a protecting hand over the sect.[1] On the other hand there was no lack of opposition to the four Bishops. On September 12th, 1653, Bagno forwarded a document of the Chapter of Angers against its Bishop and another by the Advocate Filleau against Gondrin, and on February 13th, 1654, an appeal by the Chapter of Beauvais which, notwithstanding its exemption, had been threatened by the Bishop with excommunication for giving effect to the Constitution.[2]

Up to the spring of 1654 the Jansenists had not attempted to influence opinion by means of any new publication; they were content to spread further and further their treatise on the threefold meaning of the five propositions. The confusion thus created in many minds led the new royal confessor, François Annat, to take up the cudgels against them. In a Latin work,[3] which soon appeared in French also, he showed that the five propositions were found in the works of Jansenius and that the latter was hit by the papal condemnation. The work also dealt with the Jansenists' appeal to Augustine and with the pastorals of the four Bishops.

Arnauld seemed to have waited for some publication of this kind. Within a short while he published, one after another, four books intended for the next Assembly of the Clergy, due in 1654. These books, with the exception of the fourth, were in fact laid before the Assembly. Now that Annat had fanned the flame with his publication, so Arnauld stated in his first book,[4] it was impossible to remain silent any longer. The honour of the Church was at stake for

---

[1] Angélique Arnauld, January 3, 1654, *Lettres*, II., 416. Angélique considers the impending action against Gondrin like setting fire to the house of God (letter of January 14, 1654, *ibid.*, 425).

[2] (Printed) *Lettres des doyens, chanoines et chapitre de Beauvais à N. S. P. le Pape* of December 1, 1652, *loc. cit.*

[3] " Cavilli Iansenianorum contra latam in ipsos a S. Sede sententiam seu Confutatio libelli trium columnarum."

[4] " Réponse au P. Annat " (*Œuvres*, XIX., 147 *seqq.*).

Annat ascribed to her the errors of his Society, the honour also of the Pope whom he caused to condemn as heresies what were Catholic doctrines ; the honour of St. Augustine of whom, according to Annat, the Pope had made no account ; the honour also of several Bishops, distinguished for their dignity and worth, which he trod under foot. After that Arnauld goes on to prove with all his dialectical and rhetorical skill, that the five propositions were not to be found in Jansenius ; that, in point of fact, the latter taught something very different. Though Arnauld had taken the opposite for granted in his previous apologies of Jansenius and other-wise also,[1] he ends by throwing at the Jesuits the reproach of duplicity : before the papal sentence they had discovered Calvinism in the five propositions ; at present there was no longer question of that, on the contrary, they discovered in them the condemnation of the most celebrated and the most clearly stated principles of Augustine.

A second pamphlet, which followed close on the first, endeavours to substantiate this accusation in detail.[2] According to its author, with regard to the subjects touched by the five propositions, the teaching of Jansenius is identical with that of Augustine ; if Jansenius had been condemned by the Pope, Augustine would also stand condemned. This is, briefly, the thesis of the second pamphlet. A third [3]

---

[1] [DUMAS], III., 1–42, Bossuet's opinion : " Je crois donc que les propositions sont véritablement dans Jansénius et qu'elles sont l'âme de son livre. Tout ce qu'on a dit au contraire me paraît une pure chicane et une chose inventée pour éluder le jugement de l'Église." *Letter to Marshal de Bellefonds of September 30, 1677, *Correspondance*, ed. CH. URBAIN ET E. LEVESQUE, II., Paris, 1909, 51.

[2] " Mémoires sur le dessein qu'ont les Jésuites de faire retomber la censure des cinq propositions sur la véritable doctrine de S. Augustin sous le nom de Jansénius " (*Œuvres*, XIX., 196 ss.).

[3] " Éclaircissement sur quelques nouvelles objections, . . . où il est montré que ce que les Jésuites s'efforcent de faire, ne peût qu'allumer le feu d'une très-grande division dans l'Église," *ibid.*, 208 *seqq.*

defines still more accurately the point of view which the Jansenists were determined to maintain for the future. It was impossible to believe that the Pope had ascertained whether the five theses were to be found in Jansenius, for if he had investigated the matter he would have discovered that they were simply not to be found in his writings.[1] Rome had only inquired whether the theses were true or erroneous, not whether Jansenius was their author.[2] But now, under the name of Jansenius, the most solid principles of Augustine were to be reprobated ! Let them examine whether Augustine of Ypres agrees with Augustine of Hippo ! If no such investigation is made, if Jansenius is surreptitiously condemned, nothing will be achieved.[3] A fourth pamphlet came too late to be submitted to the Assembly but in 1654 every Bishop was given a copy of the first three.

For all that Arnauld failed to prevent the Bishops from taking some steps against Jansenius. On the advice of De Marca, Mazarin decided to convene all the Bishops then in Paris for the purpose of pronouncing a joint condemnation of the threefold meaning of the five theses. However, the Assembly rejected De Marca's draft of the condemnation,[4] though on March 9th a committee of eight Bishops was chosen for the purpose of examining the affair.[5] On March 26th Aubusson of Embrun presented his report. The only question, he explained, was whether the five theses were Jansenius' and whether they had been condemned as understood by him : the answer to both questions was in the affirmative.[6] The Bishops of Beauvais and Comminges objected and on March 28th Gondrin of Sens heatedly

---

[1] *Ibid.*, 213.

[2] *Ibid.*, 220.

[3] *Ibid.*, 221.

[4] RAPIN, II., 206 *seqq.*

[5] They were Archbishops Aubusson of Embrun, Bouthillier of Tours, Harlay of Rouen, Marca of Toulouse, and Bishops Attichi of Autun, Bertier of Montauban, Mothe-Houdencourt of Rennes, and Lescot of Chartres. GERBERON, II., 225 *seqq.*

[6] *Ibid.*

advocated for two hours the cause of Augustine of Ypres and Augustine of Hippo, whose teaching must not be condemned.   But the meeting did not allow itself to be influenced.   A letter to the Pope, drawn up by De Marca, states without equivocation that they had met for the purpose of declaring, in view of the misuse of the Apostolic judgment, that the five propositions were Jansenius' and had been condemned in his sense by the Pope.[1]   A circular letter to the French Bishops, drawn up by Lescot of Chartres,[2] renewed this declaration.   "The Constitution," we read, "is as clear as possible ; it is enough to read it to judge aright the vain arguments of the opponents."   Thus, for the first time since the Council of Bâle, the French Bishops solemnly admitted the Pope's right to issue decisions on matter of faith binding in conscience, even without a Council.[3]

Curiously enough both these letters of March 28th bear the signatures of Archbishop Gondrin, Choiseul of Comminges and Choart of Beauvais.[4]   However, on April 9th Gondrin and Choiseul explained that they had only signed for the sake of peace and that they were anxious to see St. Augustine's authority safeguarded.[5]   The day after they swore once more that they had no intention of departing in any way whatever from the reverence due to the Holy See.   On April

---

[1] D'Argentré, II., 2, f. 278 ; Bourlon, 14.

[2] D'Argentré, II., 2, f. 277. Valençay (Paris, April 10, 1654), extols to the Pope Mazarin's part in bringing about the letter. There was reason to fear a schism " parmi les évêques qui peu à peu auraient glissé dans l'hérésie. Le cardinal Mazarin n'a rien négligé pour éviter ce malheur, aplanir ces difficultés et faire cesser ces dissensions spirituelles. Par ses efforts il a ramené l'union parmi les évêques." Annales de St. Louis, X. (October, 1905), 249.

[3] Thus Pallavicino (I., 186).

[4] *Excerpta, 1653-6, f. 1096, loc. cit.   The letter bears 31 signatures with the observation that 8 Bishops had left on account of the Easter festivities and therefore their names were missing.

[5] Gerberon, II., 231.

17th, 1654, they and the Bishops of Beauvais and Valence wrote once more to the Pope in justification of their conduct. They began by declaring that they accepted the Constitution without reservation, but in the conclusion they took shelter behind the name of St. Augustine, as was the customary evasion of the Jansenists. For the sake of peace they had signed, though they were uncertain whether the five propositions were Jansenius' own ; in other words, they withdrew their signature.[1] On the same day Choiseul also wrote a personal letter to the Pope though this time there is no mention of any uncertainty as to the five theses being Jansenius' ; the only thing he could be reproached with was undue attachment to Augustine and Thomas.[2] The Pope felt hurt by the letters of the four Bishops. On August 4th Gondrin and Choiseul sought to excuse themselves, though without withdrawing anything.[3]

As a matter of fact by that time Innocent X. had answered both of them by other means. By a decree of the Inquisition dated April 23rd, 1654, all Jansenist writings of the preceding four years were inserted in the list of prohibited books. They were about fifty in number, beginning with the *Augustinus* of Jansenius down to the first two pamphlets addressed by Arnauld to the Assembly of the Clergy of 1654 ; the pastoral letters of Sens and Comminges were likewise included.[4] To the Bishops of the Assembly of the Clergy the Pope addressed a most kindly Brief.[5] He praised their submission to the Constitution " in which we have condemned, under five headings, the teaching of Cornelius Jansenius contained in his book *Augustinus* ".[6] In Germany

---

[1] *Excerpta, 1653–6*, f. 1119, *loc. cit.*

[2] *Ibid.*, 1118.

[3] *Ibid.*, 1141.

[4] [DUMAS], III., *Recueil*, 82 seqq.

[5] September 29, 1654, *ibid.*, 107.

[6] " Damnavimus in quinque propositionibus Cornelii Iansenii doctrinam eius libro contentam, cui titulus Augustinus," *ibid.* Already in the decree of the Inquisition mentioned above it was

and Spain the publication of the Bull met with no opposition.[1]

Innocent X. had every reason to be satisfied with the result obtained and to reward the men who had helped in the drawing up and the publication of the Constitution. Hallier declined the See of Toul but both he and his associates were rewarded with benefices. The Augustinian Bruni who, notwithstanding the strange behaviour of his General, had faithfully fought the new doctrine,[2] was raised to the episcopate. But the most important contribution to the negotiations had come from Albizzi : " God alone knows how much I have toiled in this weighty affair " he writes himself ; " may a reward await me in heaven ! " [3] His elevation to the cardinalate was richly deserved.

(5.)

During the whole of Innocent X.'s pontificate the Jansenist teaching remained an open sore both for France and for the land of its birth.

With the accession of a new Pope hopes had arisen that a more energetic attitude towards the adherents of the Bishop of Ypres would be adopted in Flanders also. At Madrid the new nuncio, Rospigliosi, the future Pope Clement IX., worked in this sense and the King's confessor, Martinez, showed considerably greater zeal against the Jansenist teaching on grace than his predecessor, John of St. Thomas ; in Flanders the internuncio Antonio Bichi, Abbot of S. Anastasia, did all that was possible and the new Governor, Castel Rodrigo, was not unwilling to support Bichi. Yielding to Rospigliosi's repeated requests, the Inquisitor General

said : " post condemnatam sua constitutione . . . in quinque propositionibus Augustini Cornelii Iansenii episcopi Iprensis doctrinam " (ibid., 82).

[1] *Excerpta, 1653–6, f. 1213–1246, loc. cit.
[2] RAPIN, II., 138.
[3] Katholik, 1883, II., 494.

forbade the passage of Jansenius' book through the harbours
of Spain and commanded the Bishops of the peninsula to
publish Innocent X.'s Bull against the Bishop of Ypres,
whilst a royal ordinance was issued to the effect that, in
accordance with the wish of the Pope, the Bull should also
be published in the Netherlands. From Rome came Briefs
to the same effect addressed to the Bishops of Namur, Ghent,
Antwerp, Tournai, Bruges, Saint-Omer and to the Universities.[1]
The Bishops of Antwerp, Bruges and Namur obeyed the
Pope's command [2] and the University of Douai thanked him
for his Brief and promised complete submission.[3] Thus it
looked as if every one of those in authority were on the side
of the Pope, yet for all that the Jansenists had no cause for
despair. The King was weak and it was a long way from
Madrid to Brussels. One man, one moreover laid up with
gout, namely Archbishop Jacob Boonen of Malines, was
powerful enough, in conjunction with Peter Roose, President
of the Council of State, to paralyse the royal ordinance.[4]
Shortly after the receipt of the latest papal Briefs, internuncio
Bichi wrote that, to judge by certain symptoms, he thought

---

[1] RAPIN, I., 20 *seq.* Bichi, arriving at Brussels on April 8, 1642,
*reports to Rome on May 6, 1645, that he dispatched 13 Briefs
to the Bishops, for the vacant sees of Cambrai, Roermond and
Tournai to the Vicars General resp., and the one for the University
of Louvain to the Rector (*Lettere del Abbate di S. Anastasia*,
t. 29 [37], Pap. Sec. Arch.). He also communicated the Brief
to the Archbishop of Malines. Boonen seemed well disposed,
so long as he had not spoken to Van Caelen. Castel Rodrigo
presented his Brief to the State Council (*Bichi, May 13, 1645,
ibid.). On May 20 he *announces the execution of the Brief in
Antwerp and Bruges (*ibid.*). *Cf.* the Briefs in *Innocentii X.
Epist.*, I. (1644 to December, 1645, secretario Gaspare de
Simeonibus) : n. 63, to Malines ; n. 97, to Roermond, Namur,
St. Omer, Ypres, Bruges, Antwerp, Tournai, Ghent, to the
Universities of Louvain and Douai (all of February 20, 1645),
and to the Governor. Pap. Sec. Arch.

[2] RAPIN, I., 75.

[3] *May 26, 1645, *Lettere, loc. cit.*, t. 29.

[4] RAPIN, I., 4, 138.

that the Archbishop had conceived fresh hopes for the defence of Jansenism.[1]

Intellectually Boonen was of no great account. He was a mere tool in the hand of his Vicars General, Henry Van Caelen (Calenus) and Libertus Froidmont (Fromondus), who both favoured Jansenism and nourished resentment against the Pope who had refused to confirm their nomination to the sees of Roermond and Tournai.[2] Such was Fromond's prestige at the University of Louvain that he could do what he liked with it, whilst Van Caelen controlled a large part of the secular and regular clergy. Boonen and Roose were at the head of the Council of State of Flanders which played an important rôle in the execution of royal ordinances. This body favoured Jansenism.[3] One of the chief arguments with which its members were for ever intimidating the King and the Governor was the high esteem in which, they alleged, Jansenism was held in Flanders, so that it would be an exceedingly dangerous thing to provoke the people of the Low Countries whilst they were at war with France, by any measures against the Bishops.[4]

With a view to supporting the royal ordinance for the publication of the Bull, the internuncio had obtained a papal Brief for the Governor, Castel Rodrigo,[5] after which he

[1] " *Ho havuti inditii che Msgr. archivescovo di Malines pigli animo di nuovo a difesa del Jansenio sperando di poter vincere con danari a Roma et in Spagna, come ha fatto qua in beneficare i suoi adherenti. Per havere favori dal sig. Marchese di Castel Rodrigo, dice di voler impegnare de' stabili del suo arcivescovato per assistere il Re di Spagna." Bichi, July 1, 1645, *Nunziat. di Fiandra*, t. 27, Pap. Sec. Arch.

[2] RAPIN, 15, 68 ; *Letter to Bichi, April 29, 1645, *Nunziat. di Napoli*, 39 A, p. 82 *seq.*, Pap. Sec. Arch. Fromond was a personal friend of Jansenius and the excellent Latin of *Augustinus* is attributed to him. RAPIN, II., 182.

[3] A survey (from July 19, 1643, onwards), of the ensuing negotiations is given in a " *Summarium* in *Excerpta ex actis s. Officii a. 1647-1652* ", f. 434-449, *loc. cit.* (Schill).

[4] RAPIN, II., 74, 76.

[5] *March 2, 1645, *Epist.*, I.

pressed him to take action. He obtained nothing : Castel
Rodrigo explained that he was dependent on the Council
of State and that, moreover, he was so taken up with the
Hispano-French war that he had no time for anything else.[1]
The nuncio in Madrid secured a royal ordinance to the
Council of State for the publication and Innocent X. himself
caused a friend of the Governor, Cardinal Cueva, to write
to him.[2] In his reply to the Cardinal [3] Castel Rodrigo declared
that the internuncio was over-keen and allowed himself to
be too much guided by the Jesuits ; in the Low Countries
violent measures were inadvisable and the Council of State
insisted on the privileges of the country ; all the same he
hoped to settle the matter before long.

However, for the time being, Castel Rodrigo did not
dare to take a decisive step in view of the critical position
of Spanish arms in the war with France and even the internuncio, though repeatedly urged by Rome,[4] did not feel
inclined to press him in these circumstances,[5] all the more
so as the resistance of the University of Louvain, whose
prestige was considerable, seemed to him insurmountable
just then. From the first the University had led the opposition
to the Bull and only a short time after Innocent X.'s accession
it had presented to the Governor a memorial in favour of
Jansenius.[6] In its opinion the Bishop of Ypres' only fault
was his having brought to light the errors of certain modern
theologians, such as Molina, Suarez and Vasquez. Hence
the hatred of the Jesuits for him. This is why they had
obtained a Bull in which it was alleged that Jansenius had

[1] RAPIN, II., 20, 75 ; *Bichi, May 27, 1645, *Lettere, loc. cit.*

[2] RAPIN, II., 79. *Praise of Bichi's zeal in a letter of the
Secretary of State to the " Abbate di S. Anastasia " at Brussels,
July 29, 1645, *Nunziat. di Napoli*, 39 A. Papal Secret Archives.

[3] July 8, 1645, RAPIN, II., 79 *seq.*

[4] *Nunziat. di Fiandra*, t. 28, under July 29, October 21
November 4, 11, 18, 1645, etc. Pap. Sec. Arch.

[5] RAPIN, II., 80.

[6] *Cod. Preuckianus*, C. 43, f. 601–5, Library of the Anima,
Rome.

reasserted propositions that had already been condemned by
the Pope. The delegates of the University of Louvain had
failed to obtain in Rome a fresh inquiry into the question
whether Jansenius' accusations against the Jesuits were
founded on fact, though in a matter of this kind, which was
purely one of fact, the Pope was liable to err. Since the
innocence of Jansenius and the genuine teaching of St.
Augustine were being sacrificed to the violence and the
tricks of the Jesuits, the University prayed the Governor
for a hearing so that, with full knowledge of the situation,
he might obtain in Rome the inquiry which they had demanded
before this.

A second memorial of the University [1] offers to prove before
a commission that no proposition condemned by the Popes,
nor any doctrine contrary to that of Augustine, could be
found in the works of Jansenius. The minutes of the discussions
of the commission should then be laid before the Pope by
the King of Spain : if the Pope decided that the University
was in the wrong, they were prepared to accept Urban VIII.'s
Bull.

At that time only a minority of the professors of Louvain
University sided with the Pope against Jansenius, chief
among them being John Schinckel, Christian Beusecom and
William ab Angelis.[2] But after the new Pope had addressed
Briefs to the Bishops of Flanders, to Douai and to Louvain,[3]
the University decided, on May 5th, 1645, to submit
unreservedly to the papal ordinances. With this declaration
it looked as if everything were settled, but the internuncio,
in forwarding the decision to Rome,[4] expressed his misgivings

---

[1] *Ibid._, f. 609.

[2] RAPIN, I., 17.

[3] *February 20, 1645 (see above, p. 301, n. 1), Cod. Preuck.,
p. 497, loc. cit. Ibid., 495, *Letter of Bichi to the Rector of the
University, May 2, 1645.

[4] *May 6, 1645, Lettere del Abbate di S. Anastasia, t. 29 (37),
Pap. Sec. Arch. Cf. RAPIN, I., 77 seq.—*Fussero quasi tutti
concordi a concludere per l'obedienza, e solo reclamassero il
Fromondo con due o tre compagni. . . . Non resta in questa

as to whether deeds would follow words, and his doubts proved justified.

Schinckel explained to the Rector what were the practical proofs of submission on which the Roman Inquisition insisted : they were the prohibition of Jansenius' work and its with-drawal both from the trade and from the hands of the students.[1] Vernulaeus, the Rector, was prepared to submit, for though a Jansenist himself, he was a member of the Faculty of arts which was in favour of obedience to the Pope because other-wise it feared the loss of its privileges.[2] Accordingly Vernulaeus replied that, for the moment, he had put off the discussion of the decision of the University because the Jansenists threatened to interfere with it through the court and the officials.

As a matter of fact opposition came from all sides. President Roose, warned by Bichi, avoided the necessity of having to give an answer to the internuncio by going into the country, taking Innocent X.'s Brief with him.[3] Fromond spread the report that Bichi only demanded the publication of the Bull because he wanted to become a Cardinal, that the University's declaration of submission had been tampered with ; if it was authentic, the Pope should be requested to grant a delay owing to the opposition of the Council of State.[4] Now it is true that the Council of State did create difficulties, but it did so precisely because the University did not take its own submission seriously.[5] At the beginning of July

---

Nunziatura alcun sospetto d'inobedienza fuor che lui (the Archbishop) con il suo Caleno, Fromondo e pochi altri theologi di Lovanio (Bichi, June 24, 1645, *loc. cit.*). Cf. *Summarium, Excerpta, 1647–1653*, f. 434–449.

[1] *Schinkel to Bichi, May 16, 1645, *loc. cit.*

[2] RAPIN, I., 69, 75.

[3] *Ibid.*, 77 ; *Bichi, June 24, 1645, *loc. cit.*

[4] RAPIN, I., 76.

[5] *Bichi, September 30, 1645, *loc. cit.* It is false, he writes, when Sinnich speaks in Rome of the obedience of the University, for the " consegli " interfered only because " sollecitati da parti

Bichi wrote to Rome that the assurances of submission were not sincere and already by then the Council of State had forbidden the Rector and those professors who were loyal to the Pope, to obey the internuncio. A memorial by the procurator fiscal explained that on the basis of Flemish privileges, special leave from the King was necessary before the Bull could be published, hence he must put off publication until further orders from the King.[1] Bichi was instructed by Rome to investigate this Flemish privilege. He found that it had never been made use of for the purpose of prohibiting writings forbidden by Rome,[2] but his investigation did not induce the Council to withdraw its prohibition. Small wonder that just then the internuncio should have been in a despairing mood. He wrote to Rome that it would not mean dropping the Bull even if they decided to forgo immediate publication since it had been published in several dioceses in Flanders : this might be deemed sufficient.[3]

To this Rome would not consent. Accordingly Bichi wrote that the only hope lay in a formal royal ordinance strictly enjoining publication of the Bull. Such an order was in fact secured through the intervention of the Spanish nuncio, Rospigliosi,[4] and communicated to the Bishops and the

---

che vi hanno interesse. Di più mi consta, che il conseglio privato ancora ha stato sollecitato, et a nome del Università di Lovanio, non già di particolari ".

[1] Bichi, July 1, 1645, in RAPIN, I., 77. The *Summarium (see above, p. 304, n. 4) reports that on June 2, 1645, the State Council had sent to Bichi " una instanza fatta dal procuratore fiscale, affinchè risponda e fra tanto non innovi cosa alcuna ". The " instanza ", which had been sent already to Bichi's predecessor, said : " che non si venisse a publicatione d'alcuna bolla o decreto senz'il Placeto regio, e che perciò si sospendesse ogn'atto fatto sino alla risolutione di S. Maestà."

[2] RAPIN, I., 78 s. ; *Bichi, July 8, 1645, loc. cit.

[3] RAPIN, I., 78.

[4] January 30, 1646 : " Ho havuto per bene, che l'Internuntio di S. S. e suoi ministri publichino et esseguiscano la detta bolla, senza che per li miei vi si ponga alcun impedimento. . . . Ho

Universities by the Privy Council. But even so all difficulties were not yet removed. The Bishops of Antwerp and Namur indeed published the Bull a second time, but by the end of 1645 Sinnich was back from Rome and he influenced Boonen, the Archbishop of Malines, in his own sense. Armed with recommendations from Boonen, Sinnich called upon the Bishops of Ghent, Bruges and Ypres who thereupon requested their metropolitan (Boonen) to pray both Pope and King to cancel their order for publication of the Bull. Boonen agreed to this request.[1]

The royal ordinance gave great satisfaction to those professors at Louvain who were loyal to the Pope. Schinkel, though ailing, held a discussion with them at which he exerted himself so much that he died in March, 1646.[2] At a meeting of the University all objections were not considered as overcome even now, but on March 8th, 1646, Bichi published the Bull on his own initiative without meeting with any opposition.[3] The University, however, complained that the Bull lacked the royal *placet*,[4] and when Bichi had it affixed at the University, by a notary, it was at once torn down by one of the students.[5]

The internuncio now thought of applying ecclesiastical sanctions, in accordance with the Pope's orders,[6] but it was represented to him that, for the moment, minds were too excited and that if, in consequence of the unfavourable

voluto anco incaricarvi come v'incarico che diate gli ordin necessarii, perchè senza più dilatione corra questo negotio come lo dispone la detta bolla, per la publicatione della quale si darà al Internuntio l'assistenza necessaria per gli officiali, a' quali tocca." The order arrived in March. *Summarium*, *loc. cit.* ; Latin text in Claeys Boûûaert, in the *Rev. d'hist. ecclés.*, 1927, 803.

[1] Claeys Boûûaert, *loc. cit.*, 801–817.

[2] RAPIN, I., 139 *seq.*

[3] *Summarium*, *loc. cit.* ; RAPIN, I., 140.

[4] *Summarium*, *loc. cit.*

[5] RAPIN, I., 144.

[6] May 17, 1646, *Summarium*, *loc. cit.*

military situation a rising were to break out, the blame
would be laid at his door.[1]   Accordingly Bichi counselled
Rome to think of some other means of coercion. The resistance
of the University, he wrote to Pamfili,[2] came only from a
few hotheads, not one of whom was a Spanish subject.
Fromond, Van Caelen and the Rector, Pontan, hailed from
Liège, Sinnich was an Irishman and Van Werm came from
Maestricht : if the King were to expel these men there would
be peace. However, Innocent X. chose to pursue the course
he had adopted ; he accordingly urged the Spanish nuncio
to make further efforts with Philip IV.[3] Circumstances were
more favourable just then as the Council of State no longer
opposed publication ; as a matter of fact a rumour was
circulating that if there was further opposition President
Roose might be removed from his post.[4] The Governor also
showed more zeal and a last effort by the Archbishop of
Malines to win him over proved unsuccessful.[5]

But the hoped-for intervention by the King was long in
coming. It was December before Philip IV., on his return
from the campaign in Catalonia, expressed his amazement [6]
that his orders should have been so badly executed. Meanwhile
the Jansenists had pulled every imaginable string with a
view to delaying matters in Flanders. They began by pressing
to the utmost Van Caelen's candidature for the See of Roermond : by this means they hoped to occupy the internuncio

[1] RAPIN, I., 145.

[2] April 14, 1646, *ibid.*, 145 *seq.*

[3] *Ibid.*, 146.

[4] *Ibid.*, 144. On May 18 the Council of Brabant gave the
order that no obstacle be put to the publication of the Bull.,
but it added the clause : " modo fiat locis consuetis et in forma
ordinaria " (*Summarium, loc. cit.*). The clause, according to
Bichi, signified that the publication had to be made by the
Archbishop of Malines who, it was well known, would never
consent to do so. *Bichi, June 3, 1646, in *Lettere*, t. 30. Pap.
Sec. Arch.

[5] RAPIN, I., 149.

[6] December 7, 1646, in RAPIN, I., 154.

elsewhere and to distract his attention. Van Caelen personally discussed his promotion with Bichi and on January 8th, 1646, he agreed to swear obedience to the Pope.[1] However, suspicions concerning his orthodoxy were not removed even by this means and a formal judicial process was opened at which eight witnesses testified that Van Caelen held opinions condemned by the Pope. The affair was nevertheless quashed, out of consideration for the Archbishop and the President and in view of the warlike disturbances and the sensation it would have created.[2]

The University remained the chief hope of the Jansenists. At one time that body resolved [3] that Boonen should obtain a papal pronouncement to the effect that the teaching of St. Augustine had not been condemned and that Jansenius' *Augustinus* contained none of the propositions condemned by the Pope ; two days later they decided to pray the King to appoint a meeting of Bishops with Boonen as chairman.[4] But their real sentiments appeared at a gathering at Grimberghe, where they declared that they would never admit that Jansenius had taught any condemned propositions : moreover Urban VIII.'s Bull did not demand obedience since the Pope was not infallible in questions of fact.[5] When at

---

[1] *Bichi, November 4, 1645 (*Lettere*, t. 29), and January 13, 1646 (*ibid.*, t. 30, Pap. Sec. Arch.). On January 8, 1646, Van Caelen declared under oath, before the internuncio and before witnesses, that out of reverence for the Pope he would for ever refrain from reading Jansenius, but that he was still convinced that the doctrine of Jansenius was that of St. Augustine. Documentary proof of this declaration is in *Cod. Preuckianus* (without signature), f. 461 *seqq.*, Library of the Anima, Rome. On March 28, 1648, he refused to take a second oath suggested by Bichi and declined the bishopric of Roermond. *Ibid.*, f. 477.

[2] RAPIN, I., 156.

[3] June 8, 1646, *ibid.*, 150.

[4] *Ibid.*

[5] *Ibid.*, 153 ; *Bichi, September 8, 1646, *Lettere*, t. 30, *loc. cit.*— " che il Jansenio non difende le propositioni dannate nella bolla, che non sono obligati nelle cose che concernono il fatto a cattivar l'intelletto in obsequium fidei." *Ibid.*

last the letter arrived in which the King, under date of December 7th, expressed his astonishment that since January 20th of that year nothing had been done to give effect to his orders, Castel Rodrigo laid the blame on the internuncio whom he accused of lukewarmness in pushing the business. Previously to this Cardinal Cueva had complained to the Governor of the internuncio's excessive eagerness,· with the result that Bichi had been studying moderation ever since. Even now he did not dare to employ coercive means though President Roose was once more successfully delaying matters. In effect Roose acted as if he had a mind to publish the Bull himself and he caused the Governor to circularize the Bishops of Flanders for their consent. By this means time was gained and he had an explanation for the King for the delay in the publication of the Bull.[1]

Castel Rodrigo's governorship came to an end without the royal ordinance having been carried into effect.[2] Meanwhile, Jansenism had had time to consolidate itself. The Rector of Louvain University was a friend of Fromond and the Deans of all the Faculties were looked upon as Jansenists.[3] The secular clergy studied the Archbishop of Malines who allotted benefices to those who supported his views.[4] Many religious Orders favoured Jansenism, for instance the Augustinians, inasmuch as it was claimed that Jansenius was an exponent of the teaching of St. Augustine ; the Dominicans, because they believed that Jansenius' book decided in their favour the controversy on grace that had broken out during the pontificate of Clement VIII. ; other Orders because they felt that the Jansenists counterbalanced the Jesuits or because they allowed themselves to be carried away by the authority

[1] RAPIN, I., 154 seq.

[2] Only a short time before its close, on March 30, 1647, at the instigation of the internuncio, he persuaded the Privy Council to order the Rector of the University to remove a picture of Jansenius (with verses in his praise). L. VAN DER ESSEN in Bull. de la Commission Royal d'hist., Brussels, 1924, 313-18.

[3] *Bichi, September 23, 1645, Lettere, t. 29, loc. cit.

[4] RAPIN, I., 84, 151.

of influential superiors, with the result that, with the exception
of the Jesuits, hardly a single Order was free from Jansenism.[1]
A great sensation was caused by a sermon preached on the
feast of St. Dominic, in the church of the Dominicans at
Louvain, by the Augustinian Christian Le Loup : he was
reported to have drawn a parallel between the Jesuits and
the Jews who had crucified our Lord, to have denied the
Immaculate Conception and declared that though truth was
being persecuted, it would yet triumph inasmuch as God
countered the Pope's precipitancy by means of the secular
princes.[2] On Bichi's proposal the Generals of the Orders
were made to write to their subjects in Flanders but the
measure did not produce the effect that had been expected
from it.[3] Efforts were made to create sympathy for the new
teaching even among the people by setting it in rhymes which
were then spread among the masses.[4]

In view of the fact that authority was in the hands of
the Archbishop and his advisers, all of them supporters of

[1] *Ibid.*, 83 *seq.* On March 7, 1647, the Bishop of Antwerp
*writes to Innocent X. : " Videntur multi simpliciores facti
esse Ianseniani decepti specioso nomine doctrinae s. Augustini,
quo et alii abutuntur, qui Iansenianos se profitentur ex aemula-
tione contra Patres Societatis Iesu, quos in Iansenio et per
Iansenium conantur persequi, qui et hac ratione populo imponunt
asserentes tantum esse quaestionem inter opiniones Iansenii et
dictorum Patrum." Even women call themselves Jansenists.
The Bishop had accepted the Bull at once and after the order of
the King he published it a second time on May 10, 1646. *Excerpta
ex actis s. Officii a. 1647–1652.*

[2] RAPIN, I., 82 *seq.* ; *Bichi, August 20, 1645, *loc. cit.*

[3] RAPIN, I., 84 ; *Bichi, July 8, 1645, *Lettere*, t. 29, Pap.
Sec. Arch. One should try to influence especially the Provincial
of the Dominicans, because he was on friendly terms with Sinnich,
Van Caelen, and Leonardi, a Dominican professor of Louvain,
" che hora essendo de'più ferventi Janseniani e . . . da quella
fattione promosso ad esser della stretta facolta theologica, per
la quale promozione e in lite con il Schinchelio et altri obedienti
che hanno promosso Jacomo Speech prete secolare." *Ibid.*

[4] RAPIN, I., 156 ; *cf.* 179 *seq.*

Jansenism, it was inevitable that the orthodox should fall
into discouragement. In 1646 Bichi wrote that there were
some at Louvain who, until then, had sided with Schinckel
but had now joined the ranks of the rebels for the sake of
securing some benefice from the Archbishop,[1] and that when
appointments were made deserving men had been passed
over because they had rendered service to the internuncio.
The Archbishop was to blame for everything ; Spain's
attention should be drawn to these deplorable conditions
and the distribution of benefices should either be entrusted
into other hands or no prebend should be granted to anyone
who had not previously declared before the nuncio that he
accepted the Bull.[2] Baron von Rassenghien, who had been
chosen for the See of Tournai instead of Fromond, was the
object of special persecution on the part of the Archbishop
and Van Caelen.[3] On the other hand the Bishop of Namur
was strictly orthodox and there were no Jansenists in his
diocese.[4]

There seemed to be a hope of a change when Archduke
Leopold William became Governor of the Low Countries in
1647.[5] The Jansenists sought at once to win him over to
their side, but the Archduke listened to Bichi's representations.
The latter drew up a detailed account of the situation and

---

[1] *Bichi, June 3, 1646, Lettere, loc. cit. Bichi advised the Pope
to encourage and praise especially William ab Angelis. A *Brief
to him followed on July 7, 1646 (Cod. Preuck., f. 467 seq., Library
of the Anima, Rome). The modest man refused all the benefices
obtained for him (RAPIN, I., 151).

[2] *July 7, 1646, Lettere, loc. cit. " Tutto il male viene per
l'appoggio di questo arcivescovo, quale mi pare impossibile di
guadagnarlo e ridurlo." Ibid.

[3] *Bichi, July 21, September 8 and 15, and December 1, 1646,
Lettere, loc. cit.

[4] *Bichi, August 22, 1646, ibid. On August 7 the Bishop
wrote :   " Omnes, cum saeculares tum regulares, deferre
[obedientiam] decreto Apostolico " (ibid.). Cf. above, p. 301.

[5] He arrived in Flanders on April 11, 1647. *Bichi, April 13,
1647, Lettere, t. 31, Pap. Sec. Arch.

as the chief means of checking the progress of the new teaching he recommended that no benefice should be granted to any candidate who was in any way suspect of Jansenism.[1] Leopold William went even beyond this suggestion when he carried zeal so far as to demand a sworn declaration against Jansenius.[2]

Notwithstanding his goodwill, the Archduke did not at once succeed in enforcing the publication of the Bull, though orders to that effect came from Spain, the first of them shortly after the arrival of the new Governor.[3] On the occasion of the marriage of Maria Anna, daughter of the Emperor Ferdinand II. to Philip IV., in 1649, the nuncio, instructed by the Pope, prompted her to ask of her husband, as a first token of his affection, that he should publish the Bull in Flanders.[4] The fresh royal order of August 3rd, 1649, was followed by a third in a letter to the Archduke dated July 15th, 1650.[5] However, again and again the opponents' adroitness discovered ways and means to prevent their integral execution. Archduke Leopold William had made

---

[1] RAPIN, I., 176 *seq.* *Bichi to Rome, April 27, 1647 : " Hebbi commodità [April 26] di scuoprirli le arti con le quali li Janseniani si son cercati di avanzare e come alcuni di questi ministri li hanno aiutati direttamente e indirettamente, e le accennai li remedii che credevo più facili . . . e fra l'altri di non promuovere a benefitii li sequaci di quella setta." The Archduke was well disposed. *Excerpta, loc. cit.*

[2] " *Particolarmente si dogliono del giuramento che prestano quelli che aspirano a benefitii. Si vede che restano mortificati dal uso di questo giuramento, ma S. A. lo trova bene, e continua avanti di nominare ad abbatie et altri benefitii ecclesiastici da farmi avvisare, che informi se siano Janseniani." *Bichi, September 9, 1649, *Excerpta, loc. cit. Cf. ibid.* *Bichi, December 7, 1647, and January 25, 1648. Innocent X. praised the Archduke on September 9, 1647, for his zeal against the Jansenists (FRIEDENSBURG in *Quellen und Forsch.*, IV., 275).

[3] May 14, 1647, RAPIN, I., 177 *seq.* ; *Excerpta,* May 15, 1647, *loc. cit.*

[4] RAPIN, I., 387 ; *cf.* *Bichi, August 28, 1649, *Excerpta, loc. cit.*

[5] RAPIN, I., 389.

a start with the publication of the Bull, and that in Ghent, whose Bishop favoured Jansenism, but he gave up the idea of doing so in all the other towns on receipt of a letter from the Archbishop of Malines [1] in which Boonen spoke of the excitement such a measure would provoke, as well as of the great number of Jansenius' adherents and the fact that the Pope may have allowed himself to be misled when he condemned the book. Should the Archduke refuse to listen to him, Boonen prayed leave to retire to France lest he should have to witness the troubles that would befall his native land.[2] The Bishop of Ghent wrote in the same strain.[3]

Philip IV.'s first order to Leopold William demanded the suppression of Jansenius' *Augustinus* and a search in the bookshops for all Jansenist writings, for the Jansenists exercised considerable influence in the Low Countries by means of the press, especially as they distributed their publications gratuitously.[4] However, Roose knew how to oppose the execution of the order [5] and when this was achieved Fromond and Van Caelen made a show of zeal by counselling the Archduke to suppress, on his own authority, all writings on the subject of grace. Had he done so, the latter would have exceeded his powers, his ordinances would only have caused confusion and Catholic publications, of which the Jansenists disapproved, would have been suppressed. However the Archduke, who as a matter of fact showed himself at all times a sincere Catholic, listened to Bichi [6] who advised him to replace the censor of books, the Jansenist Rector of Louvain University, by a fervent Catholic, William ab

---

[1] September 17, 1647, *ibid.*, 183 *seq.*

[2] RAPIN, I., 183.

[3] *Ibid.*, 184. His *Letter of September 28, 1647, in *Excerpta, 1647–1652*, f. 103, *loc. cit.*

[4] RAPIN, I., 393.

[5] *Bichi, June 15, 1647, *Excerpta, loc. cit.*

[6] RAPIN, I., 180 *seq.* ; *Bichi, September 19, 1647, *Excerpta, loc. cit.*

Angelis.[1] Moreover the Governor gave no credence to the
calumnies by which it was sought to make Bichi's position
untenable [2] and installed the zealous Baron de Rassenghien
in the see of Tournai.[3] His conduct earned him a Brief from
Innocent X.[4] All the priests at court were made to swear
obedience to the Bull.[5] One Oratorian and three Capuchins
were stopped from preaching the new teaching in his presence.[6]
He likewise induced the University of Douai to pronounce
for the Bull and against Jansenius, a circumstance that could
not fail to bring pressure to bear on Louvain.[7] It was probably
he too who obtained the sudden recall to Spain of President
Roose in 1648.[8] After that Roose's influence in Flanders
was at an end ; he died in 1673. On his return from Spain in
1653, the nobility gave him indeed a great reception, but the
Archduke informed him publicly that the King thanked him
for his services and that he might take his retreat.[9] Roose
had been an adroit and resourceful official as well as a personal
friend of Jansenius whom he had provided with the material
for his *Mars Gallicus*.[10] For reasons of policy he opposed the
condemnation of his friend and he was wont to boast that

---

[1] RAPIN, I., 179.

[2] *Ibid.*, 180. On a " longissimum scriptum " in defence of
Jansenism to the Archduke, of which the latter took no notice,
see *Excerpta*, September 19, 1647 (Letter of Schega, S.J.,
the Archduke's confessor), *loc. cit.*

[3] RAPIN, I., 177.

[4] *Brief of September 9, 1647, *Epist.*, II.–III. (October, 1645,
to October, 1647), n. 204, Pap. Sec. Arch.

[5] *Bichi, May 2, 1648, *Excerpta, loc. cit.*

[6] RAPIN, I., 295 *seq.*

[7] *Declaration of July 27, 1648, to the Archduke, whom it
exhorts " ut pergat doctrinam illam iansenianam serio extirpare,
qua nequaquam docetur b. Augustini mens ". *Excerpta*, t. 29,
loc. cit. ; RAPIN, I., 296 *seqq.* FLEURY, LXI., 572.

[8] RAPIN, I., 299. Recalled December 4, 1648, left on October 15,
1649 (*Biogr. nat. de Belgique*, XX., 68).

[9] RAPIN, I., 536.

[10] *Biogr. nat. de Belgique*, XX., 64.

during his administration the clergy had not gained an inch
of ground.[1]

At the pressing request of the Superior of the Premonstratensians and the University of Louvain, Archbishop
Boonen had dispatched to Madrid a certain Recht with
mission to explain more fully the Archbishop's attitude
towards the Bull.   In May 1649, Philip IV. informed Boonen
that he was willing to receive the envoy and that he would
take no definite step before hearing him.   However, before
Recht's credentials reached him, in October, the order for
the publication of the Bull, which the young Queen had
obtained from her husband, had been issued on August 3rd.
Philip IV. received Recht on January 1st, 1650, though it
would seem that the latter had had a secret interview with
the King before that date, and when on that occasion Recht
asked that account should be taken of Boonen's and the
State Council's objections to the Bull, the King replied that
he was doing so in any case.   Recht promptly reported this
answer to Louvain ;   his letter arrived there at the same
time as the royal ordinance of August 3rd, 1649.[2]   The Archbishop was not slow in exploiting the new situation in the
State Council.   Since the King wished the affair to be further
examined, so he explained in a long speech, there was nothing

---

[1] RAPIN, I., 295, 299. " *Si vanta che al suo tempo li ecclesiastici non hanno acquistato un dito di terra " (Bichi, November 23,
1647, Excerpta, loc. cit. On his friendship with Jansenius, see
RAPIN, I., 4.

[2] RAPIN, I., 304, 388 ;   *Boonen to the State Council,
February 5 and 18, 1650, in Appendix to *Bichi's nunciature
report of March 17, 1650, Excerpta, loc. cit. At the audience of
January 1 the King said (according to Boonen) : " informatum
se esse, quanti ponderis esset haec causa, seseque adhibiturum,
quod et Dei et Ecclesiae servitio futurum est " (ibid.). According
to Bichi's *Despatch of April 20, 1650 (ibid.), Recht's instructions
were :   that the King should induce the Pope to have the book
of Jansenius examined by theologians, to decide the dispute
de auxiliis and to show the King the groundlessness of the prohibition. *Bichi, July 29 and August 28, 1649, ibid.

for it but to postpone the publication of the Bull.[1] Thus matters remained until the King renewed his order in the following year.[2] For the rest Leopold William only returned from the theatre of war in November.

Meanwhile the situation in Flanders had undergone a considerable change. Bichi had asked for the help of the secular arm to enforce the publication of the Bull, as otherwise he had no hope that the Jansenists would submit.[3] None the less it was his wish that the formal publication should come from him alone ; all he wanted from the secular power was support for his action.[4] The Madrid nuncio, Rospigliosi, also declared that it was necessary to publish the Bull as soon as possible,[5] to bar ecclesiastical positions to the Jansenists and to grant to the internuncio the help of the secular arm as often as he required it, whether for the purpose of searching bookshops for works forbidden by the Bull, or in order to punish those who acted in contravention of its ordinances. But this did not yet satisfy the representatives of the State. Even during Roose's presidency numerous decrees were drafted with a view to the publication of the Bull ; however, they pleased the internuncio but little and the Archduke rejected them.[6] It would seem that at that time Leopold

---

[1] RAPIN, I., 388 seq.

[2] See above, p. 313.

[3] " Vedo esser necessario che S. A. vi dia qualche ordine, altrimenti non si leva la scusa alli disobedienti." Bichi, June 13, 1648, *Excerpta, loc. cit.*

[4] " Continuai le instanze del braccio secolare . . . e con varii argomenti cercai di persuadergli che non deve far altro in questa materia che quello che io li domando " (Bichi, February 22, 1648, *ibid.*). " *Continuando le diligenze per havere l'assistenza del braccio secolare . . . et indirizzando li miei officii per haverla senza che si pubblichi editto, conforme una lettera della S. Congregatione di s. Officio de 1 febbraio " (*ibid.*).

[5] April 30, 1649, *ibid.*

[6] *Appendices to Bichi's letter to Pamfili of December 28, 1647, and May 2, 1648, *Excerpta, loc. cit.*

William's sentiments were still strictly those of a devoted son of the Church.[1]

Gradually a change came over him. At the very moment when the royal ordinance seemed to assure publication of the Bull, Madrid had shown great consideration for Boonen and his envoy Recht. A committee was formed for the purpose of discussing their objections [2] and in the order for the execution of the Bull [3] it was said that the King would request the Pope to have Jansenius' book revised and to approve it once it had been amended. Bichi was determined to insist that it was not possible to correct a book whose very root and heart were wrong, but he received instructions from Rome to say nothing on the subject.[4]

More regrettable was the circumstance that Roose's successor as President of the Council of State, D'Hovyne,[5] was an unmitigated exponent of a policy of cæsaro-papalism and that he gained great ascendency over the Archduke.[6]

---

[1] *Cf.* the *Letter of his confessor Schega to Bichi, September 16, 1648 ; the Archduke wrote to the King about Bichi : " quod ipsi tamquam ministro Ap. Sedis potissimum conveniat agere hoc negotium, quod est totum iuris ecclesiastici et concernit auctoritatem Pontificiam, quam Ill. D. V. debet prae ceteris defendere ac tueri. Deinde quod Concilium privatum in hac materia non debeat quicquam censere et iudicare, sed solum Ill. D^{ae} V^{ae}. tanquam agenti, nomine SS. D. N. porrigere brachium, saeculare, ubi opus videbitur." *Excerpta, loc. cit.*

[2] *Bichi, March 14, 1650, *ibid.*

[3] July 15, 1650, RAPIN, I., 389 *seq.* ; *Rospigliosi to Bichi, July 16, 1650, *Excerpta, loc. cit.*

[4] *Bichi, September 15, 1650, *Excerpta, loc. cit.* There also the Roman *Reply of October 12, 1650.

[5] On the form of the name *cf. Biogr. nat. de Belgique*, IX., 563.

[6] " *Quale [Hovyne] essendo in credito appresso di S. A. gli fa creder quel che vuole " (Bichi, September 16, 1651, *Excerpta, loc. cit.*). Hovyne had his son educated at Tournai in the house of Canon Fromond, a nephew of the professor ; the son had already delivered a discourse in favour of Jansenius (*Bichi to the nuncio of Madrid, September 12, 1651, *ibid.*).

Leopold William had set up a commission in connexion with
the Bull. It was composed of Counts Fuensaldaña and
Schwarzenberg and the Secretary of State Navarro[1];
they were subsequently reinforced by the Bishop of Antwerp
and the Bishop-Designate of Ypres, the Chancellor of Brabant,
Kinscot, and D'Hovyne and Bereur who were members of
the State and Privy Councils.[2] Strangely enough Boonen
himself and the Bishop of Ghent ended by obtaining a seat
in the commission.[3] The influence of cæsaro-papalism and
Jansenism was soon apparent. An ordinance of the Governor
did indeed promise the Bishops the support of the secular
power in connexion with the publication of the Bull; it
even inculcated the various clauses of the Bull and fixed
penalties for those who contravened, but all this was done
in virtue of the authority of the State and both the order
and the penalties were applicable to all, hence to the clergy
also, though this was against the principle of clerical immunity.
A letter to the Bishops charged them to publish the Bull on
March 20th and to see to it that it was complied with; to
secure this end they could have the assistance of the secular
power. The letter expressly states that the clause in Urban
VIII.'s Bull which declares that publication in Rome was
sufficient, was not to be recognized; that the King would
press for a revision of Jansenius' book, so that it might be
republished and that the Bishops must not tolerate anything
that might diminish the prestige of St. Augustine and the
Fathers. A third decree orders the Councillors of State to
have the Bull promulgated, to lend assistance to the Bishops
and to denounce them to the Governor should they fail in
their duty.[4] Thus by the terms of these drafts the Bull was
valueless unless the State published it, clerical exemption
from secular tribunals was ignored, whilst the intervention

---

[1] *Bichi, November 3, 1650, *ibid.*
[2] *Bichi, January 12, 1651, *ibid.*
[3] *Bichi, February 25, 1651, *ibid.*
[4] *Appendices to Bichi's letter to Pamfili, February 25, 1651, *ibid.*

on behalf of St. Augustine gave the Jansenists a pretext, despite every papal condemnation, for holding to their teaching which, so they claimed, was simply that of St. Augustine.

For some time already Rome had watched developments in Flanders with grave misgivings. At the end of 1647 Bichi was instructed to procure the help of the secular arm, but two months later his orders were : " simple assistance, but no edict " ; and still later " not even assistance if it cannot be had without a decree " ; and at the end of 1649 : " on no account must he give his assent to the publication of the Bull." [1] On February 23rd, 1651, the Inquisition decreed once more [2] that Bichi was not on any account to have

---

[1] The decrees are grouped together in *Bichi's letter of March 17, 1650 (*Excerpta, loc. cit.*) : December 28, 1647 : " di procurare il braccio secolare " ; February 1, 1648 : " di non far altra istanza che di una semplice assistenza del braccio secolare " and no edict ; June 6, 1648 : " che non faccia istanza di publicatione di editto, anzi vi si opponga e lassi dileguare la pretensione che si è havuta di questa assistenza, mentre non ci dia senza publicatione di editto " ; December 18, 1649 : " di non consentire in verun modo alla publicatione della bolla, e quanto alli altri mezzi per reprimere l'audacia delli Janseniani, lassi la cura a S. A., e quando debbia gastigare, non faccia atto positivo senza parteciparlo prima." The decision of the Inquisition of June 6, 1648, is found once more in the appendix of *Bichi's Letter of March 4, 1651. He finds fault with the assertion that clerics are called subjects of the King and that they are threatened with banishment. Similar " *a tergo " comments on Bichi's dispatches are frequently met with, e.g. December 28, 1647, September 9, 1649, August 18, 1650. In the *Instructions to the Spanish nuncio mention is often made of the Jansenist question in Flanders : *Nunziat. di Spagna*, 347. *Lettere al Nuntio* of March 17 and 24 and July 7, 1646, February 5 and July 13, 1647, Pap. Sec. Arch.

[2] " *Non potest ibi deveniri ad novam publicationem absque magno praeiudicio auctoritatis huius s. sedis." *Excerpta* (according to Bichi's dispatch of January 19, 1651), *loc. cit.*

anything to do with a new publication of the Bull since it had been published in Rome and had been communicated to the Bishops and had also been handed to the Louvain delegates Sinnich and Paepe before a notary and witnesses ; a fresh publication would be greatly to the prejudice of the Roman See.   If Bichi desired to reprint the Bull, he might do so though there was no need for it, but no decree about the secular arm or anything else must be added to the text. On the whole Rome would have preferred the whole affair to be dropped [1] and representations were made to Philip IV. with a view to obtaining from him what it seemed so difficult to secure from Leopold William.[2]

The internuncio failed in his attempt to persuade the Archduke to recall the decree.   The latter met Bichi's representations with the statement that the deliberations had been held in presence of four ecclesiastics and that was enough to exonerate his conscience.   D'Hovyne's answer was that the internuncio overstepped his authority and abused the kindness of the Archduke ; the decree would be issued whether Bichi liked it or not.[3]

As a matter of fact the decree was published in all the dioceses of Flanders in the last days of April.[4]   The effect

[1] On May 2, 1648, Bichi forwarded the draft of an edict of the Archduke, but " *le fu scritto sotto li 4 junio, che procurasse in ogni maniera, che quel editto non si publicasse in quella forma, anzi non facesse più instanza, ma lasci a poco a poco svanire la pretensione dell'assistenza, quando s'habbia a publicar editto ". *Summarium (see above, p. 304, n. 4).

[2] To the Spanish nuncio " si è scritto, che insista co' suoi ufficii per ottenere il decreto dell'assistenza rappresentando esser hora il tempo opportuno per la presente debbolezza de' Janseniani ".   March 6, 1649, to Bichi, *Nunziat. di Fiandra*, t. 28, Pap. Sec. Arch.

[3] *Bichi, March 4, 1651, *Excerpta, loc. cit.*

[4] The edict of February 28, 1651, in FLEURY, LXI., 750 *seq.* Bichi *reports on April 15, 1651, on the publication in Ghent, Antwerp, Bruges, Ypres, Cambrai, Tournai, Namur, Arras, Saint-Omer (*Excerpta, loc. cit.*).   The Archbishop of Malines

seemed good : Jansenius' work and the other forbidden books
were no longer bought.[1] For all that the internuncio saw
himself compelled to protest against the one-sided procedure
of the Archduke.   He was ordered to do this by Rome on
April 1st in case the edict had already been published.   In
doing so he was to use a formula bearing the date of April
20th which was sent to him from Rome.   That document
stated that it was enough if the Bull was published in Rome
and whatever was contrary to the authority and jurisdiction
of the Holy See and the Church's liberty and immunity was
null and void.[2] As a matter of fact as early as March 16th
Bichi had drawn up a similar formula on his own
authority.[3] The ministers were, of course, angry that Bichi
should not only have protested but should even have declared
the decree null and void. The Archduke ordered the Council
of Brabant to take no notice of the protest and caused the
printer to be fined.[4] One of the Councillors informed the internuncio that if he quietly accepted the intimation of the
decree of the Court of Cassation, the Council of Brabant
would take no action, whereas if he acted otherwise recourse
might be had to forcible measures.[5]

had his pastoral affixed to all the parish churches and the decree
of the Archduke to the town-halls of Brussels, Malines, and
Louvain, but the Bull nowhere. *On April 22 Bichi reports
that the Bull was published " assai negligentemente " also at
Roermond (ibid.).

[1] *Bichi, April 15, 1651, ibid.

[2] *Excerpta, Appendix to Bichi's report of March 4, 1651,
loc. cit.

[3] *Bichi, March 18, 1651, ibid.

[4] *Bichi, July 15, 1651, ibid.   The *circular of the Archduke
to the " consegli " is in the appendix of Bichi's *letter of August 12,
1651, ibid.   The Archduke did not know, however, that the
protest was made by order from Rome (*Bichi, July 29, 1651,
ibid.). The *cassation edict of the Council of Brabant, of August
31, 1651, is in the appendix of Bichi's *letter of September 16,
1651, ibid.

[5] *Bichi, July 22, 1651, ibid.

Measures of this kind had already been taken on a previous occasion. In a dispute between some convents, Bichi had given judgment without exhibiting his faculties. Accordingly the Council of Brabant caused him to be formally beleaguered in his lodgings until he withdrew his sentence.[1] The inter-nuncio was of opinion that these molestations were instigated by the Jansenists who, by this means, sought to revenge themselves for their exclusion by him from benefices and ecclesiastical offices. The Archduke, who at that time still sided with the papal envoy, advised him to yield since there was question only of the ambition of a couple of monks.[2] When Bichi withdrew his ordinance the Council likewise displayed a conciliatory disposition : it suspended its first judicial executor though the latter had done no more than carry out the decrees of the Council ; it did this on the pretext that in dealing with the internuncio, he had exceeded his powers.[3] Innocent X. protested against these proceedings, which he described as breaches of international law, but consented to consider the punishment of the judicial executor, which he ascribed to the Archduke, as a satisfaction.[4] Mean-while, on August 4th, the Council had taken another violent measure against the internuncio in connexion with a certain Canon Hughes. For the sake of his personal safety Bichi repaired to Saint-Gislain until the Archduke, through his confessor Schega, invited him to his headquarters after which he caused the proceedings to be suspended.[5]

A few months later, Innocent X. adopted a sharper tone

---

[1] *Bichi, July 15, 1649, *Lettere*, t. 33, Pap. Sec. Arch.

[2] *Bichi, July 22, 1649, *ibid.*

[3] *Bichi, July 29, 1649, *ibid.*

[4] *Brief to the Archduke of August 28, 1649, *Epist.*, IV.–VI. (May, 1648, to September, 1650, Franc. Nerlio secretario), n. 260, Pap. Sec. Arch.

[5] *Bichi, August 5 and 18, 1649, *Lettere*, loc. cit.* On April 26, 1651, acts of violence were again feared in Rome ; in that case Bichi should withdraw to Aix-la-Chapelle. *Nunziat. di Napoli*, Cifre al Nuntio, 39 A, f. 98, Pap. Sec. Arch.

towards the Archduke.[1] After praising his conduct during the first period of his administration, the Pope complained that he had allowed his advisers to induce him to issue a decree which was at variance with the Church's authority. It was an unheard of thing for ecclesiastical persons to be cited before secular tribunals. He (the Pope) had contented himself with protests and a declaration that these proceedings were null and void, but instead of amending his conduct, the Governor had allowed himself to be persuaded by his advisers to issue a fresh circular in which he sought to overthrow even the Pope's judicial power in matters of faith, for those men asserted that Urban VIII.'s decree did not bind in conscience unless it were published anew, with the royal *placet*. In justification of such conduct they had appealed to privileges and customs ; but no such privilege had ever been granted by either Pope or Council and no prince had ever claimed anything of the kind ; there could be neither custom nor prescription against papal authority, especially in matters of faith. Moreover, the Governor had been induced to declare the protest to be null and void and to punish the printer. The Archduke had become another Absalom ; if everybody was free to write against the dogmas to the faith, could the printing of a papal protest be looked upon as a crime ? As a loyal son of the Church, Leopold William should have kept an eye on his advisers, for the Pope took it for granted that the Archduke had been deceived by them. Innocent X. wrote in the same strain to Philip IV.[2] The Governor took the Brief in good part but the Privy Council raised loud protests on the plea that its tone was one that should not be adopted towards an Archduke.[3] Bichi's answer was that the language of the archducal ordinance was

---

[1] *Brief of November 11, 1651, *Epist.*, VI.–VII. (September, 1650, to September, 1652), Pap. Sec. Arch.

[2] *Brief of November 11, 1651, *ibid.*, n. 119 ; *Excerpta*, f. 645, *loc. cit.* Both Briefs were issued by the decision of the Commission for Jansenism, September 7, 1651. SCHILL in *Katholik*, 1883 ; II., 293.

[3] *Bichi, December 9 and 23, 1651, *Excerpta, loc. cit.*

undoubtedly far sharper.[1] Thereupon, Leopold William communicated the Brief to all the Provincial Councils from whom no protests against State usurpations were to be expected. Bichi [2] looked on this proceeding as a manœuvre of d'Hovyne [3] to induce the King to change his mind. The memorials of the Provincial Councils were all against the prerogatives of the Church.[4] At Madrid the King had the matter examined,[5] whilst the Spanish nuncio pressed from day to day for a decision.[6] At last Philip IV. instructed the Archduke to have the Bull carried into effect and to lend the assistance of the secular arm for the purpose.[7] Apparently the King saw in this a virtual withdrawal of the decrees but Bichi insisted on an explicit repeal.[8] To this Madrid would not agree. The Archduke, he was told, had been instructed not to encroach in any way on the Church's immunity and to maintain good relations with the inter-nuncio; by doing so they had done all that it was possible to do.[9]

(6.)

Meanwhile a fresh complication had arisen, one that had been preparing for several years. When, in 1647, Philip IV.'s

[1] *January 6, 1652, *ibid.*

[2] *Ibid.*

[3] *" Direttore principale di tutto il negotio." *Ibid.*

[4] *Bichi, February 3, 1652, *ibid.*

[5] *Bichi, August 12, 1651, *ibid.*

[6] *Rospigliosi to Bichi, October 14 and November 4, 1651, *ibid.*

[7] Rospigliosi to Bichi, December 2, 1651, *ibid.*

[8] *Bichi, December 23, 1651, *ibid.*

[9] " *Che per nessun modo diretta—o indirettamente si facesse preiuditio quantunque minimo all'immunità ecclesiastica e che se usasse ogni termine di buona corrispondenza con il ministro Apostolico ; onde pareva loro, non restare al presente da proveder di vantaggio persuadendosi che S. A. haverebbe operato che gli editti rimanghino senza osservanza." Rospigliosi, Madrid, March 16, 1652, in *Excerpta, loc. cit.*

strict injunction for the publication of the Bull arrived,
Roose looked for pretexts to put it off. Accordingly he wrote
to the Bishops requesting them to inform him why they had
not yet obeyed the royal commands.[1] The Bishop of Ghent,
Anthony von Triest, replied in a long letter dated March 20th,
1647.[2] He had not published Urban VIII.'s Bull, he states,
because it had been obtained by fraud and was unfair to
Jansenius, and its publication would only have created
confusion. When he had done with the Bull there was not
much left in it that was of any use. According to him the
Bull is wrong when it asserts that, contrary to Rome's
prohibition, Jansenius revived the dispute on grace which
had broken out under Clement VIII. ; all he did was to
expound the teaching of St. Augustine, and the prohibition
in question had neither been published nor observed. " It
was the blackest of calumnies " we read, to say that Jansenius
restated the theses of Baius ; so far from doing so, his book
ought to be crowned with laurels forasmuch as it shows the
agreement of the Holy See with St. Augustine. Not Jansenius,
but his opponents were the cause of the scandal. The Bishop
of Ypres is then extolled " as a loyal subject, a man of outstanding scholarship and exemplary conduct, an ornament
of the University ". The Privy Council subsequently consulted
the Bishops more than once.[3] Another letter of the Bishop
of Ghent [4] in answer to a question of September 1st, restates
practically the same sentiments : Jansenius is once more
described as an innocent victim ; not he is the author of
scandal but " the infamous theses and preachments of the

[1] " *Mendicando pretesti colle lunghezze, in luogo d'ordinare
che senza replica si eseguissero gl'ordini di S. M., haveva scritto
a' prelati di quelle provincie che gl'avisassero le cagioni per le
quali non havessero adempiti gl'ordini." Bichi, March 30, 1647,
Excerpta, loc. cit. RAPIN, I., 155.

[2] Excerpta, f. 402 s., loc. cit.

[3] " affinchè havessero campo l'arcivescovo di Malines e gli
altri disobedienti di scrivere, come poi han fatto." *Summarium
(see above, p. 304, n. 4, June 19, 1647).

[4] September 28, 1647, Excerpta, f. 103, loc. cit.

Jesuits ".[1] Consequently the Bull should not be made public, but they should demand a Provincial Council from the Pope. Archbishop Boonen also presented a memorial to the King at this time. In it he makes a historical survey of the questions in dispute, the object of which was, since Clement VIII., the doctrine of grace. In his opinion also the Jesuits were the cause of all the mischief. Through Molina these defended new dogmas, persecuted the Bishop of Ypres and had procured a Bull against him. In the Low Countries, Boonen claimed, there was no obligation to publish the Bull on account of that country's privileges ; in France also the better part of the clergy refused to acknowledge it.[2] Boonen's memorial and Triest's first letter were thrown to the general public in 1649 by means of the printing press.

This was not Boonen's only offence. During his visitation of the archdiocese, Van Caelen had distributed hundreds of Flemish and French copies of the Jansenist catechism of grace among women and nuns. Thereupon a Douai Doctor wrote an orthodox catechism as an " antidote " against the Jansenist product. Rome, however, prohibited even the orthodox catechism on the ground that it was forbidden to write on certain points of the doctrine of grace and because the topic was too abstruse for the people.[3] But the Archbishop thought he would give Rome a lesson ; accordingly, he wrote

---

[1] " Ex infamibus illis thesibus et concionibus Patrum Societatis ea de re petulanter habitis," *ibid.*

[2] " Rationes, ob quas Ill. et Rev. D. Archiepiscopus Mechliniensis a promulgatione bullae . . . abstinuit, ex mandato Regio allegatae ac catholicae Maiestati exhibitae. E Gallico in Latinum translatae 1649 (4º, 27 p.)." *Cf. Biogr. nat. de Belgique,* II., 705 ; RAPIN, II., 29 *seq.* The letter is dated September 17, 1647 (**Summarium, loc. cit.*). A Refutation : " **Notanda quaedam circa scriptum Ill. ac Rev. Archiepiscopi Mechliniensis* " in Bibl. Barberini, Rome, XVIII., 51, f. 163 *seqq.*

[3] **Bichi, July 14, 1650, together with the decree of the Inquisition of October 6, 1650, Excerpta, loc. cit. Cf. REUSCH, Index,* II., 471.

to the Pope [1] that he could not publish the prohibition of the two catechisms without scandal, danger to souls and grave injury to the reputation and authority of the Apostolic See, for according to that decree the reply to the Jansenist catechism was free of errors whereas Boonen endeavours to show that there were no less than fourteen errors in it. He then goes on to defend himself against the accusations that were being made against him in Rome. " Would that age and health would allow me to throw myself in person at your feet in order to exculpate myself ! " But since such a thing was out of the question, he prayed the Pope not to give credence to calumnies against himself and against so many men distinguished for virtue, learning and devotion to the Holy See, as if they were rebels against the Pope. He also prayed that the teaching of St. Augustine be at last examined with becoming impartiality.

If these words, unaccompanied as they were by deeds, were hardly calculated to soften Rome's opinion of the Archbishop, Boonen's ordinance which accompanied the publication of the Bull on March 29th, 1651, was even less likely to produce such a result.[2] The old objections against Urban VIII.'s decision are here reproduced, though not in so many words as the Archbishop's personal view, yet as the view of men " no less pious than learned ". The complaint that the Bull had been issued without adequate preliminary inquiry is also renewed in another form. Jansenius' piety and learning are extolled and the accusation of heresy against him is described as a dreadful calumny ; when it is finally stated that it was not the Pope's intention, in issuing the Bull, to trench on St. Augustine's teaching, the words can only mean that the Jansenists were free to go on defending their own peculiar views. Thus Boonen. The covering letters with which the Bishop of Ghent [3] and the Vicar General of

[1] *January 28, 1651, *Excerpta*, f. 543, *loc. cit.*

[2] Reproduced (from D'Argentré) in FLEURY, LXI., 758 *seqq.*

[3] March 26, 1651, *ibid.*, 752 *seq.* There it is stated that the observance of the Bull was commanded " saltem quantum colligere potuimus, donec et quousque Sedes Apostolica post

Ypres [1] accompanied the publication of the Bull, were in a similar strain. All three covering letters were condemned by the Inquisition together with the pamphlets with which Boonen and Triest (the latter's pamphlet is dated March 20th, 1647), sought to justify their failure to publish the Bull.[2]

The decree of the Inquisition informed those concerned that recourse would be had to ecclesiastical sanctions against them unless they exculpated themselves as soon as possible. Ypres declared its unquestioning readiness to obey the Pope [3] but the two Bishops remained silent. Accordingly, on November 18th, 1651, both were summoned to appear in Rome.[4] Unless they appeared there in six months, they were to be suspended from the exercise of episcopal functions nor would they be allowed to enter a church. On December 12th and 13th this sentence was communicated to the two prelates.[5] Archbishop Boonen replied that he had justified himself in writing and his seventy-nine years prevented him from going to Rome. Both he and the Bishop of Ghent appealed against the citation to the Royal Privy Council [6] which referred the affair to the Council of Malines ; the latter, however, declared its incompetence in the matter. Thereupon the two prelates assured the Pope of their innocence by letter,[7] and prayed that someone be appointed to judge them since their years made it impossible for them to appear

---

novum examen dicti libri sive illius revisionem, quam se . . . procuraturam edixit, . . . quatenus errores, si qui in illo inveniuntur, expurgentur et . . . quod de doctrina illius tenendum foret declarasset. . . .

[1] March 27, 1651, *ibid.*, 755 *seq.*

[2] May 11, 1651 ; see REUSCH, II., 465 ; HILGERS, 424. In the copy of the decree in FLEURY, LXI., the " Raisons " of the Bishop of Ghent are omitted.

[3] *September 19, 1651, *Excerpta*, f. 638, *loc. cit.*

[4] In FLEURY, LXI., 764 *seq.*

[5] *Bichi, December 30, 1651, *Excerpta, loc. cit.*

[6] *Bichi, February 3, 1652, *ibid.*

[7] *Triest alone on February 28, 1652, *both together on March 2, *ibid.*, f. 696, 698.

personally in Rome ; in fact they could not do so in view of
the privileges of Flanders and because as Councillors of State
they would have to obtain the King's leave. Accordingly, the
two were ordered to send a representative to Rome within two
months, to answer for them,[1] but they replied that on the
ground of the privileges òf Flanders they could not be called
to account outside their own country.[2]

Meanwhile Bichi was recalled and was succeeded by
Andrea Mangelli as internuncio as well as in the delicate task
of coming to terms with the Netherlands, ever most jealous
and susceptible where their privileges were concerned.[3]
In his very first report the internuncio had to announce that
D'Hovyne would not hear of the two Bishops going to Rome.
Mangelli vainly insisted that if the two prelates sent their
representatives to Rome someone would naturally be appointed
to make a judicial inquiry in Flanders, and that if the Pope's
judicial authority in matters of faith were circumscribed
in one country, it would also be limited and ruined in other
countries.[4] He fared no better with the Archbishop. Boonen
read to him a decree of the Council of Brabant forbidding
him to name a representative under penalty of confiscation
of his revenues. He begged for compassion ; all former Popes
had acknowledged the country's privileges and there was no
question of matters touching the faith.[5] On the other hand
the Bishop of Ghent seemed willing to submit to the Pope
but expressed a fear of giving scandal were he to appoint a
delegate.[6] However, Mangelli remained firm. He refused
to allow the appeal to the Council of Brabant ; if Boonen
had at once named a representative, he would have forestalled

[1] *To Boonen, July 26, to Trist, August 2, 1652, ibid., f. 809.

[2] *Boonen, July 28, 1652, ibid.

[3] The change was decided on by the Jansenist Congregation in
Rome (SCHILL in Katholik, 1883, II., 294). *Mangelli's credentials
for the Archduke, dated January 20, 1652, in Innocentii X.
Epist., VII.–VIII., n. 138, Pap. Secr. Arch.

[4] *Mangelli, August 31, 1652, Excerpta, loc. cit.

[5] *Ibid.

[6] *Mangelli, August 10, 1652, ibid.

the decree and there was no doubt that the question concerned
the faith. As for the Bishop of Ghent's desire to obey, Mangelli
observed that this must be proved by deeds and that the
prelate's fears were quite unfounded.[1] A certain advocate
of the name of Mortelle who, when speaking on behalf of the
Archbishop, dwelt on the scandal which the infringement
of the privileges would cause, was told that it was a much
greater scandal when an Archbishop and Primate refused
to submit to a papal decree : in this matter no Catholic,
least of all a Bishop, could appeal to any privilege. For
the rest, as internuncio, all he had to do was to carry out the
Pope's orders whilst a representative of the Bishops with the
Holy See would promote their cause far better than he could.[2]
Thereupon the two prelates excused themselves in Rome for
their inability to send a delegate,[3] but their pleading was not
admitted and the threatened penalties were now pronounced.[4]
In doing so the Pope observed that he could not tolerate that
Bishops who, at their consecration, had taken a special
oath of obedience to the Pope, should refuse submission
under such futile pretexts.[5]

The internuncio of Flanders was informed of the sentence
by the nuncio of Venice but the document itself was inter-
cepted at the frontier of Champagne by the army of Prince
de Condé,[6] and only on February 22nd, 1653, was Mangelli
able to acknowledge its reception.[7] Its execution, however,

---

[1] *Mangelli, August 10 and 31, 1652, ibid.

[2] *Mangelli to Cardinal Barberini and the Inquisition, August 3,
1652, ibid.

[3] *Mangelli, September 7, 1652, ibid.

[4] *On October 19, 1652, dispatched to Mangelli on 21st, ibid.
Text of the decree with date of December 19, 1652, in FLEURY,
LXI., 766 seq.

[5] *October 19, 1652, Excerpta, loc. cit.

[6] RAPIN, II., 31.

[7] *Excerpta ex codice S. Officii, cuius inscriptio : Acta in
Belgio circa Constitutionem damnantem 5 propositiones Iansenii
a. 1653-1656. Acta in Galliis circa Constitutionem praefatam,
a. 1653-1656 (Schill).

proved difficult. A short time before, on September 14th,
1652, Bereuil, who was the oldest member of the Archduke's
Privy Council, had informed Bichi, the then internuncio,
that the Privy Council had ordered the Bishops to forgo a
judicial procedure and to throw themselves on the Pope's
mercy and that the Bishops had consented to act accordingly.[1]
However, the letter to the Pope which they then considered,
was never written and a few months later the Council of
Brabant had changed its mind. The Archduke declared to
the internuncio that neither his archducal authority nor that
of the King would succeed in persuading the Council of
Brabant to allow the Bishops to send a delegate to Rome.
Rather than allow their privileges to be curtailed, they would
renounce all obedience to the Holy See, to the great injury
of Pope and King ; this was bound to happen if they adopted
a policy of force towards the Bishops.[2] These were strong
words ! Yet the Governor was a gentle nature and opposed
to violent measures,[3] nor was anything worse reported from
Spain than that a certain Abbate Vasquez had been commissioned to go to Flanders in connexion with the Bull and
to induce the two Bishops to obey.[4]

[1] " *Che con humilissime preghiere si gettino alli piedi di
S. S., implorando la paterna Sua misericordia, lasciando da parte
ogni altera giustificatione, che o per se stesso o per mezzo de
procuratore si potesse fare, e promettendo ubbidire ad ogni
comandamento di S. B." Ibid.

[2] " *Che nè l'autorità del Sr Archiduca nè dei ministri del
Re nè del Re medesimo bastava per indurre il Conseglio di
Brabante a permettere che si faccia dai vescovi la deputatione
del procuratore in Roma, apresa da loro per contraria e derogatoria
ai loro privilegii, e che più tosto perderanno la totale obedienza
alla Sede Apostolica con mettere in grandi fastidii non meno il
S. Pontefice che il re di Spagna, e che altro frutto non si con-
seguirà dal volere forzare con remedii più rigorosi li sudetti
vescovi. Mangelli, March 1, 1653, ibid.

[3] " *Placidissima natura con soavissime maniere " :   is not
able to act " con fervore et efficacia ". Mangelli, March 8, 1653,
ibid.

[4] *Bichi, November 9, 1652, Excerpta, a. 1647 seqq., loc. cit.

Notwithstanding the unsatisfactory reports from Brussels, Rome was determined on the execution of the decree. A notary was found who affixed it at St. Gudula's at Brussels, after which he fled with all speed.[1] The Council proposed a reward of 300 gold florins to anyone supplying information as to the identity of the person who had transcribed and affixed the decree ; on May 12th it declared the document to be false and null [2] and forbade the Bishops to present themselves in Rome.[3] Orders were given to have the decree torn down,[4] but the Archduke forbade not only their execution but a commission was convened to deliberate on the means of settling the dispute.[5] The commission found a solution of the great difficulty of safeguarding both the privileges of Flanders and the authority of the Pope [6] : this was that the two Bishops should protest their submission to the Pope, acknowledge their fault, beg the Pontiff's pardon and appeal to his clemency.[7] The commission likewise decided that the citation to Rome was not contrary to the privileges of Flanders ; consequently the Archduke should write to the Bishop and urge them to obey ; meanwhile the two prelates should abstain from pontifical functions and ask for absolution by the Pope. The Governor, moreover, was requested to order the Council of Brabant to revoke the decree of nullity of May 12th and to make their excuses to the internuncio. As for Mangelli, he might safely return from Spa whither

---

[1] RAPIN, II., 78.

[2] *Mangelli, May, 1653, *Excerpta*, a. 1653 *seqq.*, *loc. cit.*

[3] FLEURY, LXI., 768.

[4] May 22, 1653, reprint, *ibid*.

[5] *Mangelli, July 18, 1653, *Excerpta*, a. 1653 *seqq.*, *loc. cit.*

[6] The commission consisted of the Bishops of Cambrai, Bruges, Antwerp, Count Fuensaldaña, Dean Le Roy of Malines, the Secretary of State Navarro, and six Councillors of State. The reporter was the passionate Hovyne, who had said that the Pope owed satisfaction to the States. *Mangelli, July 2 and 10, 1653, *ibid*.

[7] *The same, July 10, 1653, *ibid*.

he had fled, for he had nothing to fear.[1]   Meanwhile orders
had come from Rome to the two Cathedral Chapters not to
allow the Bishops to enter their churches.[2]

Even so Archbishop Boonen seemed at first unwilling to
submit.   In the Council of Brabant he spoke against the
commission and begged the Councillors not to forsake him.
As a matter of fact the Councillors sent a message to the
Governor begging him not to give his consent to any curtail-
ment of Flanders' privileges ; otherwise the States would
refuse to pay their subsidies to the King.[3] The Archbishop
of Cambrai vainly sought to influence his colleague ; Boonen
told him he could not see that he had incurred any censures [4]
and sought to cover himself with the oath by which he had
bound himself to defend the rights of his country.

Not so the Bishop of Ghent.   From the first he seemed
prepared to seek absolution in Rome through an envoy and
these sentiments grew stronger under the influence of the
newly named Bishop of Antwerp.[5] On July 16th he informed
the internuncio at Spa that he was ready to obey the Pope
and apologized for his hesitation.[6] When Mangelli exhorted
him to give a positive proof of his submission the Bishop
sent him on July 23rd a petition in which he named the
Carmelite Isidore of St. Joseph as his representative in Rome
and asked for absolution in case he needed it.[7] After that
he called on the internuncio at Spa and assured him that
since the Brief to his Chapter he had refrained from all
episcopal functions and had urged his Chapter to elect a

---

[1] *The same, July 17, 1653, ibid.

[2] *Brief of June 28, 1653, Innocentii, X., Epist., X. (Decio
Azzolino secret.), n. 3, Pap. Sec. Arch.

[3] *Mangelli, July 10, 1653, loc. cit.

[4] *The same, July 17, 1653, ibid.

[5] *The same, July 24 and 26, 1653, ibid. ; RAPIN, II.,
79 seq.

[6] *Report of the nunciature of Brussels, t. 37 ;   *Letter of
Mangelli, July 31, 1653, Pap. Sec. Arch.

[7] *Mangelli, July 31, 1653, ibid.

Vicar whilst their Bishop was inhibited, and that this had actually been done.[1]

On July 31st, 1653, Mangelli was able to report a further success when he wrote to Rome that the Archbishop of Malines had likewise expressed his willingness to submit. On August 1st Boonen sent his nephew to the internuncio to confirm the fact that he had named a representative in Rome and that since the arrival of the Brief to his Chapter he had not officiated as Bishop.[2] On August 1st he effectively appointed a representative in Rome in the person of Canon Henri d'Othenin and wrote a letter to the Pope. After Mangelli's return to Brussels, on August 5th, both prelates called on him and renewed their assurances although the Council of Brabant had threatened the Archbishop with the suppression of his revenues if he accredited a representative in Rome.[3] On October 21st, 1653, in virtue of a papal concession, Mangelli was able to absolve the Archbishop.[4]

Boonen's recantation could not undo the evil which he had sown so long. A report by the internuncio on that period [5] draws a gloomy picture of the state of religion in the country. The chief advocates of the new teaching, Van Caelen and Fromond, in conjunction with Boonen and Triest, Mangelli writes, had spread it with so much care, caution and zeal and obtained so many adherents for it, that there was hardly a soul in those Provinces that remained untouched by it. This result was brought about by filling pastoral posts with Jansenists. As Bishops these men had the bestowal of such benefices as were in the gift of the ordinaries ; as members of the Council of State they were able to influence appointments to posts where the King enjoyed the right of patronage, with the result that there was no Chapter in any church in

---

[1] *The same, August 2, 1653, *ibid.*

[2] *Ibid.*

[3] *Ibid.*

[4] *Mangelli, October 25, 1653, *Excerpta, loc. cit.* *Brief with plenary powers for absolution, August 23, 1653, *ibid.*, f. 215.

[5] October 4, 1653, *Excerpta*, translated in RAPIN, II., 180–2.

Flanders, into which the Archbishop had not inducted some Jansenist.

In the Mendicant Orders Boonen had promoted Jansenism by the bestowal of abundant alms on its adherents and by furthering their petitions in his capacity as a member of the State Council, the Privy Council and the Council of Brabant. Almost all the Abbots who had a seat in the States General had been won over by his tricks, whilst he took advantage of the prevailing jealousy and aversion for the Society of Jesus to foster Jansenism in all the other Orders, none of which, with the exception of the Jesuits, had fought the heresy. No girl entered a convent or took the vows without being questioned on the Jansenist teaching and receiving some booklet in which it is expounded. No one was allowed to preach in the convents who was not affected by the new teaching. The Oratorians were its most dangerous as well as its most effective exponents; they considered it to be the chief duty of their Congregation to lend help to the Bishops in the pastoral ministry and they stood in sharp contrast to the Jesuits; consequently they preached the evil doctrine more openly and more zealously than the rest and they had also done greater harm in these countries. Their exemplary life and their competence in the pulpit greatly helped towards this result. It was generally believed that, more than anyone else, one of their number, Van den Linden, had induced the Archbishop to persevere in his false road and to disobey the Pope. The report goes on to describe how attacks on the Holy See went hand in hand with the spread of Jansenism. The infallibility of the Apostolic See was called in question with the assertion that in questions of fact the Pope might err and that decisions in matters of faith must come from a General Council. It was said that no Roman theologian understood the subtleties of the doctrine of grace; that the Roman clergy was as full of ignorance as the Roman court of vices.

To zeal for Jansenius, his adherents joined intolerance of the exponents of other views. Thus at Louvain, on a solemn occasion, the Dominican Alexander Sebille had put up for a disputation [1] theses which met with the displeasure of the Jansenists. They succeeded in obtaining a prohibition of the disputation whereupon Sebille appealed to Rome through the internuncio.

As a matter of fact the University of Louvain was the strongest bulwark of Jansenism in Belgium.[2] In its various Colleges it disposed of over six hundred burses, viz. foundations by which poor youths were enabled to take up study.[3] These burses attracted the youths to the Colleges but the Jansenists saw to it that the Presidents of these Colleges were always men of their party. As soon as a President had died and even before his burial, they inducted his successor ; in the College of Luxemburg a lawfully elected President was thrown out the very first night. Another means of spreading their views was the allocation of University chairs. There were nine chairs of theology ; the King had the right to nominate to four of them,[4] and over these the Jansenists had but little power, but their influence was all the greater with regard to the remaining five, viz. the so-called ordinary chairs which were endowed with thirteen benefices. The right of presentation to these belonged to the city of Louvain and on those occasions the Jansenists almost invariably got in their candidate. To this had to be added the fact that the

---

[1] *July 1, 1649, *Excerpta*, f. 253, *loc. cit.* ; RAPIN, I., 303. On July 15, 1649, the General of the Dominicans approved the theses and ordered their defence under the presidency of Sebille. *Excerpta*, f. 259, *loc. cit.*

[2] *Memorandum (of the Jesuit Schega ?), Appendix to *Mangelli's report of January 17, 1654, *Excerpta, loc. cit.*

[3] " The University possesses 13 purely theological colleges with over 300 burses, 11 mixed Colleges with over 100 burses, besides 3 Colleges of jurisprudence, 1 of medicine and 3 of humanities and the " trilingue " with their bursaries. The schools have about 800 pupils and with the " domus Standonica " over 200 burses." *Ibid.*

[4] Namely, one for catechetical instruction on Sundays and feast days, one for Holy Scripture and two for scholastic theology. *Ibid.*

examinations in theology and the conferment of theological degrees were wholly in the hands of the so-called Inner Faculty consisting of eight Doctors, each of whom had an income of eight hundred florins. This college of eight completed itself by election whenever a vacancy occurred through death. Thus once the Inner Faculty became Jansenist it was bound to remain so. Lastly the Faculty had the disposal of benefices. All this made it possible for Jansenism to take root within the space of a few years among the nobility, the scholars and even among the common people and the women. Even in the convents of nuns some of the inmates stood by the Holy See and the others, as the expression was, " with St. Augustine." In these houses the chief means of propaganda was the " Catechism of Grace ". The consequence was that from a variety of Orders, appeals reached Boonen not to suffer the teaching of Jansenius to be condemned.[1] In this connexion the attempt of the Provincial of the Augustinians, Rivius, to impose Jansenism on all his subjects by barring all influential offices to the party of the opposition, attracted a great deal of attention. But his efforts failed, chiefly owing to the opposition of Michel Paludan, also an Augustinian and a Doctor of Louvain who had also zealously defended the Pope's cause during the period of confusion in the University. The internuncio reported the matter to Innocent X. who settled the dispute through the General of the Augustinians. Rivius made his submission. In 1650 the internuncio was able to write to Rome that among the Augustinians no one dared to stand up for Jansenius and that this example was having a salutary effect on other Orders.[2] Thus the Premonstratensians had at one time been very enthusiastic for Jansenius ; eight of their Abbots had requested Boonen to prevent the execution of the Bull ;

---

[1] *Bichi, December 21, 1647, *Excerpta, loc. cit.*

[2] *The same, August 4, 1650, *ibid.* " Adesso ogni cosa è acquietata [with the Augustinians] e non vi è chi ardisca parlare per il Jansenio, come a lor esempio succede anco in diversi altri ordini religiosi." *Cf.* RAPIN, I., 302 ; II., 227.

but now a decree of the General Chapter of Verdun forbade the members of the Order to hold the opinions of Jansenius.[1]

How it was possible that teaching so appalling as that of Jansenius could have been hailed with such enthusiasm and held with so much tenacity, is in part explained by a contemporary memorial to the Archbishop of Malines.[2] On the one hand the *Augustinus* of Ypres was believed to represent the teaching of St. Augustine, the greatly venerated Bishop of Hippo. On the other hand a certain vague sentimentality, rather than intellectual reasons, may have attracted people to Jansenius. The author of the memorial referred to above writes as follows : " Two things particularly delight me in Jansenius : the first is that he so greatly exalts St. Augustine and allows himself to be taught by him, for he takes from him a teaching which is singularly calculated to humble man, to take away all reliance on ourselves and to force us to call unceasingly upon Him Who alone is able to heal humanity's wounds. Words fail me to express the delight I derived from the reading of Jansenius and how the truths of a doctrine which humbles us to such a degree, appealed to me far more than all other writings or opinions which deem it excessive that the humble will of man should be the servant of grace, and which, on the contrary, seek to give it the mastery. I quickly perceived that Augustine agrees with the Apostle Paul and I rejoiced like a thirsty man who has found a spring of refreshing water." The writer goes on to say that he could not think that the Pope had any intention of trenching on the teaching of St. Augustine,

---

[1] *Cod. Preuck.* (without signature), f. 433–7 (Libr. of the Anima, Rome), April 27, 1651. Printed sheet, Ruremond, 1651, *ibid*. On February 15, 1653, Mangelli *reports that the newly appointed Abbot of the Premonstratensians, Robert van Couwerven, of St. Michael's, Antwerp, accepted under oath the Bull of Urban VIII. on December 13, 1652, and on January 21, 1653, commanded his subjects to receive it. *Nunziat. di Fiandra*, t. 37, Pap. Sec. Arch.

[2] *November 14, 1646, *Excerpta*, a. 1647 *seqq.*, *loc. cit.*

hence he prayed the Archbishop to do his utmost so that the Bull might remain in abeyance until the Pope should be better informed, for those deceived the Holy See who said or wrote that the writings of Jansenius had given scandal ; the scandal came, on the contrary, from the teaching with which the envy of Jansenius' opponents countered his, as well as from their attempts to belittle him and even to get him out of the way altogether. The opinions of the writer of this memorial were shared by many people. From the lips of devout and learned men the Bishop of Ghent heard that they never wearied of reading Jansenius and that they derived from him a teaching which was the foundation of a solid Christian piety and humility.[1]

On the other hand, the effects of Jansenism on the people appear from a report on the archdiocese of Malines after Boonen's death (in 1655) ; there we read that throughout the archdiocese the exorbitant penances imposed by the Jansenist confessors had driven many families and nearly entire villages into the arms of Calvinism.[2]

(7.)

Although the two Bishops ended by submitting, experience with the Bull of Urban VIII. up till then showed that there was everything to fear in Flanders when, in 1653, Innocent X. published his Bull in which he solemnly condemned the famous five propositions. Even in the Netherlands many people felt the need of such a decision. Thus, a few years earlier the theological Faculty of Douai had presented a memorial to the Inquisition drawing attention to a number of passages

---

[1] *The Bishop's letter of September 28, 1647, in *Excerpta*, a. 1647 ss., " cuius [Iansenii] tamen lectione se saturari non posse, sed ex illa haurire fundamentalem doctrinam solidae christianae pietatis et humilitatis."

[2] " *Nella sola diocesi di Malines molte e molte familie e quasi villaggi intieri si sono alienati dalla religione catholica." Origine e progressi del Giansenismo, *Barb.* 3383, f. 140, Vatican Library.

in Jansenius' *Augustinus*, on which a decision was sought.[1]
At the same time the Bishop of Tournai also prayed for a
papal judgment, if not on every one of the controverted
opinions of Jansenius, then at least on the more important
ones, or at the very least on the thesis of the love of God
as a necessary condition for absolution by the priest and on
the question whether sufficient grace was given to all men and
whether Christ had died for each and all.[2] Thus the Bishop
found fault practically with the same points of Jansenius'
teaching as were subsequently condemned in Innocent X.'s
Bull on the five propositions.

Mangelli received the Bull on July 17th, 1653 : he had it
reprinted at once at Cologne and on July 31st he dispatched
it in every direction. The two rebellious Bishops had to suffer
the humiliation to see the Bull addressed not to themselves
but, over their heads, to the three Chapters of Malines, Ghent
and St. Gudula at Brussels, together with special covering
letters.[3] On July 19th the internuncio communicated it to
the ailing Archduke ; at the same time he requested support
by the State in order that it might produce its full effect
and to prevent fresh attacks on the Church's immunity and
papal inerrancy. Leopold William conceded everything [4] ; he
promised the assistance of the secular arm and urged the
Bishops to see to it that the papal decision was carried into
effect.[5]

---

[1] *May 31, 1649, *ibid.*, 1025, f. 3–6.

[2] *Excerpta* a. 1647 *seqq.*, f. 276, *loc. cit.*

[3] *Excerpta* a. 1653 *seqq. Nunziat. di Fiandra*, t. 37, July 31,
Pap. Sec. Arch.

[4] *Mangelli, July 19, 1653, *Excerpta, loc. cit.*

[5] *The same, August 2 and 9, 1653, *Nunziat. di Fiandra*,
t. 37, *loc. cit.* ; *cf.* *the same, July 26, *Excerpta, loc. cit.* *Edict
of the Archduke, August 11, 1653, to the Bishops ; they should
see to it " que les intentions de Sa Sainteté soient ponctuellement
accomplies et les diffinitions et déterminations observées et
suivies par les voies et moyens accoutumés et usités en regard
des bulles et diffinitions dogmatiques ". Mangelli, October 4,
1653, *Excerpta, loc. cit.*

As a matter of fact the Bull was received everywhere [1] ; by some with joy and unqualified submission, by others coldly and with words rather than with conviction.[2]   At Malines and Ghent the Bull was promulgated in such fashion that hardly anyone was aware of it ; at Brussels and Louvain not even that much was done, so that Mangelli expressed his displeasure ; consequently a second publication ensued and all parish priests and religious Superiors received a copy. With the exception of the Jesuits, no member of any Order had a word to say in praise of the Bull ; even among the common people the remark could be heard that the five propositions were not Jansenius', or that they had not been condemned as he understood them and that in such questions of fact the Pope was liable to error.[3] This was preached in Louvain by a Dominican and openly stated by a parish priest whilst in the very act of proclaiming the Bull.[4] " Those who were Jansenists before the Bull are likely to remain Jansenists after the Bull," Mangelli wrote.[5]

The internuncio's chief concern in this respect was the University of Louvain. No sooner had Innocent X.'s Bull been published than some of the Doctors prepared to attack it on the plea that not Jansenius but St. Augustine was the author of the five propositions.[6] On August 9th the Bull was

[1] Published in Antwerp, Tournai, Besançon on 30th, Bruges, July 31, Ghent on 1st, Cambrai 18th, Namur 22nd, St.-Omer August 23, Malines September 2, Ypres, no date.   Mangelli, October 4, 1653, *ibid.*

[2] *Mangelli, August 16, 1653, *ibid.*

[3] *Mangelli, October 4, 1653, *ibid.* ; *cf.* RAPIN, II., 181.

[4] A professor of Louvain, September 23, 1653, *Excerpta, loc. cit.*

[5] " *Tutte queste cose fanno dubitare ad alcuni, che quasi tutti quelli che erano Janseniani avanti la bolla, continuino ad essere tali doppo la promulgatione di essa." Mangelli, October 4, 1653, *ibid.*

[6] *Mangelli, July 24, 1653, *ibid.* The Louvain professors were encouraged in their objections by the Archbishop of Sens and his pastoral letter (see above, p. 291). RAPIN, II., 178.

indeed published and accepted by Vianen, the Rector ;
however, not all the Doctors had been convened, but only a
few. Others stuck to the five propositions under various
pretexts ; some said they were not Jansenius', others that
they had not been condemned as he understood them, or
again since there was question of propositions taught by
St. Augustine, the condemnation by the Bull could do no
harm whilst some expressed themselves to the effect that
only a general Council could pass judgment in such matters.[1]
Accordingly, Mangelli suggested to the Archduke to have the
Bull registered in the Acts of the University and to order all
the Doctors and students to swear to it and that this oath
should be taken before a candidate could be admitted to the
University. He also gave it as his opinion that so long as
Fromond, Sinnich, Vianen, Van Werm and Pontanus were at
the University, there would always be reason to fear that the
heresy would raise its head anew ; hence he kept urging their
removal, or at least that of most of them.[2] However, Rome
disapproved of such severity : when the men of Louvain
saw the submission of the rest, it was thought, they would
submit in their turn.[3] The Government were likewise against
sharper measures : Jansenism was finished, it was said, the
flame must be allowed to die out instead of being fanned
afresh.[4]

The University published a decree [5] which described as
false the rumours that it defended a condemned opinion.
It also stated that it received the condemnation of the five
propositions with due reverence, inasmuch as it emanated

[1] *Mangelli, August 6, 1653, *Excerpta, loc. cit.* Some of the
professors even made the remark : " che prima si lasciaranno
abbrucciare che recedere dalla doctrina di Jansenio." The same,
October 4, 1653, *ibid.*

[2] *Mangelli, August 9, 1653, *Nunziat. di Fiandra,* t. 37, Pap.
Sec. Arch. ; *August 16 and 23, *Excerpta, loc. cit.*

[3] *Marginal note in Mangelli's report of August 16, 1653 :
" per hora non cominci con rigore ect." *Ibid.*

[4] *Mangelli, April 4, 1654, *ibid.*

[5] September 29, 1653, *Mangelli, October 4, 1653, *ibid.*

from the Head of the Church and the Father of all Christians, to whom it submitted all its opinions, now as in the past. Not long afterwards it defended itself in a letter to the Pope [1] against the rumours which were being circulated about its own and Fromond's alleged insubordination. In consequence of a thesis containing an offensive clause having been defended on August 18th, Van Werm, Leonardi and Vianen called on the nuncio, on October 18th, for the purpose of offering an apology.[2] On November 3rd the University published Innocent X.'s Bull once more, together with a "splendid" introduction and an order to submit to the papal decision.[3] However, all this did not satisfy the internuncio. The splendid introduction, he said, consisted of leaves and flowers with few fruits, of sonorous words and phrases which offered little that was tangible.[4] The University, he represented to the professors, had so often shown itself rebellious to Urban VIII.'s Bull in books, letters, pamphlets and theses, that it ought to display no less zeal in its obedience, for instance by swearing to the Bull, by revoking what was done in the past, by combating errors ; the excuse that all that had been aimed at was to defend St. Augustine he refused to accept.[5] He admonished Fromond in the same strain [6] when the latter informed him, shortly before his death, that he had received the last Bull with gladness.

Meanwhile the University gave no sign of the zeal which was so greatly to be desired. Not a word was said about Jansenius. Mangelli had requested the Jesuits to report to him on the Jansenist movement, but the latter had no information to give.[7] The orthodox professor Dares wrote to the

---

[1] *October 24, 1653, Appendix to Mangelli's letter of October 25, *ibid*.

[2] *Mangelli, August 23 and October 11, 1653, *ibid*.

[3] *The same, November 15, 1653, *ibid*.

[4] *Ibid*.

[5] *Mangelli, October 11, 1653, *ibid*.

[6] *October 20, 1653, *ibid*.

[7] " *Le materie di Jansenio in Lovanio passano con sommo silentio." This is likewise attested by the Jesuits : " vigilantissimi

internuncio [1] that in former years the University disputations had invariably dealt with questions connected with Jansenius, but for the last seven months his name had not been as much as mentioned, a fact which seemed to him an ominous symptom ; he felt quite sure that Jansenius' adherents considered that his book had been unjustly condemned whilst in his teaching they saw simply that of St. Augustine. A memorial of the period [2] expresses the wish, in view of the fact that the theological Faculty properly so called was " an ever flowing spring of errors " at the University, for a thorough cleansing not by demanding an oath—for all too often the Jansenists had nullified such measures by all kinds of interpretations—but by calling the professors to account on the subject of Jansenism and by dismissing the suspects. As a matter of fact the memorial prays for a papal visitation of the University, such as had taken place in 1617.

Mangelli was in complete agreement with these suggestions. As visitors he submitted in Rome the names of the Bishops of Roermond and the Dominican Capello who had just been named Bishop of Antwerp.[3] He also insisted with the Archduke on the need of a visitation and the removal of three or four zealots.[4]   However, Rome would not hear of such stern proceedings and even forbade the internuncio all further talk of a visitation.[5]

Mangelli himself ended by admitting [6] that theses had been defended at Louvain which satisfied the orthodox Dominican Sebille and other theologians. This had been done without any reservation, in the sense that the arguments in favour of the

---

speculatori, li quali dal Provinciale a mia instanza hanno havuto strettissimi ordini in ogni città di avisare, quanto sentono et intendono in simili negotio." Mangelli, February 28, 1654, *ibid.*

[1] *February 17, 1654, *ibid.* Appendix.
[2] By SCHEGA ? (see above, p. 337, n. 2).
[3] *January 17, 1654, *Excerpta, loc. cit.*
[4] *October 17, 1654, *ibid.*
[5] *Mangelli, January 16, 1655, *ibid.*
[6] *Letter to Cardinal Albizzi, March 13, 1655, *ibid.*

condemned propositions were strongly emphasized whereas those against them were but lukewarmly stated. Undoubtedly the best thing would be if the whole dispute were buried in eternal silence. There were some, however, who never ceased to uphold and to foster the remains of Jansenism. Thus Mangelli, although he had had to make an inquiry into two very equivocal theses of Professor Van Werm.[1]

If Jansenism had struck such deep roots at the University, it is not surprising that the internuncio should have received reports of offensive utterances by a number of parish priests.[2] A few Dominicans also caused him anxiety: against these he sought the intervention of their General,[3] nor was he completely satisfied with regard to the long-standing difficulties with the Augustinians.[4] On the other hand the Professor of theology at Douai, Valentin Randoutt, received a personal Brief, praising him for his services in the Jansenist dispute.[5]

Mangelli naturally watched with special care the attitude of Archbishop Boonen of Malines. Soon after receiving Innocent X.'s Bull, the internuncio was informed from Brussels that Boonen had summoned the Jansenists to council.[6] When at the death of Fromond[7] there was question of an opponent of the Jansenists becoming Dean of St. Peter's at Louvain,[8] Boonen did not at once confirm the nomination. Mangelli kept pressing him on the ground that so long as he did not take some striking and public measure against the Jansenists, the latter would continue to boast that he was their patron. But, as so often before, this time also he was

---

[1] August 29, 1654, *Mangelli, January 16 and 23, 1655, *ibid.*

[2] *The same, October 25, November 15, December 13, 1653, and January 17, 1654, *ibid.*

[3] *The same, January 17, February 7 and March 7, 1654, *ibid.*

[4] *The same, April 4, 1654, *ibid.*

[5] *March 21, 1654, *Innocentii X. Epist.*, X. (Decio Azzolino secret.), n. 94, Pap. Sec. Arch.

[6] *Mangelli, July 16, 1653, *Nunziat. di Fiandra*, t. 37, *ibid.*

[7] October 27, 1653. Van Caelen died February 1, 1653.

[8] *Mangelli, November 15, 1653, *Excerpta, loc. cit.*

told that the Bull had been published and had encountered no opposition ; that he had never been a Jansenist and that his only wish had been that Jansenius' work should be purged from its errors.[1] Suspicion also arose out of the Archbishop's failure to intervene, in a case where this would have been necessary.[2] Acting under instructions from Rome, Mangelli demanded from him the punishment of five Jansenist priests, but all he obtained was vague promises.[3] Five drafts for a pastoral letter against the opponents of the Bull were submitted one after another, but Mangelli could not prevail on Boonen to describe the five propositions as the teaching of Jansenius.[4] Thereupon the internuncio began to discuss with the Government the advisability of giving the Archbishop a Coadjutor, a measure from which the authorities were not averse.[5] For the rest Boonen attested on oath [6] that the letter dated September 17th, 1647, and published in 1649, which had led to proceedings being taken against him, had not been written, occasioned, or published by himself and that he disapproved all that was said in that document against the Pope and the Roman authorities. Previous to this [7] an ordinance of the Inquisition had informed the internuncio that with regard to that letter and anything connected with the two Bishops, the Pope would be satisfied if they received the Bull of Urban VIII. and his own. In this respect, as well as with regard to the decree of the Inquisition of April 23rd, 1654, the Bishop of Ghent made a full submission

---

[1] *The same, November 29, 1653, *ibid.*

[2] *The same, December 13, *ibid.*

[3] *The same, February 28, March 7 and May 2, 1654, *ibid.*

[4] *The same, May 2, 1654, *ibid.*

[5] *The same, June 20, 1654, *ibid.*

[6] *May 22, 1655, *ibid.*, f. 726 : " quod libellum nunquam fecerimus aut scripserimus, nec unquam scriberemus quod fieret aut scriberetur, quodque eundem multo minus publicaverimus, improbantes proinde omnia, quae libellus iste continet contra auctoritatem S. Sedis aut honorem S. R. E. cardinalium aut officialium dictae curiae."

[7] *October 3, 1654, *ibid.*, f. 606.

whereas Boonen sought to evade doing so by various subterfuges.[1]   The Archduke showed great eagerness to root out the
new doctrines but the officials acted coldly and were inclined
to pity the Archbishop.[2]   Vigorous measures were likewise
foreign to Leopold William's gentle disposition.[3]   From
Madrid came the order to cancel the declaration of nullity
in the affair of the two Bishops, which the Council of Brabant
had pronounced against the Inquisition.   A commission
consisting of Fuensaldaña, Navarro and Hovyne, was
instructed to discuss the matter and the Archduke published
an edict dealing with it.   A further ordinance granted the
help of the secular arm in the execution of the papal Bulls.[4]

If, on the whole, Innocent X.'s Bull met with much less
resistance than that of Urban VIII., the circumstance must
undoubtedly be ascribed to the energy with which the Pamfili
Pope confronted the two Bishops.[5]

As the internuncio attests, in all these interminable quarrels,
petty personal jealousies and susceptibilities greatly obscured
the real facts.   One drawback to the activity of the Society
of Jesus in Flanders was that it gave rise to envy and jealousy
on the part of some others.[6]

---

[1] *Mangelli, January 23, 1655, *ibid.*   It was the Dominican
Capello who had induced the Bishop of Ghent to make his
submission.   RAPIN, I., 80.

[2] *Mangelli, November 29, 1653, *Excerpta, loc. cit.*

[3] *" La lenità grande dell'anima, la blandura del suo naturale
et costume, la troppa dependenza dai medesimi consegli secondo
le instruzzioni di Spagna, non le danno luogo di pensare al
rimedio " (Mangelli, October 17, 1654, *ibid.*).   *Cf.* above, p. 332, n. 3.

[4] *Edict of February 18, 1654, and *Mangelli, December 13
and 27, 1653, and February 28, 1654, *Excerpta, loc. cit.*

[5] RAPIN, II., 177.

[6] " *Li Padri della Compagnia hanno fatto e fanno continua-
mente servitii rilevantissimi alla S. Sede in queste materie, ma
l'invidia, l'emulatione et odio di tutte le communità ecclesiastiche
e di gran parte dei secolari verso di loro hanno cagionato anco
gravissimi danni in simile affare, et il lasciar correre o fomentarsi
per ventura la voce che per loro et a loro instanza la S. Sede et

In order rightly to appraise this jealousy as a powerful incentive to the rise and development of Jansenism, it is necessary to take into account the splendid condition of the Society in Flanders just then, as described by the most recent Belgian historian : " Whereas," this writer says, " the secular schools which were called into life in so great a number by the humanists of the Renaissance period, were depressingly empty, the schools of the Order literally teemed with scholars." [1]   Since the beginning of the 17th century the Society's intellectual activity " increasingly overshadowed that of the Universities ". No longer in the Faculties of the Universities but " in the Colleges and Residences of the Jesuits, scholarship sought and found shelter. Not only did the latter produce the most eminent theologians " as, for instance, Lessius in dogma and morals and the exegetist Cornelius a Lapide, " but there were to be found among them mathematicians such as D'Aiguillon and Gregory of St. Vincent, philologists such as Andrew Schott and scholars like Bollandus, Henschen, Papebroch ; they produced the most important historical work of the 17th century, viz. the collection of the *Acta Sanctorum*   The versatility of the members of the Society revealed itself even in the artistic sphere in the painter Daniel Seghers, and the excellent architect Huyssens." [2]   The works of the popular writer Poirters, " who pressed the enthusiasm, the strength and good-naturedness of the Flemish character into the service of the Catholic faith, are the best products of contemporary Flemish literature as regards originality and vigour." [3]   Moreover it is necessary to bear in mind that the few scholars here mentioned are only " the leaders of a whole army of theologians, polemists, pedagogues, preachers, grammarians

---

i suoi ministri faccino tutto, et il parlare e predicare con qualche difetto e lesione della religiosa carità non lasciano di cagionare dei nocumenti." Mangelli, January 17, 1654, *Excerpta, loc. cit.*

[1] PIRENNE, IV., 504.

[2] PIRENNE, 513.

[3] *Ibid.*, 620.

and scholars of every description ! The literary output of the Belgian Jesuits from 1600 till about 1650 is truly amazing ".[1] However, as Mangelli observed, in human life, good is strangely mixed with evil. Just as but for the splendid revival of religion in France there would have been no Port-Royal,[2] so without the efflorescence of the Society of Jesus in Flanders it is hardly likely that Jansenism would have arisen and won its tremendous successes. The scholars at the Universities deemed themselves injured in their rights when they saw themselves relegated to the second rank, hence they were only too ready to agree when Molina, Suarez, Vasquez were subjected to severe criticism in the works of Jansenius. Once called into being, hatred for the Jesuits became like a shadow dogging the new heresy's every step, like an inseparable companion. A life and death struggle was inevitable.

---

[1] *Ibid.*, 615. More particulars in A. PONCELET, *Hist. de la Compagnie de Jésus dans les anciens Pays-Bas*, I., Bruxelles, 1927, 490 *seqq.*

[2] See the present work, Vol. XXIX., 67.

CHAPTER VI.

Innocent X.'s Relations with Venice—The Pontifical
States—Death of the Pope.

(1.)

Innocent X. had always been a good Italian. On his return
from his Spanish nunciature his love for the land of his birth
broke out with irresistible force. Though it was night when
he reached Rome, he went at once to the window of his palace
in order to taste the joy of his home-coming in the contempla-
tion of the Piazza Navona and Pasquino.[1]

As an Italian he strongly resented Spain's tyranny over
Naples but during the troubles of 1647 and 1648 he was shrewd
enough not to allow himself to be drawn into an undertaking
which would have helped the restless, unreliable French,
whose power was on the increase, to secure supremacy in
Italy instead of the Spaniards.[2] As an Italian he appreciated
from the outset of his pontificate the importance of the
Republic of Venice and the value for the Holy See of good
relations with that still independent Power.

The election of the Pamfili Pope had been hailed with
enthusiasm in Venice [3] but, as a preliminary for the
establishment of good relations, the Government demanded
the restoration under the picture of " Barbarossa and
Alexander III." in the Vatican, of the inscription eulogizing
Venice which had been removed under Urban VIII. on account
of its unhistoric character.[4] So much importance was attached

---

[1] See G. Giustinian's *report of October 10, 1650 (State
Archives, Venice), used by Iusti, II., 166.

[2] See above, p. 86 *seq.*

[3] See *Avviso* of September 24, 1644, Arch. Rom., III., 17.

[4] *Cf.* our data, Vol. XXIX., 183.

to this measure in Venice that the dispatch of the customary
obbedienza embassy was made to depend on it.[1] Innocent X.
did not feel justified in alienating so powerful a State on
account of so trifling a matter ; accordingly, in November,
1644, he had the inscription restored.   Cardinal Cornaro
thanked the Pope in the name of his native city for this
" act of justice " and dispatched an account of it to Venice by a
special courier, as if there had been question of a great
diplomatic triumph.[2] The affair had a regrettable sequel :
in December 1644, the prefect of the Papal Secret Archives,
Felice Contelori, who had demonstrated the historical
inaccuracy of the inscription, lost his post, having fallen a
victim to the hatred of the Venetians and the jealousy of his
enemies in Rome : however, at a later date he recovered the
favour of Innocent X.[3] A special envoy was dispatched to
Rome to express the thanks of the Republic of Venice for
the restoration of the inscription.   The envoy was Angelo
Contarini who reached Rome in December 1644.   A cortège
of eighty carriages escorted him when he drove up for his
solemn audience.[4]

The Venetian *obbedienza* embassy was only dispatched on
April 1st, 1645. It consisted of Pier Foscarini, Giovanni Nani,
Alvise Mocenigo and Bertuccio Valiero.   It repaired amid
great display to a consistory held in the Sala Regia.   Its
reception could not have been more cordial,[5] but the Pope did
not neglect to urge the envoys to see to it that the Signoria
ceased from encroaching on the Church's jurisdiction

---

[1] See *Lettera intorno a l' iscrizione rimessa da P. Innocenzo X.
nella Sala Regia, *Barb.* 5653, p. 27 *seqq.* Vat. Libr.

[2] See Savelli's *report of November 19, 1644, State Arch.,
Vienna.   *Cf.* BELTRANI in *Arch. Rom.*, III., 17 *seqq.* A Latin
*epigram of Gregorius Portius " De inscriptione in aula regia
Vaticana suo loco et Venetis restituta ab Innocentio X. P.M."
in *Ottob.* 2434, p. 113, Vat. Lib.

[3] *Arch. Rom.*, III., 19 *seqq.*

[4] Servantius *Diaria, Papal Sec. Arch.   *Cf. Arch. Rom.*, III.,
18, 25.

[5] BERCHET, *Roma*, II., 45 *seqq.*

and immunity in its territory.[1] The nomination of an ordinary Venetian ambassador at the Curia took place on September 18th, 1645.[2] The post was entrusted to Alvise Contarini. As early as March 1645, Innocent X. had appointed Angelo Cesi, Bishop of Rimini, as nuncio to the City of the Lagoons, with special instructions to see to it that the good relations should get increasingly better now that peace had been re-established in consequence of the restoration of the inscription.[3]

The task was a particularly difficult one, for Venice stuck to its peculiar politico-ecclesiastical system whilst simultaneously making heavy demands on the Pope when, in the summer of 1645, rivalry for preponderance in the eastern section of the Mediterranean involved the Republic in a tremendous struggle with the Osmanli. The Turks' attack on Crete (Candia) was a matter of life and death for the City of the Lagoons for if she lost the few *points d'appui* which she still possessed there for her trade with the Levant, the last source of the wealth she had hitherto enjoyed would be dried up. Consequently the Republic exerted itself to its utmost to secure victory in this decisive struggle. The Turks, on their part, did not lag behind their old adversaries. Thus began a war of twenty-five years, fought by land and by sea and with varied fortune.[4]

As on former occasions, so now, the Venetians looked for help from outside, but feeling was everywhere against them. People thought it strange that Venice should expect the whole of Christendom to rally to its defence seeing that the Venetians

---

[1] See *Cifra al Nuntio di Venezia of October 14, 1645, *Nunziat. di Venezia*, 70, Papal Sec. Arch.

[2] BERCHET, *Roma*, II., 65.

[3] See *Istruttione al Vescovo di Rimini per Venezia, dated March 11, 1645, Doria-Pamfili Archives, Rome, Istruz., II. The *credentials bear the date, March 2, 1645.

[4] HAMMER, III., 259 *seq.*, 269 *seq.* ; ZINKEISEN, IV., 570 *seq.*, 730 *seq.* ROMANIN, VII. (1859), 358 *seqq.* ; L. BOSCHETTO, *Come fu aperta la guerra di Candia*, in *Ateneo Veneto*, XXXV., 1 (1913) ; JORGA, IV. (1911), 42 *seq.*

themselves had refused to lend help to others when in the same distress, as for instance, the Knights of Malta.[1]

In the days of Pius V., besides the Holy See, Spain had come to the rescue of Venice. This time also Philip IV. did not shut his eyes to the peril that threatened from the East, and though at war with France he sent a subsidy to Venice.[2] But a league of the Great Catholic Powers was out of question. French troops were fighting not only Spain but the Emperor also, and that on German soil, so that there remained only the Italian States and the Knights of Malta who were themselves more directly threatened.[3]

Innocent X., who had dispatched munitions and troops to Malta and Dalmatia already in March 1645,[4] entertained for a while the idea of forming an Italian league, but the plan failed owing to Venice's distrust, for in that city other motives were suspected behind the Pope's proposals.[5] On the other hand the Pope's offer of five galleys and 2,000 men was gratefully accepted. The Grand Duke of Tuscany and the Viceroy of Naples on their part were to furnish another five galleys each.[6] The Republic of Genoa, whose co-operation the Pope had likewise requested, made impossible conditions.[7] The Knights of Malta, though they were under an express obligation to fight the infidels, showed but little inclination

[1] See Grémonville's report in DARU, *Hist. de Venise*, IV., 525 *seq.*

[2] *Cf.* GRIMALDI, *Le trattative per una pacificazione fra la Spagna ed i Turchi in relazione con i interessi veneziani durante i primi anni della guerra di Candia* (1645–1651), Venezia, 1913.

[3] A *Parenesi o invito ai principi d'Italia contro il Turco*, 1646, in *Cod. N.*, III., 69, p. 103 *seqq.* of the Chigi Library, Rome.

[4] *Cf.* B. DAL POZZO, *Hist. della s. religione . . . detta di Malta*, II., Venezia, 1715, 105, 111 ; A. VALIERO, *Guerra di Candia*, Venezia, 1679, 119.

[5] A. BERNHARDY, *Venezia e il Turco nella seconda metà del Sec. XVII.*, Firenze, 1902, 20 *seq.*

[6] GUGLIELMOTTI, *La squadra ausiliaria* (1883), 12 *seqq.*, 18.

[7] NANI, *Storia Veneta*, II., Venezia, 1679, 49. *Cf.* the *Brief of July 12, 1645, *Epist.*, I., Papal Sec. Arch.

to come to Venice's assistance. They were also unwilling to fall in with the Pope's demand that, with a view to avoiding all disputes, the auxiliary fleet should put to sea under the banner of the Holy See.[1]

On May 4th, 1645, the Pope named Niccolò Ludovisi, Prince of Piombino, commander-in-chief of the fleet.[2] The papal ships were ready at the appointed time, but not so those of the Maltese. Giovan Battista Gori Pannelini, the Inquisitor of Malta, who also acted as papal nuncio on the island, only prevented with the utmost difficulty the indefinite postponement of the Knights' co-operation.[3] As it was, their delays caused the loss of two precious months. At length, at the beginning of August, Gori Pannelini secured the dispatch of six galleys which joined those of the Pope, of Tuscany and of the Viceroy of Naples, on August 21st; on the 29th they effected their junction with the Venetian Grand Fleet at Corfu.[4] Meanwhile bad news had come from Candia. On August 22nd, after a glorious defence, the fortress of Canea had fallen. The Pope, who was informed of the disaster about mid-September,[5] had granted to the Venetians, at the beginning of August, a subsidy of 100,000 scudi to be raised from Church property within the territory of the Republic; he had likewise sent help to the Knights of Malta [6] and dispatched war material to Ragusa.[7] The Venetian ambassador, Alvise Contarini, now suggested a league of the Catholic princes, a proposal which led the Pope to study the negotiations which had ended in the formation of such a

---

[1] P. Piccolomini, Corrispondenza fra la corte di Roma e l'inquisitore di Malta durante la guerra di Candia, 1645–1669, Firenze, 1908, 6, 10 *seq.*

[2] Guglielmotti, 14 *seq.*

[3] *Ibid.*

[4] Piccolomini, *loc. cit.*, 12.

[5] *Cifra al Nuntio di Venezia, September 16, 1645, *Nunziat. di Venezia*, 70, Papal Sec. Arch.

[6] *Bull.*, XV., 397, 400.

[7] See *Brief to Ragusa, September 12, 1645, *Epist.*, I., *loc. cit.*

coalition under Pius V.[1] But the present situation was a very
different one. The crusading spirit, which was still alive
then, was almost completely dead now[2]; the Catholic
Powers were hopelessly estranged from each other, and the
irresolute and exceedingly parsimonious Innocent X. was no
Pius V. The request of Venice for increased subsidies were
met by him with the promise that he would do what was
possible in view of the restricted means of the Holy See ;
but of what use was it if he gave them yet another ship ?
Venice should appeal to Spain and France ; Pius V. had also
availed himself of foreign help in his crusade.[3] In November
the Pope, to whom the defence of the coasts of the Papal
States occasioned considerable expenditure,[4] gave leave to
Venice to raise troops in the territory of the Church. At the
same time he did his best to hasten the peace negotiations
at Münster and addressed an urgent appeal to the King of
Poland, pressing him to mobilize the Cossacks against the
Turks.[5] Finally he wrote to the Shah of Persia [6] from whom
he looked for an attack on Bagdad. On November 20th the
Pope examined with the Cardinals what could be done in
order to obtain help for Venice from the Catholic Powers.[7]
But there was little to hope for from that quarter. France
and Spain were irreconcilable enemies, bent on injuring
each other, to the exclusion of every other consideration.
When the Signoria pressed the Spanish ambassador to work

[1] See *Cifra al Nuntio di Venezia of September 23, 1645,
loc. cit.

[2] See *Cifra al Nuntio di Venezia of February 2, 1646, loc. cit.

[3] Cf. the *instructions in code to the Venice nuncio, A. Cesi,
of October 14 and 21 and November 4, 1645, Nunziat. di Venezia,
70, Papal Sec. Arch.

[4] *Avviso of September 15, 1646, Papal Sec. Arch.

[5] *Cifre al Nuntio di Venezia of November 11 and 18, 1645,
loc. cit.

[6] *Brief of January 30, 1646, Epist., II.–III., Papal Sec.
Arch. As no reply came another *Brief was issued on August 31,
1647, ibid.

[7] Cf. *Acta consist., Barb. 2918, P. 1, Vat. Lib.

at least for an armistice at sea, so that France might be free to help Venice with all her might, the latter rejected the suggestion with the remark that he was not in the least surprised that France should take up the cause of Venice with so much enthusiasm and even seek to win over Spain for that purpose seeing that the French King was about to lay siege to Tarragona, for in these circumstances nothing could be more welcome to him than that the Spanish fleet should be prevented from relieving that town.[1] The French ambassador in Venice, Grémonville, was of opinion that Spain was playing false when she protested her willingness to join a league against the Turks, for her real object was none other than to exploit the forces thus brought together in her own interest by turning them against France. Grémonville also recalled the Venetians' jealousy of France and their selfishness : " If we found ourselves in the straits in which they are at present," he wrote, " and we had need of them as they need us, they would not give help for nothing, but would know how to get some advantage out of it." [2]

These representations were approved by Mazarin. Though towards the end of 1645 the Cardinal secretly provided the Venetians with 100,000 French thalers, of which not even Grémonville knew whether they were meant as a loan or as a present,[3] the liberality of the French minister probably had no other object than to win over the Republic for his anti-Spanish plans in Italy.[4] As for Spain, towards the end of 1645 rumours were current that discussions were on foot for a separate treaty with the Porte, with the reciprocal obligation of not making war against each other. Rome refused to believe that the Catholic King could act in such a way, and expressed the severest disapproval. The suspicion that the Pope approved these negotiations was indignantly denied in

---

[1] See ZINKEISEN, IV., 575 *seq.*

[2] DARU, *Hist. de Venise*, IV., 526.

[3] DARU, *Hist. de Venise*, IV., 524.

[4] *Cf.* BATTISTELLA's observations on G. ZULIAN, *Le relazioni tra il card. G. Mazzarino e Venezia*, Venezia, 1909/11, in *Riv. Stor.*, XXX., 193 *seqq.*

a dispatch of the Secretary of State, dated December 2nd, 1645, to the nuncio at Venice.[1] On October 30th, 1645, the Italian fleet was back in its home port. Though it had achieved

[1] " *Ma quando ciò fusse vero, che sia succeduto senza alcuna partecipatione di Sua Beat^ne, è vero come qualsivoglia articolo di fede, e quando la Santità Sua non fusse in obligo di detestare una simile risolutione, come capo della Chiesa, sarebbe stato forzato a farlo per il mero interesse politico, poichè quando il Re Cattolico si togliesse fuori della difesa comune contro il Turco, li Stati della Chiesa resterebbero facilissimamente preda delle forze Turchesche. Oltre mille altre ragioni, che si potriano addurre per levare dalla mente altrui un così spropositato sospetto . . ." (Cifra al Nuntio di Venezia, December 2, 1645, Papal Sec. Arch. BROSCH (I., 412) writes : " The Pope's relations with the Republic were bound to be profoundly troubled when the Signoria ascertained that Innocent was working on the court of Madrid with a view to inducing Spain to conclude a separate peace with Turkey, thereby securing the coast of Naples and that of the Papal States from Turkish attack. The plan aimed at the complete isolation and abandonment of Venice. A Pope who could thus deal with the Republic whilst it was at war with the infidels, could hardly expect anything from the latter except distrust and embitterment." By way of proof Brosch adds as a footnote : " The affair came to the knowledge of the Venetian ambassador in Rome through Cardinal Colonna. " Io mostrai," Giustinian writes, " di non poter credere pratiche si empie da Ministri Pontificii, et meno dal papa stesso ; ma replicò Colonna, che sono pur troppo vere." Dispatch from Rome, November 27, 1649. Venet. Arch. : *Inquisitori di St., Dispaccio dagli Amb^ori a Roma*, 1628–1649. In the present instance it is possible to demonstrate irrefutably where BROSCH'S favourite exploitation of prejudiced Venetian embassy reports leads him to. So far from countenancing Spain's intentions of taking advantage of Venice's difficulties in so indefensible a fashion (*cf.* ZINKEISEN, IV., 813 *seq.*), Innocent X. did everything in his power to dissuade Philip IV. and his ministers from such a course. On November 13, 1649, the following *instructions, in code, were dispatched by the Secretariate of State to the nuncio in Venice : Da Msgr Nuntio in Spagna si continuano le rimostranze a quella Maestà e ministri contro le proposte dello ambasciatore Turco in essecutione degli ordini di Sua Beat^ne, che li rinoverà con

nothing,[1] Innocent X. was willing to send it out in the following year.[2] In December he had given permission for the raising of troops by Venice up to 8,000 men. Further enrolments he declined at first on the ground that he himself needed soldiers for the defence of the coasts of the Pontifical States, but subsequently he allowed them in the neighbourhood of Rome.[3]

efficacia sempre maggiore in adempimento della pastorale sua cura e della paterna dilettione verso cotesta Republica, come da qui acclusa copia di cifra del medesimo Msgr. Nuntio Ella vedrà (*Nunziat. di Venezia*, 70, p. 160). The *Cifra of the Spanish nuncio, dated Madrid, October 9, 1649, is as follows : " Anche dopo la partenza di S. M^{tà} ho continuato di rappresentare a questi sig^{ri} del Consiglio di Stato le ragioni per le quali stimavo non convenire che per alcun modo si desse orecchie alle proposte dell'ambasciatore Turco, procurando specialmente di far conoscere che non erano tali che potessero accettarsi senza comprendervi gli altri principi christiani e senza prima udirne i sentimenti e particolarmente il N^{ro} Signore, e che, quando ciò si fusse lasciato da parte, sarebbe con gravissimo danno di essi et hora massima-mente della Repubblica di Venetia ; il che ripugnarebbe anche al presupposto fermissimo di Sua Maestà di non esser mai per consentire ad alcun trattato di cui potesse risultar pregiudizio benchè minimo alla christianità " (*Nunziat. di Spagna*, 99, p. 158). On November 27, 1649, the Secretary of State once more wrote to the nuncio in Venice as follows : " A Msgr Nuntio in Spagna non vi è ordinario nel quale non se gli replichino ordini efficaci in adempimento del desiderio di cotesti signori circa i negotiati dell'ambasciatore Turco ; e V. S. potrà di nuovo vederne accresciuti gli effetti nell'acclusa copia di lettera, che se le invia, di Msgr Nuntio sudetto ; al quale s'inviarà pur di nuovo il prose-guire et accrescer sempre più il calore et la premura delle instanze in beneficio della Republica " (*ibid.*, 161^b), Papal Sec. Arch.

[1] *Cf.* ROMANI, VII., 306 ; GUGLIELMOTTI, 25–39 ; PICCOLO-MINI, 12 *seq.*

[2] *Cifra al nuntio di Venezia, January 27, 1646, *Nunziat. di Venezia*, 70, *loc. cit.*

[3] See the *Instructions, in code, to the Venice nuncio of December 2, 9, 23, 30, 1645, and January 27 and February 24, 1646, *ibid.*

On February 24th, 1646, Pier Foscarini arrived in Rome as extraordinary envoy of Venice for the purpose of requesting the Pope, jointly with the ambassador Alvise Contarini, to raise the number of the pontifical ships and soldiers, and to grant large sums of money, especially to the King of Poland, to enable the latter to raise a force of Cossacks. The Pope explained that he would do his best, but that he too was short of money. He ended by granting 30,000 scudi to the Polish King,[1] and saw to it that his galleys were ready to put to sea by the end of April 1646, from Civitavecchia. A delay was caused by Ludovisi falling ill. His place was taken by Alessandro Zambeccari. Towards the end of May the Pope's ships and those of the Knights of Malta effected their junction with the Venetian fleet.[2] The galleys hitherto provided by the Grand Duke of Tuscany and the Viceroy of Naples were missing this time in consequence of Mazarin's attack on the Spaniards in Italy.

The operations of 1646 against the Turks were also unsuccessful, for the new Venetian Captain General, the weak and irresolute septuagenarian Giovanni Capello, was unequal to his task. On October 23rd, Zambeccari returned to Civitavecchia ; he died on December 21st, 1646.[3]

Already in the summer of 1646 the Venetian ambassador, Contarini, had pressed the Pope to come to the assistance of the Republic ; he was told that his demands were impossible.[4] He continued to urge his request during the first months of 1647, though on September 19th, 1646, the Pope had allowed Venice to raise a tenth to the amount of 400,000 scudi.[5] Innocent pointed out that he had to spend 40,000 scudi a month on his army, and to assist the Irish and the King of Poland. Not for lack of goodwill, but because the thing was

---

[1] See the *instructions, in code, to the Venice nuncio, March 3, 10, 17, and April 7, 1646, *ibid.*

[2] GUGLIELMOTTI, 44 *seq.*

[3] ZINKEISEN, IV., 756 ; GUGLIELMOTTI, 50 *seqq.*, 66.

[4] *Cifra al Nuntio di Venezia, of July 21, 1646, *loc. cit.*

[5] *Bull.*, XV.. 478.

utterly impossible, he was unable to provide the soldiers and the money which the ambassador demanded at every audience. He had dispatched a thousand men for the protection of Dalmatia, so that he was left with from 5,000 to 6,000 men to guard the coasts of the Pontifical States.[1] This time also the papal ships put to sea at the end of May, and together with those of the Knights of Malta, joined the Venetian armada now under the command of Battista Grimani. For three months Grimani blockaded the Turkish fleet commanded by Fasli Pasha, in the harbour of Chios, and only when the advanced season rendered a longer stay in those rough waters impossible, did Fasli Pasha succeed in escaping from that harbour and in reaching Crete with 87 galleys. Grimani, who at once set out in pursuit, could not follow quickly enough with his heavily manned ships to prevent the Pasha's landing, so he had to be content with maintaining his winter station near the island of Standia from where he dominated the harbour of Candia. In this way he was in a position to prevent the provisioning of the fortress from the sea.[2]

Notwithstanding the Pope's liberality, nuncio Angelo Cesi had had repeatedly to complain of various infringements of ecclesiastical immunity on the part of Venice.[3] When Cesi died, on September 20th, 1646, Innocent X., on December 6th, 1646, appointed the Archbishop of Pisa, Scipio Pannochieschi d'Elce, as his successor.[4] The new nuncio experienced a

---

[1] See the *instructions, in code, to the new nuncio to Venice, Scipione Pannochieschi, of January 12 and 26, February 2 and 9, March 30, April 6 and 13, 1647, loc. cit.

[2] ZINKEISEN, IV., 784 seq. ; GUGLIELMOTTI, 73 seqq.

[3] Cf. *Cifre al Cesi, of August 26 and September 30, 1645, Nunziat. di Venezia, Papal Sec. Arch.

[4] See MOLMENTI, Venezia nella metà del sec., XVII., in Atti dei Lincei, Rendiconti, 5 series, XXV. (1916/17), 187 seqq. ; there, on p. 192 seq., the Instruction of December 19, 1646, stressing the Pope's interest in the Turkish war. The *acts of Pannochieschi's nunciature, 3 parts, in the State Archives, Venice ; " *Diarium nunciaturae apud Venetos, 1646/52, in Vat. 10423, Vatican Library.

grievous interference with the Church's immunity soon after his entry upon office.[1] In September 1647, it was felt in Rome, that though Venice was for ever making fresh demands for help in its war against the Turks, the city failed in the regard due to the Pope.[2] This referred not only to the circumstance that the Government was slow in making up its mind to refuse its protection to certain apostate religious who were writing against the Pope,[3] and that when it did so at last, it was done most inadequately, but likewise to the fact that fresh demands were being made in regard to episcopal appointments within the territory of the Republic. The Signoria demanded that proposals for vacant sees should only be made in consistory by Venetian Cardinals. This the Pope could not concede ; accordingly the sees remained vacant.[4] The conflict became particularly acute when, on January 18th, 1648, Giovanni Giustinian took over the post of ambassador in Rome. His predecessor, on retiring from office, had given him the sound advice that Venice should avoid ecclesiastical disputes as much as possible, for even those Cardinals and prelates who were most favourably disposed towards the Republic, had bitterly complained of its conduct in this respect.[5] Giustinian took no notice of this advice, and in August, 1648, the Secretary of State had to complain of his pretensions.[6] In such questions as trenched on secular interests, Giustinian pursued a policy which was admirably characterized by the Secretary of State, on December 5th, 1649. In such cases, he said, the Venetians invariably professed complete ignorance and insisted on the need of investigating the affair in question ; by this means

---

[1] *Cifra al Pannochieschi, February 23, 1647, Papal Sec. Arch.

[2] *Cifra al Pannochieschi, September 14, 1647, *ibid.* *Cf.* *Cifra of May 2, 1648, *ibid.*

[3] *Cifre al Pannochieschi, November 9, December 14, 1647, *ibid.*

[4] *Cifre al Pannochieschi, October 11, December 14, 1647, May 23, July 18, 1648, *ibid.*

[5] BERCHET, *Roma*, II., 79.

[6] *Cifre al Pannochieschi, August 29, September 5. 1648, *loc. cit.*

they sought to gain time, so that the affair might fall into oblivion. Giustinian, the Secretary of State added, was for ever demanding fresh concessions, and when the Pope remarked that he had granted a great many and only got fine promises in return, the ambassador would display all his eloquence to demonstrate the contrary. However, His Holiness was well acquainted with the true state of affairs.[1]

The tension between Rome and Venice was not eased by the circumstance that, in consequence of the war of Castro, the papal fleet was unable to show itself in the Levant in 1649 and 1650, because it was needed for the protection of the jubilee pilgrims.[2]   On the other hand, in July 1649, Innocent granted Venice another subsidy from ecclesiastical revenues to the amount of 100,000 scudi.[3] The value of these concessions must appear all the greater inasmuch as the dispute over the appointment to vacant sees was still unsettled, whilst by his false reports Giustinian was doing what in him lay to poison mutual relations,[4] so much so that in August the Secretary of State formally accused him of duplicity.[5] In November the ambassador's double-dealing was revealed afresh.[6]   Though he had the effrontery to assert that Innocent X. held him in the highest esteem,[7] with a view of putting the Pope in the wrong, Giustinian would assert from time to time that Venice also had made concessions ; but when he did so he was invariably told that if a man restored part of what he had stolen he had not made adequate satisfaction.[8] When in July 1650, Giustinian lamented the misfortunes of Venice in the war, the Pope told him that he

---

[1] *Cifra al Pannochieschi, December 5, 1649, *ibid.*

[2] GUGLIELMOTTI, 106 *seqq.* There, 73 *seqq.*, on the campaign of 1647.

[3] *Bull.*, XV., 638 *seq.*

[4] *Cifre al Pannochieschi, December 19, 1648, January 2, May 22, June 5, July 10, 1649, Papal Sec. Arch.

[5] *Cifra al Pannochieschi, August 28, 1649, *ibid.*

[6] *Cifra al Pannochieschi, November 13, 1649, *ibid.*

[7] *Cifra al Pannochieschi, December 11, 1649, *ibid.*

[8] *Cifra al Pannochieschi, February 19, 1650, *ibid.*

too regretted them, but that perhaps God was punishing the Republic for its numerous encroachments on the Church's immunity, and that it was a grievous wrong to prevent the episcopal sees of the mainland and in Dalmatia from being filled because of alleged rights for which there was no foundation whatever. When Giustinian observed that it might be possible to compromise on this question, Innocent replied sharply that nothing would induce him to tolerate any restriction of the full liberty of the Church. After this remark he proceeded to complain of the ingratitude of the Republic.[1] On this point Innocent remained unshaken, however much Giustinian pressed him to yield. A general sigh of relief went up when the ambassador was recalled in November 1651.

Giustinian, who at his farewell audience demanded and obtained a number of favours, showed his gratitude by openly declaring that on his return to Venice he would do his worst against Rome ; he even went so far as to remark that the Republic would have no peace until all priests were driven from its territory ; this statement someone countered with the remark that in that case the Republic should also turn out all Catholics.[2]

---

[1] *Cifra al Pannochieschi, July 16, 1650, *ibid.*

[2] See *Cifra al Nuntio in Venezia, a dì due decembre 1651. " Il signor ambasciatore Giustiniani in questi ultimi giorni della sua dimora in Roma, ha in molti luoghi, nei quali gli è accaduto parlare, con maniere sopra modo disconvenienti, a segno di dire, che ritornato egli costà, era per operare sempre il peggio che havesse potuto negli affari di Roma, e nelle materie ecclesiastiche avrebbe ciò procurato con ogni sforzo possibile, e che in somma era per esser costì sempre un altro procuratore da Pesaro : anzi è fin giunto alcuna volta a dire che la Repubblica non farà mai cosa di profitto, se la Repubblica non manda fuori del suo dominio tutti gli ecclesiastici ; il qual concetto havendo in molti partorito estremo scandalo, ha ancora indotto qualchuno a rispondere, che era bene ancora cacciare i cattolici. Il signor ambasciatore non ha con tutto ciò lasciato di supplicar nella sua partenza Sua Beatitudine molte grazie, di gran parte delle quali ha voluto Sua Beatitudine compiacerlo, perchè nella profusione della sua

Under Giustinian's successor, Niccolò Sagredo, Innocent X. granted, in the autumn of 1653, the raising of a tenth from the Venetian clergy, and a fresh subsidy of 100,000 scudi from ecclesiastical property, for the prosecution of the war of defence against the Turks.[1] However, no improvement ensued in the ecclesiastical policy of Venice. One Order, which had rendered the highest services to the Church, and which, for that reason, had had praise and favours showered upon it by the Popes, viz. the Society of Jesus, continued to be banished from the territory of the Republic.[2] The Inquisition had only a semblance of existence and only dealt with trifling matters, yet all the time the purity of the faith was constantly in danger in the City of the Lagoons owing to the circumstance that, for purposes of trade, many Protestants, as well as other persons suspected of heresy, were allowed to reside there. The extent of the Signoria's toleration may be gauged from the fact that it conceded to the Protestants burial places in Catholic cemeteries.[3]

benignità apparisca quanto disconvenga l'uso di una si mala corrispondenza " (*Nunziat di Venezia*, 70, p. 186b, Papal Sec. Arch.). Giustinian's two reports, which BROSCH adopts uncritically, contain so many unfair judgments that RANKE (III., 176*) questions their genuineness. Ranke's statement that they are not to be found in the Venetian State Archives, is erroneous; see BERCHET, *Roma*, II., 85.

[1] *Bull.*, XV., 722 *seqq.*, 736 *seqq.* For the plan, at first enthusiastically taken up both by Sagredo and by Innocent X. and subsequently dropped, of enrolling crusaders for Venice's war from all the Franciscan convents, see VALIERO, 321 *seqq.*; WADDING, *Ann. Ord. Min.*, 1654; ZINKEISEN, IV., 819. *Cf. ibid.*, 823, on the unsuccessful plan of the Capuchin Antonio Maria di Raita of collecting money for Venice in Germany.

[2] A *Cifra of March 24, 1646, instructed the Venice nuncio to work for the return of the Jesuits, though not at first in the Pope's name; *Nunziat. di Venezia*, 70, Papal Sec. Arch.

[3] *Cf.* the interesting report addressed to the brother of nuncio Pannochieschi in MOLMENTI, *loc. cit.*, 219 *seqq.*

(2.)

From the first days of his pontificate the situation in the States of the Church had caused grave anxiety to Innocent X.[1] His first care was to get rid of the foreign soldiers whom Urban VIII. had recruited for the war of Castro, for these men had become a heavy burden on the country. To this must be added yet another inheritance of the preceding pontificate, namely, the oppressive taxation which the Pope was unable to relieve to the extent he would have wished because, notwithstanding the greatest economy, his financial situation continued unfavourable ; in fact he saw himself compelled to incur a fresh debt to the amount of three million scudi.[2] In view of the fact that the rising in Naples in the summer of 1647 might easily spread to the Pontifical States, the Pope planned a lowering of taxation, and in order to make up for the loss of revenue it was decided to reduce the rate of interest of some of the *Monti* from 7 to $4\frac{1}{2}$ per cent.[3] But even this measure proved no remedy for his financial straits. Like his predecessor, Innocent also left his successor debts which amounted to 48 million scudi. The motives which led to so heavy a burden being laid on the State were all to the honour of Innocent X., as they had been to that of his predecessors, apart from the sums wasted on the nephews. The Popes could not decline the duty of supporting the Catholic Powers in the religious struggles of the 16th and 17th centuries, and especially in the wars against the Turks, with money, troops and ships. From their predecessors

---

[1] Innocent X. confirmed on December 16, 1644, Pius V.'s Constitution on the inalienability of the Papal States ; *cf. Bull.*, XV., 333.

[2] *Cf.* the reports of A. Contarini and G. Giustinian in BERCHET, *Roma*, II., 74 *seq.*, 153 ; PALLAVICINO, I., 302 ; RANKE, III., 70 ; BROSCH, I., 413 *seq.*, who overlooks MORONI's data (LXXIV., 304). A *avviso* of February 4, 1645, already mentions measures of economy at the palace (Papal Sec. Arch.).

[3] BROSCH, I., 414. On the *monti, cf.* COPPI, *Discorso sulle finanze*, 16.

they had inherited the obligation of acting, in conjunction with Venice, as an advanced post of Christendom in Italy against the traditional enemy in the East. France, but more particularly Poland, Hungary, the Emperor, and even more than all these, Venice, demanded and received large sums of money. All the victims of persecution and spoliation in the countries of the South invariably first turned to the Popes, and as a rule they were given generous assistance.[1]

It was a calamity for everybody when in 1647, and even more so in 1648, the failure of the crops caused great scarcity and want. To this was added an inundation of the Tiber in March 1646,[2] and an even more disastrous one on December 6th, 1647, which did heavy damage.[3] The Pope, who was at all times concerned for the welfare of his subjects,

---

[1] *Cf.* with this opinion of DÖLLINGER (*Kirche und Kirchen*, 539 *seq.*), also RANKE, I., 422.

[2] See **Avviso* of March 24, 1646, which refers to the Pope's care of the poor, Papal Sec. Arch.

[3] *Cf.* Servantius, **Diaria*, who writes : " Fuerunt factae diversae provisiones ad succurrendum oppressis de necessariis alimentis, in quo multum studuerunt religiosiores Urbis praelati et praecipue Camerae clerici de ordine Papae, qui naviculis pluries regiones, praecipue Lungariae et Burgi, aliasque transfretaverunt et alimonia omnibus praebebant ; maiordomus Papae aptari iussit molendinum palatii Vaticani, nullum enim aliud moliri poterat, et triticum sine intermissione moliri ad distribuendam farinam fornariis ; et aliae provisiones necessariae factae fuerunt ; D. etiam card. Pamphilius transcurrit navicula per regionem Turris novae Ripettae et alias iuxta opus. Spectaculum fuit miserrimum, maxime eorum, qui extra Urbem domunculis rusticis morabantur, qui in quantitate non parva perierunt." Papal Sec. Arch. *Cf.* DENIS, I., 97 *seq.* ; FORCELLA, XIII., 221 ; *Savelli's *report of December 7, 1647, State Archives, Vienna ; *Diary in *Cod.* 93–46 of the Doria-Pamfili Archives, Rome. *Cod.* H. II., 43, of the Chigi Library in Rome has this passage, p. 122 *seq.* : " *Dell'antica navigazione del fiume Tevere e del modo da restituirsi. Discorso di Msgr. Bernardino abbate Biscia Romano presentato alla $S^{tà}$ di Innocenzo X., dedicato al card. Camillo Pamphilio, decembre 1653."

though all too often he was badly served by his officials,[1] did his utmost to alleviate the general misery. His alms to the poor were more generous than ever, and he bought grain for Rome wherever it could be had, with his own money.[2] How difficult this proved at times was shown by an incident which occurred at Fermo in the summer of 1648. Though there also bread was lacking, the vice-governor, the Milanese Uberto Maria Visconti, was freighting a grain ship for Rome. This operation was opposed by a section of the population ; a mutiny ensued, the Government buildings were sacked and the vice-governor killed. Thereupon troops were dispatched to Fermo and the culprits sternly punished.[3] The terror thus created stopped any inclination to rebellion in other parts of the Papal States ; Perugia alone took up a threatening

[1] DENIS, *passim*. See also BENIGNI, *Getreidepolitik*, 54 *seqq.*, also NAUDÉ in *Deutsche Literaturzeitung*, 1899, 476.

[2] See the very scarce work by F. F. MANCINI : *Compendio della vita ed azioni di P. Innocenzo X.*, 4. *Cf. Bull.*, XV., 591. Also " *Provedimenti per alimentare il popolo Romano nella carestia del 1648 ", Barb.* 3206, Vat. Libr., which gives interesting details on the organization of private relief for the 5,000 or so destitute families of Rome. On the heavy expenditure which the Pope was compelled to incur already in 1647, owing to the prevailing want in Rome, see Savelli's *report of September 12, 1648, State Archives, Vienna. *Cf.* also Albizzi's *letter to Chigi, dated Rome, May 2, 1648, *Cod.* A. III., 55, Chigi Library, Rome, and the *Diary in *Cod.* 93–46 of the Doria-Pamfili Archives in Rome.

[3] See BISACCIONI, *Hist. d. guerre civili di questi ultimi tempi*, II., Venezia, 1653, 198–208, and GUALDO, *Historia*, 149 *seq.* RANKE (III., 175*) refers to a *Memoriale presentato alla S^{tà} di N.S. Innocenzo X. dai deputati della città di Fermo per il tumulto ivi seguito alli 6 di Luglio, 1648*, but does not state where the MS. is kept. I have not been able to find it. CIAMPI (52 and 396) quotes a document in the State Archives, Rome, in connexion with this. *Cf.* also Giustinian's *dispatches quoted by BROSCH (I., 415) (State Archives, Venice), and DENIS, 176, 182 *seq.* In 1653 a fresh rising occurred at Fermo ; see DE ROSSI, *Istoria, Vat.* 8873, Vatic. Libr.

attitude, but the population ended by allowing itself to be calmed without the use of harsh measures.[1]

Fresh troubles arose in consequence of the suppression of the rising in Naples from whence individual bands fled into the States of the Church, from which they made predatory irruptions into Neapolitan territory. Even Rome beheld some sinister figures from the southern kingdom. They found protection with the French ambassador who extended the right of asylum to the neighbouring houses, where hundreds of " Masanielli ", as they were called, could be seen.[2] Grave troubles were subsequently occasioned by the conduct of Spanish recruiting agents which led to bloody encounters in the jubilee year of 1650.[3]

Such incidents were bound to cause particular pain to a man like Innocent X. whose ambition it was to preserve tranquillity and order in Rome, and not to tolerate any oppression of the weak by the strong.[4] It was felt as a public benefit when Innocent X. proceeded to compel the Barons to pay their debts. The worst offender in this respect was the youthful Duke of Parma, Ranuccio Farnese II., who refused to satisfy the creditors of his Roman loan bank (*Monti Farnesi*), the funds of which were based on the revenues of Castro and Ronciglione. This action caused serious suffering to many pious institutions, and to many widows and orphans.[5] Innocent X. was averse to warlike undertakings,[6] hence he

---

[1] BROSCH, I., 416, after Giustinian's *dispatches.

[2] IUSTI, II., 165.

[3] *Cf.* above, p. 183.

[4] See A. Contarini in BERCHET, *Roma*, II., 69 ; RANKE, III., 30 ; also CIAMPI, 108 *seq.* To preserve Rome from the plague, which was doing great havoc at Bologna (see inscription in KEYSSLER, II., 494), severe measures were taken in 1652 ; see *Editti*, V., 61, p. 99 *seqq.*, Papal Sec. Arch.

[5] See Deone (Ameyden) in RANKE, III., 30. *Cf.* also *Acta consist.*, of July 19, 1649, Papal Sec. Arch.

[6] " *S. Stà, la quale è alienissima dalla guerra e per propria natura e per la quiete d'Italia " (Savelli on July 10, 1649), State Arch., Vienna. *Cf.* *Deone (Ameyden) on July 17, 1649 : " Il

hesitated a long time before taking action, though Ranuccio's conduct was most provoking, even in purely ecclesiastical matters.[1] Whilst, as was his custom, the Pope was still considering the situation, the murder took place, on March 18th, 1649, of the newly appointed Bishop of Castro, the splendid Barnabite Cristoforo Giarda. On March 24th the Pope excommunicated the assassin and his accomplices and offered a reward of 3,000 scudi, a sum soon raised to 5,000 scudi, for the discovery of the criminals. Suspicion fell on Sansone Asinelli, by whose instigation a familiar of the Duke of Parma, the Frenchman Godefroi, had perpetrated the murder.[2]

The Pope, who in a consistory of April 12th, 1649, had protested against an assassination committed " almost before his eyes ",[3] saw himself compelled to take action, all the more so as the Duke's creditors, the so-called " Montanists ", demanded with increasing insistence that he should help them to obtain what was due to them.[4] By June Innocent could not show himself in the streets without having to hear shouts that he should give satisfaction to the Montanists who had waited for seven years for the interest on their loans.[5] The demand was a just one since the Pope was Castro's overlord, and the Curia had given leave for the foundation of the Ducal bank.

Ranuccio had no thought of yielding ; on the contrary, in May he threatened to invade the Papal States so that the Pope was forced to concentrate 4,000 infantry and 1,000 horse

Papa nel primo giorno del pontificato mi disse : Vogliamo che Roma sia allegra, ma non vogliamo soldati." Cod. 1833 (XX., III., 21), cf. Bibl. Casanatense, Rome.

[1] DEMARIA, 251.

[2] Servantius, *Diaria, Papal Sec. Arch. ; Bull., XV., 626 ; CIAMPI, 62 seqq. Cf. DEMARIA, 252 ; O. PREMOLI, C. Giarda, ultimo vescovo di Castro, Monza, 1914.

[3] See *Acta consist., Barb. 2928, p. 2, Vat. Library.

[4] Cf. Savelli's *report of April 24, 1649, State Archives, Vienna.

[5] Deone (Ameyden) in RANKE, III., 30.

on the frontier of Bologna and Ferrara.[1] However, the Duke, whom no one would assist, was not strong enough to prevent the Pope from taking action against Castro.[2] In a consistory of June 19th, Innocent X. explained to the Cardinals the necessity of intervention.[3] The siege of the fortress began in the same month, but the garrison only capitulated on September 2nd, on condition of their being granted a free departure.[4] Contrary to the expectation that only the fortifications would be razed,[5] the whole town, including the ducal palace and the churches, was levelled with the ground and a column raised on the spot with the inscription : " Here stood Castro." By a Bull of September 14th, 1649, the episcopal see was transferred to Acquapendente.[6] The Duke was compelled to sign a treaty by the terms of which the fiefs of Castro and Ronciglione passed to the Apostolic Camera with the reservation of their redemption for a large sum of money. The Camera undertook the obligation of satisfying the creditors.[7] Thus disappeared once for all the anomaly of Castro as an autonomous duchy yet a fief of the Holy See.[8] Some other small fiefs, such as those of the Malatesta of Sogliano, the Corgna, and the Malatesta of Baglione came

---

[1] Savelli's *report of May 29, 1649, *loc. cit. Cf.* DEMARIA, 254.

[2] Savelli's *report of June 5, 1649, *loc. cit.*

[3] *Acta consist., loc. cit.*

[4] Savelli's *report of September 4, 1649, *loc. cit. Cf.* CIAMPI, 67–70 ; DENIS, I., 218 *seq.*, 221, 226.

[5] *Avviso* of October 16, 1649, State Archives, Vienna.

[6] *Bull.*, XV., 641 ; CIAMPI, 71 ; CARABELLI, *Dei Farnesi*, 174 *seq.* ; detailed account of the destruction of Castro in DE ROSSI, *Istoria, Vat.* 8873, Vat. Libr. The column has disappeared, a small wood stands on the site. Of the town nothing remains except part of the church of St. Francis ; see GROTANELLI, in *Rassegna naz.*, LVIII. (1891), 278 *seq.* In justification of the Pope's severity, *cf.* PREMOLI, *loc. cit.*, 31.

[7] MORONI, X., 228 *seq.*, who gives the special bibliography ; also CARABELLI, 178 *seq.* ; *Acta consist.* of January 24, 1650, Papal Sec. Arch.

[8] CIAMPI, 326 ; DEMARIA, 256.

under the immediate sovereignty of the Pope by devolution during the reign of Innocent X.[1]

Even though Borgognone and Carlo Maratta glorified the conquest of Castro with a pompous picture now preserved in the Doria gallery, in reality the three months' siege and final capture of that small nest had nothing heroic about it ; on the contrary, the battles that took place there, as well as the conduct of Italian captains on the battlefields of Germany, threw a lurid light on the utter decadence of the art of war in Italy. The traditional warlike valour of the Roman Barons was a thing of the past. In other respects also the Roman aristocracy was in decline. The outward pomp which was still being displayed, the titles, orders and honours of every kind, the splendour of the palaces and the number of retainers, were in sharp contrast with the burden of their debts and their diminished influence.[2] True, the Roman nobility was still numerous ; there were at that time some fifty noble families three centuries old, thirty-five with a history of 200 years, and sixteen that were one century old,[3] but the financial situation of most of them was deplorable. Thus the Savelli had become impoverished and were compelled to sell Albano to the son of Camillo Pamfili at the end of 1650 [4] : the possessions of the Counts of Segni had been acquired by the Sforzas of Santa Fiora, though the latter, as well as the

---

[1] REUMONT, III., 625.

[2] *Ibid.*, 626.

[3] See ALMADEN, *Relatione di Roma*, in *Tesori*, Brussels, 1672 ; RANKE, III., 43 ; T. AMAYDEN, *La storia delle famiglio Romane*, ed. A. Bertini, 2 vols., Roma, 1910. *Cf.* also BERTUZZI, *La nobiltà Romana*, nel 1653, in *Riv. del Collegio arald.*, III. (1905), and the *Discorso sulle famiglie papali moderne che hanno fondato le loro abitationi in Roma dal tempo di Paolo III. sino al pres. tempo*, 1665, in *Barb.* 4910, Papal Sec. Arch.

[4] " *Dopo molte rivolte di esclusioni et inclusioni della vendita d'Albano, finalmente conchiusa la vendita, sendone i Savelli sforzati dalla necessità, per il figlio di Don Camillo, al quale Donna Olimpia ha fatto donatione per 400m scudi. . . ." Ameyden's Diary, December 17, 1650, *Barb.* 4819, Vat. Libr.

Frangipani, were themselves in straitened circumstances, and even the Colonna were compelled to seek to maintain themselves by means of rich marriages. At Bracciano and in their palace in the Piazza Navona, the Orsini displayed a princely magnificence, but they had lost all political significance.[1] " When I arrived in Rome," Theodore Ameyden wrote in August 1647, " Virginio Orsini was a Spaniard and on his palace he had the arms of the Catholic King. When his son died he became a Frenchman and shortly afterwards a Spaniard once more ; at present he is French again—for how long no one knows." [2] The new papal families had risen beside the old ones ; they even surpassed them and had entered into close relations with them, thus, on the one hand, the Orsini, Cesarini, Borghesi, Aldobrandini, Ludovisi, Giustiniani were allied to the Pamfili, whilst on the other the Colonna and the Barberini were also closely linked together. Donna Olimpia's reconciliation with the Barberini led to a general reunion which included all the families of some importance.[3] For the rest the Aldobrandini died out in the male line as early as 1631 and the Peretti in 1656.

Not a few families, especially such as had come from Florence and Genoa, and even from Portugal and France, had acquired their wealth by taking charge of the financial transactions of the Dataria. Even from towns in the Papal States, such as Parma, distinguished families had migrated to Rome, attracted as they were by the possibility of buying offices and the varied advantages offered by the metropolis.[4] Whereas the population of Rome had hitherto been a fluctuating one, it now became stabilized through firmly domiciled families. The way in which this change, which began with the 17th century, came about, and what elements constituted the population of Rome, appears from the registers kept by the parish priests for the purpose of controlling the fulfilment

---

[1] REUMONT, III., 2, 626 seq. ; CIAMPI, 211 seqq., 219 seq.

[2] CIAMPI, 211.

[3] RANKE, III., 41.

[4] Ibid., 43 seq.

by their parishioners of their religious duties, especially that
of the Easter Communion.[1] According to these registers the
population of Rome was made up as follows :—

Year	Population	Families	Priests	Religious	Nuns
1600	109,729	20,019	1,469	2,148	2,372
1605	99,647	20,419	1,833	1,943	2,140
1614	115,413	21,422	1,426	2,190	2,341
1619	106,050	24,380	1,956	2,455	2,887
1621	118,356	26,364	1,975	2,420	2,756
1623	111,727	26,854	1,582	2,624	2,502
1628	115,874	24,429	2,367	3,066	2,624
1644	110,608	27,274	1,742	3,414	2,726
1650	126,192	30,429	2,256	3,355	2,796
1655	122,978	30,667	2,317	3,000	2,507 [2]

That a number of shady characters should have infiltrated
into so large a population was natural enough. Attempts
to keep them at a distance [3] and to restrain immorality
were not wanting under Innocent X.[4]

(3.)

When Innocent X. ascended the Chair of St. Peter, he
was endowed with a vigour of mind and body such as is but
seldom granted to a septuagenarian. For his almost youthful
freshness, so happily shown in Mignard's portrait of him,[5]
and which he preserved for a further decade, the Pope had

---

[1] Hence the Jews are omitted ; the first statistics about them
are of 1668 ; they numbered then 4,500 persons (850 families).
Studi e docum., XII. (1891), 170.

[2] See CERASOLI in *Studi e docum.*, XII. (1891), 174 *seqq.* ;
on p. 197 *seqq.* details are given on the parishes of Rome. The
statistics given by RANKE (III., 45), on the basis of a MS. of the
Barberini Library, not fully indicated by him, are in part
erroneous. The higher number of the inhabitants in 1600 and 1650
is accounted for by the fact that these were jubilee years.

[3] *Editto contro gl'otiosi e vagabondi, of January 18, 1649,
in *Editti*, V., 66, f. 154, Papal Sec. Arch.

[4] *Editto against " donne dishoneste e loro fautori e ricetta-
tori," of March 5, 1658, *ibid.*, 60, f. 217.

[5] IUSTI, II., 180.

to thank his constitution as well as his simple and abstemious mode of life.

Innocent X. was fond of walking and took a great deal of exercise [1] but contrary to the practice of former Pontiffs, he did not make the customary sojourns in the country. Only on a few occasions during his entire pontificate did he leave the neighbourhood of the city for a short while. On October 12th, 1649, he betook himself to the Castle of San Martino al Cimino which Andrea Maidalchini had built for himself in 1625 ; he remained until the 28th in order to enjoy, amid its chestnut trees, the mountain air and the magnificent view. He made excursions to Viterbo, the Villa Bagnaia and Monte Cimino, from the crest of which a magnificent view opens on the wide campagna and the crown of hills that encircle it.[2] An excursion to Frascati in June 1652, was occasioned by the purchase of Albano for Camillo Pamfili.[3] From October 13th to November 3rd, 1653, the Pope made a second stay at San Martino.[4] In other years he sought recuperation in the magnificent Villas round Rome. Besides the Villa Pamfili before the Gate of S. Pancrazio and Donna Olimpia's garden near Ponte Rotto in the Trastevere, he particularly loved to visit the Villas Ludovisi and Borghese, especially in spring and autumn.[5]

Like most men enjoying good health, Innocent X. would

---

[1] Cf. the report of the envoy of Lucca in Studi e docum., XXII., 218.

[2] De Rossi, *Istoria, Vat. 8873, Vat. Libr. Cf. *Cod. Bolognetti, 202, Papal Sec. Arch.

[3] Denis, I., 267.

[4] Ibid., 289. An inscription in the church of the castle, beneath Innocent X.'s bust, recalls this visit. Text in Bussi (332). Ibid., 331 and 332, the inscriptions in S. Dominico at Viterbo and in the Villa Bagnaia.

[5] Servantius *Diaria on May 24, 1649 (Papal Sec. Arch.) mentions a visit of Julius III. to the Vigna. Olimpia's picturesque garden near S. Maria in Capella (cf. Ciampi, 203 seq.) was destroyed in 1887.

have nothing to do with physicians.[1] For a long period he remained completely free from the infirmities of old age and it was only towards the end of November 1647, that he had an attack of kidney trouble.   This caused at first grave anxiety, but only for a short time.[2]   In 1648 the Pope felt as well as ever, but at this time, though his action was disapproved by many, he followed the advice of the physicians and took up his residence at the Quirinal, even in winter, thus avoiding the unhealthy air of the Vatican district.[3] A bout of illness in January 1649, was quickly over.[4]   His Holiness, so a chronicler reports in July 1649, is quite well and retains an excellent memory.[5] The discovery of the falsification of Bulls by Mascambruno at the beginning of 1652 so excited the Pope as to affect his bodily health : he began to suffer from sleeplessness and a violent trembling of the right hand, so that, for a time, he was unable to say Mass, but his general condition remained robust enough to allow him even then to take long walks.[6] Even after he had entered upon his eightieth year, he still felt quite well.   In June 1654, the rapidity with which he walked in the garden whilst giving audiences, caused general surprise.[7] In July the old man suddenly began

---

[1] See Giustinian in BERCHET, Roma, II., 92.

[2] See ARNAULD, Negociat., V., 330, 332, 335, 339. On the curious remedy which a Capuchin with medical knowledge recommended to the Pope, see Ed. d'Alençon, Poudre de vipère et or potable. Consultation donnée à un Pape par un Capucin, in Étud. francisc., XXVIII. (1912), 85 seqq.

[3] *Avviso of November 27, 1649, State Archives, Vienna.

[4] Deone, *Diario, 1649, Cod. 1833 (XX., III., 21), Bibl. Casanat., Rome.

[5] Deone, *Diario, for July 17, 1649, ibid.

[6] See the report in CHANTELAUZE, Retz, II., 469. Ottob 2477, p. 587 seqq., from the pen of P. Diana, a " *Theologica dissertatio an S. N. D., qui propter tremorem manus dexterae non potest elevare calicem nec frangere hostiam, possit dispensare super hos ritus et ceremonias, ut missam celebret, et an habeat iustam causam dispensandi, et an teneatur dispensare." Vat. Libr.

[7] *Avviso, of June 17, 1654, Papal Sec. Arch.

to lose strength but he would not hear of medical assistance.[1]
Of a slight attack of illness on August 13th he took no notice
whatever. To show that he was the man that he had always
been, he had himself carried in a sedan chair to St. Mary
Major for the function on the feast of the Assumption of our
Lady, but he returned more dead than alive. Even now he
refused at first to have anything to do with the physicians,
but ended by receiving the celebrated Giovanni Giacomo
Baldino.[2] All through September the Pope's condition was
so serious that the Spaniards constantly held six couriers in
readiness. Once again he rallied. After spending 45 days in
bed, Innocent X. stultified all the predictions of physicians
and astrologers when, on October 5th, he held a consistory,
after which he called on Olimpia at the Palazzo Pamfili in the
Piazza Navona. Soon he resumed his usual walks and his
audiences.[3] In November he repeatedly inspected the building
operations at St. Agnese which he had greatly at heart.
On December 14th he had himself once more carried into
Olimpia's garden, but all of a sudden symptoms of dropsy
appeared, quickly followed by complete loss of strength.
Thereupon Olimpia put her treasures in a safe place.[4]

The grievously stricken man became a burden both to
himself and to those around him. Even Chigi found it hard
to bear with him. Trusting in his strong constitution the

[1] DE ROSSI, *Istoria*, *Vat.* 8873, Vatican Library.

[2] *Ibid.* On Innocent X.'s physicians, especially on P. Zacchia
(*ob.* 1659), see RENAZZI, III., 145 *seq.* ; CIAMPI, 228 *seq.* ; N.
Antologia, XLIV. (1893), 557 *seqq.* ; [ZAPPOLI], *Illustr. ai busti
d. medici celebri*, Roma, 1868, 89 *seqq.* ; *Bibliografia Romana*, I.
(1880), 252 *seq.* Another of Innocent X.'s physicians, Fonseca,
became famous through his sepulchre executed by Bernini in
the family chapel of S. Lorenzo in Lucina. The life-size bust
testifies to the piety of the deceased for in his right hand he clasps
his rosary, that refuge in the storms of life ; *cf.* Baldinucci,
edit. RIEGL, 215 ; BENKARD, 45 ; SOBOTKA, *Bildhauer der
Barockzeit*, Vienna, 1927, 28.

[3] DENIS, I., 311, 316, 318. CIAMPI, 173.

[4] DE ROSSI, *Istoria, loc. cit. Cf.* CIAMPI, 174.

Pope insisted in continuing his wonted mode of life. This hastened the end. Fits of delirium set in and the physicians feared he might die suddenly : Chigi accordingly had the Pope warned of the gravity of his condition by the Jesuit Oliva. The sick man received the information with wonderful calm, made his confession and received viaticum. The two nephews, Pamfili and Ludovisi, were reinstated in their offices. The Cardinals, who had been summoned to his death-bed, he exhorted to choose a worthy successor. Cardinal Sforza, who shortly before had passed over to the Spanish party, he exhorted to bear in mind that all things in this world were vanity and that the love of God alone endured for ever. To Cardinal Albizzi he said : " May your Eminence preserve the merits and virtues to which you owe your present position." The Pope's former violence now gave place to meekness. He resolved to devote the remaining days of his life exclusively to the salvation of his soul. Troublesome visitors and petitioners were refused admission by Chigi ; even the nephews, whom the Pope had exhorted to concord, were no longer allowed to see the dying man. Chigi and Fr. Oliva were alone present at his death which occurred on January 7th, 1655, at midnight, but was kept secret until morning.[1]

Innocent X.'s pontificate of ten years was neither a brilliant

---

[1] Besides PALLAVICINO, I., 208 seq., cf. on Innocent X.'s last illness DE ROSSI, *Istoria, loc. cit. ; Card. Colonna's *report to Ferdinand III., dated Rome, December 28, 1654, State Archives, Vienna ; the *reports of Girol. Albergati, dated Rome, January 2 and 5, 1655, State Archives, Bologna. Extreme Unction was administered to the Pope by the parish priest of SS. Vincent and Anastasius ; cf. *Liber in quo adnotantur obitus summorum Pontif., Archives of SS. Vincent and Anastasius, Rome ; see also GERMANO ALITINO, Relazione dell' ultima malatia e della morte del P. Innocenzo X. (sine die et anno) and the *Diario of Girolamo Pelacchi da S. Giorgio (dioc. di Fano) candatario del card. Sacchetti, in Vat. 8414, p. 10 seqq., Vat. Library. Many satirical poems on Innocent X. were also published. Cf. CIAMPI, 308 ; *Cod. 656 Q. of the Library of Monte Cassino.

nor a happy one. The thorns which had been foretold him at his accession,[1] were not wanting to him, not only as a result of the attitude of France but of that of Spain as well. There was nothing he abhorred so much as war, yet he was forced to wage one, and though he zealously worked for the restoration of peace among the Christian nations, he failed to put an end to the struggle between France and Spain. It was nothing less than a tragedy that though he lived to see the restoration of peace in Germany, he found himself forced to protest against a treaty which inflicted the most grievous injury on the Church.

A deep shadow is cast upon the pontificate of Innocent X., obscuring the Pope's good qualities and the few external successes he secured, by the almost boundless influence which Donna Olimpia exercised over the weak old man. This, as well as his own moodiness and violence, and the family quarrels to which they gave rise, created for him endless annoyances and involved him in a network of intrigues from which the ablest of his advisers were powerless to extricate him.[2] The avarice which Donna Olimpia exhibited after the Pope's death,[3] was likewise a characteristic of Camillo Pamfili. The Lombard sculptor, Ercole Ferrata, made a model of a large statue for a monument to Innocent X. ; however, the Pamfili shrank from the considerable cost on the pretext that the sculptor was too old to execute a piece of work of this kind.[4] The very plain monument which was eventually executed after a design by Giambattista Maini,[5] with the bust of the Pontiff, is so placed in St. Agnes', in the Piazza Navona, over the entrance and under the organ, that many visitors to the church fail to notice it. The monument of

[1] A. TAURELLI, *De novissima electione Innocentii X.*, Bononiae, 1644, 32.

[2] REUMONT in *Zeitschr. des Aachener Gesch. Vereins*, VII. (1885, 28 *seq.*).

[3] See above, p. 46.

[4] CIAMPI, 181.

[5] Copy in MAGNI, *Il barocco a Roma*, I., Torino, 1911, 65 ; *Annuaire pontifical*, 1916, 196 ; MUÑOZ, *Roma*, 327 ; *cf.* FERRARI.

a Pope who did so much for the adornment of the churches of Rome,[1] deserved a more honourable position.

La tomba, 156. The body was only translated from St. Peter's to S. Agnese on January 4, 1677 ; see CANCELLIERI, *Mercato*, 115 *seq.*, and **Avviso* of January 9, 1677, State Archives, Vienna.

[1] Stress is laid on this in Giacinto Gigli's **Elogio d'Innocenzo X.*, in *Sers.* 359, p. 128, of the Bibl. Vittorio Emmanuele, Rome. Besides *Elogi* there were not wanting *Pasquinate* after Innocent X.'s death ; for samples see **Cod.* 10806 of the British Museum, London.

CHAPTER VII.

INNOCENT X. AS A PATRON OF ART.

IN contrast with his cultured predecessor, who had occupied the very centre of the learned and literary life of his time, Innocent X. was merely a dry jurist whose main interest lay in practical things. Thus he encouraged the researches in Archives of the brilliant Sforza Pallavicino and the incomparable annalist, Odorico Rinaldi, whose studies were to be of the utmost benefit to the Church,[1] but for literature, not to speak of poetical products, he had little or no liking at all.[2] Of the majority of painters he made as little account as of the *beaux esprits*. Among the former, no doubt, there were some odd characters. He once observed that he did not like to have much to do with these people because they had occasioned

---

[1] On the favour shown to Pallavicino see SUSTA, *Die römische Kurie und das Konzil von Trient*, I., Vienna, 1904, ix, and *Röm. Quartalschr.*, 1902, 305 *seq.* ODORICO RINALDI (Raynaldus), the splendid continuator of Baronius' Annals, so deservedly eulogized by I. F. BÖHMER (see *Regesti* of 1198, 290 ; *Regesti* of 1241–1313, IV. ; *Regesti* of Louis of Bavaria, 218 ; *cf.* JANSSEN, *Leben Boehmers*, I., 326), RIEZLER (Vatik. Akten, I., preface), GRAUERT (*Hist. Jahrb.*, XI. 820) and HIPLER (Geschichtsauffassung, 82 *seq.*), published in 1646 the 13th vol., in 1648 the 14th, in 1652 the 15th and 16th, in 1659 the 17th, in 1663 the 18th ; volumes 19 and 20 appeared after his death in 1671. Innocent X. offered the illustrious Oratorian the post of librarian of the Vaticana ; see A. MARCHESAN, *Lettere inedite di O. Rinaldi*, Treviso, 1896, 10 *seq.*, 14 *seq.* The nomination of Luke Holste (September, 1653), as successor to L. Ricciardi at the Vatican Library, met with general approval; see *Miscell. di. stor. ital.*, XV., (1875), 199. L. Allacci received a pension from Innocent X. ; see **Barb.*, XXXVIII., 6, Vat. Libr.

[2] PALLAVICINO, *Vita di Alessandro VII.*, I., 302 ; **Poesie in lode d' Innocenzo X.*, in *Ottob.* 2896, Vat. Libr.

him nothing but annoyance and deception.[1] It would, nevertheless, be a mistake to deny to the Pamfili Pope lively appreciation and sound judgment in questions of art.[2] The historian of his pontificate has to chronicle a number of artistic creations, though they cannot stand comparison with the great works that arose under Paul V. and Urban VIII. ; however, even so they compelled the admiration of Evelyn, notwithstanding that traveller's antipapal prejudices.[3] But the decline is unmistakable, its cause being the adverse financial situation as well as the great parsimony of the Pope who considerably reduced the building personnel.[4]

The temporary disgrace of Lorenzo Bernini who, like the learned Felice Contelori,[5] as a protégé of the Barberini, had to reckon with the numerous enemies of that family, falls into the first period of Innocent X.'s reign.   Bernini gave his enemies an opening, for when under Urban VIII. a campanile had been erected over the basilica of St. Peter's, facing towards the Campo Santo, cracks appeared in the façade.   Before taking any action in the matter, Innocent X. was anxious to have the opinion of a number of experts.   One of the first to be asked for his view, in the spring of 1645, was his almoner Virgilio Spada.   The latter's memorandum was favourable to Bernini for Spada declared that the cracks were of a temporary nature and that they were due to the circumstance that the whole structure was not yet fully set.

---

[1] PASSERI, *Vite*, 112. Innocent X.'s exaggerated anxiety on the subject of undraped figures, so greatly in favour just then with many artists, is shown by the circumstance related by MALVASIA (*Felsina*, II., 269) who tells us that the Pope took offence at a nude figure of the child Jesus in a picture by Guercino in his possession ; despite his opposition, Pietro da Cortona was compelled to clothe it.

[2] IUSTI *Velasquez*, II., 168.

[3] *Cf.* C. SEGRÈ, *L'Evelyn a Roma nel 1645*, in *Nuova Antologia*, 1926, April 7.

[4] *Cf.* POLLAK in *Zeitschr. für Gesch. der Architektur*, III. (1910), 208.

[5] BELTRAMI in *Arch. Rom.*, III., 19 *seq.*

The whole matter was then discussed in detail in five sessions of the Congregation of the *Fabbrica* between March 27th, 1645, and February 23rd, 1646. The Pope assisted in person at the second and fourth session. Besides Cardinals and prelates nearly every architect of note was consulted, as, for instance, in addition to Bernini, Borromini, the two Rainaldi, Paolo Marucelli, Martino Lunghi and others. All this shows that Innocent X. was loath to abandon the work of his predecessor, but in the end, at the last session, it was decided to take down the whole of the campanile.[1] A beginning was made in April, 1646.[2] For the rest, Bernini retained his post as architect of St. Peter's but in the artistic commissions of the new Pope, preference was for a time given to his rivals, Borromini, Algardi and Rainaldi.

Bernini did not lose heart during this painful period. How much he trusted in his star is shown by the fact that simultaneously with the famous " Ecstasy of St. Teresa ", executed for Cardinal Cornaro, in S. Maria della Vittoria,[3] he was at work on an allegorical marble group " Time unveils Truth ". As a matter of fact, he succeeded already in the following year in recovering the full favour of the Pope with

[1] RIEGL (in Baldinucci's *Vita* of G. L. Bernini, 132 *seqq.*, 140 *seqq.*) first opened the question in his controversy with Fraschetti (161 *seqq.*) ; EHRLE (*Spada*, 22 *seqq.*) finally cleared it up by drawing on the Acts of the Congregation of the Fabbrica. The sittings of the Congregation were secret, a circumstance that accounts for the inaccuracy of the subjoined *report of the Florentine envoy, dated June 10, 1645 : " Fu tenuta hieri sera avanti il Papa la congregatione della Fabbrica, nella quale fu risoluto di atterrarsi il campanile di S. Pietro, alzato in tempo di Papa Urbano dal cav. Bernini ; e perchè l'aperture che si allargano nella facciata di quella Chiesa, ogni giorno più fanno temere che non basti, si discorrerà a suo tempo, se convenga demolire la facciata. State Archives, Florence.

[2] See Gigli in FRASCHETTI, 163, and the *Avviso* of April 8, 1646, recently published by DENIS (I., 35).

[3] On this work of " unheard of originality " and which was greatly misunderstood by many, see BRINCKMANN, *Barock-skulptur*, II., 240 *seqq.* ; BENKARD, 17 *seqq.*

his splendid plan for the monumental fountain in the Piazza Navona. Innocent soon gave him two further important commissions, namely that of a design for a monumental equestrian statue of the Emperor Constantine for the portico of St. Peter's and the decorations of the pillars of the six chapels in the nave of the basilica. The statue was only begun under Innocent X., but to the decoration of the pillars Bernini was able to devote himself all the more keenly as he had already made preliminary sketches at the time when he incurred the disfavour of the new Pope.[1] His plan in this work has been very diversely appraised. It is impossible to agree unreservedly with the opinion that it is simple and dignified.[2] The colours have not been happily chosen, yellow predominates too much and in particular, when compared with the decoration of the Gregorian and Clementine chapels, the general effect is unsatisfying. On the coloured marble with which he faced the pillars, Bernini affixed medallions held by *putti*. In the upper and lower ones appear the busts of holy Popes, in the middle ones the emblems of the papacy, viz. the tiara and the keys, and at the bottom, in smaller medallions, the dove with an olive branch, which was the Pamfili coat of arms.[3]

Whilst this work was proceeding Bernini's pupils executed the great stucco statues, representing the virtues, which were affixed to the arches of the pilasters of the six lateral chapels of the central nave. The Pope, who took the liveliest interest in the adornment of St. Peter's,[4] replaced the simple columns in the side chapels by 32 Cottanella columns—so

[1] RIEGL, *Baldinucci*, 155 *seqq.*

[2] BÖHN, *Bernini*, 84 ; *cf.* 65.

[3] BONANNI, *Numismata templi Vaticani*, 136, and *tab.* 57 : REYMOND, *Bernini*, 101-4 ; TH. HOFFMANN, *Entstehungsgeschichte von St. Peter* (1928) 282, 287.

[4] As early as February 3, 1647, that is during the period of Bernini's disgrace, it was reported that : " *P. Innocenzo X. si trasferì da Monte Cavallo a S. Pietro per vedere nella chiesa alcuni disegui del nuovo adornamento a pilastri e le figure a stucco nell' archi delle cappelle." Diary in Doria-Pamfili Archives, Rome.

called from a quarry near Castello di Cottanella, in the Sabine province. The splendid tints of these marble columns completed Maderno's architecture but they also modified it profoundly.[1] The Pope also commissioned Giovanni Battista Calandri to adorn the domes of the chapels with mosaics,[2] and he had placed in the interior, before the main entrance of St. Peter's, the circular slab of dark porphyry taken from the old basilica, to which clung so many memories of imperial coronations.[3]

In connexion with this was another work, namely the new mosaic floor of multi-coloured marble of the central aisle, to the designs of Bernini. An inscription of the large coat of arms in the floor states that the work was completed in the jubilee year of 1650.[4] Three years later the floor of the porch and the benediction loggia received a similar marble covering. A colossal inscription by the famous Jesuit Latinist Famiano Strada, which was placed between the inscriptions of Paul V. and Urban VIII. over the interior entrance into the basilica, together with the arms of the Pamfili Pope, informs future ages that the work on St. Peter's was brought to its conclusion by Innocent X.[5] St. Peter's basilica also owes to Innocent X. the erection of a special altar near the Madonna della Colonna for the reception of the relics of St. Leo the Great. This altar, unlike the others, was not adorned with a painting but with a gigantic relief representing the preservation of Rome from Attila by the great Pope.[6]

---

[1] RIEGL, loc. cit., 155 seq.; REYMOND, 105 seq. and Pl. 14. Cf. *Avviso of December 10, 1650, Papal Sec. Arch.

[2] PASSERI, 168.

[3] BONANNI, loc. cit.; MIGNANTI, II., 105.

[4] BONANNI, loc. cit., 137; there also, " ex libris fabricae," a note on the cost; copy in MUÑOZ, Roma, 327. The coat of arms was restored in 1928.

[5] MIGNANTI, II., 105. One medal bears this legend : " Vaticanis sacellis insignitis " (NOVAES, X., 33). The mosaics proposed by G. B. Calandra for St. Peter's failed to please the Pope hence the work was not carried out ; see BELLORI, 168.

[6] MIGNANTI, II., 105 seqq.

The relief was executed by Alessandro Algardi whose artistic activity reached its zenith under Innocent X. He began it in 1646 and with the assistance of his pupils, more especially that of Domenico Guidi, he completed it in the jubilee year of 1650. Passeri and Bellori cannot find words with which to extol the colossal work, yet it is but a " petrified picture ", divided into two sections, in the manner of the school of Bologna and for its effect it depends on the grandeur of its proportions.[1] Innocent X. presented Philip IV. of Spain with a magnificently framed silver copy based on the original model.[2] A comparison of Algardi's relief with Raphael's representation of the same subject in the *Stanze* shows the evolution that had taken place ; the work of the latter displays " effective repose ", that of the Bolognese passionate movement. The theme lent itself admirably to such treatment ; we see the holy Pontiff and the King of the Huns in dramatic contrast ; the one surrounded by his clergy, the other by warriors whose faces reflect in varying fashion the effect of the miraculous intervention of the Princes of the Apostles who are seen floating down from the clouds. The violently agitated figures spread beyond the proper field of the picture. The agitation of the heavenly helpers communicates itself to all : the garments flutter as if caught by the whirlwind.[3]

Innocent X.'s interest in the various works in St. Peter's

---

[1] PASSERI, 203 *seq.*, 207, 211 ;　BELLORI, II., 134 *seq.* *Cf.* BRINCKMANN, *Barockskulptur*, II., 256 *seq.* ;　BERGNER, 106 *seq.*

[2] IUSTI, *Velasquez*, II., 171 ; MUÑOZ, *Roma*, 306 *seq.*

[3] See POSSE in *Jahrb. der preuss. Kunstsamml.*, XXVI. (1905), 200, who, however, draws attention to the absence of skilful concentration of the scene and expresses the opinion that " Algardi had no great sense of the dramatic ". *Cf.* on this point MUÑOZ in *Annuario dell' Accad. di S. Luca*, 1912, Roma, 1913, 51. The model for the Attila relief came into the possession of the Oratorians through Virgilio Spada ; it was placed by them on the great staircase leading into their library. On a model at Dresden see BRINCKMANN, *Barock-Bozzetti*, 112.

was shown by the fact that he repeatedly inspected them [1]
and by his insistence on their completion for the jubilee
year.[2] The necessary funds were taken from the revenues of
the Spanish Cruzada, though part of these was also devoted
to the restoration of the Lateran.[3] Innocent's plans for the
gigantic development of the Piazza of St. Peter's, for which
Carlo Rainaldi furnished the designs, were not carried out.[4]
The Popes had at all times devoted much care to the basilica
of the Lateran, " the Mother and Head of all the churches of
the city and the world," but the decay of a building dating
from the time of Constantine could no more be arrested than
that of old St. Peter's. After the inadequate restoration by
Eugene IV.,[5] both Pius IV.[6] and Clement VIII. carried out
further repairs ; the latter Pope, in fact, completely altered
the transept of the basilica.[7] A similar restoration of the
nave could no longer be put off without risking its collapse.
In consequence of many fires and earthquakes it had been

---

[1] See the *Diario of Deone for February 1647, December, 1648,
and March, 1649 (Doria-Pamfili Archives), and Servantius,
*Diaria, 1649, October 28 (Innocent X. in St. Peter's : " intuitus
est res novas in Basilica peractas et deinde accessit ad videndam
Navicellam iam erectam in conspectu ingressu palatii apostolici"),
December 21 (Innocent X. in St. Peter's : viewed the " circum-
vallatio ante portam sanctam " and gave Bernini the direction
of everything), Papal Sec. Arch. On January 8, 1650, an ordinance
was published against the defilement of St. Peter's by snuff ;
see *Bull. Vat.*, III., 265 ; periodical *Roma*, IV. (1926), 412 *seq.*

[2] A. Contarini in BERCHET, *Relaz.*, Roma, II., 76.

[3] *Bull.*, XV., 674 *seqq.*, and *Nunziat. di Spagna*, 347 (Lettere
al Nunzio), Papal Sec. Arch. Giotto's navicella was given a new
place by Innocent X. ; see CASCIOLI, *La Navicella di Giotto a
S. Pietro*, Roma, 1916, 19. Innocent's arms on the Cantoria
of the Sistine Chapel show that he carried out some repairs
there.

[4] BALDINUCCI, *Rainaldi*, 362 ; HEMPEL, 24 *seq.*

[5] LAUER, 331.

[6] See our data, XIV., 395.

[7] See our data, XXIV., 475.

found necessary to erect a brick wall round all the columns
of the nave, with the exception of four, thus turning them into
octagonal brick pilasters which, linked together by arches,
were made to carry the weight of the high longitudinal walls.[1]
A plan for a complete restoration had been seriously contemplated during the last years of Urban VIII., and in 1647
he had ordered its execution and himself contributed some of
the necessary funds.[2] As supreme supervisor (*sopraintendente*)
of the work of reconstruction Innocent X. appointed his
almoner, Virgilio Spada,[3] who recommended for the restoration
Bernini's rival, Francesco Borromini, born in 1599 at Bissone,
on the Lake of Lugano,[4] and who, in 1648, was likewise
entrusted with the enlargement of the College of Propaganda.[5]
It is not surprising that so convinced and reckless an exponent
of baroque as this architect of genius was, should have planned
from the first a complete reconstruction from floor to ceiling.
Public opinion in Rome supported Borromini and only the
Lateran Chapter advocated, on religious grounds, the preservation of the existing building. Innocent X. shared this view.
It will always be his great merit that he gave orders, at the
time of the restoration of the Lateran basilica, for the

---

[1] See the valuable dissertation of H. Egger : *Fr. Borromini's
Umbau von S. Giovanni in Laterano*, in *Beiträgen zur Kunstgesch.*,
dedicated to F. Wickhoff, Vienna, 1903, 156.

[2] See the **conti* in *Cod.* 31, B 14, p. 187, 262, of the Corsini
Library, Rome. *Cf.* the **Bull.* of March 24, 1647, in *Vat.* 9313,
p. 259 *seqq.*, Vat. Library ; *Bull.*, XV., 675 ; *report of L. Pappus
to Ferdinand III., dated September 26, 1652 (on money from
fines being spent on the Lateran), State Archives, Vienna ;
Miscell. Clementis XI., t. 12, p. 23, Papal Sec. Arch.

[3] Cancellieri, *Mercato*, 52 *seq.* ; Lauer, 332 ; Pollak in
Zeitschr. für Gesch. der Architektur, IV. (1911), 204 ; Guidi,
Borromini, 99. Card. Ehrle has recently written, with his
wonted thoroughness, on Virgilio Spada : *Dalle carte e dai
disegni di V. Spada* (*ob.* 1662), Roma, 1927.

[4] Passeri, 386.

[5] The *documents on the building in Propaganda Archives,
Rome, *Fasc.* 363.

preservation of as much as possible of the old building. Accordingly its proportions remained unaltered and no walls were pulled down ; as many of the supporting pilasters remained as could be preserved as well as the whole of Constantine's eastern façade. The frescoes of Gentile da Fabriano and those of Pisanello had to be sacrificed ; on the other hand it was found possible to spare the wooden coffer ceiling executed under Pius IV. after the plan of Daniele da Volterra.[1] However, owing to the incapacity of the period to conceive the true character of antiquity and to recall it to life, after Borromini's restoration very few features of an old basilica remained.[2] Apart from this it must be granted that the result was an extraordinarily imposing and splendid interior, in the creating of which Borromini revealed his unsurpassed talent as an architect.[3]

In token of their satisfaction, the Canons of the basilica, who had at first feared for the sanctuary, decided to put up a bronze bust of Innocent X.[4] The memory of the Pamfili Pope is likewise kept alive by inscriptions and by the large coat of arms above the interior of the porch.[5]

The reconstruction of the Lateran basilica was carried

---

[1] EGGER, loc. cit., 156 seq. ; DVORAK, Fr. Borromini als Restaurator, in Kunstgesch. Jahrb. der k. k. Zentralkommission für Erforschung u. Erhaltung der Kunst- u. hist. Denkmale, I. (1907), Beibl. für Denkmalpflege, 89 seq. ; K. CASSIRER in Jahrb. der preuss. Kunstsamml., XLII. (1921), 55 seq. ; CIAMPI, 306 ; MAGNI, Il barocco a Roma, I., Torino, 1911, 93.

[2] PLATNER, III., 1, 527. Cf. BRINCKMANN, 83 ; D. FREY, Bramantes St. Peter-Entwurf, Vienna, 1915, 50. A view of the old Lateran basilica previous to Borromini's restoration, ca. 1646, in S. Martino ai Monti is reproduced in LAUER, 330, and in Mél. d'arch., V., 379 seqq. (Pl. 14).

[3] Pollak's opinion in THIEME, IV., 370. Cf. MUÑOZ, Roma, 230 seq., and Borromini, 8.

[4] *Avviso of September 7, 1647, Papal Sec. Arch.

[5] FORCELLA, VIII., 61 seqq. ; GUIDI, Borromini, 60 seqq. (with illustrations).

out with such speed [1] that it was completed, in the main,
by the beginning of the jubilee year of 1650,[2] when the pilgrims
were able to admire the high reliefs between the pilasters,
executed in stucco, after Algardi's designs, but the statues
in the niches and the pictures above them were still missing.[3]
The Pope likewise ordered the restoration of the porch [4] and
that of the precious marble floor ; this work was completed
in 1653.[5] In its execution the principle was adopted of
preserving as much of the ancient material as could be used.
Most of the sepulchral monuments were again put up in the
new basilica [6] : in this way a number of Gothic monuments,
that of Cardinal Antonio de Chiaves, Vignola's monument of
Ranuccio Farnese, and Giotto's famous fresco were preserved.
This remarkable act of piety towards the relics of antiquity
is nevertheless somewhat diminished by the circumstance
that Borromini placed the monuments in flat niches in the
walls : this led to an alteration of their former general aspect

[1] " *con celerità non credibile e senza risparmio alcuno "
we read in the marginal notes to BRUSONI, *Hist. d'Italia*, in the
Doria-Pamfili Archives, 93–46, p. 121. In like manner the *Vita
d'Innocenzo* X., *ibid.* In July, 1649, Innocent X. went to the
Lateran, " per veder la fabrica " (*Deone, in *Cod.* XX., III, 21
of Bibl. Casanat., Rome.

[2] EGGER, *loc. cit.*, 161. *Cf.* also on the work RASPONI, *De basil.
Lateran.*, Romae, 1659, 37, 39 ; CRESCIMBENI, *Stato d. chiesa
Lateran.*, Roma, 1723, 2 (*cf.* 92 on the " ringhiera " round
the baldachino with the heads of the Princes of the Apostles) ;
CIAMPI, 306 ; LAUER, 331 *seq.* ; HEMPEL, *Borromini* (1924),
94 *seq.* ; EHRLE, *Spada*, 15. *Cf.* also MAGNI, *Barocco*, 93.

[3] GUIDI, *Borromini*, 55. *Cf.* FERRARI, *Stucco*, 104 *seq.*

[4] Il " Papa havendo ristorato la chiesa di S. Giovanni Laterano,
ha ordinato che si facci parimente il portico subbito che sarà
passato l'anno santo, nel quale quella fabrica haverebbe dato
troppo impaccio per rispetto della Porta Santa. . . ." *Diario
in *Barb.* 4819, p. 132b, Vat. Library.

[5] *Cod.* 31, B 14, p. 277, of Corsini Library. Inscriptions in
CIACONIUS, IV., 649. *Cf.* ORTOLANI, *S. Giovanni in Laterano*, 36.

[6] Not all ; *cf. L'Arte*, X. (1907), 97.

and some pieces had to be removed altogether. Otherwise they underwent no modification except that they were given a magnificent new frame of a purely decorative character.[1]

Almost simultaneously with the work in St. Peter's and the Lateran, the construction of the two sister churches of the Gesù, viz. S. Andrea della Valle and S. Ignazio, advanced sufficiently to make it possible to open them for worship in the jubilee year of 1650. S. Andrea della Valle, begun in 1591 by order of Cardinal Alessandro Peretti, was continued with the aid of his nephew Francesco.[2] On September 4th, 1650, Cardinal Francesco Peretti was able to consecrate the spacious church of the Theatines [3]; only the façade was missing and this was completed in 1665.[4]

S. Ignazio had been begun by order of Cardinal Ludovisi in 1626. The façade is not by Algardi but probably by Girolamo Rainaldi.[5] Though by no means completed, this imposing church too was opened on August 7th, 1650, amid a mighty concourse of people.[6] On the following day the Pope came to see the church.[7]

In May 1645, Pietro da Cortona began the mosaic decoration

---

[1] DVORACK, *loc. cit.*, 92 *seqq.* Cf. the reproductions in *Jahrb. der preuss. Kunstsamml.*, XLII., 65. On the decoration of the Lateran baptistry, *cf.* ORTOLANI, *loc. cit.*, 104.

[2] A. BONI, *La chiesa di S. Andrea della Valle*, Roma, 1907.

[3] Servantius, **Diaria*, Papal Sec. Arch. ; **Avviso* of September 10 1650, *ibid.* ; AMEYDEN, **Diary*, in *Barb.* 4819 Vat. Libr.

[4] HEMPEL, *Rainaldi*, 55 *seq.*, who was the first to establish the part taken by Rainaldi.

[5] POLLAK, *Algardi* in *Zeitschr. für Gesch. der Architektur*, IV. (1911), 66 *seq.*, who was the first to throw light on the construction of S. Ignazio.

[6] RUGGIERI, *Annisanti*, 177.

[7] Servantius **Diaria*, Papal Sec. Arch., on August 13, 1650, Giovanni Piazza *reports : " Domenica li Padri Gesuiti apersero la loro nuova chiesa di S. Ignatio con grandissimo concorso di popolo, e la sera al 2° vespro vi si trasferì N. S. nella qual occasione la Signora Donna Olimpia pregò tre volte S. S^tà per la licenza di entrare con le dame del suo seguito a vedere il

of the dome and the tribune of the Chiesa Nuova.[1]   In 1652
the learned Luke Wadding had the Cappella Alaleona, at
S. Isidoro, decorated by Carlo Maratta.[2] At this time also the
high altar of S. Nicola da Tolentino was erected after a design
by Algardi : the cost was borne by Camillo Pamfili.[3]   An
extensive restoration was undertaken in 1650 by the General
of the Carmelites in the ancient basilica of S. Martino ai
Monti.[4]   In the same year Martino Lunghi the younger built
for Cardinal Mazarin the façade of SS. Vincent and Anastasius
which he adorned with many columns,[5] and in 1652 he erected
the national church of the Portuguese, S. Antonio, resplendent
with magnificent marbles.   At this time also, through the
generosity of Camilla Farnese, there arose at the foot of the
Janiculus, the beautiful church of the Augustinian Sisters,
Our Lady of the Seven Dolours, after a plan by Borromini [6]
who, in 1654, entered upon the last stage of the erection of
S. Andrea delle Fratte.[7]   This highly gifted master also
designed the spacious oratory adjoining Chiesa Nuova erected

collegio de' Padri, sapendo che gli era stata preparata una nobile
collatione. N. S. non rispose mai, e così la sera li Padri gli man-
darono alla casa quanto havevano provveduto per rallegrarla."
Gonzaga Archives, Mantua.

[1] See Pollak's information based on documents in *Kunstchronik.*, XXIII. (1911–12), 564 *seqq. Cf.* Voss, *Malerei*, 542 *seq.*,
and Strong, *La Chiesa Nuova*, Roma [1923], 115 *seq.*

[2] Lorenzetti, *C. Maratta*, in *L'Arte*, XVII., 147 *seq.*

[3] Pollak, *Algardi, loc. cit.*, 62 *seq.*

[4] Angeli, *Chiese*, 418.

[5] Pascoli, II., 517 ; *Inventario*, I., 53.

[6] Angeli, 53, 390 ; Gurlitt, 401 *seq.* ; Guidi, *Borromini*,
76 *seq.*   Through my intervention the church of S. Maria dei
Sette Dolori, which is most difficult of access in consequence
of the " enclosure ", was opened for O. Pollak, to enable him
to take detailed photographs. The monograph contemplated
by Pollak has been put in jeopardy by the premature death
[1915] of that scholar. Reproduction of the interior in Muñoz,
Roma, 224.

[7] Guidi, 88 *seq.*

by Virgilio Spada.[1] Here were held at one time, besides the daily evening devotions in Advent and Lent, the celebrated religious concerts to which only men were admitted. Finally, Bernini also built the church of St. Agnes in the Piazza Navona of which more will be said when we come to discuss the adjoining family palace of the Pamfili.

Innocent X.'s pontificate is likewise noteworthy by reason of several secular buildings.[2] Improved prisons are one of the achievements of our time. In this respect, as in so many others, the Popes set a good example [3] and even Innocent X.'s enemies are bound to recognize his good work in this field.[4] Besides Castel S. Angelo there were other prisons in Rome, such as those of the Borgo, the Senate, Tor di Nona on the

---

[1] P. MISCIATELLI in the periodical S. Filippo Neri, 1921, No. 1 ; STRONG, loc. cit., 143 seqq., and especially GUIDI, loc. cit., 31 seq.

[2] The Porta Portese was completed under Innocent X. ; he also repaired the city walls (cf. CIAMPI, 308 seqq. ; NIBBY, Mura di Roma, 340, 375 ; Inventario, I., 254 ; BORGATTI in Riv. di Artigleria, XVI., 386), but stopped work on Urban VIII.'s fortifications (cf. BERCHET, Relaz., Roma, II., 76), whilst on the other hand he repaired Castel S. Angelo (cf. FORCELLA, XIII., 150). Innocent's arms on the right of Ponte Nomentano also recall a restoration. An inscription on the cathedral of Frascati proclaims the fact that its erection was begun under that Pontiff ; at Viterbo the Pope's memory is kept alive by the Porta Romana with its statue of St. Rose, the patron saint of the town ; and at Ravenna by the Porta Nuova (ampliata, 1653, for that reason also described as Porta Pamfilia ; cf. CIACONIUS, IV., 651 ; KEYSSLER, II., 470 ; RICCI, Baukunst der Barockzeit, Stuttgart, 1912, 205). A most useful work was the construction of the Canale Pamfili to link Ravenna with the sea (CIAMPI, 309). At Ancona Innocent XI. saw to the restoration of the fortifications (CIACONIUS, loc. cit., and *Cod. 31, B 14, p. 243 seq. Corsini Library, Rome).

[3] Particularly in earlier times, by promoting the guilds which provided for the bodily and spiritual wants of prisoners. Cf. PLATNER, III., 3, 414.

[4] CIAMPI, 312 ; CHLEDOWSKI, II., 245.

Tiber, where the Apollo theatre was subsequently erected, and that of the Corte Savella, for the ancient family of the Savelli, besides other privileges, such as that of the dignity of Marshal to the Conclave, also enjoyed that of exercising penal jurisdiction for minor delinquencies ; hence they also had their own prison in the Via di Monserrato, near the English College.[1] These prisons were typically medieval, narrow and damp. Even at this day the inscription which Innocent X. ordered to be placed above the entrance of the new prison erected by him (*Carceri Nuovi*) sounds like a protest against the insanitary conditions and other serious evils of the Corte Savella : " Justitiæ et clementiæ, securiori ac mitiori reorum custodiæ, novum Carcerem Innocentius X. Pont. Max. posuit, Anno Domini MDCLV "—For the sake of justice and clemency and for the safer and milder custody of the guilty, Pope Innocent X. erected this new prison in 1655.[2]

Innocent X. withdrew from the Savelli their judicial powers.[3] To replace the inadequate and insanitary prisons of Corte Savella and Tor di Nona, a new and practical building arose in the Via Giulia, not far from Sangallo's Palazzo Sacchetti. Here, for the first time in Europe, the modern system of cells was introduced ; this was an immense advance on a prison system which was maintained for years to come in other places—one need only think of the famous prisons of Venice. The erection of the " New Prison ", for which the Pope furnished the funds, began in the spring of 1652 and was

[1] MORONI, IX., 266 *seq.* ; EHRLE, *Spada*, 12, who establishes the position of the Corte Savella on the basis of TEMPESTA's *Topografia* of 1593, published by H. Schück, at Upsala, 1917.

[2] FORCELLA, XIII., 132. An ordinance providing for adequate food for the prisoners was issued in 1653 ; BERTOLOTTI, *Le prigioni di Roma nei secoli*, XVI., XVII. e XVIII., Roma, 1890, 33.

[3] *1652, Settembro 22 : " Si serrano le carceri di casa Savelli e finivano li Savelli la loro giurisdittione in quel tribunale " (Diary in Doria-Pamfili Archives). *Cf.* MORONI, IX., 267 ; RATTI, *Sforza*, II., 243.

finished in 1655 under Alexander VII.[1] It is a model of practical architecture and depends for its effect exclusively on the material employed (red bricks with roughly dressed travertine), the distribution of doors and windows and the wide, recessed space which terminates the façade, above which rises the last story like an immense attic. The small gateway, with its broad, simple frame which narrows as it rises, heightens the stern character of the building.[2] The architect was Antonio del Grande, who had already given proof of his skill in the reconstruction of the Spanish Embassy in the Piazza di Spagna. In 1654 he began work on the wing of the Palazzo Colonna, which faces the Via Nazionale and houses the celebrated Calleria Grande on the ground floor.[3]

The palace on the Capitol, which in Michelangelo's plan was meant to form a counterpart to the palace of the Conservators and a museum of the antique sculptures of the City of Rome, also heralded a new epoch. The foundations were laid by Clement VIII [4]; in 1644 Innocent X. gave orders for the continuation of the building, in the great hall of which his coat of arms is still to be seen. Since there was question of a civic building, the City Council was made to bear the cost. The methods used for raising the necessary funds for the work by temporarily discharging officials and other similar measures, caused a good deal of bad blood. Carlo Rainaldi was the architect in charge.[5] The Pope took a lively interest in the building and repeatedly inspected it [in 1650 and 1654],[6] in memory whereof the Roman Senate put

---

[1] O. POLLAK, *Antonio del Grande*, in *Kunstgeschichtl. Jahrb, der K. K. Zentralkommission für Kunst.- u. hist. Denkmale*, 1909, 135 *seqq*. *Cf.* E. ROSSI in the periodical *Roma*, IV. (1926), 70 ; EHRLE, *Spada*, 11 *seq*.

[2] POLLAK, *loc. cit.*

[3] *Ibid.*, 137 *seqq.*, 152 *seq*.

[4] See our data, XXIV., 513 ; Gigli in CANCELLIERI, *Mercato*, 53; PASSERI, 222.

[5] RODOCANACHI, *Capitole*, 126 ; HEMPEL, *Rainaldi*, 94 *seq*.

[6] CANCELLIERI, *loc. cit.*, 53, n. 1.—*October 3, 1645 : " Fu levata la statua di Marforio per causa della nuova fabrica e

up a more than life-size statue of Innocent X. in the great hall of the palace of the Conservators, facing Bernini's statue of Urban VIII. The commission for the statue was given to Alessandro Algardi who, for a time, eclipsed Bernini. But his statue does not compare favourably with that of the Barberini Pope. Innocent's head is after Velasquez' painting, "the most living of contemporary portraits, but precisely the most impressive feature in the Spanish master's portrait, namely, the piercing glance which was peculiar to Innocent X., is missing in the statue," because Algardi, in order to avoid a too marked resemblance with the statue of Urban VIII., gives a side view of the Pope's face, in fact the whole artistic treatment is such as to place Algardi's work beneath that of his gifted rival.[1] He nevertheless remained the real court

posta nella piazza vicina al cavallo di bronzo per modo di provisione " (Diary in Doria-Pamfili Archives). *Ibid.*, May 9, 1647 : " Si fu accorto come la statua del cavallo di bronzo di Marco Aurelio, che sta alla piazza di Campidoglio, pendeva assai verso la chiesa d'Araceli, e la causa fu perchè si era lograto di ruzza il ferro del perno impiantato nel piede manco dietro, si che li sig. conservatori ordinando subito fosse puntellato con diligenza e fattone consapevole S. Stà ordinando a Msgr. Cessi fosse subito accomodato come fu fatto e messovi mano." May 15 : " Furono levati li puntelli della statua del cavallo di bronzo per esser stato di nuovo ricoperto di bronzo e reimbiombato e messi nuovi tasselli di marmo."

[1] Thus Posse (in *Jahrb. der preuss. Kunstsamml.*, XXVI., 193), whereas Muñoz (in Annuario dell' Accad. di S. Luca, 1912, Roma, 1913, 51 *seq.*) assigns the victory to Algardi. The statue was unveiled on March 9, 1650 (*cf.* Ruggieri, *Anni santi*, 61 *seq.*) ; a decision to that effect had been arrived at in March 1645 (*cf.* Rodocanachi, *Capitole*, 131). The following item in Deone's Diary for September 4, 1645, shows how the authorities managed in the meantime : " *Fu scavata la statua fatta far per papa Paolo IV., ch'era sotterrata nel cortile de' conservatori per ordine di P. Innocenzo X., quale essendo di buona maniera e fatta da valent'huomo serviva per la statua di S. Bne per metterla nel palazzo nuovo " (Doria-Pamfili Archives). *Cf.* Fraschetti,

sculptor of the Pamfili. It was he who created the realistic busts of the Pope for the palace of the Gonfaloniere at Bologna and the dining hall of Trinità de' Pellegrini, as well as that of Innocent X.'s brother, Benedetto, and that of Olimpia Maidalchini in the Doria Gallery, with its energetic features of the masterful head which stands out so effectively from the voluminous widows' veil.[1] In 1649, the year in which Algardi finished his tomb of Leo XI.[2] for St. Peter's, he was given a commission for the architectural fountain with the water-spouting dolphins and the relief on the face of the basin, with which Innocent X. adorned the Cortile of St. Damaso in the Vatican.[3] For the church of St. Agnes he designed a relief representing the martyrdom of the Saint.[4] The premature death of the artist (June 10th, 1654) is said to have drawn tears from the Pope whilst Camillo Pamfili, Algardi's special patron, paid him the honour of a visit as he lay dying.[5]

The large share which Algardi had in the laying out of the great park which the Cardinal nephew, Camillo Pamfili, created before the Porta S. Pancrazio, has only been established in recent times.[6]

154; STEINMANN, *Die Statuen der Päpste auf dem Kapitol*, Rome, 1924, 15 *seqq.*

[1] BELLORI, II., 139; POSSE, *loc. cit.*, 194. *Cf.* above, p. 33.

[2] *Cf.* BRINCKMANN, *Barockskulptur*, II. 255 *seq.*

[3] POLLAK, *Algardi*, in *Zeitschr. für Gesch. der Architektur*, IV. (1911), 61 *seqq.*; POSSE, *loc. cit.*, 194; MUÑOZ, *loc. cit.*, 54 *seq.*; COLASANTI, *Fontane d' Italia* (1926), 203.

[4] It found a place in the crypt. Algardi has given different presentations of the same scene; *cf.* TIETZE, *Ein Bronzerelief Algardi's* in *Kunstchronik*, 1923, No. 26-7, p. 523.

[5] BELLORI, II., 141; CANCELLIERI, *Mercato*, 113. L. Frati (*Varietà storiche artistiche, Città di Castello*, 1912) has published Algardi's will. Frati fixes 1595 as the year of Algardi's birth, instead of 1602, as has been thought up till now.

[6] Castel Gandolfo continued to be the Pope's usual holiday resort. Innocent X.'s throne is still preserved in the castle there, as well as five magnificent gobelins (The Flight to Egypt) made by order of the Pope.

In consequence of the destruction of the Villa Ludovisi and
since the Villa Borghese has become increasingly degraded
into a place of popular amusement, the Villa Pamfili, even
though it has not been spared drastic alterations, alone
conveys an idea, even at this day, of the superb Villas with
which the papal nephews of the baroque period surrounded
the Eternal City. Situate on the summit of the Janiculus,
on its western scarp, it has been rightly named by the Romans
" Belrespiro " owing to the pure, invigorating air which
prevails there even during the hottest months.[1] The terrain,
which is crossed by the ancient Via Aurelia,[2] is even more
extensive and more varied than that of the Villa Borghese
as well as exceedingly picturesque.[3]

The main entrance [4] led to a long alley with an
incomparable vista of the Vatican and the dome of St. Peter's
which appears isolated like some great shrine between green
hills. There is no other hint of the nearness of the metropolis ;
the visitor has a feeling of being in a vast solitude dominated
on the north by the purple outlines of Soracte. Here the aged
Pope was wont to seek quiet and refreshment amid his cares
and anxieties. Near the north entrance of the almost hidden
summer house, a magnificent park, divided into two sections,
stretches far away to the west. In the northern section
the characteristics of a pleasure garden were specially marked.
First there came a wide, open space which no doubt then, as
now, served as a playground. Then came copses and
orange groves adorned with a fountain and statues. Here,

---

[1] This name is already found in N. A. CAFERRIUS, *Synthema
vetustatis sive flores historiarum*, Romae, 1667.

[2] TOMASSETTI, *Campagna*, II., 466.

[3] For what follows, *cf.* above all GOTHEIN, I., 353 *seq.* See
also NOHL, *Skizzenbuch*, 175 *seq.*, 182 ; WÖLFFLIN, *Renaissance*,
177 ; GURLITT, 403 *seq.* ; BERGNER, 64 *seq.* ; V. GERSTFELDT-
STEINMANN, *Pilgerfahrten in Italien*,[4] Leipzig, 1922, 357 ;
L. DAMI, *Il giardino d'Italia*, Milano, 1924, 42, CXCIII. *seqq.* ;
COLASANTI, *loc. cit.*, 205, 207, 209.

[4] The section from the present entrance as far as " the valley
of the deer " was only added in the nineteenth century.

as in the Villa Borghese, a smaller *Casino di famiglia* stood against the wall of the terrace of the belvedere. The southern section was renowned for its pine wood. Adjoining this wood there was, as in the Villa Borghese, an extensive zoological garden with woods and meadows which, in spring, were studded with anemones. The central point was formed by an oval basin in a little dell which was subsequently transformed into a natural lake which provided an enchanting spectacle in June with its water-lilies. Following a fold in the valley, a canal, starting from this spot, cuts a straight line across the pine wood and ends in an aquatic amphitheatre above which rises a rotunda adorned with statues and a lily-shaped fountain. This artistic creation is so peculiar that some have thought it to be due to French inspiration.[1]

The summer-house in the north-eastern corner of the Villa stands on uneven ground, hence on the northern entrance there are two stories whilst on the south side, facing the garden, there are three. A pavilion rises from the terrace of the roof. Like the Villa Pia, the building is richly adorned with antique and modern sculptures. On either side open-air steps lead into the ornamental garden (*giardino segreto*), surrounded by a wall broken by niches and adorned with fruit-trees and statues. Flower-beds and fountains and flower-pots on the balustrades all around heighten the splendid and imposing impression. The beds of the *parterre* show a pattern of box arabesques filled-in with flowers—a floral tapestry of Italian invention.[2] From the *giardino segreto* two sets of steps lead to a garden at a yet lower level, adorned with flower-beds, fountains, copses and a very pretty theatre. A nymphæum stands between the steps, the so-called " Fountain of Venus " by Algardi.[3]

[1] GOTHEIN, I., 356. It is a mere legend that Le Nôtre designed the garden.

[2] *Cf. ibid.*, 354.

[3] BELLORI, II., 133 *seq.* ; POLLAK, *A. Algardi als Architekt,* in *Zeitschr. f. Gesch. der Architektur*, IV. (1911), 53 *seq.*, with numerous illustrations. *Cf.* also BRINCKMANN, *Baukunst, 7 seqq.,* and *Barockskulptur*, II., 255.

The progress of the construction can be accurately gauged by examining the account books. It was begun in the last months of 1644, and thereafter the Pope pressed for the prosecution of the work.[1] In the autumn of 1646 it became possible to begin the internal decoration. The ground floor received magnificent stucco ceilings, besides pictorial decorations of which, unfortunately, but little remains. The summer-house was finished in the beginning of 1648. Later payments of the years 1648 and 1649 concern fountains and other mason's work in the garden which was completed in 1651.[2] In 1653 the engraver, Dominique Barrière, began work on copper plates of the Villa and the antique statues. These engravings, together with some others by Falda, were gathered in a work appropriately entitled *Villa Pamphilia*.[3] The account books also supply information on Algardi's share in these splendid undertakings. It was he who procured the antique statues and restored them, designed the magnificent stucco ceilings of the ground floor and superintended the sculptural decorations of the Villa. However, the real architect was Francesco Grimaldi.[4] It is due to him that notwithstanding the great wealth of antique reliefs and busts, of stucco decoration and other charming details, the exterior of the summer-house gives an impression of simplicity and monotony, as was already felt by his contemporaries.[5] The most valuable ornaments were within, but the statues and pictures were removed to the Palazzo Doria at a later date ; however, some frescoes and the stucco ceilings of the ground floor remain to this day ; they bear witness to a profound study of antique models in the Villa Adriana and as regards their

---

[1] *Avviso* of March 7, 1646, Papal Sec. Arch.

[2] POLLAK, *loc. cit.*, who was the first to draw on the Doria-Pamfili Archives.

[3] *Villa Pamphilia eiusque Palatium cum suis prospectibus, statuae, fontes, vivaria, theatra, arcolae plantarum viarumque ordines, Romae* (*sine anno*). *Cf.* POLLAK, 56.

[4] POLLAK (57 *seqq.*) has proved this up to the hilt.

[5] PASSERI, 202.

quality, they belong to the very best Roman products of the kind in the 17th century.[1]

Even more than by the Villa Pamfili, Innocent X.'s name is kept alive in Rome by the large scale works undertaken by him in the Piazza Navona.[2] It goes without saying that the modest palace in the Piazza of that name which he had owned as a Cardinal, was enlarged after his elevation. For this purpose many adjoining houses were bought one after another and their demolition led to the discovery of a number of travertine pilasters and tiers of seats of Domitian's stadium.[3] The building turned out a somewhat plain one ; the architect was Girolamo Rainaldi, father of Carlo.[4] The Pope gave orders for the preservation, during alterations, of the paintings executed by his command by Agostino Tassi, a pupil of Paul Bril.[5] The work was pushed on with so much energy that it was hoped that the new palace might be occupied by the summer of 1646,[6] but it only approached completion in July 1648.[7]

[1] Opinion of POLLAK (*loc. cit.*, 60), who gives illustrations of two stucco soffits. *Cf.* BELLORI, II., 131 ; MUÑOZ in *Annuario dell' Accad. di S. Luca*, 1912, 56.

[2] See *Scritture concernenti le fabriche fatte nel pontificato d'Innocenzo X.* in Cod. 31, B 14, 15, and 16, of Corsini Library. *Cf.* CIAMPI, 397 *seqq.*, to which must be added the *documents in the Doria-Pamfili Archives of which Pollak intended to publish a considerable selection.

[3] CANCELLIERI, *Mercato*, 99 ; EHRLE, *Spada*, 15 *seq.* ; a *specialized list of *Acquisiti delle case che occupavano il posto del moderno palazzo in Piazza Navona*, in Doria-Pamfili Archives.

[4] PASSERI, 221 ; CANCELLIERI, *loc. cit.*, 100 ; L. DE GREGORI (see below, p. 402, n. 4), 33 *seq. Cf.* GURLITT, 381 ; BRINCKMANN, *Baukunst*, 92 *seq.*, 121.

[5] PASSERI, III. On A. Tassi, *cf.* BERTOLOTTI, *A. Tassi*, Perugia, 1877 ; GERSTENBERG, *Die ideale Landschaftsmalerei*, Halle, 1923, 88 *seq.*

[6] " Il Palazzo di Piazza Navona si tira avanti con molta diligenza et per tutta l'estate potrà esser finito." *Avviso* of March 7, 1646, Papal Sec. Arch.

[7] EHRLE, *Spada*, 16.

A number of painters were engaged on the internal decoration as, for instance, Pietro da Cortona, Giovanni Francesco Romanelli, Ciro Ferri, Andrea Camassei, Gaspard Poussin, who adorned the buildings with landscapes and scenes from Roman history. Francesco Allegrini painted biblical scenes on the soffits. Special admiration was called forth by Pietro da Cortona's scenes from Virgil's Aeneid in the long gallery. The choice of these subjects was inspired by the circumstance that the dove (which the Pamfili carried in their coat of arms), was the bird of Venus, Aeneas' mother. The most famous scene was that of Neptune chiding the winds ; for this picture the artist was rewarded with a poem by Battistini. Venus' visit to Vulcan's forge also found many admirers. For the pictures on the ceilings Cortona sought inspiration in the works of Ovid and Homer.[1] These frescoes were completed in 1654 and drawings made from them were sent to Flanders as models for tapestries,[2] whilst Carlo Cesi of Rieti made engravings of them.[3]

Closely connected with the erection of the palace was the correction of the Piazza Navona.[4] The Palazzo Aldobrandini, near S. Giacomo, which protruded too much into the piazza, was demolished [5] ; by this means the lines of the ancient stadium of Domitian were once more clearly revealed. For the centre of the piazza, a monumental fountain was to replace the existing one—a very simple one. The Pope gave

[1] CANCELLIERI, loc. cit., 102 seqq. ; FABRINI, Vita del caval. Pietro Berretini, Cortona, 1896, 102 seqq. ; VOSS, Malerei, 543 seq., 554 ; MUÑOZ, Pietro da Cortona, 10 ; M. LENZI in periodical Roma, V. (1927), 495 seq. Cf. the payments given by Pollack in Kunschronik, XXIII. (1911/12), 564 seq.

[2] CERROTI, Lettere di artisti tratte dai manoscritti d. Corsiniana, Roma, 1860, 10 seq.

[3] FABBRINI, loc. cit., 113.

[4] A view of the piazza before the alterations in P. TOTTI, Ritratto di Roma moderna (1639), 232. Cf. the excellent study by L. de Gregori : Piazza Navona prima d'Innocenzo X., Roma, 1926.

[5] Cf. Spicil. Vat., I., 117.

orders for the embodiment in the new fountain of an obelisk
of red granite of the time of the Emperor Domitian which
lay in several pieces in the *circus* of Maxentius, on the Via
Appia.   The learned Jesuit Athanasius Kircher made vain
attempts to decipher the hieroglyphs of the obelisk.[1]
Innocent X. intended to entrust the erection of the
monumental fountain in the Piazza Navona to Bernini's
rival Borromini, but the latter's design failed to please him.
Prince Nicolò Ludovisi, who had married a niece of
Innocent X., informed Bernini of the circumstance and
urged him to construct in secret a model of the proposed
work. Bernini fell in with the suggestion and the Prince so
arranged things that the Pope unexpectedly found himself
in presence of the model. On Lady Day, 1647, Innocent X.
had gone to the Minerva according to custom for the purpose
of distributing dowries to poor girls. Afterwards he repaired
to the Palazzo Pamfili.   After breakfast, Cardinal Pamfili
and Donna Olimpia escorted him through the room in which
the model stood.   The bold conception and the brilliant
execution of the design profoundly impressed the Pope. It is
said that at the end of half an hour's examination he
exclaimed : " We must give Bernini another commission,
despite the objections of his opponents : people who do not
want his works must not allow them to be brought to their
notice." [2]

Bernini was at once sent for and commissioned to carry out
the model. Thus a decisive hour of his life had struck : he
had recovered the papal favour.   Evil tongues spread the
rumour in Rome that besides the clay model, the artist had
had another made of solid silver which he had presented to the
all powerful Olimpia.[3] However, there was no need of such

---

[1] KIRCHER, *Obeliscus Pamphilius*, Romae, 1650, and *Œdippus
ægyptiacus*, 4 vols., *ibid.*, 1632-1654. *Cf* .CANCELLIERI, *Mercato*,
42 *seqq.* ; MARUCCHI, *Gli obelischi Egiziani di Roma*, Roma, 1898,
129 *seq.* ; SEURINGER, *Die Obelisken Roms*, Augsburg, 1925,
37 *seq.*

[2] *Baldinucci*, edit. RIEGL, 147 ; FRASCHETTI, 180.

[3] FRASCHETTI, *loc. cit.*

shifts to win over a connoisseur like Innocent X. Bernini had already given proofs of his mastery by his plans of fountains under Urban VIII.[1] On this occasion also he solved in superlatively brilliant fashion the difficult problem of connecting an obelisk with a fountain. But the task had not been an easy one. Some of his preliminary sketches, which have been preserved, show how he wrestled with the problem. The essential idea, that of an obelisk rising from a rock pierced by caverns, appears already in one of the earliest drawings in which armorial shields held by aquatic divinities form the link between the rock and the immense stone colossus. Another drawing, preserved at Windsor, carries this idea a step further ; here the figures of the river gods are seated at the corners ; under each of them is a fancifully modelled shell-shaped basin supported by water-spouting dolphins. In the end Bernini rejected this artificial composition ; the idea of a grotto, which was only hinted at in the earlier designs, is once more clearly emphasized in the model of the Casa Giocondi. The work was carried out according to a uniform plan in which the worlds' four great rivers were given a predominating expression.[2] To this end the river gods were executed in marble so as to form a strong and picturesque contrast to the warm tone of the cream coloured travertine employed in the construction of the grotto.[3]

This cave, situate in the centre of a circular basin enlivened by the figures of two fishes and lying a little below the level of the piazza, consists of enormous travertine blocks and is pierced on four sides. It is similarly divided into four parts at the bottom and contains the giant figures of the chief rivers of the then known four parts of the world. The Nile, the personification of Africa, veils his head to signify the obscurity which then shrouded his sources. In his right hand he holds a shell adorned with Innocent X.'s coat of arms ; to his left rises a palm-tree and a lion issues, roaring, from the grotto.

[1] *Cf.* our data, XXIX., 512.

[2] H. Voss in *Jahrb. der preuss. Kunstsamml.*, XXXI., 110.

[3] BENKARD (22) in particular draws attention to this picturesque effect. See also Muñoz, Bernini, 18 *seq.*

The Danube (Europe) leans back and looks with amazement at the obelisk ; by its side a rose grows out of a cleft in the rock. The Ganges (Asia) holds a long oar in its right hand.[1] The Rio de la Plata (America) is represented as a Moor ; by his side there are some cactuses and a number of coins symbolizing the metal wealth of the new world, and a fanciful monster.

On the summit of the rock, down whose flanks rush the waters of the Acqua Vergine, the slim, reddish obelisk rises securely and gracefully, its tip crowned with a resplendent metal cross and the Pamfili dove. Work on this grandiose scheme began in 1647. In August 1648, the obelisk was in its place. The undertaking proved as difficult as it was costly. The people began to grumble, all the more so as a fresh tax had been imposed to meet expenditure. In June 1651, the work was completed. It was still covered up when the Pope came to inspect it on the evening of June 8th. Four days later the water was turned on and the covering removed.[2] The supreme direction of the work had been in the hands of Bernini who left the execution of the figures to his pupils. They, as appears from the terracottas in the archæological museum in Venice, strictly followed the plastic models of the master. Francesco Barrata executed the figure of the Rio de la Plata, Claudio Porissimi the Ganges, Antonio Raggi the Danube and Giacomo Antonio Fancelli the Nile.[3]

The boldness of the mighty work, its majestic movement, the masterly combination of rock and water, make it impossible for the visitor to Rome ever to forget the fountain of the four rivers. With it Bernini created a new type ; here the characteristics of the element of water and its mysterious powers were for the first time given plastic expression.[4]

[1] This is now missing.

[2] See *Gigli* in CANCELLIERI, *Mercato*, 59 ; *Arch. Rom.*, II., 259.

[3] FRASCHETTI, 180 *seq.* ; VOSS, *loc. cit.*, 111 *seq.*

[4] VOSS, *loc. cit.*, 129. *Cf.* BRINCKMANN, *Barockskulptur*, II., 244 *seq.* ; BENKARD, 21 *seq.* ; W. WEISBACH, *Die Kunst des Barock in Italien*, Berlin, 1924, 31 ; FRIEDLÄNDER, *Röm. Barockbrunnen*, Leipzig, 1922, 9.

The genius of the master is likewise revealed by the exceedingly happy manner in which he correlated the fountain with its surroundings. " From whatever angle one looks at it, it presents a complete picture ; from whatever point one views it, the beholder is impressed by the grandeur of the design which, with the utmost boldness, as it were, raises the heavy mass of the obelisk into the sky above the everlasting play of the waters." [1]

The full effect of the masterpiece was especially felt on the occasion of the peculiar spectacle which, after 1652,[2] was wont to take place in the Piazza Navona during the heat of August. By stopping the pipes which carried away the water, the whole piazza was flooded. Whilst the people paddled to cool themselves, the gentry, instead of driving in the Corso, drove round the fountain, which as a matter of fact, was the centre of all the many public festivities which used to be held in this magnificent piazza. Probably no fountain in the world has enjoyed the same popularity as that of the four rivers. From the first, legends were woven around it, and charming anecdotes became connected with it. Thus it was said that on the occasion of its unveiling the Pope asked Bernini with some irony : " Is that all ? We have come to inspect a fountain, but we can see no water." Thereupon the master pleaded that the monument was still unfinished, but as the Pope was about to leave, he had the taps opened when, amid general admiration, the water began to spout and to gush forth on all sides.[3] Another legend is to the effect that Bernini's enemies having spread the rumour that the obelisk threatened to collapse, the master mingled with the populace and, in order to calm the critics for whom the catastrophe was too slow in coming, he had the

[1] BÖHN, *Benini*, 82.

[2] CIAMPI, 304. The popular rejoicings only fell into desuetude in the 'sixties of the 19th century. Old illustration in MUÑOZ, *Roma*, 322.

[3] See *Baldinucci*, edit. RIEGL, 154 *seq.* ; A. CASSIO, *Corso dell' Acque antiche*, I., Roma, 1756, 299.

obelisk fastened by thin threads to the neighbouring houses. Everybody laughed and Bernini left amid the acclamations of the crowd.[1] The symbolism of the fountain also provided matter for ironical comments ; thus it was said that the Nile veiled his head so as not to be obliged to look at Borromini's façade of the church of St. Agnes.[2]

Innocent X. had four inscriptions placed on the fountain. A medal was also struck and he forbade the disfigurement of the piazza by traders' stalls.[3] The inscription on the north side shows the survival of Sixtus V.'s idea of making the monuments of paganism subservient to Christianity.[4] It gives the following explanation of the symbolism of the dove and the cross on top of the monument : " Above Egyptian monsters (supposed to be represented by the hiero-glyphs), the guileless dove is enthroned (viz. true religion crushes superstition) ; with the olive-branch in its beak, and crowned with the lilies of the virtues,[5] it makes of the obelisk the symbol of its victory and triumph in Rome." [6] The Pope made the artist a gift of 5,000 scudi, and to his eldest son he granted a canonry at St. Peter's.[7] In 1650, he commissioned the artist to erect another family palace on the site of an antique theatre on Monte Citorio, but that building never got beyond the second story.[8]

How greatly Bernini's fame was enhanced by the fountain

---

[1] See D. Bernini in CANCELLIERI, *Mercato*, 41 ; *cf.* A. VALLE, *Una leggenda intorno alla fontana dei quattro fiumi in Piazza Navona*, Roma, 1913.

[2] The fountain was completed by 1651, whereas Borromini only undertook the erection of S. Agnese in 1653.

[3] CANCELLIERI, 44 *seq.*, 59, where there are details on the many poems occasioned by the fountain ; *cf.* also CIAMPI, 301 *seq.* ; GUIDI, *Fontane*, 77.

[4] *Cf.* our data, Vol. XXII., 240.

[5] Innocent X.'s arms show three lilies above a dove.

[6] CIACONIUS, IV., 650 ; EURINGER, *Die Obelisken Roms*, 40.

[7] See SAGGIATORE, 1844, No. 1, p. 383.

[8] FRASCHETTI, *L'esposizione Berniniana a Roma*, Roma, 1899, 12 *seq.* *Cf.* W. WEISBACH, *Kunst des Barock*, 28.

of the four rivers appears from the numerous poems it inspired at the time.[1] Someone even wrote a comedy in honour of the Pamfili and the artist. Everybody admired the fountain ; by it Bernini had made himself famous for all time, it was said.[2] " The fountain is one of the finest artistic creations in Europe," a Frenchman wrote immediately after its unveiling.[3] It has inspired a number of artists, especially French ones, as well as, at a later date, the German Schlüter's creation of the four slaves on his monument of the Grand Elector in Berlin. The latest adaption of the idea may be seen in the groups of statuary in the gardens of Versailles, Caserta, Aranjuez and Schönbrunn.[4]

When it was decided to reconstruct Gregory XIII.'s fountain opposite the Pamfili palace, it was natural to employ Bernini. He retained the existing structure, but placed in the centre the figure of a marine god holding a water-spouting dolphin. The fact that, as in the personification of Africa on the fountain of the four rivers, he gave the figure the features of a negro, was probably inspired by the reports of foreign missionaries which were very popular reading in Rome just then. The " Moro " was executed by Giovan Antonio Mari.[5]

In order to enhance the harmony and the character of the Piazza Navona,[6] Innocent X. resolved to replace by a new building the old church of St. Agnes which was hidden by houses. He also thought of transferring the fair to another locality, and of concentrating in this most centrally situated

---

[1] See above, p. 407, n. 3, and M. MENGHINI, *Le lodi e grandezze della Aguglia e Fontana di Piazza Navona. Canzonetta di Fr. Ascione* (1657), published for Nozze-Cian-Sappa-Flandinet, 1894.

[2] *Cf. Spicil. Vat.*, I., 118.

[3] DENIS, I., 263 ; *cf.* Cassiano del Pozzo's opinion in *Miscell. di stor. ital.*, XV. (1875), 194.

[4] GUIDI, *Fontane*, 78, and VOSS, *loc. cit.*, 112, also draw attention to the direct but stiff and unintelligent imitation on the Columna del Triunfo at Córdoba (1765–1781).

[5] CIAMPI, 305 ; FRASCHETTI, 201 *seq.* ; VOSS, *loc. cit.*, 124 *seq.* ; GUIDI, *Fontane*, 78 *seqq.*

[6] BRINCKMANN, *Platz und Monument*, Berlin, 1923, 92.

square the offices of the notaries and *cursori* who, until then, had been scattered all over the city, to the great inconvenience of the public.[1]

The new sacred edifice was intended to serve as a family church,[2] like the one the Borghese possessed in the Capella Paolina at St. Mary Major. Here the Pope wished to have his last resting place. A rotunda seemed to recommend itself for this purpose, all the more so as such a structure would best harmonize with the lines of the piazza.

On August 15th, 1652, Cardinal Giovan Battista Pamfili laid the foundation stone of the church of St. Agnes on which Girolamo Rainaldi and his son Carlo worked for a period of one year. The supreme direction was in the hands of the nephew Camillo Pamfili, who instructed Rainaldi to construct a flight of steps of such size as would have disfigured the whole piazza. The Pope noticed this on SS. Peter and Paul's day, 1653. He took the nephew severely to task over it, and both he and Rainaldi were dismissed from their posts of superintendents of the construction, which was thereafter entrusted to Borromini. The work was vigorously pushed forward up to the Pope's death, but it was only completed in the seventies of that century.[3]

---

[1] This appears from a memorial of Propaganda to Innocent X. in 1652, Propaganda Archives, 363, p. 65.

[2] For this reason the cardinalitial title was transferred to S. Agnese fuori le Mura on October 5, 1654.

[3] CANCELLIERI, *Mercato*, 109 *seqq.*, 111, 113 ; HEMPEL, *Rainaldi*, 29 *seq*. DE ROSSI reports (*Istoria*, Vat. 8873, p. 115 *seqq.*, Vat. Libr.) : " Passò dunque [il Papa], come dicemmo, e vidde con ammirazione che i cimenti della fabrica, secondo il disegno datone dal cav. Carlo Raynaldi, si estendevano in occupare non poco spazio di Piazza Navona. Sua S^{tà} che per render questa più ampia e disbrigata, haveva già fatto buttare a terra le case contigue a S. Jacopo de' Spagnuoli, et oltre al nobile edificio dell'istesso palazzo riceveva la Piazza Navona abbellimento si grande della bellissima guglia e fontana fattevi collocare, quando vidde la sproportione e l'ingombro della fabrica, dimandò subito adiratamente, con quali ordini et autorità fosse stato introdotto.

The church of St. Agnes is a Greek cross with an apse ;
its sides are entirely faced with white marble up to the frieze
where gilt stucco and paintings begin.   The effect of the
interior is pleasing and imposing, whilst the exterior has met
with the approval of the severest critics.   It recalls the
impression made by the basilica of St. Peter's with Maderna's
towers.   The detached campaniles harmonize wonderfully
with the cupola and dominate the spacious piazza.[1]   The
church is a perfect example of Borromini's style, both in
the slim, pointed shape of the cupola, and the façade which
dominates the piazza.

The constructions of the Pamfili in the Piazza Navona
and their Villa on the Janiculus are among the most remarkable
artistic creations of papal nepotism in the 17th century,
and their splendour helps us in part to forget the darker
side and the weakness of such a system.   Nevertheless, however

Gli fu risposto che D. Camillo l'haveva comandato ;   sono in-
esplicabili i risentimenti che ne fece anco in publico, e condottosi
poscia alle sue stanze ne sbraviò con tal vehemenza di sdegno
il nipote che esso all'incontro non si potè contenere di non
esprimere il desiderio che aveva di vedersi una volta disciolto
dei continui rancori, nei quali per l'incontri del zio si trovava.
Per molti giorni fece il Papa soprasedere la fabrica e poi deputò
il chierico di Camera Msgr. Franzoni, toltane ogni incumbenza
a D. Camillo per sopraintendervi e proveduto di nuovo architetto,
del Borromino."   Cf. CANCELLIERI, Mercato, 111 ;   GUIDI, Borromini, 81 seqq.   An *Avviso of January 23, 1672, refers to the
consecration of S. Agnese :   On Sunday Cardinal Gualtieri consecrated the church of S. Agnese in Navona :   " fatta fabricare
da fondamenti dalla f. m. d'Innocenzo X. molto vaga et bella
ornata di oro e di fini marmi con bellissime colonne et statue,
e gl'altari tutti di basso rilievo di marmi, sicome sarà l'altare
maggiore con superbissimo organo, mancandovi di dipingere la
cuppola, e di farvi il deposito di domino Papa da esservi trasportato
dalla Basilica di S. Pietro."   Papal Sec. Arch.

[1] BERGNER, 60. Cf. MUÑOZ, Roma, 234 seq., and Borromini, 8 ;
MAGNI, 16, 63, 64 ;   BRIGGS, 24 ;   HEMPEL, loc. cit., 35, and
GURLITT'S praise (393 seq.), who still ascribed everything to
Rainaldi.

much we may be compelled to value the continued patronage of the arts, and to pay our tribute of admiration to what was then achieved, the historian of the Church cannot overlook the harm done by the excessive favour shown by Innocent X. and Urban VIII. to their relatives, and the great loss of prestige which the Holy See suffered in consequence. Like his predecessors, Paul III. and IV., Innocent X. also realized this fact in his more thoughtful moments. However, the aged Pontiff was no longer possessed of sufficient energy to do away with an abuse to which an end was only put at a later period by Innocent XII.

APPENDIX

OF

UNPUBLISHED DOCUMENTS

AND

EXTRACTS FROM ARCHIVES

APPENDIX

1. The Cardinal Secretary of State to the Spanish Nuncio [1]

Rome, December 17, 1650.

Il sig^r D. Diego de Silva Velasquez della Camera di Sua Maestà Cattolica, il quale, havendo qui dimorato lungo tempo per servitio della M^{tà} Sua, ha non solo in esso adempito intieramente le sue parti, ma mostrato ancora straordinario valore nel fare il ritratto di Nostro Signore medesimo ha porto materia lui, per lo che mi ha imposto di scrivere a V. Sig^{ia} che nella alla S^{tà} Sua d'inclinare benignamente ad ogni giovamento di pretensione, che egli ha, di conseguire da Sua M^{tà} uno de' tre habiti militari, Ella promuova con ogni efficacia l'istanza del sig^r D. Diego. Et io havendo ancora particolari cagioni di desiderare a lui sodisfazioni et augumento, sono ad accertar V. Sig^{ia} che recherò a mio debito verso Lei tutto ciò ch'Ella sarà per operare in vantaggio di lui. E le prego dal Sig^{re} Dio vera prosperità.

2. The Holy See and the Peace of Westphalia [2]

The material for Chigi's activity as a mediator at the Peace Congress of Westphalia, and the Curia's policy at the time is extraordinarily plentiful, and it has been preserved in its entirety. Whatever Chigi wrote, read or had on his table during his stay at Münster, is almost completely before us.

One part of the documents is in the Papal Secret Archives, another and no less valuable a section is in the Chigi Library. In the Papal Secret Archives (*Nunziatura di paci*, 16–28) are preserved the decoded copies of Chigi's reports from Münster and Aix-la-Chapelle : a complete series, together with his letters *en clair*, and lastly the replies and instructions of the Secretary of State in cypher. Steinberger has made use of these documents, though only for the specialized purpose of

---

[1] Page 29, n. 2.
[2] Page 94, n. 1.

his valuable work on the Jesuits and the question of peace, whilst he unfortunately had no access to the material in the Chigi Library. The first to give some account of this were GACHARD (*La bibliothèque des Princes de Chigi*) and CIAMPI in his essay *L'epistolario inedito di Fabio Chigi poi Papa Alessandro VII*, in *Atti dei Lincei*, Cl. di scienze morali, Serie III., vol. i (1877). BROM used them in the measure in which his particular purpose required it, in the third volume of his *Archivalia*.

When in 1905, in my capacity as Director of the Austrian Historical Institute, I resolved to examine the part played by the Holy See in the great peace negotiations of the 17th and 18th century, the Westphalian Peace Congress was entrusted to the Prague historian, Dr. W. Kybal, who had the co-operation of a number of members of the Institute, especially that of Dr. von Löhr, Dr. Martin, Dr. Stolz, Dr. Haid and Dr. Grosz. It was of the utmost advantage for us that Prince Mario Chigi (*ob*. 1915), who, since 1879, had most liberally seconded my research work in the Archives, gave permission to use all the material preserved in his library. How rich this is appears from the following extract from the catalogue of MSS. :

A I 1. Registro di lettere scritte in Munster per la pace generale al sacro collegio, a Papa Innocenzo X., a'signori cardinali Panzirolo e Pamfilo, dal 1644 al 1645.—Cod. chart., ipsis annis scriptus. In fol.

A I 2—5. Registro ed abbozzo di lettere in confuso a diversi, in IV tomi divisi, dall'a. 1631 al 1644.—Codd. chart. praedictis annis exarati. In fol.

A I 6. [Fabio Chigi] Lettere scritte da 22 di Dicembre 1644 fino a 26 di Ottobre del 1649.—Eorum, ad quos missae sunt, secundum litterarum seriem, index praecurrit.—C. ch., praedicto tempore exaratus. In fol.

A I 7. [Fabio Chigi] Lettere italiane scritte dal 16 di Novembre di 1649, fino tutto il 31 di Dicembre del 1650.—Sequuntur : Lettere latine scritte da' 12 di Dicembre del 1649 fino tutto il 31 di Dicembre del 1650.—Utriusque linguae epistolis index litterarum ordine praecedit.—C. ch., scr. praedictus annis. In fol.

A I 9–13. Scripturarum ad pontificium secretum missarum et per numeros expressarum acta, cum litteris separatis Fabii

Chisii, Nuntii apostolici ordinarii ad tractus Rheni, et extra-ordinarii Monasterii pro pace generali. ab a. 1644 ad a. 1650.— Quinque voluminibus comprehenduntur : nonnullae italo sermone et gallico exaratae miscentur ; singulis voluminibus materiarum index praefixus.—*Codd. ch.*, scr. saec. XVII. In fol.

A I 14–18. [Fabio Chigi] Registro di lettere e cifre scritte a Palazzo, mentr'era Nunzio ordinario al Reno e straordinario per la pace generale a Munster di Vestfalia, dal 1646 al 1651, che fu il suo ritorno in Italia, comprese in V tomi.—*C. ch.*, scr. praedicto tempore. In fol.

A I 21. [Fabio Chigi] Registro di lettere a M^or Macchiavelli, patriarca di Constantinopoli, e vescovo di Ferrata, poi cardinale, dal 1641 al 1652.—*C. ch.*, praedictis annis exaratus. In fol.

A I 22. [Fabio Chigi] Registro di lettere scritte a monsignor Albizzi, assessore del Sant'Offizio, dal 1639 al 1651.—*C. ch.*, scr. praedictis annis. In fol.

A I 23. [Fabio Chigi] Registro di lettere scritte da Munster di Vestfalia..., e poi da Aquisgrano, a monsignor Camillo Meltio, arciv^o di Capoa e Nunzio della Santa Sede appresso l'Imperatore, dal 1644 al 1652.—*C. ch.*, praedictis annis. In fol.

A I 24. [Fabio Chigi] Registro di lettere scritte da Munster di Vestfalia dal congresso per la pace generale, e poi da Aquisgrano, dal 1644 fino al 1651, a monsignor Niccolò de' conti Guido, Nunzio al Re Cristianissimo Luigi XIV.— *C. ch.*, scr. praedictis annis. In fol.

A I 25. [Fabio Chigi] Registro di lettere a monsignor d'Elci, arcivescovo di Pisa e Nunzio apostolico in Venezia, dal 1647 al 1651, e a monsignor Rospigliosi, Nunzio in Madrid, dal 1644 al 1652.—*C. ch.*, scr. saec. XVII. In fol.

A I 26. [Fabio Chigi] Negoziato del 1632 fatto da M. Corsini et da M. Chigi, commissari sopra le controversie tra la Sede Ap^ca e la Rep^ca di Venezia per li confini di Aviano e di Loreo.— *C. ch.*, scr. saec. XVII. In fol.

A I 31. [Fabio Chigi] Lettere a familiarj, dal 1632 al 1647.— *C. ch., anep., autogr.*, scr. saec. XVII. In fol.

A I 32. [Fabio Chigi] Lettere a diversi, dal 1626 al 1643.— *C. ch.*, titulo carens. *autogr.*, praed. ann. In fol.

A I 39. [Fabio Chigi] Lettere a Don Augusto e Don Agostino Chigi, dal 1648 al 1654.—*C. ch., autogr.*, praed. In fol.

A I 40. [Fabio Chigi] Lettere a Don Mario Chigi, dal 1649 al 1654.—*C. ch.*, *autogr.*, ips. annorum. In 8⁰.

A I 42. [Fabio Chigi] Memorie, note e polizze circa i trattati della pace in Munster dal 1644 al 1649.—*C. ch.*, *autogr.*, saec. XVII. In 4⁰. (Cfr. p. quoted as Diarium.)

A II 27–29. [Fabio Chigi] Registro di lettere scritte a varj personnaggi, dal 1632 al 1652, raccolte in tre tomi.—Virorum index singulis libris praemittitur.—*Codd. ch.*, dictis annis scr. In fol.

A I 44–45. [Fabio Chigi] Epistolarum latinarum ab a. 1639 ad a. 1649 variis ex locis datarum acta, in duo volumina divisa : utrique ecrum, ad quos litterae scriptae sunt, iuxta litteras index praecurrit ; intermiscentur quaedam italico et gallico sermone exarata.—*Cod. ch.*, *anep.*, scr. praedictis annis. In 4⁰.

A II 36–46. Lettere e cifre di Palazzo a monsignor [Fabio Chigi], vescovo di Nardi. Nunzio per la pace generale a Munster in Vestfalia, dal 1629 al 1651, in XI tomi raccolte.— Viri, qui scribunt, singulos tomos praecedunt.—*Codd. ch.*, *autogr.*, scr. saec. XVII. In fol.

A II 47. Registro di cifre di Segretaria di Stato a monsignor Chigi, arcivescovo [!] di Nardi e Nunzio apostolico al Reno, dal 1646 al 1651.—Scribentium index praemissus.—*C. Ch.*, scr. saec. XVII. In fol.

A II 49. Lettere della Congregazione del Sant'Offizio a monsignor [Fabio Chigi] Nunzio di Colonia, ed in specie circa il matrimonia del duca di Lorena, il Giansenio e le missioni di Olanda, dal 1639 al 1648. Aliquae latiae et galliae immistae.— *C. ch.*, *autogr.*, scr. saec. XVII. In fol.

A II 51 52, III 53–69, B I 1–3. Lettere su varie materie scritte in diversi tempi ad Alexandrum VII, dal 1620 al 1654, in XII tomi raccolte.—*C. ch.*, *scr. saec.* XVII. In fol.

B I 4. Contarini, Alvise, Venetae reipublicae ad Romanam aulam legatus : Lettere scritte, da' 13 agosto 1649 a' 29 luglio 1650, ad Alessandro VII, mentre era Nunzio in Colonia.— *C. ch.*, scr. saec. XVII. In fol.

Q II 46–49. Lettere a varj personnaggi, brevi, decreti, relazioni, e scritture su varie materie politiche, dal 1643 al 1644, ripartite in IV tomi. Alia latine, alia gallice scripta ; singulis tomis materiarum index praefixus. Index IV. tomi est Fabii Chisii manu exaratus. Epistolas et orationes

aliquorum virorum litteris illustrium mistas reperies.—*Codd.*
ch., anep., scr. saec. XVII. In fol.

Q II 54. Scritture diverse spettanti al trattato della pace di
Colonia e di Munster.—Materiarum index praecedit : haec
italo, illa gallico sermone exarata.—Saec. XVII. In 4⁰.

Q III 57. Scritture per la pace generale delle due corone di
Francia e di Spagna in Munster, dall'a. 1644 al 1649. Legenda
nota praemissa et aliae passim insertae manu Fabii Chisii.—
Saec. XVII. In fol.

Q III 58. Scritture per la pace tra l'Imperatore e il Re
di Francia in Munster dall'a. 1644 al 1649. Legendae notae
scriptae manu Fabii Chisii, pleraque gallico et latino scripta
sermone.—Saec. XVII. In fol.

Q III 59. Generanda, comes et Hispaniarum Regis legatus
et arbiter in pace Monasterii firmanda : Lettere spagnuole per
la pace di Munster, dal 1654 al 1649, a Fabio Chigi. Accedunt
nonnullae Imperatoris et Galli ministri epistolae ad eundem.—
In fol.

Q III 60–63. Scritture diverse del trattato di Munster, dal
1649 al 1650, raccolte in IV protocolli. Praecedunt nonnulla
ab a. 1638 ad 1643. Omnia latine, itale e gallice exarata.—
Scr. saec. XVII. In fol.

Q III 65–66. Trattati, concordati e lettere diverse per la
pace di Munster, dall'a. 1610 al 1646, raccolte in due tomi.
Singulis materiarum index praemissus.—Scr. saec. XVII.—
In 4⁰.

Q III 69–77. Scritture, trattati, editi, articoli, rimonstranze,
proteste, lettere e cose simili per la pace di Munster, dall'a.
1644 al 1649, divise in IX volumi. Alia latina, alia itala, alia
gallica. In I⁰ vol. interseruntur nonnulla poetica et aliqua in
hoc et in ultimo Fabii Chisii manu scripta ; praeter quatuor
prima, cetera indicem materiarum habent praefixum.—Saec.
XVII. In 4⁰.

When all the material had been examined, that is both that
in the Chigi Library and that in the Papal Secret Archives,
Professor Dr. Kybal, who had bestowed the utmost diligence
on the task, began to have all the more important pieces
copied. In this he was assisted by the Austrian Ministry of
Education. The work had so far progressed that in his book
Das Oesterreichische Historische Institut in Rom 1901–1913
(Vienna, 1914), Dengel was able to express the hope that

publication would begin in the near future. But then the World War broke out. I still hope that somehow, with the coming of better times, the publication on which Professor Kybal has bestowed so much toil, will be realized. Out of consideration for him I have refrained from printing some of the reports.

3.   PAOLO CASATI S.J. ON THE CONVERSION OF QUEEN
CHRISTINE OF SWEDEN [1]

November 19th, 1655.

Al M. R. P. in Christo P. Franco Bonelli della Compagnia di Giesù.

Non posso lasciare di sodisfare alla giusta curiosità di V. R. che ha desiderato di sapere in ristretto e brevemente, con qual progresso sia andata la resolutione della Serma Regina di Svetia di lasciare il regno e farsi cattolica. Ecco dunque brevemente il fatto. Cominciò la Regina internamente a dubitare di molte cose della setta Luterana, e tanto più, quanto meno le vedeva spiegate dalli suoi Pastori (che così chiamano colà li predicanti e ministri), onde con maggior attentione e diligenza studiando ne' libri di quella setta, tanto più si confermò ne' suoi dubii, e perciò con sollecitudine e straordinaria agitatione di mente si diede ad informarsi di quante sette sono mai state, e per trovar se in alcuna potesse acquietarsi, et in questo occupò lo spatio di cinque anni continui non mancando di conferire con più dotti homini, che colà capitassero, anche da lei chiamati ; ma non ritrovando sodisfattione in alcuna, si risolse di seguire quella, in cui era allevata, stimando che dal canto suo bastasse nell'opre seguire in tutto il dettame della ragione, nè far cosa, di cui potesse giamai arrossirsi ; parvele di haver trovato quiete, e così stette due anni in circa ; ma il Signore Iddio, che vedeva la sua buona volontà, volle illuminarla nell'intelletto con eccitar di nuovo la sollecitudine per trovar la vera fede. Stava in questa anzietà, quando

---

[1] *Cf.* this work, p. 343 *seqq.* Extracts in RANKE, III., 61 *seq.*, 183* *seq.* For Casati see ARCKENHOLTZ, I., 471 ; SOMMERVOGEL, II., 799 *seq.* ; IX., 2 *seq.*

giunse a Stockolm un'ambasciatore di Portogallo, che seco conduceva due Padri della Comp. di Giesù, uno de' quali era il P. Antonio Macedo, che serviva d'interprete all'ambasciatore con sua M.^{tà} ; quest'occasione di trattare col Padre fece che la Regina lo scoprisse per huomo prudente e fidato : onde assicurandosi della di lui secretezza, ne sperando d'haver mai più simile occasione, s'indusse a persuaderlo di partir nascostamente, et all'improviso alla volta di Roma, consegnandoli sue lettere indirizzate al P. Franc. Piccolomini Generale della Compagnia, nelle quali lo richiedeva che mandasse doi Padri, e nominatamente li voleva Italiani, co' quali potesse conferire alcune cose di religione, dando intentione di farsi cattolica, reconosciuta ch' havesse la verità. Giunse il P. Macedo a Roma sul fine di Ottobre del 1651, dove trovando morto il P. Piccolomini, diede le lettere al P. Vicario, che hora è Generale. Egli le aprì, et essendo quelle in lingua francese familiarissima alla Regina, le confidò al P. Anat Assistente di Francia, col quale e col P. Assistente d'Italia e P. Segretario consultò per elettione di chi dovea mandarsi, et a me toccò questa buona fortuna ; e si scrisse acciò da Torino si spiccasse il P. Franc. de Malines, e venisse a trovarmi nel luogo assegnato. Partii alli 22 di Novembre di quell'anno 1651, et accompagnatomi per strada col P. Malines arrivammo a Stockolm il giorno di S. Matthia 1652, circa il qual tempo S. M.^{tà} ci stava aspettando, conforme a quello che da Roma se l'era scritto. Furono frequentissimi e di molte hore per volta li colloquii (trovando la prudenza di S. M.^{tà} l'opportunità del tempo e del luogo) et assicuro V. R. che ho visto con evidenza gli effetti della divina bontà, la quale immediatamente scioglieva i nodi inestricabili che tenevano impegnata la mente della Regina, et operava molto più nel cuore di quello di fuori apparisse. Ella havea tanta cognizione delle cose della religione cattolica, che non havea mestieri d'istruzione, sgombrate le nebbie de' dubii che haveva intorno ad alcune cose particolari ; e la perspicacia del suo ingegno, aiutata da una singolar gratia dello Spirito Santo, facea che in un colloquio si potesse discorrere di molte dificoltà, alle quali date che havevamo le risposte, che il Sig.^r Iddio ci suggeriva proportionate alle interrogationi, lasciavamo che il Sig.^o Iddio pefettionasse l'opra che havea cominciata. Ella finalmente alla fine d'aprile si risolse d'abbracciare la santa fede cattolica, e perchè già molto prima havea pensato a ciò, ch'ella dovesse fare in evento che a ciò si risolvesse et, in caso che senza pericolo della sua salute non potesse congiungere allo stato reale la vera fede, vedendo non esser possibile introdurre nel regno la religione cattolica, nè fermarsi nel governo di essa senza pericolo di far cosa ripugnante alla protestatione della vera fede, chiaramente disse, che voleva rinunciare al regno, e dissegnatone il modo, subito spedì me verso Roma, acciò per mezzo del P. nostro Generale si rappresentasse a Nostro Sig^re Innocentio X di fel. mem. et acciò io pigliassi alcune informationi spettanti a questo. Partii di Stockolm con suo passaporto sul principio di Maggio di quell'anno, ma non potendomi dar lettera per Sua Santità, poichè non era gionto certo corriere, ch'ella aspettava, mi commandò le aspettassi in Nambourg, ma tardando l'arrivo del corriere, con lettera delli 21 di Maggio m'impose, che partissi con una sola sua lettera al P. Generale, ch'era lettera di credenza a quello, che io haverei esposto, ma con espressa riserva di non parlarne con N^ro Sig^re, sinchè non ricevessi le lettere ch'ella mi havria mandato a Roma per mezzo del P. Malines, che pensava doversi spedire dopo 15 giorni. Non comparve mai il P. Malines, nè le lettere, onde spediti gl'altri negotii commessimi, et havute le informationi necessarie, parte delle quali s'hebbero dall'E^mo Chigi ora N^ro Sig^re Alessandro VII, il quale unicamente era consapevole del butto sin da principio, partii sul fine di Settembre da Roma, et essendomi per strada per varie contingenze trattenuto, giunsi alla fine del 1652 a Nambourg. Ivi trovai lettere di S. M^tà che m'ingiongevano di non passar avanti : avvisai del mio arrivo e ricevei ordine di mandare le informationi portate e d'aspettare il P. Malines ; ma tardandoe questi, finalmente hebbi licenza di tornarmene in Italia circa la metà di Marzo 1653, et il penultimo di Giugno giunsi di ritorno a Roma.

Mentre nell'estate del 1653 io era di ritorno a Roma, giunse a Stockolm il Sig^r D. Antonio Pimentel inviato dal Re di Spagna, che seco havea il P. Carlo Manderscheidt della nostra Compagnia, et ambedue riconobbero il P. Malines già da loro conosciuto in Fiandra molt'anni prima. In progresso di tempo S. M^tà prese confidenza nella prudenza del Pimentel, e communicatagli la risolutione di lasciare il regno per farsi cattolica, e che prima di venire a Roma volea ritirarsi nelli stati di S. M^tà Catt^ca, dovea D. Antonio andare in Hispagna a rappresentarlo al Re. Ma non potendo egli all'hora andare, si prese ispediente d'inviare un Padre Domenicano Spagnuolo, il quale, quand'io era in Svetia, stava in Coppenhagen cappellano del conte di Rebogliedo ambasciatore di Spagna appresso il Re di Danimarca. Se questo Padre fosse chiamato a posta o ivi si trovasse a caso, non lo so, perchè già erano molti mesi che m'ero partito ; a lui, come a Religioso prudente che havria guardato il segreto, fu communicata la risolutione già presa dalla Regina, e fu spedito in Spagna, dovendo poco dopo seguitare D. Antonio ; ma questi tardando la sua partenza, al Padre Malines, che al fine di Marzo dovea venire per ritornare meco in Italia, mandò la Regina ordine di passare in Spagna, d'onde fu di ritorno a Roma al fine di Giugno 1653.

Non stava la Regina otiosa per l'essecutione de' suoi dissegni, e già inviava la sua biblioteca, come m'avvisò con lettera di Agosto 1653, e con altre lettere scritte al P. Generale mostrava grandissimo desiderio di venire a fine de' suoi dissegni, sempre assicurandoci della sua costanza e della prontezza per superare ogni difficoltà. Quando finalmente con una delli 26 di Febbraio 1654 scritta da Upsal tutta piena d'allegrezza mi avvisò di haver conchiuso la sua rinoncia del regno, e che con pretesto delle acque di Spah saria venuta in Fiandra—il che s'esseguì com'è noto a tutti. Si trattenne qualche tempo in Anversa, poi andata a Bruselles immediatamente avanti la festa di Natale l'istesso anno 1654 alla presenza del Ser^{mo} Arciduca Leopoldo, del General conte Montecuccoli, chiamato da Vienna dalla stessa Regina, di D. Antonio Pimentel e D. Antonio de la Cueva fece privatamente la professione della fede cattolica. E perchè molto si premeva che la cosa si còmmunicasse a quanti meno si poteva, giudicorno di non chiamare altra persona ecclesiastica, havendosi ottenute le necessarie facoltà per il Padre Domenicano, ricondotto di Spagna dal Pimentelli per segretario suo dell'ambasciata ; e questi poi ha sempre segretamente servito la Regina da cappellano e di confessore. Quest'estate poi del 1655 scrisse la Regina a N^{ro} Sig^{re} Alessandro settimo dando a Sua Sta parte della risolutione e di venirsene a Roma, e si concertò che uscita da luoghi mescolati d'eretici, in Inspruck facesse publica professione della fede cattolica, com'ella ha fatto alli 3 di Novembre, con quelle circostanze che per esser note a V. R. non giudico di replicare, bastandomi con questo sémplice e breve racconto di haver soddisfatto al desiderio che ho di dichiararmi.

D. V. R.

dal Collegio Romano li 19 Novembre 1655.

Umilissimo servo nel Sig^re
Paolo Casati
della Compagnia di Giesù ".

[Contemporary copy in the State Archives, Modena, *Documenti di Stati Esteri, Svezia*, B^ta I.]

4. MEMORANDUM OF P. SFORZA PALLAVICINO FOR ALEXANDER VII. ON THE BENEFICES OF THE NEPHEWS [1]

May 9th, 1656.

He thanks the Pope for his confidence. He discusses the reasons for and against calling the nephews. He then proceeds :

" Per evitar i narrati incomodi dell'una e dell'altra parte io non veggo altro modo se non quello che le accennai nell'ultima àudienza, cioè che la S^tà V. col publicare la risolutione di chiamare i signori suoi parenti promulgasse anche una bolla giurata ad lei e da tutti i cardinali, la qual è necessaria a due cose : l'una da assicurar il mondo della sua futura moderazione, della quale non si fidarà mai in altra maniera, havendo veduto questo primo passo ed anche l'esempio degli antecessori, ciascun de' quali ha cominciato protestando di voler esser moderato e poi ha dato in eccessi. L'altra, obligare i successori all'imitazione, già che un motivo principale della chiamata è lasciare un esempio imitabile.

In questa bolla si potrebbe prescrivere quello che i Papi al più dovessero dar a i loro parenti, non già con tanta strettezza quanta V. S^tà disegna rispetto a se, perchè io stimo che a questa i pontefici non siano obligati, ma dentro a quei concetti, tra quali si custodisse insieme la discrezione e la edificazione, aggiugnendosi che quando fusser più il successore, debba ritorlo con tutte le altre cautele, per le quali habbiamo vedute osservate le bolle di Pio e di Sisto.

Oltre a ciò dovrebbe contenere la medesima bolla che non debbano i Papi promuover al cardinalato alcun de' loro parenti

---

[1] *Cf.* Vol. XXXI., p. 22.

se non dopo tanto tempo di vita clericale e di prelatura, il che sarebbe di grand'edificazione per molti capi e terrebbe in offizio fra tanto quello, il qual suol poi esser l'arbitro del pontificato e darebbe commodità al Papa et agli altri di conoscerlo nell'esperienza. E se V. S^{tà} non provede a questo con bolla da se giurata, non potrà difendersi ella medesima dalle violenti istanze de' principi, i quali pensaranno di guadagnarsi il signor D. Flavio con strappar dalle mani di V. Sta in poche settimane un cappello per lui. E pure la sua gioventù e l'essere stato fin hora secolare non par che lo renda maturo a questa dignità nè secondo l'idea di Christo nè secondo di quella della S^{tà} V. E finalmente converrebbe statuire in questa bolla che a sì fatti cardinali non si potesse dar più che una entrata ragionevole, per esempio di 12^m scudi, il che sarebbe di gran consolatione al Collegio.

Terzo potrebbe V. Sta ordinare che i signori suoi congiunti trattassero con assai minor altura che non hanno usata i passati nepoti de' Papi. Il che cagionarebbe edificazione et amore. E ciò senza verun pregiudizio, perchè non essendo quella magnifica scena de' nipoti de' Papi durabile dopo la morte del zio, è meglio metterli in posto d'onde poi non debban calare.

Quarto. Potrebbe dichiararsi la S. V. publicamente in concistoro che da' cardinali, i quali elle è per fare in sua vita, non richiede per gratitudine che ne' conclavi futuri seguano altri che Cristo, anzi che riputerà ingrati a lei quelli che procederanno ivi con altro rispetto.

Con questi concettini la chiamata di quei signori può riuscire utile e non dannosa al governo nè scandalosa al cristianesimo, anzi d'edificazione."

[Chigi Library, Rome, C. III, 70, p. 156–9.]

5. Instruction for Baldeschi, Nuncio in Switzerland [1]
1665.

" . . . Quelli Pontefici che mossi da smisurato zelo stabilirono che sotto pena di scomunica non si dovesse pratticar cogli eretici, non ebbero mai la mira d'includer coloro che dovevano affaticarsi alla lora conversione : et in fatti come è possibile

---

[1] *Cf.* Vol. XXXI., p. 148.

di tirar gl'heretici alla nostra fede, se non si pratticano, se non si conversa con essi loro ?

Io non dico che V. S. entri a trattato alcuno con i Cantoni protestanti, nè comunicar con i loro deputati ; ma bensì di levarsi ogni scrupulo di conversar con i loro particolari, et è certo che quei Nuntii, che sono stati li più retinenti a far ciò, sono quelli che hanno meglio riuscito ne' negotiati e che hanno rotto e non risarcito i trattati.''

Conviene conoscer prima gl'humori particolari degl'huomini, chi vuol ben negotiare cogl'huomini publici delle nationi ; che però il conversar di quando in quando con le persone civili dei Cantoni protestanti e l'ordinare alli suoi domestici che faccino lo stesso, non può portar che grandi avvantaggi alla sua Nunziatura, perchè in questa maniera imparerà a conoscere li loro humori ; sopra di che le sarà più facile di fondare quel tanto che deve negotiare.

Oltre a questo, conversando V. S. li protestanti con quella gentilezza e prudenza che sono state sempre naturali alla sua persona, portarà un gran beneficio alla nostra religione medesima et aprirà tanto maggiormente la strada alla conversione di quei popoli, quali hanno impresso nell'animo, come ancora tutti gl'altri protestanti del mondo, il cattivo concetto che noi habbiamo di loro e l'avversione che verso di loro hanno i nostri popoli, che si muovono, se non per altra, per questa ragione ad odiarci e a star costanti alla loro durezza ; onde bisogna con la frequentatione disingannarli a puoco a puoco della opinione che hanno che noi li odiamo, e fargli conoscere che il nostro humore è contrario alla loro imaginatione. Così, se una volta saranno spogliati della avversione che hanno per noi, si renderà facile il modo d'istruirli nella nostra dottrina, particolarmente nei punti che essi ignorano e che noi siamo obligati di farli conoscere.

Non sono 20 anni che alcuni deputati d'un certo luogo del..., che non voglio nomare per qualche consideratione, andarono per negotiare nella corte d'un principe d'alto grido, ma quello ch'è più curioso, essi avevano intrapreso la deputatione con ferma speranza di guadagnar tutto, perchè s'imaginavano questa corte piena d'huomini di puoca esperienza, et accettuatone un solo, mettevano tutti gl'altri alla dozzena ; e pure li ministri di questa corte per lungo spatio di tempo si erano assuefatti nel trattare con li ministri di molti principi negl'affari e negotiati più importanti dell'Europa ; et essi non havevano mai negotiato altro che qualche cause civile di diece scudi, o per lo più essercitati a condannare alcuna puttanella alla frusta ; tanto più che essendo restati puoco men che due mesi in detta corte, si viddero loro stessi ligati con quei medesimi lacci, con i quali credevano ligar gl'altri, e posti in un labirinto, di dove non poterono svilupparsi che con puoca loro riputazione e con danno notabile del loro principe.

Somigliante cosa successe ad un nostro Monsignore assai bene conosciuto da V. S., il quale nel pontificato di Urbano VIII fu eletto per essercitar la Nuntiatura nella Svissa, che abbracciò volentieri, havendo ancor egli negl'affari politici maggior fumo che arrosto, essendosi posto in testa di poter ridurre in breve tutta la parte heretica in cattolica e tutta la cattolica obligar a riconoscere il Pontifice per arbitro sovrano di tutti gl'affari civili e criminali de' Cantoni. Fondava questi suoi pensieri e ventose intraprese sopra alcune historie vecchie lette da lui e sopra certi rapporti interessati riferiti più tosto per ridere che per altro, quali gli havevano preoccupato lo spirito e ridottolo a credere che gli Svisseri erano huomini di grosso legname, mercenarii della loro vita istessa da loro ordinariamente venduta per denari, ignoranti di lettere, puoco assidui nella lettura dei buoni libri e costumati ad imbriacarsi dalla mattina fino alla sera ; che però stimava egli facile di guadagnar tutto sopra lo spirito di huomini si fatti ; onde nel viaggio in quelle parti andava dicendo ad alcuni suoi più confidenti che sperava in breve di poter mettere i Svisseri tutt'insieme in un fiasco.

Ma giunto alla giurisditione della sua Nuntiatura, trovò le cose molto diverse da quello egli si era immaginate, et in cambio di mettere li Svizzeri in un fiasco, si vidde egli medesimo posto dagli Svizzeri in una scatola, e in tre anni di Nuntiatura non potè mai spuntare alcuna cosa che fusse favorevole alla Sede Apost., e pure i Svizzeri spuntarono molti punti in loro favore et in detrimento di Roma, che non havevano mai potuto ottenere in tempo dell'altro Nuntio. Onde, ritornato doppo questo pur buon ministro a Roma, andava dicendo per tutto, che " gli Svizzeri erano grossolani di nome, ma non d'effetti " ; et è certo che questa carica lo fece perder molto di stima, e non per altro forse se non perché si era addormentato sopra la speranza di dover trattare con popoli rozzi e di puoco valore ; che è un grand'errore proprio a far perdee molti ministri, quali devono sempre immaginarsi di dover negotiar con huomini molto più esperti di loro, perché questa immaginatione l'oblighera a studiar sempre più le maniere di ben negotiare.

Sono veramente li Svisseri puoco inclinati alle lettere, perché il loro mestiere principale è quello dell'armi ; ad ogni modo vi trattengono di buonissime università publiche, dalle quali sono usciti sapientissimi huomini, ma in picciolo numero, essendo vero che generalmente il loro spirito non è delli più sottili del mondo nè dei più speculativi della terra, conservando non so che di rozzo, che si crede generato dall'asprezze di tante montagne che circondano quel paese. Ma, sia come si voglia, havendo da qualche tempo in quà introdotto il costume di far viaggiar la gioventù, hanno dato con questo quasi un'altra natura a quel luogo, e con la prattica delle nationi straniere si sono così bene assottigliati che al presente sorpassano nella finezza quasi tutti gl'altri popoli di Europa. Onde un certo ministro di sperimentato valore che haveva lungamente negotiato con quelli Cantoni, si lasciò intendere che questi popoli erano divenuti tanto sottili, che bisognava stracciare i fogli di tutti quei libri che li descrivevano per grossolani. Et io ho inteso dire ad un Francese, che al presente era più facile d'ingannare un cattivo Spagnuolo che un buon Svizzero. Et in questi sentimenti s'accordano molti altri ministri che negotiano con dette Cantoni.

Bisogna di necessità confessare esser questi popoli molto prudenti et accorti nel maneggiare i loro interessi, e dicano gl'altri quello che voglioni, giachè hanno saputo mantenersi per sì lungo tempo in libertà e vivere nel mezzo d'una diversità si grande di religioni con tanta quiete tra di loro, oltre che sanno così ben fare i fatti loro, che i più grandi principi d'Europa con solenni ambasciate li ricercano per confederarsi con essi loro, e li trattengono con buone somme di danaro, e tra tante rotture tra Francia e Spagna hanno saputo benissimo e con molto ingegno mantenersi con ambe le parti, cavar dall'una e dall'altra immensi tesori, e ben spesso per ragion di politica si sono dati a contrapesar la bilancia, potendosi dire che la liberta dell'Italia è stata più volte mantenuta dal valore e prudenza delli Svisseri ; nè queste cose si operano che da

grandi giudicii ; essendo vero che sotto una cattiva scorza si nasconde spesso un dolce frutto. . . ."
[Papal Sec. Arch. *Nunziat. diverse*, 242 *seq.*, 341–4.]

" . . . La malitia humana è cresciuta et avvanzata sì oltre, che molti principi e senati de' più cattolizzanti si vanno allontanando con ogni industria da quella continua obbedienza che doverebbero prestare alla Sede Apost., e per lo più tengono a gloria di allontanare il Pontefice da tutti li loro negotiati, et, in cambio di sottomettersi a' suoi consigli paterni, non vogliono neanche communicarli quel tanto che da loro stessi havranno negotiato con altri, scusandosi con dire che il Pontefice non deve ingerirsi nelle materie di stato, ma in quelle cose che riguardano l'anima solamente, come se non fosse l'anima quella che dee condurre il corpo ad oprar bene, o che fusse possibile la divisione di queste due parti ; e già si sa che ultimamente nel trattato di pace tra Francia e Spagna li plenipotentiarii da per loro accommodarono tutti gl'articoli e, quel che più importa, anco in ciò dove vi andava l'interesse del Papa, senza che gliene participassero cosa immaginabile, essempio invero di molto pregiuditio alla grandezza della Sede Apost. et alla Maestà pontificia, perchè dicono gl'altri : Se il Mazarino, che era cardinale e per conseguenza obligato a portar inanzi gl'interessi del Pontefice et a render la Maestà di questo di maggior riputatione, non volse nè meno che si sapesse che egli havesse parte alcuna a' trattati di quella pace procurata molto tempo prima dal zelo dello stesso Pontefice, perchè permetteremo noi che detto Papa s'introduca a' maneggi politici de' nostri stati e consigli ?

Li Cantoni protestanti, che sanno molto bene questa puoco buona dispositione de' principi cattolica verso la Sede Apost., ne godono sommamente, essendo un punto di gran conseguenza al loro mantenimento che la Maestà del Pontefice perda di concetto nel mondo e che la corte di Roma non sia chiamata a parte di alcun maneggio ; onde, come già ne ho toccato qualche cosa, studiano ogni industria per divertire i Cantoni cattolici e farli risolvere a fare le cose da per loro, senza mescolarvi l'autorità del Papa ; e fortificano questi loro consigli con gl'essempii de'principi cattolici medesimi. Che però V. S. deve star con gl'occhi aperti in questo particolare, perchè, se una volta s'impossessa qualche sinistro concetto del Papa nella mente delli Svisseri, potrebbesi in breve rin-versare tutta la religione in quei paesi. Certo è che tra tutti li principi del christianesimo non se ne trova alcuno che sia più ossequioso delli Svisseri verso la Sede Apost., onde bisogna saperli conservare procurandoli qualche avvantaggio col fargli vedere che l'intentione di Roma non batte ad altro che ad avvantaggiare sopra tutti gl'altri i loro interessi, et in fatti converrà mostrarlo con l'opere.

Fra le mani de'Cantoni protestanti vi sono un'infinità di beni ecclesiastici alienati e venduti da' loro magistrati a molti particolari, che li godono come proprii e che conviene a nostro dispetto, per così dire, lasciarglieli godere, non trovandosi alcun rimedio sino a che la Providenza Divina non disponga le cose in altra forma e non gli dia altra faccia.

Il parlar di racquistar tali beni, ciò sarebbe il metter tutta la Svissa in rivolta, et in questo s'interessarebbero gl'Olandesi e tutte le altre città de'protestanti, per le conseguenze che da ciò ne risultarebbero a lor detrimento. Ben è vero che tra li confini d'alcuni Cantoni cattolici e protestanti vi sono certe cure e beni di monasterii, che essi protestanti godono, quan-tunque confinanti con i territorii de' cattolici ; in che potrebbe V. S. adoprarsi per la restitutione, se non in altra forma, almeno con la compra di detti beni, quando però volessero consentire per levargli dalle lor mani. . . ."

[*Ibid.*, 242 *seq.*, 345–6.]

6. THE " VITA DI ALESSANDRO VII " OF SFORZA PALLAVICINO.

At the time of Alexander VII's election, Sforza Pallavicino's famous *History of the Council of Trent*, the first volume of which appeared in 1656, was almost complete in MS. But now he undertook another historical task when he began a biography of the reigning Pope whose friend he had been from his youth.[1] Unfortunately, the work was never completed. The cause was not, as Muratori affirms (*ad a.* 1656) and as was long believed, that his pen fell from his hand when he saw the Pope's nepotism, for he has left a full account precisely of this incident.[2] His account reaches the year 1659. On

---

[1] *Cf.* MACCHIA, *Relazioni fra il P. Sf. Pallavicino e Fabio Chigi*, Torino, 1907.

[2] *Cf.* above, XXXI., p. 22 *seqq.*

November 10th of that year Pallavicino was raised to the purple, so that there can be but little doubt that this event was the cause of the interruption of the work, for Pallavicino was as conscientious a historian as he was a conscientious Cardinal. His duties as such were more weighty than those of a historian, hence the latter were put on one side. To this must be added the infirmities of age.[1] The continuation of the *Vita* was put off. It was only a fragment when Pallavicino died on June 5th, 1667, at the age of 60.[2] Though no one thought of publishing it, it was widely spread in manuscript, though often enough with many errors. We find it in the Papal Secret Archives (*Cod. Bolognetti*, 246–7) and in the Vatican Library (*Cod. Ottob.* 2574–5, as well as in the MSS. collections of the Altieri, Albani, Barberini,[3] Corsini,[4] Chigi, and in the Alessandrina.[5] Affò[6] mentions copies at Mantua and Turin, and Novaes one in the library of the Roman Jesuits.[7] Many of these MSS. are so fragmentary that Ciaconius thought

---

[1] On July 12, 1664, Pallavicino writes to Ang. Correr : " La sterilità della mia età e della mia complessione mi predicano che l'ultimo volume della mia istoria, pur uscito ora a luce, sarà l'ultimo della mia penna " (*Lettere*, III., Roma, 1848, 171). After that Pallavicino wrote his splendid introduction to Christian life and thought (*Arte della perfezione cristiana*) which appeared in July, 1665, inasmuch as he felt an obligation " di scriver alcuna cosa indirizzata meramente ad onor di Dio " (*Lettere*, I., 29). Here also he speaks of his many duties. *Cf.* Luigi Rossi Da Lucca in *La Provincia di Teramo*, 1902, No. 42.

[2] His funeral inscription, of classic simplicity, on the floor of S. Andrea al Quirinale, in FORCELLA, IX., 120.

[3] *Cod.*, LIV., 54 e 55. Latin translation entitled " Alexandri VII. de vita propria liber primus et tertius cum fragmentis libri secundi " in *Barb.* 2575, Vat. Lib. *Cf.* RANKE, III., App. No. 130, who, as usual, gives no reference. This whole passage in Ranke, as Reumont (*Hist. Jahrbuch*, V., 636) already observed, has not been altered in subsequent editions so that it is wholly out of date.

[4] *Cod.*, 173–4, 729–731.

[5] *Cod.*, II., L., 9.

[6] *Memorie degli scrittori Parmigiani*, V., 158 *seq*

[7] NOVAES, X., 195.

that there was no question of a *Vita* but merely of a collection
of notes for private use, for the purpose of fixing the more
important events.[1]   In reality, Pallavicino's *Vita di
Alessandro VII.* is a finely executed biography of great
historical value. At first only selections from it were published,
as in 1837 the description of the plague in Rome,[2] and in the
following year the Chapter on Queen Christine of Sweden.[3]
The first complete edition appeared in 1839 at Prato, followed
by a reprint at Milan in 1843.

Although the Prato edition has for its sub-title " tratta dei
migliori manoscritti esistenti nelle biblioteche di Roma ",
it teems with inaccuracies, so that it was only right that
Ottavio Gigli, the editor of other works of Pallavicino, should
prepare a new edition based on a better manuscript.[4] Unfortunately, as a result of the storms of the revolution, only 240
pages of the first volume appeared, that is the first Book and
part of Book II, up to Chapter V. The text breaks off abruptly
at the account of Astalli's elevation to the cardinalate.[5]

---

[1] CIACONIUS, IV., 741.

[2] Descrizione del contagio che da Napoli si communicò a
Roma nell'anno 1656 e de' saggi provvedimenti ordinati allora
da Alessandro VII., estratta dalla vita del medesimo che con-
servasi manoscritta nella biblioteca Albani, opera inedita del
card. Sf. Pallavicino, Roma, 1837.

[3] Descrizione del primo viaggio fatto a Roma dalla regina di
Svezia Cristina Maria . . . e delle accoglienze quivi avute sino
alla sua partenza, opera inedita del p. Sf. Pallavicino, tratta da
un manoscritto della biblioteca Albani, Roma, 1838. The publication gave rise to the erroneous notion, still held by CLARETTA
(*Christina X.*), that Pallavicino had written a special history of
the Queen of Sweden.

[4] *Vita di Alessandro VII., Opera inedita, pubblicata secondo
la lezione del codice chigiano*, tomo i, Roma, Tipografia della
Società Editrice Romana, 1849 (*Opere edite ed inedite del cardinale
Sforza Pallavicino*, tomo xiv, 1849 : *Biblioteca classica sacra
o sia Raccolta di opere religiose di celebri autori edite ed inedite
del secolo* xiv *al* xix, *ordinata e pubblicata da* OTTAVIO GIGLI,
secolo xvii, tomo xxxi).

[5] At the words : " Fu d'infinita ammirazione alla qual non
vedea nel " (Prato edition, 155).

It has become very rare. Giuseppe Cugnoni, Professor at the Roman University and head of the Biblioteca Chigiana up to the time of his death, had planned a new edition, but he failed to find a publisher. Much of his material was given by him to Professor Luigi Rossi Da Lucca for the latter's excellent articles on " Sforza Pallavicino prosatore ", unfortunately published in a little-known periodical (*La Provincia di Teramo*, 1902, No. 27–52 ; 1903, 1–13). I too owe much valuable information to Cugnoni not only for the present dissertation but for the whole of my presentment of Alexander VII.

The Chigi Library has the following MSS. of Pallavicino's *Vita di Alessandro VII.*

(1) E I 1–5. Five small volumes, in 4⁰.

(2) D III 46 and 47. Two volumes in folio, probably the copy mentioned by Affò, *loc. cit.*, which had belonged to Cardinal Imperiali and of which there are several copies in the Chigiana.

(3) D III 49. One volume in folio, incomplete.

(4) Unsigned : " Vita di Alessandro Papa settimo fino alla sua elezione in pontefice, cioè fino a tutto il secondo libro."

(5) D III 42. Latin translation of the *Vita*, but incomplete.

The first of these MSS. is undoubtedly the best. It is the real original MS. which Pallavicino left by will to Cardinal Flavio,[1] who consigned it to the Roman family library. There the MS. remained long unnoticed, until Luigi Maria Rezzi first drew attention to it.[2] Gigli also recognized its value and based his edition upon it, whereas the Prato edition is for the most part based on the less satisfactory copy in the Albani library.

The Codices E I 1–5 are by different hands, though this should not create any difficulties, for as Pallavicino himself informed the Pope, he had his work written out by copyists, on account of his own extraordinarily bad handwriting.[3] That this text is the best of all is proved by the corrections of the

[1] Affò, *Vita del card. Sf. Pallavicino*, Roma, 1845, 133.

[2] *Cf.* Pietro Giordani al celeb. Mons. A. Mai, 1820 (*Scritti editi e postumi*, III., 404).

[3] *Cod.* C III., 63, p. 231, of Bibl. Chigi, Rome. Pallavicino's bad handwriting may be seen in his letters in the Bibl. Casanat., Rome.

author which mingle with corrections from the hand of
Alexander VII. himself, for Pallavicino submitted to the Pope
the various parts of his work as they were completed.
Alexander VII.'s corrections are for the most part concerned
with dates and names, and at times with the text itself.[1]
These corrections are either in the text or on the margin,
unfortunately some of them were written in pencil and have
become illegible.   As a result of the Pope's corrections,
Pallavicino himself altered many passages and added others.
How closely the Pope revised the work appears from the fact
that he corrected even minor mistakes.[2]

There can be no doubt of the high value of Pallavicino's
biography of Alexander VII., seeing that it was, as it were,
written under the very eyes of the Pope and by one of his
oldest and most intimate friends, who had been, for the most
part, an ocular and auricular witness [3] of what he recounts
and whose advice the Pope had often taken in the most
important questions.[4]   In his preface he himself says that
during a period of thirty years he had enjoyed the confidence
of Alexander VII. to such a degree (as proved by oral and
written communications), that he believed he knew all that
the Pope did, and even what he thought.   Even after his
elevation to the Chair of Peter, Alexander continued to communicate to him all the secrets which he needed to know for
his work.[5]   The correspondence between Pallavicino and
Alexander VII. (*Cod. Chigi*, C III, 63) reveals the intimate
relations between the two men, as well as the fact that
Pallavicino turned to his friend on the papal throne for

[1] Thus the sentence on Chigi's stay at Münster : " e neppure "
up to " Spagnuoli " (I., 132), is an addition by the Pope.

[2] Thus in IV., 9 (Prato edition, II., 73) he changed " nipote "
into ' cugino " and " zio " into " cugino ". In IV., 16, Pallavicino
had given " Andrea " as Cremonino's Christian name ; this was
changed into " Cesare " by the Pope. The Prato edition (II., 125)
has this correction.

[3] See the opinion of LUIGI ROSSI DA LUCCA in *Provincia di
Teramo*, 1902, No. 38.

[4] *Cf.* Pallavicino's letters to Alexander VII. in MACCHIA,
67 *seqq.*, 82 *seqq.*

[5] *Vita*, I., 20 ; *cf.* II., 171.

information for his work.[1] They corresponded not only on the contents of the *Vita*, but on the style and even the orthography. How carefully Pallavicino prepared himself for his task is shown by his preliminary studies, many of which are still preserved in the family Archives at Ariccia. The value of the work is further enhanced by the fact that, as appears from several passages,[2] many parts were written at the time when the events took place. Subsequently also no changes were made ; thus the curious passage on youthful Louis XIV. was retained,[3] though the subsequent conduct of that monarch did not confirm it.

Real errors occur extremely rarely in the biography,[4] and with few exceptions the author's judgments may be accepted.[5] The freedom with which he describes the shadows in Innocent X.'s rule is worthy of notice. If there are none such in that of Alexander VII., the reason is that the first five years of his pontificate gave no room for criticism. That Pallavicino did not approve of the subsequent lapse into nepotism is shown by his sharp comments before his death.[6] However sincere an admirer of his hero Pallavicino may have been, he never falls into flattery or untruths, for he was aware that a falsehood would have been the surest means to forfeit the favour of the Pope.[7]

If we compare Pallavicino's presentment with the many new documents that we now possess, we find it fully confirmed.[8] Hence it is most regrettable that he only described

---

[1] See *letters in *Codex* S. 22, 26, 46.

[2] *Vita*, II., 90.

[3] " Ludovico XIV. giovane di 16 anni candido e pio di costumi " (*Vita*, II., 296).

[4] Thus Mazarin is described as " piccolo gentilhuomo di Sicilia " whereas he was born at Pescina in the Abruzzi ; see ORLANDINI, *La patria e la famiglia del card. Mazarino*, in *Riv. Abruzzese*, IX. (1911).

[5] Thus (I., 272), Adrian VI. is as wrongly judged as he is in the History of the Council of Trent ; *cf.* our data IX., 226 *seq.*

[6] *Arch. stor. ital.*, App. VI., 394 *seqq.*

[7] *Vita*, I., 21.

[8] This has been pointed out by SCARABELLI in *Arch. stor. ital.*, App. VI., 389, who also shows that where A. Corer disagrees with

the first five years of the pontificate. The passages concerning Queen Christine prove that Pallavicino had access to the very best sources and that he sometimes quotes them textually, If chronological data are less prominent in his narrative, the fault is one that Pallavicino shares with his contemporaries. But there are no inaccuracies. The narrative is as detailed as it is lively, and connoisseurs such as Luigi Rossi Da Lucca praise his style.[1] Certain obscurities are due to the circumstance that the printed edition is not based on the original manuscript.

7. BARGELLINI TO ROSPIGLIOSI [2]

Paris, September 25, 1668.[3]

" Con mia estrema mortificatione et infinito dispiacere hieri in occasione di vedere monsieur di Lionne a San Germano, e questa mattina in casa sua propria,ho conosciuti avverati i miei sospetti. Dolendomi confidentemente, e rappresentando a S. Ecc^{za} ciò che hebbi l'honore di portare coll'ultima mia cifra a V. E., mi ha risposto che, quando i quattro vescovi habbino fatto un processo verbale, e che stia nascosto, la Chiesa non deve giudicare delle cose occulte ; che hanno imitato l'esempio di quarant'altri, de' quali non si è parlato, e che le pareva di havermene dato motivo una volta nel bel principio che si fece la prima propositione a V. E. Ho risposto che assolutamente non mi è stato parlato di processo verbale o di altra cosa che potesse intorbidare la pura signatura, e mostrata la copia della lettera scritta a V. E. il primo giugno, ricordato quante volte io mi sono dichiarato che la sotto-scrittione doveva essere sincera, S. Ecc^{za} mi ha replicato che

Pallavicino, the latter is more credible. Scarabelli singles out in Pallavicino's *Vita* " la parsimonia delle lodi e delle frasi affettuose, si che proprio non trovi che ciò che l'encomiato non avrà potuto comandare all'amico di togliere ".

[1] *La Provincia di Teramo*, 1902, No. 39. " Bartoli, Pallavicino and Segneri," Wiseman writes (*Recollections of the last four Popes*, II.) " were the only ones who were not affected by the bad taste of the period."

[2] Vol. XXXI., p. 388.

[3] Decoded October 18.

questo colpo era inevitabile, che quando li commissarii havessero proceduto contro li quattro vescovi, li medesimi havrebbero prodotta la loro signatura sincera e libera in questa maniera ; ma con il processo verbale a parte e che all'hora trattandosi giuridicamente, Roma era in necessità o di lasciarla passare, o di proceder contro quarant'altri, e che hora si può dissimular saperlo, e dar la pace alla Chiesa..."

[Papal Sec. Arch., *Nunziat. di Francia*, 137, f. 339.]

8. To Bargellini [1]

Rome, October 11th, 1668.

1.

" Sentitasi dalla S^{tà} di N. S^{re} la forma tenuta da V. S. nel rispondere alle lettere che a lei scrissero li quattro vescovi, quando le dettero ragguaglio della sottoscrittione che dicevano haver fatto del formulario, delle quali risposte ha ella inviata copia con le sue lettere delli 18 scorso, come anco il contenuto di tre sue cifre scritte sotto li 21 e 25 del medesimo, me ha comandato la S^{tà} Sua di scrivere a V. S. ch'ella insista per haver l'atto autentico della sottoscrittione del formulario, qual sottoscrittione non importa che in alcuna scrittura sia chiamata libera, ma sarà veramente e qui si stimerà libera e sincera, quando sotto la formula data dalla Sede Apost. si saranno in effetto sottoscritti i detti vescovi senza restrittione nè limitatione alcuna. Mostri però V. S. di haver creduto meglio di non dar parte qua delli processi verbali, che possano esser stati fatti, o possano farsi intorno a quest'atto da i quattro vescovi, et haver ella così operato anche in riguardo del consiglio datole dal signor di Lionne, e perché in realtà si come la Sede Apost. non ha voluto altro da i quattro vescovi che la sottoscrittione pura del formulario, così essendo questa seguita, et asserendosi tale da i quattro vescovi medesimi e da quelli che hanno trattato a nome loro nello scrivere a S. S^{tà}, ella deve presumere, o che non vi sia alcun processo verbale, o che essendovi non sia punto contrario alla sottoscrittione sincera, nè appartenere a lei hora il cercar altro. Si dichiari però col sig^r di Lionne, che se mai apparirà in qualunque modo

---

[1] Vol. XXXI., p. 390.

essersi da' quattro vescovi fatto processo verbale che pregiudichi alla sincerità della sottoscrittione, V. S. sarà obligata a scrivere a S. S^tà, e saranno gl'inconvenienti maggiori di prima."

[Papal Sec. Arch., *Nunziat. di Francia*, 137, f. 64b.]

2.

" Procuri V. S. di sapere con la maggior destrezza ch'ella potrà non da monsù di Lionne nè da alcuno di quelli che han trattato a nome de' quattro vescovi, ma con somma cautela e per quella via per la quale potrà ella più assicurarsi della segretezza, e che non sia penetrato da alcuna persona, benchè sua confidente, e particolarmente ministro della corte, se i processi verbali che hanno fatti i sudetti vescovi nell'atto della sottoscrittione, siano stati da loro fatti nel sinodo in modo che siano parte degli atti del medesimo sinodo, e però publici a segno che non possa mostrarsene ignoranza.

Sarà anco opportuno ch'ella s'informi se ne' processi verbali fatti da i quattro vescovi vi sia stata fatta o inserita cosa contraria alla libera e sincera sottoscrittione del formulario, con avvisar poi qua ciò che ne havrà riportato di vero e di sussistente, ma senza mostrare a persona veruna di haver fatta tal diligenza."

[*Ibid.*, f. 65b.]

3.

" Sarà molto opportuno che V. S. dica a monsù di Lionne ch'ella ha stimato meglio di non scriver qua cosa alcuna de' processi verbali fatti da' quattro vescovi, perchè essendosi N. S^re in questo punto mosso ad operare ad instanza del Re e riposando nell'autorità e nel zelo di S. M^tà e dell'istesso signor di Lionne, ha ella stimato che sia il maggior vantaggio di S. S^tà l'haver sicurezza della sincera sottoscrittione del formulario dalla parola di S. M^tà e dell'istesso signor di Lionne, senza cercar di più, supponendo che cosa sì grave e che importa egualmente all'interesse et alla pietà di S. M^tà che all'autorità del Papa, non possa S. S^tà temer di esser defraudata, mentre si è appoggiata alla fede della M^{tà} Sua e di monsù di Lionne medesimo, e per conseguenza vi va dell'honour della M^{tà} Sua, che non possa mai dirsi essersi in questo punto mancato a S. B^{ne}."

[Ibid., f. 66 b.]

9. SESSION OF THE INQUISITION OF DECEMBER 23RD, 1668 [1]

" Ginetti : Quatuor episcopos satisfecisse plene. Ottoboni : likewise ; neque obstare voces et scripturas informes, quibus dicitur subscripsisse cum reservationibus circa quaestionem facti et iuris et circa materiam gratiae efficacis, quia cum constet per publica documenta de sincera subscriptione, et de contrario non constet nisi de auditu et per scripturas informes, non videtur insistendum pro alia declaratione, maxime cum immineant maxima et gravissima pericula." The four must not be praised " ne elati, ubi sunt audacissimi, ostentent in Galliis favorem et gratiam Santitatis Suae ". Borromeo dixit, convenire cum Ottoboni et praecipue quia a principio semper protestatus fuit, quod in rebus facti non potest SS. Pontifex obligare fideles ad actus internos et nunc versemus in quaestione facti quoad illam partem formularii, in qua dicitur : iuxta sensum ab auctore intentum. Albizzi dixit, actum esse de religione in Gallia et de infallibilitate SS. Pontificis, si quando ex constanti rumore et notorietate necnon ex depositionibus canonicorum cathedralis Apamiensis constat de restrictionibus appositis in subscriptione, SS. Pontifex iis postpositis respondet episcopis et declarat, ipsos satisfecisse mandatis Sedis Apostolicae, praecipue cum declaratio episcopi Chalon. sit de voluntate alterius et archiepiscopus Rothomagensis explicet praedictam declarationem iuxta ipsiusmet mentem. Quare addidit, consulendum esse Pontificem [sic !], ut emissa nova Constitutione confirmet condemnationes factas per Innocentium X et Alexandrum VII fel. rec., necnon omnes et singulas prohibitiones tam mandamentorum quam aliarum scripturarum emanatarum adversus praedictas condemnationes. Chisius : Incumbendum esse in exhibitione processuum verbalium et subscriptionibus. Quatenus vero alii EE. DD. aliter censeant, debere responsum [dari] per

[1] Vol. XXXI., p. 394.

breve, in quo S. D. N. dicat, episcopos pure et simpliciter subscripsisse. Rasponus : Esse in voto cum Chisio, sed praecipue animadvertendum, ut in brevi non apponantur verba, ex quibus possit dubitari, quod SS. Pontifex non fuerit certior factus de sincera subscriptione ad formam Constitutionum. Rospigliosi : Respondendum esse ad formam declarationis episcopi Chalon. et Antonii Arnaldi, necnon iuxta declarationes archiepiscopi Rothomagensis, quia ex carum tenore clare percipitur, quod si episcopi contumaces subscripserunt eo modo, ut declarant episcopus et Arnauld necnon Rothomagensis, plene satisfactum fuit mandatis Sedis Apostolicae, nec amplius potest expeti a quocunque episcopo catholico, cum sub illa generalitate remaneant attrita mandamenta et processus verbales, necnon omnia, quae in contrarium adduci unquam possent. Azzolini riepilogando omnia dicta et adhaerendo sententiae Rospigliosi dicit : Respondendum omnino neque protrahendum amplius tam grande negotium, perpendenda tamen esse verba responsionis. Celsius dixit : Si constaret de sincera subscriptione quatuor episcoporum, utique conveniret cum DD., vero pia confessio subscriptionis non est subscriptio, ideo instandum, ut episcopi doceant de reali subscriptione facta in synodis. Tunc em. Ottobonus respondit. regulam procedere in actibus producentibus obligationem, non in casu praesenti. Et em. Borromaeus dixit : Ubi agitur de declaratione animi tantum, sufficit quaecunque manifestatio. Em. tamen Celsius perstitit in sua sententia.

Omnes igitur, exceptis em. Albizzi et Celsio, dixerunt : Respondendum esse episcopis, firmetur minuta brevis ; revideatur primum per em. Azzolinium, deinde communicetur omnibus em. cardinalibus Congregationis particularis et mittatur Nuntio iuxta mentem cardinalis Rospigliosi.

Eadem die hora prima noctis retuli S. D. N° omnia acta et gesta in s. Congregatione, necnon singula suffragia EE. DD. et minuta Constitutionis faciendae iuxta sententiam em. Albizzi [he had himself handed in the draft], quibus auditis Sanctitas Sua praecepit mihi Assessori, ut componerem minutam brevis illamque traderem R. P. D. archiepiscopo Florentino, necnon agerem cum em. Rospigliosi et Azzolini, ut quam primum expediantur responsa danda in Galliis, ut cito rediret ad suos tabellarius.

An anonymous letter from a French Jesuit also lay before the meeting.

[From codex : *Iansenio e Formulario* of the Holy Office. Biblioteca Angelica, Rome, S. 3. 1, p. 448 *seqq.*]

There follow in the codex various drafts of the Brief and Albizzi's objections :

" Albizzi : Di più avendo i medesimi vescovi publicato non solamente nei loro sinodi che N. S. Clemente IX meglio informato della dotrina del Jansenio haveva approvati i loro mandamenti ed era receduto dalle Constitutioni de' suoi predecessori, ma fatto ciò publicare per mezzo dei loro adherenti per tutta l'Europa, come si vede dalle relazioni e dalle gazette di Parigi, d'Amsterdam e di Bruxelles, non pareva rimedio bastante per salvare l'onore e la fama di N. S. e l'autorità della S. Sede, di passarlo con una risposta alla lettera dei quattro vescovi, la quale se si manderà alle mani del Nuntio per preservarla [presentarla ?], impegnato a sostenere il suo inganno, Dio sa, che non vi faccia difficoltà in porla nelle mani dei quattro vescovi, e mandi in lungo il negotio che pure fa di mediari [mestieri ?] di finire prestamente. Se poi si manderà a dirittura ai vescovi, o negheranno d'haverla ricevuta, o la glosseranno o la falsificheranno, come hanno falsificata la mente di N. S. . . .

Io prego V. S. a leggere per disteso questo mio voto a N. S., affinchè io resti sicuro d'haver adempieto quell'obligo, che mi corre come cardinale di s. Chiesa, persuadendomi che S. S. possa avere a me qualche credito più degli altri, perchè per le mie mani è passata la materia del Jansenismo nel suo nascimento e nel suo progresso, nè posso sopportare, che si voglia far parere al mundo esser estinta quest'eresia, mentre nella sua pretesa estintione si vede più che mai rinovata. [January 6th, 1669.]

Celsi was also decidedly against a Brief : Dico dunque brevemente, che o li vescovi suddetti hanno sottoscritto al detto formolario, o no. Se hanno sottoscritto, è necessario che apparisca detta sottoscrittione, et in tal caso forse sarà luogo alle dichiarazioni da essi fatte, di aver sottoscritto puramente e sinceramente. O non hanno sottoscritto, e non può la Sede Apost. senza gran discapito recedere da bolle, decreti e tanti altri fatti. The declarations are inadequate, perchè colui che

deve esseguire un atto, non basta il dire d'averlo fatto, se
non consta effet tivamente l'adempimento di esso. Piccolomini,
who had not been present, was also opposed to the dispatch of
a Brief.

[*Ibid.*, p. 860.]

10.   ROSPIGLIOSI TO BARGELLINI [1]

January 20, 1669.

1.

" La dichiaratione fatta a V. S. da monsignor di Chalons in
assenza degli altri due vescovi mediatori, sottoscritta da
monsù Arnauld e confermata poi dall'arcivescovo di Sens, le
certificationi autentiche a lei inviate parimente in scritto da i
quattro vescovi di haver sinceramente sottoscritto e fatto
sottoscrivere il formulario, e le sicurezze che monsù di Lionne
ha di ciò date a V. S. con quel di più che l'arcivescovo di
Roano et altri ne hanno attestato, pare a N. Sᴿᵉ che costi-
tuiscano una prova, la qual prevaglia di gran lunga per ogni
ragione a quanto si era sparso in contrario su qualche foglietto
et avviso particolare del contenuto de' processi verbali, onde
possa e deva la Sᵗᵃ Sua su la fede del Re e de' sudetti gravi e
replicati testimonii ben appoggiar la sua credenza dell'effettiva
et intiera obedienza de' quattro vescovi e della sincera sottoscrittione fatta da loro del formulario.

Ha però S. Bⁿᵉ risposto a i medesimi vescovi nella forma che
V. S. vedrà dalla copia del breve che se le manda per loro, la
quale V. S. dovrà ben considerare in ogni parte e prenderne a
mente il tenore per poter conformarsi ad esso anco ne' discorsi
ch'ella havrà occasione di far con chiunque bisogni nella
materia. Si è stimato necessario l'accennar nel breve ciò che
nell'animo di S. Sᵗᵃ havevano eccitato gli avvisi e le scritture
uscite circa i processi verbali, et insieme l'impulso havuto
dalle nuove e gravi testimonianze giunte a S. Sᵗᵃ della sincera
sottoscrittione e della piena sommissione et obedienza de'
quattro vescovi, perchè essendo questo il fondamento, al
quale s'appoggia la giustificatione della clemenza che S. Bⁿᵉ
usa hora verso di loro, chiunque vedrà mai ciò vegga insieme la
ragione che porge a S. Bⁿᵉ giusto motivo di farlo e riconosca
haver la Santa Sede ricercato per una risolutione di tanto peso
ciò che conveniva per condescendervi.

[1] XXXI., p. 398.

Se per li riguardi altre volte considerati costì di sottrarre a gli spiriti inquieti ogni materia di nuovo cimento, e per conservar più stabilmente l'unione e la pace si stimerà conveniente il non dar fuori copia del breve scritto da S. B^{ne} a i quattro vescovi, potrà V. S. non darla nè far altro per sua parte che possa interpretarsi ad ostentatione e propalatione non necessaria di quanto è seguito.

Ma in termini gravi e generali non lascerà ella di dire ove bisogni, haver S. B^{ne}, sodisfatta dell'intiera obedienza de' quattro vescovi, usati verso di loro gli atti della sua clemenza.

Non è già dovere per la libertà che prenda alcun cervello inquieto di spargere o scriver cose contro la verità di questo successo, far publiche dichiarationi e racconti della serie di esso, ma quando si procedesse veramente con doppiezza (il che non si crede, nè si ha hora cagione di credere) e si volesse in pregiuditio dell'autorità della Santa Sede e del candore e decoro col quale si è di qua operato, divulgar menzogne che facessero apparir minore la piena obedienza che si è professato di rendere a S. S^{tà}, sarà necessario dar fuori non solo la copia de' brevi, ma quant'altro appartiene al fatto per sincera testimonianza del vero. Onde V. S. dovrà col signor di Lionne fermar bene questo punto per non esser ridotta a simile necessità, nella quale però quando pur ella si trovi, sarà bene che potendo darne avviso qua e riceverne ordini in tempo, lo faccia, schivando di prender impegno, quando non vi sia necessità, per quelle ragioni delle quali si lascia il giuditio alla sua prudenza."

[Papal Sec. Arch., *Nunziat. di Francia*, 137 f., 94 f.]

2.

"Non si è stimato che convenga, nominando nel breve il formulario, aggiungervi la parola ' di fede ', perchè essendosi preteso da chi ha havuta sinistra intentione che il formulario havesse due parti, l'una di fede che riguarda il jus, e l'altra non di fede che riguarda il fatto, poteva quell'aggiunta interpretarsi per tassativa e restrettiva nel significato sudetto. Il che si partecipa a V. S. non perchè ella formalizzi o faccia nuova contestatione sopra quella parola, ma perchè sappia tutto ciò che può intendervisi da altri, benchè hora convenga dissimularlo et intenderla a nostro modo.

Sarebbe stato molto gradito il sapere, quali fossero le due parole che l'arcivescovo di Sens haveva lasciate nella dichiaratione sottoscritta, che poi ha egli mandata intiera, essendo in questa materia sì grave importantissima ogni minuzia."

[*Ibid.*, f. 97ᵇ.]

11. To the Spanish Nuncio [1]

Rome, August 31st, 1669.

" La pace fra le corone ; la parola ottenuta dal Re Christᵐᵒ di non offender cotesta per quest'anno ; le concessioni e le proroghe di gratie notabilissime d'impositioni nuove sopra il clero, che ben sa V. S. quanto siano gravi a chi le soffre e questo in tempo non di guerre con gl'infedeli, su le quali eran fondate molte di esse, ma di leghe con essi e di pace con tutti ; la tranquillità ultimamente ristabilita in cotesta monarchia con maniera di tanto impegno e pericolo per Sua Stᵃ, che ogn'altro secondo il solito di qui haverebbe fuggite ; e finalmente la riserva spontanea d'un cardinalato, nel modo e nelle circostanze che il mondo e la corte di Roma ha veduto con ammiratione, mostrano, qual sia la tenerezza di S. Stᵃ verso cotesta corona. E l'havere impegnate in Candia le armi del Re Christᵐᵒ e fattele servire a defender l'antemurale di Sicilia e di Napoli contro il Turco, fa vedere che, se Sua Stᵃ ha fatto un cardinale alla Francia per averne ottenuta un'armata intiera marittima e terrestre pagata per tutto quest'anno contro il Turco, l'ha fatto per mantener con questo mezzo la pace alla Spagna e difendere gli stati di essa con l'armi di Francia. Il che piaccia a Dio che non apparisca pur troppo vero dall'effettiva incursione di questi barbari nel regno di Sicilia dopo che Candia si sarà perduta. Nel rimanente la mia gita in Francia sa il mondo et i ministri medesimi qui del Re Cattᶜᵒ non essere stata per altro che per procurar di fermar l'armi del Re Christᵐᵒ dall'inoltrarsi in Fiandra, e se ciò non mi fu permesso, rimasero almeno incaminate le cose al trattato d'Aquisgrana et impegnato il Re a consentir non solo alla pace, ma a prometter che per ragioni delle nuove conquiste non se ne sarebbe impedita l'esecutione. Onde se ben si riguarda costì, sarà facile il ravvisare, in ogni passo che Nʳᵒ Sigʳᵉ ha dato verso la Francia, una particolare intenzione

---

[1] *Cf.* XXXI., p. 341.

e volontà di giovare a cotesta corona, la quale, se per la condizione de' tempi ha in tante cose stimato ella medesima di dover cedere alla fortuna e deferire alle sodisfattioni del Re Christ^mo, quanto più deve conoscer la necessità che preme S. Beat^ne come padre comune di tenersi in buona corrispondenza con chi può influir tanto al bene del christianesimo e della pace, e di conservarsi in stato di poter sostentarla, et esser di profitto alla Spagna medesima nell'occasioni.

All'incontro a Napoli si tengono in sequestro ai vescovi l'entrate, si fa violenza d'oppositione alle decime e pregiudicio insoffribile coll'istessa permissione del farle esigere ; si suscitano pretensioni sopra le lumiere con una insolita novità senza esempio e riservata solo al pontificato di N. S^re ; si nega l'Exequatur agli appaltatori della Camera Apost. per vender l'alume nel regno. Ciò è stato sentito da S. S^tà vivissimamente e V. S. non potrà dolersene a bastanza costì, perchè è un sommo torto, che si fa alla S. Sede il metter solo in discorso la pretensione d'aprir lumiere nel regno di Napoli ; ma il proceder de facto a negar l'Exequatur agli appaltatori della Camera Apost., dopo il possesso ch'essa ha in contrario, non mai interrotto nè controverso, è un'apparente violazione del giusto et un'aperta volontà di togliere alla Sede Apostolica quel che è suo senza riguardo di ragione.

Le stravaganze del Cappellano Maggiore e tant'altri pregiuditii della immunità e giurisdittione ecclesiastica, le innovationi fatte qui nella Dateria non sono inventioni del sigr. cardinale Litta, il zelo del quale è solo di sostenere i dritti della Chiesa, e non può conseguirlo con tutta la sua virtù. . . .

[Papal Sec. Arch., *Nunziat. di Spagna*, 136 f., 124–6.]

12. To the Spanish Nuncio [1]

Rome, August 13th, 1672.

" I due discorsi fatti con V. S. dal conte di Peneranda e dall'ambasciatore di Francia sono ben ingegnosi, essendosi ciascheduno di essi prescritto il fine di tirar il Papa ne' proprii interessi, l'uno esagerandone la necessità, l'altro proponendone la gloria.

Quando il Re Christ^mo opprime gl' eretici, fa risorger la fede sepolta in quelle provincie ed accresce il figliuoli e i suddetti

[1] *Cf.* XXXI., p. 635.

all'autorità spirituale della S. Sede ; non può Sua Beat^{ne} se non render gratie a Dio di sì felici successi. All'incontro con simil paragone i pregiuditii che si ricevono in Fiandra dal conte di Montereij dopo la disapprovata permissione data agli Olandesi, nelle gravezze che vuole imporre a i mendicanti, per trarre dalle loro povere sostanze gl' aiuti da sostenere i ribelle a Dio ed alla religione cattolica, sono troppo sensibili, e prevale tanto nel paterno cuore di Sua S^{tà} il bene delle anime ad ogni altra qual sia forte consideratione, che non saprebbe dar luogo ai motivi dei pericoli o dei vantaggi temporali, senza un vehemente dubbio di derogare al obligo del suo quasi divino ministero.

È verissimo che i principi uniti potrebbono non solamente resistere, ma assalire i Turchi per imprese assai più vantaggiose che non sono quelle, le quali risultano dalle guerre che tra essi si rimovono e si coltivano di tempo in tempo ; ma quanto sia difficile di comporne l'unione, l'esperienza l'ha dimostrato. Ciò che hora conviene è di pregare la bontà divina che faccia risplendere il zelo del Re nella mortificazione degli Olandesi e nella restitutione della libertà ai fedeli, non permettendo che il fuoco più oltre si stenda che a consumar gl' eretici, nel qual caso tutte le nazioni cattoliche rimarranno obligate alle opere grandi del Re, e sarà glorificato Dio nelle prosperità di esse. Gli Spagnuoli havranno in Fiandra migliori vicini ; l'eresia non sarà fomentata altrove, ed i Turchi saranno meno arditi, quando tra i cattolici sarà mancata la contradittione e la disunione del credere la verità di fede, che rende i principi meno atti a congregare le forze ed a tentare gl' acquisti dell'Oriente. . . ."

[Papal Sec. Arch., *Nunziat. di Spagna*, 139 f., 49 f.]

13. CARDINAL ALTIERI TO CARDINAL NERLI [1]
Rome, July, 11th, 1673.

" Fra le cose, che nel corse di pochi mesi si sono attentate con esempio inaudito in cotesta corte a pregiudizio della Sede Apostolica, non ha certamente l'ultimo luogo l'editto per la creazione degli ufficii di banchieri e spedizionieri per la corte di Roma e legazione d'Avignone, non solo perchè con quello viene a restringersi a' fedeli la libertà di ricorrere al loro padre

---

[1] *Cf.* XXXI., p. 495.

commune per li bisogni e direttione delle coscienze, ma perchè lo stesso editto si avanza a dichiarare nulli e di niun effetto li rescritti et atti apostolici in altra maniera ottenuti ; onde, conosciutasi questa verità, in una congregazione di cardinali unita per ordine di N^{ro} S^{re}, fu in quella risoluta che Sua Beat^{ne} non potea in modo alcuno permettere si fatta innovazione e che dovea, come perniciosa e di pessimo esempio alla cristianità tutta, annullarla e irritarla ; ma in ogni modo, volendo la S^{tà} Sua procedere in questo affare con la solita mansuetudine, et apprendendo che quei che hanno suggerito la pubblicazione di un simile editto, siano poco istrutti della rilevanza di esso e di ciò ch'è succeduto in altri tempi, quando si è voluto attentare, volse col mezzo d'un suo Breve significare i suoi sensi alla M^{tà} del Re, sperando che dalla pietà e giustizia d'un principe sì religioso fusse potuto togliere affatto questo scandalo dal cristianesimo, e ciò s'induceva a sperarlo tanto più facilmente, quanto che, per le notizie havute, s'era conos-siuto ch', essendosi in diversi tempi per l'avidità d'alcuni banchieri solo intenti al proprio interesse fatti intorno a ciò alcuni regolamenti, erano sempre stati a richiesta del clero, giustamente interessato nella libertà ecclesiastica, rivocati et annullati, come si credeva che potesse succedere di presente per i rincontri datine da V. E. Hora, vedendosi che non solo si è proceduto alla deputazione de' spedizionieri, ma che se n'è publicato l'editto, si è giudicato bene di dirle che assoluta-mente qui non si potrà più soffrire un attentato sì pernicioso ; in conseguenza di che sarà obbligato Sua Beat^{ne} con sommo suo dispiacere a praticare quelle risoluzioni, che in casi simili meditavano di fare i suoi antecessori, e con tutto che si tenghi per infallibile che le pessime conseguenze, che ne deriveranno a pregiudizio de' sudditi di Sua Maestà e a profitto solamente dell'avarizia di pochi, daranno motivo alla Maestà Sua di ritrattar quest'editto e di lasciar che nelle spedizioni si osservi l'antica libertà, in ogni modo non deve Sua Beatitudine aspettare che succedino scandali così inevitabili, ma deve, per quanto puote, prevenirli, come fa col mezzo di questa, incari-cando a V. E. di applicar tutto lo spirito nell'imprimere a' cotesti ministri, che Nostro Signore è costituito in questa obligazione e che deve in tutti i modi adempirla.

[Papal Sec. Arch., *Nunziat. di Francia*, 432, f. 174 s. (now 148-9).]

14. CLEMENT X. TO LOUIS XIV.

Carissimo in Christo filio Ludovico Francorum Regi Christianissimo Clemens PP. X.

1.

Carissime in Christo fili Noster salutem etc. Strenua Traiecti superioris expugnatio per nobilem virum Ducem Destroeum Maiestatis tuae nomine nuntiata Nobis eximiae iure merito tibi ab Apostolica Sede laudes comparat, cuius profecto praeclara incrementa sunt victoriae tuae. Invisam enim dum Superis gentem, arcibus munitissimis obvallatam atque in multitudine divitiarum suarum gloriantem de sacrilega dominatione deturbas, antiqua coeli iura restituis subiugatisque Ecclesiae perduellibus nationes edoces universas, non execrandum tantummodo, sed infelix quoque tandem scelus esse impiam ab orthodoxa matre defectionem. Excelsos itaque invictae fortitudini tuae et pontificio solio plausus excitantes, te, carissime fili, natum ad palmas, educatum ad triumphos, amantissime in Domino complectimur, indefinitam inclytis conatibus tuis gloriae metam auspicamur, omniumque bonorum authorem Deum accuratissimis precibus obsecramus, ut apostolicam benedictionem, quam Maiestati tuae ex omni cordis Nostri sensu impertimur, profusis ipse quoque beneficentiae thesauris cumulate confirmet.

Datum Romae apud Sanctam Mariam Maiorem sub annulo piscatoris die XXVI. Iulii 1673, pontificatus Nostri anno 4º. Papal Sec. Arch., *Clementis X. epist. ad principes, Arm.* IV–V., f. 28 *seq.*[1]

2.

Carissime in Christo fili Noster salutem. Iucundum admodum accidit Nobis praeclarum testimonium, quod de egregie gesta a dilecto filio Nostro Francisco cardinali Nerlio apud Maiestatem tuam Apostolici Nuntii provincia necnon de ipsius virtutibus ac promeritis accuratis ad Nos litteris dedisti ; gavisi enim magnopere sumus impensam eidem praecipuis documentis voluntatem Nostram luculenter tanti regis suffragio comprobatam esse. Eximiae insuper argumentum

---

[1] *Cf.* XXXI., p. 497.

laetitiae sumpsimus cum ex iisdem litteris tum ex voce praedicti dilecti filii Nostri, qui filialem ergo Nos atque Sanctam hanc Sedem observantiam tuam disertis coram significationibus prosecutus est ; effervescentibus autem vicissim in Nobis erga Maiestatem tuam paternae caritatis ardoribus, te ortho-doxae religionis decus totiusque christianae reipublicae orna-mentum intimi amoris sensu in Domino complectimur, meritum tibi pro Traiecto superiori expugnato ex apostolica statione iterum iterumque plausum damus ac pontificiam benedic-tionem amantissime impertimur.

Datum Romae apud S. Mariam Maiorem sub annulo piscatoris die XXII. Augusti 1673, pontificatus Nostri anno quarto.

[*Ibid.*, f. 36.]

15. BIOGRAPHIES OF POPE INNOCENT XI.

For a long time we were reduced to a few small works for the life of Innocent XI.[1] The first is by Giovanni Battista Pistoni, *Vita d'Innocenzo* XI. (Venice, 1891 ; new edition, 1716). The work cannot offer much, were it only by reason of its brevity. Not much more is to be found in the *Vita* by GIOVANNI ALBIZZI, Venice, 1695. More detailed are the writings of Fr. CACCIA, O.F.M. ; *Leben Innozenz XI.* (Neyss, 1696 ; Frankfurt, 1697), and FILIPPO BONAMICI's book dedicated to Pius VI. : *De vita et rebus gestis venerabilis servi Dei Innocentii XI. Pont. Max. commentarius*, Romae, 1776, printed in NAT. ALEXANDER, *Hist. eccl. suppl.*, III., 48–92 (without the introduction), and in BERTHIER, *Innocentii XI. Epistolae*, I., ix–lii (complete). The value of BONAMICI's work, written in elegant Latin, lies chiefly in the circumstance that he was able to make use of the notes of Marracci, Innocent XI's confessor. LEBRET gave a German translation of Bonamici's work (Frankfurt and Leipzig, 1791), with anti-Jesuit remarks in keeping with the superficial " enlightenment " of the period.[2]

[1] The bizarre work of GASPER SAZ : *Ecos sagrados de la fama gloriosa de Innocencio XI. S.P.O.M. Panegyrico ecometrico*, Madrid, 1681, is of no historical value.

[2] The *Vita Innocentii XI.* by COMES A TURRE REZZONICO has remained in MS. in the Monti Archives, Como.

Three other biographies of Innocent XI. only became known through the Dominican BERTHIER (*Vita d'Innocenzo XI.*, Roma, 1889), to whom we also owe an edition of the Latin letters of the Pontiff ; they are :

1. An anonymous biography, composed in the year of the Pope's death (BERTHIER, 258–277), but which is wrong on several points and, as a matter of fact, does not give much that is new.

2. The *Vita Innocentii XI. exarata a P. Ludovico Marracci, qui ipsi fuit a confessionibus* (BERTHIER, 240–258), sincere, most trustworthy, and giving much that is new but no real biography.[1]

3. The *Vita del servo di Dio Papa Innocentio XI. raccolta in tre libri per Mattia Giuseppe Lippi*. The original of this biography, which fills a whole volume (BERTHIER, 1–203), is preserved in the Odescalci Archives, Rome. Copies are found in the Bibl. Vallicelliana (K 48) and in Bibl. Corsini, Rome. A third copy, of the year 1719, I found in the Ricci Archives, Rome, and a fourth is in *Cod.* 6306 of the State Library, Vienna. RANKE (III., 202) gives a short extract of this work, whose author remained unknown to him. He quotes in his own peculiar fashion as " Ms. Rom." : he probably used the MS. of the Corsini Library (39 D 3).

Lippi's *Vita* is divided into three books : the first treats of the antecedents of the Pope : the second of his government, with the exception of his efforts for the Turkish war ; to this, Innocent XI.'s greatest effort, the whole of the third book is devoted, ending with his death and an account of the veneration of which he became the object after his death. The work is of very great value in many ways, for it is that of a contemporary (composed 1693), who kept his eyes open and who had the assistance of well-informed men, such as Cardinal Colloredo and the Oratorian Carafini. Naturally enough, Lippi was not initiated into the details of diplomatic negotiations ; for this we depend on the documents preserved in the Archives. Moreover there are shadows on which Lippi does not dwell. Lippi is completely mistaken with regard to the government

[1] MARRACCI also wrote a book entitled : *L'Ebreo preso per le buone overo discorsi famigliari et amichevoli fatti con i Rabbini di Roma intorno al Messia*, Roma, 1701.

of the Jesuit General Gonzalez (p. 55), but it is his merit to have adopted from the first a critical attitude towards the legends which quickly gathered round the person of the Pope (p. 184).

An apology, obviously written in view of the eventual canonization of the Pontiff, has for its author the learned Dominican and friend of Benedict XIV., Tommaso Maria Mamachi (*Pro Innocentio XI. Pont. Max. liber singularis*).[1] There is a copy in the Odescalchi Archives and in those of the Roman Dominicans. In his Appendix, Berthier has given a few passages from this refutation of the unfounded accusations of which Innocent XI. has been the object. Berthier also quotes the Acts of the process of beatification, but without indicating that important sections of them had already been printed in the *Analecta juris pontificii*, 11th series (1872), 271–327.

New light has been thrown upon Innocent XI.'s aims by the Briefs published by Berthier,[2] and by the partial publication of the nunciature reports.[3] The best recent presentment is that in IMMICH'S monograph (1900), but the latter limits himself to the Pope's political activity ; where he touches on his ecclesiastical activity, he commits more than one blunder.

MICHAUD'S book, *Louis XIV. et Innocent XI.* (4 vols., Paris, 1882) is valuable for the unpublished documents we find in its pages ; for the rest it is a tendentious piece of work (see XXXII, p. 126, n. 2).

16. Instruction for A. Pignatelli, Nuncio in Germany (Innocent XII.) [4]

1668.

. . . Dalla maggior parte de' politici si crede hoggidì che tra tutte le Nuntiature quella di Germania sia la meno faticosa e

---

[1] *Cf.* MORONI, XLII., 95 *seqq.*

[2] The text is faithfully but uncritically printed.

[3] To the data collected by IMMICH (p. 9) on this publication must be added the recent but incomplete work of Bojani, though it is not free from grave defects, *cf. Röm. Quartalschrift*, 1914, 59* *seqq.* ; *Rev. d'hist. ecclés.*, XII., 127 *seqq.* ; *Hist. Jahrbuch*, XXXI., 814 *seqq.* ; *Rev. d'hist. de l'Église de France*, V., 392 *seqq.*

[4] *Cf.* XXXII., 572.

la più facile da reggere con somma riputazione della Sede Apost., in che pare che vi si trovi qualche fondamento non mediocre, perchè nella Francia ordinariamente il Nuntio trova inviluppi così grandi rispetto a' privilegi della chiesa Gallicana, alla libertà del Parlamento et alle maniere ardite de' popoli, che quasi non sa come svilupparsene. In Spagna s'incontrano difficoltà non ordinarie per la libertà, la gravità del Consiglio di Stato, per le pretentioni de' Spagnoli e per il troppo zelo del Cattolico Re, in che fidati li Nuntii credono di poter ottenere tutto quello che vogliono, ma si trovano ingannati, perchè il Re non cerca altro che a scuotersi da quel predominio che gli ecclesiastici hanno preso sopra di lui e de' suoi Stati, quali esendo amplissimi, danno sempre differenti materie di dispareri, che servono a moltiplicar le fatiche dei Nuntii.

Di Venetia non dico nulla, mentre si sa benissimo dalla corte che questa Nuntiatura serve al Nuntio di prigione, e non bisogna andarvi con una testa di cristallo, perché non vi sarà molto a guadagnare, e portandosene una di ferro, è pure pericoloso, non potendo mai far bene duro con duro ; onde fa di mestieri cercar la strada di mezzo, che non è senza pericolo, havendo da due lati i precipitii et abissi. Quali ragioni non militano nella corte dell'Imperatore, riconoscendo questo, come vogliono questi politici, la sua grandezza dalla grandezza di Roma, essendo obligato per il dovere del suo scettro di conservare et augmentare la maestà della Sede Apost., la quale cosa rende ai Nuntii molto più facili li negotiati, già che Cesare istesso è obbligato di procurar le sodisfattioni del Papa.

Io ad ogni modo non ardisco affermare nè sottoscrivermi a questa opinione, anzi io trovo che non vi è Nuntiatura piè difficile da maneggiare di quella della Germania, perchè l'Imperatore in tempo di pace ha limitata la sua autorità dalla Dieta elettorale, et in tempo di guerra, riconoscendo la sua autorità dalla forza dell'armi, puoco cura di humiliarsi alle dimande di Roma. Ogni trattato si rende nella corte imperiale difficile, contrastando insieme i privilegi degl'Elettori e la suprema M^{tà} dell'Imperatore, gl'uni volendo far dell'impero una republica, e l'altro pretendendo far della republica elettorale una sovranità particolare. Onde per lo più non si sa a qual partito appigliarsi, tanto più che i partiti di Roma danno al presente una gelosia troppo grande agl'interessi della Germania.

Tuttavia dirò con buona ragione che V. S. I. truova aperta una porta, perdove entrando, se gli renderanno facilissimi i negotiati ; et in fatti la Nuntiatura di Polonia è una scuola de' primi durimenti della Nuntiatura di Germania. Qui s'imparano le prime regole di quei grandi studii che conviene essercitare nella corte imperiale. In Polonia si celebrano le vigilie, et in Germania le feste, trovandosi molti trattati quasi di una medesima specie, costumandosi pian piano il Nuntio nella corte di Polonia a riconoscere la differenza che si trova di vivere in Roma o in altri regni fra huomini d'una stessa religione, e di conversare, anzi trattare con politici di credenza, e però havendo con tanta sodisfattione de' Polonesi, del Re Casimiro e della Sede Apost. esercitata V. S. I. quella Nuntiatura, certo è che non si trovarà alcuna difficoltà di essercitare quella della Germania, servendosi dell'esperienza e prattiche di fresco passate.

Veramente, se non si avesse da negotiare che con il solo imperatore o che questo fosse monarca di disponere ogni cosa a suo beneplacito, i negotiati si renderebbono i più facili che si potessero mai desiderare ; mentre Cesare conservando quel naturale zelo di religione, anzi quello ossequio e riverenza verso la Sede Apost., che sono tanto conaturalizzate nella case di Austria, procurarebbe di far cadere il tutto in sodisfattione del Papa. Ma il male è che si trovano molti traversi, et il numero grande de' protestanti interessati nella corte imperiale rompono per lo più ogni buon disegno, et all'hora appunto quando si crede di haver per guadagnato e vinto qualche punto, sia di religione o di politica, conviene perdere il tutto a ricominciar quasi da capo il trattato, perdendosi molto tempo a rompere i disegni di quelli che non hanno altra mira che a rinversare ogni cosa. . . .

[Papal Sec. Archives, *Nunziat. diverse*, 242, f. 353–5.]

[Means for helping the Church in Germany.]

. . . Il primo è l'aggrandimento et il perpetuo stabilimento dell'imperio in una case cattolica. Il 2º l'unione de' principi cattolici con il partito di Cesare. Il 3º la propagatione della religione Romana. Il 4º la riputatione dell'autorità apostolica e il ristoro della immunità e giurisdittione ecclesiastica. Et

il 5º la riforma de' costumi del clero e della disciplina ecclesiastica . . .

[*Ibid.*, f. 358]

. . . Questo era lo scudo delli Nuntii, quando bisognava star
nelle difese ; ma al presente per la di Dio gratia noi siamo a
cavallo, perchè sicome i cattolici nei tempi andati temevano
gli avvanzi dei protestanti, hora al contrario i protestanti
temono gli avvanzi dei cattolici e si guardano più di noi che noi
di loro, e questo vuol dir che pensano più tosto a difendersi da'
nostri colpi che a tirar verso di noi quei colpi che ci hanno dato
per l'addietro.

Corre fama che si tratti da' Calvinisti l'unione delle due
religioni Luterana e Calvinista, e benchè questa sia un'opera
più tosto da desiderarsene che da vedersene la loro essecutione,
con tutto ciò sarà bene d'invigilar negl'andamenti degl'uni e
degl'altri, perchè, quando questo si potesse mettere in effetto,
la religione Romana correrebbe rischio di vedersi in peggiori
calamità di quelle in che si vidde nel tempo di Gustavo Adolfo.

La Francia ad ogni modo dalla sua parte si sforzarebbe di
romper tali disegni, quando si vedessero in campo, per non
render gl'Ugonotti di quel regno troppo appoggiati nel di
fuori ; onde la rottura de' trattati sarà facile, tanto più che
materie simili non si possono trattare in segreto ; pure non
bisogna addormentarsi sopra la speranza dell'impossibile, per
non restar da se stesso ingannato e malamente deluso.

In quanto al 4º potrei dir molte cose, ma sceglierò il più
necessario, che pure servirà per istruttione del 3º punto di
sopra accennato. E veramente l'autorità apostolica e giurisdittione ecclesiastica hanno sofferto ferite sensibilissime nella
Germania, che però sarà bene procurarne la guarigione. Dovrà
dunque V. S. I. proteggere e far proteggere con ardente zelo
dall'Imperatore tutte le università de' cattolici, acciochè
alla gioventù non s'insegnino false dottrine, parimente moltiplicar sempre più il numero de' parrochi cattolici in tutte le
città imperiali come ancora in altri luoghi dipendenti
dall'imperio, e sopra tutto che vi sia buon numero di maestri
di scuola tutti cattolici, e far continuare con assiduità l'uso
de' catechismi. Sarebbe da desiderare che nelle città imperiali,
e particolarmente nelle più considerabili, non vi fussero altri
librari che cattolici, e laddove il numero degli heretici è

troppo grande e potente, ottenere che vi sia trai librari heretici alcuno cattolico che habbia buona provisione di libri concernenti la nostra religione. Ben è vero che i librari di questi tempi sono tanto mercenarii, che si fanno lecito di vender libri contro Christo per tirar dalle mani di un scelerato dieci quadrini. Onde esorti V. S. I. allo spesso Sua Maestà Cesarea, acciò da' suoi commissarii si visitino per tutto tutte le stampe di quando in quando e librarie degli heretici et ancora de' cattolici, acciochè non mettino in publico l'opere degl'empii autori.

Per far rilucere la autorità apostolica non vi è mezzo più efficace che la moltiplicatione de' Gesuiti, che sono veramente quelli che non solo hanno difesa, ma di più propagata la maestà del Pontefice. Quindi è che, conoscendo gli heretici il zelo, bontà, valore e virtù di questi Padri, temono più della dottrina di mezza dozzena di detti religiosi che di tutto il resto della frateria ; onde procurano con tutte le massime più diaboliche di screditarli nel mondo, per levarsi dinanzi gl'occhi questo ostacolo, dal quale preveggono il loro sterminio ; che però conviene che V. S. se la tenghi con essi loro e gli esorti a moltiplicar le missioni, le prediche e le loro opere, le facci correr per tutto e conservi il lor credito nella corte di Cesare e nella mente di tutti.

Si guardi di tener la mano a questi rimedii con troppo rigore, benchè coperto di zelo, e non permetta che usi mai contro gl'heretici la forza o far gran strepito, perchè con questo si potrebbe commover tutta la Germania e metter di nuovo l'armi nelle lor mani, mentre gli heretici ci stanno all'erta, e basta la persecutione d'un solo per dare all'armi, come se fusse una guerra di religione ; ma conviene procedere a puoco a puoco conforme la qualità de' popoli e con l'ardor suave e la piace volezza ardente che suole usare nelle opere sue lo Spirito Santo. E piacesse a Dio che V. S. havesse tanto di gratia che per opera di Lei et a suo tempo si cominciasse a stender nelle parti più heresiarche la cattolica religione ; che certo con l'autorità pietosa di Sua Maestà unita al suo zelo e con le preghiere di Sua Santità se ne potrebbe sperare ottimo fine. . . .

[*Ibid.*, f. 360 s.]

. . . Esorti li prelati a continuare le visite per le loro diocesi et a tenere la mano alla vergognosa vita degli ecclesiastici et in particolare dei monasterii. Ma sopra l'altre cose egli è mestiere, per la grandissima penuria che vi è di sacerdito e di operarii cattolici, il ritorno indietro a far di nuovo e rimettere in piedi i seminarii et i collegii de' poveri, et il fondarne di nuovo, assegnando a quelli per mantenerli li beni ecclesiastici alienati et occupati dagli heretici, che si dovrebbero con ogni studio ricuperare ; e non meno da questi che da' beneficii più grossi si potrebbe ancora cavare il modo di andare alimentando i poveri convertiti alla fede. . . .

[Ibid., f. 362.]

. . . In quanto poi al pratticare degli heretici, chè un punto tanto essentiale per le cose della Germania, dirò che non conviene dar segno di aborrirli, come hanno fatto altri, tanto che oltre all'usato l'habbiamo ad odiare maggiormente. V. S. ad ogni modo farà maggiore opera, per facilitarne l'essecutione della sua carica, a mostrare di havere loro anzi compassione che odio, e cercarà con la dolcezza del trattare e con termini di benevolenza di renderseli confidenti più tosto che avversi, perchè potrà con questo assicurarsi che non gli riuscirà inutile all'ufficio intrapreso una cotal destrezza di operare, come lo vedrà per esperienza.

Quando occorrono dispute particolari tra gentilhuomini cattolici e protestanti, non dia mai segno nel sentirne discorrere di dipendere, prima delle necessarie informationi, dalla parte de' cattolici ; ma con dovuti termini tenga la parte della ragione e non dia motivo con parole ingiuriose o altro a' protestanti di crederlo troppo appassionato, e, se si può, scusi la debolezza dei protestanti, anco quando conosce il torto esser tutto dalla lor banda. . . .

[Ibid., f. 378.]

INDEX OF NAMES IN VOL. XXX.

457